Scotland's Golf Courses

KEY
1. ST ANDREWS
2. CARNOUSTIE
3. ROYAL DORNOCH
4. MUIRFIELD
5. TURNBERRY
6. TROON
7. PRESTWICK
8. LOCH LOMOND
9. GLENEAGLES
10. MACHRAHANISH
11. DURNESS
12. SOUTHERNESS

Vic Robbie

# Scotland's Golf Courses

## The Complete Guide

## Foreword by Bernard Gallacher

MAINSTREAM
PUBLISHING

EDINBURGH AND LONDON

First published in Great Britain in 2002 by
MAINSTREAM PUBLISHING COMPANY (EDINBURGH) LTD
7 Albany Street
Edinburgh EH1 3UG


ISBN 1 84018 442 6

A catalogue record for this book is available from the British Library

Typeset in AGaramond and Gill
Printed and bound in Great Britain by Mackays of Chatham

# CONTENTS

Map of Scotland                              2

Acknowledgements                             7

Foreword by Bernard Gallacher, OBE           9

Preface by Sandy Jones                       10

Introduction                                 11

The Open Championship in Scotland            14

How to use this guide                        17

Directory of Clubs                           18

Index                                        465

# ACKNOWLEDGEMENTS

The compilation of this completely updated and revised edition of *Scotland's Golf Courses: The Complete Guide* has taken many willing hands without whose assistance it would not have been possible, and I owe them my sincere thanks. To the club secretaries, captains, professionals and members who have provided the information about their beloved courses; and to those who have allowed me to hack around them in my research. To Bernard Gallacher, Sandy Jones (PGA), the SGU, and eminent golf correspondent Michael McDonnell. To Andy Hooper, Stan Hunter and Brian Morgan for their magnificent photographs, which capture perfectly the beauty of our Scottish courses. To Bill Bowyer for his technical expertise. To Christine, Gabrielle and Kirstie for all their hard work, good-humoured support and encouragement. To Maia for her inspiration and to my regular playing partner Nick, who has shown me how some of these great courses should be played. And last, but not least, to the many golfers around the world, whose interest in *Scotland's Golf Courses: The Complete Guide* when it was first published in 1997 led to the birth of www.scotlands-golf-courses.com.

# FOREWORD

BY BERNARD GALLACHER, OBE
THREE TIMES RYDER CUP CAPTAIN

I am privileged, as a professional golfer, in being able to travel around the world and play in tournaments in many exotic and exciting locations, such as Augusta and Valderrama. As Ryder Cup captain, I took the European team to the Ocean Course at Kiawah Island, The Belfry and Oak Hill at Rochester, where I experienced one of the greatest moments of my career when we defeated the United States to win the Cup. For 20 years I was Head Professional at Wentworth in Surrey, yet it still gives me a thrill to return to play in my homeland. Scotland is very much the home of golf and my golfing roots are there.

I learned to play the game as a boy at Bathgate Golf Club, near Edinburgh, and progressed through the junior ranks, representing Scotland and going on to become a Tour professional. No matter where golf takes me, however, I jump at the chance to get out my clubs and return to Scotland where there is the greatest variety of courses in the world.

That is why this book is essential reading for anyone planning to play in Scotland or just wanting to know more about the Scottish game. Apart from containing a history of the game in Scotland and carrying marvellous colour photographs showing the true beauty of some of our courses, it includes a comprehensive list of Scottish clubs – giving all the information you need to plan your round – and provides a card of the course and diagrams of the signature hole of many of the top courses.

Good golfing!

# PREFACE

BY SANDY JONES
EXECUTIVE DIRECTOR OF THE PROFESSIONAL GOLFERS' ASSOCIATION

As Executive Director of the PGA, may I say how honoured I am to be writing an introduction for this excellent guide. It is the result of months of tireless work and, knowing the author as I do, much of it taking place on the taxing but ultimately satisfying 19th hole.

The PGA can offer anyone visiting Scottish courses a vast range of benefits and information. Our members, the PGA Professionals at each club, are trained to give you the best advice in every aspect of golf. On arrival at your chosen course, why not visit the pro shop where you will receive a warm welcome from the course professional and be able to view the massive range of golfing equipment and apparel? PGA Professionals throughout Scotland guarantee to give you the right advice and the right equipment at the right price.

You could also book a lesson or two and add that little something to your Scottish golfing experience. Expert tuition will give you a whole new way of looking at the game. If you are travelling to a course on your own, our member can fix you up with a partner, possibly even himself at a nominal fee. We really can satisfy your every golfing need and whichever courses you visit you can be safe in the knowledge that you willl be treated in exactly the same way as any seasoned course member.

At the PGA we are committed to the premise that golf is a sport for everybody, and we hope that as you make your way around the courses you will gain a good impression of our organisation and its members. The scenery around many courses in Scotland is outstanding, but we hope that doesn't put you off carding respectable scores as you 'bag' your courses like Munros (the only difference being that golf is rarely an uphill slog in Scotland).

Finally, let me express my congratulations to Vic Robbie for a superb book charting the courses in my homeland of Scotland. Many of those listed hold very happy memories for me personally and I hope they will provide you with many hours of fantastic experiences. Scotland is a truly beautiful nation and our golf courses encapsulate perfectly that beauty.

# INTRODUCTION

Imagine a fine summer's day. The turf is lush beneath your feet. A breeze emphasises the purity of the air. The fairways are ablaze with the colour of purple heather and yellow gorse, and mountains provide an impressive backdrop. All about you there is an overwhelming atmosphere of history – you know you are walking in the footsteps of the greats who made golf the game it is today.

Behind are successes and disasters in equal measure; ahead, a battle between your skills as a golfer and the subtle intricacies of a course laid down many years before and made more difficult by the wind and water of the Scottish climate. It is an experience many have tried to replicate around the world. Over the years millions upon millions of pounds have been spent in this quest, most actively in America and Japan. Yet they cannot achieve that goal.

Scotland is the undoubted home of golf. No matter what standard golfers are, they have to make the pilgrimage to Scotland, where there are more than 500 spectacular and beautiful courses. Otherwise they feel they haven't played the game at all. The most popular and famous, of course, are the links courses that have evolved on sandy coastal strips which, centuries ago, were beneath the sea. Here nature is the architect, the course being fashioned out of the natural terrain rather than having design imposed upon it. Then there are the magnificent inland courses, which provide just as challenging a test.

Be it St Andrews, where you can almost see the ghosts of the past marching down the wide, undulating fairways; or Prestwick, the birthplace of golf's most prestigious prize, the Open Championship; or the great Open courses of Muirfield, Turnberry, Carnoustie and Royal Troon; or the splendour of Royal Dornoch and Loch Lomond or some humbler course – there is no finer country in which to play golf.

The stamp of greatness is everywhere. Almost every club has some link with the traditions of the sport. Everyone has a tale to tell of the great men who were the founding fathers of a great game. Scotland's rich history is peopled with giants like Allan Robertson, probably the first professional and certainly the first man to reduce St Andrews to fewer than 80 strokes; Old Tom Morris, the most famous name in Scottish golf; and his son, Tom, the only man to win the Open Championship four times in succession (the first time at the age of 17). Other greats include Willie Park, the first winner of the Open, and James Braid, who won the Open five times and laid down hundreds of courses. Braid's trademark was the most devilish of bunkers and his great rival, J.H. Taylor, said on seeing one of his bunkers at Prestwick: 'The man who made it should be buried here with a niblick through his heart.'

The origins of golf remain a mystery. There have been claims that the game was invented elsewhere. Play golf in Scotland and you realise that cannot be true. All civilisations have stick-and-ball games. As early as 200 BC the Chinese were supposed to have had some such game, as were the Romans. The Dutch played a game called *Kolven* or *Kolf,* but it was more akin to ice hockey, and the Belgians and French had *Chole.*

The first mention of golf in Scotland was in 1457 when King James II declared that it be banned lest men be tempted not to practise their archery, which was more useful in the defence of the kingdom against the English. In 1491 James IV's parliament ordered: 'In na place of the Realme there be used Fute-ball, Golfe, or uther sik unproffitable sportis.' But some historians claim that golf was played at St Andrews some two centuries earlier when shepherds, who grazed their flocks on the common land along the coast, took to hitting pebbles with sticks at targets to alleviate their boredom – the name 'golf' coming from 'to gowff', a verb in the Scottish dialect meaning 'to hit'. James was eventually won over by the game and by 1513 was reportedly ordering some golf clubs to be made for him.

In 1553, the people of the Auld Grey Toon, St Andrews, were given the rights by Archbishop John Hamilton to play golf on the links. Fourteen years later Mary, Queen of Scots perhaps set the trend for fanatical golfers by playing there only hours after the murder of her husband, Lord Darnley. Legend has it that in 1641 Charles I escaped an injudicious defeat at Leith Links. He was trailing by six holes with eight to play when news came of the Irish rebellion. Of course, he had to take leave of his opponent immediately to attend to matters of State. Such was the growing popularity of the game that those who put a round of golf ahead of a sermon on a Sunday morning could be fined 40 shillings for incurring the minister's displeasure.

As with all games, there came a time when the participants wanted more than just the challenge matches with hundreds of pounds at stake. They needed champions and in 1744 The Honourable Company of Edinburgh Golfers, who then played on Leith Links and now reside at Muirfield, petitioned the Edinburgh Council to provide a Silver Club for competition. John Rattray, a surgeon and a partner of Bonnie Prince Charlie in more serious issues such as the Jacobite rebellion, was the first winner. He escaped a beheading, some say, because of his prowess as a golfer. And, not far from Leith, the first ladies' competition was staged in Musselburgh in 1810.

The early days of golf were an expensive affair. It was played with the feathery ball, which was made of a top-hatful of feathers stuffed into a hand-stitched leather casing. At half a crown [12½p], it was more expensive than a club and deterred many from getting involved. Allan Robertson made a good living manufacturing the balls in the kitchen of his home at St Andrews, aided by his assistant Old Tom Morris, but when the rubber-moulded gutta-percha ball came on the market in 1848, Robertson declared: 'It's nae gowff.'

It was the gutty which started the golf boom in Scotland. More began to play and its popularity really took off with the launching of the Open Championship by the Prestwick Club in 1860, which turned the top golfers of the day into national heroes. By that time Old Tom Morris had moved to Prestwick as greenkeeper, on the salary of £50 a year, and he was favourite to win. His mentor Allan Robertson had been regarded as the champion player and he and Morris featured as partners in many foursomes matches played for stakes as high as £400. Yet they never played each other in competition.

Old Tom, an impressive figure with a full beard, was beaten in the inaugural championship by a 'foreigner from the East Coast', Willie Park, but he made his mark over the next seven years, winning it four times. Then he handed over to his son, Young Tom, who in winning his first Open recorded the first hole in one and unbelievably reduced the then 578-yard first at Prestwick to three strokes with a gutty ball and hickory shafts.

Young Tom made the Championship Belt his own by winning three years in succession. In 1871 there was no championship, and then a year later today's Claret Jug was put up as the trophy and he won that too. What Young Tom might have achieved is anyone's guess. His father once said, 'I could cope with Allan [Robertson] masel', but never wi' Tommy.' Tragically, Young Tom died – some say of a broken heart – on Christmas morning 1875 at the age of 24, three months after his wife had died giving birth.

Scotland's grip on the Open lasted 30 years before an English amateur, John Ball, broke the sequence. If any Scotsman took over the mantle of the Morrises, it would have been the Fife-born James Braid, who formed the great triumvirate with Harry Vardon and J.H. Taylor. He won five times between 1901 and 1910. But since those days only five Scots have won the Championship: Jock Hutchison and Tommy Armour (who were by then American citizens), George Duncan, Sandy Lyle and most recently Aberdeen's Paul Lawrie at Carnoustie in 1999. Lawrie came from ten shots back in the final round to force a three-way play-off with France's Jean Van de Velde and American Justin Leonard. His triumph was the first by a Scot on home soil since Willie Auchterlonie in 1893.

Although the ultimate prize has eluded generations of Scottish golfers down the years, there have been many fine exponents of the game in John Panton, Eric Brown, Brian Barnes, Bernard Gallacher (who went on to captain the Ryder Cup team three times), and today's superstars Sam Torrance, captain of the 2002 European Ryder Cup team, and Colin Montgomerie, who was Europe's No.1 for a record seven years. They are the direct descendants of a great golfing tradition in which you can participate by playing the finest courses in the world.

# THE OPEN CHAMPIONSHIP IN SCOTLAND

(36 holes until 1892)

| Year | Winner | Runner-up | Venue | Score |
|------|--------|-----------|-------|-------|
| 1860 | W. Park | T. Morris Snr | Prestwick | 174 |
| 1861 | T. Morris Snr | W. Park | Prestwick | 163 |
| 1862 | T. Morris Snr | W. Park | Prestwick | 163 |
| 1863 | W. Park | T. Morris Snr | Prestwick | 168 |
| 1864 | T. Morris Snr | A. Strath | Prestwick | 167 |
| 1865 | A. Strath | W. Park | Prestwick | 162 |
| 1866 | W. Park | D. Park | Prestwick | 169 |
| 1867 | T. Morris Snr | W. Park | Prestwick | 167 |
| 1868 | T. Morris Jnr | R. Andrew | Prestwick | 157 |
| 1869 | T. Morris Jnr | T. Morris Snr | Prestwick | 154 |
| 1870 | T. Morris Jnr | R. Kirk, D. Strath | Prestwick | 149 |
| 1871 | No championship | | | |
| 1872 | T. Morris Jnr | D. Strath | Prestwick | 166 |
| 1873 | T. Kidd | J. Anderson | St Andrews | 179 |
| 1874 | M. Park | T. Morris Jnr | Musselburgh | 159 |
| 1875 | W. Park | B. Martin | Prestwick | 166 |
| 1876 | R. Martin | D. Strath | St Andrews | 176 |
|      | [Strath refused to play-off] | | | |
| 1877 | J. Anderson | R. Pringle | Musselburgh | 160 |
| 1878 | J. Anderson | R. Kirk | Prestwick | 157 |
| 1879 | J. Anderson | J. Allan, A. Kirkaldy | St Andrews | 169 |
| 1880 | R. Ferguson | P. Paxton | Musselburgh | 162 |
| 1881 | R. Ferguson | J. Anderson | Prestwick | 170 |
| 1882 | R. Ferguson | W. Fernie | St Andrews | 171 |
| 1883 | W. Fernie | R. Ferguson | Musselburgh | 159 |
|      | [Won play-off 158 to 159] | | | |
| 1884 | J. Simpson | D. Rolland, W. Fernie | Prestwick | 160 |
| 1885 | R. Martin | A. Simpson | St Andrews | 171 |
| 1886 | D. Brown | W. Campbell | Musselburgh | 157 |
| 1887 | W. Park Jnr | R. Martin | Prestwick | 161 |
| 1888 | J. Burns | D. Anderson, B. Sayers | St Andrews | 171 |
| 1889 | W. Park Jnr | A. Kirkaldy | Musselburgh | 155 |
|      | [Won play-off 158 to 163] | | | |
| 1890 | J. Ball | W. Fernie | Prestwick | 164 |
| 1891 | H. Kirkaldy | A. Kirkaldy | St Andrews | 166 |
| 1892 | H.H. Hilton | J. Ball, H. Kirkaldy, A. Herd | Muirfield | 305 |

| 1893 | W. Auchterlonie | J.E. Laidlay | Prestwick | 322 |
|---|---|---|---|---|
| 1895 | J.H. Taylor | A. Herd | St Andrews | 322 |
| 1896 | H. Vardon | J.H. Taylor | Muirfield | 316 |
| | [Won play-off 157 to 159] | | | |
| 1898 | H. Vardon | W. Park Jnr | Prestwick | 307 |
| 1900 | J.H. Taylor | H. Vardon | St Andrews | 309 |
| 1901 | J. Braid | H. Vardon | Muirfield | 309 |
| 1903 | H. Vardon | T. Vardon | Prestwick | 300 |
| 1905 | J. Braid | R. Jones, J.H. Taylor | St Andrews | 318 |
| 1906 | J. Braid | J.H. Taylor | Muirfield | 300 |
| 1908 | J. Braid | T. Ball | Prestwick | 291 |
| 1910 | J. Braid | A. Herd | St Andrews | 299 |
| 1912 | E. Ray | H. Vardon | Muirfield | 295 |
| 1914 | H. Vardon | J.H. Taylor | Prestwick | 306 |
| 1915–19 | No championship | | | |
| 1921 | J. Hutchison | R.H. Wethered | St Andrews | 296 |
| | [Won play-off 150 to 159] | | | |
| 1923 | A.G. Havers | W. Hagen | Troon | 295 |
| 1925 | J. Barnes | E. Ray, | Prestwick | 300 |
| | | A. Compston | | |
| 1927 | R.T. Jones Jnr | A. Boomer, | St Andrews | 285 |
| | | F. Robson | | |
| 1929 | W. Hagen | J. Farrell | Muirfield | 292 |
| 1931 | T. Armour | J. Jurado | Carnoustie | 296 |
| 1933 | D. Shute | C. Wood | St Andrews | 292 |
| | [Won play-off 149 to 154] | | | |
| 1935 | A. Perry | A.H. Padgham | Muirfield | 283 |
| 1937 | T.H. Cotton | R.A. Whitcombe | Carnoustie | 290 |
| 1939 | R. Burton | J. Bulla | St Andrews | 290 |
| 1940–45 | No championship | | | |
| 1946 | S. Snead | A.D. Locke, J. Bulla | St Andrews | 290 |
| 1948 | T.H Cotton | F. Daly | Muirfield | 284 |
| 1950 | A.D. Locke | R. de Vicenzo | Troon | 279 |
| 1953 | B. Hogan | F.R. Stranaham, | Carnoustie | 282 |
| | | A. Cerda, | | |
| | | P.W. Thomson, | | |
| | | D.J. Rees | | |
| 1955 | P.W. Thomson | J. Fallon | St Andrews | 281 |
| 1957 | A.D. Locke | P.W. Thomson | St Andrews | 279 |
| 1959 | G. Player | F. van Donck, | Muirfield | 284 |
| | | F. Bullock | | |
| 1960 | K.D.G. Nagle | A. Palmer | St Andrews | 278 |
| 1962 | A. Palmer | K.D.G. Nagle | Troon | 276 |
| 1964 | A. Lema | J. Nicklaus | St Andrews | 279 |
| 1966 | J. Nicklaus | D.C. Thomas, | Muirfield | 282 |
| | | D. Sanders | | |
| 1968 | G. Player | J. Nicklaus, | Carnoustie | 289 |

|      |                |                      |             |     |
|------|----------------|----------------------|-------------|-----|
|      |                | R.J. Charles         |             |     |
| 1970 | J. Nicklaus    | D. Sanders           | St Andrews  | 283 |
|      | [Won play-off 72 to 73] |            |             |     |
| 1972 | L. Trevino     | J. Nicklaus          | Muirfield   | 278 |
| 1973 | T. Weiskopf    | N.C. Coles,          | Troon       | 276 |
|      |                | J. Miller            |             |     |
| 1975 | T. Watson      | J. Newton            | Carnoustie  | 279 |
|      | [Won play-off 71 to 72] |            |             |     |
| 1977 | T. Watson      | J. Nicklaus          | Turnberry   | 268 |
| 1978 | J. Nicklaus    | S. Owen,             | St Andrews  | 281 |
|      |                | R. Floyd,            |             |     |
|      |                | B. Crenshaw, T. Kite |             |     |
| 1980 | T. Watson      | L. Trevino           | Muirfield   | 271 |
| 1982 | T. Watson      | P. Oosterhuis,       | Troon       | 284 |
|      |                | N. Price             |             |     |
| 1984 | S. Ballesteros | B. Langer,           | St Andrews  | 276 |
|      |                | T. Watson            |             |     |
| 1986 | G. Norman      | G.J. Brand           | Turnberry   | 280 |
| 1987 | N. Faldo       | R. Davis, P. Azinger | Muirfield   | 279 |
| 1989 | M. Calcavecchia | G. Norman,          | Royal Troon | 275 |
|      |                | W. Grady             |             |     |
|      | [Won play-off over four holes] |      |             |     |
| 1990 | N. Faldo       | M. McNulty,          | St Andrews  | 270 |
|      |                | P. Stewart           |             |     |
| 1992 | N. Faldo       | J. Cook              | Muirfield   | 272 |
| 1994 | N. Price       | J. Parnevik          | Turnberry   | 268 |
| 1995 | J. Daly        | C. Rocca             | St Andrews  | 272 |
|      | [Won play-off over four holes] |      |             |     |
| 1997 | J. Leonard     | D. Clarke, J. Parnevik | Troon     | 272 |
| 1999 | P. Lawrie      | J. Leonard,          | Carnoustie  | 290 |
|      |                | J. Van de Velde      |             |     |
|      | [Won play-off over four holes] |      |             |     |
| 2000 | T. Woods       | E. Els, T. Bjorn     | St Andrews  | 269 |

# HOW TO USE THIS GUIDE

This book aims to give the visitor to Scotland and also the Scottish golfer a comprehensive guide to a great range of courses, which are listed by town in geographical areas and alphabetically by club in the index. Where possible all the contact information you need is listed – addresses, telephone numbers, fax numbers, e-mail addresses and websites along with the names of the secretary and professional. There are also directions and suggestions for accommodation.

To give you an idea of what to expect from the course, we detail the number of holes, yardages – in most cases from the championship or medal tees – par, standard scratch score (SSS) and course record. In some cases, there is also a card of the course and a description and diagram of the club's signature hole. Clubs operate different restrictions and wherever possible these are detailed along with green fees. We also state whether clubs have a bar and catering services, and list the facilities they provide, such as motorised buggies and the hire of trolleys, clubs and caddies, changing-rooms, putting green, pro shop, practice ground, driving range, coaching clinics and the availability of membership.

While every effort has been made to compile an accurate and complete guide to Scotland's golf courses, the publisher and author cannot be responsible for any errors, omissions or changes of details. We would welcome any information on any course that may not have been included in the guide. It is worth noting that clubs can change their rates at any time; if you are planning to visit a Scottish golf course, it is worth telephoning the club in advance to determine playing times and green fees.

# DIRECTORY OF CLUBS

## LOTHIANS INCLUDING EDINBURGH

| | | | |
|---|---|---|---|
| Aberlady | Kilspindie Golf Club | 18 | Links |
| | Luffness New Golf Club | 18 | Links |
| Bathgate | Balbardie Park Golf Club | 9 | Parkland |
| | Bathgate Golf Club | 18 | Parkland |
| Bonnyrigg | Broomieknowe Golf Club Ltd | 18 | Parkland |
| Dalkeith | Newbattle Golf Club Ltd | 18 | Parkland |
| Dalmahoy | Marriott Dalmahoy Hotel Golf & Country Club | 36 | Parkland |
| Dunbar | Dunbar Golf Club | 18 | Links |
| | Winterfield Golf Club | 18 | Links |
| Edinburgh | Baberton Golf Club | 18 | Parkland |
| | Braid Hills Golf Club | 36 | Heathland |
| | Carrick Knowe Course | 18 | Parkland |
| | Craigentinny Golf Course | 18 | Parkland |
| | Craigmillar Park Golf Club | 18 | Parkland |
| | Duddingston Golf Club | 18 | Parkland |
| | Kingsknowe Golf Club | 18 | Parkland |
| | Liberton Golf Club | 18 | Parkland |
| | Lothianburn Golf Club | 18 | Parkland |
| | Merchants of Edinburgh Golf Club | 18 | Parkland |
| | Mortonhall Golf Club | 18 | Moorland |
| | Murrayfield Golf Club Ltd | 18 | Parkland |
| | Portobello Golf Club | 9 | Parkland |
| | Prestonfield Golf Club | 18 | Parkland |
| | Ravelston Golf Club | 9 | Parkland |
| | Royal Burgess Golfing Society of Edinburgh | 18 | Parkland |
| | Silverknowes Golf Club | 18 | Parkland |
| | Swanston Golf Club | 18 | Parkland |
| | The Bruntsfield Links Golfing Society Ltd | 18 | Parkland |
| | Torphin Hill Golf Club | 18 | Heathland |
| | Turnhouse Golf Club | 18 | Parkland |
| Fauldhouse | Greenburn Golf Club | 18 | Moorland |
| Gifford | Castle Park Golf Club | 9 | Parkland |
| | Gifford Golf Club | 9 | Parkland |
| Gorebridge | Vogrie Country Park Golf Club | 9 | Parkland |
| Gullane | Gullane Golf Club | 54 | Links |
| | Muirfield (The Honourable Company of Edinburgh Golfers) | 18 | Links |

| | | | |
|---|---|---|---|
| Haddington | Haddington Golf Club | 18 | Parkland |
| Lasswade | Kings Acre Golf Course | 18 | Parkland |
| | Melville Golf Centre | 9 | Parkland *email 1-2* |
| Linlithgow | Bridgend & District Golf Club | 9 | Parkland |
| | Linlithgow Golf Club | 18 | Parkland *email 1-2* |
| | The West Lothian Golf Club | 18 | Parkland |
| Livingston | Deer Park Golf & Country Club | 18 | Parkland |
| Longniddry | Longniddry Golf Club | 18 | Links/Parkland *email 1-2* |
| Musselburgh | Musselburgh Links, The Old Course | 9 | Links |
| | The Musselburgh Golf Club | 18 | Parkland |
| Newbridge | Gogarburn Golf Club | 12 | Parkland |
| North Berwick | Jane Connachan Golf Centre | 9 | Parkland |
| | Glen Golf Club | 18 | Links *emailed 11-13* |
| | North Berwick Golf Club | 18 | Links *emailed 11-13* |
| | Whitekirk Golf Club | 18 | Heathland *email 11-26* |
| Penicuik | Glencorse Golf Club | 18 | Parkland |
| Prestonpans | Royal Musselburgh Golf Club | 18 | Parkland *email 11-26* |
| Pumpherston | Pumpherston Golf Club | 9 | Parkland |
| Ratho | Ratho Park Golf Club | 18 | Parkland |
| South Queensferry | Dundas Parks Golf Club | 9 | Parkland |
| Uphall | Uphall Golf Club | 18 | Parkland |
| West Calder | Harburn Golf Club | 18 | Moorland |
| West Linton | Rutherford Castle Golf Club | 18 | Parkland *email 1-2* |
| | West Linton Golf Club | 18 | Moorland |
| Whitburn | Polkemmet Country Park | 9 | Parkland |
| Winchburgh | Niddry Castle Golf Club | 9 | Parkland |

## HIGHLANDS INCLUDING INVERNESS

| | | | |
|---|---|---|---|
| Alness | Alness Golf Club | 18 | Parkland *email 12-17* |
| Arisaig | Traigh Golf Course | 9 | Links *email 1-2-05* |
| Beauly | Aigas Golf Course | 9 | Parkland |
| Boat of Garten | Boat of Garten Golf Club | 18 | Heathland |
| Bonar Bridge | Bonar Bridge/Ardgay Golf Club | 9 | Heathland |
| Brora | Brora Golf Club | 18 | Links |
| Carrbridge | Carrbridge Golf Club | 9 | Parkland *email 1-2* |
| Dornoch | Carnegie Club (Skibo Castle) | 27 | Links |
| | Royal Dornoch Golf Club | 36 | Links |
| Durness | Durness Golf Club | 9 | Links *email 11-23* |
| Elgin | Elgin Golf Club *on the way* | 18 | Parkland *email 12-16* |
| Forres | Forres Golf Club | 18 | Parkland |
| Fort Augustus | Fort Augustus Golf Club | 9 | Moorland |
| Fort William | Fort William Golf Club | 18 | Heathland |
| Fortrose | Fortrose & Rosemarkie Golf Club | 18 | Links |
| Gairloch | Gairloch Golf Club | 9 | Links |
| Garmouth | Garmouth & Kingston Golf Club | 18 | Links |
| Golspie | Golspie Golf Club | 18 | Links |

| | | | |
|---|---|---|---|
| Grantown-on-Spey | Craggan Golf Course | 18 | Parkland |
| | Grantown-on-Spey Golf Club | 18 | Parkland |
| Helmsdale | Helmsdale Golf Club | 9 | Heathland |
| Hopeman | Hopeman Golf Club | 18 | Links |
| Invergordon | Invergordon Golf Club | 18 | Parkland |
| Inverness | Inverness Golf Club | 18 | Parkland |
| | Loch Ness Golf Course | 18 | Parkland |
| | Torvean Golf Club | 18 | Parkland |
| Kingussie | Kingussie Golf Club | 18 | Moorland |
| Kinloss | Kinloss Country Golf Course | 9 | Parkland |
| Kyle of Lochalsh | Kyle of Lochalsh Golf Course | 9 | Meadowland |
| Lochcarron | Lochcarron Golf Club | 9 | Links |
| Lossiemouth | Covesea Golf Course | 12 | Links |
| | Moray Golf Club | 36 | Links |
| Lybster | Lybster Golf Club | 9 | Heathland |
| Muir of Ord | Muir of Ord Golf Club | 18 | Heathland |
| Nairn | Cawdor Castle Golf Club | 9 | Parkland |
| | Nairn Dunbar Golf Club | 18 | Links |
| | The Nairn Golf Club | 27 | Links |
| Nethy Bridge | Abernethy Golf Club | 9 | Moorland |
| Newtonmore | Newtonmore Golf Club | 18 | Parkland |
| Portmahomack | Tarbat Golf Club | 9 | Links |
| Reay | Reay Golf Club | 18 | Links |
| Skye (Isle of) | Isle of Skye Golf Club | 9 | Parkland |
| | Skeabost Golf Club | 9 | Parkland |
| Spean Bridge | Spean Bridge Golf Club | 9 | Parkland |
| Spey Bay | Spey Bay Golf Club | 18 | Links |
| Strathpeffer | Strathpeffer Spa Golf Club | 18 | Moorland |
| Tain | Tain Golf Club | 18 | Links |
| Thurso | Thurso Golf Club | 18 | Parkland |
| Tiree (Isle of) | Vaul Golf Club | 9 | Parkland |
| Ullapool | Ullapool Golf Club | 9 | Moorland |
| Wick | Wick Golf Club | 18 | Links |

## GRAMPIAN INCLUDING ABERDEEN

| | | | |
|---|---|---|---|
| Aberdeen | Auchmill Golf Club | 18 | Heathland |
| | Balnagask Golf Course | 18 | Links |
| | Craibstone Golf Centre | 18 | Parkland |
| | Deeside Golf Club | 27 | Parkland |
| | Hazlehead Public Courses | 45 | Parkland |
| | King's Links | 24 | Links |
| | Murcar Golf Club | 27 | Links |
| | Royal Aberdeen Golf Club | 36 | Links |
| | Westhill Golf Club | 18 | Heathland |
| Aboyne | Aboyne Golf Club | 18 | Parkland |

| | | | |
|---|---|---|---|
| Alford | Alford Golf Club | 18 | Parkland ~~email 12/15~~ |
| Auchenblae | Auchenblae Golf Course | 9 | Parkland |
| Ballater | Ballater Golf Club | 18 | Heathland email 11-26 |
| Balmedie | East Aberdeenshire Golf Centre Ltd | 24 | Parkland email 12-16 |
| Banchory | ~~Banchory~~ Golf Club | 18 | Parkland email 11-29 |
| | Inchmarlo Golf Club | 9 | Parkland |
| | Lumphanan Golf Club | 9 | Heathland |
| Banff | Duff House Royal Golf Club | 18 | Parkland email 11-29 |
| Braemar | Braemar Golf Club | 18 | Parkland email 11-26 |
| Buckie | Buckpool Golf Club | 18 | Links email 11-26 |
| | Strathlene Golf Club | 18 | Links email 12-13 |
| ~~Cruden Bay~~ | Cruden Bay Golf Club | 27 | Links |
| ~~Cullen~~ | Cullen Golf Club | 18 | Links email 11-15 |
| ~~Dufftown~~ | Dufftown Golf Club | 18 | Parkland |
| Dunecht | Dunecht House Golf Club | 9 | Parkland |
| Ellon | McDonald Golf Club | 18 | Parkland |
| Fraserburgh | Fraserburgh Golf Club | 27 | Links |
| Huntly | Huntly Golf Club | 18 | Parkland |
| Insch | Insch Golf Club | 18 | Parkland email 11-15 |
| Inverallochy | Inverallochy Golf Club | 18 | Links email 11-29 |
| Inverurie | Inverurie Golf Club | 18 | Parkland email 11-29 |
| Keith | Keith Golf Club | 18 | Parkland |
| Kemnay | Kemnay Golf Club | 18 | Parkland email 11-29 |
| Kintore | Kintore Golf Club | 18 | Moorland |
| Longside | Longside Golf Club | 18 | Parkland |
| ~~Macduff~~ | Royal Tarlair Golf Club | 18 | Parkland |
| ~~Newburgh~~ | Newburgh-on-Ythan Golf Club | 18 | Links |
| ~~Newmachar~~ | Newmachar Golf Club | 36 | Heathland |
| Oldmeldrum | Meldrum House Golf Club | 18 | Parkland |
| | Oldmeldrum Golf Club | 18 | Parkland email 12-16 |
| Peterculter | Peterculter Golf Club | 18 | Parkland email 12-13 |
| ~~Peterhead~~ | Peterhead Golf Club | 27 | Links |
| Portlethen | Portlethen Golf Club | 18 | Parkland |
| Rosehearty | Rosehearty Golf Club | 9 | Links |
| Rothes | Rothes Golf Club | 9 | Moorland |
| Stonehaven | Stonehaven Golf Club | 18 | Parkland |
| Tarland | Tarland Golf Club | 9 | Parkland |
| Torphins | Torphins Golf Club | 9 | Parkland |
| Turriff | Turriff Golf Club | 18 | Parkland |

**TAYSIDE INCLUDING DUNDEE AND PERTH**

| | | | |
|---|---|---|---|
| Aberfeldy | Aberfeldy Golf Club | 18 | Parkland email 12/15 |
| Aberuthven | Whitemoss Golf Club | 18 | Parkland email 11-26 |
| Alyth | Glenisla Golf Centre | 18 | Parkland email 11-29 |
| | Strathmore Golf Centre | 27 | Parkland email 11-29 |
| | ~~The~~ Alyth Golf Club | 18 | Heathland |
| Arbroath | Arbroath Links Golf Course | 18 | Links |

21

|  | Letham Grange Hotel & Golf Course | 36 | Parkland |
| Auchterarder | Auchterarder Golf Club | 18 | Parkland |
|  | The Gleneagles Hotel Golf Courses | 63 | Moorland |
| Barry | Panmure Golf Club | 18 | Links |
| Blair Atholl | Blair Atholl Golf Club | 9 | Parkland |
| Blairgowrie | Blairgowrie Golf Club | 45 | Heathland |
| Brechin | Brechin Golf Club | 18 | Parkland |
| Carnoustie | Carnoustie – Championship Course | 18 | Links |
|  | Carnoustie Golf Links – Buddon Links | 18 | Links |
|  | Carnoustie Golf Links – Burnside Course | 18 | Links |
| Comrie | Comrie Golf Club | 9 | Heathland |
| Crieff | Crieff Golf Club Ltd | 27 | Parkland |
|  | Crieff Hydro Golf Centre | 15 | Parkland |
|  | Foulford Inn Golf Course | 9 | Heathland |
| Dundee | Caird Park Golf Club | 18 | Parkland |
|  | Camperdown Golf Club | 18 | Parkland |
|  | Downfield Golf Club | 18 | Parkland |
|  | Monifieth Golf Links | 36 | Links |
| Dunkeld | Dunkeld & Birnam Golf Club | 18 | Heathland |
| Dunning | Dunning Golf Club | 9 | Parkland |
| Edzell | The Edzell Golf Club | 18 | Heathland |
| Forfar | Forfar Golf Club | 18 | Heathland |
| Glenalmond | Glenalmond Golf Course | 9 | Moorland |
| Glenshee | Dalmunzie Golf Course | 9 | Upland |
| Kenmore | Kenmore Golf Course | 9 | Moorland |
|  | Taymouth Castle Golf Club | 18 | Parkland |
| Kirriemuir | Kirriemuir Golf Club | 18 | Parkland |
| Montrose | Montrose Links Trust | 36 | Links |
| Muthill | Muthill Golf Club | 9 | Parkland |
| Perth | Craigie Hill Golf Club | 18 | Parkland |
|  | King James VI Golf Club | 18 | Parkland |
|  | Murrayshall Golf Course | 36 | Parkland |
|  | North Inch Golf Course | 18 | Links |
| Pitlochry | Pitlochry Golf Course Ltd | 18 | Parkland |
| St Fillans | St Fillans Golf Club | 9 | Parkland |
| Strathtay | Strathtay Golf Club | 9 | Parkland |
| Tayport | Scotscraig Golf Club | 18 | Links |

## FIFE INCLUDING ST ANDREWS

| Aberdour | Aberdour Golf Club | 18 | Parkland |
| Anstruther | Anstruther Golf Club | 9 | Links |
| Burntisland | Burntisland Golf House Club | 18 | Parkland |
| Cardenden | Auchterderran Golf Club | 9 | Parkland |
| Colinsburgh | Charleton Golf Club | 27 | Parkland |
| Cowdenbeath | Cowdenbeath Golf Club | 9 | Parkland |
| Crail | Crail Golfing Society | 36 | Links |

| Crosshill | Lochore Meadows Golf Course | 9 | Parkland |
| Cupar | Cupar Golf Club | 9 | Parkland |
| | Elmwood Golf Course | 18 | Parkland |
| Dunfermline | Canmore Golf Club | 18 | Parkland |
| | Dunfermline Golf Club | 18 | Parkland |
| | Pitreavie Golf Club | 18 | Parkland |
| Elie | The Golf House Club, Elie | 18 | Links |
| | Elie Sports Club | 9 | Links |
| Falkland | Falkland Golf Club | 9 | Parkland |
| Glenrothes | Glenrothes Golf Course | 18 | Parkland |
| Kinghorn | Kinghorn Golf Club | 18 | Links |
| Kinnesswood | Bishopshire Golf Club | 9 | Heathland |
| Kinross | Kinross Golf Club | 36 | Parkland |
| Kirkcaldy | Dunnikier Park Golf Club | 18 | Parkland |
| | Kirkcaldy Golf Club | 18 | Parkland *email 12-18* |
| Ladybank | Ladybank Golf Club | 18 | Heathland |
| Leslie | Leslie Golf Club | 9 | Parkland |
| Leuchars | Drumoig Hotel & Golf Course | 18 | Parkland |
| | St Michael's Golf Club | 18 | Parkland *email 12-12* |
| Leven | Leven Links Golf Club | 18 | Links |
| | Scoonie Golf Club | 18 | Parkland |
| Lochgelly | Lochgelly Golf Club | 18 | Parkland |
| Lundin Links | Lundin Golf Club | 18 | Links |
| | Lundin Ladies Golf Club | 9 | Parkland |
| Markinch | Balbirnie Park Golf Club | 18 | Parkland |
| Milnathort | Milnathort Golf Club Ltd | 9 | Parkland |
| Saline | Saline Golf Club | 9 | Parkland |
| St Andrews | St Andrews – The Old Course | 18 | Links |
| | St Andrews – Balgove Course | 9 | Links |
| | St Andrews – Eden Course | 18 | Links |
| | St Andrews – Jubilee Course | 18 | Links |
| | St Andrews – New Course | 18 | Links |
| | St Andrews – Strathtyrum Course | 18 | Links |
| | The Duke's Course | 18 | Parkland |
| | Kingsbarns Golf Links | 18 | Links |
| Thornton | Thornton Golf Club | 18 | Parkland |

## CENTRAL INCLUDING STIRLING

| Aberfoyle | Aberfoyle Golf Club | 18 | Parkland |
| Alloa | Alloa Golf Club | 18 | Parkland |
| | Braehead Golf Club | 18 | Parkland |
| Alva | Alva Golf Club | 9 | Parkland |
| Balfron | Shian Golf Course | 9 | Parkland |
| Bonnybridge | Bonnybridge Golf Club | 9 | Heathland |
| Bridge of Allan | Bridge of Allan Golf Club | 9 | Moorland |
| Callander | Callander Golf Club | 18 | Parkland |
| Dollar | Dollar Golf Club | 18 | Parkland |

| | | | |
|---|---|---|---|
| Drymen | Buchanan Castle Golf Club | 18 | Parkland |
| | Strathendrick Golf Club | 9 | Parkland |
| Dunblane | Dunblane New Golf Club | 18 | Parkland |
| Falkirk | Falkirk Golf Club | 18 | Parkland |
| | Polmont Golf Club Ltd | 9 | Parkland |
| Grangemouth | Grangemouth Golf Club | 18 | Parkland |
| Killin | Killin Golf Club | 9 | Parkland |
| Kincardine | Tulliallan Golf Club | 18 | Parkland |
| Larbert | Falkirk Tryst Golf Club | 18 | Links |
| | Glenbervie Golf Club | 18 | Parkland |
| Muckhart | Muckhart Golf Club Ltd | 27 | Heathland |
| Stirling | Airthrey Golf Course (University of Stirling) | 9 | Parkland |
| | Brucefields Family Golf Centre Ltd | 9 | Parkland |
| | Stirling Golf Club | 18 | Parkland |
| Tillicoultry | Tillicoultry Golf Club | 9 | Parkland |

## STRATHCLYDE INCLUDING AYR AND GLASGOW

| | | | |
|---|---|---|---|
| Abington | Arbory Brae Golf Club | 9 | Parkland |
| Airdrie | Airdrie Golf Club | 18 | Parkland |
| | Easter Moffat Golf Club | 18 | Moorland |
| Alexandria | Vale of Leven Golf Club | 18 | Parkland |
| Arran (Isle of) | Brodick Golf Club | 18 | Parkland |
| | Corrie Golf Club | 9 | Moorland |
| | Lamlash Golf Club | 18 | Heathland |
| | Lochranza Golf Club | 18 | Parkland |
| | Machrie Bay Golf Club | 9 | Links |
| | Shiskine Golf & Tennis Club | 12 | Links |
| | Whiting Bay Golf Club | 18 | Links |
| Ayr | Belleisle Seafield Golf Courses | 36 | Parkland |
| | Dalmilling Golf Club | 18 | Meadowland |
| Balloch | Cameron House Hotel & Country Estate | 9 | Parkland |
| Barrhead | Fereneze Golf Club | 18 | Moorland |
| Beith | Beith Golf Club | 18 | Parkland |
| Bellshill | Bellshill Golf Club | 18 | Parkland |
| Biggar | Biggar Golf Club | 18 | Parkland |
| Bishopton | Erskine Golf Club | 18 | Parkland |
| Bothwell | Bothwell Castle Golf Club | 18 | Parkland |
| Bridge of Weir | The Old Course Ranfurly Golf Club | 18 | Moorland |
| | The Ranfurly Castle Golf Club Ltd | 18 | Moorland |
| Bute (Isle of) | Bute Golf Club | 9 | Links |
| | Port Bannatyne Golf Club | 13 | Parkland |
| | Rothesay Golf Club | 18 | Moorland |
| Campbeltown | Dunaverty Golf Club | 18 | Links |
| | Machrihanish Golf Club | 18 | Links |
| Cardross | Cardross Golf Club | 18 | Parkland |

24

| | | | |
|---|---|---|---|
| Carluke | Carluke Golf Club | 18 | Parkland |
| Carnwath | Carnwath Golf Club | 18 | Parkland |
| Carradale | Carradale Golf Club | 9 | Heathland |
| Clydebank | Clydebank & District Golf Club | 18 | Parkland |
| | Clydebank Municipal Course | 18 | Parkland |
| Coatbridge | Coatbridge Golf Club | 18 | Parkland |
| | Drumpellier Golf Club | 18 | Parkland |
| Colonsay (Isle of) | Colonsay Golf Club | 18 | Links |
| Cumbernauld | Palacerigg Golf Club | 18 | Parkland |
| | Westerwood Hotel Golf & Country Club | 18 | Moorland |
| Cumbrae (Isle of) | Millport Golf Club | 18 | Heathland |
| Dalmally | Dalmally Golf Club | 9 | Parkland |
| Douglas Water | Douglas Water Golf Club | 9 | Parkland |
| Dullatur | Dullatur Golf Club | 36 | Parkland *email 11-28* |
| Dumbarton | Dumbarton Golf Club | 18 | Parkland |
| Dunoon | Cowal Golf Club | 18 | Heathland *email 12-10* |
| East Kilbride | East Kilbride Golf Club | 18 | Parkland |
| | Langlands Golf Course | 18 | Moorland |
| | Torrance House Golf Course | 18 | Parkland |
| Elderslie | Elderslie Golf Club | 18 | Parkland |
| Galston | Loudoun Gowf Club | 18 | Parkland |
| Gigha (Isle of) | Isle of Gigha Golf Club | 9 | Meadowland |
| Girvan | Brunston Castle Golf Club | 18 | Parkland |
| | Girvan Golf Course | 18 | Links/Parkland |
| Glasgow | Alexandra Park Golf Course | 9 | Parkland |
| | Bearsden Golf Club | 16 | Parkland *email 11-29* |
| | Bishopbriggs Golf Club | 18 | Parkland |
| | Blairbeth Golf Club | 18 | Parkland |
| | Bonnyton Golf Club | 18 | Moorland |
| | Cambuslang Golf Club | 9 | Parkland |
| | Cathcart Castle Golf Club | 18 | Parkland |
| | Cathkin Braes Golf Club | 18 | Moorland *email 11-28* |
| | Cawder Golf Club | 36 | Parkland |
| | Clober Golf Club | 18 | Parkland |
| | Cowglen Golf Club | 18 | Parkland |
| | Crow Wood Golf Club | 18 | Parkland |
| | Douglas Park Golf Club | 18 | Parkland |
| | Esporta Dougalston Golf Club | 18 | Parkland |
| | ~~Glasgow Golf Club (Killermont)~~ | 18 | Parkland |
| | Haggs Castle Golf Club | 18 | Parkland |
| | Hilton Park Golf Club | 36 | Moorland |
| | Kirkhill Golf Club | 18 | Meadowland |
| | Knightswood Golf Course | 9 | Parkland |
| | Lenzie Golf Club | 18 | Parkland |
| | Lethamhill Golf Course | 18 | Parkland |
| | Linn Park Golf Club | 18 | Parkland |

|  | Littlehill Golf Club | 18 | Parkland |
|  | Milngavie Golf Club | 18 | Moorland |
|  | Mount Ellen Golf Club | 18 | Parkland |
|  | Pollok Golf Club | 18 | Parkland |
|  | Rouken Glen Golf Centre | 18 | Parkland |
|  | Sandyhills Golf Club | 18 | Parkland |
|  | The East Renfrewshire Golf Club | 18 | Moorland |
|  | The Eastwood Golf Club | 18 | Moorland |
|  | Whitecraigs Golf Club | 18 | Parkland |
|  | Williamwood Golf Club | 18 | Parkland |
|  | Windyhill Golf Club | 18 | Parkland |
| Gleddoch | Gleddoch Golf & Country Club | 18 | Parkland |
| Gourock | Gourock Golf Club | 18 | Moorland |
| Greenock | Greenock Whinhill Golf Club | 18 | Heathland |
|  | The Greenock Golf Club | 27 | Moorland |
| Hamilton | Hamilton Golf Club | 18 | Parkland |
|  | Strathclyde Park Golf Course | 9 | Parkland |
| Helensburgh | Helensburgh Golf Club | 18 | Moorland |
| Hollandbush | Hollandbush Golf Club | 18 | Parkland |
| Innellan | Innellan Golf Club | 9 | Moorland |
| Inveraray | Inveraray Golf Club | 9 | Parkland |
| Irvine | Glasgow Gailes | 18 | Links |
|  | Irvine Golf Club | 18 | Heathland /Links |
|  | Ravenspark Golf Club | 18 | Parkland |
|  | Western Gailes Golf Club | 18 | Links |
| Islay (Isle of) | Islay Golf Club | 18 | Links |
| Johnstone | Cochrane Castle Golf Club | 18 | Parkland |
| Kilbirnie | Kilbirnie Place Golf Club | 18 | Parkland |
| Kilmacolm | Kilmacolm Golf Club | 18 | Moorland |
| Kilmarnock | Annanhill Golf Club | 18 | Parkland |
|  | Caprington Golf Club | 18 | Parkland |
| Kilsyth | Kilsyth Lennox Golf Club | 18 | Moorland |
| Kirkintilloch | Hayston Golf Club | 18 | Parkland |
|  | Kirkintilloch Golf Club | 18 | Parkland |
| Lanark | Lanark Golf Club | 27 | Moorland |
| Largs | Inverclyde National Golf Training Centre | 6 | Parkland |
|  | Largs Golf Club | 18 | Parkland |
|  | Routenburn Golf Club | 18 | Heathland |
| Larkhall | Larkhall Golf Club | 9 | Parkland |
| Leadhills | Leadhills Golf Club | 9 | Moorland |
| Lennoxtown | Campsie Golf Club | 18 | Parkland |
| Lochgilphead | Lochgilphead Golf Club | 9 | Parkland |
| Lochgoilhead | Drimsynie Golf Course | 9 | Parkland |
| Lochwinnoch | Lochwinnoch Golf Club | 18 | Parkland |
| Luss | Loch Lomond Golf Club | 18 | Parkland |

| Mauchline | Ballochmyle Golf Club | 18 | Parkland *email 12-10* |
|-----------|----------------------|----|----------|
| Maybole | Maybole Golf Club | 9 | Parkland |
| Motherwell | Colville Park Golf Club | 18 | Parkland |
| Muirkirk | Muirkirk Golf Club | 9 | Moorland |
| Mull (Isle of) | Craignure Golf Club | 9 | Links |
| | Tobermory Golf Club | 9 | Parkland |
| New Cumnock | New Cumnock Golf Club | 9 | Parkland |
| Oban | Glencruitten Golf Club | 18 | Parkland |
| | Isle of Eriska Golf Course | 6 | Links |
| | Isle of Seil Golf Club | 9 | Links |
| Paisley | Barshaw Golf Club | 18 | Parkland |
| | Ralston Golf Club | 18 | Parkland |
| | The Paisley Golf Club | 18 | Moorland |
| Patna | Doon Valley Golf Club | 9 | Parkland |
| Port Glasgow | Port Glasgow Golf Club | 18 | Moorland |
| ~~Prestwick~~ | Prestwick Golf Club | 18 | Links |
| | Prestwick St Cuthbert Golf Club | 18 | Parkland |
| | Prestwick St Nicholas Golf Club | 18 | Links |
| Renfrew | Renfrew Golf Club | 18 | Parkland |
| Shotts | Shotts Golf Club | 18 | Moorland |
| Skelmorlie | Skelmorlie Golf Club | 18 | Moorland |
| Stevenston | Ardeer Golf Club | 18 | Parkland |
| | Auchenharvie Golf Club | 9 | Parkland |
| Strathaven | Strathaven Golf Club | 18 | Parkland |
| Strone | Blairmore & Strone Golf Club | 9 | Moorland |
| Tarbert | Tarbert Golf Club | 9 | Heathland |
| Taynuilt | Taynuilt Golf Club | 9 | Parkland |
| Tighnabruaich | Kyles of Bute Golf Club | 9 | Moorland |
| Torrance | Balmore Golf Club Ltd | 18 | Parkland |
| Troon | Kilmarnock (Barassie) Golf Club | 27 | Links *email 11-21-04* |
| | ~~Royal Troon Golf Club~~ | 36 | Links |
| | Troon Municipal Golf Courses | 54 | Links |
| | (Lochgreen, Darley and Fullarton) | | |
| ~~Turnberry~~ | Turnberry Hotel Golf Courses | 36 | Links |
| Uddingston | Calderbraes Golf Club | 9 | Parkland |
| Uplawmoor | Caldwell Golf Club Ltd | 18 | Parkland *email 11-23* |
| West Kilbride | West Kilbride Golf Club | 18 | Links *email 11-23* |
| Wishaw | Wishaw Golf Club | 18 | Parkland |

## BORDERS INCLUDING HAWICK

| Ashkirk | The Woll Golf Course | 9 | Parkland |
|---------|---------------------|----|----------|
| Coldstream | The Hirsel Golf Club | 18 | Parkland |
| Duns | Duns Golf Club | 18 | Parkland *email 12-10* |
| Eyemouth | Eyemouth Golf Club | 18 | Links |
| Galashiels | Galashiels Golf Club | 18 | Parkland |
| | Torwoodlee Golf Club | 18 | Parkland *email 11-29* |
| Hawick | Hawick Golf Club | 18 | Moorland |

| | | | |
|---|---|---|---|
| Innerleithen | Innerleithen Golf Club | 9 | Parkland |
| Jedburgh | Jedburgh Golf Club | 9 | Parkland |
| Kelso | Kelso Golf Club | 18 | Parkland |
| | The Roxburghe Hotel & Golf Course | 18 | Parkland |
| Lauder | Lauder Golf Club | 9 | Moorland |
| Melrose | Melrose Golf Club | 9 | Parkland |
| Minto | Minto Golf Club | 18 | Parkland |
| Newcastleton | Newcastleton Golf Club | 9 | Moorland |
| Peebles | Peebles Golf Club | 18 | Parkland |
| Selkirk | Selkirk Golf Club | 9 | Heathland |
| St Boswells | St Boswells Golf Club | 9 | Parkland |

## DUMFRIES & GALLOWAY INCLUDING DUMFRIES & STRANRAER

| | | | |
|---|---|---|---|
| Annan | Powfoot Golf Club | 18 | Links |
| Castle Douglas | Castle Douglas Golf Club | 9 | Parkland |
| Colvend | Colvend Golf Club | 18 | Parkland |
| Dumfries | Crichton Golf Club | 9 | Parkland |
| | Dumfries & County Golf Club | 18 | Parkland |
| | Dumfries & Galloway Golf Club | 18 | Parkland |
| | The Pines Golf Centre | 18 | Parkland |
| Ecclefechan | Hoddom Castle Golf Club | 9 | Parkland |
| Gatehouse of Fleet | Cally Palace Hotel Golf Course | 18 | Parkland |
| | Gatehouse of Fleet Golf Club | 9 | Parkland |
| Gretna | Gretna Golf Club | 9 | Parkland |
| Kirkcudbright | Kirkcudbright Golf Club | 18 | Parkland |
| Langholm | Langholm Golf Club | 9 | Parkland |
| Lochmaben | Lochmaben Golf Club | 18 | Parkland |
| Lockerbie | Lockerbie Golf Club | 18 | Parkland |
| Moffat | The Moffat Golf Club | 18 | Moorland |
| Monreith | St Medan Golf Club | 9 | Links |
| New Galloway | New Galloway Golf Club | 9 | Moorland |
| Newton Stewart | Newton Stewart Golf Club | 18 | Parkland |
| | Wigtownshire County Golf Club | 18 | Links |
| Portpatrick | Lagganmore Golf Club | 18 | Parkland |
| | Portpatrick (Dunskey) Golf Club | 27 | Links |
| Sanquhar | Sanquhar Golf Club | 9 | Parkland |
| Southerness | Solway Links Golf Course | 11 | Links |
| | Southerness Golf Club | 18 | Links |
| Stranraer | Stranraer Golf Club | 18 | Parkland |
| Thornhill | Thornhill Golf Club | 18 | Heathland |
| Wigtown | Wigtown & Bladnoch Golf Club | 9 | Parkland |

## THE NORTHERN ISLES

| | | | |
|---|---|---|---|
| Orkney Isles | Orkney Golf Club | 18 | Parkland *e mail 11-29* |
| | Stromness Golf Club | 18 | Parkland *email 12-10* |
| | Westray Golf Club | 9 | Links |
| Shetland Isles | Shetland Golf Club | 18 | Moorland *e mail 11-29* |
| | Whalsay Golf Club | 18 | Moorland *e email* |

## THE WESTERN ISLES

| | | | |
|---|---|---|---|
| Barra (Isle of) | Barra Golf Club | 9 | Links |
| Harris (Isle of) | Isle of Harris Golf Club | 9 | Links |
| Lewis (Isle of) | Stornoway Golf Club | 18 | Parkland *email 11-29* |
| North Uist (Isle of) | Benbecula Golf Club | 9 | Parkland |
| South Uist (Isle of) | Askernish Golf Club | 9 | Meadowland |

# LOTHIANS INCLUDING EDINBURGH

# ABERLADY

## KILSPINDIE GOLF CLUB

### COURSE DESCRIPTION:
Taking up golf can be a daunting process. Pick the wrong course for your maiden voyage and it can end in tears with a vow never to repeat the experience. Select the right one and it can be an experience that lives with you for the rest of your golfing days. Kilspindie could fit perfectly into the latter category. Edinburgh and its environs abound with magnificent golf courses to meet any taste. Many golfers drive east of the city on their way to the world-famous Muirfield, Gullane and North Berwick not realising that a little gem is hidden away in the village of Aberlady. At 5,480 yards with a par of 69, this typical Scottish links is short enough to encourage the beginner but tight enough with well-bunkered holes to trouble the most accomplished when the wind blows. The 1st, played almost from the steps of the clubhouse, is a 167-yard par 3 with a generous green and it sets the mood before the course gets down to serious business. The 2nd is one of four holes bordering the Forth estuary: at 515 yards it is the longest which, like the 413-yard 3rd, is a challenge when the wind gets up. As on the 1st, the 18th green is so close to the clubhouse you could end up in the changing-rooms if you over-club from the tee 252 yards away. When my son was ten, I took him to Kilspindie for his first taste of golf. Armed only with a cut-down 7-iron and using my putter, he so enjoyed the experience that golf was to become his sport and he graduated to the US college circuit. As then, you can be assured of a friendly welcome on and off the course. Kilspindie are planning to open a second course in the near future.
18 holes, 5,480 yards, par 69 (SSS 66). Amateur record 60. Pro record 59.

### SIGNATURE HOLE:
EIGHTH (162 yards, par 3) From a new elevated tee, you play across Gosford Bay – after which it is named – to a far from generous green, close to a barrier of sleepers that provide protection from the tide. It is guarded by bunkers to the front and left, and there is little to spare at the back. On a calm day you could take a wedge but later, when the wind gets up, it might need a full-blooded driver.

### COURSE CARD

| HOLE | MEDAL YDS | PAR | LADIES YDS | PAR | HOLE | MEDAL YDS | PAR | LADIES YDS | PAR |
|------|-----------|-----|------------|-----|------|-----------|-----|------------|-----|
| 1 | 167 | 3 | 156 | 3 | 10 | 155 | 3 | 145 | 3 |
| 2 | 515 | 5 | 490 | 5 | 11 | 295 | 4 | 266 | 4 |
| 3 | 413 | 4 | 369 | 4 | 12 | 269 | 4 | 265 | 4 |
| 4 | 365 | 4 | 336 | 4 | 13 | 185 | 3 | 152 | 3 |
| 5 | 290 | 4 | 282 | 4 | 14 | 339 | 4 | 294 | 4 |
| 6 | 279 | 4 | 268 | 4 | 15 | 436 | 4 | 420 | 5 |

| | | | | | | | | | |
|---|---|---|---|---|---|---|---|---|---|
| 7 | 384 | 4 | 350 | 4 | 16 | 412 | 4 | 379 | 4 |
| 8 | 162 | 3 | 144 | 3 | 17 | 276 | 4 | 259 | 4 |
| 9 | 286 | 4 | 280 | 4 | 18 | 252 | 4 | 240 | 3 |
| Yds Out | 2,861 | | 2,675 | | Yds In | 2,619 | | 2,420 | |
| Total Yds | 5,480 | | 5,095 | | | | | | |
| Total Par | 69 | | | | | | | | |

ADDRESS: The Clubhouse, Aberlady, East Lothian EH32 0QD.
TELEPHONE: +44 (0)1875 870358.
SECRETARY: Bob McInnes.
PROFESSIONAL: Graham Sked +44 (0)1875 870695
VISITORS: After 9.15 a.m. weekdays. After 10.30 a.m. weekends.
GREEN FEES: £27.50 per round weekdays, £44 per day. £33 per round weekends, £55 per day.
CATERING: Full catering facilities and bar snacks available.
FACILITIES: Trolley hire, putting green, pro shop, practice ground.
LOCATION: 24 miles east of Edinburgh on A198.
LOCAL HOTELS: Cringletie House Hotel, Dalhousie Castle & Spa Hotel, Greywalls, Kilspindie House Hotel, Marine Hotel, The Goldenstones, The Golf Hotel, The Nether Abbey.

## LUFFNESS NEW GOLF CLUB

COURSE DESCRIPTION:
Championship links course. Final qualifying course when the Open is held at Muirfield.

18 holes, 6,122 yards, par 69 (SSS 70). Amateur record R. Winchester 63. Pro record C. O'Connor 62.

SIGNATURE HOLE:
THIRD (196 yards, par 3) Challenging. 6-iron to 3-wood depending on the wind.

COURSE CARD

| HOLE | YDS | PAR | HOLE | YDS | PAR |
|---|---|---|---|---|---|
| 1 | 332 | 4 | 10 | 176 | 3 |
| 2 | 420 | 4 | 11 | 445 | 4 |
| 3 | 196 | 3 | 12 | 336 | 4 |
| 4 | 531 | 5 | 13 | 393 | 4 |
| 5 | 326 | 4 | 14 | 435 | 4 |
| 6 | 155 | 3 | 15 | 346 | 4 |
| 7 | 293 | 4 | 16 | 163 | 3 |
| 8 | 383 | 4 | 17 | 349 | 4 |

| 9 | 427 | 4 | 18 | 416 | 4 |
|---|---|---|---|---|---|
| Yds | 3,063 | | Yds | 3,059 | |
| Out | | | In | | |
| Total Yds | 6,122 | | | | |
| Total Par | 69 | | | | |

ADDRESS: Aberlady, East Lothian EH32 0QA.
TELEPHONE: +44 (0)1620 843336.
FAX: +44 (0)1620 842933.
SECRETARY: Lt.-Col. Ian Tedford.
VISITORS: Weekdays, except public holidays.
GREEN FEES: £37.50 per round, £55 per day.
CATERING: Restaurant and bar.
FACILITIES: Motorised buggies, trolleys, putting green, pro shop, practice ground.
LOCATION: Between Aberlady and Gullane on A198.
LOCAL HOTELS: Cringletie House Hotel, Dalhousie Castle & Spa Hotel, Greywalls, Kilspindie House Hotel, Mallard Hotel, Marine Hotel, Old Aberlady Inn, The Goldenstones, The Golf Hotel, The Nether Abbey.

# BATHGATE

## BALBARDIE PARK GOLF CLUB

COURSE DESCRIPTION:
Challenging par 3 course with good greens.
    9 holes, 2,474 yards.

ADDRESS: Balbardie Park, Bathgate, West Lothian EH48 4LE.
TELEPHONE: +44 (0)1506 776790.
VISITORS: Any time.
GREEN FEES: £3.25 weekdays, juniors £1.75. £4.60 weekends.
CATERING: Snacks only.
FACILITIES: Practice green.
LOCATION: North side of Bathgate off Torphichen Road.
LOCAL HOTELS: Dreadnought Hotel, Fairway Hotel, Kaim Park Hotel.

## BATHGATE GOLF CLUB

COURSE DESCRIPTION:
Pleasant parkland easy-walking course, which has produced two Ryder Cup captains, Bernard Gallacher and Eric Brown.
    18 holes, 6,326 yards, par 71 (SSS 70). Course record Sam Torrance 58.

## COURSE CARD

| HOLE | YDS | PAR | HOLE | YDS | PAR |
|------|-----|-----|------|-----|-----|
| 1 | 476 | 5 | 10 | 398 | 4 |
| 2 | 451 | 4 | 11 | 175 | 3 |
| 3 | 329 | 4 | 12 | 505 | 5 |
| 4 | 216 | 3 | 13 | 215 | 3 |
| 5 | 480 | 5 | 14 | 429 | 4 |
| 6 | 400 | 4 | 15 | 504 | 5 |
| 7 | 373 | 4 | 16 | 337 | 4 |
| 8 | 145 | 3 | 17 | 142 | 3 |
| 9 | 346 | 4 | 18 | 405 | 4 |
| *Yds Out* | 3,216 | | *Yds In* | 3,110 | |
| *Total Yds* | 6,326 | | | | |
| *Total Par* | 71 | | | | |

ADDRESS: Edinburgh Road, Bathgate EH48 1BA.
SECRETARY: W. Osborne +44 (0)1506 630505.
PROFESSIONAL: Sandy Strachan +44 (0)1506 630553.
VISITORS: Welcome any time. Societies on weekdays.
GREEN FEES: £17 per round weekdays, £22 per day. £33 per day weekends.
CATERING: Full catering and bar service all week.
FACILITIES: Trolley/buggy hire, club hire, putting green, pro shop, practice ground.
LOCATION: 5 minutes' walk from town and train station.
LOCAL HOTELS: Dreadnought Hotel, Fairway Hotel, Kaim Park Hotel.

# BONNYRIGG

## BROOMIEKNOWE GOLF CLUB LTD

COURSE DESCRIPTION:
Interesting mature parkland course. Elevated with good views.
18 holes, 6,150 yards, par 70 (SSS 70). Course record 65.

## COURSE CARD

| HOLE | YDS | PAR | HOLE | YDS | PAR |
|------|-----|-----|------|-----|-----|
| 1 | 316 | 4 | 10 | 402 | 4 |
| 2 | 347 | 4 | 11 | 183 | 3 |
| 3 | 369 | 4 | 12 | 441 | 4 |
| 4 | 321 | 4 | 13 | 430 | 4 |
| 5 | 167 | 3 | 14 | 408 | 4 |
| 6 | 401 | 4 | 15 | 153 | 3 |

| 7 | 468 | 4 | 16 | 297 | 4 |
| 8 | 470 | 5 | 17 | 309 | 4 |
| 9 | 350 | 4 | 18 | 318 | 4 |
| *Yds* *Out* | 3,209 | | *Yds* *In* | 2,941 | |
| *Total* *Yds* | 6,150 | | | | |
| *Total* *Par* | 70 | | | | |

ADDRESS: 36 Golf Course Road, Bonnyrigg EH19 2HZ.
TELEPHONE: +44 (0)131 663 9317.
FAX: +44 (0)131 663 2152.
SECRETARY: John White.
PROFESSIONAL: Mark Patchett +4 (0)131 660 2035.
VISITORS: Midweek after 9.30 a.m.
GREEN FEES: £19 per round weekdays, £25 per day. £28 per round weekends.
CATERING: Bar snacks, lunches, high teas Tuesday to Sunday.
FACILITIES: Trolley hire, putting green, pro shop, practice ground. Independent
   driving range next to course.
LOCATION: 1½ miles west of roundabout on A7/A6094.
LOCAL HOTELS: Dalhousie Castle & Spa Hotel, Esbank Hotel.

# DALKEITH

## NEWBATTLE GOLF CLUB LTD

COURSE DESCRIPTION:
Undulating wooded parkland course. Beware the River Esk, which comes into play
on the 2nd and 17th holes.
   18 holes, 6,025 yards, par 69 (SSS 70). Course record 61.

ADDRESS: Abbey Road, Dalkeith EH22 3AD.
TELEPHONE: +44 (0)131 663 2123 or 663 1819.
PROFESSIONAL: Scott McDonald +44 (0)131 660 1631.
VISITORS: Weekdays before 4 p.m., except public holidays. Societies welcome.
GREEN FEES: £17 per round, £25 per day.
CATERING: Yes. Bar.
FACILITIES: Trolley hire, putting green, pro shop, practice ground.
LOCATION: South-west of town off A68.
LOCAL HOTELS: Dalhousie Castle & Spa Hotel, Esbank Hotel, Parliament House
   Hotel, Peebles Hotel Hydro

# DALMAHOY

## MARRIOTT DALMAHOY HOTEL GOLF & COUNTRY CLUB

**COURSE DESCRIPTION:**
Set in over 1,000 acres of fine Scottish woodland and almost in the shadow of the Pentland Hills, Dalmahoy, designed by James Braid in 1927, offers something special for every golfer. A regular European Tour venue, it is only seven miles from Edinburgh. There are two outstanding courses, meandering around the lake and across picturesque streams. The West Course is the easier of the two and features some spectacular crossings of the Gogar Burn. The trickier East Course is a greater challenge.

*East course* (card below) – 18 holes, 6,642 yards, par 72 (SSS 72). Amateur record M. Backhausen, F. Jacobsen 65. Pro record Brian Barnes 62.

*West course* – 18 holes, 5,168 yards, par 68 (SSS 66). Amateur record D. Brown, H. McConkey, J. Still 66.

**SIGNATURE HOLE:**
FIFTEENTH (150 yards, par 3) Called 'The Wee Wrecker' and not without reason.

**COURSE CARD**

| HOLE | MEDAL YDS | PAR | FORWARD YDS | PAR | LADIES YDS | PAR | HOLE | MEDAL YDS | PAR | FORWARD YDS | PAR | LADIES YDS | PAR |
|---|---|---|---|---|---|---|---|---|---|---|---|---|---|
| 1 | 496 | 5 | 478 | 5 | 403 | 5 | 10 | 505 | 5 | 486 | 5 | 384 | 4 |
| 2 | 406 | 4 | 380 | 4 | 390 | 4 | 11 | 433 | 4 | 426 | 4 | 416 | 5 |
| 3 | 427 | 4 | 412 | 4 | 408 | 5 | 12 | 409 | 4 | 396 | 4 | 391 | 4 |
| 4 | 143 | 3 | 138 | 3 | 126 | 3 | 13 | 425 | 4 | 407 | 4 | 351 | 4 |
| 5 | 304 | 4 | 301 | 4 | 296 | 4 | 14 | 457 | 4 | 444 | 4 | 407 | 5 |
| 6 | 392 | 4 | 385 | 4 | 359 | 4 | 15 | 150 | 3 | 140 | 3 | 137 | 3 |
| 7 | 204 | 3 | 347 | 4 | 331 | 4 | 16 | 423 | 4 | 416 | 4 | 403 | 5 |
| 8 | 354 | 4 | 347 | 4 | 331 | 4 | 17 | 305 | 4 | 300 | 4 | 295 | 4 |
| 9 | 480 | 5 | 471 | 4 | 448 | 5 | 18 | 329 | 4 | 289 | 4 | 208 | 4 |
| Yds Out | 3,206 | | 3,085 | | 2,894 | | Yds In | 3,436 | | 3,304 | | 2,993 | |
| Total Yds | 6,642 | | 6,389 | | 5,887 | | | | | | | | | |
| Total Par | 72 | | 71 | | 75 | | | | | | | | | |

**ADDRESS:** Kirknewton, Midlothian EH27 8EB.
**TELEPHONE:** +44 (0)131 333 1845.
**FAX:** +44 (0)131 333 1433.
**E-MAIL:** golf.dalmahoy@marriotthotels.co.uk
**DIRECTOR OF GOLF & COUNTRY CLUB:** Iain Burns.
**SECRETARY:** Jennifer Bryans.

VISITORS: Weekdays.

GREEN FEES: East Course: £69 per round weekdays, £85 weekends (Hotel residents £49/£65). West Course: £49 per round weekdays, £65 weekends (Hotel residents £39/£49).

CATERING: Excellent facilities in Country Club (Terrace Restaurant & Club Bar).

FACILITIES: Trolley/buggy hire, club hire, changing-rooms, putting green, pro shop, practice ground, floodlit driving range.

LOCATION: South-west of Edinburgh off A71. Travelling from Glasgow, leave M8 at junction 3, using A599 to link with A71.

LOCAL HOTELS: Marriott Dalmahoy Hotel & Country Club, Parliament House Hotel.

# DUNBAR

## DUNBAR GOLF CLUB

### COURSE DESCRIPTION:

Championship links. Became an Open qualifying course in 1992. Club dates back to 1856 but some records suggest it may have been founded in 1794. Old Tom Morris designed the first 15 holes. The sea is a lateral water hazard on some holes and when windy it is a formidable test for even the best of golfers.

18 holes, 6,426 yards, par 71 (SSS 71). Course record 64.

### COURSE CARD

| HOLE | YDS | PAR | HOLE | YDS | PAR |
|------|-----|-----|------|-----|-----|
| 1 | 477 | 5 | 10 | 202 | 3 |
| 2 | 494 | 5 | 11 | 417 | 4 |
| 3 | 172 | 3 | 12 | 459 | 4 |
| 4 | 349 | 4 | 13 | 378 | 4 |
| 5 | 148 | 3 | 14 | 433 | 4 |
| 6 | 350 | 4 | 15 | 343 | 4 |
| 7 | 386 | 4 | 16 | 166 | 3 |
| 8 | 369 | 4 | 17 | 339 | 4 |
| 9 | 507 | 5 | 18 | 437 | 4 |
| Yds Out | 3,252 | | Yds In | 3,174 | |
| Total Yds | 6,426 | | | | |
| Total Par | 71 | | | | |

ADDRESS: East Links, Dunbar EH42 1LT.

TELEPHONE: +44 (0)1368 862317.

FAX: +44 (0)1368 865202.

SECRETARY: Colin McWhannell.

PROFESSIONAL: Jacky Montgomery +44 (0)1368 862086.

VISITORS: Yes, except Thursdays.
GREEN FEES: £32 per round weekdays, £42 per day. £38 per round weekends.
CATERING: Yes. Bar.
FACILITIES: Trolley hire, putting green, pro shop, practice ground.
LOCATION: 27 miles east of Edinburgh. Off the A1.
LOCAL HOTELS: Dalhousie Castle & Spa Hotel, Hillside Hotel, Royal Mackintosh Hotel.

## WINTERFIELD GOLF CLUB

COURSE DESCRIPTION:
Seaside links course relatively flat but undulating. Greens are quite fast.
    18 holes, 5,220 yards, par 65 (SSS 64).

ADDRESS: North Road, Dunbar EH42 1AY.
TELEPHONE: +44 (0)1368 865119.
PROFESSIONAL: Kevin Phillips +44 (0)1368 863562.
VISITORS: Contact in advance.
GREEN FEES: £14.50 per round weekdays, £19 per day. £16.50 per round weekends, £25 per day.
CATERING: Bar. Available April to September.
LOCATION: West of town, off A1087.
LOCAL HOTELS: Bayswell Hotel, Dalhousie Castle & Spa Hotel.

# EDINBURGH

## BABERTON GOLF CLUB

COURSE DESCRIPTION:
Inland parkland course designed by Willie Park Jnr.
    18 holes, 6,123 yards, par 69 (SSS 70). Amateur record D. Beveridge Jnr, R. Bradly, B. Tait 64. Pro record Brian Barnes 62.

SIGNATURE HOLE:
THIRTEENTH (383 yards, par 4) A fine driving hole. Trees to the right and left of the landing area. The second shot is to an elevated, two-tiered green.

COURSE CARD

| HOLE | YDS | PAR | HOLE | YDS | PAR |
|------|-----|-----|------|-----|-----|
| 1 | 404 | 4 | 10 | 342 | 4 |
| 2 | 494 | 5 | 11 | 212 | 3 |
| 3 | 357 | 4 | 12 | 472 | 4 |
| 4 | 304 | 4 | 13 | 383 | 4 |
| 5 | 230 | 3 | 14 | 125 | 3 |
| 6 | 369 | 4 | 15 | 487 | 5 |

| 7 | 393 | 4 | 16 | 464 | 4 |
|---|-----|---|----|-----|---|
| 8 | 199 | 3 | 17 | 152 | 3 |
| 9 | 319 | 4 | 18 | 417 | 4 |
| *Yds* *Out* | 3,069 | | *Yds* *In* | 3,054 | |
| *Total* *Yds* | 6,123 | | | | |
| *Total* *Par* | 69 | | | | |

ADDRESS: 50 Baberton Avenue, Juniper Green, Edinburgh EH14 5DU.
TELEPHONE: +44 (0)131 453 4911.
SECRETARY: Eric Horberry.
PROFESSIONAL: Ken Kelly +44 (0)131 453 3555.
VISITORS: Monday to Friday 9.30 a.m. to 3.30 p.m and weekends.
GREEN FEES: £22 per round weekdays, £32 per day. £25 per round weekends, £35 per day.
CATERING: Available. Bar.
FACILITIES: Trolley hire, putting green, pro shop, practice ground.
LOCATION: 5 miles south-west of city centre off A70.
LOCAL HOTELS: Braids Hills Hotel, Royal Scot Hotel.

## BRAID HILLS GOLF CLUB

COURSE DESCRIPTION:
Municipal heathland course. Can be hard physically with lots of hills to climb. The No. 2 course is even higher. Good views of Edinburgh and the Firth of Forth.
   *Course 1* – 18 holes, 6,172 yards, par 70 (SSS 68). Course record 62.
   *Course 2* – 18 holes, 4,832 yards, par 65 (SSS 63).

ADDRESS: Braid Hills Approach, Edinburgh EH10 6JZ.
TELEPHONE: +44 (0)131 452 9408.
PROFESSIONAL: +44 (0)131 447 6666.
VISITORS: May not play on Saturday mornings. Closed on Sundays. No. 2 Course open seven days a week from April to September.
GREEN FEES: £10 per round, £12.50 at weekends.
CATERING: Full range at Braid Hills Hotel.
FACILITIES: Trolley hire, putting green, pro shop, practice ground.
LOCATION: 2½ miles south of city centre off A702.
LOCAL HOTELS: Braid Hills Hotel, Cringletie House Hotel, Parliament House Hotel.

## CARRICK KNOWE COURSE

COURSE DESCRIPTION:
Municipal flat parkland course with a few groups of trees and a number of testing holes. Said to be one of the busiest courses in Europe.
   18 holes, 6,299 yards, par 71 (SSS 70).

ADDRESS: Glendevon Park, Edinburgh EH12 5UZ.
TELEPHONE: +44 (0)131 337 1096.
VISITORS: May be restricted at weekends.
GREEN FEES: £10 per round, £12.50 at weekends.
CATERING: No.
FACILITIES: Trolley hire, small practice ground.
LOCATION: 3 miles west of city centre, south of A8.
LOCAL HOTELS: Forte Posthouse.

## CRAIGENTINNY GOLF COURSE

COURSE DESCRIPTION:
Municipal course. Generally flat, although some hillocks with gentle slopes. Good views of Arthur's Seat.
    18 holes, 5,418 yards, par 67 (SSS 65).

ADDRESS: Fillyside Road, Lochend EH7 6RG.
TELEPHONE: +44 (0)131 554 7501.
VISITORS: Any time.
GREEN FEES: £10 per round weekdays, £12.50 weekends.
FACILITIES: Trolley hire, practice ground.
LOCATION: North-east side of city between Leith and Portobello.
LOCAL HOTELS: King James Thistle Hotel, Parliament House Hotel

## CRAIGMILLAR PARK GOLF CLUB

COURSE DESCRIPTION:
Founded in 1896 and designed by James Braid. Parkland course, set around Blackford Hill, the site of the Royal Observatory, with panoramic views over Edinburgh.
    18 holes, 5,851 yards, par 70 (SSS 69). Course record 64.

SIGNATURE HOLE:
SIXTEENTH (402 yards, par 4) Played into prevailing west wind and requires an accurate tee shot and a well-hit second to a well-trapped green.

COURSE CARD

| HOLE | YDS | PAR | HOLE | YDS | PAR |
|---|---|---|---|---|---|
| 1 | 351 | 4 | 10 | 351 | 4 |
| 2 | 269 | 4 | 11 | 128 | 3 |
| 3 | 254 | 3 | 12 | 411 | 4 |
| 4 | 465 | 4 | 13 | 150 | 3 |
| 5 | 424 | 4 | 14 | 505 | 5 |
| 6 | 284 | 4 | 15 | 168 | 3 |
| 7 | 206 | 3 | 16 | 402 | 4 |
| 8 | 297 | 4 | 17 | 493 | 5 |
| 9 | 331 | 4 | 18 | 362 | 4 |

| | | | |
|---|---|---|---|
| *Yds* | 2,881 | *Yds* | 2,970 |
| *Out* | | *In* | |
| *Total* | 5,851 | | |
| *Yds* | | | |
| *Total* | 70 | | |
| *Par* | | | |

**ADDRESS:** 1 Observatory Road, Edinburgh EH9 3HG.
**TELEPHONE:** +44 (0)131 667 0047.
**SECRETARY:** Tom Lawson.
**PROFESSIONAL:** Brian McGhee +44 (0)131 667 2850.
**VISITORS:** Yes.
**GREEN FEES:** £18 per round weekdays, £26 per day. £25 per round weekends.
**CATERING:** Bar lunches, high teas, à la carte available.
**FACILITIES:** Trolley hire, putting green, pro shop, practice ground.
**LOCATION:** 10 minutes from city centre. A71 to Cameron Toll roundabout, right up Esslemont Road, past King's Buildings and course is on the left.
**LOCAL HOTELS:** Iona Hotel.

## DUDDINGSTON GOLF CLUB

**COURSE DESCRIPTION:**
Undulating parkland, semi-seaside course with stream. Easy walking and windy.
18 holes, 6,647 yards, par 72 (SSS 72).

**ADDRESS:** Duddingston Road West, Duddingston, Edinburgh EH15 3QD.
**TELEPHONE:** +44 (0)131 661 7688.
**PROFESSIONAL & FAX:** Alastair McLean +44 (0)131 661 4301.
**VISITORS:** May not play weekends. Societies Tuesdays and Thursdays only.
**GREEN FEES:** £29 per round, £36 per day.
**CATERING:** Bar.
**FACILITIES:** Pro shop.
**LOCATION:** 2½ miles south-east of city centre off A1.
**LOCAL HOTELS:** Parliament House Hotel.

## KINGSKNOWE GOLF CLUB

**COURSE DESCRIPTION:**
Well-kept undulating parkland course.
18 holes, 5,979 yards, par 69 (SSS 69). Course record 69.

**SIGNATURE HOLE:**
SIXTEENTH (460 yards, par 4) Slight dogleg down valley. Long drive required to get home in two. Tree plantations both sides. Green well bunkered.

## COURSE CARD

| HOLE | YDS | PAR | HOLE | YDS | PAR |
|------|------|-----|------|------|-----|
| 1 | 168 | 3 | 10 | 392 | 4 |
| 2 | 303 | 4 | 11 | 149 | 3 |
| 3 | 488 | 5 | 12 | 316 | 4 |
| 4 | 364 | 4 | 13 | 422 | 4 |
| 5 | 432 | 4 | 14 | 307 | 4 |
| 6 | 326 | 4 | 15 | 230 | 3 |
| 7 | 345 | 4 | 16 | 460 | 4 |
| 8 | 416 | 4 | 17 | 335 | 4 |
| 9 | 223 | 3 | 18 | 303 | 4 |
| *Yds* *Out* | 3,065 | | *Yds* *In* | 2,914 | |
| *Total* *Yds* | 5,979 | | | | |
| *Total* *Par* | 69 | | | | |

ADDRESS: 326 Lanark Road, Edinburgh EH14 2JD.
TELEPHONE: +44 (0)131 441 1145.
FAX: +44 (0)131 441 2079.
E-MAIL: kingsknowe.golfclub@virgin.net
SECRETARY: Katie Swinton.
PROFESSIONAL: Chris Morris +44 (0)131 441 4030.
VISITORS: Yes.
GREEN FEES: £22 per round weekdays, £30 per day. £35 per round weekends.
CATERING: Restaurant and bar. No catering Tuesdays. Functions catered for.
FACILITIES: Motorised buggies, trolley hire, changing-rooms, putting green, pro shop, practice ground, driving nets, coaching clinics.
LOCATION: South-west outskirts of Edinburgh on A70.
LOCAL HOTELS: Forte Posthouse, Orwell Lodge, Royal Ettrick Hotel

# LIBERTON GOLF CLUB

COURSE DESCRIPTION:
Pleasant parkland course with five par 3s. Wooded and undulating with tightly bunkered greens.
18 holes, 5,306 yards, par 67 (SSS 66). Course record 61.

SIGNATURE HOLE:
EIGHTH (193 yards par 3) Played alongside clubhouse from elevated tee.

ADDRESS: Kingston Grange, 297 Gilmerton Road, Edinburgh EH16 5OJ.
TELEPHONE: +44 (0)131 664 3009.
FAX: +44 (0)131 666 0853.
SECRETARY: Tom Watson.
PROFESSIONAL: Iain Seath +44 (0)131 664 1056.

VISITORS: No societies at weekends.
GREEN FEES: £20 per round weekdays. £30 per round weekends.
CATERING: Full catering facilities.
FACILITIES: Practice ground.
LOCATION: 3 miles from city centre on A7.
LOCAL HOTELS: Eskbank Hotel, Parliament House Hotel.

## LOTHIANBURN GOLF CLUB

### COURSE DESCRIPTION:
Wooded hillside course in the Pentland foothills. The course, which was designed by James Braid in 1929, rises from the clubhouse 300 feet to its highest point at the 13th green. Testing when windy. A reputation for good greens – some of which, it is claimed, are faster than those at the Augusta National, home of the US Masters.
    18 holes, 5,662 yards, par 71 (SSS 68). Amateur record 66.

### SIGNATURE HOLE:
SEVENTEENTH ('The Valley' 302 yards, par 4) Into prevailing wind with gorse on both sides of tight fairway to a well-protected plateau green.

### COURSE CARD

| HOLE | MEDAL YDS | PAR | FORWARD YDS | PAR | LADIES YDS | PAR | HOLE | MEDAL YDS | PAR | FORWARD YDS | PAR | LADIES YDS | PAR |
|---|---|---|---|---|---|---|---|---|---|---|---|---|---|
| 1 | 270 | 4 | 236 | 4 | 263 | 4 | 10 | 109 | 3 | 106 | 3 | 99 | 3 |
| 2 | 162 | 3 | 144 | 3 | 122 | 3 | 11 | 278 | 4 | 267 | 4 | 256 | 4 |
| 3 | 437 | 4 | 427 | 4 | 424 | 5 | 12 | 300 | 4 | 293 | 4 | 290 | 4 |
| 4 | 414 | 4 | 407 | 4 | 359 | 4 | 13 | 243 | 4 | 228 | 4 | 209 | 4 |
| 5 | 312 | 4 | 295 | 4 | 231 | 4 | 14 | 580 | 5 | 558 | 5 | 558 | 5 |
| 6 | 143 | 3 | 135 | 3 | 135 | 3 | 15 | 351 | 4 | 303 | 4 | 293 | 4 |
| 7 | 476 | 5 | 460 | 5 | 447 | 5 | 16 | 320 | 4 | 306 | 4 | 293 | 4 |
| 8 | 354 | 4 | 355 | 4 | 302 | 4 | 17 | 302 | 4 | 307 | 4 | 180 | 3 |
| 9 | 335 | 4 | 314 | 4 | 325 | 5 | 18 | 276 | 4 | 281 | 4 | 222 | 3 |
| Yds Out | 2,903 | | 2,773 | | 2,608 | | Yds In | 2,759 | | 2,649 | | 2,350 | |
| Total Yds | 5,662 | | 5,422 | | 4,958 | | | | | | | | |
| Total Par | 71 | | 71 | | 70 | | | | | | | | |

ADDRESS: 106A Biggar Road, Fairmilehead, Edinburgh EH10 7DU.
TELEPHONE: +44 (0)131 445 5067.
SECRETARY: W.F.A. Jardine.
PROFESSIONAL: Kurt Mungall +44 (0)131 445 2288.
VISITORS: Yes, weekdays and some weekends.
GREEN FEES: £16.50 per round weekdays, £22.50 per day. £22.50 per round weekends, £27.50 per day. Special offer: one round Mondays between 9 a.m. and 3 p.m., £10.

CATERING: Bar and meals. Functions catered for. Members' club – no catering on Wednesdays.

FACILITIES: Trolley hire, club hire, changing-rooms, putting green, pro shop, practice ground, memberships available.

LOCATION: From the Edinburgh city bypass, take the Lothianburn exit and proceed south on the A702 Abington/Carlisle road for approximately 200 metres. Clubhouse and course on the right.

LOCAL HOTELS: Braid Hills Hotel, Cringletie House Hotel, Parliament House Hotel.

## MERCHANTS OF EDINBURGH GOLF CLUB

### COURSE DESCRIPTION:

Shot-testing course, a mixture of hills and parkland. Some hidden greens.
18 holes, 4,889 yards, par 65 (SSS 64). Course record 59.

### SIGNATURE HOLE:

THIRTEENTH (208 yards, par 3) Elevated tee with shot to a well-bunkered green below. Splendid views.

### COURSE CARD

| HOLE | YDS | PAR | HOLE | YDS | PAR |
|------|------|-----|------|-------|-----|
| 1 | 244 | 3 | 10 | 289 | 4 |
| 2 | 246 | 4 | 11 | 175 | 3 |
| 3 | 174 | 3 | 12 | 163 | 3 |
| 4 | 400 | 4 | 13 | 208 | 3 |
| 5 | 253 | 4 | 14 | 328 | 4 |
| 6 | 406 | 4 | 15 | 254 | 4 |
| 7 | 118 | 3 | 16 | 369 | 4 |
| 8 | 406 | 4 | 17 | 160 | 3 |
| 9 | 414 | 4 | 18 | 282 | 4 |
| *Yds Out* | 2,661 | | *Yds In* | 2,228 | |
| *Total Yds* | 4,889 | | | | |
| *Total Par* | 65 | | | | |

ADDRESS: 10 Craighill Gardens, Edinburgh EH10 5PY

TELEPHONE: +44 (0)131 447 1219.

SECRETARY: A. Montgomery.

PROFESSIONAL: Neil Colquhoun +44(0)131 447 8709.

VISITORS: Yes, but not weekends or after 4 p.m. weekdays.

GREEN FEES: £15 per round, £20 per day.

CATERING: Yes, but not Wednesday afternoons or all day Thursdays.

FACILITIES: Trolley hire, putting green, pro shop.

LOCATION: 2 miles south-west of city centre off A702.

LOCAL HOTELS: Braid Hills Hotel, Cringletie House Hotel, Parliament House Hotel.

## MORTONHALL GOLF CLUB

COURSE DESCRIPTION:
Moorland course with views over Edinburgh.
    18 holes, 6,557 yards, par 72 (SSS 71). Course record 66.

ADDRESS: 231 Braid Road, Mortonhall, Edinburgh EH10 6PB.
TELEPHONE: +44 (0)131 447 6974.
FAX: +44 (0)131 447 8712.
PROFESSIONAL: Douglas Horn +44 (0)131 447 5185.
VISITORS: Contact in advance. Societies may not play at weekends.
GREEN FEES: £30 per round weekdays/weekends, £40 per day.
CATERING: Full service. Bar.
FACILITIES: Trolley hire, putting green, pro shop, practice ground.
LOCATION: 3 miles south of city centre off A702.
LOCAL HOTELS: Braid Hills Hotel, Cringletie House Hotel, Parliament House Hotel.

## MURRAYFIELD GOLF CLUB LTD

COURSE DESCRIPTION:
Hilly parkland course just three miles from Edinburgh city centre. Picturesque
with good views.
    18 holes, 5,765 yards, par 70 (SSS 69).

ADDRESS: 43 Murrayfield Road, Edinburgh EH12 6EU.
TELEPHONE: +44 (0)131 337 3478.
FAX: +44 (0)131 313 0721.
MANAGER: Mrs M.K.Thomson.
PROFESSIONAL: J.J. Fisher.
VISITORS: Limited weekdays. Not on weekends.
GREEN FEES: On application.
CATERING: Bar and meals.
FACILITIES: Trolley hire, club hire, changing-rooms, putting green, pro shop.
LOCATION: 3 miles from city centre, near Murrayfield rugby ground. Approximately
    5 miles from Edinburgh Airport.
LOCAL HOTELS: Braid Hills Hotel, Cringletie House Hotel, Ellersly House, Murrayfield
    Hotel.

## PORTOBELLO GOLF CLUB

COURSE DESCRIPTION:
Municipal parkland course with some trees and no hazards. Easy walking.
    9 holes, 4,800 yards (for 18 holes), par 64 (SSS 64).

ADDRESS: Stanley Street, Portobello, Edinburgh EH15 1JJ.
TELEPHONE: +44 (0)131 669 4361.

VISITORS: May not play Saturdays between 8.30 a.m. and 10 a.m. and between 12.30 p.m. and 2 p.m. and on competition days.
GREEN FEES: £4.35 for 9 holes weekdays, £4.85 weekends.
FACILITIES: Trolley hire.
LOCATION: 3 miles east of city centre off A1.
LOCAL HOTELS: Donmaree Hotel, Parliament House Hotel

## PRESTONFIELD GOLF CLUB

COURSE DESCRIPTION:
Parkland course with good views. Busy club with 850 members.
 18 holes, 6,212 yards, par 70 (SSS 70). Amateur record A. Dun 62 (1976).

COURSE CARD

| HOLE | YDS | PAR | HOLE | YDS | PAR |
|------|------|-----|------|------|-----|
| 1 | 290 | 4 | 10 | 366 | 4 |
| 2 | 151 | 3 | 11 | 440 | 4 |
| 3 | 551 | 5 | 12 | 436 | 4 |
| 4 | 451 | 4 | 13 | 145 | 3 |
| 5 | 179 | 3 | 14 | 353 | 4 |
| 6 | 377 | 4 | 15 | 370 | 4 |
| 7 | 508 | 5 | 16 | 256 | 4 |
| 8 | 432 | 4 | 17 | 436 | 4 |
| 9 | 146 | 3 | 18 | 325 | 4 |
| *Yds Out* | 3,085 | | *Yds In* | 3,127 | |
| *Total Yds* | 6,212 | | | | |
| *Total Par* | 70 | | | | |

ADDRESS: 6 Priestfield Road North, Edinburgh EH16 5HS.
TELEPHONE: +44 (0)131 667 9665.
WEBSITE: www.prestonfieldgolfclub.co.uk
PROFESSIONAL: John Macfarlane +44 (0)131 667 8597.
VISITORS: Yes, unrestricted weekdays. Saturdays not available between 8 a.m. and 10. 30 a.m. and between 12 noon and 1.30 p.m. Sundays not available before 11 a.m.
GREEN FEES: £20 per round weekdays, £30 per day. £30 per round weekends, £40 per day.
CATERING: Full range. Bar.
FACILITIES: Motorised buggies (£12), trolley hire, club hire (£7.50), putting green, pro shop.
LOCATION: 1 mile south of city centre on A7.
LOCAL HOTELS: Arthur View Hotel, Parliament House Hotel, Prestonfield House.

## RAVELSTON GOLF CLUB

### COURSE DESCRIPTION:
Parkland course, designed by James Braid in 1912, set on the north-east slopes of Corstorphine Hill in the west of Edinburgh. Panoramic views of Fife, the Firth of Forth and Edinburgh Castle.

9 holes, 5,218 yards (for 18 holes), par 66 (SSS 65). Amateur record 64. Pro record 67.

### SIGNATURE HOLE:
SECOND (236 yards, Par 3) Long uphill par 3 to plateau green.

### COURSE CARD

| HOLE | MEDAL YDS | PAR | LADIES YDS | PAR |
|---|---|---|---|---|
| 1 | 337 | 4 | 334 | 4 |
| 2 | 236 | 3 | 232 | 4 |
| 3 | 315 | 4 | 306 | 4 |
| 4 | 348 | 4 | 312 | 4 |
| 5 | 124 | 3 | 120 | 3 |
| 6 | 406 | 4 | 391 | 5 |
| 7 | 329 | 4 | 306 | 4 |
| 8 | 394 | 4 | 387 | 4 |
| 9 | 120 | 3 | 116 | 3 |
| *Yds Out* | 2,609 | | 2,508 | |
| *Total Yds* | 2,609 | | | |
| *Total Par* | 33 | | | |

ADDRESS: 24 Ravelston Dykes Road, Edinburgh EH4 3NZ
TELEPHONE & FAX: +44 (0)131 315 2486.
SECRETARY: Jim Lowrie.
VISITORS: Parties of no more than 12 accepted. Weekdays, no weekends.
GREEN FEES: £15 per round weekdays.
CATERING: Snacks.
FACILITIES: Trolleys, changing-rooms.
LOCATION: A90 Queensferry Road. Turn into Strachan Road at Kwik-Fit garage. Cross junction with Craigcrook Road and clubhouse is on the right.
LOCAL HOTELS: Dalhousie Castle & Spa Hotel, Holiday Inn.

## ROYAL BURGESS GOLFING SOCIETY OF EDINBURGH

### COURSE DESCRIPTION:
Instituted in 1735, this is the oldest golfing society in the world. If you are interested in the history of golf, you should visit. A pleasant parkland course, it was first set out

in 1895 on the advice of Old Tom Morris and it remained largely unaltered until 1945 when James Braid made a number of alterations. His devilish bunker locations on the left of the 4th, the right of the 7th green, and the angle of the green and bunker placements at the 13th are perfect examples of 'Braid's brawest'. Alhough it is a gentlemen's golfing society, ladies are welcome to play and enjoy the dining facilities; but changing accommodation is limited for ladies.

18 holes, 6,494 yards, par 71 (SSS 71). Visitors 6,111 yards, par 68 (SSS 69). Course record 66.

ADDRESS: 181 Whitehouse Road, Edinburgh EH4 6BY.
TELEPHONE: +44 (0)131 339 2075.
FAX:+44 (0)131 339 3712.
E-MAIL: secretary@royalburgess.co.uk
WEBSITE: www.royalburgess.co.uk
PROFESSIONAL: George Yuille +44 (0)131 339 6474.
VISITORS: Yes but should arrange tee time through the professional or secretary.
GREEN FEES: £42 per round weekdays, £55 per day. £65 per round weekends (After 5 p.m. weekday rate applies).
CATERING: Dining-room and bar. Lunches served daily with the exception of Mondays and Saturdays. Buffet lunches, high teas and dinners can be arranged for golfing parties.
FACILITIES: Trolley hire (manual and electric), club hire, changing-rooms, putting green, pro shop, practice ground.
LOCATION: 5 miles west of city centre off A90.
LOCAL HOTELS: Barnton Thistle Hotel, Dalhousie Castle & Spa Hotel, Parliament House Hotel.

## SILVERKNOWES GOLF CLUB

COURSE DESCRIPTION:
Municipal generally flat parkland course with a links feel. Reasonably new, having been opened in 1947. Little trouble off the tees but accurate second shots needed. On the coast overlooking the Firth of Forth.

18 holes, 6,298 yards, par 71 (SSS 70).

ADDRESS: Parkway, Silverknowes, Edinburgh EH4 5ET.
TELEPHONE: +44 (0)131 336 3843.
VISITORS: Restricted Saturdays and Sundays. Advance booking recommended.
GREEN FEES: £10 per round, £12.50 at weekends.
CATERING: Full range at nearby hotel.
FACILITIES: Trolley hire, putting green, pro shop, practice ground.
LOCATION: 4 miles north-west of city centre. North of A902.
LOCAL HOTELS: Ben Doran Guest House, Dalhousie Castle & Spa Hotel, Parliament House Hotel, Quality Commodore Hotel.

## SWANSTON GOLF CLUB

COURSE DESCRIPTION:
Hillside course with banked greens, situated in Swanston Village overlooking Robert Louis Stevenson's house. Steep climb at the 12th and 13th holes.

18 holes, 5,024 yards, par 66 (SSS 65).

ADDRESS: 111 Swanston Road, Fairmilehead, Edinburgh EH10 7DS.
TELEPHONE: +44 (0)131 445 2239.
VISITORS: Contact in advance. No visitors to tee-off after 4 p.m. on Fridays.
GREEN FEES: £15 per round weekdays, £20 weekends.
CATERING: Full service. Bar.
FACILITIES: Pro shop.
LOCATION: 4 miles south of city centre, off B701.
LOCAL HOTELS: Braid Hills Hotel, Cringletie House Hotel, Parliament House Hotel.

## THE BRUNTSFIELD LINKS GOLFING SOCIETY LTD

COURSE DESCRIPTION:
Fifth oldest club in the world, having been in existence since 1761. Mature parkland course, originally designed by Willie Park Jnr. Magnificently situated with views over the Firth of Forth to the Fife coast. A great variety of trees ensures the golfer cannot believe he is so near to the city centre. Many challenging holes with arguably the 11th (see below) and the 10th, a short (339 yards) dogleg par 4 which demands accuracy and the right weight of approach shot to hold the green, vying for the title of Signature Hole.

18 holes, 6,407 yards, par 71 (SSS 71). Amateur record 67. Pro record 68.

SIGNATURE HOLE:
ELEVENTH (415 yards, par 4) Scenic beauty and historic value. The prevailing westerly wind is very challenging. Tricky contoured green. Dogleg left with out of bounds on left and trees right.

COURSE CARD

| HOLE | MEDAL YDS | PAR | FORWARD YDS | PAR | HOLE | MEDAL YDS | PAR | FORWARD YDS | PAR |
|------|-----------|-----|-------------|-----|------|-----------|-----|-------------|-----|
| 1 | 419 | 4 | 410 | 4 | 10 | 339 | 4 | 325 | 4 |
| 2 | 381 | 4 | 366 | 4 | 11 | 415 | 4 | 392 | 4 |
| 3 | 487 | 5 | 448 | 4 | 12 | 168 | 3 | 158 | 3 |
| 4 | 549 | 5 | 529 | 5 | 13 | 455 | 4 | 445 | 4 |
| 5 | 205 | 3 | 195 | 3 | 14 | 493 | 5 | 479 | 5 |
| 6 | 332 | 4 | 317 | 4 | 15 | 170 | 3 | 160 | 3 |
| 7 | 157 | 3 | 142 | 3 | 16 | 373 | 4 | 355 | 4 |
| 8 | 382 | 4 | 345 | 4 | 17 | 381 | 4 | 370 | 4 |
| 9 | 354 | 4 | 336 | 4 | 18 | 347 | 4 | 337 | 4 |
| Yds Out | 3,266 | | 3,088 | | Yds In | 3,141 | | 3,021 | |

| Total 6,407 Yds | 6,109 | |
|---|---|---|
| Total 71 Par | 70 | |

**ADDRESS:** The Clubhouse, 32 Barnton Avenue, Edinburgh EH4 6JH.
**TELEPHONE:** +44 (0)131 336 1479.
**FAX:** +44 (0)131 336 5538.
**SECRETARY:** Cdr. David Sandford.
**PROFESSIONAL:** Brian Mackenzie +44 (0)131 336 4005.
**VISITORS:** Yes, telephone to arrange time.
**GREEN FEES:** £42 per round weekdays, £60 per day. £47 per round weekends, £65 per day.
**CREDIT CARDS ACCEPTED:** Visa/Mastercard.
**CATERING:** Yes. Restaurant and bar. Carvery lunch, high tea/dinner by arrangement. Functions by arrangement. Gentlemen must wear a jacket and tie in the clubhouse.
**FACILITIES:** Motorised buggies (£12), trolley hire (£2), changing-rooms, putting green, pro shop, practice ground, driving range, coaching clinics, ten-year waiting list for membership.
**LOCATION:** Situated at Davidson's Mains, 3 miles north-west of city centre, 6 miles from the Forth Road Bridge and Edinburgh Airport, off A90.
**LOCAL HOTELS:** Dalhousie Castle & Spa Hotel, Parliament House Hotel, The Barnton Thistle Hotel.

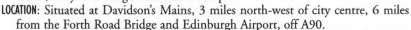

# TORPHIN HILL GOLF CLUB

**COURSE DESCRIPTION:**
Hillside heathland course with fine views of Edinburgh and the Forth estuary. 18 holes, 5,038 yards, par 67 (SSS 66). Course record 64.

**ADDRESS:** Torphin Road, Colinton, Edinburgh EH13 0PG.
**TELEPHONE:** +44 (0)131 441 1100.
**PROFESSIONAL:** Jamie Browne +44 (0)131 441 4061.
**VISITORS:** Contact in advance.
**GREEN FEES:** £12 per round weekdays, £18 per day. £20 per round weekends.
**CATERING:** Full service. Bar.
**FACILITIES:** Putting green, pro shop, practice ground.
**LOCATION:** 5 miles south-west of city centre, south of A720.
**LOCAL HOTELS:** Learney Arms Hotel.

## TURNHOUSE GOLF CLUB

COURSE DESCRIPTION:
Interesting parkland course with some hills.
18 holes, 6,171 yards, par 69 (SSS 70). Amateur record 64. Pro record 63.

### COURSE CARD

| HOLE | YDS | PAR | HOLE | YDS | PAR |
|---|---|---|---|---|---|
| 1 | 400 | 4 | 10 | 450 | 4 |
| 2 | 278 | 4 | 11 | 106 | 3 |
| 3 | 380 | 4 | 12 | 455 | 4 |
| 4 | 478 | 5 | 13 | 347 | 4 |
| 5 | 234 | 3 | 14 | 373 | 4 |
| 6 | 440 | 4 | 15 | 160 | 3 |
| 7 | 445 | 4 | 16 | 340 | 4 |
| 8 | 405 | 4 | 17 | 250 | 3 |
| 9 | 145 | 3 | 18 | 485 | 5 |
| Yds Out | 3,205 | | Yds In | 2,966 | |
| Total Yds | 6,171 | | | | |
| Total Par | 69 | | | | |

ADDRESS: 154 Turnhouse Road, Edinburgh EH12 0AD.
TELEPHONE: +44 (0)131 339 1014.
SECRETARY: A. Hay.
PROFESSIONAL: John Murray +44 (0)131 339 7701.
VISITORS: Yes, certain times during week. Not at weekends.
GREEN FEES: £18 per round, £26 per day.
CATERING: Available. Bar.
FACILITIES: Trolley hire, putting green, pro shop, practice ground.
LOCATION: West of city on A9080 near Edinburgh Airport.
LOCAL HOTELS: Parliament House Hotel, Royal Scot Hotel.

# FAULDHOUSE

## GREENBURN GOLF CLUB

COURSE DESCRIPTION:
Set in moorland. Features include railway, which bisects the course, and water hazards.
18 holes, 6,046 yards, par 71 (SSS 71). Course record 64.

ADDRESS: 6 Greenburn Road, Fauldhouse, West Lothian EH47 9HG.
TELEPHONE: +44 (0)1501 770292.

E-MAIL: secretary@greenburngolfclub.fsnet.uk
SECRETARY: Derek Watson +44 (0)1501 744334.
PROFESSIONAL: Malcolm Leighton +44 (0)1501 771187.
VISITORS: Yes, casual by arrangement with pro. Parties by arrangement with secretary. No visitors on competition days.
GREEN FEES: £17 per round weekdays, £25 per day. £20 per round weekends, £30 per day.
CATERING: Yes. Bar.
FACILITIES: Trolley/buggy hire, putting green, pro shop, practice ground.
LOCATION: 5 miles south of Bathgate junction off M8.
LOCAL HOTELS: Dreadnought Hotel.

# GIFFORD

## CASTLE PARK GOLF CLUB

### COURSE DESCRIPTION:
Undulating parkland course surrounded by mature woodland on a site that was formerly the deer park for the nearby Yester Castle. Breathtaking scenery with views to the Lammermuir Hills. Fun golf in peaceful surroundings. Opened in 1994, it will be extended to 18 holes by May 2002.

9 holes, 5,744 yards (for 18 holes), par 68 (SSS 68). Amateur record 71. Pro record 70.

### SIGNATURE HOLE:
THIRD ('The Well' 173 yards, par 3) Play over a pond to an elevated green.

### COURSE CARD

| HOLE | MEDAL YDS | PAR | LADIES YDS | PAR | HOLE | MEDAL YDS | LADIES PAR |
|------|-----------|-----|------------|-----|------|-----------|------------|
| 1 | 400 | 4 | 364 | 4 | 10 | 400 | 4 |
| 2 | 380 | 4 | 286 | 4 | 11 | 380 | 4 |
| 3 | 173 | 3 | 157 | 3 | 12 | 173 | 3 |
| 4 | 359 | 4 | 343 | 4 | 13 | 359 | 4 |
| 5 | 300 | 4 | 277 | 4 | 14 | 300 | 4 |
| 6 | 317 | 4 | 302 | 4 | 15 | 317 | 4 |
| 7 | 163 | 3 | 156 | 3 | 16 | 233 | 3 |
| 8 | 352 | 4 | 339 | 4 | 17 | 352 | 4 |
| 9 | 393 | 4 | 339 | 4 | 18 | 393 | 4 |
| Yds Out | 2,837 | | 2,600 | Yds In | | 2,907 | |
| Total Yds | 5,744 | | | | | | |
| Total Par | 68 | | | | | | |

ADDRESS: Castlemains, Gifford, Haddington, East Lothian EH41 4PL.
TELEPHONE: +44 (0)1620 810733.
FAX: +44 (0)1620 810723.
E-MAIL: stuartfortune@aol.com
WEBSITE: www.castleparkgolfclub.co.uk
MANAGER: Stuart Fortune.
PROFESSIONAL: Derek Small.
VISITORS: Welcome at all times, apart from monthly medal day.
GREEN FEES: £12 per round weekdays, £18 per day. £14 per round weekends, £22 per day.
CREDIT CARDS ACCEPTED: Visa/Mastercard.
CATERING: Restaurant and bar. Maximum of 20–24 for outings.
FACILITIES: Motorised buggies (£14), trolley hire (£2), club hire (£5), changing-rooms, putting green, practice ground, driving range, coaching clinics, memberships available.
LOCATION: 2 miles south of Gifford on the Longyester road.
LOCAL HOTELS: Goblin Ha' Hotel, Tweeddale Arms Hotel

## GIFFORD GOLF CLUB

COURSE DESCRIPTION:
Gently undulating parkland course in the foothills of the Lammermuir Hills. Maintained to the highest standards with first-class greens. The Speedy Burn meanders through the course and comes into play on four holes.

9 holes, 6,243 yards (for 18 holes), par 71 (SSS 70). Amateur record 64.

### COURSE CARD

| HOLE | YDS | PAR | HOLE | YDS | PAR |
|------|-----|-----|------|-----|-----|
| 1 | 362 | 4 | 10 | 172 | 3 |
| 2 | 365 | 4 | 11 | 365 | 4 |
| 3 | 324 | 3 | 12 | 324 | 4 |
| 4 | 365 | 4 | 13 | 365 | 4 |
| 5 | 153 | 3 | 14 | 216 | 3 |
| 6 | 412 | 4 | 15 | 412 | 4 |
| 7 | 319 | 4 | 16 | 319 | 3 |
| 8 | 407 | 4 | 17 | 407 | 4 |
| 9 | 478 | 5 | 18 | 478 | 5 |
| *Yds Out* | 3,185 | | *Yds In* | 3,058 | |
| *Total Yds* | 6,243 | | | | |
| *Total Par* | 71 | | | | |

ADDRESS: Edinburgh Road, Gifford EH41 4JE.
TELEPHONE & FAX: +44 (0)1620 810267.
SECRETARY: Pete Blyth.

VISITORS: Yes, but not after 4 p.m. on Tuesdays, Wednesdays and Saturdays, and midday Sundays. Closed on first Sunday of the month from April to October.
GREEN FEES: £12 per round weekdays/weekends. £15 per day.
CATERING: 2 hotels 500 yards from club.
FACILITIES: Trolley hire, putting green, practice ground.
LOCATION: 4 miles from A1, Haddington exit.
LOCAL HOTELS: Goblin Ha' Hotel, Tweeddale Arms Hotel.

# GOREBRIDGE

## VOGRIE COUNTRY PARK GOLF CLUB

COURSE DESCRIPTION:
Municipal course with wide fairways.
9 holes, 5,060 yards (for 18 holes), par 66.

ADDRESS: Vogrie Estate Country Park, Gorebridge EH 23 4NU.
TELEPHONE: +44 (0)1875 821986.
VISITORS: Book 24 hours in advance.
GREEN FEES: £6 for 9 holes weekdays.
LOCATION: Off B6372.
LOCAL HOTELS: Johnstounburn House Hotel.

# GULLANE

## GULLANE GOLF CLUB

COURSE DESCRIPTION:
The East Lothian Golf Club first played here in 1854. Three superb links courses open throughout the year. No. 1 is a real test, especially when the wind gets up. Has been used for pre-qualifying for the Open Championship.
   *Course No. 1* – (course card below) Established in 1884. The well-maintained greens, the links grasses and the numerous bunkers make it a unique challenge.
   18 holes, 6,466 yards, par 71 (SSS 70). Course record 65.
   *Course No. 2* – Completed in 1898, with the 1st and 18th holes on the south side of the A198. The course runs alongside No. 1 for the first seven holes and then sweeps down towards Aberlady Bay before turning back towards the clubhouse. This course features quality short holes, especially the 11th.
   18 holes 6,244 yards, par 71 (SSS 70).
   *Course No.3* – Completed in 1910, the first three and last three holes are on the south side of the A198. It may be short but this is a real test of accurate shot-making.
   18 holes, 5,252 yards, par 68 (SSS 66).

SIGNATURE HOLE:
No. 1 Course: NINTH ('Corbie' 151 yards, par 3) Well bunkered with a tricky, sloping green.

COURSE CARD

| HOLE | MEDAL YDS | PAR | FORWARD YDS | PAR | HOLE | MEDAL YDS | PAR | FORWARD YDS | PAR |
|------|-----------|-----|-------------|-----|------|-----------|-----|-------------|-----|
| 1 | 302 | 4 | 287 | 4 | 10 | 466 | 4 | 434 | 4 |
| 2 | 379 | 4 | 334 | 4 | 11 | 471 | 4 | 427 | 4 |
| 3 | 496 | 5 | 479 | 5 | 12 | 480 | 5 | 423 | 5 |
| 4 | 144 | 3 | 134 | 3 | 13 | 170 | 3 | 160 | 3 |
| 5 | 450 | 4 | 436 | 4 | 14 | 435 | 4 | 409 | 4 |
| 6 | 324 | 4 | 299 | 4 | 15 | 537 | 5 | 497 | 5 |
| 7 | 398 | 4 | 398 | 4 | 16 | 186 | 3 | 177 | 3 |
| 8 | 332 | 4 | 322 | 4 | 17 | 390 | 4 | 390 | 4 |
| 9 | 151 | 3 | 141 | 3 | 18 | 355 | 4 | 338 | 4 |
| *Yds Out* | 2,976 | | 2,830 | | *In* | *Yds* 3,490 | | 3,245 | |
| *Total Yds* | 6,466 | | 6,075 | | | | | | |
| *Total Par* | 71 | | 71 | | | | | | |

ADDRESS: West Links Road, Gullane, East Lothian EH31 2BB.
TELEPHONE: +44 (0)1620 842255.
FAX: +44 (0)1620 842327.
E-MAIL: bookings@gullanegolfclub.com
WEBSITE: www.gullanegolfclub.com
SECRETARY: Stan Owram.
PROFESSIONAL: Jimmy Hume.
VISITORS: Weekdays 10.30 a.m. to 12 noon, 2.30 p.m. to 4 p.m. Advance booking recommended.
GREEN FEES: Course No. 1 – £60 per round weekdays, £90 per day. £75 per round weekends. Course No. 2 – £28 per round weekdays, £40 per day. £33 per round weekends, £50 per day. Course No. 3 – £16 per round weekdays, £25 per day. £22 per round weekends, £33 per day.
CREDIT CARDS ACCEPTED: Amex/Visa/Mastercard.
CATERING: Restaurant and bar. Functions catered for.
FACILITIES: Trolley hire, club hire, caddies (£25+), changing-rooms, putting green, pro shop, practice ground, driving range, coaching clinics.
LOCATION: From A1 to A198.
LOCAL HOTELS: Cringletie House Hotel, Dalhousie Castle & Spa Hotel, Greywalls Hotel, Kilspindie House Hotel, Marine Hotel, The Goldenstones, The Golf Hotel, The Nether Abbey Hotel.

# MUIRFIELD
# (THE HONOURABLE COMPANY OF EDINBURGH GOLFERS)

### COURSE DESCRIPTION:

This links venue for the 2002 Open Championship, in the lee of Gullane Hill, almost 20 miles from Edinburgh, is simply one of the best courses in the world. The home of the Honourable Company of Edinburgh Golfers, it was designed in 1891 by Old Tom Morris and, including 2002, has hosted 15 Open Championships since 1892, the Amateur Championship on numerous occasions and the Ryder, Walker and Curtis Cups.

From the championship tees, the course stretches to a formidable 6,970 yards and still adds up to a par 70 6,601 yards off the medal tees. Although the thick rough and cavernous bunkers, of which there are 151, can make it a very severe test, it is a course which invokes respect from all who have tangled with it. Henry Cotton called it 'cruelly fair'. Tom Watson said there was 'not a weak hole on the course'. Jack Nicklaus, who won in 1966, was so impressed that he gave its name to his golf complex in Ohio, Muirfield Village.

The course is laid out in two separate undulating loops, with the back nine forming an inner circle, which ensures that the golfer will not have to contend with the same wind direction on more than a few holes.

Muirfield starts with a bang. There is no lulling you into a false sense of security. Right from the off you have to battle for par. But it is perhaps its four par 3s which present the biggest danger to a golfer's card. Each has raised greens, which are tight targets. Miss them and you are just as likely to end up in a seriously deep bunker, where sideways or even backwards is often the only way to escape.

You get the idea as early as the 174-yard 4th which has four bunkers in front – and is one of the most dangerous holes on the course. The 151-yard 7th is similar in design to the 4th but runs in the opposite direction, into the prevailing wind, and offers an exposed elevated green guarded by four bunkers. Nicklaus regards the 146-yard 13th as a truly great par 3 and a golfing gem. It runs uphill to a narrow green with deep bunkers on both sides. Beware – you could spend the day here. The final par 3 is the 16th, at 181 yards the longest of the four short holes. There are seven bunkers to contend with, the slope of the terrain taking any shot played to the left side into the traps. In addition to the short holes, Muirfield demands accuracy everywhere else, especially on the 436-yard par-4 6th which doglegs left to a split-level fairway. You must be right to get that second shot close. Someone once said they thought Muirfield had a bunker for every day of the week and it certainly seems so on the 8th. This 439-yard par 4 has 12 bunkers and starts a run of three very challenging holes. The 9th (460 yards, par 4) has out of bounds all along the left and a bunker called 'Simpson's Folly' 40 yards short of the green. The 350-yard 11th has the only blind drive at Muirfield and, of course, the tricky green is surrounded by bunkers.

It hardly needs repeating that two of the characteristics of Muirfield are the bunkers and the long grasses of the rough. When Nicklaus won in 1966, the grass had been allowed to grow so long that the philosophical Doug Sanders reportedly remarked that he didn't mind about the championship as long as he could have the hay concession.

18 holes, 6,601 yards (Championship 6,970), par 70 (SSS 73). Championship course record R. Davis, I. Aoki 63.

### SIGNATURE HOLE:

FIRST (447 yards, par 4) Jack Nicklaus says it 'is as tough an opening hole as there is anywhere in championship golf'. One of many large bunkers dominates the left of the fairway, which is narrow. Stray off it and you are in severe rough. The green slopes from front to back.

### COURSE CARD

| HOLE | CHAMPIONSHIP YDS | PAR | HOLE | YDS | PAR |
|------|------|-----|------|-----|-----|
| 1 | 447 | 4 | 10 | 475 | 4 |
| 2 | 351 | 4 | 11 | 385 | 4 |
| 3 | 379 | 4 | 12 | 381 | 4 |
| 4 | 180 | 3 | 13 | 159 | 3 |
| 5 | 559 | 5 | 14 | 449 | 4 |
| 6 | 469 | 4 | 15 | 417 | 4 |
| 7 | 185 | 3 | 16 | 188 | 3 |
| 8 | 444 | 4 | 17 | 550 | 5 |
| 9 | 504 | 5 | 18 | 448 | 4 |
| *Yds Out* | 3,518 | | *Yds In* | 3,452 | |
| *Total Yds* | 6,970 | | | | |
| *Total Par* | 71 | | | | |

ADDRESS: Gullane, East Lothian EH31 2BB.
TELEPHONE: +44 (0)1620 842123.
SECRETARY: Group Captain J. A. Prideaux.
VISITORS: Tuesdays and Thursdays only. Visiting groups of no more than 12 on these days. Evening clubs of no more than 40. Contact in advance. Must have handicap certificate (limits of 18 for men, 24 for women).
GREEN FEES: £90 per round, £120 per day.
CATERING: Full service (ladies may not lunch in the clubhouse). Bar.
FACILITIES: Trolley/ buggy hire, putting green, practice area.
LOCATION: Duncur Road, Gullane. Off A198 on north-east side of village.
LOCAL HOTELS: Cringletie House Hotel, Dalhousie Castle & Spa Hotel, Greywalls, Kilspindie House Hotel, Marine Hotel, The Goldenstones, The Golf Hotel, The Nether Abbey.

# HADDINGTON

## HADDINGTON GOLF CLUB

COURSE DESCRIPTION:
Inland, tree-lined parkland course by the River Tyne. Not hilly but bunkered and not as easy as it looks.

18 holes, 6,317 yards, par 71 (SSS 70).

COURSE CARD

| HOLE | MEDAL YDS | PAR | FORWARD YDS | PAR | LADIES YDS | PAR | HOLE | MEDAL YDS | PAR | FORWARD YDS | PAR | LADIES YDS | PAR |
|------|-----------|-----|-------------|-----|------------|-----|------|-----------|-----|-------------|-----|------------|-----|
| 1 | 340 | 4 | 332 | 4 | 324 | 4 | 10 | 393 | 4 | 381 | 4 | 369 | 4 |
| 2 | 458 | 4 | 421 | 4 | 399 | 5 | 11 | 513 | 5 | 506 | 5 | 466 | 5 |
| 3 | 281 | 4 | 269 | 4 | 258 | 4 | 12 | 375 | 4 | 368 | 4 | 361 | 4 |
| 4 | 360 | 4 | 356 | 4 | 347 | 4 | 13 | 520 | 5 | 514 | 5 | 463 | 5 |
| 5 | 347 | 4 | 308 | 4 | 296 | 4 | 14 | 140 | 3 | 134 | 3 | 125 | 3 |
| 6 | 375 | 4 | 324 | 4 | 316 | 4 | 15 | 442 | 4 | 413 | 4 | 406 | 5 |
| 7 | 345 | 4 | 332 | 4 | 311 | 4 | 16 | 360 | 4 | 326 | 4 | 276 | 4 |
| 8 | 154 | 3 | 148 | 3 | 105 | 3 | 17 | 141 | 3 | 139 | 3 | 126 | 3 |
| 9 | 367 | 4 | 353 | 4 | 336 | 4 | 18 | 406 | 4 | 397 | 4 | 384 | 4 |
| Yds Out | 3,027 | | 2,843 | | 2,692 | | Yds In | 3,290 | | 3,178 | | 2,976 | |
| Total Yds | 6,317 | | 6,021 | | 5,568 | | | | | | | | |
| Total Par | 71 | | 71 | | 73 | | | | | | | | |

ADDRESS: Amisfield Park, Haddington EH41 4PT.
TELEPHONE: +44 (0)1620 823627.
FAX: +44 (0)1620 826580.
E-MAIL: hadd.golf1@tesco.net
WEBSITE: www.haddingtongolf.co.uk
PROFESSIONAL: John Sandilands +44 (0)1620 822727.
VISITORS: May not play between 7 a.m. and 10 a.m. and between noon and 2 p.m. at weekends. Contact in advance.
GREEN FEES: £18 per round weekdays, £26 per day. £23 per round weekends, £32 per day.
CATERING: Full service. Bar.
FACILITIES: Motorised buggies, trolley hire, club hire, changing-rooms, putting green, practice ground, pro shop.
LOCATION: East side of town, off A613.
LOCAL HOTELS: Goblin Ha' Hotel, Tweeddale Arms Hotel.

# LASSWADE

## KINGS ACRE GOLF COURSE

### COURSE DESCRIPTION:

A challenging parkland course, designed by Graeme Webster, situated in lush countryside and hilly in places. Featuring over 50 bunkers and water hazards, the course boasts excellent large, undulating greens built to USGA specifications. Although opened in June 1997, it has an established feel to it, helped by the planting of 1,000 trees in 1999. There's a good variety of holes that call for considered shot-making. One of the outstanding features is the Golf Academy with 30 covered bays; two fully equipped teaching bays with the latest computer-aided video system, allowing you not only to identify the flaws in your game but also to compare your own swing with the world's top players. There are six target greens, ten bunkers and three lakes to give you the ultimate in practice. Several touring pros have made this their practice base. Owners John and Tom King say: 'Golf should be interesting and enjoyable, whether you are playing on the course or hitting balls on the range.' There is also a four-hole course for juniors under 18.

18 holes, 5,935 yards, par 70 (SSS 70).

### SIGNATURE HOLE:

EIGHTEENTH (361 yards, par 4) Fittingly called the 'Last Splash' because it is easy to misjudge your approach to the green. The tiger line is over the first lake with a carry of around 213 yards. With the pin usually tucked in on the left of the green, it requires a well-placed approach over a second lake to an undulating green.

### COURSE CARD

| HOLE | MEDAL YDS | PAR | FORWARD YDS | PAR | LADIES YDS | PAR | HOLE | MEDAL YDS | PAR | FORWARD YDS | PAR | LADIES YDS | PAR |
|------|-----------|-----|-------------|-----|------------|-----|------|-----------|-----|-------------|-----|------------|-----|
| 1 | 327 | 4 | 318 | 4 | 308 | 4 | 10 | 378 | 4 | 352 | 4 | 322 | 4 |
| 2 | 449 | 5 | 440 | 5 | 402 | 5 | 11 | 186 | 3 | 171 | 3 | 157 | 3 |
| 3 | 553 | 5 | 545 | 5 | 522 | 5 | 12 | 506 | 5 | 484 | 5 | 417 | 5 |
| 4 | 153 | 3 | 145 | 3 | 118 | 3 | 13 | 343 | 4 | 322 | 4 | 295 | 4 |
| 5 | 367 | 4 | 357 | 4 | 352 | 4 | 14 | 177 | 3 | 169 | 3 | 162 | 3 |
| 6 | 198 | 3 | 184 | 3 | 173 | 3 | 15 | 501 | 5 | 498 | 5 | 474 | 5 |
| 7 | 356 | 4 | 346 | 4 | 314 | 4 | 16 | 217 | 3 | 202 | 3 | 177 | 3 |
| 8 | 172 | 3 | 133 | 3 | 101 | 3 | 17 | 302 | 4 | 294 | 4 | 286 | 4 |
| 9 | 389 | 4 | 366 | 4 | 342 | 4 | 18 | 361 | 4 | 340 | 4 | 313 | 4 |
| Yds Out | 2,964 | | 2,834 | | 2,612 | | Yds In | 2,971 | | 2,832 | | 2,603 | |
| Total Yds | 5,935 | | 5,666 | | 5,215 | | | | | | | | |
| Total Par | 70 | | 70 | | 70 | | | | | | | | |

ADDRESS: Lasswade, Midlothian EH18 1AU.

TELEPHONE: +44 (0)131 663 3456 or 663 7076.

OWNERS: John and Tom King.

PROFESSIONAL: Alan Murdoch (PGA professional coach: Adam Hunter).

VISITORS: Welcome, pay as you play.

GREEN FEES: £17 per round weekdays (excluding public holidays); £24 weekends.

CATERING: Full service and bar in superbly restored sandstone clubhouse and new conservatory with views of the course. Restaurant: last orders 5.30 p.m. Tuesday to Friday; 6.30 p.m. Saturday and Sunday. Monday is chef's day off.

FACILITIES: Buggies, trolleys, club hire, practice area, putting green, driving range.

LOCATION: 6 miles from Edinburgh city centre and 2 minutes from the city by-pass.

LOCAL HOTELS: Dalhousie Castle & Spa Hotel.

## MELVILLE GOLF CENTRE

COURSE DESCRIPTION:

Although nine holes, has an 18-hole feel. Twisting fairways and a good test.

9 holes, 4,604 yards (for 18 holes), par 66. Course record 61.

SIGNATURE HOLE:

THIRD (151 yards, par 3) Steep hill to a green surrounded by bunkers.

ADDRESS: South Melville, Lasswade, Midlothian EH18 1AN.

TELEPHONE: +44 (0)131 654 0224.

FAX: +44 (0) 131 654 0814

EMAIL: golf@melvillegolf.co.uk

WEBSITE: www.melvillegolf.co.uk

PROPRIETORS: Colin and Morag Macfarlane.

PROFESSIONAL: Garry Carter.

VISITORS: Yes.

GREEN FEES: £8 per nine holes weekdays, £10 weekends. £14 for 18 holes weekdays. £18 weekends.

CATERING: Hot and cold drinks. Snacks.

FACILITIES: Trolleys, club/shoe hire, putting green, pro shop, practice ground, floodlit driving range, 4-hole practice course.

LOCATION: South of Edinburgh. Off A7 Galashiels road.

LOCAL HOTELS: Dalhousie Castle & Spa Hotel, Eskbank Hotel.

# LINLITHGOW

## BRIDGEND & DISTRICT GOLF CLUB

COURSE DESCRIPTION:

A relatively new nine-hole parkland course opened in 1999.

9 holes, 5,580 yards (for 18 holes), par 68 (SSS 67).

ADDRESS: Bridgend, near Linlithgow, West Lothian EH49 6NW.

TELEPHONE: +44 (0)1506 834140.

FAX: +44 (0)1506 834706.

VISITORS: Welcome except during competitions.

GREEN FEES: £8 per round weekdays, £15 per day. £10 per round weekends, £18 per day.

CATERING: Restaurant and bar.

CREDIT CARDS ACCEPTED: Visa.

FACILITIES: Trolleys, changing-rooms, memberships available.

LOCATION: Three miles east of Linlithgow and 15 miles west of Edinburgh, just off B9080.

LOCAL HOTELS: West Port Hotel, Star & Garter Hotel.

## LINLITHGOW GOLF CLUB

### COURSE DESCRIPTION:

A short but testing, undulating, parkland course with panoramic views of historic Linlithgow and the Forth Valley. Within easy reach of the M8 and M9 motorways. Excellent drainage of the course goes back to the Ice Age when glaciers receded, depositing soil and boulders. The original course was laid out in 1913 by Carnoustie professional Robert Simpson of which the first four holes still survive. The club publishes a map of the course which details the abundance of flora and fauna that can be seen on the various holes.

18 holes, 5,729 yards, par 70 (SSS 68).

### SIGNATURE HOLE:

SEVENTEENTH (169 yards, par 3) Next to the Union Canal and drops 50 feet to a postage-stamp green which needs no bunkers.

### COURSE CARD

| HOLE | MEDAL YDS | PAR | FORWARD YDS | PAR | LADIES YDS | PAR | HOLE | MEDAL YDS | PAR | FORWARD YDS | PAR | LADIES YDS | PAR |
|---|---|---|---|---|---|---|---|---|---|---|---|---|---|
| 1 | 312 | 4 | 296 | 4 | 304 | 4 | 10 | 232 | 3 | 220 | 3 | 220 | 3 |
| 2 | 384 | 4 | 324 | 3 | 317 | 4 | 11 | 315 | 4 | 311 | 4 | 311 | 4 |
| 3 | 279 | 4 | 268 | 4 | 268 | 4 | 12 | 477 | 5 | 435 | 5 | 435 | 5 |
| 4 | 376 | 4 | 372 | 4 | 350 | 4 | 13 | 490 | 5 | 475 | 5 | 474 | 5 |
| 5 | 282 | 4 | 272 | 4 | 272 | 4 | 14 | 273 | 4 | 267 | 4 | 214 | 4 |
| 6 | 250 | 4 | 237 | 4 | 224 | 4 | 15 | 278 | 4 | 246 | 4 | 246 | 4 |
| 7 | 168 | 3 | 168 | 3 | 158 | 3 | 16 | 446 | 4 | 406 | 4 | 434 | 5 |
| 8 | 169 | 3 | 152 | 3 | 152 | 3 | 17 | 169 | 3 | 154 | 3 | 154 | 3 |
| 9 | 417 | 4 | 363 | 4 | 363 | 4 | 18 | 412 | 4 | 399 | 4 | 399 | 5 |
| Yds Out | 2,637 | | 2,452 | | 2,408 | | Yds In | 3,092 | | 2,913 | | 2,887 | |
| Total Yds | 5,729 | | 5,365 | | 5,296 | | | | | | | | |
| Total Par | 70 | | 70 | | 72 | | | | | | | | |

ADDRESS: Braehead, Linlithgow, West Lothian, EH49 6QF.
TELEPHONE: +44 (0)1506 842585.
FAX: +44 (0)1506 842764.
E-MAIL: info@linlithgowgolf.co.uk
WEBSITE: www.linlithgowgolf.co.uk
GENERAL MANAGER: David Roy.
VISITORS: Yes. Not Saturdays.
GREEN FEES: £15 per round weekdays, £23 per day. £23 per round Sundays, £30 per day.
CATERING: Yes.
FACILITIES: Trolley hire, putting green, pro shop, practice ground, coaching clinics.
LOCATION: Travelling west along Linlithgow High Street, take a left onto the A706. After approximately half a mile, the club is signposted to the left, by the Maltings.
LOCAL HOTELS: West Port Hotel, Star & Garter Hotel.

## THE WEST LOTHIAN GOLF CLUB

COURSE DESCRIPTION:
Undulating parkland course with superb views of the Forth Valley.
    18 holes, 6,406 yards, par 71 (SSS 71). Course record 64.

ADDRESS: Airngath Hill, Linlithgow, West Lothian EH49 7RH.
TELEPHONE: +44 (0)1506 826030.
PROFESSIONAL: Neil Robertson +44 (0)1506 825060.
VISITORS: Weekends by arrangement. Contact in advance.
GREEN FEES: £17 per round weekdays, £23 per day. £23 per round weekends, £30 per day.
CATERING: Full service. Bar.
FACILITIES: Trolley hire, putting green, pro shop, practice ground.
LOCATION: 1 mile south of Linlithgow, off A706.
LOCAL HOTELS: Earl O'Moray Inn.

# LIVINGSTON

## DEER PARK GOLF & COUNTRY CLUB

COURSE DESCRIPTION:
Championship course. Flat first nine, hilly second nine. Hosted regional qualifying for the Open and Scottish Professional Championship.
    18 holes, 6,688 yards, par 72 (SSS 72). Amateur record D. Thomson 67. Pro record Colin Brooks 65.

SIGNATURE HOLE:
FOURTEENTH (par 5) Long, uphill hole. Oxygen mask required.

ADDRESS: Golf Course Road, Livingston, West Lothian E54 8AD.
TELEPHONE: +44 (0)1506 431037.
PROFESSIONAL: Bill Yule.
VISITORS: Yes, any time.
GREEN FEES: £24 per round weekdays, £36 weekends.
CATERING: All week.
FACILITIES: Trolley/buggy hire, putting green, pro shop, practice ground.
LOCATION: Off M8, junction 3.
LOCAL HOTELS: Cringletie House Hotel, Deer Park Beefeater.

# LONGNIDDRY

## LONGNIDDRY GOLF CLUB

### COURSE DESCRIPTION:
The course, a mixture of links and parkland, was constructed on the south side of the Firth of Forth in 1921 and many thousands of Scots pines were removed at the western end. Part of the course is tree-lined, whereas part is very open and exposed to the prevailing winds. It was designed by Harry S. Colt but has since been altered by James Braid, Mackenzie Ross and recently Donald Steel. There are no par 5s (for the men) but a number of long par 4s which are very testing if the wind blows. The SSS reflects the degree of difficulty at two over par. Accuracy is essential because there are out of bounds to the left of 11 holes. Relatively flat and easily walked with superb views to Fife, up the Forth to Edinburgh and the Pentlands. Superb greens.

18 holes, 6,186 yards, par 68 (SSS 70). Amateur record R. Russell, J. Noon 63. Pro record C Hardin 63.

### SIGNATURE HOLE:
SEVENTH (427 yards, par 4) Trees, rough and out of bounds to the left. Trees to the right. A long accurate drive is essential, the right of centre, or else the ball finds the trees.

### COURSE CARD

| HOLE | MEDAL YDS | PAR | FORWARD YDS | PAR | LADIES YDS | PAR | HOLE | MEDAL YDS | PAR | FORWARD YDS | PAR | LADIES YDS | PAR |
|------|-----------|-----|-------------|-----|------------|-----|------|-----------|-----|-------------|-----|------------|-----|
| 1 | 396 | 4 | 396 | 4 | 385 | 4 | 10 | 364 | 4 | 356 | 4 | 352 | 4 |
| 2 | 412 | 4 | 384 | 4 | 400 | 5 | 11 | 329 | 4 | 320 | 4 | 316 | 4 |
| 3 | 459 | 4 | 450 | 4 | 442 | 5 | 12 | 378 | 4 | 367 | 4 | 301 | 4 |
| 4 | 195 | 3 | 185 | 3 | 167 | 3 | 13 | 172 | 3 | 172 | 3 | 152 | 3 |
| 5 | 314 | 4 | 305 | 4 | 299 | 4 | 14 | 401 | 4 | 384 | 4 | 397 | 5 |
| 6 | 168 | 3 | 160 | 3 | 151 | 3 | 15 | 423 | 4 | 411 | 4 | 380 | 5 |
| 7 | 427 | 4 | 418 | 4 | 420 | 5 | 16 | 142 | 3 | 136 | 3 | 129 | 3 |
| 8 | 371 | 4 | 364 | 4 | 359 | 4 | 17 | 432 | 4 | 379 | 4 | 358 | 4 |
| 9 | 373 | 4 | 364 | 4 | 347 | 4 | 18 | 430 | 4 | 418 | 4 | 387 | 5 |

| Yds | 3,115 | 3,026 | 2,970 | Yds | 3,071 | 2,943 | 2,772 |
| Out | | | | In | | | |
| Total Yds | 6,186 | 5,969 | 5,742 | | | | |
| Total Par | 68 | 68 | 73 | | | | |

ADDRESS: Links Road, Longniddry, East Lothian EH32 0NL.
SECRETARY: Neil Robertson +44 (0)1875 852141.
FAX: +44 (0)1875 853371.
PROFESSIONAL: John Gray +44 (0)1875 852228.
E-MAIL: secretary@longniddrygolfclub.co.uk
WEBSITE: www.longniddrygolfclub.co.uk
VISITORS: Welcome but limited at weekends. Advance booking recommended.
GREEN FEES: £35 per round weekdays, £50 per day. £45 per round weekends.
CREDIT CARDS ACCEPTED: Amex/Visa/Mastercard.
CATERING: Restaurant and bar. Functions catered for.
FACILITIES: Motorised buggies (£15), trolley hire (£2), club hire (£15), caddies (£25),
    changing-rooms, putting green, pro shop, practice ground, coaching clinics.
LOCATION: 12 miles east of Edinburgh. From south and north, access from A1. Take
    slip road, signposted Cockenzie (A198) to Longniddry. Golf course access via
    Links Road.
LOCAL HOTELS: Cringletie House Hotel, Dalhousie Castle & Spa Hotel, Kilspindie
    House Hotel.

# MUSSELBURGH

## MUSSELBURGH LINKS, THE OLD COURSE

### COURSE DESCRIPTION:

There's nothing like the experience of playing a Scottish links course, but to see it through the eyes of the pioneers of the sport, that's something else. Here at Musselburgh you have the chance to step back in history and try to emulate local man Willie Park Jnr, who won the second of his Open titles over the Old links in 1889. To some, the Old Course may be just a 2,808-yard nine-hole links course encircled by a racecourse. Others claim it was possibly the first proper golf course in the world. Golf was played at the links as far back as 1672, although it is suggested that Mary, Queen of Scots, enjoyed playing golf at the Old Course in 1567. So what challenges did they face? See for yourself. Musselburgh, which hosted the Open Championship on six occasions between 1874 and 1889, hire out hickory-shafted clubs and gutta-percha balls. The locals claim that playing with the old equipment gives you a better understanding of the course because the bunkers tend to come into play more. Some prefer the gutta-percha balls because high approach shots stop quicker on the greens. History is all around. The first three holes run eastwards alongside the Links Road – and because many sliced their shots and had to play back to the links from the road, the brassie, a wood with a brass plate on the sole, was invented in 1885. 'The Graves', the 344-yard 2nd, is so named because it may have been a burial ground for soldiers who died at the Battle of Pinkie in 1547 and were buried there to discourage golfers. The course has been home to a number of prestigious golf clubs over the years, including the Honourable Company, Royal Burgess and Bruntsfield Golf Club. At one time over 60 clubs played at the course.

9 holes, 5,616 yards (for 18 holes), par 68 (SSS 68). Course record 67.

### SIGNATURE HOLE:

FOURTH (424 yards, par 4) Known as 'Mrs Forman's' because her hostelry was behind the green. This was a most popular resting place on the course and drinks used to be served to golfers through a window adjacent to the green.

### COURSE CARD

| HOLE | YDS | PAR |
|---|---|---|
| 1 | 146 | 3 |
| 2 | 344 | 4 |
| 3 | 314 | 4 |
| 4 | 424 | 4 |
| 5 | 178 | 3 |
| 6 | 323 | 4 |
| 7 | 476 | 5 |
| 8 | 237 | 3 |
| 9 | 366 | 4 |
| *Yds Out* | 2,808 | |
| *Total Yds* | 2,808 | |
| *Total Par* | 34 | |

ADDRESS: Musselburgh Links, Millhill, Musselburgh EH21 7SB.
RESIDENT CLUB: Musselburgh Old Course Golf Club +44 (0)131 665 6981.
E-MAIL: mocgc@breathmail.net
TELEPHONE/FAX: +44 (0)131 665 5438.
E-MAIL: info@musselburgholdlinks.co.uk
WEBSITE: www.musselburgholdlinks.co.uk
VISITORS: Always welcome. Course closed three hours prior to first race on race days.
GREEN FEES: Adult £8 (9 holes); OAP/Juv £4.50 (9 holes)
CATERING: Hot and cold drinks plus confectionery available from the starter's hut. Bar and light meals available Saturday and Sunday only from the clubhouse or by arrangement.
FACILITIES: Hickory club hire (£20 + £20 deposit), modern club hire, trolley hire, souvenirs, full range of memberships.
LOCATION: 5 miles from Edinburgh city centre to the east of Musselburgh. Follow the signs for Musselburgh from the A1 and then the signs for the racecourse and golf course.

LOCAL HOTELS: Donmaree Hotel, Parliament House Hotel.

## THE MUSSELBURGH GOLF CLUB

COURSE DESCRIPTION:
Testing parkland course with natural hazards, including a burn.
   18 holes, 6,614 yards, par 71 (SSS 73). Course record 65.

ADDRESS: Monktonhall, Musselburgh EH21 6SA.
TELEPHONE: +44 (0)131 665 2005.
PROFESSIONAL: Fraser Mann +44 (0)131 665 7055.
VISITORS: Contact in advance.
GREEN FEES: £18 per round weekdays, £26 per day. £22 per round weekends, £31 per day.
CATERING: Full service. Bar.
FACILITIES: Trolley/buggy hire, putting green, pro shop, practice ground.
LOCATION: 1 mile south of Musselburgh on B6415.
LOCAL HOTELS: Donmaree Hotel, Parliament House Hotel.

# NEWBRIDGE

## GOGARBURN GOLF CLUB

COURSE DESCRIPTION:
Founded in 1975, a challenging 12-hole parkland course close to Edinburgh Aiport.
   12 holes, 5,070 yards.

ADDRESS: Hanley Lodge, Newbridge, Midlothian EH28 8NN.
TELEPHONE: +44 (0)131 333 4110.
STARTER: +44 (0) 131 333 4718.
VISITORS: Yes, by prior arrangement.
GREEN FEES: £12 per round weekdays, £16 per round weekends.
CATERING: Restaurant and bar.
LOCATION: Off Edinburgh–Glasgow road (A8).
LOCAL HOTELS: Dalhousie Castle & Spa Hotel.

# NORTH BERWICK

## JANE CONNACHAN GOLF CENTRE

COURSE DESCRIPTION:
   9 holes, 530 yards, par 27.

ADDRESS: Dirleton Road, North Berwick, East Lothian.
TELEPHONE: +44 (0)1620 850475.
VISITORS: Yes.
GREEN FEES: £3 per adults, £2 for children.
FACILITIES: Driving range, practice bunkers, putting green, shop, catering.
LOCAL HOTELS: Belhaven Hotel, Cringletie House Hotel, Dalhousie Castle & Spa Hotel, Kilspindie House Hotel, Marine Hotel.

## GLEN GOLF CLUB

COURSE DESCRIPTION:
Combination of links and inland with magnificent panoramic views of the Forth estuary, the Bass Rock and the town. Offers all-year-round golf. Designed originally as a nine-hole course in 1894 by Ben Sayers and James Braid.

18 holes, 6,043 yards, par 69 (SSS 69). Amateur record 64.

SIGNATURE HOLE:
THIRTEENTH ('Sea Hole' 144 yards, par 3) Bounded on three sides by the Firth of Forth, it is a semi-blind tee shot from an elevated tee to a green below. Club selection is crucial according to the elements, can vary from a 2-iron to a pitching wedge.

### COURSE CARD

| HOLE | MEDAL YDS | PAR | FORWARD YDS | PAR | LADIES YDS | PAR | HOLE | MEDAL YDS | PAR | FORWARD YDS | PAR | LADIES YDS | PAR |
|---|---|---|---|---|---|---|---|---|---|---|---|---|---|
| 1 | 333 | 4 | 328 | 4 | 331 | 4 | 10 | 346 | 4 | 341 | 4 | 339 | 4 |
| 2 | 373 | 4 | 358 | 4 | 351 | 4 | 11 | 321 | 4 | 300 | 4 | 295 | 4 |
| 3 | 349 | 4 | 302 | 4 | 299 | 4 | 12 | 464 | 4 | 409 | 4 | 402 | 5 |
| 4 | 184 | 3 | 175 | 3 | 163 | 3 | 13 | 144 | 3 | 133 | 3 | 128 | 3 |
| 5 | 369 | 4 | 362 | 4 | 363 | 4 | 14 | 370 | 4 | 336 | 4 | 327 | 4 |
| 6 | 476 | 5 | 432 | 5 | 419 | 5 | 15 | 397 | 4 | 399 | 4 | 344 | 4 |
| 7 | 381 | 4 | 366 | 4 | 364 | 4 | 16 | 191 | 3 | 186 | 3 | 182 | 3 |
| 8 | 357 | 4 | 350 | 4 | 325 | 4 | 17 | 416 | 4 | 395 | 4 | 382 | 4 |
| 9 | 207 | 3 | 254 | 3 | 224 | 4 | 18 | 365 | 4 | 365 | 4 | 359 | 4 |
| Yds Out | 3,029 | | 2,927 | | 2,839 | | Yds In | 3,014 | | 2,864 | | 2,759 | |
| Total Yds | 6,043 | | 5,791 | | 5,598 | | | | | | | | |
| Total Par | 69 | | 69 | | 72 | | | | | | | | |

ADDRESS: East Links, Tantallon Terrace, North Berwick, East Lothian EH39 4LE.
TELEPHONE: +44 (0)1620 892726.
FAX: +44 (0)1620 895447.
E-MAIL: secretary@glengolfclub.co.uk
WEBSITE: glengolfclub.co.uk
SECRETARY: Kevin Fish.

VISITORS: Yes, at all times. No restrictions, but advance booking recommended.

GREEN FEES: £20 per round weekdays, £30 per day. £27 per round weekends, £38 per day. Weekly ticket £75.

CREDIT CARDS ACCEPTED: Visa/Mastercard.

CATERING: Restaurant and bar, seven days a week. Functions catered for.

FACILITIES: Trolley hire (£2), club hire (£10), caddies (£25+), changing-rooms, putting green, pro shop, practice ground, memberships available.

LOCATION: From A1 take A198 to North Berwick. Follow directions to harbour. Turn right and follow signs for East Links golf course.

LOCAL HOTELS: Belhaven Hotel, Cringletie House Hotel, Dalhousie Castle & Spa Hotel, Greywalls, Kilspindie House Hotel, Marine Hotel, Goldenstones, Golf Hotel, Nether Abbey.

## NORTH BERWICK GOLF CLUB

### COURSE DESCRIPTION:

Some claim that golf was being played at this Championship course even before St Andrews. The many interesting hazards include the beach, light rough, walls intersecting fairways and streams crossing three of the fairways. Rich variety of holes, including the 14th, aptly named 'Perfection' because your approach has to be perfect otherwise you end up on the shingle of the beach. The 16th is a 381-yard par 4 with only a ditch some 200 yards from the tee to manoeuvre; but it is the long three-tiered green, with what can only be described as a valley in the middle of it, that is the fatal attraction – hit the wrong part of it and a six-putt is not impossible. To finish, the 18th , which stretches a mere 274 yards, tempts you to drive the green. Like many others, it's on a plateau and you could find your ball skipping through and ending on the welcome mat of the clubhouse.

OUT OF BOUNDS

18 holes, 6,420 yards, par 71 (SSS 71). Amateur record Gordon Sherry, George Cochrane 66. Pro record Nick Job 64.

### SIGNATURE HOLE:

FIFTEENTH (192 yards, par 3) 'Redan' is played across a hummocky valley to an angled plateau green guarded by a formidable bunker in front and 20 feet below the flag. To the right are three bunkers.

## COURSE CARD

| HOLE | YDS | PAR | HOLE | YDS | PAR |
|------|------|-----|------|------|-----|
| 1 | 328 | 4 | 10 | 176 | 3 |
| 2 | 431 | 4 | 11 | 550 | 5 |
| 3 | 464 | 4 | 12 | 389 | 4 |
| 4 | 175 | 3 | 13 | 365 | 4 |
| 5 | 373 | 4 | 14 | 376 | 4 |
| 6 | 162 | 3 | 15 | 192 | 3 |
| 7 | 354 | 4 | 16 | 381 | 4 |
| 8 | 495 | 5 | 17 | 425 | 4 |
| 9 | 510 | 5 | 18 | 274 | 4 |
| *Yds Out* | 3,292 | | *Yds In* | 3,128 | |
| *Total Yds* | 6,420 | | | | |
| *Total Par* | 71 | | | | |

ADDRESS: Beach Road, North Berwick, East Lothian EH39 4BB.

TELEPHONE: +44 (0)1620 895040.

FAX: +44 (0)1620 890312.

ADVANCE BOOKINGS +44 (0)1620 892135.

SECRETARY: N.A.Wilson.

PROFESSIONAL: David Huish +44(0)1620 893233.

VISITORS: Yes, from 10 a.m.

GREEN FEES: £42 per round weekdays, £65 per day. £65 per round weekends.

CREDIT CARDS ACCEPTED: Visa/Mastercard.

CATERING: Restaurant and bar.

FACILITIES: Trolley hire, club hire, caddies, changing-rooms, putting green, pro shop, practice ground.

LOCATION: From Edinburgh, A1 to Meadowmill turn-off, then A198. From the South, A1 to A198 at Biel Gates.

LOCAL HOTELS: Belhaven Hotel, Cringletie House Hotel, Dalhousie Castle & Spa Hotel, Fairway Guest House, Greywalls, Kilspindie House Hotel, Marine Hotel, Goldenstones, Golf Hotel, Nether Abbey.

# WHITEKIRK GOLF CLUB

### COURSE DESCRIPTION:

A traditional Scottish heathland course with lush fairways, natural water hazards, gorse-covered banks and greens built to USGA specifications, two miles from the coast. Designed by Cameron Sinclair and opened in 1995, the course shows no sign of its youth. Sits on a hill overlooking North Berwick with commanding views over East Lothian and past the famous landmarks of the Bass Rock, Berwick Law and Tantallon Castle. Host venue to PGA Mastercard Tour.

18 holes, 6,526 yards, par 72 (SSS 72). Amateur record 74. Pro record James Knight (Sandford Springs) 64 (1998).

SIGNATURE HOLE:
FIFTH ('Cameron's Test' 420 yards, par 4) Stroke index 1 and a real thriller. Dogleg left with strategically placed bunkers to catch the errant drive that drifts right. Well-bunkered green.

COURSE CARD

| | MEDAL | | FORWARD | | LADIES | | | MEDAL | | FORWARD | | LADIES | |
|---|---|---|---|---|---|---|---|---|---|---|---|---|---|
| HOLE | YDS | PAR | YDS | PAR | YDS | PAR | HOLE | YDS | PAR | YDS | PAR | YDS | PAR |
| 1 | 492 | 5 | 481 | 5 | 435 | 5 | 10 | 360 | 4 | 345 | 4 | 263 | 4 |
| 2 | 276 | 4 | 268 | 4 | 236 | 4 | 11 | 389 | 4 | 377 | 4 | 322 | 4 |
| 3 | 435 | 4 | 393 | 4 | 335 | 4 | 12 | 518 | 5 | 512 | 5 | 448 | 5 |
| 4 | 359 | 4 | 344 | 4 | 307 | 4 | 13 | 499 | 5 | 459 | 5 | 451 | 5 |
| 5 | 420 | 4 | 411 | 4 | 363 | 4 | 14 | 160 | 3 | 154 | 3 | 135 | 3 |
| 6 | 167 | 3 | 160 | 3 | 123 | 3 | 15 | 572 | 5 | 512 | 5 | 411 | 5 |
| 7 | 365 | 4 | 355 | 4 | 326 | 4 | 16 | 358 | 4 | 343 | 4 | 301 | 4 |
| 8 | 149 | 3 | 139 | 3 | 119 | 3 | 17 | 220 | 3 | 212 | 3 | 173 | 3 |
| 9 | 378 | 4 | 369 | 4 | 297 | 4 | 18 | 409 | 4 | 391 | 4 | 346 | 4 |
| *Yds Out* | 3,041 | | 2,920 | | 2,541 | | *Yds In* | 3,485 | | 3,305 | | 2,850 | |
| *Total Yds* | 6,526 | | 6,225 | | 5,391 | | | | | | | | |
| *Total Par* | 72 | | 72 | | 72 | | | | | | | | |

ADDRESS: Whitekirk, near North Berwick, East Lothian EH39 5PR.
TELEPHONE: +44 (0)1620 870300.
FAX: +44 (0)1620 870330.
E-MAIL: golf@whitekirk.u-net.com
WEBSITE: www.whitekirk.com
MANAGER: David Brodie.
PROFESSIONAL: Paul Wardell.
VISITORS: Yes, seven days a week.
GREEN FEES: £20 per round weekdays, £30 per day. £25 per round weekends, £40 per day.
CREDIT CARDS ACCEPTED: Visa/Mastercard.
CATERING: Restaurant and bar overlooking the 9th and 18th greens.
FACILITIES: Motorised buggies(£15 per round, £25 per day), trolley hire (£2), club hire (£10), changing-rooms, putting green, pro shop, practice ground, driving range, coaching clinics, memberships available.
LOCATION: 3 miles east of North Berwick. Off the A1 (Edinburgh–Berwick-upon-Tweed road) on the A198.
LOCAL HOTELS: Belhaven Hotel, Cringletie House Hotel, Dalhousie Castle & Spa Hotel, Fairway Guest House, Greywalls, Kilspindie House Hotel, Marine Hotel, Goldenstones, Golf Hotel, Nether Abbey, Whitekirk Mains Bed & Breakfast.

# PENICUIK

## GLENCORSE GOLF CLUB

### COURSE DESCRIPTION:
A picturesque inland parkland course with trees. Burn affects ten holes. Eight par 3s – only one under 200 yards.

18 holes, 5,217 yards, par 64 (SSS 66). Amateur record N. Shillinglaw 60. Pro record C. Brooks 60.

### SIGNATURE HOLE:
FIFTH ('Forrester's Rest' 237 yards, par 3) Spectacular hole from an elevated tee with a 200-yard carry over a burn. One of the most difficult in the country.

### COURSE CARD

| HOLE | YDS | PAR | HOLE | YDS | PAR |
|------|------|-----|------|------|-----|
| 1 | 225 | 3 | 10 | 335 | 4 |
| 2 | 355 | 4 | 11 | 211 | 3 |
| 3 | 208 | 3 | 12 | 211 | 3 |
| 4 | 451 | 4 | 13 | 434 | 4 |
| 5 | 237 | 3 | 14 | 329 | 4 |
| 6 | 273 | 4 | 15 | 236 | 3 |
| 7 | 308 | 4 | 16 | 375 | 4 |
| 8 | 164 | 3 | 17 | 215 | 3 |
| 9 | 331 | 4 | 18 | 319 | 4 |
| *Yds Out* | 2,552 | | *Yds In* | 2,665 | |
| *Total Yds* | 5,217 | | | | |
| *Total Par* | 64 | | | | |

ADDRESS: Milton Bridge, Penicuik, Midlothian EH26 0RD.
TELEPHONE: +44 (0)1968 677189.
FAX: +44 (0)1968 674399.
E-MAIL: Glencorsegc@glencorse.penicuik.fsnet.co.uk
SECRETARY: Bill Oliver.
PROFESSIONAL: Cliff Jones +44(0)1968 676481.
VISITORS: Yes, Monday to Thursday and Sunday afternoons.
GREEN FEES: £20 per round weekdays, £26 per day. £26 per round Sundays. Special offer: two rounds plus food £35.
CREDIT CARDS ACCEPTED: Visa/Mastercard at pro shop only.
CATERING: Restaurant and bar.
FACILITIES: Trolley hire (£2), club hire (£7.50), caddies (£10), changing-rooms, putting green, pro shop, driving range (quarter-mile from the course), coaching clinics.

LOCATION: 9 miles south of Edinburgh on the A701 Peebles road.
LOCAL HOTELS: Cringletie House Hotel, Peebles Hotel Hydro, Roslin Glen Hotel, Royal Hotel.

# PRESTONPANS

## ROYAL MUSSELBURGH GOLF CLUB

COURSE DESCRIPTION:
Secluded tree-lined parkland course, opened in 1926 and designed by James Braid. Fairly flat overlooking the Firth of Forth with excellent sea views.
18 holes, 6,237 yards, par 70 (SSS 70). Course record 64.

SIGNATURE HOLE:
FOURTEENTH ('The Gully' 149 yards, par 3) Drive over a gully to a green surrounded by bunkers.

COURSE CARD

| HOLE | MEDAL YDS | PAR | FORWARD YDS | PAR | LADIES YDS | PAR | HOLE | MEDAL YDS | PAR | FORWARD YDS | PAR | LADIES YDS | PAR |
|---|---|---|---|---|---|---|---|---|---|---|---|---|---|
| 1 | 349 | 4 | 309 | 4 | 293 | 4 | 10 | 356 | 4 | 343 | 4 | 330 | 4 |
| 2 | 295 | 4 | 280 | 4 | 269 | 4 | 11 | 370 | 4 | 351 | 4 | 331 | 4 |
| 3 | 368 | 4 | 349 | 4 | 306 | 4 | 12 | 362 | 4 | 329 | 4 | 300 | 4 |
| 4 | 365 | 4 | 352 | 4 | 335 | 4 | 13 | 452 | 4 | 435 | 4 | 413 | 5 |
| 5 | 329 | 4 | 311 | 4 | 292 | 4 | 14 | 149 | 3 | 127 | 3 | 118 | 3 |
| 6 | 176 | 3 | 147 | 3 | 128 | 3 | 15 | 440 | 4 | 419 | 4 | 409 | 5 |
| 7 | 391 | 4 | 363 | 4 | 350 | 4 | 16 | 176 | 3 | 148 | 3 | 141 | 3 |
| 8 | 420 | 4 | 410 | 4 | 359 | 4 | 17 | 352 | 4 | 334 | 4 | 300 | 3 |
| 9 | 477 | 5 | 465 | 5 | 460 | 5 | 18 | 410 | 4 | 377 | 4 | 369 | 5 |
| Yds Out | 3,170 | | 2,986 | | 2,792 | | Yds In | 3,067 | | 2,863 | | 2,711 | |
| Total Yds | 6,237 | | 5,849 | | 5,503 | | | | | | | | |
| Total Par | 70 | | 70 | | 73 | | | | | | | | |

ADDRESS: Prestongrange House, Prestonpans, near Edinburgh EH32 9RP.
TELEPHONE & FAX : +44 (0) 1875 810276.
E-MAIL: Royalmusselburgh@btinternet.com
WEBSITE: www.royalmusselburgh.co.uk
SECRETARY: T.H. Hardie.
PROFESSIONAL: John Henderson.
VISITORS: Yes, by arrangement with management secretary. Restricted at certain times.
GREEN FEES: £22 per round weekdays, £35 per day. No weekly tickets. Special arrangements with management secretary.

CATERING: Restaurant and bar.

FACILITIES: Motorised buggies (£15 for round, £25 for day), trolley hire (£2), club hire (£10 for round), caddies on request to pro (£25 per round), changing-rooms, putting green, pro shop, practice ground, coaching clinics.

LOCATION: B1361 to North Berwick. Course west of Prestonpans, off A59.

LOCAL HOTELS: Cringletie House Hotel, Dalhousie Castle & Spa Hotel, Kilspindie House Hotel.

# PUMPHERSTON

## PUMPHERSTON GOLF CLUB

### COURSE DESCRIPTION:
Short, undulating parkland course with trees, bunkers and a pond providing hazards.

9 holes, 5,434 yards (for 18 holes), par 66 (SSS 66). Amateur record P. Drake 64 (1996).

### SIGNATURE HOLE:
SIXTH (251 yards, par 4) Green built in the pond, leaving only a seven-yard wide entrance. Three bunkers short of the pond. Out of bounds from tee to green on the left and a lateral water hazard on the right.

### COURSE CARD

| HOLE | YDS | PAR |
|------|------|-----|
| 1 | 410 | 4 |
| 2 | 440 | 4 |
| 3 | 184 | 3 |
| 4 | 340 | 4 |
| 5 | 185 | 3 |
| 6 | 251 | 4 |
| 7 | 165 | 3 |
| 8 | 302 | 4 |
| 9 | 440 | 4 |
| Yds Out | 2,717 | |
| Total Yds | 2,717 | |
| Total Par | 33 | |

ADDRESS: Drumshoreland Road, Pumpherston EH53 0LF.

TELEPHONE: +44 (0)1506 432869.

SECRETARY: A. Docharty.

VISITORS: No casual visitors. Societies Monday to Thursday.

GREEN FEES: £4 with member, £11 without.

CATERING: Snack meals.
FACILITIES: Putting green, practice ground.
LOCATION: 2 miles east of Pumpherston, between A71 and A89.

# RATHO

## RATHO PARK GOLF CLUB

COURSE DESCRIPTION:
Flat parkland course.
    18 holes, 5,900 yards, par 69 (SSS 68). Course record 62.

ADDRESS: Ratho, Newbridge, Midlothian EH28 8NX.
TELEPHONE & FAX: +44 (0)131 333 1752.
PROFESSIONAL: Alan Pate.
VISITORS: Contact in advance.
GREEN FEES: £25 per round weekdays, £35 weekends.
CATERING: Restaurant and bar +44 (0)131 333 2566.
FACILITIES: Trolley hire, putting green, pro shop, practice ground.
LOCATION: 8 miles west of Edinburgh on A71. Adjacent to Edinburgh Airport.
LOCAL HOTELS: Dalhousie Castle & Spa Hotel, Forte Posthouse.

# SOUTH QUEENSFERRY

## DUNDAS PARKS GOLF CLUB

COURSE DESCRIPTION:
Moderately undulating parkland course.
    9 holes, 6,024 yards (for 18 holes), par 70 (SSS 69). Course record 66.

ADDRESS: Dundas Castle Estate, South Queensferry, West Lothian EH30 9SP.
SECRETARY: +44 (0)131 331 5603.
VISITORS: Contact in advance.
GREEN FEES: £8 per round.
FACILITIES: Putting green, practice ground, bunker and driving bay.
LOCATION: 1 mile south on A8000.
LOCAL HOTELS: Forth Bridges Hotel.

# UPHALL

## UPHALL GOLF CLUB

COURSE DESCRIPTION:
Parkland course. As it is relatively short it is ideal for golf societies. Picturesque with some great character-building holes.

18 holes, 5,600 yards, par 69 (SSS 67). Course record 62.

ADDRESS: Houston Mains, Uphall EH52 6JT.
TELEPHONE: +44 (0)1506 856404.
FAX: +44 (0)1506 855358.
PROFESSIONAL: Gordon Law +44 (0)1506 855553.
VISITORS: Yes.
GREEN FEES: £14 per round weekdays, £19 per day. £18 per round weekends, £26 per day.
CATERING: Á la carte, bar meals, suppers, golf outings and functions catered for.
FACILITIES: Trolley/buggy hire, putting green, pro shop, practice ground.
LOCATION: Junction 3 off M8. 10 miles from Edinburgh, 30 miles from Glasgow.
LOCAL HOTELS: Houston House Hotel.

# WEST CALDER

## HARBURN GOLF CLUB

COURSE DESCRIPTION:
Moorland course laid out on a slope 600 feet above sea level. Reasonably flat, some tree-lined holes and water hazards.

18 holes, 5,921 yards, par 69 (SSS 69). Course record 62.

ADDRESS: Harburn Village, West Calder EH55 8RS.
TELEPHONE: +44 (0)1506 871131.
FAX: +44 (0) 1506 870286
PROFESSIONAL: Stephen Mills.
VISITORS: Contact in advance. No visitors on Wednesdays. Limited at weekends.
GREEN FEES: £18 per round weekdays, £23 per round weekends and bank holidays.
CATERING: Restaurant and bar.
FACILITIES: Motorised buggies (£15), trolley hire, club hire, changing-rooms, putting green, pro shop, practice ground, coaching clinics.
LOCATION: Two miles south of West Calder on B7008.
LOCAL HOTELS: The Hilcroft Hotel.

# WEST LINTON

## RUTHERFORD CASTLE GOLF CLUB

**COURSE DESCRIPTION:**
Set amongst 150 acres of rolling parkland beneath the Pentland Hills, this course with its natural water hazards and mature trees challenges golfers of all standards. A good combination of tough par 3s, exciting par 4s and formidable par 5s, coupled with majestic scenery, will satisfy most.
   18 holes, 6,525 yards, par 72 (SSS 71).

**SIGNATURE HOLE:**
SIXTH (375 yards, par 4) The hardest hole on the course.

**COURSE CARD**

| HOLE | MEDAL YDS | PAR | LADIES YDS | PAR | HOLE | MEDAL YDS | PAR | LADIES YDS | PAR |
|------|-----------|-----|------------|-----|------|-----------|-----|------------|-----|
| 1 | 386 | 4 | 351 | 4 | 10 | 167 | 3 | 137 | 3 |
| 2 | 389 | 4 | 372 | 4 | 11 | 410 | 4 | 338 | 4 |
| 3 | 375 | 4 | 342 | 4 | 12 | 509 | 5 | 432 | 5 |
| 4 | 193 | 3 | 168 | 3 | 13 | 515 | 5 | 448 | 5 |
| 5 | 488 | 5 | 442 | 5 | 14 | 279 | 4 | 224 | 4 |
| 6 | 375 | 4 | 333 | 4 | 15 | 426 | 4 | 397 | 4 |
| 7 | 555 | 5 | 506 | 5 | 16 | 396 | 4 | 351 | 4 |
| 8 | 339 | 4 | 268 | 4 | 17 | 406 | 4 | 370 | 4 |
| 9 | 180 | 3 | 162 | 3 | 18 | 137 | 3 | 128 | 3 |
| *Yds Out* | 3,280 | | 2,944 | | *Yds In* | 3,245 | | 2,825 | |
| *Total Yds* | 6,525 | | 5,769 | | | | | | |
| *Total Par* | 72 | | 72 | | | | | | |

**ADDRESS:** West Linton, Peeblesshire EH46 7AS.
**TELEPHONE & FAX:** +44 (0)1968 661233.
**E-MAIL:** info@ruth-castlegc.co.uk
**WEBSITE:** www.ruth-castlegc.co.uk
**MANAGER:** Wendy Mitchell.
**VISITORS:** Yes, at all times.
**GREEN FEES:** £10 per round weekdays, £15 per day. £25 per round weekends, £35 per day. Group packages available.
**CREDIT CARDS ACCEPTED:** Visa/Mastercard.
**FACILITIES:** Motorised buggies (£10), trolley hire (£2), changing-rooms, pro shop, memberships available.
**CATERING:** Bar, pro shop and bar snacks available.

LOCATION: From Edinburgh city by-pass, Lothianburn exit. It is 15 minutes south on the A702 between West Linton and Carlops.

LOCAL HOTELS: Cringletie House Hotel, Dalhousie Castle & Spa Hotel, Peebles Hotel Hydro, The Allan Ramsay.

# WEST LINTON GOLF CLUB

### COURSE DESCRIPTION:
Scenic moorland course with views of the Pentland Hills and Moorfoot Hills. Although the fairways are generous, the rough is punitive and it is a real challenge of golf.

18 holes, 6,132 yards, par 69 (SSS 70). Amateur record S. Walker 63. Pro record Bernard Gallacher 71.

### SIGNATURE HOLE:
EIGHTEENTH (230 yards, par 3) Uphill tee shot over a gully to a small green with out of bounds on the right.

### COURSE CARD

| HOLE | YDS | PAR | HOLE | YDS | PAR |
|------|-----|-----|------|-----|-----|
| 1 | 307 | 4 | 10 | 348 | 4 |
| 2 | 143 | 3 | 11 | 469 | 4 |
| 3 | 353 | 4 | 12 | 203 | 3 |
| 4 | 525 | 5 | 13 | 295 | 4 |
| 5 | 470 | 4 | 14 | 376 | 4 |
| 6 | 360 | 4 | 15 | 503 | 5 |
| 7 | 330 | 4 | 16 | 415 | 4 |
| 8 | 447 | 4 | 17 | 196 | 3 |
| 9 | 162 | 3 | 18 | 230 | 3 |
| *Yds* *Out* | 3,097 | | *Yds* *In* | 3,035 | |
| *Total Yds* | 6,132 | | | | |
| *Total Par* | 69 | | | | |

ADDRESS: Medwyn Road, West Linton. Peeblesshire EH46 7HN.
TEL: +44 (0)1968 660256
SECRETARY: G. Scott.
PROFESSIONAL: Ian Wright.
VISITORS: Weekdays, except on medal days. Weekends, non-medal days after 1 p.m.
GREEN FEES: £18 per round weekdays, £27 per day. £28 per round weekends.
CATERING: Full service.
FACILITIES: Trolley/buggy hire, putting green, pro shop, practice ground.
LOCATION: 18 miles south-west of Edinburgh on A702.
LOCAL HOTELS: Cringletie House Hotel, Dalhousie Castle & Spa Hotel, Gordon Arms Hotel.

# WHITBURN

## POLKEMMET COUNTRY PARK

COURSE DESCRIPTION:
Public parkland course surrounded by mature woodland. River Almond bisects the course.
  9 holes, 6,496 yards (for 18 holes), par 74 (SSS 74).

ADDRESS: Polkemmet Country Park, Whitburn EH47 0AD.
TELEPHONE: +44 (0)1501 743905.
VISITORS: Any time.
GREEN FEES: £4.50 per nine holes; £5.25 on Sundays.
CATERING: Restaurant and bar.
FACILITIES: Trolley hire, practice ground, driving range.
LOCATION: 2 miles west, off B7066.
LOCAL HOTELS: The Hilcroft Hotel.

# WINCHBURGH

## NIDDRY CASTLE GOLF CLUB

COURSE DESCRIPTION:
Wooded, parkland course. Tight with small greens.
  9 holes, 5,514 yards, par 70 (SSS 67).

ADDRESS: Castle Road, Winchburgh EH52 6RQ.
TELEPHONE: +44 (0)1506 891097.
VISITORS: Contact at weekends. Restricted during competitions.
GREEN FEES: £13 per round weekdays, £19 weekends.
FACILITIES: Full clubhouse facilities.
LOCATION: 9 miles west of Edinburgh between Kirkliston and Linlithgow.

# HIGHLANDS INCLUDING INVERNESS

# ALNESS

## ALNESS GOLF CLUB

### COURSE DESCRIPTION:
A beautifully situated parkland course, overlooking the Cromarty Firth and surrounding hills of Easter Ross and the Black Isle. The last five holes run alongside the River Averon, offering a contrast from the previous holes. The course was extended from 9 to 18 holes in 1997 and offers a challenge to all levels of golfer. Not a long course, 4,886 yards, but tight – and the small greens can test and promote skilful approach shots. The new clubhouse was officially opened in 2000 and offers all facilities. The comfortable lounge has views over the town of Alness, known for its floral displays which regularly win Britain in Bloom and Scotland in Bloom trophies.

18 holes, 4,886 yards, par 67 (SSS 64).

### SIGNATURE HOLE:
TENTH (307 yards, par 4) Downhill with trouble on the left. Panoramic views.

### COURSE CARD

| HOLE | YDS | PAR | HOLE | YDS | PAR |
|------|-----|-----|------|-----|-----|
| 1 | 365 | 4 | 10 | 307 | 4 |
| 2 | 102 | 3 | 11 | 286 | 4 |
| 3 | 368 | 4 | 12 | 322 | 4 |
| 4 | 304 | 4 | 13 | 94 | 3 |
| 5 | 510 | 5 | 14 | 406 | 4 |
| 6 | 265 | 4 | 15 | 140 | 3 |
| 7 | 328 | 4 | 16 | 101 | 3 |
| 8 | 176 | 3 | 17 | 279 | 4 |
| 9 | 369 | 4 | 18 | 164 | 3 |
| *Yds Out* | 2,787 | | *Yds In* | 2,099 | |
| *Total Yds* | 4,886 | | | | |
| *Total Par* | 67 | | | | |

ADDRESS: Ardross Road, Alness, Ross-shire IV17 0QA.
TELEPHONE: +44 (0)1349 883877.
E-MAIL: info@alnessgolfclub.co.uk
WEBSITE: www.alness.com
SECRETARY: Mrs Betty Taylor.

VISITORS: Any time, except competition days. Visiting parties are very welcome. Prior notice required and discounts for large parties.

GREEN FEES: £13 per round.

CATERING: Bar snacks, teas and coffees.

FACILITIES: Trolley hire, club hire, changing-rooms, practice ground, disabled facilities.

LOCATION: 23 miles north of Inverness on main A9. From the south, turn off the A9 and follow the signs for Alness, which take you to the High Street. Halfway along, turn left onto Ardross Road (turn right if you are arriving from the north). You will find the club half a mile on the left.

LOCAL HOTELS: Bunchrew House Hotel, Commercial Hotel, Mansfield House Hotel, Morven House Hotel, Station Hotel.

# ARISAIG

## TRAIGH GOLF COURSE

COURSE DESCRIPTION:

Seaside links course lying beside sandy beaches and rocky islets, featuring a line of grassy hills which used to be sand dunes. Golf has been played here since 1900, but the course was enlarged and improved in the early 1990s. Spectacular views over Traigh Sands and the Sound of Sleat to the islands of Eigg, Rum and Skye. The word Traigh – pronounced 'Try' – means 'beach' in Gaelic.

9 holes, 4,912 yards (for 18 holes), par 68 (SSS 65). Amateur record 69.

SIGNATURE HOLE:

NINTH (180 yards, par 3) Elevated tee down to a challenging green. Depending on the wind, it can be anything from a full driver to an easy 9-iron. Spectacular views to the islands.

COURSE CARD

| HOLE | MEDAL YDS | PAR | FORWARD YDS | PAR |
|------|------|-----|------|-----|
| 1 | 130 | 3 | 130 | 3 |
| 2 | 452 | 5 | 452 | 5 |
| 3 | 173 | 3 | 173 | 3 |
| 4 | 257 | 4 | 249 | 4 |
| 5 | 135 | 3 | 125 | 3 |
| 6 | 283 | 4 | 264 | 4 |
| 7 | 479 | 5 | 446 | 5 |
| 8 | 367 | 4 | 337 | 4 |
| 9 | 180 | 3 | 170 | 3 |
| Yds Out | 2,456 | | 2,346 | |

| Total Yds | 2,456 |
|---|---|
| Total Par | 34 |

ADDRESS: Arisaig, by Mallaig, Inverness-shire PH39 4NT.
TELEPHONE: +44 (0)1687 450337.
WEBSITE: www.traighgolf.co.uk
MANAGER: W. Henderson +44 (0)1687 450645.
VISITORS: Any time. Course open all year.
GREEN FEES: £12 per day. £45 per week.
CATERING: Soft drinks, coffee and snacks. Clubhouse is open from April to October.
FACILITIES: Trolley hire.
LOCATION: West Highlands. On A830 Fort William–Mallaig road. Course 3 miles north of Arisaig.
LOCAL HOTELS: Arisaig House Hotel, Arisaig Hotel, Invercreran Country House Hotel, Marine Hotel, Morar Hotel, West Highland Hotel.

# BEAULY

## AIGAS GOLF COURSE

COURSE DESCRIPTION:
Opened in 1993, a challenging undulating parkland course with large greens set in Strathglass beside the River Beauly.
9 holes, 4,878 yards (for 18 holes), par 66 (SSS 63).

SIGNATURE HOLE:
THIRD ('Farmhouse' 401 yards, par 4) A challenging hole played into the prevailing wind and rising up to a small elevated green with strategically placed bunkers.

COURSE CARD

| HOLE | MEDAL | | FORWARD | | LADIES | |
|---|---|---|---|---|---|---|
| | YDS | PAR | YDS | PAR | YDS | PAR |
| 1 | 524 | 5 | 515 | 5 | 507 | 5 |
| 2 | 142 | 3 | 140 | 3 | 132 | 3 |
| 3 | 401 | 4 | 395 | 4 | 357 | 5 |
| 4 | 202 | 3 | 190 | 3 | 173 | 3 |
| 5 | 132 | 3 | 126 | 3 | 120 | 3 |
| 6 | 339 | 4 | 323 | 4 | 296 | 4 |
| 7 | 153 | 3 | 140 | 3 | 122 | 3 |
| 8 | 287 | 4 | 270 | 4 | 262 | 4 |
| 9 | 259 | 4 | 270 | 4 | 243 | 4 |
| Yds | 2,439 | | 2,352 | | 2,242 | |

| Out | |
| --- | --- |
| Total Yds | 2,439 |
| Total Par | 33 |

ADDRESS: Mains of Aigas, by Beauly, Inverness-shire IV4 7A.
TELEPHONE: +44 (0)1463 782942.
FAX: +44 (0)1463 782423.
E-MAIL: aigas@cali.co.uk
WEBSITE: www.cali.co.uk/aigas
GREEN FEES: £7 for 9 holes weekdays, £11 for 18. £15 for day. £9 for 9 holes weekends, £13 for 18. £18 for day. Weekly ticket £45.
CATERING: Coffee shop. Clubhouse is open from April to October for light refreshments.
FACILITIES: Trolley hire (£1), club hire (£3.50), new practice green adjacent to clubhouse.
LOCAL ACCOMMODATION: Mains of Aigas.

# BOAT OF GARTEN

## BOAT OF GARTEN GOLF CLUB

COURSE DESCRIPTION:
Heathland course, designed by James Braid, with demanding birch-lined fairways beside the River Spey and spectacular views of the Cairngorm Mountains' snow-capped peaks.
   18 holes, 5,866 yards, par 69 (SSS 69). Amateur record 67.

SIGNATURE HOLE:
TWELFTH (349 yards, par 4) Tricky but not too difficult. From an elevated tee you drive down an avenue of silver birches. The two-tiered green is guarded by bunkers and an over-hit approach shot will find deep rough.

COURSE CARD

| HOLE | YDS | PAR | HOLE | YDS | PAR |
| --- | --- | --- | --- | --- | --- |
| 1 | 188 | 3 | 10 | 271 | 4 |
| 2 | 360 | 4 | 11 | 379 | 4 |
| 3 | 163 | 3 | 12 | 349 | 4 |
| 4 | 514 | 5 | 13 | 432 | 4 |
| 5 | 333 | 4 | 14 | 323 | 4 |
| 6 | 403 | 4 | 15 | 307 | 4 |
| 7 | 386 | 4 | 16 | 168 | 3 |
| 8 | 355 | 4 | 17 | 344 | 4 |
| 9 | 154 | 3 | 18 | 437 | 4 |

| | | | | |
|---|---|---|---|---|
| *Yds* | 2,856 | | *Yds* | 3,010 |
| *Out* | | | *In* | |
| *Total Yds* | 5,866 | | | |
| *Total Par* | 69 | | | |

**ADDRESS:** Boat of Garten, PH24 3BQ.
**TELEPHONE:** +44 (0)1479 831282.
**FAX:** +44 (0)1479 831523.
**E-MAIL:** boatgolf@enterprise.net
**WEBSITE:** www.boatgolf.com
**SECRETARY:** Paddy Smyth.
**SHOP MANAGER:** James Ingram.
**VISITORS:** Weekdays 9.30 a.m. to 6 p.m., weekends 10 a.m. to 4 p.m.
**GREEN FEES:** £23 per round weekdays, £28 per day. £28 weekends, £33 per day. Weekly ticket £110.
**CATERING:** Restaurant and bar.
**CREDIT CARDS ACCEPTED:** Visa/Mastercard/Diners Club.
**FACILITIES:** Motorised buggies, trolley hire, club hire, caddies by prior arrangement, changing-rooms, putting green, pro shop, practice ground.
**LOCATION:** 30 miles south of Inverness just off the A9.
**LOCAL HOTELS:** Bunchrew House Hotel, Glen Mhor Hotel, Greenlawns, Skye of Curr Hotel, Boat Hotel, Craigard Hotel, Links Hotel, Moorfield House Hotel.

# BONAR BRIDGE

## BONAR BRIDGE/ARDGAY GOLF CLUB

### COURSE DESCRIPTION:
A heath and moorland course. Undulating, narrow, tree-lined fairways favour the accurate rather than the long hitter, and there are some small, difficult-to-read, greens. Rough is not fierce and the course is suitable for high-handicap players and the visitor in search of family golf. Easy walking, great views and the chance to see and hear a huge variety of wildlife.

9 holes, 5,284 yards (for 18 holes), par 68 (SSS 66). Amateur record 66.

### SIGNATURE HOLE:
THIRD ('Pond' 171 yards, par 3) Played from an elevated tee to a generous green with a pond at the rear. Ranked among the less demanding holes: a birdie is a distinct possibility and aces have been known. The views down to Loch Migdale and the dramatic hills form the backdrop to this picturesque hole.

## COURSE CARD

| HOLE | MEDAL YDS | PAR | FORWARD YDS | PAR | LADIES YDS | PAR |
|------|-----------|-----|-------------|-----|------------|-----|
| 1 | 339 | 4 | 339 | 4 | 312 | 4 |
| 2 | 297 | 4 | 297 | 4 | 223 | 4 |
| 3 | 171 | 3 | 171 | 3 | 171 | 3 |
| 4 | 352 | 4 | 352 | 4 | 352 | 4 |
| 5 | 576 | 5 | 438 | 5 | 438 | 5 |
| 6 | 174 | 3 | 174 | 3 | 174 | 3 |
| 7 | 285 | 4 | 285 | 4 | 240 | 4 |
| 8 | 137 | 3 | 137 | 3 | 137 | 3 |
| 9 | 311 | 4 | 311 | 4 | 275 | 4 |
| Yds Out | 2,642 | | 2,504 | | 2,322 | |
| Total Yds | 2,642 | | | | | |
| Total Par | 34 | | | | | |

ADDRESS: Migdale Road, Bonar Bridge, Sutherland IV24 3EJ.
TELEPHONE: +44 (0)1863 766375.
FAX: +44 (0)1863 766738.
E-MAIL: secbbagc@aol.com
WEBSITE: www.bonarbridgegolfclub.co.uk
SECRETARY: Frank Mussard.
VISITORS: Any time.
GREEN FEES: £12 per day. Weekly ticket £60.
CATERING: Limited catering, May to September.
FACILITIES: Trolley hire (£2), club hire (£10), changing-rooms, putting green, memberships available.
LOCATION: From south, immediately after crossing the bridge, go straight on up hill (Migdale Road) for half a mile. Course on right.
LOCAL HOTELS: Royal Hotel.

# BRORA

## BRORA GOLF CLUB

COURSE DESCRIPTION:
The club was established in 1891 and this traditional links course was designed by James Braid in 1923. Australia's Peter Thomson, five times Open Champion, says it is 'the most natural links anywhere in the world'. And *Today's Golfer* magazine voted it Best Value Course in Britain. Offers all the challenges of links with a host of interesting and testing holes. Maintained in traditional fashion. Noted for fast, true greens.

18 holes, 6,110 yards, par 69 (SSS 69). Amateur record J. Miller 61.

SIGNATURE HOLE:
TWELFTH (362 yards, par 4) Rolling fairway. The perfect drive is down the right, but beware of out of bounds. If you choose the left, the second shot has to contend with bunkers.

## COURSE CARD

| HOLE | MEDAL YDS | PAR | FORWARD YDS | PAR | LADIES YDS | PAR | HOLE | MEDAL YDS | PAR | FORWARD YDS | PAR | LADIES YDS | PAR |
|---|---|---|---|---|---|---|---|---|---|---|---|---|---|
| 1 | 297 | 4 | 280 | 4 | 276 | 4 | 10 | 435 | 4 | 425 | 4 | 395 | 4 |
| 2 | 344 | 4 | 334 | 4 | 323 | 4 | 11 | 412 | 4 | 412 | 4 | 383 | 4 |
| 3 | 447 | 4 | 447 | 4 | 413 | 5 | 12 | 362 | 4 | 314 | 4 | 273 | 4 |
| 4 | 325 | 4 | 313 | 4 | 277 | 4 | 13 | 125 | 3 | 108 | 3 | 108 | 3 |
| 5 | 428 | 4 | 418 | 4 | 378 | 4 | 14 | 334 | 3 | 305 | 3 | 282 | 4 |
| 6 | 174 | 3 | 164 | 3 | 153 | 3 | 15 | 430 | 4 | 399 | 4 | 324 | 4 |
| 7 | 350 | 4 | 340 | 4 | 333 | 4 | 16 | 345 | 3 | 335 | 4 | 256 | 4 |
| 8 | 501 | 5 | 501 | 5 | 430 | 5 | 17 | 438 | 4 | 438 | 4 | 386 | 4 |
| 9 | 162 | 3 | 149 | 3 | 141 | 3 | 18 | 201 | 3 | 190 | 3 | 142 | 3 |
| Yds Out | 3,028 | | 2,946 | | 2,724 | | Yds In | 3,082 | | 2,926 | | 2,549 | |
| Total Yds | 6,110 | | 5,872 | | 5,273 | | | | | | | | |
| Total Par | 69 | | 69 | | 70 | | | | | | | | |

ADDRESS: Golf Road, Brora, Sutherland KW9 6QS.
TELEPHONE: +44 (0)1408 621417.
FAX: +44 (0)1408 622157.
E-MAIL: secretary@broragolf.co.uk
SECRETARY: James Fraser.
VISITORS: Yes, seven days a week.
GREEN FEES: £25 per round weekdays, £35 per day. £30 per round weekends, £40 per day. Weekly tickets by arrangement.
CREDIT CARDS ACCEPTED: Visa/Mastercard.
CATERING: Restaurant and bar. Functions catered for.
FACILITIES: Trolley hire (£2), club hire (£7), caddies (£20), changing-rooms, putting green, pro shop, practice ground, memberships available.
LOCATION: 5 miles north of Golspie on A9. 52 miles from Inverness. Turn right in the centre of the village to seaside car park.
LOCAL HOTELS: Mansfield House Hotel, Nigg Ferry Hotel, Royal Marine Hotel, The Links Hotel.

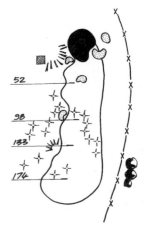

# CARRBRIDGE

## CARRBRIDGE GOLF CLUB

**COURSE DESCRIPTION:**
Short but challenging part-parkland, part-heathland course with water on every hole. Course rises 300 feet to about 1,000 feet at its highest point. Good greens. Superb views of Cairngorm Mountains. Founded in 1980.

9 holes, 5,402 yards (for 18 holes), par 71 (SSS 68). Amateur record 64.

**SIGNATURE HOLE:**
EIGHTH (174 yards, par 3) Elevated tee to a green surrounded by bunkers with a ditch behind. A gorse-covered bank punishes wayward shots to the right; cottage gardens on the left are out of bounds.

**COURSE CARD**

| HOLE | MEDAL YDS | PAR | FORWARD YDS | PAR | LADIES YDS | PAR | HOLE | MEDAL YDS | PAR | FORWARD YDS | PAR | LADIES YDS | PAR |
|---|---|---|---|---|---|---|---|---|---|---|---|---|---|
| 1 | 480 | 4 | 446 | 4 | 473 | 5 | 10 | 480 | 5 | 446 | 4 | 473 | 5 |
| 2 | 334 | 4 | 334 | 4 | 334 | 4 | 11 | 334 | 4 | 334 | 4 | 334 | 4 |
| 3 | 342 | 4 | 331 | 4 | 285 | 5 | 12 | 342 | 4 | 331 | 4 | 285 | 4 |
| 4 | 331 | 4 | 227 | 4 | 233 | 4 | 13 | 331 | 4 | 227 | 4 | 233 | 3 |
| 5 | 258 | 4 | 226 | 4 | 241 | 4 | 14 | 258 | 4 | 226 | 4 | 241 | 4 |
| 6 | 270 | 4 | 238 | 4 | 243 | 3 | 15 | 270 | 4 | 238 | 4 | 243 | 4 |
| 7 | 262 | 4 | 262 | 4 | 218 | 4 | 16 | 262 | 4 | 262 | 4 | 218 | 4 |
| 8 | 174 | 3 | 158 | 3 | 165 | 3 | 17 | 174 | 3 | 158 | 3 | 168 | 3 |
| 9 | 231 | 3 | 231 | 3 | 209 | 4 | 18 | 269 | 4 | 269 | 4 | 209 | 4 |
| *Yds* Out | 2,682 | | 2,453 | | 2,401 | | *Yds* In | 2,720 | | 2,491 | | 2,401 | |
| Total Yds | 5,402 | | 4,944 | | 4,802 | | | | | | | | |
| Total Par | 71 | | 69 | | 72 | | | | | | | | |

**ADDRESS:** Inverness Road, Carrbridge, Inverness-shire PH23 3AU.
**TELEPHONE:** +44 (0)1479 841623 or 841506.
**E-MAIL:** enquiries@carrbridgegolf.com
**WEBSITE:** www.carrbridgegolf.com
**SECRETARY:** Mrs Anne Baird.
**VISITORS:** Yes, but not Wednesdays after 5 p.m. and most Sundays until mid-afternoon. Check availability.
**GREEN FEES:** £12 per day weekdays, £13 July to September. £15 per day weekends. Weekly ticket £55, juniors £27.50.
**CATERING:** Tea, coffee, snacks April to October. No bar.
**FACILITIES:** Trolley hire (£1), club hire (£3.50), changing-rooms, putting green,

memberships available.

**LOCATION:** 7 miles north of Aviemore. 27 miles south of Inverness. Off A9.

**LOCAL HOTEL:** Skye of Curr Hotel

# DORNOCH

## CARNEGIE CLUB (SKIBO CASTLE)

### COURSE DESCRIPTION:

Greg Norman, who knows a thing or two about golf courses, said of this magnificent links: 'There is nothing better in life than a dream come true – and this is definitely that dream.' Whatever the delights of this 7,500-acre estate on the banks of the Firth of Dornoch, it is the course that is Skibo's brightest gem. Once owned by Andrew Carnegie, the course fell into disrepair until Peter de Savary bought the Castle – now famous for Madonna's wedding – and its grounds for £5.6 million and spent more than £10 million renovating it. He set about with Donald Steel's help building a testing, but fair, championship course which is a delight in every sense. With such magnificent scenery of the estuarial waters of the Firth on three sides, and the hills of Sutherland and Ross-shire all around, this could never be a good walk spoiled. Almost

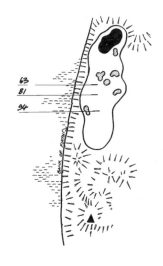

as welcoming as the firm and fast and gently rolling fairways, pockmarked with bunkers, is the friendly Golf House where you can sit and gaze out through huge picture windows at an amazing panorama. The last three holes loop around the Golf House and three eminent gentlemen of my acquaintance enjoyed them so much that after a drink they went out and played the final three again. They then retired for refreshment and repeated the exercise. This was done until they lost count of how many holes, drinks or shots had been taken. From the 1st – a 449-yard par 4 – you know that whatever success and disaster lie ahead, it will be an experience enjoyed. Usually playing downwind, you drive into the throat of a valley from which you will play your second to a green which, if you misjudge your approach, will sweep the ball away to the left and into one of those bunkers. Naming a Signature Hole at Carnegie is like professing a preference for one of your offspring, but for me it would have to be the par-4 17th (see below). It's one of those intriguing holes which force the golfer to think; make a mess of it, then just enjoy being there and look all around you at the Struie Hill to the west, the Castle and the Estate to the north and the rest of the course to the south and the east. The course has a wide range of tees to suit all standards of play and is a typical Scottish links course. Has been voted No. 1 new golf course by *Golf World* magazine.

18 holes, 6,671 yards, par 71 (SSS 72). Amateur record 70. Pro record 69.
*Monk's Walk* – 9 holes, parkland.

## SIGNATURE HOLE:

SEVENTEENTH (267 yards, par 4) A teasing short par 4 which rewards accuracy and severely punishes poor shots. It takes a 250-yard drive to reach the front of the green, which is in range on a good day. The angled green rewards anyone who plays tight to the beach on the left. Large fairway bunkers must be carried and a deep greenside bunker is to be avoided. The scenery is magnificent.

## COURSE CARD

| HOLE | YDS | PAR | HOLE | YDS | PAR |
|------|------|-----|------|------|-----|
| 1 | 449 | 4 | 10 | 509 | 5 |
| 2 | 412 | 4 | 11 | 155 | 3 |
| 3 | 152 | 3 | 12 | 555 | 5 |
| 4 | 311 | 4 | 13 | 217 | 3 |
| 5 | 359 | 4 | 14 | 461 | 4 |
| 6 | 215 | 3 | 15 | 189 | 3 |
| 7 | 398 | 4 | 16 | 468 | 4 |
| 8 | 448 | 4 | 17 | 267 | 4 |
| 9 | 549 | 5 | 18 | 557 | 5 |
| *Yds Out* | 3,293 | | *Yds In* | 3,378 | |
| *Total Yds* | 6,671 | | | | |
| *Total Par* | 71 | | | | |

ADDRESS: Skibo Castle, Dornoch, Sutherland IV25 3RQ.
TELEPHONE: +44 (0)1862 894600.
FAX: +44 (0)1862 894601.
E-MAIL: skibo@carnegieclubs.com
WEBSITE: www.carnegieclub.co.uk
SECRETARY: Andrew McPherson.
PROFESSIONAL: David Thomson.
VISITORS: Weekdays preferably, only between 11 a.m. and 12 noon.
GREEN FEES: £140 per round, including three-course set lunch.
CREDIT CARDS ACCEPTED: Amex/Visa/Mastercard/Diners Club.
CATERING: Restaurant and bar. Lunch £35. Soup and sandwiches £12.50.
FACILITIES: Free trolleys, club hire (£30), caddies (£25 + tip), changing-rooms, putting green, driving range, pro shop, coaching clinics, memberships available.
LOCATION: 45 miles north of Inverness. A9 towards Wick. After crossing Dornoch Firth, first left signposted Meikle Ferry. 5 miles from Royal Dornoch.
LOCAL HOTELS: Bunchrew House Hotel, Glen Mhor Hotel, Golf View Hotel, Greenlawns, Mansfield House Hotel, Morangie Hotel, Nigg Ferry, Royal Golf Hotel, Skibo Castle Hotel, Royal Hotel, Skye of Curr Hotel.

# ROYAL DORNOCH GOLF CLUB

### COURSE DESCRIPTION:

Ask any knowledgeable golfer to name his top ten courses in the world and it is almost certain that Royal Dornoch will feature high among them. This outstanding links, originally the work of Old Tom Morris, is a championship course of the highest order and encapsulates everything a golfer seeks in the most satisfying of rounds – a beautiful setting, a tough but fair test of skill and fast, tricky greens.

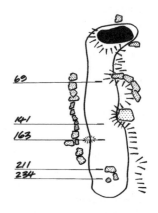

Bordered by the Dornoch Firth with views of the mountains of Sutherland and the gorse ablaze with yellow in early summer, the purity of the air and the surroundings ensure you feel good, no matter what your score. At 6,514 yards, it is not long by modern standards, but you have to think your way around the bunkers, sandhills, hummocks, knolls and swales that can punish the unfortunate shot. Imagine a saucer and upend it and you have a typical Dornoch green. If you manage to keep your ball on the putting surface, you are undoubtedly faced with a putt that will have to take account of a host of subtle contours.

When we last played it on three successive days in the summer, it was a completely different course each time. The first day was still and the course benign. The next day the wind blew from behind on the first eight holes and into our faces on the homeward ten that skirt the sandy beaches of Dornoch Bay, making club selection difficult. And just in case we'd worked out how to play it, the wind turned around for the final day, making many a shot guesswork.

Five-times Open champion Tom Watson says of this magnificent links: 'It was the most fun I've had playing golf in my whole life.' Dornoch's remoteness has prevented it from hosting its fair share of major championships, but that remoteness adds to its charisma, and while golfers often bite their tongues for sharing the secret of Dornoch with acquaintances, they can console themselves that its distance of 600 miles from London and 49 miles from Inverness (Britain's most northerly city) prevents many from sharing its delights.

At 331 yards, the 1st could lull you into a false sense of security, but the 177-yard 2nd sets the standard for the rest of your round. It's one of those saucer greens falling away to both sides and at the rear. Play it short and a grassy mound will carry your ball into either of two cavernous bunkers.

The 5th, a favourite of Tom Watson's, starts a run of four tricky holes and is played from an elevated tee. Ahead some 170 yards away is a great mound which has to be carried. A bunker awaits the shot to the right and gorse to the left. Naturally, it has a plateau green.

The 163-yard 6th is another devilish par 3 and one of the hardest in the world. Again you have to be almost inch perfect. Miss it to the left and three bunkers and thick grass await; go right and you plummet down a steep slope.

The 7th, a 463-yard par 4, is rated the hardest hole on the course, but it is not as interesting as the 8th, which is the last of the outward stretch. You drive over a precipice about 200 yards out and the second shot has to negotiate a series of humps and bumps. At the 9th (496 yards, par 5) you turn for the clubhouse. The beach is down the left, there is long grass and gorse to the right and the wind is probably in your face. The 10th is another par 3, demanding pinpoint accuracy to hold the green. The last is a long par 4, 456 yards, along the top of a ridge. Bunkers 30 yards out await the under-hit approach shot to the green, which has a grassy swale in front.

The influence of Royal Dornoch can be seen in many American courses. Donald Ross, who was born in Dornoch in 1872 and learned his golf there and his trade as a greenkeeper and professional under Old Tom at St Andrews, emigrated to America in 1898 and became one of the greatest architects of golf courses. He designed more than 500 courses – including the famous Pinehurst No. 2 Course and the Seminole Course in Florida – using much of what he had learned at Dornoch. Now many American courses have features which are reminiscent of Dornoch at its best.

Golf was first played here in 1616 and about that time Sir Robert Gordon wrote: 'About this town along the sea coast are the fairest and largest links or green fields of any pairt of Scotland.' Back in 1616, the subscription was two shillings and sixpence; it costs a bit more nowadays but it's an experience worth every penny.

18 holes, 6,514 yards, par 70 (SSS 73). Amateur record C. Christie 66. Championship record 62.

*Struie Course* – 18 holes, 5,438 yards, par 69 (SSS 66).

SIGNATURE HOLE:
FOURTEENTH (445 yards, par 4) 'Foxy', on the Championship Course, was reckoned by Harry Vardon to be the most natural hole in golf. There are no man-made obstacles; instead, on your right, there is a succession of hillocks running up to a raised narrow green of subtle contours.

COURSE CARD

| HOLE | CHAMPIONSHIP YDS | PAR | FORWARD YDS | PAR | LADIES YDS | PAR | HOLE | CHAMPIONSHIP YDS | PAR | FORWARD YDS | PAR | LADIES YDS | PAR |
|---|---|---|---|---|---|---|---|---|---|---|---|---|---|
| 1 | 331 | 4 | 300 | 4 | 266 | 4 | 10 | 147 | 3 | 142 | 3 | 137 | 3 |
| 2 | 177 | 3 | 167 | 3 | 163 | 3 | 11 | 446 | 4 | 434 | 4 | 425 | 5 |
| 3 | 414 | 4 | 398 | 4 | 380 | 4 | 12 | 507 | 5 | 489 | 5 | 472 | 5 |
| 4 | 427 | 4 | 403 | 4 | 391 | 4 | 13 | 166 | 3 | 148 | 3 | 137 | 3 |
| 5 | 354 | 4 | 317 | 4 | 311 | 4 | 14 | 445 | 4 | 439 | 4 | 401 | 5 |
| 6 | 163 | 3 | 163 | 3 | 135 | 3 | 15 | 319 | 4 | 298 | 4 | 288 | 4 |
| 7 | 463 | 4 | 423 | 4 | 412 | 5 | 16 | 402 | 4 | 395 | 4 | 387 | 4 |
| 8 | 396 | 4 | 386 | 4 | 380 | 4 | 17 | 405 | 4 | 390 | 4 | 364 | 4 |
| 9 | 496 | 5 | 447 | 5 | 435 | 5 | 18 | 456 | 4 | 446 | 4 | 442 | 5 |
| Yds Out | 3,221 | | 3,004 | | 2,882 | | Yds In | 3,293 | | 3,181 | | 3,074 | |
| Total Yds | 6,514 | | 6,185 | | 5,958 | | | | | | | | |
| Total Par | 70 | | 70 | | 76 | | | | | | | | |

ADDRESS: Golf Road, Dornoch, Sutherland IV25 3LW.

TELEPHONE: +44 (0)1862 810219 or 811220.

FAX: +44 (0)1862 810792.

E-MAIL: rdgc@royaldornoch.com

WEBSITE: www.royaldornoch.com

SECRETARY/MANAGER: John Duncan.

PROFESSIONAL: Andrew Skinner.

VISITORS: Yes. All days, but limited times on Saturdays. Gentlemen must have handicap of 24 and ladies 39 for the Championship Course.

GREEN FEES: *Championship Course* – £60 per round weekdays, £70 Sundays. Combination tickets (one round on each course) £65 Monday to Saturday; £75 on Sundays.

    *Struie Course* – £18 per round, £25 per day, £100 weekly ticket.

CATERING: Restaurant and bar. Full service daily. Functions catered for.

FACILITIES: Motorised buggies hire for those with medical requirements (£20), trolley hire (£2), club hire (£10–£15), caddies (£20–£30), changing-rooms, putting green, pro shop, practice ground, coaching clinics on request.

LOCATION: 49 miles north of Inverness off A9, north of Dornoch. Signposted from square in Dornoch.

LOCAL HOTELS: Balnagown, Bunchrew House Hotel, Burghfield House Hotel, Glen Mhor Hotel, Glenmorangie, Golf View Hotel, Greenlawns, Holiday Inn Express, Mallin House Hotel, Mansfield House Hotel, Nigg Ferry Hotel, Royal Golf Hotel, Skye of Curr Hotel, The Castle Hotel.

# DURNESS

## DURNESS GOLF CLUB

### COURSE DESCRIPTION:

The most northerly course on the British mainland. Varied links course with some inland holes, including the beautiful par-5 6th bordering on Loch Lanlish. Short but very testing with a variety of holes. Spectacular scenery and an abundance of flora and fauna in very peaceful surroundings.

9 holes but 18 tees, 5,555 yards (for 18 holes), par 70 (SSS 69). Course record 69.

### SIGNATURE HOLE:

EIGHTEENTH (155 yards, par 3) One of the most spectacular holes in Scottish golf. Not for the faint-hearted. You have to play across a gully about 100 yards wide to a green protected by three bunkers with the wind always a hazard. When the tide is in, you are hitting over the Atlantic Ocean.

## COURSE CARD

| HOLE | MEDAL YDS | PAR | LADIES YDS | PAR | HOLE | MEDAL YDS | PAR | LADIES YDS | PAR |
|---|---|---|---|---|---|---|---|---|---|
| 1 | 296 | 4 | 242 | 4 | 10 | 282 | 4 | 221 | 4 |
| 2 | 321 | 4 | 276 | 4 | 11 | 311 | 4 | 280 | 4 |
| 3 | 408 | 4 | 368 | 4 | 12 | 391 | 4 | 354 | 4 |
| 4 | 287 | 4 | 280 | 4 | 13 | 323 | 4 | 287 | 4 |
| 5 | 344 | 4 | 300 | 4 | 14 | 312 | 4 | 280 | 4 |
| 6 | 443 | 5 | 413 | 5 | 15 | 505 | 5 | 429 | 5 |
| 7 | 178 | 3 | 154 | 3 | 16 | 154 | 3 | 131 | 3 |
| 8 | 377 | 4 | 360 | 4 | 17 | 360 | 4 | 322 | 4 |
| 9 | 108 | 3 | 100 | 3 | 18 | 155 | 3 | 108 | 3 |
| *Yds* Out | 2,762 | | 2,473 | | *In* | 2,793 | | 2,383 | |
| Total Yds | 5,555 | | 4,856 | | | | | | |
| Total Par | 70 | | 70 | | | | | | |

**ADDRESS:** Balnakeil, Durness, Sutherland IV27 4PN.
**TELEPHONE:** +44 (0)1971 511364.
**SECRETARY:** Lucy Mackay.
**VISITORS:** Yes, at any time except Sundays before noon.
**GREEN FEES:** £15 per day. £50 for weekly ticket. Special discounts for parties of four plus.
**CATERING:** Snacks available May to September.
**FACILITIES:** Trolley hire (£2), club hire (£5), changing-rooms, putting green, memberships available.
**LOCATION:** 57 miles north-west of Lairg on A838.
**LOCAL HOTELS:** Cape Wrath Hotel, Glen Golly Bed & Breakfast, Melvich Hotel, Parkhill Hotel, Portnacon Guest House, Rhiconick Hotel, Smoo Falls Guest House. Amenities

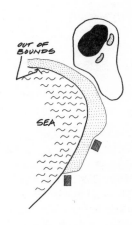

# ELGIN

## ELGIN GOLF CLUB

### COURSE DESCRIPTION:
Relatively flat, parkland course with some tree-lined holes. Rated by many as the best inland course in the North. Undulating greens and tight holes that demand accuracy. Only one par 5, but several long par 4s make it a test for all abilities. Host to the PGA Northern Open four times in the last 20 years. Panoramic views.

18 holes, 6,416 yards, par 69 (SSS 71). Amateur record N. Grant 65. Pro record Kevin Stables 64.

SIGNATURE HOLE:
SIXTH (222 yards, par 3) Standing on the elevated tee, the challenge is easy to see. Any shot which lacks height, and which is short, will be swept to the right of the target. Too strong and a quarry, dwarfed by towering pine trees, awaits.

## COURSE CARD

| HOLE | MEDAL YDS | PAR | FORWARD YDS | PAR | LADIES YDS | PAR | HOLE | MEDAL YDS | PAR | FORWARD YDS | PAR | LADIES YDS | PAR |
|---|---|---|---|---|---|---|---|---|---|---|---|---|---|
| 1 | 459 | 4 | 441 | 4 | 423 | 5 | 10 | 438 | 4 | 431 | 4 | 403 | 5 |
| 2 | 438 | 4 | 410 | 4 | 383 | 4 | 11 | 375 | 4 | 368 | 4 | 356 | 4 |
| 3 | 368 | 4 | 335 | 4 | 330 | 4 | 12 | 278 | 4 | 271 | 4 | 254 | 4 |
| 4 | 155 | 3 | 148 | 3 | 137 | 3 | 13 | 325 | 4 | 297 | 4 | 285 | 4 |
| 5 | 484 | 5 | 458 | 5 | 427 | 5 | 14 | 462 | 4 | 439 | 4 | 393 | 4 |
| 6 | 222 | 3 | 215 | 3 | 213 | 4 | 15 | 188 | 3 | 181 | 3 | 162 | 3 |
| 7 | 167 | 3 | 160 | 3 | 145 | 3 | 16 | 417 | 4 | 410 | 4 | 405 | 4 |
| 8 | 453 | 4 | 446 | 4 | 434 | 5 | 17 | 334 | 4 | 327 | 4 | 208 | 4 |
| 9 | 408 | 4 | 397 | 4 | 375 | 4 | 18 | 445 | 4 | 429 | 4 | 405 | 5 |
| Yds Out | 3,154 | | 3,010 | | 2,870 | | Yds In | 3,262 | | 3,153 | | 2,991 | |
| Total Yds | 6,416 | | 6,163 | | 5,631 | | | | | | | | |
| Total Par | 69 | | 69 | | 74 | | | | | | | | |

ADDRESS: Hardhillock, Birnie Road, Elgin, Moray IV30 8SX.
TELEPHONE: +44 (0)1343 542338.
FAX: +44 (0)1343 542341.
E-MAIL: secretary@elgingolfclub.com
WEBSITE: www.elgingolfclub.com
SECRETARY: David Black.
PROFESSIONAL: Ian Rodger +44 (0)1343 542884.
VISITORS: Yes, any day usually after 9.30 a.m. Telephone secretary for details.
GREEN FEES: £24 per round weekdays/weekends, £30 per day.
CATERING: Restaurant and bar.
FACILITIES: Trolley hire (£3), club hire (£10), caddies (£30), changing-rooms, putting green, pro shop, practice ground, driving range, coaching clinics, memberships available.
LOCATION: South of Elgin on A941 (Rothes road) and turn into Birnie Road.
LOCAL HOTELS: Craigellachie Hotel, Eight Acres Hotel, Glen Mhor Hotel, Greenlawns, Laichmoray Hotel, Mansfield House Hotel, Rothes Glen, St Leonards, Sunninghill Hotel, The Links Hotel, The Mansion House Hotel, The Old Coach House Hotel.

# FORRES

## FORRES GOLF CLUB

COURSE DESCRIPTION:
All-year parkland course in wooded countryside with spectacular views. Some holes flat, others gently undulating. Easy walking despite some hilly holes. Hosted the Northern Open in 2000.

Founded in 1889, the original nine holes were designed by James Braid. In 1912, Willie Park converted the course to 18 holes.

18 holes, 6,236 yards, par 70 (SSS 70). Amateur record 63. Pro record 64.

SIGNATURE HOLE:
SIXTEENTH (322 yards, par 4) Aptly named 'The Pond', which provides a watery grave for many a stray golf ball.

ADDRESS: Muiryshade, Forres, Moray IV36 2RD.
TELEPHONE & FAX: +44 (0)1309 672250.
E-MAIL: sandy@forresgolfclub.fsnet.co.uk
WEBSITE: www.forresgolfclub.fsnet.co.uk
MANAGER & PROFESSIONAL: Sandy Aird.
VISITORS: Welcome, most days.
GREEN FEES: £19 per round, £27 per day weekdays/weekends. Weekly ticket (Mondays to Fridays) £66.
CREDIT CARDS ACCEPTED: Visa/Mastercard.
CATERING: Restaurant and bar. Functions catered for.
FACILITIES: Motorised buggies, trolley hire, club hire, changing-rooms, putting green, pro shop, practice ground, memberships available, coaching clinics.
LOCATION: On A96, 25 miles east of Inverness. South-east of town centre, off B9010.
LOCAL HOTELS: Ramnee, Sunninghill Hotel, Links Hotel, Old Coach House Hotel.

# FORT AUGUSTUS

## FORT AUGUSTUS GOLF CLUB

COURSE DESCRIPTION:
Moorland course set in the beauty and quiet of the countryside and bordered by the Caledonian Canal. Its tight fairways provide a good challenge to golfers of all standards.

9 holes (18 tees), 5,454 yards (for 18 holes), par 67 (SSS 67). Amateur record P. MacDonald 67.

SIGNATURE HOLE:
FIRST (321 yards, par 4) Drive towards picturesque Ben Teigh, but the scenery is forgotten if you are wayward. Out of bounds to the left and a water hazard on the right. If the second shot to an elevated green is short, it runs downhill into a bunker. A short but testing par 4.

**COURSE CARD**

| HOLE | YDS | PAR | HOLE | YDS | PAR |
|------|-----|-----|------|-----|-----|
| 1 | 321 | 4 | 10 | 313 | 4 |
| 2 | 438 | 4 | 11 | 455 | 4 |
| 3 | 349 | 4 | 12 | 363 | 4 |
| 4 | 172 | 3 | 13 | 150 | 3 |
| 5 | 160 | 3 | 14 | 193 | 3 |
| 6 | 550 | 5 | 15 | 493 | 5 |
| 7 | 233 | 3 | 16 | 253 | 4 |
| 8 | 352 | 4 | 17 | 336 | 4 |
| 9 | 131 | 3 | 18 | 192 | 3 |
| *Yds* *Out* | 2,706 | | *Yds* *In* | 2,748 | |
| *Total* *Yds* | 5,454 | | | | |
| *Total* *Par* | 67 | | | | |

ADDRESS: Markethill, Fort Augustus, Inverness-shire PH32 4DP.
TELEPHONE: +44 (0)1320 366660.
SECRETARY: Hugh Fraser.
VISITORS: At all times, except Saturday afternoons (1 p.m to 4 p.m.) and occasional Sunday afternoons.
GREEN FEES: £10 per day. £35 per week (5 days).
CATERING: Lounge bar, but no meals.
FACILITIES: Trolley hire, club hire.
LOCATION: One mile west of Fort Augustus on A82.
LOCAL HOTEL: Invercreran Country House Hotel, Lovat Arms Hotel.

# FORT WILLIAM

## FORT WILLIAM GOLF CLUB

COURSE DESCRIPTION:
Sitting at the foot of Ben Nevis, Britain's highest mountain, this heathland course, built in 1975, is ideal for both the beginner and the experienced golfer. Major improvements to the course were made in 1995.

18 holes, 6,217 yards, par 72 (SSS 71). Course record 67.

SIGNATURE HOLE:
SIXTH (125 yards, par 3) A wide inviting green surrounded by a highland burn, with trees flanking the hole. Trouble if you are short.

## COURSE CARD

| HOLE | MEDAL YDS | PAR | FORWARD YDS | PAR | LADIES YDS | PAR | HOLE | MEDAL YDS | PAR | FORWARD YDS | PAR | LADIES YDS | PAR |
|---|---|---|---|---|---|---|---|---|---|---|---|---|---|
| 1 | 339 | 4 | 287 | 4 | 284 | 4 | 10 | 479 | 5 | 377 | 4 | 376 | 5 |
| 2 | 385 | 4 | 310 | 4 | 307 | 4 | 11 | 387 | 4 | 387 | 4 | 298 | 4 |
| 3 | 110 | 3 | 110 | 3 | 91 | 3 | 12 | 183 | 3 | 183 | 3 | 140 | 3 |
| 4 | 566 | 5 | 393 | 4 | 390 | 5 | 13 | 284 | 4 | 284 | 4 | 147 | 3 |
| 5 | 482 | 5 | 385 | 4 | 353 | 5 | 14 | 407 | 4 | 407 | 4 | 376 | 4 |
| 6 | 125 | 3 | 125 | 3 | 96 | 3 | 15 | 262 | 3 | 262 | 4 | 191 | 3 |
| 7 | 464 | 4 | 336 | 4 | 333 | 4 | 16 | 156 | 3 | 156 | 3 | 133 | 3 |
| 8 | 372 | 4 | 372 | 4 | 338 | 4 | 17 | 357 | 4 | 357 | 4 | 283 | 4 |
| 9 | 527 | 5 | 401 | 4 | 398 | 5 | 18 | 332 | 4 | 332 | 4 | 316 | 4 |
| Yds Out | 3,370 | | 2,719 | | 2,590 | | Yds In | 2,847 | | 2,745 | | 2,280 | |
| Total Yds | 6,217 | | 5,464 | | 4,850 | | | | | | | | |
| Total Par | 72 | | 68 | | 71 | | | | | | | | |

ADDRESS: Torlundy, Fort William, Inverness-shire PH33 6SN.
TELEPHONE: +44 (0)1397 704464.
SECRETARY: Gordon Bales +44 (0)1397 702404.
VISITORS: Very welcome at all times, including Saturdays and Sundays.
GREEN FEES: £17 per round, £20 per day weekdays/weekends.
CREDIT CARDS ACCEPTED: Amex/Visa/Mastercard/Diners Club.
CATERING: Bar and snacks.
FACILITIES: Trolley hire (£2), club hire (£6), caddies on request, changing-rooms, putting green, memberships available.
LOCATION: 3 miles north of Fort William on A82 (Fort William–Inverness road).
LOCAL HOTELS: Invercreran Country House Hotel, Moorings Hotel.

# FORTROSE

## FORTROSE & ROSEMARKIE GOLF CLUB

COURSE DESCRIPTION:
Seaside links course, set on the Chanonry Point peninsula with sea on three sides. Designed by James Braid and founded in 1888. Easy walking, good views. What it may lack in yardage is more than compensated for by its small, deceptive greens and strategically placed bunkers – challenges which are multiplied by a public road dissecting the course, the proximity of the sea to eight of the holes and the dense

inland gorse. Many interesting holes, including the 132-yard 5th which, depending on wind direction, can be anything from a flick with a wedge to a full-blooded 3-iron. Breathtaking scenery and a dolphin colony in the adjacent firth are additional attractions.

18 holes, 5,875 yards, par 71 ( SSS 69). Course record N. Hampton 64.

### SIGNATURE HOLE:

FOURTH ('Lighthouse' 455 yards, par 5) Two full shots for position below an elevated green leaves a wedge shot and two putts for your par.

### COURSE CARD

| HOLE | MEDAL YDS | PAR | FORWARD YDS | PAR | LADIES YDS | PAR | HOLE | MEDAL YDS | PAR | FORWARD YDS | PAR | LADIES YDS | PAR |
|---|---|---|---|---|---|---|---|---|---|---|---|---|---|
| 1 | 331 | 4 | 325 | 4 | 311 | 4 | 10 | 322 | 4 | 315 | 4 | 311 | 4 |
| 2 | 412 | 4 | 400 | 4 | 389 | 4 | 11 | 381 | 4 | 352 | 4 | 331 | 4 |
| 3 | 314 | 4 | 292 | 4 | 284 | 4 | 12 | 394 | 4 | 377 | 4 | 365 | 4 |
| 4 | 455 | 5 | 446 | 4 | 438 | 5 | 13 | 308 | 4 | 301 | 4 | 253 | 4 |
| 5 | 132 | 3 | 123 | 3 | 104 | 3 | 14 | 267 | 4 | 254 | 4 | 240 | 4 |
| 6 | 469 | 5 | 419 | 4 | 410 | 5 | 15 | 293 | 4 | 255 | 4 | 286 | 4 |
| 7 | 309 | 4 | 255 | 4 | 245 | 4 | 16 | 336 | 4 | 330 | 4 | 321 | 4 |
| 8 | 389 | 4 | 382 | 4 | 368 | 4 | 17 | 355 | 4 | 345 | 4 | 332 | 4 |
| 9 | 196 | 3 | 189 | 3 | 181 | 3 | 18 | 212 | 3 | 195 | 3 | 190 | 3 |
| *Yds Out* | 3,007 | | 2,831 | | 2,730 | | *Yds In* | 2,868 | | 2,724 | | 2,629 | |
| *Total Yds* | 5,875 | | 5,555 | | 5,369 | | | | | | | | | |
| *Total Par* | 71 | | 69 | | 71 | | | | | | | | | |

ADDRESS: Ness Road East, Fortrose, Ross-shire IV10 8SE.
TELEPHONE: +44 (0)1381 620529.
FAX: +44 (0)1381 621328.
E-MAIL: secretary@fortrosegolfclub.co.uk
WEBSITE: www.fortrosegolfclub.co.uk
SECRETARY: Mrs.Margaret Collier.
VISITORS: Yes, outwith members' times which are 9 to 10.15 a.m., 1 to 2.15 p.m., 4.45 to 6.30 p.m.
GREEN FEES: £21 per round weekdays, £32 per day. £26 per round weekends, £37 per day. 5-day ticket (Monday to Friday): £75.
CREDIT CARDS ACCEPTED: Visa/Mastercard (for shop and green fees through shop only).
CATERING: Bar and meals.
FACILITIES: Motorised buggies (£15), trolley hire (£1.50), club hire (£5), changing-rooms, putting green, practice ground, pro shop, memberships available.
LOCATION: A832 to Fortrose off A9 at Tore roundabout. North of Inverness. Turn right at police station, then first left to golf clubhouse.
LOCAL HOTELS: Bunchrew House Hotel, Heathmount Hotel, Mansfield House Hotel, Redcroft Guest House, Royal Hotel.

# GAIRLOCH

## GAIRLOCH GOLF CLUB

**COURSE DESCRIPTION:**
Seaside links course with some interesting par 3s. A good test of golf, particularly in windy conditions. Superb views to the Inner Hebrides and the Isle of Skye.
9 holes, 4,514 yards (for 18 holes), par 63 (SSS 64). Amateur record 62.

**SIGNATURE HOLE:**
EIGHTH ('Traigh Mor' 526 yards, par 5) Requires accuracy from the tee with deep rough and Gairloch Sands on the left. Trouble awaits the wayward second shot, too. Has been described as one of the most natural par 5s in Scotland.

**COURSE CARD**

| HOLE | MEDAL YDS | PAR | FORWARD YDS | PAR | LADIES YDS | PAR | HOLE | MEDAL YDS | PAR | FORWARD YDS | PAR | LADIES YDS | PAR |
|---|---|---|---|---|---|---|---|---|---|---|---|---|---|
| 1 | 320 | 4 | 312 | 4 | 266 | 4 | 10 | 327 | 4 | 312 | 4 | 376 | 5 |
| 2 | 185 | 3 | 179 | 3 | 155 | 3 | 11 | 182 | 3 | 179 | 3 | 298 | 4 |
| 3 | 162 | 3 | 152 | 3 | 129 | 3 | 12 | 184 | 3 | 153 | 3 | 140 | 3 |
| 4 | 233 | 3 | 209 | 3 | 196 | 3 | 13 | 244 | 4 | 209 | 3 | 147 | 3 |
| 5 | 317 | 4 | 312 | 4 | 292 | 4 | 14 | 423 | 4 | 312 | 4 | 376 | 4 |
| 6 | 194 | 3 | 187 | 3 | 151 | 3 | 15 | 194 | 3 | 187 | 3 | 151 | 3 |
| 7 | 91 | 3 | 88 | 3 | 88 | 3 | 16 | 143 | 3 | 89 | 3 | 89 | 3 |
| 8 | 526 | 5 | 488 | 5 | 408 | 5 | 17 | 526 | 5 | 488 | 5 | 409 | 5 |
| 9 | 119 | 3 | 119 | 3 | 116 | 3 | 18 | 144 | 3 | 119 | 3 | 116 | 3 |
| Yds Out | 2,147 | | 2,046 | | 1,802 | | Yds In | 2,367 | | 2,047 | | 1,803 | |
| Total Yds | 4,514 | | 4,093 | | 3,605 | | | | | | | | |
| Total Par | 63 | | 62 | | 62 | | | | | | | | |

**ADDRESS:** Gairloch, Ross-shire IV21 2BE.
**TELEPHONE & FAX:** +44 (0)1445 712407.
**E-MAIL:** secretary@gairlochgc.freeserve.co.uk
**SECRETARY:** A. W. Sherlock.
**VISITORS:** Any time. Societies by arrangement.
**GREEN FEES:** £15 per day. £49 per week.
**CREDIT CARDS ACCEPTED:** Visa/Mastercard.
**CATERING:** Bar and light refreshments. Functions catered for.
**FACILITIES:** Trolley hire (£2), club hire (£5), changing-rooms, memberships available.
**LOCATION:** 75 miles west of Inverness on A832.
**LOCAL HOTELS:** Gairloch Hotel, Myrtle Bank Hotel, The Old Inn. Also self-catering accommodation within easy reach of course.

# GARMOUTH

## GARMOUTH & KINGSTON GOLF CLUB

### COURSE DESCRIPTION:
Flat links course, situated on the west bank at the mouth of the River Spey between the twin villages of Garmouth and Kingston. The River Spey's ever-changing estuary has recently reclaimed part of the 14th hole and a new course layout with three new holes has been opened. There is an abundance of wild life, including osprey.

18 holes, 5,935 yards, par 69 (SSS 69). Amateur record 65.

### SIGNATURE HOLE:
EIGHTH ('Road' 328 yards, par 4) The fairway is bounded by a ditch on either side with the ditch on the left being out of bounds for the length of the hole. Requires an accurate drive and approach shot.

### COURSE CARD

| HOLE | MEDAL YDS | PAR | FORWARD YDS | PAR | LADIES YDS | PAR | HOLE | MEDAL YDS | PAR | FORWARD YDS | PAR | LADIES YDS | PAR |
|---|---|---|---|---|---|---|---|---|---|---|---|---|---|
| 1 | 365 | 4 | 355 | 4 | 324 | 4 | 10 | 268 | 4 | 237 | 4 | 210 | 4 |
| 2 | 374 | 4 | 362 | 4 | 363 | 4 | 11 | 171 | 3 | 144 | 3 | 147 | 3 |
| 3 | 419 | 4 | 393 | 4 | 419 | 5 | 12 | 386 | 4 | 367 | 4 | 349 | 4 |
| 4 | 184 | 3 | 124 | 3 | 129 | 3 | 13 | 419 | 4 | 396 | 4 | 392 | 4 |
| 5 | 376 | 4 | 335 | 4 | 340 | 4 | 14 | 419 | 4 | 407 | 4 | 410 | 5 |
| 6 | 389 | 4 | 360 | 4 | 383 | 4 | 15 | 384 | 4 | 377 | 4 | 353 | 4 |
| 7 | 339 | 4 | 316 | 4 | 314 | 4 | 16 | 167 | 3 | 156 | 3 | 155 | 3 |
| 8 | 328 | 4 | 321 | 4 | 297 | 4 | 17 | 531 | 5 | 517 | 5 | 442 | 5 |
| 9 | 268 | 4 | 256 | 4 | 254 | 4 | 18 | 148 | 3 | 122 | 3 | 141 | 3 |
| Yds Out | 3,042 | | 2,822 | | 2,802 | | Yds In | 2,893 | | 2,723 | | 2,599 | |
| Total Yds | 5,935 | | 5,545 | | 5,401 | | | | | | | | |
| Total Par | 69 | | 69 | | 71 | | | | | | | | |

ADDRESS: Spey Street, Garmouth, Fochabers, Grampian IV32 7NJ.
TELEPHONE & FAX: +44 (0)1343 870388.
SECRETARY: A. Robertson.
VISITORS: Yes, except when club competitions are arranged.
GREEN FEES: £16 per round weekdays, £18 per day. £20 per round/day weekends. Over 60s and juniors half price.
CATERING Dining-room and bar. Functions catered for.
FACILITIES: Trolley hire (£2), club hire (£2), changing-rooms, practice ground, shop, memberships available.

LOCATION: Follow B9015 from the A96 at Mosstodloch crossroads to the mouth of the River Spey (west bank).
LOCAL HOTELS: Garmouth Hotel, Glen Mhor Hotel, Greenlawns, Sunninghill Hotel, The Old Coach House Hotel.

# GOLSPIE

## GOLSPIE GOLF CLUB

COURSE DESCRIPTION:
Founded in 1889, Golspie is a mixture of links, heath and parkland, offering a challenge to all standards of golfer. When the wind blows, the course offers a true test of shot-making. Stunning views over the Dornoch Firth on one side and majestic Ben Bhraggie on the other. An easy-walking course and a friendly relaxed atmosphere in the clubhouse.
18 holes, 5,836 yards, par 68 (SSS 68).

SIGNATURE HOLE:
TENTH ('The Lochy' 148 yards, par 3) with water hazard.

ADDRESS: Ferry Road, Golspie KW10 6ST.
TELEPHONE: +44 (0)1408 633266.
FAX: +44 (0)1408 633393.
E-MAIL: info@golspie-golf-club.co.uk
WEBSITE: www.golspie-golf-club.co.uk
SECRETARY: Mrs Marie Macleod.
VISITORS: Parties must pre-book.
GREEN FEES: £20 per round weekdays/weekends, £25 per day.
CATERING: Yes.
FACILITIES: Trolley hire, putting green, pro shop, practice ground.
LOCATION: 10 miles north of Dornoch on A9. 1 hour north of Inverness.
LOCAL HOTELS: Bunchrew House Hotel, Golf Link Hotel, Mansfield House Hotel, Royal Hotel, Sutherland Arms.

# GRANTOWN-ON-SPEY

## CRAGGAN GOLF COURSE

COURSE DESCRIPTION:
Designed by Bill Mitchell of the PGA, the first 9 holes were opened in 1995 and the extension in 2000. A parkland course situated beside the River Spey, it has magnificent views of the Cairngorm Mountains and up and down Strathspey. Although it is not long, it is suitable for all golfers whether beginner of expert.

There are plenty of hazards and great pride is taken in the condition of the greens. It is a test of a golfer's short game with holes ranging from the 51-yard 16th to the 209-yard 11th.

18 holes, 2,406 yards, par 54.

SIGNATURE HOLE:
TWELFTH (162 yards, par 3) Downhill over a small pond and onto a two-tiered green with the River Spey as a backdrop.

ADDRESS: Craggan, Grantown-on-Spey, Moray PH26 3NT.
TELEPHONE: +44 (0)1479 872120.
FAX: +44 (0)1479 872325.
SECRETARY: F. Laing.
VISITORS: Advance booking is recommended for large parties but has not yet been necessary for small groups of golfers. Clubhouse open from 10 a.m. to 6 p.m., seven days a week.
GREEN FEES: £10 per day weekdays. Weekly ticket £60.
CATERING: Hot and cold drinks, snacks and ice creams from 10 a.m. to 6 p.m.
FACILITIES: Trolley hire (£1), club hire (£5) putting green, balls, tees etc. on sale in clubhouse, memberships available.
LOCATION: 1 mile outside Grantown-on-Spey beside the A95 Grantown–Aviemore road.
LOCAL HOTELS: Bendarroch House Hotel, Bunchrew House Hotel, Glen Mhor Hotel, Greenlawns, Heathmount Hotel, Skye of Curr Hotel, The Links Hotel.

# GRANTOWN-ON-SPEY GOLF CLUB

COURSE DESCRIPTION:
Parkland/woodland course, designed by Willie Park, with generally easy walking, providing a fair test for every calibre of golfer. Scenically beautiful.

18 holes, 5,710 yards, par 70 (SSS 68). Amateur record G. Bain 60. Pro record D. Webster 62.

SIGNATURE HOLE:
NINTH (275 yards, par 4) Downhill, which tempts the longer hitters. Fairway is lined with heather and pine trees and the Cromdale Hills provide a backdrop. Even if you are expert enough to hit the green with your tee shot, you may not get your birdie because the surface is severely undulating.

COURSE CARD

| HOLE | YDS | PAR | HOLE | YDS | PAR |
|------|-----|-----|------|-----|-----|
| 1 | 287 | 4 | 10 | 367 | 4 |
| 2 | 441 | 4 | 11 | 191 | 3 |
| 3 | 401 | 4 | 12 | 413 | 4 |
| 4 | 308 | 4 | 13 | 295 | 4 |
| 5 | 359 | 4 | 14 | 388 | 4 |
| 6 | 475 | 5 | 15 | 265 | 4 |

| 7 | 380 | 4 | 16 | 137 | 3 |
|---|-----|---|----|-----|---|
| 8 | 161 | 3 | 17 | 277 | 4 |
| 9 | 275 | 4 | 18 | 290 | 4 |
| Yds Out | 3,087 | | Yds In | 2,623 | |
| Total Yds | 5,710 | | | | |
| Total Par | 70 | | | | |

ADDRESS: Golf Course Road, Grantown-on-Spey, Morayshire PH26 3HY.
TELEPHONE: +44 (0)1479 872079.
FAX: +44 (0)1479 873725.
E-MAIL: secretary@grantownonspeygolfclub.co.uk
WEBSITE: www.grantownonspeygolfclub.co.uk
SECRETARY: James Matheson.
VISITORS: Any time except weekends before 10 a.m. Essential to book in advance.
GREEN FEES: £20 per day weekdays. £25 per day weekends.
CREDIT CARDS ACCEPTED: Visa/Mastercard in shop only.
CATERING: Restaurant and bar.
FACILITIES: Motorised buggies (£10 per round), trolley hire (£2 per day), club hire (£7 per round), changing-rooms, putting green, pro shop, practice ground, memberships available.
LOCATION: South-east side of town centre.
LOCAL HOTELS: Bendarroch House Hotel, Bunchrew House Hotel, Glen Mhor Hotel, Greenlawns, Heathmount Hotel, Skye of Curr Hotel, The Links Hotel.

# HELMSDALE

## HELMSDALE GOLF CLUB

COURSE DESCRIPTION:
Testing, undulating heathland course with a fair expanse of gorse and bracken, bordered by a hill on the north and the A897 on the south. Tight fairways.
9 holes, 3,720 yards (for 18 holes), par 62 (SSS 61).

SIGNATURE HOLE:
NINTH (192 yards, par 3) Elevated tee, giving a panoramic view of the Moray Firth to the east and the Strath of Kildonan to the west. Misjudge this one at your peril. Numerous hazards await the wayward shot.

ADDRESS: Strath Road, Helmsdale KW8 6JA.
TELEPHONE: +44 (0)1431 821650.
VISITORS: Any time by prior arrangement.
GREEN FEES: £6 per round, £12 per day, £30 per week. Country membership

available on application.

**LOCATION:** From A9 junction in Helmsdale, follow A897. Course is on right on outskirts of Village.

**LOCAL HOTELS:** The Links Hotel.

# HOPEMAN

## HOPEMAN GOLF CLUB

### COURSE DESCRIPTION:
Links-type course with beautiful seaside views over the Moray Firth.

18 holes, 5,590 yards, par 68 (SSS 67). Course record 64.

### SIGNATURE HOLE:
TWELFTH ('Prieshach' 152 yards, par 3) Drop of 100 feet from tee to the green alongside the shore. It can require anything from a wedge to a wood depending on the wind.

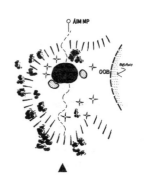

### COURSE CARD

| HOLE | YDS | PAR | YDS | PAR | YDS | PAR | HOLE | YDS | PAR | YDS | PAR | YDS | PAR |
|------|-----|-----|-----|-----|-----|-----|------|-----|-----|-----|-----|-----|-----|
| 1 | 371 | 4 | 342 | 4 | 351 | 4 | 10 | 299 | 4 | 296 | 4 | 299 | 4 |
| 2 | 352 | 4 | 301 | 4 | 344 | 5 | 11 | 365 | 4 | 348 | 4 | 344 | 4 |
| 3 | 174 | 3 | 165 | 3 | 168 | 3 | 12 | 152 | 3 | 135 | 3 | 135 | 3 |
| 4 | 471 | 5 | 460 | 5 | 463 | 5 | 13 | 344 | 4 | 339 | 4 | 339 | 4 |
| 5 | 342 | 4 | 334 | 4 | 334 | 4 | 14 | 383 | 4 | 371 | 4 | 376 | 4 |
| 6 | 397 | 4 | 361 | 4 | 365 | 4 | 15 | 106 | 3 | 91 | 3 | 97 | 3 |
| 7 | 198 | 3 | 179 | 3 | 198 | 3 | 16 | 384 | 4 | 354 | 4 | 375 | 4 |
| 8 | 346 | 4 | 341 | 4 | 344 | 4 | 17 | 194 | 3 | 194 | 3 | 194 | 3 |
| 9 | 302 | 4 | 271 | 4 | 260 | 4 | 18 | 410 | 4 | 383 | 4 | 383 | 5 |
| Yds Out | 2,953 | | 2,754 | | 2,847 | | Yds In | 2,637 | | 2,511 | | 2,543 | |
| Total Yds | 5,590 | | 5,265 | | 5,390 | | | | | | | | |
| Total Par | 68 | | 68 | | 72 | | | | | | | | |

**ADDRESS:** Hopeman IV30 5YA.

**TELEPHONE:** +44 (0)1343 830578.

**FAX:** +44 (0)1343 830152.

**E-MAIL:** hopemangc@aol.com

**WEBSITE:** www.hopeman-golf-club.co.uk

**SECRETARY:** Jim Fraser.

VISITORS: Yes, all year round.

GREEN FEES: £13 per round weekdays, £18 per day. £18 per round weekends, £23 per day. 5-day ticket, £60. Generous discounts for parties of ten or more.

CATERING: Restaurant and bar.

FACILITIES: Motorised buggy, trolley hire, changing-rooms, small practice ground, putting green, shop, memberships available.

LOCATION: A96 from Inverness to Elgin. Take left turn at Forres onto the B9011. Take the B9012 from Elgin. Left onto the B9040 Lossiemouth–Hopeman road.

LOCAL HOTELS: Glen Mhor Hotel, Greenlawns, Station Hotel, Sunninghill Hotel, The Links Hotel, The Old Coach House Hotel.

# INVERGORDON

## INVERGORDON GOLF CLUB

### COURSE DESCRIPTION:

Parkland with moderate slopes on some holes. An 11-hole extension was completed in 1994. Mature trees/rhododendrons on old holes. Many young trees on the new.

18 holes, 6,030 yards, par 69 (SSS 69). Amateur record 66.

### SIGNATURE HOLE:

EIGHTH (123 yards, par 3) One of the new holes created in 1994. Although the shortest of the par 3s, it is often played into the prevailing wind and is just about all carry. Trees and whins line the left, while on the right is a pond which cuts into the fairway and has to be carried if the pin is on the right of the green. Rhododendrons lie to the right of the pond and there are more bushes and trees behind the green.

### COURSE CARD

| HOLE | YDS | PAR | HOLE | YDS | PAR |
|------|------|-----|------|------|-----|
| 1 | 134 | 3 | 10 | 166 | 3 |
| 2 | 275 | 4 | 11 | 425 | 4 |
| 3 | 456 | 4 | 12 | 383 | 4 |
| 4 | 374 | 4 | 13 | 371 | 4 |
| 5 | 506 | 5 | 14 | 387 | 4 |
| 6 | 430 | 4 | 15 | 195 | 3 |
| 7 | 376 | 4 | 16 | 340 | 4 |
| 8 | 123 | 3 | 17 | 385 | 4 |
| 9 | 387 | 4 | 18 | 317 | 4 |
| *Yds* | 3,061 | | *Yds* | 2,969 | |
| *Out* | | | *In* | | |

| Total Yds | 6,030 |
| Total Par | 69 |

ADDRESS: King George Street, Invergordon, Ross-shire IV18 0BD.
TELEPHONE: +44 (0)1349 852715.
FAX: +44 (0)1349 884800.
SECRETARY: N. Paterson +44 (0)1349 882693.
VISITORS: Yes. Club competitions are held on Tuesday/Thursday evenings and Saturday mornings. These should be avoided, but check club noticeboard.
GREEN FEES: £15 per round, £20 per day. Discounts for groups of 20 plus.
CATERING: Bar snacks/meals. Tuesday/Thursday/Friday evenings after 7 p.m. Weekends normal bar hours.
FACILITIES: Trolley hire (£2), club hire (£5), putting green, practice ground.
LOCATION: A9 north from Inverness, then B817 entering town from west along the High Street. Turn left at Albany Road and left again over the railway bridge (Cromlet Drive). Continue to the end of the road.
LOCAL HOTELS: Kincraig Hotel, Mansfield House Hotel, Marine Hotel, Nigg Ferry Hotel, Royal Hotel.

# INVERNESS

## INVERNESS GOLF CLUB

### COURSE DESCRIPTION:
Fairly flat but challenging parkland tree-lined championship course with the Mill Burn crossing parts of the course. Although not long, its lush fairways ensure it plays to its full length. Well-bunkered short holes require accuracy as they are usually played into the prevailing wind.

18 holes, 6,226 yards, par 69 (SSS 70).

### SIGNATURE HOLE:
FOURTEENTH (475 yards, par 4) Dogleg to the right from the tee with a carry of 180 yards over trees and the corner of the burn, which runs the full length of the hole. Requires an accurate tee shot and approach through an extremely narrow entrance to a small green.

### COURSE CARD

| | MEDAL | | FORWARD | | LADIES | | | MEDAL | | FORWARD | | LADIES | |
| HOLE | YDS | PAR | YDS | PAR | YDS | PAR | HOLE | YDS | PAR | YDS | PAR | YDS | PAR |
|---|---|---|---|---|---|---|---|---|---|---|---|---|---|
| 1 | 308 | 4 | 301 | 4 | 288 | 4 | 10 | 406 | 4 | 405 | 4 | 391 | 4 |
| 2 | 161 | 3 | 141 | 3 | 123 | 3 | 11 | 423 | 4 | 394 | 4 | 390 | 4 |
| 3 | 487 | 5 | 444 | 4 | 434 | 4 | 12 | 394 | 4 | 339 | 4 | 330 | 4 |
| 4 | 463 | 4 | 444 | 4 | 456 | 5 | 13 | 190 | 3 | 154 | 3 | 142 | 3 |

| 5 | 478 | 5 | 464 | 4 | 456 | 5 | 14 | 475 | 4 | 435 | 4 | 430 | 5 |
| 6 | 313 | 4 | 291 | 4 | 290 | 4 | 15 | 176 | 3 | 147 | 3 | 144 | 3 |
| 7 | 197 | 3 | 169 | 3 | 154 | 3 | 16 | 380 | 4 | 356 | 4 | 362 | 4 |
| 8 | 373 | 4 | 343 | 4 | 330 | 4 | 17 | 333 | 4 | 326 | 4 | 290 | 4 |
| 9 | 208 | 3 | 179 | 3 | 162 | 3 | 18 | 461 | 4 | 446 | 4 | 447 | 5 |
| Yds Out | 2,988 | | 2,776 | | 2,712 | | Yds In | 3,238 | | 3,002 | | 2,916 | |
| Total Yds | 6,226 | | 5,778 | | 5,628 | | | | | | | | | |
| Total Par | 69 | | 67 | | 72 | | | | | | | | | |

ADDRESS: Culcabock Road, Inverness IV2 3XQ.

TELEPHONE & FAX: +44 (0)1463 239882.

E-MAIL: igc@freeuk.com

WEBSITE: www.invernessgolfclub.co.uk

SECRETARY: J.S.Thomson.

PROFESSIONAL: Alistair Thomson +44 (0)1463 231989.

VISITORS: Can pre-book 10 a.m. to noon and 2 p.m. to 4 p.m. Mondays, Tuesdays, Wednesdays, Fridays. Thursdays sometimes ladies' day. Available Saturdays. Restricted Sundays after 10.30 a.m.

GREEN FEES: £29 per round weekdays, weekends £39 per day. Discounts on parties of ten or more.

CATERING: Restaurant and bar. Best to arrange meals with caterers before teeing off.

FACILITIES: Trolley hire, club hire, caddies by arrangement, changing-rooms, putting green, pro shop, practice ground, coaching clinics by arrangement, waiting list for memberships.

LOCATION: 1 mile south of town centre on Culcabock Road. 6 miles from Inverness Airport.

LOCAL HOTELS: Bunchrew House Hotel, Craigmonie Hotel, Glen Mhor Hotel, Greenlawns, Heathmount Hotel, Mansfield House Hotel, Marriott Kingsmills Hotel, Nigg Ferry Hotel, Royal Hotel, Skye of Curr Hotel, The Links Hotel.

## LOCH NESS GOLF COURSE

COURSE DESCRIPTION:

Parkland course with generous fairways, opened in June 1996, offering a challenge to all levels of golfer. Planning extra holes and a 6-hole par 3 course.
18 holes, 6,722 yards, par 73 (SSS 72).

SIGNATURE HOLE:

FOURTEENTH ('Chance' 76 yards, par 3) Nothing between you and the green except a deep gully with a burn at the bottom. Usually played into the prevailing wind, it catches out many players.

## COURSE CARD

| HOLE | MEDAL YDS | PAR | FORWARD YDS | PAR | LADIES YDS | PAR | HOLE | MEDAL YDS | PAR | FORWARD YDS | PAR | LADIES YDS | PAR |
|---|---|---|---|---|---|---|---|---|---|---|---|---|---|
| 1 | 323 | 4 | 310 | 4 | 296 | 4 | 10 | 510 | 5 | 485 | 5 | 391 | 5 |
| 2 | 557 | 5 | 546 | 5 | 471 | 5 | 11 | 208 | 3 | 190 | 3 | 177 | 4 |
| 3 | 154 | 3 | 144 | 3 | 134 | 3 | 12 | 400 | 4 | 376 | 4 | 367 | 4 |
| 4 | 444 | 4 | 425 | 4 | 419 | 5 | 13 | 457 | 4 | 445 | 4 | 435 | 5 |
| 5 | 405 | 4 | 391 | 4 | 364 | 4 | 14 | 76 | 3 | 76 | 3 | 72 | 3 |
| 6 | 431 | 4 | 420 | 4 | 416 | 4 | 15 | 520 | 5 | 498 | 5 | 490 | 5 |
| 7 | 339 | 4 | 326 | 4 | 312 | 4 | 16 | 371 | 4 | 350 | 4 | 330 | 4 |
| 8 | 296 | 4 | 282 | 4 | 264 | 4 | 17 | 503 | 5 | 477 | 5 | 471 | 5 |
| 9 | 439 | 4 | 424 | 4 | 412 | 5 | 18 | 339 | 4 | 328 | 4 | 315 | 4 |
| *Yds Out* | 3,388 | | 3,268 | | 3,072 | | *Yds In* | 3,384 | | 3,225 | | 3, 088 | |
| *Total Yds* | 6,772 | | 6,493 | | 6,150 | | | | | | | | |
| *Total Par* | 73 | | 73 | | 76 | | | | | | | | |

ADDRESS: Fairways Leisure, Castle Heather, Inverness IV2 6AA.
TELEPHONE: +44 (0)1463 713335.
FAX: +44 (0)1463 712695.
E-MAIL: info@golflochness.com
WEBSITE: www.golflochness.com
SECRETARY: Neil Hampton.
PROFESSIONAL: Martin Piggot +44 (0)1463 713334.
VISITORS: Yes, at all times.
GREEN FEES: £20 per day weekdays, £25 per day weekends.
CREDIT CARDS ACCEPTED: Visa/Mastercard.
CATERING: Restaurant and bar. Full service all day, every day.
FACILITIES: Motorised buggies (£15), trolley hire (£2), club hire (£5), caddies by arrangement, changing-rooms, putting green, pro shop, 20-bay floodlit driving range, coaching clinics, memberships available.
LOCATION: 1½ miles from Inverness city centre.
LOCAL HOTELS: Bunchrew House Hotel, Glen Mhor Hotel, Greenlawns, Heathmount Hotel, Nigg Ferry Hotel, Royal Hotel, Skye of Curr Hotel, The Links Hotel.

## TORVEAN GOLF CLUB

COURSE DESCRIPTION:
Municipal parkland course surrounded by trees with three ponds coming into play. Close to Loch Ness and the Caledonian Canal. Easy walking. It boasts one of the longest par 5s in the North, the 5th at 565 yards.

18 holes, 5,784 yards, par 69 (SSS 68). Amateur record men, P. Savage 64; Ladies, C. Macleod 70. Pro record R. Weir 70.

SIGNATURE HOLE:
SEVENTEENTH ('Kilvean' 164 yards, par 3) Carry of 164 yards over water to the green with only ten yards between the pond and the green.

## COURSE CARD

| HOLE | YDS | PAR | HOLE | YDS | PAR |
|------|-----|-----|------|-----|-----|
| 1 | 194 | 3 | 10 | 286 | 4 |
| 2 | 358 | 4 | 11 | 526 | 5 |
| 3 | 273 | 4 | 12 | 400 | 4 |
| 4 | 270 | 4 | 13 | 410 | 4 |
| 5 | 565 | 5 | 14 | 338 | 4 |
| 6 | 277 | 4 | 15 | 174 | 3 |
| 7 | 157 | 3 | 16 | 471 | 3 |
| 8 | 277 | 4 | 17 | 164 | 3 |
| 9 | 220 | 4 | 18 | 424 | 4 |
| *Yds Out* | 2,591 | | *Yds In* | 3,193 | |
| *Total* Yds | 5,784 | | | | |
| *Total Par* | 69 | | | | |

ADDRESS: Glenurquhart Road, Inverness IV3 8JN.
TELEPHONE: +44 (0)1463 231248.
SECRETARY: Mrs K. Gray +44 (0)1463 225651 (and fax).
VISITORS: Yes, book direct at clubhouse or on +44 (0)1463 711434. Group bookings through the Highland Council +44 (0)1463 724224.
GREEN FEES: £13 per round weekdays, £15 per day. £16.50 per round weekends, £18.70 per day.
CATERING: Weekends only, except by prior arrangement with the secretary.
FACILITIES: Trolley hire, putting green.
LOCATION: On A82 Fort William road, approximately 1 mile from Inverness city centre.
LOCAL HOTELS: Bunchrew House Hotel, Glen Mhor Hotel, Heathmount Hotel, Loch Ness House Hotel.

# KINGUSSIE

## KINGUSSIE GOLF CLUB

COURSE DESCRIPTION:
Hilly moorland course designed by Harry Vardon and opened in 1891. Very scenic in the heart of the Highlands and 1,000 feet above sea level at its highest point. River Gynack comes into play on five holes.

18 holes, 5,615 yards, par 67 (SSS 68). Amateur record 63. Pro record 66.

COURSE CARD

| | MEDAL | | FORWARD | | LADIES | | | MEDAL | | FORWARD | | LADIES | |
|---|---|---|---|---|---|---|---|---|---|---|---|---|---|
| HOLE | YDS | PAR | YDS | PAR | YDS | PAR | HOLE | YDS | PAR | YDS | PAR | YDS | PAR |
| 1 | 230 | 3 | 219 | 3 | 214 | 3 | 10 | 189 | 3 | 177 | 3 | 165 | 3 |
| 2 | 431 | 4 | 419 | 4 | 407 | 4 | 11 | 346 | 4 | 320 | 4 | 295 | 4 |
| 3 | 362 | 4 | 350 | 4 | 308 | 4 | 12 | 399 | 4 | 387 | 4 | 377 | 4 |
| 4 | 475 | 5 | 459 | 5 | 390 | 5 | 13 | 422 | 4 | 410 | 4 | 400 | 5 |
| 5 | 321 | 4 | 309 | 4 | 307 | 4 | 14 | 439 | 4 | 424 | 4 | 411 | 5 |
| 6 | 325 | 4 | 316 | 4 | 290 | 4 | 15 | 105 | 3 | 95 | 3 | 90 | 3 |
| 7 | 151 | 3 | 140 | 3 | 137 | 3 | 16 | 202 | 3 | 194 | 3 | 194 | 3 |
| 8 | 128 | 3 | 124 | 3 | 121 | 3 | 17 | 385 | 4 | 384 | 4 | 343 | 4 |
| 9 | 426 | 4 | 413 | 4 | 400 | 5 | 18 | 279 | 4 | 271 | 4 | 242 | 4 |
| Yds Out | 2,849 | | 2,749 | | 2,574 | | Yds In | 2,766 | | 2,662 | | 2,517 | |
| Total Yds | 5,615 | | 5,411 | | 5,091 | | | | | | | | |
| Total Par | 67 | | 67 | | 73 | | | | | | | | |

ADDRESS: Gynack Road, Kingussie PH21 1LR.
TELEPHONE: +44 (0)1540 661600.
FAX: +44 (0)1540 662066.
E-MAIL: kinggolf@globalnet.co.uk
WEBSITE: www.kingussie-golf.co.uk
SECRETARY: Norman MacWilliam.
VISITORS: Yes.
GREEN FEES: £18 per round weekdays, £20 per day. £20 per round weekends, £25 per day. Weekly ticket £60.
CATERING: Restaurant and bar.
FACILITIES: Motorised buggies, trolley hire, club hire, changing-rooms, putting green, pro shop, memberships available.
LOCATION: Half-a-mile from High Street. Turn at Duke of Gordon Hotel and continue to the end of the road.
LOCAL HOTELS: Bendarroch House Hotel, Columba House Hotel, Skye of Curr Hotel.

# KINLOSS

## KINLOSS COUNTRY GOLF COURSE

COURSE DESCRIPTION:
Parkland course which provides year-round golf and can be challenging even for the experienced golfer. Situated on the Moray coast which, with its low rainfall, makes for a favourable golfing climate.

9 holes, 5,070 yards (for 18 holes), par 68.

SIGNATURE HOLE:
THIRD ('Firth View' 178 yards, par 3) A small target from an elevated tee and panoramic views of the surrounding countryside and the Caithness mountains in the distance.

COURSE CARD

| | MEDAL | | LADIES | |
| HOLES | YDS | PAR | YDS | PAR |
|---|---|---|---|---|
| 1 | 344 | 4 | 259 | 4 |
| 2 | 78 | 3 | 68 | 3 |
| 3 | 178 | 3 | 170 | 3 |
| 4 | 319 | 4 | 308 | 4 |
| 5 | 138 | 3 | 120 | 3 |
| 6 | 506 | 5 | 412 | 5 |
| 7 | 338 | 4 | 324 | 4 |
| 8 | 287 | 4 | 275 | 4 |
| 9 | 347 | 4 | 339 | 4 |
| Yds Out | 2,535 | | 2,275 | |
| Total Yds | 2,535 | | | |
| Total Par | 34 | | | |

ADDRESS: Kinloss, Forres, Moray IV36 2UA.
TELEPHONE: +44 (0)1343 850585, +44 (0)1343 850242.
E-MAIL: braeside@miltonhill.demon.co.uk
WEBSITE: www.miltonhill.demon.co.uk
SECRETARY: Sylvia Verner.
VISITORS: Yes, all year round.
GREEN FEES: On application. Weekly ticket £45.
CREDIT CARDS ACCEPTED: Visa/Mastercard.
CATERING: Hot and cold drinks. Ice cream and confectionery.
FACILITIES: Motorised buggies (£8), trolley hire (£1), club hire (£3), changing-rooms, putting green, practice ground, pro shop, memberships available.
LOCATION: On B9089 approximately 2 miles east of Kinloss.
LOCAL HOTELS: Sunninghill Hotel, The Links Hotel, The Old Coach House Hotel.

# KYLE OF LOCHALSH

## KYLE OF LOCHALSH GOLF COURSE

### COURSE DESCRIPTION:
Tight and quite testing meadowland course, set on the Plock of Kyle, with elevated tees and eight par 3s and the last, a par 4. Take your camera, for there

are great views to the Isle of Skye. The course fell into disuse until it was reborn in 1985.

9 holes, 966 yards, par (for 18 holes) 56.

SIGNATURE HOLE:
NINTH (245 yards, par 4) The only par 4 on the course, and it's uphill.

ADDRESS: 7 Lochalsh Road, Kyle of Lochalsh, Ross-shire IV40 8RP.
TELEPHONE & FAX: +44 (0)1599 534581.
VISITORS: Yes.
GREEN FEES: £6 per day.
CATERING: None.
FACILITIES: Club hire.

# LOCHCARRON

## LOCHCARRON GOLF CLUB

COURSE DESCRIPTION:
Lochside links course with some parkland. Short, but great accuracy needed especially at high tide. Set in beautiful surroundings by the head of a sea loch with mountains around. Excellent course for beginners and family groups to enjoy an unhurried game. Planning permission granted for new clubhouse.

9 holes, 3,578 yards (for 18 holes), par 62 (SSS 60). Course record 60.

SIGNATURE HOLE:
SECOND ('Johnny's Seat' 209 yards, par 4) A tight hole between the sea to the right and the graveyard to the left. The drive must carry a water hazard that can be greatly enlarged at high tide.

COURSE CARD

| HOLE | YDS | PAR |
|------|-------|-----|
| 1 | 201 | 3 |
| 2 | 209 | 4 |
| 3 | 284 | 4 |
| 4 | 225 | 4 |
| 5 | 158 | 3 |
| 6 | 144 | 3 |
| 7 | 178 | 3 |
| 8 | 125 | 3 |
| 9 | 265 | 4 |
| Yds Out | 1,789 | |
| Total Yds | 1,789 | |

| Total | 31 |
|-------|----|
| Par   |    |

**ADDRESS:** East End, Strathcarron, Lochcarron, Highlands IV54 8YL.
**SECRETARY:** Alastair Beattie +44 (0)1520 766211.
**VISITORS:** Yes, except Saturday afternoons.
**GREEN FEES:** £10 per day. Weekly ticket £40.
**CATERING:** Bar meals available at local hotels.
**FACILITIES:** Club hire (£3.50 from Lochcarron Hotel), memberships available (£75 local, £60 country).
**LOCATION:** By A896 road, approximately half a mile east of Lochcarron village towards Strathcarron station. From south or east, go to A890/A896 junction and continue towards Lochcarron for 1½ miles.
**LOCAL HOTELS:** Bank House, Lochcarron Hotel, Strathcarron Hotel.

# LOSSIEMOUTH

## COVESEA GOLF COURSE

**COURSE DESCRIPTION:**
Friendly, fun, although quite challenging, links par-3 course.
12 holes, 1,533 yards, par 36.

**COURSE CARD**

| HOLE | YDS | PAR | HOLE | YDS | PAR |
|------|-----|-----|------|-----|-----|
| 1 | 157 | 3 | 10 | 79 | 3 |
| 2 | 95 | 3 | 11 | 115 | 3 |
| 3 | 212 | 3 | 12 | 80 | 3 |
| 4 | 135 | 3 | | | |
| 5 | 166 | 3 | | | |
| 6 | 111 | 3 | | | |
| 7 | 83 | 3 | | | |
| 8 | 212 | 3 | | | |
| 9 | 88 | 3 | | | |
| Yds Out | 1,259 | | Yds In | 274 | |
| Total Yds | 1,533 | | | | |
| Total | 36 | | | | |

**ADDRESS:** Covesea, Lossiemouth, Moray, IV30 5QS.
**TELEPHONE:** +44 (0)1343 814124.
**VISITORS:** Yes, open 9 a.m. to 9 p.m.
**GREEN FEES:** £5 per round/day weekdays/weekends.
**CATERING:** Light refreshment.

FACILITIES: Club hire, toilets.
LOCATION: On the B9040 Hopeman to Lossiemouth road.
LOCAL HOTELS: Greenlawns, The Links Hotel, The Old Coach House Hotel.

# MORAY GOLF CLUB

### COURSE DESCRIPTION:
Two fine Scottish championship links courses, situated on the Moray Firth. Mild weather. Like St Andrews, the Old Course's first and last holes are part of the town. A test at the best of times, when the wind blows prepare yourself for a battle. New Moray is shorter but is tighter with smaller greens and a lot of gorse.

*Old Moray* – 18 holes, 6,578 yards, par 71 (SSS 73).
*New Moray* – 18 holes, 6,004 yards, par 69 (SSS 69).

### SIGNATURE HOLE:
EIGHTEENTH ('Home' 406 yards, par 4) Probably Moray's most photographed hole. Out of bounds all the way down the right and the left is protected by revetted bunkers and long rough. A good straight drive is a must, which will set up a long-to mid-iron to a large elevated green.

### COURSE CARD

| HOLE | MEDAL YDS | PAR | FORWARD YDS | PAR | LADIES YDS | PAR | HOLE | MEDAL YDS | PAR | FORWARD YDS | PAR | LADIES YDS | PAR |
|---|---|---|---|---|---|---|---|---|---|---|---|---|---|
| 1 | 332 | 4 | 321 | 4 | 311 | 4 | 10 | 312 | 4 | 261 | 4 | 251 | 4 |
| 2 | 494 | 5 | 483 | 5 | 444 | 5 | 11 | 423 | 4 | 400 | 4 | 413 | 5 |
| 3 | 397 | 4 | 391 | 4 | 384 | 4 | 12 | 389 | 4 | 377 | 4 | 354 | 4 |
| 4 | 197 | 3 | 197 | 3 | 197 | 3 | 13 | 421 | 4 | 395 | 4 | 386 | 4 |
| 5 | 416 | 4 | 404 | 4 | 387 | 4 | 14 | 409 | 4 | 398 | 4 | 400 | 5 |
| 6 | 145 | 3 | 138 | 3 | 130 | 3 | 15 | 184 | 3 | 146 | 3 | 139 | 3 |
| 7 | 434 | 4 | 428 | 4 | 420 | 5 | 16 | 351 | 4 | 341 | 4 | 235 | 4 |
| 8 | 452 | 4 | 438 | 4 | 434 | 5 | 17 | 506 | 5 | 495 | 4 | 450 | 5 |
| 9 | 310 | 4 | 279 | 4 | 294 | 4 | 18 | 406 | 4 | 400 | 4 | 373 | 4 |
| Yds | 3,177 | | 3,079 | | 3,001 | | Yds | 3,401 | | 3,213 | | 3,102 | |
| Total Yds | 6,578 | | 6,292 | | 6,103 | | | | | | | | |
| Total Par | 71 | | 70 | | 75 | | | | | | | | |

ADDRESS: Stotfield Road, Lossiemouth, Moray IV31 6QS.
TELEPHONE: +44 (0)1343 812018.
FAX: +44 (0)1343 815102.
E-MAIL: secretary@moraygolf.co.uk
WEBSITE: www.moraygolf.co.uk
SECRETARY: Boyd Russell.
PROFESSIONAL: Alistair Thomson.
VISITORS: Yes, after 10 a.m.
GREEN FEES: Old Moray: £30 per round weekdays, £45 per day. £40 per round

weekends, £60 per day.

**NEW MORAY:** £20 per round weekdays, £30 per day. £25 per round weekends, £35 per day.

**WEEKLY TICKETS:** Old £125, New £90.

**CREDIT CARDS ACCEPTED:** Amex/Visa/Mastercard/Diners Club.

**CATERING:** Restaurant and bar. Functions catered for.

**FACILITIES:** Motorised buggies, trolley hire, club hire, caddies, changing-rooms, putting green, pro shop, practice ground.

**LOCATION:** From Inverness, take A96 through Nairn into Elgin. Follow signpost for Lossiemouth Golf Course on West Beach. From Aberdeen, take A96 through Elgin and follow as above.

**LOCAL HOTELS:** Greenlawns, Laverock Bank Hotel, Rock House Hotel, Stotfield Hotel, Sunninghill Hotel, The Links Hotel, The Old Coach House Hotel.

# LYBSTER

## LYBSTER GOLF CLUB

**COURSE DESCRIPTION:**
Short heathland/moorland course with views over Moray Firth. Easy walking.
9 holes, 3,796 yards (for 18 holes), par 62 (SSS 62).

**ADDRESS:** Main Street, Lybster KW1 6BL.
**TELEPHONE:** +44 (0)1593 721308.
**VISITORS:** Any time.
**GREEN FEES:** £7 per day weekdays/weekends (honesty box).
**LOCATION:** East of village on A9, 13 miles south of Wick.
**LOCAL HOTELS:** Melvich Hotel, Portland Arms Hotel.

# MUIR OF ORD

## MUIR OF ORD GOLF CLUB

**COURSE DESCRIPTION:**
Established 1875 and designed in part by James Braid. Heathland course with tight fairways and good greens. Easy walking. Road and railway line cuts course into three.
18 holes, 5,557 yards, par 68 (SSS 68).

**ADDRESS:** Great North Road, Muir of Ord IV6 7SX.
**TELEPHONE:** +44 (0)1463 870825.
**FAX:** +44 (0)1463 871867.
**E-MAIL:** muirgolf@supanet.com

**VISITORS:** Not before 11 a.m. weekends without prior agreement and during club competitions.

**GREEN FEES:** £16 per round weekdays, £18 per day. £20 per round weekends, £22 per day.

**CATERING:** Yes, bar meals at weekends and by prior arrangement.

**CREDIT CARDS ACCEPTED:** Visa/Mastercard in shop only.

**FACILITIES:** Motorised buggies (£12), trolley hire (£2), club hire (£6), changing-rooms, putting green, shop, practice ground, memberships available.

**LOCATION:** 14 miles north of Inverness on the A832.

**LOCAL HOTELS:** Bunchrew House Hotel, Glen Mhor Hotel, Heathmount Hotel, Priory Hotel.

# NAIRN

## CAWDOR CASTLE GOLF CLUB

**COURSE DESCRIPTION:**
Inland course, opened in 1976, covering 25 acres of mature parkland. Cawdor Castle has been associated with Macbeth but it was built in 1370 and it is impossible for King Duncan to have lost any blood, or Lady Macbeth much sleep, in this particular house.

9 holes, 1,429 yards, par 31. Course record 28.

**COURSE CARD**

| HOLE | YDS | PAR |
|------|------|-----|
| 1 | 76 | 3 |
| 2 | 159 | 3 |
| 3 | 109 | 3 |
| 4 | 144 | 3 |
| 5 | 115 | 3 |
| 6 | 168 | 4 |
| 7 | 182 | 4 |
| 8 | 212 | 4 |
| 9 | 273 | 4 |
| Yds Out | 1,429 | |
| Total Yds | 1,429 | |
| Total Par | 31 | |

**ADDRESS:** Cawdor Castle, near Nairn IV12 5RD.
**TELEPHONE:** +44 (0)1667 404615.
**FAX:** +44 (0)1667 404674.
**E-MAIL:** info@cawdorcastle.com

WEBSITE: www.cawdorcastle.com
VISITORS: Yes, May to second Sunday in October (10 a.m. to 5 p.m.)
GREEN FEES: £5 per round.
CATERING: Licensed restaurant in castle; snack bar in grounds. Functions catered for.
FACILITIES: Club hire (£1.50 – £2), putting green (£1), memberships available.
LOCATION: On B9090 road, off the A96 between Inverness and Nairn.
LOCAL HOTELS: Black Bull Thistle Hotel, Bunchrew House Hotel, Claymore Hotel, Clifton Hotel, Glen Mhor Hotel, Golf View Hotel, Greenlawns, Heathmount Hotel, Mansfield House Hotel, Newton Hotel, Royal Hotel, Skye of Curr Hotel, Sunninghill Hotel, The Links Hotel, Windsor Hotel.

## NAIRN DUNBAR GOLF CLUB

COURSE DESCRIPTION:
Championship links with gorse- and whin-lined fairways. Medium greens.
   18 holes, 6,720 yards, par 72 (SSS 73). Pro record 64. Amateur record 66.

SIGNATURE HOLE:
SEVENTH (395 yards, par 4) Encircled by gorse, bushes and trees with Minister's Loch waiting for your tee shot off the left. A raised green with deep bunkers either side.

COURSE CARD

| HOLE | YDS | PAR | HOLE | YDS | PAR |
|------|-----|-----|------|-----|-----|
| 1 | 418 | 4 | 10 | 414 | 4 |
| 2 | 333 | 4 | 11 | 126 | 3 |
| 3 | 189 | 3 | 12 | 381 | 4 |
| 4 | 448 | 4 | 13 | 529 | 5 |
| 5 | 453 | 4 | 14 | 346 | 4 |
| 6 | 419 | 4 | 15 | 161 | 3 |
| 7 | 395 | 4 | 16 | 503 | 5 |
| 8 | 163 | 3 | 17 | 442 | 4 |
| 9 | 501 | 5 | 18 | 499 | 5 |
| Yds Out | 3,319 | | Yds In | 3,401 | |
| Total Yds | 6,720 | | | | |
| Total Par | 72 | | | | |

ADDRESS: Lochloy Road, Nairn IV12 5AE.
TELEPHONE: +44 (0)1667 452741.
FAX: +44 (0)1667 456897.
E-MAIL: secretary@nairndunbar.com
SECRETARY: Scott Falconer.
PROFESSIONAL: David Torrance +44 (0)1667 453964.
VISITORS: Yes. Weekdays preferred. Normally 9.30 a.m. to 4 p.m.

GREEN FEES: £33 per round weekdays, £42 per day. £40 per round weekends, £53 per day.

CATERING: Restaurant and bar.

CREDIT CARDS ACCEPTED: Visa/Mastercard.

FACILITIES: Motorised buggies, trolley hire, club hire, caddies, changing-rooms, putting green, pro shop, practice ground, memberships available.

LOCATION: Off A96.

LOCAL HOTELS: Bunchrew House Hotel, Claymore Hotel, Glen Mhor Hotel, Golf View Hotel, Greenlawns, Heathmount Hotel, Mansfield House Hotel, Royal Hotel, Skye of Curr Hotel, Sunninghill Hotel, The Links Hotel.

## THE NAIRN GOLF CLUB

### COURSE DESCRIPTION:

An outstanding championship links course with fast greens, on the shores of the Moray Firth. After Great Britain & Ireland defeated the United States to win the 37th Walker Cup here in 1999, the vanquished team's captain Danny Yates said 'The golf course was spectacular. The conditioning, the set-up couldn't have been better. This has been a special place and the people have been so wonderful.' Founded in 1887 and extended by Old Tom Morris, James Braid and Archie Simpson, it has played host to many golfing greats.

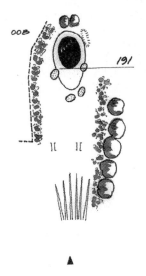

*Championship Course* – 18 holes, 6,705 yards (championship tees), par 72 (SSS 74). Medal 6,430 yards, par 71.

*Newton Course* – 9 holes, 3,542 yards (for 18 holes), par 58 (SSS 57).

### SIGNATURE HOLE:

FOURTEENTH ('Kopjes' 219 yards, par 3) out of bounds on the left. From the championship tee, 191 yards to the front of the undulating two-tiered green, which is guarded by bunkers right and left. Picturesque hole.

### COURSE CARD

| HOLE | MEDAL YDS | PAR | FORWARD YDS | PAR | HOLE | MEDAL YDS | PAR | FORWARD YDS | PAR |
|---|---|---|---|---|---|---|---|---|---|
| 1 | 395 | 4 | 383 | 4 | 10 | 496 | 5 | 495 | 5 |
| 2 | 463 | 4 | 453 | 4 | 11 | 160 | 3 | 152 | 3 |
| 3 | 373 | 4 | 361 | 4 | 12 | 444 | 4 | 401 | 4 |
| 4 | 144 | 3 | 135 | 3 | 13 | 423 | 4 | 412 | 4 |
| 5 | 377 | 4 | 371 | 4 | 14 | 211 | 3 | 195 | 3 |
| 6 | 183 | 3 | 175 | 3 | 15 | 306 | 4 | 281 | 4 |
| 7 | 495 | 5 | 488 | 5 | 16 | 417 | 4 | 403 | 4 |

| 8 | 326 | 4 | 307 | 4 | 17 | 377 | 4 | 337 | 4 |
|---|---|---|---|---|---|---|---|---|---|
| 9 | 324 | 4 | 301 | 4 | 18 | 516 | 5 | 490 | 5 |
| *Yds* | 3,080 | | 2,974 | | *Yds* | 3,350 | | 3,166 | |
| *Out* | | | | | *In* | | | | |
| *Total* 6,430 | | 6,140 | | | | | | | |
| *Yds* | | | | | | | | | |
| *Total* | 71 | | 71 | | | | | | |
| *Par* | | | | | | | | | |

ADDRESS: Seabank Road, Nairn IV12 4HB.
TELEPHONE: +44 (0)1667 453208.
FAX: +44 (0)1667 456328.
E-MAIL: bookings@nairngolfclub.prestel.co.uk
WEBSITE: www.nairngolfclub.co.uk
SECRETARY: James Somerville.
PROFESSIONAL: Robin Fyfe.
VISITORS: Yes, subject to availability.
GREEN FEES: £70 per round weekdays and weekends.
CREDIT CARDS ACCEPTED: Amex/Visa/Mastercard/Diners Club.
CATERING: Restaurant and bar open all year round in a magnificent new clubhouse built in 1990. Functions catered for.
FACILITIES: Trolley hire (£2), club hire (£12), caddies may be requested but cannot be guaranteed, changing-rooms, putting green, pro shop, practice ground, driving range, coaching clinics.
LOCATION: 15 miles east of Inverness. From Inverness, turn left at church with tower and go along Seabank Road. From Aberdeen, on A96, turn right at church.
LOCAL HOTELS: Altonburn Hotel, Bunchrew House Hotel, Claymore House Hotel, Glen Mhor Hotel, Golf View Hotel, Greenlawns, Heathmount Hotel, Mansfield House Hotel, Newton Hotel, Royal Hotel, Skye of Curr Hotel, Sunninghill Hotel, The Links Hotel, Windsor Hotel.

# NETHYBRIDGE

## ABERNETHY GOLF CLUB

COURSE DESCRIPTION:
A traditional Highland course, built on natural moorland, surrounded by majestic pine trees. Founded in 1893, it offers a great variety of shot-making for the accomplished or casual golfer. The short 2nd is played across some bogland and a B-class road to a two-tiered green. The small and fast greens are the most undulating in the valley. The Abernethy Forest lies on its boundary and from many parts of the course there are splendid views of Strathspey.

9 holes, 5,038 yards (for 18 holes), par 66 (SSS 66). Amateur record I. Murray 61.

SIGNATURE HOLE:
SEVENTH ('Balnagowan' 414 yards, par 4) Most challenging on the course. A dogleg played around a boundary of fine old Caledonian pines with the second shot to a green with wonderful contours.

## COURSE CARD

| HOLE | MEDAL YDS | PAR | FORWARD YDS | PAR | LADIES YDS | PAR |
|------|-----------|-----|-------------|-----|------------|-----|
| 1 | 301 | 4 | 286 | 4 | 296 | 4 |
| 2 | 115 | 3 | 113 | 3 | 113 | 3 |
| 3 | 304 | 4 | 292 | 4 | 298 | 4 |
| 4 | 315 | 4 | 269 | 4 | 310 | 4 |
| 5 | 217 | 3 | 166 | 3 | 213 | 4 |
| 6 | 303 | 4 | 280 | 4 | 291 | 4 |
| 7 | 414 | 4 | 378 | 4 | 364 | 4 |
| 8 | 231 | 3 | 210 | 3 | 228 | 4 |
| 9 | 319 | 4 | 301 | 4 | 307 | 4 |
| Yds Out | 2,519 | | 2,295 | | 2,420 | |
| Total Yds | 2,519 | | | | | |
| Total Par | 33 | | | | | |

ADDRESS: Nethy Bridge, Inverness-shire PH25 3EG.
TELEPHONE: +44 (0)1479 821305.
E-MAIL: bob_robbie@compuserve.com
WEBSITE: www.nethybridge.com/golfclub.htm
SECRETARY: R.H. Robbie.
VISITORS: Are always welcome. At weekends phone beforehand to check whether the course is closed for a club competition. Tee reservation is often unnecessary.
GREEN FEES: £13 per day weekdays. £16 per day weekends. Weekly ticket £70.
CATERING: The clubhouse serves refreshments, snacks and home baking and is unlicensed. It is open from April to October.
FACILITIES: Trolley hire, club hire, changing-rooms, practice facilities.
LOCATION: ½ mile north of Nethy Bridge on the B970 Grantown-on-Spey–Coylumbridge road.
LOCAL HOTELS: Heatherbrae Hotel, Mountview Hotel, Nethy Hotel, Newton House Hotel, Skye of Curr Hotel.

# NEWTONMORE

## NEWTONMORE GOLF CLUB

COURSE DESCRIPTION:
Flat parkland course beside the River Spey. Beautiful views and easy walking.
18 holes, 6,029 yards, par 70 (SSS 68). Course record 68.

COURSE CARD

| HOLE | MEDAL YDS | PAR | FORWARD YDS | PAR | LADIES YDS | PAR | HOLE | MEDAL YDS | PAR | FORWARD YDS | PAR | LADIES YDS | PAR |
|---|---|---|---|---|---|---|---|---|---|---|---|---|---|
| 1 | 252 | 4 | 239 | 4 | 230 | 4 | 10 | 518 | 5 | 404 | 4 | 394 | 5 |
| 2 | 373 | 4 | 260 | 4 | 258 | 4 | 11 | 254 | 4 | 248 | 3 | 245 | 4 |
| 3 | 409 | 4 | 398 | 4 | 395 | 4 | 12 | 417 | 4 | 389 | 4 | 383 | 5 |
| 4 | 303 | 4 | 292 | 4 | 288 | 4 | 13 | 392 | 4 | 384 | 4 | 374 | 4 |
| 5 | 373 | 4 | 340 | 4 | 330 | 4 | 14 | 406 | 4 | 317 | 4 | 310 | 4 |
| 6 | 332 | 4 | 308 | 4 | 306 | 4 | 15 | 155 | 3 | 149 | 3 | 145 | 3 |
| 7 | 403 | 4 | 384 | 4 | 378 | 4 | 16 | 389 | 4 | 335 | 4 | 333 | 4 |
| 8 | 163 | 3 | 131 | 3 | 119 | 3 | 17 | 194 | 3 | 157 | 3 | 150 | 3 |
| 9 | 365 | 4 | 356 | 4 | 347 | 4 | 18 | 331 | 4 | 309 | 4 | 304 | 4 |
| Yds Out | 2,973 | | 2,708 | | 2,651 | | Yds In | 3,056 | | 2,692 | | 2,638 | |
| Total Yds | 6,029 | | 5,400 | | 5,289 | | | | | | | | |
| Total Par | 70 | | 67 | | 73 | | | | | | | | |

ADDRESS: Golf Course Road, Newtonmore PH20 1AT.
TELEPHONE: +44 (0)1540 673328.
FAX: +44 (0)1540 673878.
E-MAIL: golfclub@newtonmore.com
WEBSITE: www.newtonmore.com/golfclub/
PROFESSIONAL: Bob Henderson.
VISITORS: Contact in advance.
GREEN FEES: £15 per round weekdays, £18 per day. £17 per round weekends, £23 per day.
CATERING: Full service. Bar.
FACILITIES: Trolley/buggy hire, putting green, pro shop, practice ground.
LOCATION: East of town, off A9.
LOCAL HOTELS: Skye of Curr Hotel, The Scot House Hotel.

# PORTMAHOMACK

## TARBAT GOLF CLUB

### COURSE DESCRIPTION:
Links course overlooking the Dornoch Firth and Moray Firth. Magnificent backdrop of mountains.

9 holes, 5,082 yards (for 18 holes), par 67 (SSS 65). Amateur record 67.

### SIGNATURE HOLE:
EIGHTH (302 yards, par 4) Approach to an elevated green is protected by undulating land for some 100 yards before the green.

### COURSE CARD

| HOLE | YDS | PAR | HOLE | YDS | PAR |
|------|-----|-----|------|-----|-----|
| 1 | 290 | 4 | 10 | 290 | 4 |
| 2 | 324 | 4 | 11 | 324 | 4 |
| 3 | 414 | 4 | 12 | 385 | 4 |
| 4 | 265 | 4 | 13 | 180 | 3 |
| 5 | 177 | 3 | 14 | 177 | 3 |
| 6 | 355 | 4 | 15 | 355 | 4 |
| 7 | 166 | 3 | 16 | 130 | 3 |
| 8 | 302 | 4 | 17 | 302 | 4 |
| 9 | 323 | 4 | 18 | 323 | 4 |
| Yds Out | 2,616 | | Yds In | 2,466 | |
| Total Yds | 5,082 | | | | |
| Total Par | 67 | | | | |

ADDRESS: Portmahomack, Ross-shire IV20 1SL.
TELEPHONE: +44 (0)1862 871598.
E-MAIL: motol@clara.co.uk
SECRETARY: Morag Lane.
VISITORS: Any time, except Saturday mornings when there are competitions.
GREEN FEES: £12 per day.
CATERING: No, but local pubs and restaurant.
FACILITIES: Practice ground.
LOCATION: East side of village.
LOCAL HOTELS: Caledonian Hotel, Castle Hotel.

# REAY

## REAY GOLF CLUB

**COURSE DESCRIPTION:**
This beautiful seaside course alongside Sandside Bay is the most northerly 18-hole links on the British mainland. It has excellent greens and contoured fairways, providing enjoyable golf for high and low handicappers alike. Many interesting and challenging holes, including the 4th ('Sahara' 581 yards, par 5), which requires a solid tee shot and fairway wood to set up an approach to a sheltered green protected by a burn. Commanding views of the Pentland Firth and Orkney Isles.

18 holes, 5,831 yards, par 69 (SSS 69). Course record 64.

**SIGNATURE HOLE:**
SEVENTH ('Pilkington' 196 yards, par 3) Played across Reay Burn to a raised green.

**COURSE CARD**

| HOLE | MEDAL YDS | PAR | LADIES YDS | PAR | HOLE | MEDAL YDS | PAR | LADIES YDS | PAR |
|------|-----------|-----|------------|-----|------|-----------|-----|------------|-----|
| 1 | 235 | 3 | 165 | 3 | 10 | 351 | 4 | 340 | 4 |
| 2 | 428 | 4 | 409 | 5 | 11 | 406 | 4 | 320 | 4 |
| 3 | 369 | 4 | 337 | 4 | 12 | 348 | 4 | 333 | 4 |
| 4 | 581 | 5 | 434 | 5 | 13 | 305 | 4 | 238 | 4 |
| 5 | 144 | 3 | 139 | 3 | 14 | 476 | 5 | 429 | 5 |
| 6 | 477 | 5 | 419 | 5 | 15 | 136 | 3 | 127 | 3 |
| 7 | 196 | 3 | 131 | 3 | 16 | 314 | 4 | 268 | 4 |
| 8 | 399 | 4 | 383 | 4 | 17 | 328 | 4 | 292 | 4 |
| 9 | 176 | 3 | 162 | 3 | 18 | 162 | 3 | 141 | 3 |
| Yds Out | 3,005 | | 2,579 | | Yds In | 2,826 | | 2,488 | |
| Yds Total | 5,831 | | 5,057 | | | | | | |
| Total Par | 69 | | 70 | | | | | | |

**ADDRESS:** The Club House, Reay, Caithness KW14 7RE.
**TELEPHONE:** +44 (0)1847 811288.
**FAX:** +44 (0)1847 894189.
**E-MAIL:** info@reaygolfclub.co.uk
**WEBSITE:** www.reaygolfclub.co.uk
**SECRETARY:** Bill McIntosh.
**VISITORS:** Any time.
**GREEN FEES:** £15 per round or day. £45 per week.
**CATERING:** Bar. Catering by arrangement with secretary. Functions catered for.

FACILITIES: Trolley hire, club hire, changing-rooms, putting green, practice ground, full and country memberships available.
LOCATION: 11 miles west of Thurso on A836.
LOCAL HOTELS: Forss Hotel, Melvich Hotel.

# ISLE OF SKYE

## ISLE OF SKYE GOLF CLUB

### COURSE DESCRIPTION:
Seaside parkland course. Magnificent views.
9 holes, 4,677 yards (for 18 holes), par 66 (SSS 64). Amateur record 62.

### COURSE CARD

| HOLE | YDS | PAR | HOLE | YDS | PAR |
|------|-----|-----|------|-----|-----|
| 1 | 288 | 4 | 10 | 307 | 4 |
| 2 | 447 | 4 | 11 | 417 | 4 |
| 3 | 153 | 3 | 12 | 129 | 3 |
| 4 | 280 | 4 | 13 | 280 | 4 |
| 5 | 162 | 3 | 14 | 122 | 3 |
| 6 | 349 | 4 | 15 | 349 | 4 |
| 7 | 146 | 3 | 16 | 142 | 3 |
| 8 | 294 | 4 | 17 | 276 | 4 |
| 9 | 268 | 4 | 18 | 268 | 4 |
| Yds Out | 2,387 | | Yds In | 2,290 | |
| Total Yds | 4,677 | | | | |
| Total Par | 66 | | | | |

ADDRESS: Sconser, Isle of Skye IV48 8TD.
TELEPHONE & FAX: +44 (0)1478 650414.
E-MAIL: isleofskye.golfclub@btinternet.com
SECRETARY: I. Macmillan +44 (0)1478 650414
VISITORS: Any time. Avoid 10 a.m. to 11 a.m. on Saturdays.
GREEN FEES: £15 per day. Juniors £7.50 per day.
CATERING: Yes.
FACILITIES: Trolley hire (£2), club hire (£7), practice area, changing rooms, shower.
LOCATION: On main road from Skye Bridge to Portree, but be prepared for exorbitantly high tolls on the bridge.

## SKEABOST GOLF CLUB

COURSE DESCRIPTION:
Wooded, taxing seaside course in the grounds of the 26-bedroom Skeabost House Hotel. Tight fairways and greens. Constructed on the site of a mortal feud between the MacDonalds and MacLeods.

9 holes, 3,114 yards (for 18 holes), par 62 (SSS 60). Course record 58.

### COURSE CARD

| HOLE | YDS | PAR | HOLE | YDS | PAR |
|------|------|-----|------|------|-----|
| 1 | 103 | 3 | 10 | 103 | 3 |
| 2 | 256 | 4 | 11 | 205 | 4 |
| 3 | 252 | 4 | 12 | 288 | 4 |
| 4 | 91 | 3 | 13 | 91 | 3 |
| 5 | 225 | 4 | 14 | 225 | 4 |
| 6 | 125 | 3 | 15 | 144 | 3 |
| 7 | 258 | 4 | 16 | 258 | 4 |
| 8 | 119 | 3 | 17 | 100 | 3 |
| 9 | 150 | 3 | 18 | 121 | 3 |
| *Yds Out* | 1,579 | | *Yds In* | 1,535 | |
| *Total Yds* | 3,114 | | | | |
| *Total Par* | 62 | | | | |

ADDRESS: Skeabost House Hotel, Skeabost Bridge, Isle of Skye IV51 9NP.
TELEPHONE: +44 (0)1470 532202.
FAX: +44 (0)1470 532454.
E-MAIL: skeabost@sol.co.uk
WEBSITE: www.sol.co.uk/s/skeabost
VISITORS: Contact in advance.
GREEN FEES: £10 per day.
CATERING: Restaurant (in hotel) and bar.
FACILITIES: Trolley hire, club hire, putting green, pro shop, practice ground.
LOCATION: 6 miles out of Portree on Dunvegan road.
LOCAL HOTELS: Skeabost House Hotel.

# SPEAN BRIDGE

## SPEAN BRIDGE GOLF CLUB

COURSE DESCRIPTION:
Interesting inland course.
9 holes, 4,406 yards (for 18 holes), par 63.

ADDRESS: Station Road, Spean Bridge, near Fort William PH34 4EU.
TELEPHONE: +44 (0)1397 704594.
VISITORS: Yes, by arrangement.
GREEN FEES: £10 per round.
CATERING: Snacks available.
FACILITIES: Trolley hire, club hire.
LOCATION: 8 miles north of Fort William on the A82.

# SPEY BAY

## SPEY BAY GOLF CLUB

COURSE DESCRIPTION:
Undulating links course.
   18 holes, 6,092 yards, par 70 (SSS 69). Course record 66.

SIGNATURE HOLE:
SIXTEENTH (517 yards, par 5) Bounded by gorse and the beach, this hole poses problems for the wayward.

ADDRESS: Spey Bay, Fochabers, Moray IV32 7PJ.
TELEPHONE: +44 (0)1343 820424.
PROFESSIONAL: Hamish McDonald.
VISITORS: Contact in advance.
GREEN FEES: £10 per round weekdays, £15 per day. £13 per round weekends, £18 per day.
CATERING: Meals and bar all day.
FACILITIES: Trolley hire, putting green, practice ground, driving range.
LOCATION: 4½ miles north of Fochabers on B9104.
LOCAL HOTELS: Glen Mhor Hotel, Greenlawns, Mill House Hotel, Spey Bay Hotel, Sunninghill Hotel, The Old Coach House Hotel.

# STRATHPEFFER

## STRATHPEFFER SPA GOLF CLUB

COURSE DESCRIPTION:
Testing hilly upland course, designed in 1888 by Old Tom Morris. Many natural hazards, including burns and three lochans. Only three bunkers. Panoramic views down the Peffery Valley to the Black Isle and from the upper end of the course to the Fannich hills.
   18 holes, 4,794 yards, par 65 (SSS 64). Course record 60.

SIGNATURE HOLE:
FIRST ('Castle Leod' 297 yards, par 4) The drive from tee to green is the longest drop on any course in Scotland. Drive left of the mound to allow a clear pitch to the green. Out-of -bounds all the way down the right and behind the green.

## COURSE CARD

| HOLE | YDS | PAR | HOLE | YDS | PAR |
|------|-----|-----|------|-----|-----|
| 1 | 297 | 4 | 10 | 162 | 3 |
| 2 | 257 | 4 | 11 | 231 | 4 |
| 3 | 199 | 3 | 12 | 279 | 4 |
| 4 | 211 | 3 | 13 | 306 | 4 |
| 5 | 120 | 3 | 14 | 151 | 3 |
| 6 | 183 | 3 | 15 | 419 | 4 |
| 7 | 287 | 4 | 16 | 369 | 4 |
| 8 | 316 | 4 | 17 | 271 | 4 |
| 9 | 430 | 4 | 18 | 306 | 4 |
| Yds Out | 2,300 | | Yds In | 2,494 | |
| Total Yds | 4,794 | | | | |
| Total Par | 65 | | | | |

ADDRESS: Golf Course Road, Strathpeffer, Ross-shire, IV14 9AS.
TELEPHONE: +44 (0)1997 421219.
FAX: +44 (0) 1997 421011
E-MAIL: mail@strathpeffergolf.co.uk
WEBSITE: www.strathpeffergolf.co.uk
HON. SECRETARY: Norman Roxburgh +44 (0)1997 421396.
VISITORS: Welcome without reservation. Advisable to check tee availability in advance. Some restrictions on competition days (Tuesdays, Fridays and Saturdays).
GREEN FEES: £15 per round, £21 per day weekdays/weekends. £60 per week (Monday to Friday).
CATERING: Bar and catering available seven days a week. Catering restricted on Mondays and Tuesdays unless previously booked with club steward.
CREDIT CARDS ACCEPTED: Visa/Mastercard.
FACILITIES: Trolley hire(£2), club hire (£10), caddies by arrangement, changing-rooms, putting green, pro shop, practice ground, memberships available.
LOCATION: ½ mile north of village, off A834.
LOCAL HOTELS: Brunstane Lodge Hotel, Highland Hotel, Holly Lodge Hotel, Richmond Hotel, Strathpeffer Hotel.

# TAIN

## TAIN GOLF CLUB

**COURSE DESCRIPTION:**
Part inland, part links course with fast greens, designed by Old Tom Morris in 1890. River Tain winds through the course at three holes. Tain is also the home of the Glenmorangie malt whisky and the distillery is worth a visit.

18 holes, 6,404 yards, par 70 (SSS 71).

**SIGNATURE HOLE:**
ELEVENTH (380 yards, par 4) The green is hidden behind two huge sand hills. The pin position must be checked on indicator board on the tee.

**COURSE CARD**

| HOLE | MEDAL YDS | PAR | FORWARD YDS | PAR | LADIES YDS | PAR | HOLE | MEDAL YDS | PAR | FORWARD YDS | PAR | LADIES YDS | PAR |
|------|-----------|-----|-------------|-----|------------|-----|------|-----------|-----|-------------|-----|------------|-----|
| 1 | 382 | 4 | 371 | 4 | 343 | 4 | 10 | 403 | 4 | 380 | 4 | 320 | 4 |
| 2 | 391 | 4 | 351 | 4 | 381 | 4 | 11 | 380 | 4 | 374 | 4 | 370 | 5 |
| 3 | 435 | 4 | 416 | 4 | 385 | 4 | 12 | 386 | 4 | 372 | 4 | 325 | 4 |
| 4 | 542 | 5 | 532 | 5 | 478 | 5 | 13 | 501 | 5 | 492 | 5 | 486 | 5 |
| 5 | 181 | 3 | 167 | 3 | 150 | 3 | 14 | 438 | 4 | 397 | 4 | 392 | 5 |
| 6 | 309 | 4 | 309 | 4 | 282 | 4 | 15 | 346 | 4 | 330 | 4 | 320 | 4 |
| 7 | 377 | 4 | 369 | 4 | 345 | 4 | 16 | 147 | 3 | 139 | 3 | 127 | 3 |
| 8 | 189 | 3 | 179 | 3 | 179 | 3 | 17 | 215 | 3 | 211 | 3 | 208 | 4 |
| 9 | 355 | 4 | 349 | 4 | 346 | 4 | 18 | 427 | 4 | 371 | 4 | 286 | 4 |
| *Yds* Out | 3,161 | | 3,043 | | 2,811 | | *Yds* In | 3,243 | | 3,066 | | 2,844 | |
| *Total Yds* | 6,404 | | 6,109 | | 5,655 | | | | | | | | |
| *Total Par* | 70 | | 70 | | 73 | | | | | | | | |

**ADDRESS:** Chapel Road, Tain, Ross-shire IV19 1JE.
**TELEPHONE:** +44 (0)1862 892314.
**FAX:** +44 (0)1862 892099.
**E-MAIL:** tgc@cali.co.uk
**SECRETARY:** Mrs K. Ross.
**VISITORS:** Whenever tee is available. Pre-booking required.
**GREEN FEES:** £30 per round weekdays, £36 per day. £36 per round weekends, £46 per day.
**CATERING:** Yes.
**FACILITIES:** Trolley hire, putting green, pro shop, practice ground.
**LOCATION:** 35 miles north of Inverness. ½ mile from the town centre on B9174.
**LOCAL HOTELS:** Bunchrew House Hotel, Carnegie Lodge Hotel, Heathmount Hotel,

Mansfield House Hotel, Morangie House Hotel, Nigg Ferry Hotel, Royal Hotel, The Links Hotel.

# THURSO

## THURSO GOLF CLUB

**COURSE DESCRIPTION:**
Parkland course with fine views of Pentland Firth and Orkney Isles. Tends to be windy and most fairways are tree-lined. Several holes have tight drives and out of bounds features on ten holes. The course also has areas of gorse and heather and, although relatively short, is a test of straight hitting.

18 holes, 5,853 yards, par 69 (SSS 69). Amateur record 63.

**SIGNATURE HOLE:**
THIRTEENTH ('Lintles Pool' 279 yards, par 4) Can be driven under the right conditions, but when played into the wind it can be daunting. Has heather on the left, rough on the right and a bunker protecting the green.

**COURSE CARD**

| HOLE | MEDAL YDS | PAR | LADIES YDS | PAR | HOLE | MEDAL YDS | PAR | LADIES YDS | PAR |
|------|------|-----|------|-----|------|------|-----|------|-----|
| 1 | 406 | 4 | 406 | 5 | 10 | 419 | 4 | 410 | 5 |
| 2 | 371 | 4 | 366 | 4 | 11 | 368 | 4 | 357 | 4 |
| 3 | 186 | 3 | 179 | 3 | 12 | 223 | 4 | 198 | 3 |
| 4 | 504 | 5 | 398 | 5 | 13 | 279 | 4 | 211 | 4 |
| 5 | 200 | 3 | 195 | 3 | 14 | 161 | 3 | 156 | 3 |
| 6 | 345 | 4 | 241 | 4 | 15 | 356 | 4 | 346 | 4 |
| 7 | 492 | 5 | 372 | 4 | 16 | 440 | 4 | 440 | 5 |
| 8 | 263 | 4 | 263 | 4 | 17 | 370 | 4 | 296 | 4 |
| 9 | 158 | 3 | 158 | 3 | 18 | 312 | 4 | 301 | 4 |
| Yds Out | 2,925 | | 2,678 | | Yds In | 2,928 | | 2,706 | |
| Total Yds | 5,853 | | 5,384 | | | | | | |
| Total Par | 69 | | 71 | | | | | | |

**ADDRESS:** Newlands of Geise, Thurso, Caithness KW14 7XD.
**TELEPHONE:** +44 (0)1847 893807.
**VISITORS:** Yes, any time.
**GREEN FEES:** £15 per day. Outside summer, pay in honesty box. Weekly ticket £40.
**CATERING:** Bar and meals (available during the day from June to August).
**FACILITIES:** Trolley hire, club hire, changing-rooms, putting green, memberships available.

LOCATION: 2 miles west of Thurso off unmarked road to Reay and B874 road to Halkirk.
LOCAL HOTELS: John O'Groats Hotel, MacKays Hotel, Melvich Hotel, Ormlie Hotel, Park Hotel, Pentland Hotel, Royal Hotel, Weigh Inn Motel.

# ISLE OF TIREE

## VAUL GOLF CLUB

COURSE DESCRIPTION:
Seaside course with lovely views of magnificent sand beaches. No trees, no water hazards, but has its own difficulties.
9 holes, 5,674 yards (for 18 holes), par 71 (SSS 71).

ADDRESS: Vaul, Isle of Tiree, PA77 6XH.
TELEPHONE: +44 (0)1879 220334.
VISITORS: Tees closed to visitors on Saturdays between 1 p.m. and 4 p.m. No golf on Sundays.
GREEN FEES: £8 per round weekdays/weekends.
LOCATION: ¾ mile from Lodge Hotel and two miles from Scarinish.
LOCAL HOTELS: Lodge Hotel.

# ULLAPOOL

## ULLAPOOL GOLF CLUB

COURSE DESCRIPTION:
A picturesque new nine-hole moorland course, opened in 1998 by Prince Andrew, which blends with the surrounding Highland landscape and stretches down to the shores of Loch Broom. It can be testing for both beginner and experienced alike with a variety of holes, some skirting the shores of Loch Broom, some lined with gorse and others open and grassy. Outstanding views of Loch Broom and the Summer Isles.
9 holes, 5,338 yards (for 18 holes), par 70 (SSS 66).

SIGNATURE HOLE:
FOURTH ('Summer Isles' 151 yards, par 3) Tee shot needs to clear gorse bushes and avoid the beach. Beautiful view out to the Summer Isles.

COURSE CARD

| | MEDAL | | FORWARD | | LADIES | |
|------|-----|-----|-----|-----|-----|-----|
| HOLE | YDS | PAR | YDS | PAR | YDS | PAR |
| 1 | 323 | 4 | 309 | 4 | 298 | 4 |

| 2 | 135 | 3 | 128 | 3 | 120 | 3 |
|---|-----|---|-----|---|-----|---|
| 3 | 338 | 4 | 272 | 4 | 261 | 4 |
| 4 | 151 | 3 | 137 | 3 | 125 | 3 |
| 5 | 251 | 4 | 236 | 3 | 188 | 4 |
| 6 | 288 | 4 | 270 | 4 | 262 | 4 |
| 7 | 408 | 4 | 398 | 4 | 389 | 5 |
| 8 | 477 | 5 | 438 | 4 | 406 | 5 |
| 9 | 296 | 4 | 289 | 4 | 280 | 4 |
| *Yds* | 2,669 | | 2,477 | | 2,329 | |
| *Out* | | | | | | |
| *Total* | 2,669 | | | | | |
| *Yds* | | | | | | |
| *Total* | 35 | | | | | |
| *Par* | | | | | | |

ADDRESS: Morefield, Ullapool, Ross-shire IV26 2TH.
TELEPHONE & FAX: +44 (0)1854 613323.
E-MAIL: info@ullapool-golf.co.uk
WEBSITE: www.ullapool-golf.co.uk
VISITORS: Very welcome.
GREEN FEES: £12 per round/day weekdays; £15 per round/day weekends. £40 per week (Monday to Friday). Juniors: £6 per day, £20 per week.
CATERING: Bar. Functions catered for.
FACILITIES: Trolley hire (£2), club hire (£6), changing-rooms, practice ground, memberships available.
LOCATION: Take A835 north from Inverness (59 miles). Course located on left side of North Road as you are leaving the village.
LOCAL HOTELS: Arch Inn, Cruachan Bed & Breakfast, Riverside Hotel.

# WICK

## WICK GOLF CLUB

COURSE DESCRIPTION:
Challenging, typical Scottish links course. Nine holes out and nine back parallel to the sand dunes. An extension to the course, which will increase the yardage to 6,200 yards – and include changes to the 2nd, 3rd, 15th, 16th, 17th and 18th holes – is planned.

18 holes, 5,976 yards, par 69 (SSS 69). Amateur record 63.

SIGNATURE HOLE:
THIRTEENTH ('Cup', 390 yards, par 4) Accurate drive required through a narrow valley and an approach shot to a two-tier green.

## COURSE CARD

| HOLE | MEDAL YDS | PAR | LADIES YDS | PAR | HOLE | MEDAL YDS | PAR | LADIES YDS | PAR |
|------|-----------|-----|------------|-----|------|-----------|-----|------------|-----|
| 1 | 286 | 4 | 279 | 4 | 10 | 403 | 4 | 389 | 5 |
| 2 | 353 | 4 | 328 | 4 | 11 | 171 | 3 | 164 | 3 |
| 3 | 352 | 4 | 332 | 4 | 12 | 416 | 4 | 364 | 4 |
| 4 | 203 | 3 | 192 | 3 | 13 | 390 | 4 | 368 | 4 |
| 5 | 423 | 4 | 407 | 5 | 14 | 149 | 3 | 144 | 3 |
| 6 | 375 | 4 | 325 | 4 | 15 | 291 | 4 | 283 | 4 |
| 7 | 389 | 4 | 373 | 4 | 16 | 188 | 3 | 149 | 3 |
| 8 | 507 | 5 | 440 | 5 | 17 | 549 | 5 | 534 | 5 |
| 9 | 152 | 3 | 140 | 3 | 18 | 379 | 4 | 296 | 4 |

*Yds* 3,040    2,824    *Yds* 2,936    2,691
*Out*                   *In*

*Total* 5,976    5,515
*Yds*

*Total* 69    71
*Par*

ADDRESS: Reiss, Wick, Caithness KW1 4RW.

TELEPHONE: +44 (0)1955 602726.

SECRETARY: D. Shearer.

VISITORS: At all times.

GREEN FEES: £20 per round and day weekdays and weekends. Weekly ticket: £60.

CATERING: Bar and meals. Parties catered for by arrangement.

FACILITIES: Motorised buggies (£10), trolleys (£2), club hire (£5), changing-rooms, putting green, practice ground, memberships available.

LOCATION: 3½ miles north of Wick, on A9.

LOCAL HOTELS: Mackays Hotel, Melvich Hotel.

# GRAMPIAN INCLUDING ABERDEEN

# ABERDEEN

## AUCHMILL GOLF CLUB

COURSE DESCRIPTION:
Tough municipal heathland course with narrow tree-lined fairways. Three holes are quite hilly, but the rest are flat. Good views of Aberdeen.
18 holes, 5,883 yards, par 70 (SSS 69).

SIGNATURE HOLE:
EIGHTEENTH (455 yards, par 4) Dogleg left with out of bounds on right leading to a driving range.

ADDRESS: Bonnyview Road West, Hetheryfold, Aberdeen AB2 7FQ.
TELEPHONE: +44 (0)1224 715214.
STARTER: +44 (0)1224 714577.
VISITORS: Members have priority Saturdays and Wednesdays for competitions. Societies contact Aberdeen Leisure +44 01224 647647.
GREEN FEES: £9 per round weekdays (visitors £11.25; juniors £4.50). £11.25 per round weekends (visitors £14; juniors £5.75).
CATERING: Yes. Bar.
FACILITIES: Putting green, practice ground.
LOCATION: 5 miles north of Aberdeen on A96 Aberdeen–Inverness road.
LOCAL HOTELS: Aberdeen Patio Hotel, Raemoir House Hotel, Simpson's Hotel, Bar/Brasserie, Stakis Craigendarroch Hotel & Country Club, The White Horse Inn.

## BALNAGASK GOLF COURSE

COURSE DESCRIPTION:
Very undulating municipal links course without trees. Used by the Nigg Bay Club. Founded in 1955.
18 holes, 5,986 yards, par 70 (SSS 69).

SIGNATURE HOLE:
SIXTH (432 yards, par 4) Dogleg left with a blind tee shot over a hill.

**COURSE CARD**

| HOLE | YDS | PAR | HOLE | YDS | PAR |
|------|-----|-----|------|-----|-----|
| 1 | 368 | 4 | 10 | 483 | 5 |
| 2 | 447 | 4 | 11 | 367 | 4 |
| 3 | 406 | 4 | 12 | 296 | 4 |
| 4 | 360 | 4 | 13 | 265 | 4 |

| 5 | 133 | 3 | 14 | 210 | 3 |
| 6 | 432 | 4 | 15 | 358 | 4 |
| 7 | 310 | 4 | 16 | 336 | 4 |
| 8 | 316 | 4 | 17 | 338 | 4 |
| 9 | 345 | 4 | 18 | 216 | 3 |
| *Yds* *Out* | 3,117 | | *Yds* *In* | 2,869 | |
| *Total* *Yds* | 5,986 | | | | |
| *Total* *Par* | 70 | | | | |

ADDRESS: St Fitticks Road, Aberdeen AB1 3QT.
TELEPHONE: +44 (0)1224 876407.
VISITORS: No restrictions. Societies contact Aberdeen Leisure +44 (0)1224 647647.
GREEN FEES: £9 per round weekdays (visitors £11.25; juniors £4.50). £11.25 per round weekends (visitors £14; juniors £5.75).
CATERING: Bar.
LOCATION: 2 miles east of city centre.
FACILITIES: Putting green.
LOCATION: Two miles south-east of Aberdeen.
LOCAL HOTELS: Aberdeen Patio Hotel, Caledonian Hotel, Raemoir House Hotel, Simpson's Hotel, Bar/Brasserie, Stakis Craigendarroch Hotel & Country Club, The White Horse Inn.

## CRAIBSTONE GOLF CENTRE

COURSE DESCRIPTION:
Parkland course, opened in 2000, attached to the Scottish Agricultural College. It offers some excellent, scenic golf overlooking Aberdeen. Although a new course, it has an established feel about it with the back nine flanked by woodland. Good greens.
18 holes, 5,613 yards, par 69 (SSS 69).

SIGNATURE HOLE:
ELEVENTH ('Gruesome Glen' 362 yards, par 4) Resembles a links hole. A narrow fairway with banks on both sides uphill to a long, narrow green. You can hit your tee shot anywhere but right on this hole.

ADDRESS: Craibstone Estate, Bucksburn, Aberdeen AB21 9YA
TELEPHONE: +44 (0)1224 716777.
FAX: +44 (0)1224 711298.
E-MAIL: golf@ab.sac.ac.uk
WEBSITE: www.craibstone.com
SECRETARY: G. Paterson.
VISITORS: Yes, seven days a week.
GREEN FEES: £16 per round weekdays, £22 weekends; £20 per round weekends, £26 per day.

CREDIT CARDS ACCEPTED: Visa/Mastercard.

CATERING: Restaurant and bar. Functions catered for. Everyone welcome.

FACILITIES: Trolley hire (£3), club hire (£10), changing-rooms, practice ground (£4).

LOCATION: Take the A96 to Inverness and Airport. Just before the Craibstone roundabout take the Forril Brae road (on the left if leaving Aberdeen, or on the right if approaching Aberdeen).

LOCAL HOTELS: Craibstone Halls of Residence, Speedbird Inn, Airport Thistle Hotel. Aberdeen Patio Hotel, Glen Lui Hotel, Raemoir House Hotel, Simpson's Hotel, Bar/Brasserie, Stakis Craigendarroch Hotel & Country Club, The White Horse Inn.

## DEESIDE GOLF CLUB

COURSE DESCRIPTION:

Picturesque riverside, tree-lined, parkland courses with a stream coming into play on nine of the holes on the main course.

18 holes, 5,971 yards, par 71 (SSS 69). Amateur record 64. Pro record 63.

Also reasonable nine-hole course.

ADDRESS: Golf Road, Bieldside, Aberdeen AB15 9DL.

TELEPHONE: +44 (0)1224 869457.

PROFESSIONAL: Frank Coutts +44 (0)1224 861041.

VISITORS: At certain times, contact in advance. Societies on Thursdays, noon to 3.30 p.m.

GREEN FEES: £35 per day weekdays. £45 weekends and holidays.

CATERING: Full service. Bar.

FACILITIES: Trolley/buggy hire, putting green, pro shop, practice ground.

LOCATION: 3 miles west of the city centre on A93. Off North Deeside Road, first left beyond Bieldside Inn on Aberdeen–Culter road.

LOCAL HOTELS: Aberdeen Patio Hotel, Airport Thistle Hotel, Glen Lui Hotel, Raemoir House Hotel, Simpson's Hotel, Bar/Brasserie, Speedbird Inn, Stakis Craigendarroch Hotel & Country Club, The White Horse Inn.

## HAZLEHEAD PUBLIC COURSES

COURSE DESCRIPTION:

*No. 1* – Fully mature wooded, parkland course. It offers a challenging round of golf, having been influenced by Dr Alister Mackenzie, the creator of Augusta National, home of the US Masters.

18 holes, 6,204 yards, par 70 (SSS 70).

*No. 2* – Parkland.

18 holes, 5,801 yards, par 67 (SSS 68).

*No. 3* – Parkland.

9 holes, 5,540 yards (for 18 holes), par 70 (SSS 68).

ADDRESS: Hazlehead Park, Groats Road, Aberdeen AB15 8BD.

TELEPHONE: +44 (0)1224 310711.

STARTER: +44 (0)1224 321830.
PROFESSIONAL: Alistair Smith.
VISITORS: Yes. No advance bookings.
GREEN FEES: £9 per round weekdays, £11.25 weekends.
CATERING: At adjacent club. Bar.
FACILITIES: Trolley/buggy hire, putting green, pro shop, practice ground.
LOCATION: Off Queens Road, Hazlehead Park, 4 miles north-west of the city centre.
LOCAL HOTELS: Aberdeen Patio Hotel, Airport Thistle Hotel, Belvedere Hotel, Caledonian Hotel, Glen Lui Hotel, Queens Hotel, Raemoir House Hotel, Simpson's Hotel, Bar/Brasserie, Speedbird Inn, Stakis Craigendarroch Hotel & Country Club, The White Horse Inn, Treetops Hotel.

## KING'S LINKS

COURSE DESCRIPTION:
Very windy municipal links course on Aberdeen sea front with no trees and plenty of bunkers and fast greens – hence some testing holes. Only minutes from the city centre, and next door to Aberdeen Football Club's ground at Pittodrie, this site has played host to golf since at least the sixteenth century. Playable all year. The Bon Accord Club, Caledonian Club and Northern Club play over this course.

18 holes, 6,270 yards, par 71 (SSS 71).

Also a six-hole course. Next door is the King's Links Golf Centre, which offers 58 floodlit driving bays, video monitoring equipment and teaching from PGA professionals.

SIGNATURE HOLE:
TENTH (183 yards, par 3) Tee shot to elevated green which can vary from anything from a 6-iron to a driver depending on the wind. Large bunker on left of the green

COURSE CARD

| HOLE | YDS | PAR | HOLE | YDS | PAR |
|------|------|-----|------|-------|-----|
| 1 | 358 | 4 | 10 | 183 | 3 |
| 2 | 364 | 4 | 11 | 374 | 4 |
| 3 | 171 | 3 | 12 | 280 | 4 |
| 4 | 482 | 5 | 13 | 404 | 4 |
| 5 | 393 | 4 | 14 | 425 | 4 |
| 6 | 409 | 4 | 15 | 495 | 5 |
| 7 | 502 | 5 | 16 | 177 | 3 |
| 8 | 293 | 4 | 17 | 402 | 4 |
| 9 | 364 | 4 | 18 | 194 | 3 |
| Yds Out | 3,336 | | Yds In | 2,934 | |
| Total Yds | 6,270 | | | | |
| Total Par | 71 | | | | |

ADDRESS: 22 Golf Road, Aberdeen AB2 1NR.

TELEPHONE: +44 (0)1224 632269

VISITORS: Contact Starter's Box +44 (0)1224 632269 to book tee times. Societies contact Aberdeen Leisure +44 (0)1224 647647.

GREEN FEES: £9 per round weekdays (visitors £11.25; juniors £4.50). £11.25 per round weekends (visitors £14; juniors £5.75).

CATERING: No

LOCATION: ¾ mile north-east of the city centre.

LOCAL HOTELS: Aberdeen Patio Hotel, Airport Thistle Hotel, Belvedere Hotel, Glen Lui Hotel, Queens Hotel, Raemoir House Hotel, Simpson's Hotel, Bar/Brasserie, Speedbird Inn, Stakis Craigendarroch Hotel & Country Club, The White Horse Inn, Treetops Hotel.

## MURCAR GOLF CLUB

### COURSE DESCRIPTION:

Traditional Scottish links course with undulating fairways, set amid towering sand dunes. There are many steep-sided gullies and sharp falls away from greens and tees. The front nine runs northwards, close to the shore, and although the inward nine moves away from the sea and is shorter, it provides several testing par 4s, two fine short holes and a short par 5 which needs careful positioning of the tee shot. Designed by Archie Simpson in 1909, Murcar is rated amongst the top 100 courses in the UK and has hosted many major championships. Each hole offers a different challenge. Elevated tees take advantage of the views to the North Sea and Aberdeen.

18 holes, 6,287 yards, par 71 (SSS 71). Course record 65.

*Strabathie Course* – 9 holes, 3,000 yards, par 35.

### SIGNATURE HOLE:

SIXTH (447 yards, par 4) Dogleg to the left. Most challenging, particularly if wind against. Difficult to judge the second shot to the green from an undulating fairway.

### COURSE CARD

| HOLE | MEDAL YDS | PAR | FORWARD YDS | PAR | LADIES YDS | PAR | HOLE | MEDAL YDS | PAR | FORWARD YDS | PAR | LADIES YDS | PAR |
|------|-----------|-----|-------------|-----|------------|-----|------|-----------|-----|-------------|-----|------------|-----|
| 1 | 322 | 4 | 300 | 4 | 296 | 4 | 10 | 402 | 4 | 385 | 4 | 382 | 4 |
| 2 | 367 | 4 | 340 | 4 | 340 | 4 | 11 | 338 | 4 | 312 | 4 | 294 | 4 |
| 3 | 401 | 4 | 380 | 4 | 348 | 4 | 12 | 155 | 3 | 144 | 3 | 142 | 3 |
| 4 | 489 | 5 | 423 | 5 | 423 | 5 | 13 | 386 | 4 | 365 | 4 | 351 | 4 |
| 5 | 162 | 3 | 152 | 3 | 142 | 3 | 14 | 482 | 5 | 442 | 5 | 412 | 5 |
| 6 | 447 | 4 | 421 | 4 | 417 | 5 | 15 | 351 | 4 | 332 | 4 | 295 | 4 |
| 7 | 423 | 4 | 411 | 4 | 356 | 4 | 16 | 160 | 3 | 139 | 3 | 129 | 3 |
| 8 | 383 | 4 | 362 | 4 | 348 | 4 | 17 | 367 | 4 | 307 | 4 | 293 | 4 |
| 9 | 323 | 4 | 280 | 4 | 264 | 4 | 18 | 329 | 4 | 314 | 4 | 297 | 4 |
| *Yds Out* | 3,317 | | 3,069 | | 2,934 | | *Yds In* | 2,970 | | 2,740 | | 2,600 | |

| | | | |
|---|---|---|---|
| *Total* Yds | 6,287 | 5,809 | 5,534 |
| *Total* Par | 71 | 69 | 72 |

ADDRESS: Bridge of Don, Aberdeen AB23 8BD.
TELEPHONE: +44 (0)1224 704354.
FAX: +44 (0)1224 704370.
SECRETARY: R. Matthews.
PROFESSIONAL: Gary Forbes +44 (0)1224 704370.
VISITORS: Mondays and Tuesdays after 12.30 p.m. Wednesdays before 12 noon. Thursdays, Fridays and Saturdays after 4 p.m. Sundays after 12 noon.
GREEN FEES: £30 per round weekdays, £40 per day. £35 per round weekends, £45 per day.
CATERING: Full catering and bar service.
FACILITIES: Trolley hire, changing-rooms, putting green, pro shop, practice ground.
LOCATION: Approximately 5 miles north-east of Aberdeen off A92 Peterhead–Fraserburgh road.
LOCAL HOTELS: Aberdeen Patio Hotel, Airport Thistle Hotel, Belvedere Hotel, Glen Lui Hotel, Queens Hotel, Raemoir House Hotel, Simpson's Hotel, Bar/Brasserie, Speedbird Inn, Stakis Craigendarroch Hotel & Country Club, The White Horse Inn, Treetops Hotel.

## ROYAL ABERDEEN GOLF CLUB

### COURSE DESCRIPTION:
Founded in 1780, this is the sixth oldest golf club in the world. The Balgownie Links is a challenging championship course set amongst hill, sand and sea. Not for the faint-hearted, it is a perfect example of the exacting nature of links courses. If you are a competent player, be prepared for a test of your ability. If not, bring a bag of balls. Many of the great names of golf – Morris, Hagen, Cotton, Lema, Jacklin and Norman to name a few – have played here.

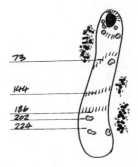

18 holes, 6,624 yards (championship tees), par 70 (SSS 73).

*Silverburn Course* – 18 holes, 4,066 yards, par 60 (SSS 60).

### SIGNATURE HOLE:
EIGHTEENTH (434 yards, par 4) One of the best finishing holes in Scottish golf. The tee is modestly elevated, displaying the hole and its dangers. Bunkers, long links grasses, thick gorse. Then, for a second shot, a long iron to a plateau green.

## COURSE CARD

| HOLE | MEDAL YDS | PAR | HOLE | YDS | PAR |
|------|-----------|-----|------|-----|-----|
| 1 | 409 | 4 | 10 | 342 | 4 |
| 2 | 530 | 5 | 11 | 175 | 3 |
| 3 | 223 | 3 | 12 | 404 | 4 |
| 4 | 436 | 4 | 13 | 375 | 4 |
| 5 | 326 | 4 | 14 | 390 | 4 |
| 6 | 486 | 5 | 15 | 341 | 4 |
| 7 | 375 | 4 | 16 | 389 | 4 |
| 8 | 147 | 3 | 17 | 180 | 3 |
| 9 | 453 | 4 | 18 | 434 | 4 |
| *Yds Out* | 3,385 | | *Yds In* | 3,030 | |
| *Total Yds* | 6,415 | | | | |
| *Total Par* | 70 | | | | |

ADDRESS: Balgownie Links, Links Road, Bridge of Don, Aberdeen AB23 8AT.
TELEPHONE: +44 (0)1224 702571.
FAX: +44 (0) 1224 826591.
E-MAIL: admin@royal-aberdeen.demon.co.uk
VISITORS: During the week.
GREEN FEES: £65 per round on weekdays, £90 per day. £75 per round weekends.
CATERING: Dining-room holds a maximum of 36. Lounge and bar.
CREDIT CARDS ACCEPTED: Visa/Mastercard.
FACILITIES: Trolley/buggy hire, clubhire, caddies on request, changing-rooms, putting green, pro shop, practice ground, membership available.
LOCATION: Northbound on the main road from Aberdeen (A92 to Fraserburgh). Turn right at traffic lights after crossing the Bridge of Don.
LOCAL HOTELS: Aberdeen Patio Hotel, Airport Thistle Hotel, Glen Lui Hotel, Marcliffe Hotel, Raemoir House Hotel, Simpson's Hotel, Bar/Brasserie, Speedbird Inn, Stakis Craigendarroch Hotel & Country Club, The White Horse Inn.

# WESTHILL GOLF CLUB

COURSE DESCRIPTION:
Inland course with a mix of undulating heathland and parkland holes, but easy walking. Greens usually fast.
    18 holes, 5,921 yards, par 69 (SSS 69). Course record 65.

ADDRESS: Westhill Heights, Skene, Aberdeen AB32 6RY.
TELEPHONE: +44 (0)1224 742567.
PROFESSIONAL: George Bruce +44 (0)1224 740159.
VISITORS: Contact in advance.

GREEN FEES: £12 per round weekdays, £16 per day. £16/£22 weekends.
CATERING: Full service. Bar.
FACILITIES: Trolley/buggy hire, putting green, pro shop, practice ground.
LOCATION: 6 miles north-west of city centre off A944.
LOCAL HOTELS: Aberdeen Patio Hotel, Airport Thistle Hotel, Glen Lui Hotel, Raemoir House Hotel, Simpson's Hotel, Bar/Brasserie, Speedbird Inn, Stakis Craigendarroch Hotel & Country Club, The White Horse Inn, Westhill Inn.

# ABOYNE

## ABOYNE GOLF CLUB

COURSE DESCRIPTION:
First nine is well-maintained parkland with the back nine over hilly, almost heathland. Two lochs with beautiful views. Finishes with two par 3s. Founded 1883.
18 holes, 5,975 yards, par 69 (SSS 68). Course record 62.

ADDRESS: Formaston Park, Aboyne AB34 5HP.
TELEPHONE: +44 (0)1339 886328.
SECRETARY: +44 (0)1339 887078.
VISITORS: Any time. Contact in advance.
GREEN FEES: £19 per round weekdays, £25 per day. £23 per round weekends, £30 per day.
CATERING: Full service. Bar.
FACILITIES: Trolley hire, putting green, pro shop, practice ground.
LOCATION: East of village, north of A93.
LOCAL HOTELS: Birse Lodge, Callater Lodge, Glen Lui Hotel, Huntly Arms, Raemoir House Hotel, Stakis Craigendarroch Hotel & Country Club.

# ALFORD

## ALFORD GOLF CLUB

COURSE DESCRIPTION:
Flat inland, parkland course, surrounded by the hills of Donside and divided by a road, railway and a burn. Challenging without being physically demanding. Lush fairways with areas of mature and semi-mature trees.
18 holes, 5,290 yards, par 69 (SSS 66). Course record 64.

## COURSE CARD

| HOLE | YDS | PAR | HOLE | YDS | PAR |
|------|-----|-----|------|-----|-----|
| 1 | 275 | 4 | 10 | 271 | 4 |
| 2 | 371 | 4 | 11 | 273 | 4 |
| 3 | 165 | 3 | 12 | 190 | 3 |
| 4 | 328 | 4 | 13 | 503 | 5 |
| 5 | 372 | 4 | 14 | 320 | 4 |
| 6 | 132 | 3 | 15 | 299 | 4 |
| 7 | 280 | 4 | 16 | 150 | 3 |
| 8 | 293 | 4 | 17 | 291 | 4 |
| 9 | 394 | 4 | 18 | 383 | 4 |
| *Yds* *Out* | 2,610 | | *Yds* *In* | 2,680 | |
| *Total Yds* | 5,290 | | | | |
| *Total Par* | 69 | | | | |

ADDRESS: Montgarrie Road, Alford, Aberdeenshire AB33 8AE.

TELEPHONE & FAX: +44 (0)1975 562178.

VISITORS: Contact in advance.

GREEN FEES: £13 per round weekdays, £19 per day. £21 per round weekends, £27 per day.

CATERING: Full meals and snacks. Bar.

FACILITIES: Trolley hire, pro shop, practice ground.

LOCATION: 25 miles west of Aberdeen on A944.

LOCAL HOTELS: Aberdeen Patio Hotel, Airport Thistle Hotel, Forbes Arms Hotel, Glen Lui Hotel, Kildrummy Castle, Raemoir House Hotel, Simpson's Hotel, Bar/Brasserie, Speedbird Inn, Stakis Craigendarroch Hotel & Country Club, The White Horse Inn.

# AUCHENBLAE

## AUCHENBLAE GOLF COURSE

COURSE DESCRIPTION:

Undulating parkland course. Picturesque views.

9 holes, 4,348 yards (for 18 holes), par 64 (SSS 60). Course record 60.

ADDRESS: Auchenblae, Laurencekirk, Aberdeenshire AB30 1TP.

TELEPHONE: +44 (0)1561 320002.

MANAGER: Mrs Jenny Thomson.

VISITORS: Any time other than Wednesday and Friday evenings during summer.

GREEN FEES: £10 per round/day weekdays, £12 per round/day weekends.

CATERING: Small shop selling refreshments.

FACILITIES: Trolley hire, changing area, waiting list for membership.

LOCATION: Inland from A90. From south: after Laurencekirk by-pass, turn left at sign for Auchenblae. From north: after Drumlithie turn-off, turn right at sign for Auchenblae.

LOCAL HOTELS: Aberdeen Patio Hotel, Airport Thistle Hotel, Drumtochty Hotel, Glen Lui Hotel, Raemoir House Hotel, Simpson's Hotel, Bar/Brasserie, Speedbird Inn, Stakis Craigendarroch Hotel & Country Club, The White Horse Inn, Thistle Hotel.

# BALLATER

## BALLATER GOLF CLUB

### COURSE DESCRIPTION:

Ballater was founded in 1892 and the course was expanded from nine to eighteen holes in 1905. From the clubhouse the course looks quite flat, but you soon discover plenty of rolling hills and humps. This medium-length course is situated in one of the most beautiful parts of upper Deeside. Several holes lie close to the River Dee. Ballater and the course lie within a circle of hills which protect it from bad weather.

18 holes, 6,112 yards, par 70 (SSS 69).

### SIGNATURE HOLE:

FIFTH (186 yards, par 3) Arguably the best hole on the course. It demands the perfect tee shot with a very tight approach to a semi-plateau green. Miss the raised green, which has a large bunker on the front-right and a drop of five feet on the left, and you could be in a lot of trouble.

### COURSE CARD

| HOLE | MEDAL YDS | PAR | FORWARD YDS | PAR | LADIES YDS | PAR | HOLE | MEDAL YDS | PAR | FORWARD YDS | PAR | LADIES YDS | PAR |
|------|-----------|-----|-------------|-----|------------|-----|------|-----------|-----|-------------|-----|------------|-----|
| 1 | 464 | 5 | 394 | 4 | 384 | 4 | 10 | 392 | 4 | 375 | 4 | 373 | 4 |
| 2 | 422 | 4 | 413 | 4 | 400 | 5 | 11 | 477 | 5 | 420 | 4 | 417 | 5 |
| 3 | 223 | 3 | 180 | 3 | 183 | 3 | 12 | 403 | 4 | 365 | 4 | 363 | 4 |
| 4 | 419 | 4 | 409 | 4 | 390 | 5 | 13 | 161 | 3 | 157 | 3 | 155 | 3 |
| 5 | 186 | 3 | 177 | 3 | 121 | 3 | 14 | 319 | 4 | 310 | 4 | 269 | 4 |
| 6 | 368 | 4 | 338 | 4 | 277 | 4 | 15 | 368 | 4 | 337 | 4 | 330 | 4 |
| 7 | 509 | 5 | 457 | 5 | 457 | 5 | 16 | 346 | 4 | 318 | 4 | 314 | 4 |
| 8 | 333 | 4 | 324 | 4 | 291 | 4 | 17 | 167 | 3 | 153 | 3 | 153 | 3 |
| 9 | 220 | 3 | 208 | 3 | 193 | 3 | 18 | 335 | 4 | 303 | 4 | 237 | 4 |
| *Yds* Out | 3,144 | | 2,900 | | 2,696 | | *Yds* In | 2,968 | | 2,738 | | 2,611 | |
| *Total Yds* | 6,112 | | 5,638 | | 5,307 | | | | | | | | |
| *Total Par* | 70 | | 67 | | 71 | | | | | | | | |

ADDRESS: Victoria Road, Ballater, Aberdeenshire AB35 5QX.
TELEPHONE: +44 (0)1339 755567.
FAX: +44 (0)1339 755057.
E-MAIL: sec@ballatergolfclub.co.uk
WEBSITE: www.ballatergolfclub.co.uk
SECRETARY: Sandy Barclay.
PROFESSIONAL: Bill Yule +44 (0)1339 755658.
VISITORS: No restrictions except during medal competitions.
GREEN FEES: £19 per round weekdays, £28 per day. £22 per round weekends, £32 per day. Weekly ticket, £90.
CREDIT CARDS ACCEPTED: Visa/Mastercard.
CATERING: Restaurant and bar. Functions catered for.
FACILITIES: Motorised buggies, trolley hire, club hire, caddies possible, changing-rooms, putting green, pro shop, practice ground, coaching clinics, country memberships available.
LOCATION: On A93, 42 miles west of Aberdeen.
LOCAL HOTELS: Callater Lodge, Glen Lui Hotel, Raemoir House Hotel, Simpson's Hotel, Bar/Brasserie, Stakis Craigendarroch Hotel & Country Club.

# BALMEDIE

## EAST ABERDEENSHIRE GOLF CENTRE LTD

COURSE DESCRIPTION:
Testing parkland course over 130 acres of former Buchan farmland. It was opened in the Spring of 1999 and designed as two loops of nine holes, each starting and finishing outside the clubhouse. Its par-3 holes have in a short time gained a reputation as being as good as any in the north of Scotland. The large, contoured, well-bunkered greens have been designed to USPGA specifications and are playable on the wettest of days. In all, there are 71 bunkers on the course. On the top holes the panoramic views – stretching from Peterhead in the north, to south of Aberdeen Bay – have to be seen to be appreciated. The driving range with nine manufactured greens is designed to give you the feeling that you are playing on a golf course. Also a six-hole course for beginners.

18 holes, 6,276 yards, par 71 (SSS 71). Course record 72.

SIGNATURE HOLE:
SEVENTEENTH (208 yards, par 3) Named 'Cresser's Best' after the course's designer Ian Creswell, it is challenging, with strategically placed bunkers left and right of the green, which is on a higher level than the tee. It demands a full carry over a ditch and a drystone dyke. A par at this hole can feel like a birdie.

COURSE CARD

| HOLE | MEDAL YDS | PAR | FORWARD YDS | PAR | LADIES YDS | PAR | HOLE | MEDAL YDS | PAR | FORWARD YDS | PAR | LADIES YDS | PAR |
|---|---|---|---|---|---|---|---|---|---|---|---|---|---|
| 1 | 274 | 4 | 258 | 4 | 221 | 4 | 10 | 411 | 4 | 399 | 4 | 282 | 4 |
| 2 | 451 | 5 | 426 | 4 | 381 | 4 | 11 | 382 | 4 | 356 | 4 | 253 | 4 |
| 3 | 183 | 3 | 165 | 3 | 160 | 3 | 12 | 350 | 4 | 322 | 4 | 311 | 4 |
| 4 | 384 | 4 | 359 | 4 | 328 | 4 | 13 | 339 | 4 | 321 | 4 | 306 | 4 |
| 5 | 218 | 3 | 199 | 3 | 134 | 3 | 14 | 170 | 3 | 138 | 3 | 109 | 3 |
| 6 | 485 | 5 | 450 | 4 | 438 | 5 | 15 | 515 | 5 | 503 | 5 | 435 | 5 |
| 7 | 334 | 4 | 281 | 4 | 231 | 4 | 16 | 390 | 4 | 363 | 4 | 334 | 4 |
| 8 | 384 | 4 | 364 | 4 | 337 | 4 | 17 | 208 | 3 | 177 | 3 | 136 | 3 |
| 9 | 418 | 4 | 393 | 4 | 323 | 4 | 18 | 380 | 4 | 349 | 4 | 326 | 4 |
| *Yds Out* | 3,131 | | 2,895 | | 2,553 | | *Yds In* | 3,145 | | 2,928 | | 2,492 | |
| *Total Yds* | 6,276 | | 5,823 | | 5,045 | | | | | | | | |
| *Total Par* | 71 | | 69 | | 70 | | | | | | | | |

ADDRESS: Millden, Balmedie, Aberdeenshire AB23 8YY.

TELEPHONE: +44 (0)1358 742111.

FAX: +44 (0)1358 742123.

E-MAIL: info@eagolf.com

WEBSITE: www.eagolf.com

MANAGER: Kevin Forrest.

PROFESSIONAL: Ian Bratton.

VISITORS: Yes, at all times.

GREEN FEES: £15 per round weekdays, £25 per day (includes buggy for one round). £20 per round weekends, £30 per day. Lunchtime special (Mondays to Fridays, 12 noon to 2 p.m.) £4.50 for a bucket of balls, soup and sandwiches.

CREDIT CARDS ACCEPTED: Visa/Mastercard.

CATERING: Restaurant and public bar. Functions catered for. Also hosts various entertainments.

FACILITIES: Motorised buggies (£15), trolley hire (£2), club hire (£7.50), caddies (£15 + tip), changing-rooms, putting green, practice ground, pro shop, driving range (£2.50), coaching clinics, memberships available.

LOCATION: From Aberdeen, head north on the A92 for 5 miles. Take a left from the dual carriageway at the sign for Millden and you will find the clubhouse at the top of the hill.

LOCAL HOTELS: Aberdeen Patio Hotel, Airport Thistle Hotel, Glen Lui Hotel, Raemoir House Hotel, Simpson's Hotel, Bar/Brasserie, Speedbird Inn, Stakis Craigendarroch Hotel & Country Club, The White Horse Inn.

# BANCHORY

## BANCHORY GOLF CLUB

### COURSE DESCRIPTION:
Founded in 1905, but this parkland course has been recently extensively remodelled by John Souter. Set above the bonnie banks of the River Dee. Short, easy walking, but strategically placed bunkers, mature native trees and the river provide obstacles that can test all standards of player.

18 holes, 5,781 yards, par 69 (SSS 68). Amateur record Angus Cowie 65. Pro record Craig Roland 67.

### SIGNATURE HOLE:
SIXTEENTH ('Doo'cot' 88 yards, par 3) A short iron to an elevated green set above the ancient river bank with the distinctive dovecote a main feature.

### COURSE CARD

| | MEDAL | | FORWARD | | LADIES | | | MEDAL | | FORWARD | | LADIES | |
|---|---|---|---|---|---|---|---|---|---|---|---|---|---|
| HOLE | YDS | PAR | YDS | PAR | YDS | PAR | HOLE | YDS | PAR | YDS | PAR | YDS | PAR |
| 1 | 315 | 4 | 315 | 4 | 312 | 4 | 10 | 514 | 5 | 501 | 5 | 433 | 5 |
| 2 | 224 | 4 | 220 | 3 | 220 | 4 | 11 | 353 | 4 | 342 | 4 | 349 | 4 |
| 3 | 125 | 3 | 125 | 3 | 121 | 3 | 12 | 183 | 3 | 173 | 3 | 158 | 3 |
| 4 | 444 | 4 | 430 | 4 | 439 | 5 | 13 | 420 | 4 | 376 | 4 | 365 | 4 |
| 5 | 354 | 4 | 289 | 4 | 286 | 4 | 14 | 302 | 4 | 292 | 4 | 286 | 4 |
| 6 | 485 | 5 | 465 | 5 | 452 | 5 | 15 | 521 | 5 | 491 | 5 | 458 | 5 |
| 7 | 188 | 3 | 170 | 3 | 170 | 3 | 16 | 88 | 3 | 80 | 3 | 85 | 3 |
| 8 | 326 | 4 | 312 | 4 | 255 | 4 | 17 | 430 | 4 | 412 | 4 | 351 | 4 |
| 9 | 155 | 3 | 134 | 3 | 120 | 3 | 18 | 354 | 4 | 354 | 4 | 340 | 4 |
| *Yds* Out | 2,616 | | 2,460 | | 2,375 | | *Yds* In | 3,165 | | 3,021 | | 2,825 | |
| *Total* *Yds* | 5,781 | | 5,481 | | 5,200 | | | | | | | | |
| *Total* *Par* | 69 | | 68 | | 71 | | | | | | | | |

ADDRESS: Kinneskie Road, Banchory, Kincardineshire AB31 5TA.
TELEPHONE: +44 (0)1330 822365.
FAX: +44 (0)1330 822491.
WEBSITE: www.banchorygolfclub.co.uk
SECRETARY: W.Crighton.
PROFESSIONAL: D. Naylor.
VISITORS: Yes, 7 days, but restricted on Tuesdays and weekends.
GREEN FEES: £18 per round weekdays, £25 per day. £21 per round weekends. Weekly ticket £75.
CREDIT CARDS ACCEPTED: Visa.

CATERING: Restaurant and bar. Functions catered for.

FACILITIES: Motorised buggies, trolley hire, club hire, caddies, changing-rooms, putting green, pro shop, practice ground, coaching clinics can be arranged, waiting list for membership.

LOCATION: 18 miles south-west of Aberdeen on the A93 road to Royal Deeside.

LOCAL HOTELS: Aberdeen Patio Hotel, Banchory Lodge, Burnett Arms, Glen Lui Hotel, Raemoir House Hotel, Simpson's Hotel, Speedbird Inn, Stakis Craigendarroch Hotel & Country Club, The Stag Hotel, The White Horse Inn.

## INCHMARLO GOLF CLUB

COURSE DESCRIPTION:

Quality parkland course set amidst dramatic scenery.

9 holes, 4,300 yards (for 18 holes), par 66 (SSS 64).

ADDRESS: Inchmarlo, Banchory, Aberdeenshire, AB31 4BQ.

TELEPHONE: +44 (0)1330 822557.

VISITORS: Always welcome. Parties and outings by prior arrangement.

GREEN FEES: On application.

CATERING: Restaurant and bar.

FACILITIES: Putting green, pro shop, 30-bay floodlit driving range.

LOCATION: Half a mile west side of Banchory on the A93.

LOCAL HOTELS: Aberdeen Patio Hotel, Glen Lui Hotel, Raemoir House Hotel, Simpson's Hotel, Stakis Craigendarroch Hotel & Country Club, The White Horse Inn.

## LUMPHANAN GOLF CLUB

COURSE DESCRIPTION:

Testing hilly heathland course with narrow fairways and small greens.

9 holes, 3,176 yards (for 18 holes), par 56 (SSS 59).

ADDRESS: Main Road, Lumphanan, Banchory, Aberdeenshire, AB31 4PW.

TELEPHONE: +44 (0)1339 883480.

VISITORS: Course unmanned, so you have to leave your green fee in the honesty box.

GREEN FEES: £10 per round weekdays and weekends.

CATERING: Bar.

FACILITIES: Changing-rooms, putting green.

# BANFF

## DUFF HOUSE ROYAL GOLF CLUB

COURSE DESCRIPTION:
Flat parkland course. Large two-tier greens. Lush tree-lined fairways. Bunkers well positioned on fairways and around greens. Founded 1909.
    18 holes, 6,161 yards, par 68 (SSS 69).

SIGNATURE HOLE:
NINTH (172 yards, par 3) Too long and pulled and you're in the river. Too short and you're bunkered.

COURSE CARD

| HOLE | YDS | PAR | HOLE | YDS | PAR |
|------|-----|-----|------|-----|-----|
| 1 | 314 | 4 | 10 | 403 | 4 |
| 2 | 366 | 4 | 11 | 214 | 3 |
| 3 | 392 | 4 | 12 | 498 | 5 |
| 4 | 367 | 4 | 13 | 175 | 3 |
| 5 | 330 | 4 | 14 | 434 | 4 |
| 6 | 139 | 3 | 15 | 468 | 4 |
| 7 | 460 | 4 | 16 | 242 | 3 |
| 8 | 381 | 4 | 17 | 462 | 4 |
| 9 | 172 | 3 | 18 | 344 | 4 |
| *Yds* | 2,921 | | *Yds* | 3,240 | |
| *Out* | | | *In* | | |
| *Total* | 6,161 | | | | |
| *Yds* | | | | | |
| *Total* | 68 | | | | |
| *Par* | | | | | |

ADDRESS: The Barnyards, Banff AB45 3SX.
TELEPHONE: +44 (0)1261 812062.
FAX: +44 (0) 1261 812224.
E-MAIL: Duff-House-Royal@btinternet.com
PROFESSIONAL: Bob Strachan +44 (0)1261 812075.
VISITORS: Welcome. Restricted during competitions.
GREEN FEES: £18 per round weekdays, £24 per day. £25 per round weekends, £30 per day.
CATERING: Full catering available during season. Bar.
CREDIT CARDS ACCEPTED: Visa/Mastercard.
FACILITIES: Motorised buggies (£10), trolleys (£1.50), putting green, pro shop, practice ground, driving nets.
LOCATION: On Moray Firth coast, in centre of Banff. On A96 Aberdeen–Inverness road.

LOCAL HOTELS: Banff Springs Hotel, County Hotel, Fife Lodge Hotel, The Old Coach House Hotel.

# BRAEMAR

## BRAEMAR GOLF CLUB

### COURSE DESCRIPTION:
Parkland course situated in the bottom of Glen Clunie with the River Clunie running through the centre. Highest 18-hole course in Scotland, but easy walking. Founded in 1902.

18 holes, 4,935 yards, par 65 (SSS 64). Amateur record 61. Pro record 64.

### SIGNATURE HOLE:
SECOND (369 yards, par 4) Because the green is 40 feet above the fairway, it plays a lot longer. The River Clunie cuts in and out the whole length of the right side of the fairway and the rough does the same on the left. A ditch runs across the fairway at about 250 yards.

### COURSE CARD

| HOLE | YDS | PAR | HOLE | YDS | PAR |
|------|------|-----|------|------|-----|
| 1 | 375 | 4 | 10 | 409 | 4 |
| 2 | 369 | 4 | 11 | 277 | 4 |
| 3 | 185 | 3 | 12 | 334 | 4 |
| 4 | 403 | 4 | 13 | 173 | 3 |
| 5 | 231 | 3 | 14 | 310 | 4 |
| 6 | 103 | 3 | 15 | 421 | 4 |
| 7 | 207 | 3 | 16 | 261 | 4 |
| 8 | 253 | 4 | 17 | 245 | 4 |
| 9 | 257 | 4 | 18 | 122 | 3 |
| Yds Out | 2,383 | | Yds In | 2,552 | |
| Total | 4,935 | | | | |
| Yds Total Par | 65 | | | | |

ADDRESS: Cluniebank Road, Braemar, Aberdeenshire AB35 5XX.
TELEPHONE: +44 (0)1339 741618.
SECRETARY: John Pennet +44 (0)1224 704471.
VISITORS: Any time by phoning club day before play. Societies by phoning secretary.
GREEN FEES: £14 per round weekdays, £20 per day. £17 per round weekends, £25 per day.

CATERING: Full catering available. Bar.
FACILITIES: Trolley hire, pro shop.
LOCATION: ½ mile from village centre.
LOCAL HOTELS: Callater Lodge, Glen Lui Hotel, Invercauld Arms Hotel, Fife Arms, Moorfield House Hotel, Raemoir House Hotel, Simpson's Hotel Bar/Brasserie, Stakis Craigendarroch Hotel & Country Club.

# BUCKIE

## BUCKPOOL GOLF CLUB

COURSE DESCRIPTION:
Seaside links course overlooking Moray Firth. Whin and broom line the fairways. Can be windy, but easy walking.
 18 holes, 6,257 yards, par 70 (SSS 70). Course record 64.

ADDRESS: Barrhill Road, Buckpool AB56 1DU.
TELEPHONE & FAX: +44 (0)1542 832236.
VISITORS: Apply in advance.
GREEN FEES: £12 per round weekdays, £15 per day. £15 per round weekends, £20 per day.
CATERING: Yes. Bar.
FACILITIES: Trolley hire, putting green, practice area.
LOCATION: Off A98.
LOCAL HOTELS: Buckie Hotel, Marine Hotel, Sunninghill Hotel, The Old Coach House Hotel.

## STRATHLENE GOLF CLUB

COURSE DESCRIPTION:
Undulating seaside links course, founded 1877. Good views over Moray Firth. Windy with raised greens, which can cause problems.
 18 holes, 5,980 yards, par 69 (SSS 69). Course record 65.

ADDRESS: Strathlene Road, Buckie AB56 1DJ.
TELEPHONE: +44(0)1542 831798.
VISITORS: Book at weekends. Societies telephone for Mondays to Fridays and write for weekends.
GREEN FEES: £13 per round weekdays, £20 per day. £20 per round weekends, £25 per day.
CATERING: Yes. Bar.
FACILITIES: Trolley hire, putting green, pro shop, practice area.
LOCATION: 3 miles east on A942.
LOCAL HOTELS: Buckie Hotel, Marine Hotel, Sunninghill Hotel, The Old Coach House Hotel.

# CRUDEN BAY

## CRUDEN BAY GOLF CLUB

### COURSE DESCRIPTION:

When you gaze out from Cruden Bay's splendid clubhouse you are faced with a magnificent panorama of what is one of the finest examples of a traditional Scottish links course. There before you lies a never-to-be-forgotten test of golf with a rich variety of demanding holes wending their way between towering dunes and knee-high rough. If that is not enough to give you a nightmare then the brooding presence of the ruins of Slains Castle might. They dominate the first three holes and reportedly were the inspiration for Bram Stoker's *Dracula* novel.

At 6,395 yards – short for a championship course nowadays – this par 70 makes every shot count, especially when the wind gets up. The first two holes are steady par 4s. Then the fun starts. 'Claypits', the 3rd at 286 yards, encourages you to drive the green, but you have to pick the right line over a distant mound. Get it right and everything runs down to the green in a hollow. If you don't get a birdie here, you feel cheated. 'Bluidy Burn', a 529-yard par 5, can take even the biggest hitters three full-blooded shots – with the burn waiting for those who don't get it quite right.

The 7th, 'Whaupshank', is an intriguing dogleg uphill, the 8th a short par 4 at only 258 yards to a treacherous green. Then the course seems to step out of character with a sapping climb to what is really a parkland hole. But the climb is worth it. From the tenth tee on the edge of a cliff the view is magnificent and on a clear day you feel that you can drive forever. But beware, the burn awaits that rush of adrenaline. Then comes a variety of holes to please the most demanding golfer: a short tricky par 3; a driveable par 4 with the wind behind; a 550-yard par 5, and then a narrow par 4 with the sea on the right and thick rough on the left and the green in a hole in the ground.

The aptly named 15th, the 'Blin' Dunt', is a par 3 with your tee shot needing to be drawn through a canyon between a hill and the dunes 239 yards to the green at the base of the dunes. There's a great sense of relief when you emerge from the canyon to find your ball.

Cruden Bay also boasts some of the best practice facilities around with a putting green, large pitching green, practice ground, driving nets and a ten-bay driving range – plus the nine-hole St Olaf course. The 1999 Open Champion, Paul Lawrie, has been known to practise here.

18 holes, 6,395 yards, par 70 (SSS 72) Amateur record 67. Pro record 65.

*St Olaf Course* – 9 holes, 5,106 yards (for 18 holes), par 64 (SSS 65).

### SIGNATURE HOLE:

FOURTH (193 yards, par 3) One of the most challenging as well as one of the most picturesque. Water and out of bounds on left. The mounds on the right can cause you to underestimate the strength of the wind and blow off course your long shot to a plateau green.

COURSE CARD

| HOLE | MEDAL YDS | PAR | FORWARD YDS | PAR | LADIES YDS | PAR | HOLE | MEDAL YDS | PAR | FORWARD YDS | PAR | LADIES YDS | PAR |
|------|-----------|-----|-------------|-----|------------|-----|------|-----------|-----|-------------|-----|------------|-----|
| 1 | 416 | 4 | 386 | 4 | 386 | 4 | 10 | 385 | 4 | 366 | 4 | 339 | 4 |
| 2 | 339 | 4 | 319 | 4 | 313 | 4 | 11 | 149 | 3 | 139 | 3 | 138 | 3 |
| 3 | 286 | 4 | 270 | 4 | 266 | 4 | 12 | 320 | 4 | 305 | 4 | 288 | 4 |
| 4 | 193 | 3 | 183 | 3 | 141 | 3 | 13 | 550 | 5 | 540 | 5 | 491 | 5 |
| 5 | 454 | 4 | 444 | 4 | 424 | 5 | 14 | 397 | 4 | 362 | 4 | 358 | 4 |
| 6 | 529 | 5 | 507 | 5 | 507 | 5 | 15 | 239 | 4 | 225 | 3 | 210 | 3 |
| 7 | 392 | 4 | 355 | 4 | 349 | 4 | 16 | 182 | 3 | 175 | 3 | 170 | 3 |
| 8 | 258 | 4 | 225 | 4 | 220 | 4 | 17 | 428 | 4 | 396 | 4 | 386 | 5 |
| 9 | 462 | 4 | 430 | 4 | 393 | 5 | 18 | 416 | 4 | 395 | 4 | 382 | 4 |
| Yds Out | 3,329 | | 3,119 | | 2,999 | | Yds In | 3,066 | | 2,903 | | 2,762 | |
| Total Yds | 6,395 | | 6,022 | | 5,761 | | | | | | | | |
| Total Par | 70 | | 70 | | 73 | | | | | | | | |

ADDRESS: Aulton Road, Cruden Bay, Peterhead AB42 0NN.
TELEPHONE: +44(0)1779 812285.
FAX: +44 (0)1779 812945.
E-MAIL: cbaygc@aol.com
WEBSITE: www.crudenbaygolfclub.co.uk
SECRETARY: Mrs Rosemary Pittendrigh.
PROFESSIONAL: Robbie Stewart +44(0)1779 812414.
VISITORS: Welcome. Parties on weekdays only.
GREEN FEES: £50 per round weekdays; £70 per day. £60 per round weekends. St Olaf: £15 weekdays, £25 weekends.
CATERING: Full bar and catering facilities in a modern well-appointed clubhouse with panoramic views over the course.
FACILITIES: Trolley hire, pro shop, and splendid practice facilities with putting green, large pitching green, practice ground, driving nets, driving range.
LOCATION: 7 miles south of Peterhead, 23 miles north-east of Aberdeen, just off A92.
LOCAL HOTELS: Raemoir House Hotel, Simpson's Hotel, Bar/Brasserie, The Udny Arms Hotel, The White Horse Inn.

# CULLEN

## CULLEN GOLF CLUB

COURSE DESCRIPTION:
Traditional seaside links course with elevated section. Natural rock landscaping – stacks of red sandstone – comes into play at several holes. Beach (out of bounds) on several holes. On elevated section of the course there are panoramic views of

the coastline, Cullen Bay and rural hinterland. Several tricky par 3s. Founded 1879.

18 holes, 4,610 yards, par 63 (SSS 62). Amateur record B. Main (1979) 58.

## SIGNATURE HOLE:

SEVENTH (231 yards, par 3) Elevated tee to green some 80–100 feet below. Subject to wind and weather, this hole can play havoc with your score. Club selection can vary from driver to a mid-iron.

## COURSE CARD

| HOLE | YDS | PAR | HOLE | YDS | PAR |
|------|-----|-----|------|-----|-----|
| 1 | 344 | 4 | 10 | 309 | 4 |
| 2 | 130 | 3 | 11 | 245 | 3 |
| 3 | 236 | 3 | 12 | 182 | 3 |
| 4 | 129 | 3 | 13 | 149 | 3 |
| 5 | 360 | 4 | 14 | 207 | 3 |
| 6 | 172 | 3 | 15 | 510 | 5 |
| 7 | 231 | 3 | 16 | 348 | 4 |
| 8 | 275 | 4 | 17 | 262 | 4 |
| 9 | 194 | 3 | 18 | 327 | 4 |
| *Yds Out* | 2,071 | | *Yds In* | 2,539 | |
| *Total Yds* | 4,610 | | | | |
| *Total Par* | 63 | | | | |

ADDRESS: The Links, Cullen, Buckie, Banffshire AB56 2UU.
TELEPHONE: +44 (0)1542 840685.
SECRETARY: Ian Findlay +44 (0)1542 840174.
VISITORS: Welcome. May be restrictions on Wednesdays due to club competitions.
GREEN FEES: £12 per round weekdays, £16 per day. £16 per round weekends, £20 per day.
CATERING: Full catering April to October. Other months by arrangement with caterer.
FACILITIES: Putting green, practice ground.
LOCATION: On west boundary of burgh off A98 midway between Aberdeen and Inverness on Moray Firth coast.
LOCAL HOTELS: Bayview Hotel, Cullen Bay Hotel, Grant Arms, Royal Oak Hotel, Seafield Arms Hotel, Sunninghill Hotel, The Old Coach House Hotel, Three Kings Hotel, Waverley Hotel.

# DUFFTOWN

## DUFFTOWN GOLF CLUB

### COURSE DESCRIPTION:
A scenic parkland course with superb views of surrounding countryside. Has small hills in parts, and the highest section of the course is 1,000 feet above sea level. From the 10th there is a marvellous view of Glen Rinnes.

18 holes, 5,308 yards, par 67 (SSS 67). Amateur record 65.

### SIGNATURE HOLE:
TENTH ('Glenfiddich' 462 yards, par 4) Very impressive view from its high plateau tee with a 339-feet drop to the green. A daunting drive to start the inward nine.

### COURSE CARD

| HOLE | MEDAL YDS | PAR | FORWARD YDS | PAR | LADIES YDS | PAR | HOLE | MEDAL YDS | PAR | FORWARD YDS | PAR | LADIES YDS | PAR |
|------|------|-----|------|-----|------|-----|------|------|-----|------|-----|------|-----|
| 1 | 288 | 4 | 244 | 4 | 288 | 4 | 10 | 462 | 4 | 340 | 4 | 462 | 5 |
| 2 | 285 | 4 | 159 | 3 | 285 | 4 | 11 | 290 | 4 | 247 | 3 | 247 | 4 |
| 3 | 333 | 4 | 333 | 4 | 333 | 4 | 12 | 222 | 3 | 222 | 3 | 222 | 4 |
| 4 | 367 | 4 | 367 | 4 | 367 | 4 | 13 | 359 | 4 | 319 | 4 | 319 | 4 |
| 5 | 143 | 3 | 143 | 3 | 143 | 3 | 14 | 397 | 4 | 342 | 4 | 342 | 4 |
| 6 | 345 | 4 | 293 | 4 | 293 | 4 | 15 | 200 | 3 | 200 | 3 | 200 | 3 |
| 7 | 103 | 3 | 67 | 3 | 103 | 3 | 16 | 325 | 4 | 325 | 4 | 325 | 4 |
| 8 | 276 | 4 | 276 | 4 | 276 | 4 | 17 | 411 | 4 | 411 | 4 | 411 | 5 |
| 9 | 305 | 4 | 305 | 4 | 305 | 4 | 18 | 197 | 3 | 197 | 3 | 197 | 3 |
| Yds Out | 2,445 | | 2,187 | | 2,393 | | Yds In | 2,863 | | 2,603 | | 2,725 | |
| Total Yds | 5,308 | | 4,790 | | 5,118 | | | | | | | | |
| Total Par | 67 | | 64 | | 70 | | | | | | | | |

ADDRESS: Tomintoul Road, Dufftown, Keith, Moray AB55 4BS.
TELEPHONE & FAX: +44 (0)1340 820325.
E-MAIL: marion_dufftowngolfclub@yahoo.com
WEBSITE: www.speyside.moray.org/dufftown/golfclub
ADMINISTRATOR: Marion Swann.
VISITORS: Yes, seven days a week.
GREEN FEES: £12 per round weekdays/weekends, £15 per day. Weekly tickets £40.
CATERING: Restaurant and bar. Functions catered for. All by prior reservation.
FACILITIES: Trolley hire (£1.50), club hire (£5), changing-rooms, putting green.
LOCATION: 1 mile south of Dufftown on Tomintoul road (B9009).
LOCAL HOTELS: Callater Lodge, The Old Coach House Hotel.

# DUNECHT

## DUNECHT HOUSE GOLF CLUB

COURSE DESCRIPTION:
Inland wooded parkland course, founded in 1925.
   9 holes, 6,270 yards (for 18 holes), par 70 (SSS 70).

ADDRESS: Dunecht House, Skene, Aberdeenshire AB3 7AX.
TELEPHONE: +44 (0)1330 860223.
VISITORS: Can play only with a member.
LOCATION: On B994 to Dunecht.

# ELLON

## McDONALD GOLF CLUB

COURSE DESCRIPTION:
Tight tree-lined inland parkland course with streams and a pond. Finishes with two long par 4s.
   18 holes, 5,991 yards, par 70 (SSS 69). Amateur record 65. Pro record 63.

SIGNATURE HOLE:
SEVENTEENTH (452 yards, par 4) A dogleg to the left. Drive has to be accurately positioned to the right of a gap in mature trees.

### COURSE CARD

| HOLE | YDS | PAR | HOLE | YDS | PAR |
|------|------|-----|------|-------|-----|
| 1 | 291 | 4 | 10 | 321 | 4 |
| 2 | 329 | 4 | 11 | 166 | 3 |
| 3 | 379 | 4 | 12 | 205 | 3 |
| 4 | 484 | 5 | 13 | 260 | 4 |
| 5 | 378 | 4 | 14 | 262 | 4 |
| 6 | 389 | 4 | 15 | 147 | 3 |
| 7 | 201 | 3 | 16 | 313 | 4 |
| 8 | 403 | 4 | 17 | 452 | 4 |
| 9 | 580 | 5 | 18 | 431 | 4 |
| Yds Out | 3,434 | | Yds In | 2,557 | |
| Total Yds | 5,991 | | | | |
| Total Par | 70 | | | | |

ADDRESS: Hospital Road, Ellon, Aberdeenshire AB41 9AW.
TELEPHONE: +44 (0)1358 720576.
FAX: +44 (0)1358 720001.
SECRETARY: George Ironside.
PROFESSIONAL: Ronnie Urquhart +44 (0)1358 722891.
VISITORS: At all times.
GREEN FEES: £14 per round weekdays, £20 per day. Saturdays, £16 per round, £24 per day. Sundays, £20 per round, £30 per day.
CATERING: Full service, except on Mondays, in new clubhouse. Bar.
FACILITIES: Trolley hire, putting green, pro shop.
LOCATION: 16 miles north of Aberdeen on A90.
LOCAL HOTELS: Buchan Hotel, New Inn, Station Hotel, The White Horse Inn.

# FRASERBURGH

## FRASERBURGH GOLF CLUB

### COURSE DESCRIPTION:
Testing natural seaside links course, much of which was designed by James Braid in 1922. Records show that the club was in existence in 1780; and in parish records of 1613 a youth, John Burnett, received a punishment for playing golf on a Sunday. The main features of the course are the tricky par 3s, of which there are four. Rosehill, set on flat land, offers a contrast to Corbie Hill, but has many interesting holes.

    *Corbie Hill* – 18 holes, 6,278 yards, par 70 (SSS 70). Amateur record 65.

    *Rosehill* – 9 holes, 5,000 yards (for 18 holes), par 64 (SSS 64).

### SIGNATURE HOLE:
Corbie Hill: SEVENTH ('The Well' 165 yards, par 3) Elevated tee to a green which slopes from back to front and is guarded by bunkers with a steep bank at the back. If you get a par here, you won't be disappointed.

### COURSE CARD

| HOLE | MEDAL YDS | PAR | FORWARD YDS | PAR | LADIES YDS | PAR | HOLE | MEDAL YDS | PAR | FORWARD YDS | PAR | LADIES YDS | PAR |
|------|-----------|-----|-------------|-----|------------|-----|------|-----------|-----|-------------|-----|------------|-----|
| 1 | 434 | 4 | 404 | 4 | 398 | 4 | 10 | 322 | 4 | 277 | 4 | 271 | 4 |
| 2 | 391 | 4 | 363 | 4 | 361 | 4 | 11 | 357 | 4 | 310 | 4 | 305 | 4 |
| 3 | 332 | 4 | 295 | 4 | 293 | 4 | 12 | 389 | 4 | 364 | 4 | 314 | 4 |
| 4 | 328 | 4 | 307 | 4 | 301 | 4 | 13 | 315 | 4 | 305 | 4 | 265 | 4 |
| 5 | 183 | 3 | 180 | 3 | 139 | 3 | 14 | 198 | 3 | 189 | 3 | 160 | 3 |
| 6 | 528 | 5 | 497 | 5 | 452 | 5 | 15 | 508 | 5 | 508 | 5 | 398 | 5 |
| 7 | 165 | 3 | 131 | 3 | 125 | 3 | 16 | 378 | 4 | 345 | 4 | 330 | 4 |
| 8 | 368 | 4 | 360 | 4 | 274 | 4 | 17 | 189 | 3 | 154 | 3 | 118 | 3 |
| 9 | 458 | 4 | 450 | 4 | 443 | 5 | 18 | 435 | 4 | 378 | 4 | 371 | 5 |
| *Yds* Out | 3,187 | | 2,987 | | 2,786 | | *Yds* In | 3,091 | | 2,830 | | 2,532 | |

| | | | |
|---|---|---|---|
| *Total* 6,278 | 5,817 | 5,318 | |
| *Yds* | | | |
| *Total* 70 | 70 | 74 | |
| *Par* | | | |

**ADDRESS:** Philorth Road, Fraserburgh, Aberdeenshire AB43 8TL.
**TELEPHONE:** +44 (0)1346 516616 (office), 517898 (shop), 518287 (bar).
**FAX:** +44 (0)1346 516616.
**E-MAIL:** fburgh@aol.com
**SECRETARY:** James Mollison.
**VISITORS:** Yes, no restrictions.
**GREEN FEES:** £17 per round weekdays, £22 per day. £22 per round weekends, £27 per day.
**CATERING:** Restaurant and bar. European and Thai cuisine. Functions catered for.
**FACILITIES:** Trolley hire, club hire, caddies with notice, changing-rooms, putting green, pro shop, practice ground, memberships available.
**LOCATION:** 1 mile south-east of town on B9033.

# HUNTLY

## HUNTLY GOLF CLUB

**COURSE DESCRIPTION:**
A rolling inland parkland course between the rivers Deveron and Bogie with a burn cutting across four holes. Huntly Castle backs onto the second green. Founded 1892.

18 holes, 5,399 yards, par 67 (SSS 66).

**SIGNATURE HOLE:**
EIGHTH (406 yards, par 4) Regarded as the toughest hole on the course with a well-bunkered green.

**COURSE CARD**

| HOLE | YDS | PAR | HOLE | YDS | PAR |
|---|---|---|---|---|---|
| 1 | 366 | 4 | 10 | 393 | 4 |
| 2 | 154 | 3 | 11 | 387 | 4 |
| 3 | 158 | 3 | 12 | 350 | 4 |
| 4 | 389 | 4 | 13 | 333 | 4 |
| 5 | 294 | 4 | 14 | 187 | 3 |
| 6 | 107 | 3 | 15 | 336 | 4 |
| 7 | 334 | 4 | 16 | 389 | 4 |
| 8 | 406 | 4 | 17 | 163 | 3 |
| 9 | 369 | 4 | 18 | 284 | 4 |
| *Yds* *Out* | 2,577 | | *Yds* *In* | 2,822 | |

| Total | 5,399 |
|-------|-------|
| Yds |  |
| Total | 67 |
| Par |  |

**ADDRESS:** Cooper Park, Huntly, Aberdeenshire AB54 4SH.
**TELEPHONE:** +44 (0)1466 792643.
**PROFESSIONAL:** +44 (0)1466 794181.
**VISITORS:** Any day after 8 a.m. Societies by arrangement with secretary.
**GREEN FEES:** £12 per round weekdays, £18 per day.
**CATERING:** Yes, in recently refurbished clubhouse. Bar.
**FACILITIES:** Pro shop, practice area.
**LOCATION:** 39 miles north-west of Aberdeen on A96. On north side of Huntly.
**LOCAL HOTELS:** Huntly Arms.

# INSCH

## INSCH GOLF CLUB

**COURSE DESCRIPTION:**
Recently extended to 18 holes. Original parkland course in natural woodland with water hazards and large contoured greens. New holes are testing. One hole steep, but there are excellent panoramic views over the local hills and village.
18 holes, 5,414 yards, par 69 (SSS 69).

**SIGNATURE HOLE:**
NINTH ('The Lang Line' 536 yards, par 5) An extremely long hole requiring an accurate drive into the prevailing wind. Final approach will be slightly uphill to a green set into the slope.

**COURSE CARD**

| HOLE | MEDAL YDS | PAR | FORWARD YDS | PAR | LADIES YDS | PAR | HOLE | MEDAL YDS | PAR | FORWARD YDS | PAR | LADIES YDS | PAR |
|------|-----------|-----|-------------|-----|------------|-----|------|-----------|-----|-------------|-----|------------|-----|
| 1 | 425 | 4 | 371 | 4 | 424 | 5 | 10 | 276 | 4 | 258 | 4 | 211 | 4 |
| 2 | 360 | 4 | 321 | 4 | 312 | 4 | 11 | 296 | 4 | 283 | 4 | 262 | 4 |
| 3 | 362 | 4 | 354 | 4 | 325 | 4 | 12 | 315 | 4 | 258 | 4 | 315 | 4 |
| 4 | 296 | 4 | 280 | 4 | 267 | 4 | 13 | 158 | 3 | 146 | 3 | 126 | 3 |
| 5 | 422 | 4 | 396 | 4 | 385 | 4 | 14 | 289 | 4 | 289 | 4 | 256 | 4 |
| 6 | 168 | 3 | 148 | 3 | 149 | 3 | 15 | 285 | 4 | 270 | 4 | 279 | 4 |
| 7 | 264 | 4 | 253 | 4 | 231 | 4 | 16 | 493 | 5 | 482 | 5 | 417 | 5 |
| 8 | 180 | 3 | 128 | 3 | 153 | 3 | 17 | 131 | 3 | 116 | 3 | 112 | 3 |
| 9 | 536 | 5 | 525 | 5 | 482 | 5 | 18 | 158 | 3 | 150 | 3 | 133 | 3 |
| Yds Out | 3,013 |  | 2,776 |  | 2,728 |  | Yds In | 2,401 |  | 2,252 |  | 2,111 |  |
| Total | 5,414 |  | 5,028 |  | 4,839 |  |  |  |  |  |  |  |  |

| *Yds* | | | |
|---|---|---|---|
| *Total* | 69 | 69 | 70 |
| *Par* | | | |

**ADDRESS:** Golf Terrace, Insch, Aberdeenshire AB52 6JY.
**TELEPHONE & FAX:** +44 (0)1464 820363.
**E-MAIL:** inschgolf@euphony.net
**SECRETARY/MANAGER:** Douglas Cumming.
**VISITORS:** Yes, telephone to book tee time.
**GREEN FEES:** On application.
**CATERING:** Bar and meals. Functions catered for. Check with bar staff/caterer for availability.
**FACILITIES:** Trolley hire (£2), practice facilities.
**LOCATION:** North-west of Aberdeen on the main A96 Inverness road. Follow the signs to Insch. The golf course is situated within the village.

# INVERALLOCHY

## INVERALLOCHY GOLF CLUB

**COURSE DESCRIPTION:**
Typical seaside links course, founded in 1888, with great grassy dunes and several tricky par 3s. Runs parallel to picturesque beach.
   18 holes, 5,237 yards, par 64 (SSS 65). Course record 59.

**SIGNATURE HOLE:**
SEVENTEENTH (418 yards, par 4) Tee shot has to be fairly long but short of a burn which runs diagonally across the fairway. Second shot to a small elevated green.

**COURSE CARD**

| HOLE | YDS | PAR | HOLE | YDS | PAR |
|---|---|---|---|---|---|
| 1 | 384 | 4 | 10 | 239 | 4 |
| 2 | 203 | 3 | 11 | 192 | 3 |
| 3 | 371 | 4 | 12 | 442 | 4 |
| 4 | 319 | 4 | 13 | 335 | 4 |
| 5 | 184 | 3 | 14 | 157 | 3 |
| 6 | 454 | 4 | 15 | 322 | 4 |
| 7 | 200 | 3 | 16 | 190 | 3 |
| 8 | 147 | 3 | 17 | 418 | 4 |
| 9 | 282 | 4 | 18 | 398 | 4 |
| *Yds* | 2,544 | | *Yds* | 2,693 | |
| *Out* | | | *In* | | |
| *Total Yds* | 5,237 | | | | |

*Total* 64
*Par*

**ADDRESS:** Cairnbulg, Inverallochy, near Fraserburgh AB43 5YL.
**TELEPHONE:** +44 (0)1346 582000.
**SECRETARY:** Ian Watt.
**VISITORS:** Any time by prior arrangement.
**GREEN FEES:** £10 weekdays. £15 weekends.
**CATERING:** Bar in new clubhouse.
**FACILITIES:** Putting green, pro shop, small practice ground.
**LOCATION:** 4 miles south-east of Fraserburgh.
**LOCAL HOTELS:** Tufted Duck Hotel.

# INVERURIE

## INVERURIE GOLF CLUB

**COURSE DESCRIPTION:**
Course layout has changed and been developed over the years since the golf club was founded in 1923. Now a well-established course which poses a pleasant, interesting challenge to all standards of golfer. There are parkland holes to give an open, varied start; a series of shorter holes around the town, which demand accurate iron play; followed by a testing, picturesque, tree-lined section to finish.

18 holes, 5,711 yards, par 69 (SSS 68). Course record 65.

**SIGNATURE HOLE:**
SIXTEENTH ('Lang Chauve' 444 yards, par 4) If you manage to hit the fairway, you are not home and dry. Another accurate wood or long iron is required to give yourself a chance of a par.

**COURSE CARD**

| HOLE | MEDAL YDS | PAR | FORWARD YDS | PAR | LADIES YDS | PAR | HOLE | MEDAL YDS | PAR | FORWARD YDS | PAR | LADIES YDS | PAR |
|------|-----------|-----|-------------|-----|------------|-----|------|-----------|-----|-------------|-----|------------|-----|
| 1 | 294 | 4 | 284 | 4 | 276 | 4 | 10 | 128 | 3 | 123 | 3 | 105 | 3 |
| 2 | 346 | 4 | 336 | 4 | 330 | 4 | 11 | 304 | 4 | 304 | 4 | 300 | 4 |
| 3 | 401 | 4 | 371 | 4 | 386 | 5 | 12 | 322 | 4 | 316 | 4 | 312 | 4 |
| 4 | 196 | 3 | 186 | 3 | 180 | 3 | 13 | 257 | 4 | 247 | 4 | 140 | 3 |
| 5 | 512 | 5 | 502 | 5 | 423 | 5 | 14 | 369 | 4 | 354 | 4 | 313 | 4 |
| 6 | 348 | 4 | 338 | 4 | 332 | 4 | 15 | 183 | 3 | 163 | 3 | 145 | 3 |
| 7 | 184 | 3 | 174 | 3 | 167 | 3 | 16 | 444 | 4 | 440 | 4 | 336 | 4 |
| 8 | 365 | 4 | 355 | 4 | 349 | 4 | 17 | 407 | 4 | 364 | 4 | 354 | 4 |
| 9 | 301 | 4 | 286 | 4 | 296 | 4 | 18 | 350 | 4 | 340 | 4 | 334 | 4 |
| *Yds* *Out* | 2,947 | | 2,832 | | 2,739 | | *Yds* *In* | 2,764 | | 2,651 | | 2,339 | |

| Total Yds | 5,711 | 5,483 | 5,078 |
|---|---|---|---|
| Total Par | 69 | 69 | 69 |

ADDRESS: Blackhall Road, Inverurie, Aberdeenshire AB51 5JB.
TELEPHONE: +44 (0)1467 624080.
FAX: +44 (0)1467 621051.
E-MAIL: administrator@inveruriegc.co.uk
WEBSITE: www.inveruriegc.co.uk
SECRETARY: Mrs Barbara Rogerson.
PROFESSIONAL: Mark Lees +44 (0) 1467 620193.
VISITORS: All year upon request.
GREEN FEES: £14 per round weekdays, £18 per day. £18 per round weekends, £24 per day.
CATERING: Bar and meals. Warm clubhouse where visitors are made welcome. Functions catered for.
CREDIT CARDS ACCEPTED (in pro shop only): Amex/Visa/Mastercard/Diners Club.
FACILITIES: Motorised buggy (one for health reasons), trolley hire (£2), club hire (£10), changing-rooms, putting green, practice ground, pro shop, coaching clinics, waiting list for membership.
LOCATION: 16 miles north-west of Aberdeen. The course is easily accessible from the Blackhall roundabout off the A96 by-pass.
LOCAL HOTELS: Kintore Arms, Pittodrie House Hotel, Raemoir House Hotel, Simpson's Hotel, Bar/Brasserie, Strathburn Hotel, Thainstone House Hotel, The White Horse Inn.

# KEITH

## KEITH GOLF CLUB

COURSE DESCRIPTION:
Undulating parkland course with greens renowned for their texture and consistency. Panoramic views of surrounding countryside.
18 holes, 5,802 yards, par 69 (SSS 68).

SIGNATURE HOLE:
SEVENTH (232 yards, par 3) out of bounds to the left and behind the small green, which has a bunker to the right and slopes to the left.

ADDRESS: Fife Park, Keith, Banffshire AB55 5DF.
TELEPHONE: +44 (0)1542 882469.
SECRETARY: Denis Shepherd.
VISITORS: Any time. By appointment.
GREEN FEES: £10 per round weekdays, £12 per day. £12 per round weekends, £15 per

day.

CATERING: Bar.

FACILITIES: Trolley hire, putting green, practice ground.

LOCATION: Leave A96 at Keith, taking Dufftown road. Turn first right and first left, then left again.

LOCAL HOTELS: Callater Lodge, Fife Arms, Grampian Hotel, Royal Hotel, The Old Coach House Hotel, Ugie House Hotel.

# KEMNAY

## KEMNAY GOLF CLUB

### COURSE DESCRIPTION:

Flat parkland course surrounded by mature trees. A stream crosses four holes. Superb views.

18 holes, 5,903 yards, par 70 (SSS 69). Amateur record 69. Pro record 72.

### COURSE CARD

| HOLE | YDS | PAR | HOLE | YDS | PAR |
|------|-----|-----|------|-----|-----|
| 1 | 352 | 4 | 10 | 308 | 4 |
| 2 | 282 | 4 | 11 | 326 | 4 |
| 3 | 340 | 4 | 12 | 208 | 3 |
| 4 | 180 | 3 | 13 | 498 | 5 |
| 5 | 374 | 4 | 14 | 403 | 4 |
| 6 | 386 | 4 | 15 | 420 | 4 |
| 7 | 348 | 4 | 16 | 356 | 4 |
| 8 | 160 | 3 | 17 | 170 | 3 |
| 9 | 488 | 5 | 18 | 304 | 4 |
| Yds Out | 2,910 | | Yds In | 2,993 | |
| Total Yds | 5,903 | | | | |
| Total Par | 70 | | | | |

ADDRESS: Monymusk Road, Kemnay, Aberdeenshire AB51 5RA.

TELEPHONE: +44 (0)1467 643746.

SECRETARY: Doug Imrie.

PROFESSIONAL: Ronnie McDonald +44 (0)1467 642225.

VISITORS: Yes. Book through shop.

GREEN FEES: £17 per round weekdays, £24 per day. £19 per round weekends, £28 per day.

CATERING: Full catering in new clubhouse.

FACILITIES: Trolley/buggy hire, pro shop.

LOCATION: From A96 main Aberdeen–Inverness road, take B994 signposted Kemnay.

LOCAL HOTELS: Burnett Arms Hotel, Grant Arms, Park Hill Lodge Hotel, Raemoir House Hotel, Simpson's Hotel, Bar/Brasserie, The White Horse Inn.

# KINTORE

## KINTORE GOLF CLUB
COURSE DESCRIPTION:
Founded in 1911 as a nine-hole course, it was thoughtfully extended to eighteen in 1992. It covers a large area from the Don Basin, overlooked by the clubhouse, to mature woodland at the far perimeter with excellent drainage (resulting in very few days of lost play). The interest lies in the contrast between the old and the new nines: having climbed the hill at the 2nd and completed the 3rd, you embark on the latter which, by virtue of being lined with trees and criss-crossed by burns, produces some very testing and some delightful holes. Returning to the old nine, the remaining six holes are short and relatively hilly with the balance between triumph and disaster depending on club selection, accuracy and a certain amount of luck. Your reward will be spectacular views over the River Don, stretching away to the Bennachie hills to the north.

18 holes, 6,019 yards, par 70 (SSS 69). Amateur record 64. Pro record 62.

SIGNATURE HOLE:
SEVENTH ('Burnside' 378 yards, par 4) Well bunkered. Open ditch running diagonally across the fairway close to the green. Demands an accurate second shot.

COURSE CARD

| HOLE | MEDAL YDS | PAR | FORWARD YDS | PAR | LADIES YDS | PAR | HOLE | MEDAL YDS | PAR | FORWARD YDS | PAR | LADIES YDS | PAR |
|---|---|---|---|---|---|---|---|---|---|---|---|---|---|
| 1 | 230 | 3 | 213 | 3 | 230 | 4 | 10 | 145 | 3 | 135 | 3 | 135 | 3 |
| 2 | 453 | 5 | 418 | 5 | 418 | 5 | 11 | 508 | 5 | 426 | 5 | 426 | 5 |
| 3 | 407 | 4 | 370 | 4 | 335 | 4 | 12 | 337 | 4 | 283 | 4 | 283 | 4 |
| 4 | 490 | 5 | 484 | 5 | 373 | 4 | 13 | 380 | 4 | 369 | 4 | 262 | 4 |
| 5 | 453 | 4 | 389 | 4 | 389 | 4 | 14 | 240 | 3 | 200 | 3 | 190 | 3 |
| 6 | 175 | 3 | 130 | 3 | 169 | 3 | 15 | 300 | 4 | 290 | 4 | 290 | 4 |
| 7 | 378 | 4 | 263 | 4 | 263 | 4 | 16 | 275 | 4 | 237 | 4 | 234 | 4 |
| 8 | 367 | 4 | 326 | 4 | 326 | 4 | 17 | 152 | 3 | 136 | 3 | 132 | 3 |
| 9 | 424 | 4 | 351 | 4 | 351 | 4 | 18 | 305 | 4 | 303 | 4 | 303 | 4 |
| Yds Out | 3,377 | | 2,944 | | 2,854 | | Yds In | 2,642 | | 2,379 | | 2,255 | |
| Total Yds | 6,019 | | 5,323 | | 5,109 | | | | | | | | | |
| Total Par | 70 | | 70 | | 70 | | | | | | | | | |

ADDRESS: Balbithan Road, Kintore, Aberdeenshire AB51 0UR.
TELEPHONE & FAX: +44 (0)1467 632631.

SECRETARY: Mrs Vicki Graham.
VISITORS: All-year round. Pre-booking advisable during the season.
GREEN FEES: £13 per round weekdays, £18 per day. £19 per round weekends, £24 per day.
CATERING: Restaurant and bar.
FACILITIES: Motorised buggies (£10), trolley hire (£1.50), changing-rooms, putting green, practice ground, memberships available.
LOCATION: 16 miles north of Aberdeen off the A96. Turn to Kintore at Broomhill roundabout, turn right in village centre to Hatton of Fintry. Cross railway line and river.
LOCAL HOTELS: Crown Hotel, Raemoir House Hotel, Toryburn Hotel, Simpson's Hotel Bar/Brasserie, Thanestone Hotel, The White Horse Inn.

# LONGSIDE

## LONGSIDE GOLF CLUB

COURSE DESCRIPTION:
Short, flat, inland parkland course with small greens.
18 holes, 5,225 yards, par 66 (SSS 66).

ADDRESS: West End Main Street, Longside, Peterhead, AB42 4XJ.
TELEPHONE: +44 (0)1779 821558.
VISITORS: Not on Wednesday evenings or on Sundays before 10.30 a.m.
GREEN FEES: £12 per round weekdays, £16 Saturdays, £18 Sundays.
CATERING: Restaurant and bar.
FACILITIES: Changing-rooms, practice area.
LOCATION: 6 miles west of Peterhead on A950.
LOCAL HOTELS: The Old Coach House Hotel.

# MACDUFF

## ROYAL TARLAIR GOLF CLUB

COURSE DESCRIPTION:
Seaside cliff-top parkland course, which presents a challenge for the more serious golfer and an idyllic setting for the not so serious. The greens are said to be the envy of many courses in the area. There are spectacular views of the coastline.
18 holes, 5,866 yards, par 71 (SSS 68). Amateur record 62.

SIGNATURE HOLE:
THIRTEENTH ('Clivet' 125 yards, par 3) Dramatic cliff-side setting and testing tee shot over a gully. Some reckon it rivals the 7th at Pebble Beach.

COURSE CARD

| HOLE | MEDAL YDS | PAR | FORWARD YDS | PAR | LADIES YDS | PAR | HOLE | MEDAL YDS | PAR | FORWARD YDS | PAR | LADIES YDS | PAR |
|------|-----------|-----|-------------|-----|------------|-----|------|-----------|-----|-------------|-----|------------|-----|
| 1 | 292 | 4 | 353 | 4 | 265 | 4 | 10 | 353 | 4 | 340 | 4 | 308 | 4 |
| 2 | 365 | 4 | 355 | 4 | 255 | 4 | 11 | 345 | 4 | 348 | 4 | 334 | 4 |
| 3 | 125 | 3 | 120 | 3 | 106 | 3 | 12 | 331 | 4 | 319 | 4 | 321 | 4 |
| 4 | 477 | 5 | 476 | 5 | 409 | 5 | 13 | 152 | 3 | 144 | 3 | 129 | 3 |
| 5 | 289 | 4 | 292 | 4 | 278 | 4 | 14 | 276 | 4 | 271 | 4 | 270 | 4 |
| 6 | 410 | 4 | 402 | 4 | 306 | 4 | 15 | 363 | 4 | 353 | 4 | 284 | 4 |
| 7 | 176 | 3 | 167 | 3 | 161 | 3 | 16 | 477 | 5 | 454 | 5 | 391 | 5 |
| 8 | 483 | 5 | 483 | 5 | 476 | 5 | 17 | 221 | 3 | 214 | 3 | 215 | 4 |
| 9 | 351 | 4 | 334 | 4 | 277 | 4 | 18 | 380 | 4 | 374 | 4 | 367 | 4 |
| Yds Out | 2,968 | | 2,899 | | 2,635 | | Yds In | 2,898 | | 2,817 | | 2,579 | |
| Total Yds | 5,866 | | 5,716 | | 5,214 | | | | | | | | |
| Total Par | 71 | | 71 | | 74 | | | | | | | | |

ADDRESS: Buchan Street, Macduff, Aberdeenshire AB44 1TA.

TELEPHONE: +44 (0)1261 832897.

FAX: +44 (0)1261 833455.

E-MAIL: info@royaltarlair.co.uk

WEBSITE: www.royaltarlair.co.uk

SECRETARY: Mrs C. Davidson.

VISITORS: Very welcome. No problem weekdays. Advance booking for weekends.

GREEN FEES: £10 per round weekdays, £15 per day. £15 per round weekends, £20 per day. April to September (Monday to Friday): 2 rounds of golf and full-day catering, £20.

CATERING: Bar and meals. Functions catered for.

FACILITIES: Trolley hire (£1), club hire, changing-rooms, putting green, pro shop, memberships available, including international membership.

LOCATION: 45 miles north of Aberdeen. On the A98 Fraserburgh–Inverness road, east of Macduff.

# NEWBURGH

## NEWBURGH-ON-YTHAN GOLF CLUB

COURSE DESCRIPTION:

Seaside links course founded in 1888. River Ythan cuts through the course, which is adjacent to a bird sanctuary. The outward nine is characterised by greater undulations and hills with elevated tees and greens demanding a range of shot making which challenges both the experienced golfer and novice. The inward nine, although longer, is slightly easier but demands accurate golf from tee to green. A greater number of blind shots are called for, from the tee or into the greens that may be small but have subtle borrows.

18 holes, 6,162 yards, par 72 (SSS 70).

COURSE CARD

| HOLE | YDS | PAR | HOLE | YDS | PAR |
|------|-----|-----|------|-----|-----|
| 1 | 385 | 4 | 10 | 338 | 4 |
| 2 | 224 | 3 | 11 | 390 | 4 |
| 3 | 467 | 5 | 12 | 428 | 4 |
| 4 | 285 | 4 | 13 | 316 | 4 |
| 5 | 201 | 3 | 14 | 347 | 4 |
| 6 | 343 | 4 | 15 | 305 | 4 |
| 7 | 288 | 4 | 16 | 148 | 3 |
| 8 | 313 | 4 | 17 | 354 | 4 |
| 9 | 482 | 5 | 18 | 548 | 5 |
| Yds Out | 2,988 | | Yds In | 3,174 | |
| Total Yds | 6,162 | | | | |
| Total Par | 72 | | | | |

ADDRESS: Newburgh Links, Newburgh AB41 0FD.
TELEPHONE: +44 (0)1358 789786 or 789436.
FAX: +44 (0)1358 789956.
SECRETARY: +44 (0)1358 789084.
VISITORS: Contact in advance.
GREEN FEES: £16 per day weekdays. £22 weekends.
CATERING: Restaurant and bar.
FACILITIES: Practice ground, changing-rooms, pro shop, coaching.
LOCATION: East of village on A975.
LOCAL HOTELS: Udny Arms Hotel, The White Horse Inn, Ythan Hotel.

# NEWMACHAR

## NEWMACHAR GOLF CLUB

COURSE DESCRIPTION:
Hawkshill is championship-standard heathland, known as 'the thinking man's course'. Highly praised for its testing layout and use of water hazards, which come into play on seven of the holes. Mature silver birch and Scots pines line the strategically bunkered fairways and greens. Opened in 1990, it was designed by Dave Thomas. It has been the venue for the Scottish Seniors' Championship.

18 holes, 6,623 yards, par 72 (SSS 74). Course record 65.

Swailend, which opened in 1997, is rolling parkland. It does not have as much water or as many trees as the Hawkshill, but it is more exposed to the wind.

18 holes, 6,388 yards, par 72 (SSS 71).

## HAWKSHILL COURSE CARD

| HOLE | MEDAL YDS | PAR | FORWARD YDS | PAR | LADIES YDS | PAR | HOLE | MEDAL YDS | PAR | FORWARD YDS | PAR | LADIES YDS | PAR |
|------|-----------|-----|-------------|-----|------------|-----|------|-----------|-----|-------------|-----|------------|-----|
| 1 | 390 | 4 | 370 | 4 | 352 | 4 | 10 | 337 | 4 | 299 | 4 | 255 | 4 |
| 2 | 543 | 5 | 500 | 5 | 471 | 5 | 11 | 381 | 4 | 367 | 4 | 345 | 4 |
| 3 | 331 | 4 | 313 | 4 | 274 | 4 | 12 | 428 | 4 | 412 | 3 | 365 | 4 |
| 4 | 378 | 4 | 354 | 4 | 327 | 4 | 13 | 399 | 4 | 384 | 4 | 351 | 4 |
| 5 | 320 | 4 | 320 | 4 | 267 | 4 | 14 | 362 | 4 | 343 | 4 | 311 | 4 |
| 6 | 170 | 3 | 170 | 3 | 138 | 3 | 15 | 210 | 3 | 197 | 3 | 129 | 3 |
| 7 | 405 | 4 | 380 | 4 | 336 | 4 | 16 | 504 | 5 | 487 | 5 | 410 | 5 |
| 8 | 493 | 5 | 493 | 5 | 442 | 5 | 17 | 432 | 4 | 422 | 4 | 398 | 5 |
| 9 | 181 | 3 | 143 | 3 | 96 | 3 | 18 | 359 | 4 | 359 | 4 | 336 | 4 |
| *Yds* *Out* | 3,211 | | 3,043 | | 2,703 | | *Yds* *In* | 3,412 | | 3,270 | | 2,900 | |
| *Total* *Yds* | 6,623 | | 6,313 | | 5,603 | | | | | | | | |
| *Total* *Par* | 72 | | 72 | | 73 | | | | | | | | |

ADDRESS: Swailend, Newmachar, Aberdeenshire AB21 7UU.
TELEPHONE: +44 (0)1651 863002.
FAX: +44 (0)1651 863055.
E-MAIL: newmachargolfclub@compuserve.com
WEBSITE: www.newmachargolfclub.co.uk
SECRETARY/MANAGER: George McIntosh.
PROFESSIONAL: Gordon Simpson.
VISITORS: Yes, 7 days a week. Must have handicap certificate.
GREEN FEES: *Hawkshill:* £30 per round weekdays, £45 per day. £40 per round weekends. *Swailend:* £15 per round weekdays, £25 per day. £20 per round weekends, £30 per day. One round on each course: £35 weekdays, £45 weekends. Special offer: 36 holes on Swailend + full catering, £22.
CREDIT CARDS ACCEPTED: Visa/Mastercard.
CATERING: Restaurant and bar. Functions catered for.
FACILITIES: Motorised buggies (£15), trolley hire (£2), club hire, changing-rooms, putting green, pro shop, practice ground, driving range, coaching clinics, memberships available.
LOCATION: 12 miles north-west of Aberdeen, off A947.
LOCAL HOTELS: Dunavon House Hotel, Glen Lui Hotel, Kirkhill Hotel, Marriott Hotel, Simpson's Hotel, Stakis Craigendarroch Hotel & Country Club.

# OLDMELDRUM

## MELDRUM HOUSE HOTEL AND GOLF COURSE

**COURSE DESCRIPTION:**
Parkland course in the attractive grounds of Meldrum House Hotel, which is a thirteenth-century baronial mansion.

18 holes, 6,379 yards, par 70 (SSS 72).

**ADDRESS:** Meldrum House Hotel, Oldmeldrum, Aberdeenshire.
**TELEPHONE:** +44 (0)1651 873553.
**VISITORS:** Members and residents only.
**GREEN FEES:** £35 per round weekdays, £40 weekends.
**CATERING:** Restaurant and bar.
**FACILITIES:** Trolley/buggy hire, pro shop, golf academy.
**LOCAL HOTELS:** Meldrum House Hotel, Meldrum Arms, Raemoir House Hotel, Redgarth Hotel, Simpson's Hotel, The White Horse Inn

## OLDMELDRUM GOLF CLUB

**COURSE DESCRIPTION:**
Challenging and undulating parkland course with tree-lined fairways and water features and small and tricky greens. At the side of the 12th fairway can be seen the 'Groaner Stone' which dates back to the days of Robert the Bruce. The original holes are over 100 years old and nine of the holes are reasonably new.

18 holes, 5,988 yards, par 70 (SSS 69). Amateur record D.H. Clark 66.

**SIGNATURE HOLE:**
ELEVENTH (196 yards, par 3) Over two ponds to a small green surrounded on three sides by bunkers.

### COURSE CARD

| HOLE | MEDAL YDS | PAR | FORWARD YDS | PAR | LADIES YDS | PAR | HOLE | MEDAL YDS | PAR | FORWARD YDS | PAR | LADIES YDS | PAR |
|------|-----------|-----|-------------|-----|------------|-----|------|-----------|-----|-------------|-----|------------|-----|
| 1 | 260 | 4 | 261 | 4 | 205 | 4 | 10 | 466 | 4 | 404 | 4 | 390 | 4 |
| 2 | 482 | 5 | 437 | 4 | 429 | 5 | 11 | 196 | 3 | 170 | 3 | 114 | 3 |
| 3 | 192 | 3 | 180 | 3 | 156 | 3 | 12 | 440 | 4 | 392 | 4 | 378 | 4 |
| 4 | 417 | 4 | 362 | 4 | 350 | 4 | 13 | 425 | 4 | 414 | 4 | 393 | 4 |
| 5 | 274 | 4 | 258 | 4 | 247 | 4 | 14 | 295 | 4 | 280 | 4 | 271 | 4 |
| 6 | 476 | 5 | 408 | 4 | 396 | 4 | 15 | 301 | 4 | 294 | 4 | 290 | 4 |
| 7 | 148 | 3 | 139 | 3 | 134 | 3 | 16 | 301 | 4 | 289 | 4 | 288 | 4 |
| 8 | 410 | 4 | 328 | 4 | 299 | 4 | 17 | 163 | 3 | 163 | 3 | 153 | 3 |
| 9 | 423 | 4 | 376 | 4 | 357 | 4 | 18 | 319 | 4 | 307 | 4 | 300 | 4 |
| *Yds* *Out* | 3,082 | | 2,749 | | 2,583 | | *Yds* *In* | 2,906 | | 2,713 | | 2,577 | |

| Total Yds | 5,988 | 5,462 | 5,160 |
|---|---|---|---|
| Total Par | 70 | 68 | 69 |

ADDRESS: Kirk Brae, Oldmeldrum, Aberdeenshire AB51 0DJ.
TELEPHONE: +44 (0)1651 872648.
FAX: +44 (0)1651 873555.
WEBSITE: www.oldmeldrumgolf.freeserve.co.uk
SECRETARY: John Page +44 (0)1651 872315.
VISITORS: With the reputation of being a friendly club, visitors are welcome except when there are club competitions.
GREEN FEES: £14 per round/day weekdays. £20 per round weekends, £24 per day. Weekly ticket £50 (Monday to Friday).
CATERING: Restaurant and bar. Functions catered for.
FACILITIES: Trolley hire, club hire, changing-rooms, putting green, pro shop, practice ground, coaching clinics, memberships available.
LOCATION: 17 miles north of Aberdeen on A947.
LOCAL HOTELS: Meldrum House Hotel, Meldrum Arms, Raemoir House Hotel, Redgarth Hotel, Simpson's Hotel, The White Horse Inn.

# PETERCULTER

## PETERCULTER GOLF CLUB

COURSE DESCRIPTION:
Tight and undulating inland parkland course laid out on two tiers on the banks of the River Dee. The lower tier is sheltered from the wind which can sweep down the Dee Valley (of which there are spectacular views). Founded in 1989, the course has matured to offer all standards of player a good golfing experience.

18 holes, 5,947 yards, par 68 (SSS 68). Course record 68.

ADDRESS: Oldtown, Burnside Road, Peterculter, Aberdeenshire AB14 0LN.
TELEPHONE: +44 (0)1224 735245.
FAX: +44 (0)1224 735580.
E-MAIL: info@petercultergolfclub.co.uk
WEBSITE: www.petercultergolfclub.co.uk
SECRETARY: Keith Anderson.
PROFESSIONAL: Dean Vannet +44 (0)1224 734994.
VISITORS: Any time. No outings at weekends.
GREEN FEES: £16 per round weekdays, £22 per day. £20 per round weekends, £26 per day.
CREDIT CARDS ACCEPTED: Visa/Mastercard.
CATERING: Full bar and catering facilities, apart from Mondays.
FACILITIES: Trolley/buggy hire, putting green, pro shop, practice ground.

LOCATION: 8 miles west of Aberdeen on main Deeside Road (A93).
LOCAL HOTELS: Callater Lodge, Golden Arms Hotel, Raemoir House Hotel.

# PETERHEAD

## PETERHEAD GOLF CLUB

COURSE DESCRIPTION:
Not so many golfers know about this splendid natural links course between grassy dunes bounded by the sea and the River Ugie. It can match many of its more illustrious neighbours as a challenging test of golf.

*Old Course* – 18 holes, 6,173 yards, par 70 (SSS 71). Course record 64.

*New Course* – 9 holes, 4,456 yards (for 18 holes), par 62 (SSS 62).

ADDRESS: Craigewan Links, Peterhead, Aberdeenshire AB42 6LT.
TELEPHONE: +44 (0)1779 472149.
FAX: +44 (0)1779 480725.
VISITORS: Contact in advance. Competition day Saturdays. Societies not weekends.
GREEN FEES: Old Course: £18 per round weekdays, £24 per day. £22 per round weekends, £30 per day. New Course: £10 per round/day.
CATERING: Yes. Bar.
FACILITIES: Practice ground.
LOCATION: North of town, off A952.
LOCAL HOTELS: Palace Hotel, Raemoir House Hotel, Simpson's Hotel, The White Horse Inn, Waterside Inn.

# PORTLETHEN

## PORTLETHEN GOLF CLUB

COURSE DESCRIPTION:
Rolling parkland course, which has several long-driving holes with water hazards. Founded in 1986.

18 holes, 6,707 yards, par 72 (SSS 72). Amateur record J. Murray 67 (1995). Pro record D. Vannet 62 (1996).

SIGNATURE HOLE:
EIGHTEENTH (506 yards, par 5) out of bounds left, with a burn crossing the fairway 140 yards short of the green.

### COURSE CARD

| HOLE | YDS | PAR | HOLE | YDS | PAR |
|------|-----|-----|------|-----|-----|
| 1 | 384 | 4 | 10 | 237 | 3 |

| 2 | 498 | 5 | 11 | 334 | 4 |
|---|-----|---|----|-----|---|
| 3 | 418 | 4 | 12 | 188 | 3 |
| 4 | 485 | 5 | 13 | 538 | 5 |
| 5 | 135 | 3 | 14 | 371 | 4 |
| 6 | 382 | 4 | 15 | 399 | 4 |
| 7 | 431 | 4 | 16 | 367 | 4 |
| 8 | 178 | 3 | 17 | 418 | 4 |
| 9 | 438 | 4 | 18 | 506 | 5 |
| *Yds* *Out* | 3,349 | | *Yds* *In* | 3,358 | |
| *Total* *Yds* | 6,707 | | | | |
| *Total* *Par* | 72 | | | | |

ADDRESS: Badentoy Road, Portlethen, Aberdeenshire AB12 4YA.
TELEPHONE & FAX: +44 (0)1224 781090.
SECRETARY: B. Mole.
PROFESSIONAL: Muriel Thomson +44 (0)1224 782571.
VISITORS: Yes. Weekdays 9.30 to 4.30 p.m. Saturdays as available. Sundays after 1 p.m.
GREEN FEES: £15 per round weekdays, £22 per day. £22 per round weekends, £31 per day. Advance booking advised.
CATERING: Yes, full clubhouse facilities. Bar.
FACILITIES: Trolley hire, putting green, pro shop, practice ground.
LOCATION: 6 miles south of Aberdeen on A90.
LOCAL HOTELS: Aberdeen Patio Hotel, The White Horse Inn.

# ROSEHEARTY

## ROSEHEARTY GOLF CLUB

COURSE DESCRIPTION: Very tricky, tight links course which demands straight hitting with out-of-bounds on almost every hole. Starts with a difficult 188-yard par 3. Course very seldom played to par.

9 holes, 4,394 yards (for 18 holes), par 62 (SSS 62).

ADDRESS: Castle Street, Rosehearty, Aberdeenshire AB43 4JP.
TELEPHONE: +44 (0)1346 571250.
VISITORS: Any time.
GREEN FEES: £10 per day weekdays; £12 weekends.
FACILITIES: Pro shop, changing-rooms, club hire.
CATERING: via Masons Arms Hotel.
LOCATION: 3 miles north-west of Fraserburgh.

LOCAL HOTELS: Mason Arms Hotel.

# ROTHES

## ROTHES GOLF CLUB

### COURSE DESCRIPTION:

Constructed in 1990 from derelict farmland, this moorland course has magnificent views over the River Spey and Rothes Castle from its elevated position between woodland and a distillery. Challenging for all abilities.

9 holes, 4,972 yards (for 18 holes), par 68 (SSS 65).

### SIGNATURE HOLE:

SIXTH (145 yards, par 3) Although one of the shortest holes, it is very close to a steep drop into the valley. Narrow green. Accuracy rather than power is required.

### COURSE CARD

| HOLE | YDS | PAR |
|------|-----|-----|
| 1 | 345 | 4 |
| 2 | 306 | 4 |
| 3 | 372 | 4 |
| 4 | 116 | 3 |
| 5 | 404 | 4 |
| 6 | 145 | 3 |
| 7 | 290 | 4 |
| 8 | 252 | 4 |
| 9 | 256 | 4 |
| Yds Out | 2,486 | |
| Total Yds | 2,486 | |
| Total Par | 34 | |

ADDRESS: Blackhall, Rothes, Moray AB38 7AN.
TELEPHONE: +44 (0)1340 831443.
SECRETARY: J. Tilley +44 (0)1340 831277.
VISITORS: Yes, weekdays. Weekends by arrangement.
GREEN FEES: £12 per day weekdays; £15 weekends.
CATERING: By arrangement for parties only. Bar.
LOCATION: 9 miles south of Elgin on A941. Turn off at Glen Spey Distillery entrance.
LOCAL HOTELS: Benaigen Hotel, Craigellachie Hotel, Eastbank Hotel, Rothes Glen Hotel, Sunninghill Hotel.

# STONEHAVEN

## STONEHAVEN GOLF CLUB

**COURSE DESCRIPTION:**
Parkland course with three gullies, founded in 1888. It is set on cliffs overlooking Stonehaven Bay and affords magnificent views over the North Sea and along the coast. When in the area visit the spectacular Dunnottar Castle.

18 holes, 5,103 yards, par 66 (SSS 65). Amateur record R. Forbes, F. McCarron 61.

**SIGNATURE HOLE:**
FIFTEENTH (161 yards, par 3) A very challenging hole which is all carry over a gully 75 feet deep to a well-bunkered green with gorse on the left. Club selection can vary due to wind conditions.

**COURSE CARD**

| HOLE | YDS | PAR | HOLE | YDS | PAR |
|------|-----|-----|------|-----|-----|
| 1 | 305 | 4 | 10 | 329 | 4 |
| 2 | 203 | 3 | 11 | 272 | 4 |
| 3 | 331 | 4 | 12 | 416 | 4 |
| 4 | 364 | 4 | 13 | 252 | 4 |
| 5 | 376 | 4 | 14 | 169 | 3 |
| 6 | 190 | 3 | 15 | 161 | 3 |
| 7 | 170 | 3 | 16 | 482 | 5 |
| 8 | 159 | 3 | 17 | 315 | 4 |
| 9 | 398 | 4 | 18 | 211 | 3 |
| *Yds Out* | 2,496 | | *Yds In* | 2,607 | |
| *Total Yds* | 5,103 | | | | |
| *Total Par* | 66 | | | | |

**ADDRESS:** Cowie, Stonehaven, AB39 3RH.
**TELEPHONE:** +44 (0)1569 762124.
**FAX:** +44 (0) 1569 765973.
**VISITORS:** Yes, except Saturdays.
**GREEN FEES:** £15 weekdays. £20 weekends.
**CATERING:** Full catering facilities.
**FACILITIES:** Trolleys, putting green, practice ground.
**LOCATION:** North of the town.

LOCAL HOTELS: County Hotel, Crown Hotel, Heugh Hotel, Raemoir House Hotel, Station Hotel.

# TARLAND

## TARLAND GOLF CLUB

### COURSE DESCRIPTION:
An exceptional parkland course, founded in 1908 and designed by Old Tom Morris in a beautiful natural setting. Lengthened recently. Easy walking but very difficult. A reputation for always being maintained in the best condition.
9 holes, 5,875 yards (for 18 holes), par 67 (SSS 68). Course record 65.

### SIGNATURE HOLE:
FIRST (309 yards, par 4) Looks an easy start but you must drive straight. Have to be careful with your approach as you could roll through into a large bunker.

### COURSE CARD

| HOLE | YDS | PAR | HOLE | YDS | PAR |
|------|-----|-----|------|-----|-----|
| 1 | 309 | 4 | 10 | 311 | 4 |
| 2 | 350 | 4 | 11 | 350 | 4 |
| 3 | 171 | 3 | 12 | 221 | 3 |
| 4 | 373 | 4 | 13 | 379 | 4 |
| 5 | 236 | 4 | 14 | 208 | 3 |
| 6 | 450 | 4 | 15 | 415 | 4 |
| 7 | 172 | 3 | 16 | 211 | 3 |
| 8 | 437 | 4 | 17 | 486 | 5 |
| 9 | 398 | 4 | 18 | 398 | 4 |
| *Yds Out* | 2,896 | | *Yds In* | 2,979 | |
| *Total Yds* | 5,875 | | | | |
| *Total Par* | 67 | | | | |

ADDRESS: Aberdeen Road, Tarland, Aberdeenshire AB34 4TB.
TELEPHONE: +44 (0)1339 881000.
SECRETARY: Mrs L. O. Ward.
VISITORS: Yes, but check availability at weekends.
GREEN FEES: £14 per day weekdays. £18 per day weekends.
CATERING: Bar and lunches.
FACILITIES: Trolley hire(£2), changing-rooms, putting green, membership available, practice ground.
LOCATION: 5 miles north of Aboyne, off B9119.
LOCAL HOTELS: Aberdeen Arms Hotel, Callater Lodge, Commercial Hotel, Glen Lui

Hotel, Raemoir House Hotel, Stakis Craigendarroch Hotel & Country Club.

# TORPHINS

## TORPHINS GOLF CLUB

COURSE DESCRIPTION:
Hilly inland parkland course with some blind holes and magnificent views of the Highlands. Excellent greens.
9 holes, 4,738 yards (for 18 holes), par 64 (SSS 64). Course record 63.

ADDRESS: Bog Road, Torphins, Aberdeenshire AB31 4JU.
TELEPHONE: +44 (0)1339 882115 or 882402.
FAX: +44 (0) 1339 882402.
E-MAIL: stuart@macgregor.fsnet.co.uk
SECRETARY: Stuart MacGregor.
VISITORS: Weekdays and weekends on non-competition days.
GREEN FEES: £12 per round/day weekdays; £14 per round/day weekends.
CATERING: Meals at weekends only. No bar.
FACILITIES: Changing-rooms, putting green, membership available.
LOCATION: 1½ miles west of Torphins towards Lumphanan. Signpost to the right.
LOCAL HOTELS: Callater Lodge, Learney Arms Hotel, Raemoir House Hotel, Stakis Craigendarroch Hotel & Country Club.

# TURRIFF

## TURRIFF GOLF CLUB

COURSE DESCRIPTION:
Parkland course alongside River Deveron. Founded in 1896.
18 holes, 6,145 yards, par 69 (SSS 68). Course record 63.

ADDRESS: Rosehall, Aberdeenshire AB53 7HB.
TELEPHONE: +44 (0)1888 562982.
PROFESSIONAL: Robin Smith +44 (0)1888 563025.
VISITORS: Not before 10 a.m. at weekends. Contact in advance. Handicap certificates required.
GREEN FEES: £16 per round weekdays, £20 per day. £21 per round weekends, £27 per day.
CATERING: Bar.
FACILITIES: Trolley hire, putting green, pro shop, practice ground.
LOCATION: 1 mile west off B9024.
LOCAL HOTELS: Union Hotel, White Heather Hotel.

# TAYSIDE INCLUDING DUNDEE AND PERTH

# ABERFELDY

## ABERFELDY GOLF CLUB

### COURSE DESCRIPTION:
Founded in 1895, this is a pleasant, flat parkland course set on the north and south banks of the River Tay, incorporating some of the best scenery of highland Perthshire. Tricky but not too demanding a test.

18 holes, 5,283 yards, par 68 (SSS 66). Amateur record 62.

### SIGNATURE HOLE:
THIRTEENTH ('Waterloo' 309 yards, par 4) Sharp dogleg to the right. A 4-iron and wedge for the cautious or a driver to carry the trees for the brave – but beware, the Tay awaits a slice.

### COURSE CARD

| HOLE | MEDAL YDS | PAR | FORWARD YDS | PAR | LADIES YDS | PAR | HOLE | MEDAL YDS | PAR | FORWARD YDS | PAR | LADIES YDS | PAR |
|------|-----------|-----|-------------|-----|------------|-----|------|-----------|-----|-------------|-----|------------|-----|
| 1 | 229 | 3 | 170 | 3 | 223 | 4 | 10 | 174 | 3 | 164 | 3 | 169 | 3 |
| 2 | 337 | 4 | 276 | 4 | 333 | 4 | 11 | 305 | 4 | 293 | 4 | 300 | 4 |
| 3 | 382 | 4 | 376 | 4 | 379 | 5 | 12 | 309 | 4 | 291 | 4 | 254 | 4 |
| 4 | 515 | 5 | 492 | 5 | 501 | 5 | 13 | 309 | 4 | 299 | 4 | 304 | 4 |
| 5 | 335 | 4 | 316 | 4 | 323 | 4 | 14 | 163 | 3 | 157 | 3 | 106 | 3 |
| 6 | 280 | 4 | 269 | 4 | 275 | 4 | 15 | 289 | 4 | 238 | 4 | 240 | 4 |
| 7 | 142 | 3 | 111 | 3 | 116 | 3 | 16 | 363 | 4 | 349 | 4 | 360 | 4 |
| 8 | 308 | 4 | 297 | 4 | 303 | 4 | 17 | 367 | 4 | 356 | 4 | 365 | 4 |
| 9 | 361 | 4 | 349 | 4 | 355 | 4 | 18 | 115 | 3 | 100 | 3 | 108 | 3 |
| Yds Out | 2,889 | | 2,656 | | 2,808 | | Yds In | 2,394 | | 2,247 | | 2,206 | |
| Total Yds | 5,283 | | 4,903 | | 5,014 | | | | | | | | |
| Total Par | 68 | | 67 | | 70 | | | | | | | | |

ADDRESS: Taybridge Road, Aberfeldy, Perthshire, PH15 2BH.
TELEPHONE & FAX: +44 (0)1887 820535.
SECRETARY: Peter Woolley.
VISITORS: Very welcome all year round.
GREEN FEES: £16 per round weekdays, £26 per day. £21 per round weekends, £29 per day.
CREDIT CARDS ACCEPTED: Visa/Mastercard.
CATERING: Bar and meals.
FACILITIES: Motorised buggies, trolley hire, club hire, changing-rooms, putting green,

memberships available.

LOCATION: Take B846 north for about a ¼ mile from the main crossroads in Aberfeldy. Course is on the edge of town.

LOCAL HOTELS: Ballathie House Hotel, Balrobin Hotel, Bendarroch House Hotel, Crown Hotel, Kinloch House Hotel, Palace Hotel, The Poplars.

# ABERUTHVEN

## WHITEMOSS GOLF CLUB

COURSE DESCRIPTION:
Opened in 1994, the course has matured to become an interesting and challenging test of golf, with five par 3s and two par 5s. Lying in the heart of beautiful Perthshire countryside, it is ideal for the beginner or experienced player.

18 holes, 5,968 yards, par 69 (SSS 69).

SIGNATURE HOLE:
SIXTEENTH ('Agricola's Urn' 147 yards, par 3) The course is built on ground steeped in history and around this hole relics from Roman times have been found.

### COURSE CARD

| HOLE | MEDAL YDS | PAR | FORWARD YDS | PAR | LADIES YDS | PAR | HOLE | MEDAL YDS | PAR | FORWARD YDS | PAR | LADIES YDS | PAR |
|------|-----------|-----|-------------|-----|------------|-----|------|-----------|-----|-------------|-----|------------|-----|
| 1 | 420 | 4 | 416 | 4 | 412 | 5 | 10 | 200 | 3 | 197 | 3 | 195 | 3 |
| 2 | 199 | 3 | 193 | 3 | 189 | 3 | 11 | 381 | 4 | 369 | 4 | 346 | 4 |
| 3 | 448 | 5 | 438 | 5 | 403 | 5 | 12 | 411 | 4 | 407 | 3 | 378 | 4 |
| 4 | 162 | 3 | 160 | 3 | 132 | 3 | 13 | 202 | 3 | 197 | 3 | 189 | 3 |
| 5 | 377 | 4 | 368 | 4 | 359 | 4 | 14 | 275 | 4 | 256 | 4 | 238 | 4 |
| 6 | 366 | 4 | 342 | 4 | 318 | 4 | 15 | 368 | 4 | 332 | 4 | 305 | 4 |
| 7 | 383 | 4 | 361 | 4 | 356 | 4 | 16 | 147 | 3 | 145 | 3 | 143 | 3 |
| 8 | 348 | 4 | 315 | 4 | 313 | 4 | 17 | 358 | 4 | 355 | 4 | 353 | 4 |
| 9 | 617 | 5 | 588 | 5 | 427 | 5 | 18 | 306 | 4 | 302 | 4 | 295 | 4 |
| Yds Out | 3,320 | | 3,181 | | 2,909 | | Yds In | 2,648 | | 2,560 | | 2,442 | |
| Total Yds | 5,968 | | 5,741 | | 5,351 | | | | | | | | | |
| Total Par | 69 | | 69 | | 71 | | | | | | | | | |

ADDRESS: Whitemoss Road, Aberuthven PH2 0QX.

TELEPHONE & FAX: +44 (0)1738 730300.

SECRETARY: V. Westwood.

VISITORS: Yes.

GREEN FEES: £15 per round, £20 per day.

CATERING: All meals – homemade food and baking.

FACILITIES: Trolley hire, practice range, green/chipping area, practice net.
LOCATION: ½ mile from A9, 10 miles south of Perth, 20 miles north of Stirling.
LOCAL HOTELS: Balrobin Hotel, Breadalbane Hotel, Croft-na-caber Hotel, Crown Hotel, Guinach House Hotel, Meness Country Club, Newton House Hotel, Palace Hotel, Parklands Hotel & Restaurant, Queens Hotel, Tayside Hotel, The Gleneagles Hotel.

# ALYTH

## GLENISLA GOLF CENTRE

### COURSE DESCRIPTION:
Set amidst 180 acres of beautiful, undulating parkland in Perthshire, the course features more than 40 bunkers and five water hazards. All holes are of modern design and complement each other to create an attractive golfing environment.

18 holes, 6,402 yards, par 71 (SSS 71). Amateur record J.White 66. Pro record Andrew Crerar 64.

### SIGNATURE HOLE:
EIGHTEENTH ('Lindsay's Hame' 342 yards, par 4) Fronted by the Alyth Burn, which makes the second shot daunting. A great finishing hole with the clubhouse behind offering panoramic views

ADDRESS: Pitcrocknie, Alyth, near Blairgowrie PH11 8JJ.
TELEPHONE: +44 (0)1828 632445.
FAX: +44 (0)1828 633749.
E-MAIL: info@golf-glenisla.co.uk
WEBSITE: www.golf-glenisla.co.uk
GOLF ADMINISTRATOR: Ewan Wilson.
VISITORS: Yes, welcome seven days a week by arrangement.
GREEN FEES: £22 per round weekdays, £33 per day. £26 per round weekends, £39 per day. Composite tickets available with nearby Alyth and Strathmore courses.
CREDIT CARDS ACCEPTED: Visa/Mastercard/Diners Club.
CATERING: Restaurant and bar open all day. Functions and conferences catered for. Glenisla also has B&B and self-catering cottages overlooking the course.
FACILITIES: Motorised buggies (£15 per round), trolley hire (£2 per round, £3 per day), club hire (£10), caddies on request, changing-rooms, putting green, pro shop, memberships available.
LOCATION: B954 by Alyth, 15 miles north-east of Dundee, 20 miles north-west of Perth.
LOCAL HOTELS: Airlie Arms Hotel, Alyth Hotel, Ballathie House Hotel, Carlogie House Hotel, Parklands Hotel & Restaurant, Queens Hotel, Tayside Hotel, The Poplars (Hotel).

# STRATHMORE GOLF CENTRE

## COURSE DESCRIPTION:
*Rannaleroch Course* – Opened in 1996. Challenging but forgiving with generous fairways and good greens. Rolling parkland with views over the valley of Strathmore.

18 holes, 6,454 yards, par 72 (SSS 72). Course record 68 (men), 73 (ladies).
*Leiftie Links* – Ideal for beginners or older golfers.

9 holes, 1,666 yards, par 29 (SSS 29).

## SIGNATURE HOLE:
SIXTH (122 yards, par 3) A challenging short hole.

## COURSE CARD

| HOLE | MEDAL YDS | PAR | FORWARD YDS | PAR | LADIES YDS | PAR | HOLE | MEDAL YDS | PAR | FORWARD YDS | PAR | LADIES YDS | PAR |
|---|---|---|---|---|---|---|---|---|---|---|---|---|---|
| 1 | 514 | 5 | 484 | 5 | 463 | 5 | 10 | 286 | 4 | 272 | 4 | 257 | 4 |
| 2 | 361 | 4 | 326 | 4 | 307 | 4 | 11 | 313 | 4 | 280 | 4 | 259 | 4 |
| 3 | 337 | 4 | 301 | 4 | 279 | 4 | 12 | 547 | 5 | 496 | 5 | 475 | 5 |
| 4 | 188 | 3 | 173 | 3 | 156 | 3 | 13 | 159 | 3 | 145 | 3 | 130 | 3 |
| 5 | 468 | 4 | 400 | 4 | 386 | 4 | 14 | 469 | 4 | 433 | 4 | 409 | 5 |
| 6 | 122 | 3 | 111 | 3 | 98 | 3 | 15 | 337 | 4 | 323 | 4 | 307 | 4 |
| 7 | 399 | 4 | 367 | 4 | 347 | 4 | 16 | 341 | 4 | 326 | 4 | 314 | 4 |
| 8 | 450 | 4 | 394 | 4 | 380 | 4 | 17 | 224 | 4 | 198 | 3 | 189 | 3 |
| 9 | 414 | 4 | 379 | 4 | 360 | 4 | 18 | 525 | 5 | 440 | 4 | 423 | 5 |
| Yds Out | 3,253 | | 2,935 | | 2,776 | | Yds In | 3,201 | | 2,913 | | 2,763 | |
| Total Yds | 6,454 | | 5,848 | | 5,539 | | | | | | | | | |
| Total Par | 72 | | 70 | | 72 | | | | | | | | | |

ADDRESS: Leroch, Alyth, Blairgowrie, Perthshire PH11 8NZ.
TELEPHONE: +44 (0)1828 633322.
FAX: +44 (0)1828 633533.
E-MAIL: enquiries@strathmoregolf.com
WEBSITE: www.strathmoregolf.com
SECRETARY/MANAGER: Jane Taylor/Jeremy Barron.
PROFESSIONAL: Colin Smith.
VISITORS: Yes, always welcome.
GREEN FEES: *Rannaleroch*: £20 per round weekdays, £30 per day. £25 per round weekends, £37.50 per day. Midweek 5-day ticket, £90. Weekly ticket, £120.
    *Leitfie*: £8 per day weekdays, £10 per day weekends.
CREDIT CARDS ACCEPTED: Visa/Mastercard.
CATERING: Restaurant and bar. Functions catered for.
FACILITIES: Motorised buggies (£20), trolley hire (£2), club hire (£8), changing-rooms, putting green, pro shop, practice ground, floodlit driving range,

coaching clinics, memberships available (from £295).

**LOCATION:** 2 miles off A926 Blairgowrie–Alyth road, 2 miles west of Alyth.

**LOCAL HOTELS:** Airlie Arms Hotel, Alyth Hotel, Ballathie House Hotel, Carlogie House Hotel, Kinloch House Hotel, Queens Hotel, Tayside Hotel, The Poplars (Hotel).

## THE ALYTH GOLF CLUB

### COURSE DESCRIPTION:
Precision golf required on this heathland course with tricky rollercoaster greens set within pines, silver birch and heather. In this tranquil setting it is easy to lose yourself in a layout so conceived that you barely notice other groups of golfers. Designed by James Braid and founded in 1894.

18 holes, 6,205 yards, par 70 (SSS 71). Amateur record Mark Cameron 64. Pro record Ian Young 64.

### SIGNATURE HOLE:
FIFTH (325 yards, par 4) A difficult par 4 with out of bounds on the right. A dogleg with criss-cross burn leaving a second shot to plateau green with out of bounds at the rear.

### COURSE CARD

| HOLE | YDS | PAR | HOLE | YDS | PAR |
|------|------|-----|------|-------|-----|
| 1 | 398 | 4 | 10 | 436 | 4 |
| 2 | 417 | 4 | 11 | 504 | 5 |
| 3 | 155 | 3 | 12 | 308 | 4 |
| 4 | 368 | 4 | 13 | 318 | 4 |
| 5 | 325 | 4 | 14 | 198 | 3 |
| 6 | 388 | 4 | 15 | 446 | 4 |
| 7 | 130 | 3 | 16 | 545 | 5 |
| 8 | 255 | 4 | 17 | 202 | 3 |
| 9 | 456 | 4 | 18 | 356 | 4 |
| *Yds Out* | 2,892 | | *Yds In* | 3,313 | |
| *Total Yds* | 6,205 | | | | |
| *Total Par* | 70 | | | | |

**ADDRESS:** Pitcrocknie, Alyth, Perthshire PH11 8HF.

**TELEPHONE:** +44 (0)1828 632268.

**FAX:** +44 (0)1828 633491.

**E-MAIL:** mansec@alythgolfclub.co.uk

**WEBSITE:** www.alythgolfclub.co.uk

**MANAGING SECRETARY:** Jim Docherty.

**PROFESSIONAL:** Tom Melville.

**VISITORS:** Most days.

**GREEN FEES:** £22 per round weekdays, £33 per day. £30 per round weekends, £45 per day.

**CATERING:** Full range from bar snacks to dinner.

**FACILITIES:** Motorised buggies, trolley hire, club hire, caddies on request, changing-rooms, putting green, pro shop, practice ground, driving range, coaching clinics, waiting list of memberships.

**LOCATION:** From Glasgow/Edinburgh, motorway to Perth. Follow signs to Coupar Angus then to Meigle/Forfar. Signposted from there on. From Aberdeen, follow A90 to Forfar turn-off and turn right, signposted Coupar Angus.

**LOCAL HOTELS:** Airlie Arms Hotel, Alyth Hotel, Ballathie House Hotel, Carlogie House Hotel, Kinloch House Hotel, Lands of Loyal Hotel, Parklands Hotel & Restaurant, Queens Hotel, Tayside Hotel, The Poplars (Hotel).

# ARBROATH

## ARBROATH LINKS GOLF COURSE

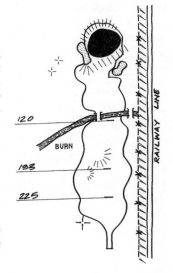

### COURSE DESCRIPTION:

Testing links course, designed by James Braid, with heavily sand-trapped, undulating greens. Flat fairways. The strong holes are in the back nine where the 12th has a difficult approach shot if you are coming in from the right. There's the 13th (see below) and the 14th is a very good par 3 with large bunkers to the front and water beyond the green.

18 holes, 6,185 yards, par 70 (SSS 70). Amateur record 64. Pro record 66.

### SIGNATURE HOLE:

THIRTEENTH ('Dowrie' 412 yards, par 4) Railway line and out of bounds down the right. A burn crosses the fairway 120 yards from the green, leaving a tricky second shot to the smallest green on the course.

### COURSE CARD

| HOLE | MEDAL YDS | PAR | FORWARD YDS | PAR | LADIES YDS | PAR | HOLE | MEDAL YDS | PAR | FORWARD YDS | PAR | LADIES YDS | PAR |
|------|-----------|-----|-------------|-----|------------|-----|------|-----------|-----|-------------|-----|------------|-----|
| 1 | 367 | 4 | 360 | 4 | 347 | 4 | 10 | 407 | 4 | 399 | 4 | 406 | 5 |
| 2 | 481 | 5 | 444 | 4 | 401 | 5 | 11 | 326 | 4 | 313 | 4 | 309 | 4 |
| 3 | 348 | 4 | 334 | 4 | 289 | 4 | 12 | 316 | 4 | 290 | 4 | 269 | 4 |
| 4 | 166 | 3 | 153 | 3 | 114 | 3 | 13 | 412 | 4 | 368 | 4 | 363 | 4 |
| 5 | 405 | 4 | 389 | 4 | 341 | 4 | 14 | 239 | 3 | 200 | 3 | 189 | 3 |
| 6 | 375 | 4 | 364 | 4 | 348 | 4 | 15 | 355 | 4 | 343 | 4 | 318 | 4 |

| 7 | 159 | 3 | 155 | 3 | 135 | 3 | 16 | 182 | 3 | 151 | 3 | 128 | 3 |
| 8 | 372 | 4 | 354 | 4 | 326 | 4 | 17 | 495 | 5 | 447 | 4 | 406 | 5 |
| 9 | 373 | 4 | 363 | 4 | 335 | 4 | 18 | 407 | 4 | 399 | 4 | 360 | 4 |
| Yds Out | 3,046 | | 2,916 | | 2,636 | | Yds In | 3,139 | | 2,910 | | 2,748 | |
| Total Yds | 6,185 | | 5,826 | | 5,384 | | | | | | | | |
| Total Par | 70 | | 68 | | 71 | | | | | | | | |

ADDRESS: Elliot, Dundee Road, Arbroath, Angus DD11 2PE.
TELEPHONE & FAX: +44 (0)1241 875837.
E-MAIL: golfshop@fsmail.net
SECRETARY: Rab Crawford.
PROFESSIONAL: Lindsay Ewart.
VISITORS: All week. Starting times bookable at weekends.
GREEN FEES: £18 per round weekdays, £24 per day. £24 per round weekends, £32 per day.
CREDIT CARDS ACCEPTED: Visa/Mastercard/Diners Club.
CATERING: Restaurant and bar. Functions for members and guests catered for. 120-seater clubhouse with showers and locker rooms.
FACILITIES: Trolley hire, club hire, changing-rooms, putting green, pro shop, practice ground, coaching clinics, memberships available.
LOCATION: A92 Dundee road to Arbroath heading north. Before Elliot turn right.
LOCAL HOTELS: Airlie Arms Hotel, Carlogie House Hotel, Cliffburn Hotel, Five Gables Hotel, Letham Grange Hotel, Rosely Country House Hotel, Seaforth Hotel, Viewfield Hotel.

# LETHAM GRANGE HOTEL & GOLF COURSE

COURSE DESCRIPTION:
An open parkland championship course, often referred to as the Augusta of Scotland, wooded with water hazards.
*Old Course* – 18 holes, 6,632 yards, par 73 (SSS 73). Course record 68.
*Glens* – Open parkland. 18 holes, 5,528 yards, par 68 (SSS 68). Course record 63.

ADDRESS: Letham Grange, Colliston, Arbroath DD11 4RL.
TELEPHONE: +44 (0)1241 890373.
FAX: +44 (0)1241 890725.
E-MAIL: lethamgrange@sol.co.uk
WEBSITE: lethamgrange.co.uk
VISITORS: No visitors at weekends before 9.30 a.m.; Old Course before 10 a.m. on Tuesdays; and Glens before 10 a.m. on Fridays.
GREEN FEES: Old Course: £40 per round weekdays, £45 per day. £45 per round weekends, £55 per day. Glens: £18 per round weekdays, £25 per day. £23 per round weekends, £28 per day. Combination of one round on each course £40

(Monday to Friday), £45 weekends.

CREDIT CARDS ACCEPTED: Amex/Visa/Mastercard/Diners Club.

CATERING: Restaurant and bar. Meals should be booked in advance. Functions catered for.

FACILITIES: Motorised buggies, trolley hire, club hire, changing-rooms, putting green, pro shop, practice ground, coaching clinics, memberships available.

LOCATION: 4 miles north of Arbroath on A933.

LOCAL HOTELS: Letham Grange Hotel, Airlie Arms Hotel, Carlogie House Hotel, Cliffburn Hotel, Rosely Country House Hotel, Seaforth Hotel, Viewfield Hotel.

# AUCHTERARDER

## AUCHTERARDER GOLF CLUB

COURSE DESCRIPTION:

Flat parkland course, part woodland with fine examples of pine, larch and silver birch. Adjacent to the more famous Gleneagles, but with a character all of its own. Short it may be, but it can be tricky, with cunning doglegs and guarded greens meaning that accuracy brings more rewards than sheer power. With great views across to Glendevon, it has an attractive wooded stretch from the 6th to the 13th.

18 holes, 5,775 yards, par 69 (SSS 68). Course record 64.

SIGNATURE HOLE:

FOURTEENTH (211 yards, par 3) Auchterarder has four par 3s on the back nine but the 'Punchbowl', if not the longest, is perhaps the trickiest. A blind tee shot needs to be hit accurately over the left edge of the cross bunker to a long and narrow green. Miss the target and you face a difficult downhill chip shot from deep rough.

COURSE CARD

| HOLE | YDS | PAR | HOLE | YDS | PAR |
|------|-----|-----|------|-----|-----|
| 1 | 380 | 4 | 10 | 359 | 4 |
| 2 | 303 | 4 | 11 | 339 | 4 |
| 3 | 343 | 4 | 12 | 167 | 3 |
| 4 | 142 | 3 | 13 | 291 | 4 |
| 5 | 406 | 4 | 14 | 211 | 3 |
| 6 | 476 | 5 | 15 | 513 | 5 |
| 7 | 365 | 4 | 16 | 225 | 3 |
| 8 | 151 | 3 | 17 | 438 | 4 |
| 9 | 478 | 5 | 18 | 188 | 3 |
| *Yds* *Out* | 3,044 | | *Yds* *In* | 2,731 | |
| *Total* *Yds* | 5,775 | | | | |

| Total | 69 |
|-------|-----|
| Par | |

ADDRESS: Orchil Road, Auchterarder PH3 1LS.
TELEPHONE & FAX: +44 (0)1764 662804.
SECRETARY: W. Campbell.
PROFESSIONAL: Gavin Baxter +44 (0)1764 663711.
VISITORS: Weekdays and weekends. Restricted on Sundays and competition days.
GREEN FEES: £20 per round weekdays, £28 per day. £25 per round weekends, £36 per day.
CATERING: Full catering and bar.
FACILITIES: Trolley hire, putting green, pro shop, practice ground.
LOCATION: A9 to south-west of town.
LOCAL HOTELS: Cairn Lodge, Colliearn House Hotel, Duchally Hotel, Gleneagles Hotel.

# THE GLENEAGLES HOTEL GOLF COURSES

## COURSE DESCRIPTION:

One of the foremost golfing centres in the country, offering three championship, undulating moorland courses set alongside this five-star hotel. The courses were the inspiration of five-times Open champion James Braid (King's and Queen's) and probably the greatest golfer ever Jack Nicklaus (PGA Centenary). Surrounded by the Grampian Mountains, the Trossachs and the Ochil Hills, the views are spectacular.

*PGA Centenary Course* – American-style championship course, which staged the 2001 Scottish PGA Championship. From the championship tees, it measures 7,088 yards, the longest inland course in Scotland. There are five tees at each hole making it a fair test for all abilities. Fittingly, the course, formally known as the Monarch's begins by playing south-east towards the glen sweeping up the Ochil Hills to the summit of the pass below Ben Shee which joins it to Glendevon. Everywhere there are spectacular views.

18 holes, 6,559 yards (medal), par 72 (SSS 73).

*King's Course* – Opened in 1919, it is one of the most beautiful courses in Scotland, with springy moorland turf and holes that require a combination of thought and skill. The 17th is appropriately named 'Warslin' Lea' (Wrestling Ground), which just about sums up the problems many golfers have with this long par 4.

18 holes, 6,471 yards, par 70 (SSS 73).

*Queen's Course* – A challenging course which threads through high ridges on the north and west sides of Gleneagles and offers woodland settings, lochans and ditches as water hazards. At 3,192 yards, the first nine can be deceptive with a fresh south-westerly breeze making par difficult to achieve. Alan Shepard, the only man to hit a golf shot on the moon, has played here.

18 holes, 5,965 yards, par 68 (SSS 70).

*Wee Course* – 9 holes, par 27. A little light relief for beginners and experts alike. It recalls the original nine-hole course at Gleneagles, constructed in 1928 by the head greenkeeper, George Alexander, and staff from the hotel.

**SIGNATURE HOLE:**
PGA CENTENARY: SIXTEENTH ('Lochan Loup' 543 yards, par 5) The name means 'Leap over the small loch'. From the medal tee, it is 25 yards shorter but your second shot should be short of the loch and in a central position, leaving a short, middle-iron third shot. Don't be too aggressive here as you could be left with a nasty pitch back down to the green, which has a slight step in the back left corner and small undulations.

**PGA CENTENARY COURSE CARD**

| HOLE | MEDAL YDS | PAR | FORWARD YDS | PAR | LADIES YDS | PAR | HOLE | MEDAL YDS | PAR | FORWARD YDS | PAR | LADIES YDS | PAR |
|---|---|---|---|---|---|---|---|---|---|---|---|---|---|
| 1 | 394 | 4 | 363 | 4 | 349 | 4 | 10 | 190 | 3 | 160 | 3 | 145 | 3 |
| 2 | 501 | 5 | 472 | 5 | 456 | 5 | 11 | 326 | 4 | 307 | 4 | 276 | 4 |
| 3 | 388 | 4 | 369 | 4 | 318 | 4 | 12 | 484 | 5 | 470 | 5 | 425 | 5 |
| 4 | 211 | 3 | 187 | 3 | 177 | 3 | 13 | 436 | 4 | 417 | 4 | 392 | 4 |
| 5 | 423 | 4 | 386 | 4 | 360 | 4 | 14 | 178 | 3 | 160 | 3 | 146 | 3 |
| 6 | 176 | 3 | 160 | 3 | 160 | 3 | 15 | 436 | 4 | 404 | 4 | 375 | 4 |
| 7 | 358 | 4 | 338 | 4 | 329 | 4 | 16 | 518 | 5 | 490 | 5 | 440 | 5 |
| 8 | 342 | 4 | 316 | 4 | 277 | 4 | 17 | 179 | 3 | 167 | 3 | 144 | 3 |
| 9 | 535 | 5 | 505 | 5 | 505 | 5 | 18 | 484 | 5 | 470 | 5 | 429 | 5 |
| *Yds* Out | 3,328 | | 3,096 | | 2,931 | | *Yds* In | 3,231 | | 3,045 | | 2,773 | |
| *Total Yds* | 6,559 | | 6,141 | | 5,704 | | | | | | | | |
| *Total Par* | 72 | | 72 | | 72 | | | | | | | | |

**ADDRESS:** Gleneagles Hotel, Auchterarder, Perthshire PH3 1NF.
**TELEPHONE:** +44 (0)1764 662231. Freefone: 0800 704705 (UK only).
**FAX:** +44 (0)1764 662134.
**E-MAIL:** resort.sales@gleneagles.com
**WEBSITE:** www.gleneagles.com
**PROFESSIONAL:** Sandy Smith +44 (0)1764 694453.
**VISITORS:** All courses open to day visitors, hotel guests and members. Advisable to give as much notice as possible.
**GREEN FEES:** PGA Centenary, King's and Queen's: £110 per round. Wee Course: £25 per round.
**CATERING:** Full service and bar available at the Dormy Clubhouse Bar & Restaurant, which overlooks the 18th greens of the King's and Queen's courses.
**FACILITIES:** Motorised buggies available for PGA Centenary Course (£30), trolley hire (£5), club hire (£30 per round, £45 per day, for Wee Course £22), shoe hire (£15), putting green, pro shop, practice ground, driving range, caddies (£30).
**LOCATION:** 2 miles south-west of A823

LOCAL HOTELS: Gleneagles Hotel, Alyth Hotel, Ballathie House Hotel, Cairn Lodge, Colliearn House Hotel, Duchally Hotel, Kinloch House Hotel, Parklands Hotel & Restaurant, Queens Hotel, Tayside Hotel, The Sporting Laird Hotel.

# BARRY

## PANMURE GOLF CLUB

COURSE DESCRIPTION:
Traditional tight links course, established in 1845 and designed by St Andrews architect. Requires accuracy.

18 holes, 6,317 yards. SSS 71. Amateur record 66.

ADDRESS: Burnside Road, Barry, by Carnoustie DD7 7RT.
TELEPHONE: +44 (0)1241 855120.
FAX: +44 (0)1241 859737.
PROFESSIONAL: Neil Mackintosh +44 (0)1241 852460.
VISITORS: Any time, except after 4 p.m. Not Saturdays
GREEN FEES: £35 per round, £50 per day.
CATERING: Yes.
FACILITIES: Pro shop, practice ground.
LOCATION: 9 miles east of Dundee, 1 mile west of Carnoustie.
LOCAL HOTELS: Airlie Arms Hotel, Alyth Hotel, Ballathie House Hotel, Carlogie House Hotel, Kinloch House Hotel, Old Manor Hotel, Queens Hotel, Panmure Hotel, Rosely Country House Hotel, Station Hotel, The Sporting Laird Hotel, Woodlands Hotel.

# BLAIR ATHOLL

## BLAIR ATHOLL GOLF CLUB

COURSE DESCRIPTION:
Inland flat parkland course established in 1896. Easy walking. River runs by three holes.

9 holes, 6,246 yards (for 18 holes), par 69 (SSS 69). Course record 64.

ADDRESS: Blair Atholl, Perthshire PH18 5TG.
TELEPHONE: +44 (0)1796 481407.
SECRETARY: J. McGregor.
VISITORS: Any time
GREEN FEES: £13 per day, weekdays. £16 per day weekends.
CATERING: Yes. Bar.
FACILITIES: Trolley/buggy hire, practice ground.

LOCATION: Leave A9 north of Pitlochry at sign for Blair Atholl. Enter village and turn left at Tilt Hotel.
LOCATION: Atholl Arms Hotel, Balrobin Hotel, The Poplars (Hotel), Tilt Hotel.

# BLAIRGOWRIE

## BLAIRGOWRIE GOLF CLUB

COURSE DESCRIPTION:
Two wooded heathland courses – the Rosemount, founded in 1889, and the Lansdowne, founded 1974 – with pines, silver birch, gorse, broom and heather. In 1977 Greg Norman won his first European Tour event on the Rosemount. Also a nine-hole course.
  *Rosemount Course* – 18 holes, 6,588 yards, par 72 (SSS 72).
  *Lansdowne Course* – 18 holes, 6,895 yards, par 72 (SSS 73).
  *Wee Course* – 9 holes, 4,654 yards (for 18 holes), par 64 (SSS 63).

ADDRESS: Golf Course Road, Rosemount, Blairgowrie PH10 6LG.
TELEPHONE: +44 (0)1250 872622.
FAX: +44 (0)1250 875451.
PROFESSIONAL: Charles Dernie +44 (0)1250 873116.
VISITORS: Contact in advance. Must have handicap certificate. Restricted Wednesdays, Fridays and weekends.
GREEN FEES: *Rosemount*: £50 per round weekdays, £55 per round weekends.
  *Lansdowne:* £40 per round weekdays, £45 per round weekends.
  *Wee Course:* £20 per day.
CATERING: Full service. Bar +44 (0)1250 875527.
FACILITIES: Putting green, pro shop, practice ground.
LOCATION: 2 miles south of A93.
LOCAL HOTELS: Airlie Arms Hotel, Altamount House Hotel, Alyth Hotel, Angus Hotel, Ballathie House Hotel, Balrobin Hotel, Bendarroch House Hotel, Callater Lodge, Carlogie House Hotel, Kinloch House Hotel, Moorfield House Hotel, Newton House Hotel, Parklands Hotel & Restaurant, Queens Hotel, Royal Hotel, Tayside Hotel, The Poplars (Hotel).

# BRECHIN

## BRECHIN GOLF CLUB

COURSE DESCRIPTION:
Excellent parkland course with superb views of the Grampian Hills. Scenic and relatively flat. A good test of golf. Founded in 1893 and designed by James Braid.
  18 holes, 6,096 yards, par 72 (SSS 70).

SIGNATURE HOLE:

EIGHTH ('Wee Well' 301 yards, par 4) You have a choice of playing over a row of trees between the tee and the green or through a gap. The green is on two levels and there is out of bounds to the left.

COURSE CARD

| HOLE | MEDAL YDS | PAR | FORWARD YDS | PAR | LADIES YDS | PAR | HOLE | MEDAL YDS | PAR | FORWARD YDS | PAR | LADIES YDS | PAR |
|---|---|---|---|---|---|---|---|---|---|---|---|---|---|
| 1 | 429 | 4 | 407 | 4 | 395 | 4 | 10 | 172 | 3 | 170 | 3 | 170 | 3 |
| 2 | 317 | 4 | 306 | 4 | 297 | 4 | 11 | 282 | 4 | 259 | 4 | 251 | 4 |
| 3 | 129 | 3 | 120 | 3 | 120 | 3 | 12 | 259 | 4 | 201 | 3 | 201 | 4 |
| 4 | 492 | 5 | 430 | 4 | 420 | 5 | 13 | 215 | 3 | 206 | 3 | 197 | 3 |
| 5 | 183 | 3 | 168 | 3 | 128 | 3 | 14 | 486 | 5 | 450 | 4 | 447 | 5 |
| 6 | 389 | 4 | 358 | 4 | 348 | 4 | 15 | 429 | 4 | 417 | 4 | 363 | 4 |
| 7 | 487 | 5 | 472 | 5 | 419 | 5 | 16 | 494 | 5 | 479 | 5 | 445 | 5 |
| 8 | 301 | 4 | 288 | 4 | 242 | 4 | 17 | 277 | 4 | 264 | 4 | 260 | 4 |
| 9 | 437 | 4 | 348 | 4 | 339 | 4 | 18 | 318 | 4 | 294 | 4 | 279 | 4 |
| Yds Out | 3,164 | | 2,897 | | 2,708 | | Yds In | 2,932 | | 2,740 | | 2,613 | |
| Total Yds | 6,096 | | 5,637 | | 5,321 | | | | | | | | |
| Total Par | 72 | | 69 | | 72 | | | | | | | | |

ADDRESS: Trinity, by Brechin, Angus DD9 7PD.

TELEPHONE: +44 (0)1356 622383.

FAX: +44 (0)1356 626925.

SECRETARY: Ian Jardine.

PROFESSIONAL: Stephen Rennie +44 (0)1356 625270.

VISITORS: Yes.

GREEN FEES: £17 per round weekdays, £25 per day. £22 per round weekends, £30 per day. Midweek package: 2 rounds of golf, bacon roll, soup and sandwiches lunch and high tea, £28 (groups of 8 to 40).

CATERING: Restaurant and bar.

FACILITIES: Motorised buggies, trolley hire, club hire, changing-rooms, putting green, practice ground, pro shop, coaching clinics, memberships available.

LOCATION: Turn off A94 (Perth–Aberdeen road) at Brechin. Course is 1 mile from Brechin.

LOCAL HOTELS: Airlie Arms Hotel, Carlogie House Hotel, Glenesk Hotel, Kinloch House Hotel, Northern Hotel, Rosely Country House Hotel.

# CARNOUSTIE

## CARNOUSTIE GOLF LINKS – CHAMPIONSHIP COURSE

### COURSE DESCRIPTION:

In 1999 the Open Championship returned to Carnoustie and the course lived up to its reputation as the toughest links in the world. Most of the world's top players struggled to tame the 7,361-yard monster. Not since 1975 had the Open been held at Carnoustie and that year, Tom Watson came from nowhere to win. On its return it was perhaps fitting that a local hero, Paul Lawrie from Aberdeen, should win after a four-hole play-off with American Justin Leonard and France's Jean Van de Velde. Lawrie's winning score of 290 – six over par – is testimony to the degree of difficulty.

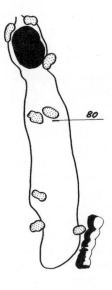

Carnoustie has been called the killer links and Walter Hagen described it as the greatest course in the British Isles. When the wind blows, it changes from a sleeping giant into a terror. Even from the club's medal tees, 6,941 yards, it is still formidable. Even before Lawrie's sensational win, Carnoustie's pedigree as an Open venue was without question, producing great champions in Tommy Armour (1931), Henry Cotton (1937), Ben Hogan (1953), Gary Player (1968) and Tom Watson (1975) – every one a great Championship.

Perhaps Player's triumph in 1968 – his second Open win – was the most spectacular. Under pressure from Billy Casper, Bob Charles and Jack Nicklaus by the par-5 14th, the little South African found himself behind the 'Spectacles', two large bunkers set in the face of a ridge that runs across the fairway less than 80 yards from the green. If ever he needed a good second shot, it was now. He struck a 3-wood. From where he played, he could not see the green and, as he scrambled up the bank, he heard a roar from the crowd. It was not until he reached the green that he saw he was only two feet from the hole. That gave him an eagle three and, more importantly, the advantage to win.

Armour's victory in 1931 was a popular one because he was a Scot who had emigrated to America. Henry Cotton saw off the victorious American Ryder Cup team for the second of his three Opens. The great Ben Hogan played in only one Open Championship – and won it at Carnoustie in foul weather with a final-round 68 which many regard as the true Carnoustie Open record (even though Jack Newton bettered it by three shots to force an 18-hole play-off with Watson in 1975). Each of Hogan's four rounds was lower than the one before.

As early as the sixteenth century, golf was played on the adjoining Barry links. There are now six clubs playing over the links, but the first official club was founded in 1842 when a tract of land was bought from the Earl of Dalhousie and ten holes were designed by Allan Robertson.

In 1867 Old Tom Morris extended it to 18 holes and Willie Park Jnr improved on it. But today's great test of golf is down to James Braid, who remodelled the course in 1926.

What is it that makes Carnoustie such a challenge to the very best? Basically a flat course it demands accuracy. If you are wayward, there is a heavy price to pay. The wind is a forever-changing rival, as the course is laid out in a square which means that no more than two consecutive holes, every one individual in character, run in the same direction. There are far more trees than you would expect on a links and, of course, there are the burns.

The Barry Burn and Jocky's Burn cross the fairways in the most inconvenient spots, usually just in front of greens and in areas you'd like to drive to. Jocky's Burn comes into play on the 2nd, 3rd, 5th and 6th and the more famous Barry Burn on the 1st, 10th, 11th, 17th and 18th. But it is the finishing stretch of the final five holes that makes Carnoustie a course of the highest calibre. The famous Spectacles (see below) is the start of the run-in. Then there is the 459-yard 15th, whose green is set into a bowl. A bit of a breathing space before the terrors to follow. The 245-yard 16th is a tough par 3 that demands a powerful, accurate tee shot to a small plateau green guarded by six bunkers. Jack Nicklaus once needed a driver followed by an 8-iron to get up. When Watson won in 1975, he never once managed to hit the green.

That old adversary, the Barry Burn, crosses the 17th fairway three times, earning it the name of 'The Island'. The trick is to land your drive on the 'island' between the first and second loop – not many carry both – and having done that you face a long second shot over bumps and bunkers. The burn lies in wait for you again on the home hole (444 yards, par 4) and you have to carry it with your tee shot to set up an intriguing second as the burn again guards the green. Do you go for it or lay up? The decision is yours.

18 holes, 6,941 yards (medal tees), par 72 (SSS 75). Course record A. Tait, C. Montgomerie 64.

SIGNATURE HOLE:
FOURTEENTH (483 yards, par 5) Beware the famous 'Spectacles', two large and deep bunkers in the face of a ridge guarding the green about 80 yards from the flag. The tee shot is critical, for there is out of bounds on the left and a wood to the right and bunkers sited to catch and punish the smallest error. The tee shot must be long and perfectly placed to have any chance of carrying the Spectacles with the second shot.

COURSE CARD

| HOLE | MEDAL YDS | PAR | FORWARD YDS | PAR | HOLE | MEDAL YDS | PAR | FORWARD YDS | PAR |
|---|---|---|---|---|---|---|---|---|---|
| 1 | 401 | 4 | 391 | 4 | 10 | 446 | 4 | 425 | 4 |
| 2 | 435 | 4 | 412 | 4 | 11 | 362 | 4 | 352 | 4 |
| 3 | 337 | 4 | 316 | 4 | 12 | 479 | 5 | 462 | 4 |
| 4 | 375 | 4 | 374 | 4 | 13 | 161 | 3 | 141 | 3 |

| 5 | 387 | 4 | 375 | 4 | 14 | 483 | 5 | 468 | 4 |
| 6 | 520 | 5 | 500 | 5 | 15 | 459 | 4 | 442 | 4 |
| 7 | 394 | 4 | 373 | 4 | 16 | 245 | 3 | 235 | 3 |
| 8 | 167 | 3 | 157 | 3 | 17 | 433 | 4 | 421 | 4 |
| 9 | 413 | 4 | 420 | 4 | 18 | 444 | 4 | 428 | 4 |
| *Yds* Out | 3,429 | | 3,318 | | *Yds* In | 3,512 | | 3,374 | |
| *Total Yds* | 6,941 | | 6,692 | | | | | | |
| *Total Par* | 72 | | 70 | | | | | | |

ADDRESS: Links Parade, Carnoustie DD7 7JE.
TEE RESERVATIONS: +44 (0)1241 853789.
FAX: +44 (0)1241 852720.
STARTER: +44 (0)1241 853249.
SECRETARY: E. Smith.
PROFESSIONAL: Lee Vannet.
VISITORS: Yes. Must have handicap certificate – men 28, ladies 36. Weekdays and Saturdays after 2 p.m. Sundays after 11.30 a.m. Contact in advance for availability.
GREEN FEES: £80 per round. Juniors half price. Combination ticket (round on championship course + one other) £85.
CATERING: Full clubhouse facilities.
FACILITIES: Trolley hire, caddies, putting green.
LOCATION: South-west side of town off A930.
LOCAL HOTELS: Airlie Arms Hotel, Alyth Hotel, Ballathie House Hotel, Carlogie House Hotel, Carnoustie Golf Course Hotel, Kinloch House Hotel, Old Manor Hotel, Queens Hotel, Rosely Country House Hotel, Sporting Laird Hotel.

# CARNOUSTIE GOLF LINKS – BUDDON LINKS

COURSE DESCRIPTION:
18 holes, 5,420 yards, par 66 (SSS 66).

## COURSE CARD

| HOLE | YDS | PAR | HOLE | YDS | PAR |
|------|-----|-----|------|-----|-----|
| 1 | 284 | 4 | 10 | 138 | 3 |
| 2 | 427 | 4 | 11 | 366 | 4 |
| 3 | 172 | 3 | 12 | 382 | 4 |
| 4 | 390 | 4 | 13 | 175 | 3 |
| 5 | 160 | 3 | 14 | 409 | 4 |
| 6 | 332 | 4 | 15 | 165 | 3 |
| 7 | 405 | 4 | 16 | 498 | 5 |
| 8 | 164 | 3 | 17 | 165 | 3 |
| 9 | 369 | 4 | 18 | 419 | 4 |

| | | | | | |
|---|---|---|---|---|---|
| *Yds* | 2,703 | | *Yds* | 2,717 | |
| *Out* | | *In* | | | |
| *Total* *Yds* | 5,420 | | | | |
| *Total* *Par* | 66 | | | | |

ADDRESS: Links Parade, Carnoustie DD7 7JE.
TEE RESERVATIONS: +44 (0)1241 853789.
STARTER: +44 (0)1241 853249.
SECRETARY: E. Smith.
PROFESSIONAL: Lee Vannet.
FACILITIES: Trolley hire, putting green.
CATERING: Full clubhouse facilities.
VISITORS: Weekdays. Saturdays after 11 a.m. Sundays after 11 a.m.
GREEN FEES: £20 per round.
LOCATION: South-west side of town off A930.
LOCAL HOTELS: Airlie Arms Hotel, Alyth Hotel, Ballathie House Hotel, Carlogie House Hotel, Carnoustie Golf Course Hotel, Kinloch House Hotel, Old Manor Hotel, Queens Hotel, Rosely Country House Hotel, The Sporting Laird Hotel.

## CARNOUSTIE GOLF LINKS — BURNSIDE COURSE

COURSE DESCRIPTION:
18 holes, 6,020 yards, par 68 (SSS 69). Course record A Tait 62.

COURSE CARD

| HOLE | YDS | PAR | HOLE | YDS | PAR |
|---|---|---|---|---|---|
| 1 | 324 | 4 | 10 | 336 | 4 |
| 2 | 450 | 4 | 11 | 375 | 4 |
| 3 | 175 | 3 | 12 | 386 | 4 |
| 4 | 460 | 4 | 13 | 382 | 4 |
| 5 | 158 | 3 | 14 | 228 | 3 |
| 6 | 348 | 4 | 15 | 500 | 5 |
| 7 | 360 | 4 | 16 | 163 | 3 |
| 8 | 432 | 4 | 17 | 473 | 4 |
| 9 | 163 | 3 | 18 | 307 | 4 |
| *Yds* *Out* | 2,870 | | *Yds* *In* | 3,150 | |
| *Total* *Yds* | 6,020 | | | | |
| *Total* *Par* | 68 | | | | |

ADDRESS: Links Parade, Carnoustie DD7 7JE.
TEE RESERVATIONS: +44 (0)1241 853789.

STARTER: +44 (0)1241 855344
SECRETARY: E. Smith.
PROFESSIONAL: Lee Vannet.
VISITORS: Weekdays. Saturdays after 2 p.m. Sundays after 11.30 a.m.
GREEN FEES: £25 per round.
CATERING: Full clubhouse facilities.
FACILITIES: Trolley hire, putting green.
LOCATION: South-west side of town off A930.
LOCAL HOTELS: Airlie Arms Hotel, Alyth Hotel, Ballathie House Hotel, Carlogie House Hotel, Carnoustie Golf Course Hotel, Kinloch House Hotel, Old Manor Hotel, Queens Hotel, Rosely Country House Hotel, Sporting Laird Hotel.

# COMRIE

## COMRIE GOLF CLUB

COURSE DESCRIPTION:
Very beautiful scenery. Slightly hilly heathland course with some testing holes. The 'Quarry' and 'Happy Valley' are two notably tricky par 3s. Founded 1891.
    9 holes, 6,040 yards (for 18 holes), par 70 (SSS 70). Amateur record 62.

SIGNATURE HOLE:
FIFTH (173 yards, par 3) Play over rocks to an elevated green surrounded by bunkers.

COURSE CARD

| HOLE | YDS | PAR |
|------|-----|-----|
| 1 | 344 | 4 |
| 2 | 261 | 4 |
| 3 | 174 | 3 |
| 4 | 400 | 4 |
| 5 | 173 | 3 |
| 6 | 493 | 5 |
| 7 | 368 | 4 |
| 8 | 369 | 4 |
| 9 | 438 | 4 |
| Yds Out | 3,020 | |
| Total Yds | 3,020 | |
| Total Par | 35 | |

ADDRESS: Laggan Braes, Comrie PH6 2LR.

**TELEPHONE:** +44 (0)1764 670055
**SECRETARY:** Steve Van der Walt +44 (0)1764 670941.
**VISITORS:** Any time except Monday and Tuesdays from 4.30 p.m.
**GREEN FEES:** £15 per day weekdays. £20 per day weekends. Weekly ticket: £50 from Monday to Friday.
**CATERING:** Meals and refreshments.
**FACILITIES:** Trolley hire, putting green.
**LOCATION:** Seven miles west of Crieff on A85.
**LOCAL HOTELS:** Comrie Hotel, Royal Hotel, The Gleneagles Hotel.

# CRIEFF

## CRIEFF GOLF CLUB LTD

### COURSE DESCRIPTION:

At first sight, Crieff looks a sporting course, not too testing with reasonably wide fairways, no heavy rough and always the chance of a shot no matter how wayward. Opened in 1980, it incorporates in its present form some of the old holes designed by Robert Simpson of Carnoustie in 1913 and 11 new holes laid out on the policies of Ferntower House. On a summer's day with the turf lush beneath your feet, breathing in the highland air and panoramic views of the Strathearn Valley, this undulating parkland course is a delightful golfing experience. But it can be deceptive. When the wind gets up and the rains set in, Crieff could be renamed grief. The last time we played here was such a day. My partner, accustomed to hitting 280-yard drives, found it took him driver, 3-wood and 4-iron into the teeth of the gale to reach the green on the 454-yard par 4 7th. But it's not just the weather that makes this course an intriguing test of golf. It has a rich variety of holes that make the golfer think about what he is doing. There are three par 5s on the front nine but it is perhaps the two par 3s that catch out many. From your very first shot you have to get it right. The 1st is a deceptive par 3, the tee alongside the unusual rotunda professional shop. It is slightly uphill, with bunkers guarding the green right and left, but only 163 yards, with trees behind the green making it look even closer. If the pro had a pound for every tee shot that was short, he'd be a wealthy man. The aptly named 'Wee Knock', the 124-yard 4th, is another tester. Uphill to a well-bunkered green front and back with trees all around, it is all carry and you have to be spot on or else it can be costly.

*Ferntower* – 18 holes, 6,402 yards, par 71 (SSS 71). Course record 65.
*Dornock* – 9 holes, 4,774 yards (for 18 holes), par 64 (SSS 63).

### SIGNATURE HOLE:

TWELFTH (467 yards, par 4) Perhaps Crieff's toughest. There is a gentle dogleg to the right. Your tee shot needs to be placed perfectly on the left side of the fairway or else the ball runs to the right and trees can block your long second shot to the green. There is a narrow entrance to a small two-tiered green, guarded by bunkers left and right. Accuracy is paramount or you're likely to be in three-putt territory.

## COURSE CARD

| HOLE | YDS | PAR | HOLE | YDS | PAR |
|------|------|-----|------|------|-----|
| 1 | 163 | 3 | 10 | 414 | 4 |
| 2 | 380 | 4 | 11 | 379 | 4 |
| 3 | 418 | 4 | 12 | 467 | 4 |
| 4 | 124 | 3 | 13 | 191 | 3 |
| 5 | 532 | 5 | 14 | 353 | 4 |
| 6 | 482 | 5 | 15 | 377 | 4 |
| 7 | 454 | 4 | 16 | 412 | 4 |
| 8 | 303 | 4 | 17 | 139 | 3 |
| 9 | 511 | 5 | 18 | 303 | 4 |
| *Yds Out* | 3,367 | | *Yds In* | 3,035 | |
| *Total Yds* | 6,402 | | | | |
| *Total Par* | 71 | | | | |

ADDRESS: Ferntower, Perth Road, Crieff PH7 3LR.
TELEPHONE: +44 (0)1764 652909.
FAX: +44 (0)1764 655096.
SECRETARY: J. Miller +44(0)1764 652397.
PROFESSIONAL: David Murchie.
VISITORS: Welcome at any time. Handicap certificates usually required.
GREEN FEES: Ferntower: Winter rates: £14 per round. £22 per round weekdays March/April/October; £25 per round July/August. £32 per round weekends March/April/October; £37 May/September; £42 July/August. Dornock: £12 per round weekdays/ weekends (£8 for nine holes).
CATERING: Full service in restaurant and bar in the clubhouse opened in 1991 – the centenary of the club.
FACILITIES: Trolley/buggy hire, putting green, pro shop, practice ground.
LOCATION: On A85 between Stirling and Perth.
LOCAL HOTELS: Balrobin Hotel, Bendarroch House Hotel, Crieff Hydro, Foulford Inn, Murray Park Hotel, Parklands Hotel, Queens Hotel, Tayside Hotel, The Gleneagles Hotel.

## CRIEFF HYDRO GOLF CENTRE

COURSE DESCRIPTION:
Culcrieff Course is testing parkland.

9 holes, 4,520 yards (for 18 holes), par 64. There is also a par-3 course – 6 holes, 645 yards, par 18.

ADDRESS: Crieff Hydro Hotel, Crieff PH7 3LQ.

TELEPHONE: +44 (0)1764 651615.
MANAGER: P. Milroy.
VISITORS: Welcome.
GREEN FEES: £12 per round, £15 per day. Seven-day ticket £40.
PAR-3 COURSE: £3.
CATERING: Licensed clubhouse and all-day restaurant.
FACILITIES: Trolley/buggy hire, driving range.
LOCAL HOTELS: Balrobin Hotel, Bendarroch House Hotel, Crieff Hydro, Foulford Inn,
Murray Park Hotel, Parklands Hotel, Queens Hotel, Tayside Hotel, The
Gleneagles Hotel.

# FOULFORD INN GOLF COURSE

### COURSE DESCRIPTION:
A challenge for the experienced golfer as well as the beginner. Enjoyable heathland
test of your short game. Water hazards, stocked with trout, come into play on
several holes. Terrific views of the Perthshire hills.

9 holes, 916 yards, par 27 (SSS 27). Amateur record 24.

### SIGNATURE HOLE:
FOURTH ('Buchanty Spout' 90 yards, par 4) Played from a roadside tee to a very
tight green on a peninsula in a pond.

### COURSE CARD

| HOLE | YDS | PAR |
|------|-----|-----|
| 1 | 94 | 3 |
| 2 | 86 | 3 |
| 3 | 116 | 3 |
| 4 | 90 | 3 |
| 5 | 86 | 3 |
| 6 | 130 | 3 |
| 7 | 126 | 3 |
| 8 | 86 | 3 |
| 9 | 102 | 3 |
| *Yds Out* | 916 | |
| *Total Yds* | 916 | |
| *Total Par* | 27 | |

ADDRESS: Foulford Inn, by Crieff, Perthshire PH7 3LN.
TELEPHONE & FAX: +44 (0)1764 652407.
E-MAIL: foulford@btclick.com
WEBSITE: www.fouldordinn.co.uk
SECRETARY/MANAGER: B. Beaumont.
VISITORS: Yes, any time.

GREEN FEES: £3 per round, £5 per day. Hotel residents play free.
CREDIT CARDS ACCEPTED: Visa/Mastercard.
CATERING: Restaurant and bar. Functions catered for. Family-run hotel/restaurant adjacent to golf course.
FACILITIES: Club hire (£1), changing-rooms, putting green.
LOCATION: Leave Crieff on A85 in Perth direction. Turn left onto A822 at Gilmerton. Course 3 miles north.
LOCAL HOTELS: Foulford Inn, Balrobin Hotel, Bendarroch House Hotel, Crieff Hydro, Murray Park Hotel, Parklands Hotel, Queens Hotel, Tayside Hotel, The Gleneagles Hotel.

# DUNDEE

## CAIRD PARK GOLF CLUB

COURSE DESCRIPTION:
Municipal inland parkland course. Founded in 1926.
    18 holes, 5,494 yards, par 69 (SSS 68).

ADDRESS: Mains Loan, Dundee DD4 9BX .
TELEPHONE: +44 (0)1382 453606.
STARTER: +44 (0)1382 438871.
WEBSITE: www.dundeecity.gov.uk/golf
PROFESSIONAL: J. Black.
VISITORS: Any time. Societies contact Dundee Council +44 (0)1382 223141.
GREEN FEES: £17 per round, £28 day ticket. £60 for a five-round multi-card.
CATERING: Bar.
FACILITIES: Pro shop.
LOCATION: 1½ miles north of city centre, off A972.
LOCAL HOTELS: Airlie Arms Hotel, Alyth Hotel, Ballathie House Hotel, Carlogie House Hotel, Kingsway Hotel, Kinloch House Hotel, Newton House Hotel, Old Manor Hotel, Rosely Country House Hotel, Swallow Hotel.

## CAMPERDOWN GOLF CLUB

COURSE DESCRIPTION:
Public parkland course just over 40 years old.
    18 holes, 6,561 yards, par 71 (SSS 72). Course record J. Flynn Jnr 67.

SIGNATURE HOLE:
ELEVENTH (505 yards, par 5) Narrow, tree-lined fairway. Dogleg. Spectacular view of River Tay and Fife.

## COURSE CARD

| HOLE | YDS | PAR | HOLE | YDS | PAR |
|------|-----|-----|------|-----|-----|
| 1 | 410 | 4 | 10 | 403 | 4 |
| 2 | 513 | 5 | 11 | 505 | 5 |
| 3 | 377 | 4 | 12 | 392 | 4 |
| 4 | 156 | 3 | 13 | 193 | 3 |
| 5 | 361 | 4 | 14 | 358 | 4 |
| 6 | 523 | 5 | 15 | 300 | 4 |
| 7 | 216 | 3 | 16 | 469 | 3 |
| 8 | 413 | 4 | 17 | 160 | 3 |
| 9 | 399 | 4 | 18 | 413 | 4 |
| *Yds Out* | 3,368 | | *Yds In* | 3,193 | |
| *Total Yds* | 6,561 | | | | |
| *Total Par* | 71 | | | | |

ADDRESS: Camperdown House, Dundee DD2 4TF.
TELEPHONE: +44 (0)1382 623398.
STARTER: +44 (0)1382 432688.
WEBSITE:www.dundeecity.gov.uk/golf
SECRETARY: Ronald Gordon.
PROFESSIONAL: Roddy Brown.
VISITORS: Yes, all week.
GREEN FEES: £17 per round, £28 day ticket. £60 for a five-round multi-card.
CATERING: On request.
FACILITIES: Trolley hire, putting green, pro shop, practice ground.
LOCATION: Three miles north-west of city centre off A923.
LOCAL HOTELS: Airlie Arms Hotel, Alyth Hotel, Ballathie House Hotel, Carlogie House Hotel, Invercarse Hotel, Jolly's Hotel, Kingsway Hotel, Kinloch House Hotel, Newton House Hotel, Old Manor Hotel, Premier Lodge, Rosely Country House Hotel, Swallow Hotel, Woodlands Hotel.

# DOWNFIELD GOLF CLUB

### COURSE DESCRIPTION:

Championship undulating parkland course with the Gelly Burn providing a hazard on a number of holes. One of the most challenging yet fair courses. It is a test for the top golfer, yet remains playable for the novice. There are many good par 3s and 4s, but it is the clutch of five fantastic par 5s which separate Downfield from most courses, and with trees and water features in evidence on most holes it is a beautiful place to play. Downfield has hosted the Scottish Amateur and Professional Championships but it was the hosting of the 1999 Final Open Qualifying that put it firmly on the golfing map. It is now being recognised as one of the finest inland courses in the UK and was recently named in the Top 20 golf courses in the country.

18 holes, 6,803 yards, par 73 (SSS 73). Pro record Andy Crerar 65 (1995).

SIGNATURE HOLE:
ELEVENTH ('Paddlers Joy' 498 yards, par 5 ) A great par 5 with a pond and a stream at the front of the green. The big hitters can come to grief if they go for the green in two and come up short. Even when you lay up, the pitch over the hazards is extremely nerve-wracking.

COURSE CARD

| HOLE | MEDAL YDS | PAR | FORWARD YDS | PAR | LADIES YDS | PAR | HOLE | MEDAL YDS | PAR | FORWARD YDS | PAR | LADIES YDS | PAR |
|---|---|---|---|---|---|---|---|---|---|---|---|---|---|
| 1 | 425 | 4 | 385 | 4 | 409 | 5 | 10 | 434 | 4 | 382 | 4 | 331 | 4 |
| 2 | 408 | 4 | 398 | 4 | 380 | 4 | 11 | 498 | 5 | 434 | 4 | 428 | 5 |
| 3 | 228 | 3 | 210 | 3 | 180 | 3 | 12 | 182 | 3 | 148 | 3 | 128 | 3 |
| 4 | 538 | 5 | 507 | 5 | 486 | 5 | 13 | 480 | 5 | 446 | 4 | 400 | 5 |
| 5 | 393 | 4 | 361 | 4 | 359 | 4 | 14 | 515 | 5 | 481 | 5 | 444 | 5 |
| 6 | 177 | 3 | 151 | 3 | 127 | 3 | 15 | 326 | 4 | 322 | 4 | 276 | 4 |
| 7 | 491 | 5 | 438 | 4 | 426 | 5 | 16 | 352 | 4 | 326 | 4 | 305 | 4 |
| 8 | 407 | 4 | 363 | 4 | 344 | 4 | 17 | 151 | 3 | 140 | 3 | 109 | 3 |
| 9 | 414 | 4 | 389 | 4 | 389 | 4 | 18 | 384 | 4 | 366 | 4 | 318 | 4 |
| Yds Out | 3,481 | | 3,202 | | 3,100 | | Yds In | 3,322 | | 3,045 | | 2,739 | |
| Total Yds | 6,803 | | 6,247 | | 5,839 | | | | | | | | |
| Total Par | 73 | | 70 | | 74 | | | | | | | | |

ADDRESS: Turnberry Avenue, Dundee, Tayside DD2 3QP.
TELEPHONE: +44 (0)1382 889246.
FAX: +44 (0)1382 813111.
E-MAIL: downfieldgc@ukonline.co.uk
WEBSITE: www.downfieldgolf.com
SECRETARY: Margaret Stewart.
PROFESSIONAL: Kenny Hutton.
VISITORS: Mondays to Fridays 9.30 a.m. to 11.45 p.m. and 2.15 p.m. to 3.45 p.m. Sundays from 2 p.m.
GREEN FEES: £31 per round weekdays, £45 per day. £34 per round weekends. Two rounds and meals package, £49.
CREDIT CARDS ACCEPTED: Visa/Mastercard.
CATERING: Restaurant and bar. Functions catered for.
FACILITIES: Motorised buggies, trolley hire, club hire, caddies (sometimes), changing-rooms, putting green, practice ground, pro shop, coaching clinics.
LOCATION: Follow A90 through Dundee and follow signs for Clatto Country Park until Downfield is found on the left.
LOCAL HOTELS: Airlie Arms Hotel, Alyth Hotel, Ballathie House Hotel, Carlogie House Hotel, Kingsway Hotel, Kinloch House Hotel, Newton House Hotel, Old Manor Hotel, Rosely Country House Hotel, Swallow Hotel.

## MONIFIETH GOLF LINKS

### COURSE DESCRIPTION:

Two courses running along the Tay Estuary. The Medal Course has been the venue for Open Championship qualifying and provides a good challenge for the experienced golfer. Seaside links course with tree plantations. The Dundee–Aberdeen railway line provides the main hazard over the first few holes. The Ashludie is more suited to those who prefer a compact course where an accurate short game is essential.

*Medal Course* – 18 holes, 6,655 yards, par 71 (SSS 72). Amateur record 63. Pro record 64.

*Ashludie Course* – 18 holes, 5,123 yards, par 66 (SSS 66).

### SIGNATURE HOLE:

Medal Course FOURTH ('Featherbed' 456 yards, par 4) The green is surrounded by trees and guarded on the right by a large mound and bunker. A very accurate second shot is required. Probably the most scenic hole on the course.

### MEDAL COURSE CARD

| HOLE | MEDAL YDS | PAR | FORWARD YDS | PAR | LADIES YDS | PAR | HOLE | MEDAL YDS | PAR | FORWARD YDS | PAR | LADIES YDS | PAR |
|---|---|---|---|---|---|---|---|---|---|---|---|---|---|
| 1 | 338 | 4 | 312 | 4 | 305 | 4 | 10 | 369 | 4 | 350 | 4 | 354 | 4 |
| 2 | 414 | 4 | 405 | 4 | 396 | 5 | 11 | 183 | 3 | 173 | 3 | 164 | 3 |
| 3 | 429 | 4 | 419 | 4 | 381 | 4 | 12 | 374 | 4 | 364 | 4 | 265 | 4 |
| 4 | 456 | 4 | 445 | 4 | 405 | 5 | 13 | 432 | 4 | 428 | 4 | 378 | 4 |
| 5 | 191 | 3 | 182 | 3 | 168 | 3 | 14 | 158 | 3 | 143 | 3 | 139 | 3 |
| 6 | 382 | 4 | 370 | 4 | 340 | 4 | 15 | 376 | 4 | 370 | 4 | 316 | 4 |
| 7 | 417 | 4 | 406 | 4 | 362 | 4 | 16 | 340 | 4 | 330 | 4 | 328 | 4 |
| 8 | 284 | 4 | 273 | 4 | 267 | 4 | 17 | 435 | 4 | 424 | 4 | 349 | 4 |
| 9 | 547 | 5 | 536 | 5 | 478 | 5 | 18 | 530 | 5 | 519 | 5 | 496 | 5 |
| *Yds* Out | 3,458 | | 3,348 | | 3,102 | | *Yds* In | 3,197 | | 3,111 | | 2,789 | |
| Total Yds | 6,655 | | 6,459 | | 5,891 | | | | | | | | |
| Total Par | 71 | | 71 | | 73 | | | | | | | | |

ADDRESS: Princes Street, Monifieth, Angus DD5 4AW.
TELEPHONE & FAX: +44 (0)1382 535553.
RESERVATIONS: +44 (0)1382 532767.
SECRETARY: Sandy Fyffe.
PROFESSIONAL: Ian McLeod +44(0)1382 532945.
E-MAIL: monifiethgolf@freeuk.com
WEBSITE: www.monifiethgolf.co.uk
VISITORS: Yes, daily.
GREEN FEES: Medal: £30 per round weekdays, £39 weekends. Ashludie: £15 per round weekdays, £16 weekends, £22 per day. Special offer: one round on each

course + catering £49.

**CREDIT CARDS ACCEPTED:** Visa/Mastercard.

**CATERING:** Restaurant and bar. Functions catered for.

**FACILITIES:** Trolley hire (£2), changing-rooms, putting green, pro shop, practice ground.

**LOCATION:** From Dundee take coastal route to Carnoustie. In Monifieth village, a finger sign indicates Panmure Hotel. The Links car park is behind hotel.

**LOCAL HOTELS:** Airlie Arms Hotel, Alyth Hotel, Ballathie House Hotel, Carlogie House Hotel, Kingsway Hotel, Kinloch House Hotel, Newton House Hotel, Old Manor Hotel, Panmure Hotel, Rosely Country House Hotel, Swallow Hotel, Woodlands Hotel.

# DUNKELD

## DUNKELD AND BIRNAM GOLF CLUB

### COURSE DESCRIPTION:

Founded in 1892, this heathland course was laid out during the First World War and has recently been extended to 18 holes. Panoramic views and adjacent loch is home to nesting ospreys.

18 holes, 5,511 yards (for 18 holes), par 70 (SSS 67).

### COURSE CARD

| HOLE | YDS | PAR | HOLE | YDS | PAR |
|------|-----|-----|------|-----|-----|
| 1 | 285 | 4 | 10 | 508 | 5 |
| 2 | 281 | 4 | 11 | 141 | 3 |
| 3 | 140 | 3 | 12 | 274 | 4 |
| 4 | 442 | 5 | 13 | 325 | 4 |
| 5 | 376 | 4 | 14 | 417 | 4 |
| 6 | 303 | 4 | 15 | 396 | 4 |
| 7 | 271 | 4 | 16 | 274 | 4 |
| 8 | 393 | 4 | 17 | 195 | 3 |
| 9 | 367 | 4 | 18 | 123 | 3 |
| *Yds Out* | 2,858 | | | 2,653 | |
| *Total Yds* | 5,511 | | | | |
| *Total Par* | 70 | | | | |

**ADDRESS:** Fungarth, Dunkeld PH8 0HU.

**TELEPHONE:** +44 (0)1350 727524.

**FAX:** +44 (0)1350 728660.

**SECRETARY:** Richard D. Barrance.

**VISITORS:** Welcome and booked parties.

GREEN FEES: £18 per round weekdays, £21 per round weekends.
CATERING: Full bar and catering facilities available in new clubhouse.
FACILITIES: Trolley hire, putting green, shop, practice ground, memberships available.
LOCATION: Take A923 a mile north of Dunkeld.
LOCAL HOTELS: Ballathie House Hotel, Bendarroch House Hotel, Kinloch House Hotel, Royal Dunkeld Hotel, Stakis Dunkeld House Resort, Tayside Hotel.

# DUNNING

## DUNNING GOLF CLUB

### COURSE DESCRIPTION:
Parkland course, which has five stone bridges across the same stream.
9 holes, 5,000 yards (for 18 holes), par 66 (SSS 63). Amateur record 62.

ADDRESS: Rollo Park, Dunning, Perthshire PH2 0RJ.
TELEPHONE: +44 (0)1764 684747.
SECRETARY/MANAGER: J.R. Stockley +44 (0)1764 684237.
VISITORS: Weekdays and Sundays.
GREEN FEES: £14 per round weekdays/weekends.
CATERING: Meals by prior arrangement. Soft and hot drinks.
FACILITIES: Trolley hire, club hire, changing-rooms, putting green, practice ground.
LOCATION: 9 miles south-west of Perth, 2½ miles from A9.
LOCAL HOTELS: Balrobin Hotel, Newton House Hotel, Parklands Hotel & Restaurant, Queens Hotel, Tayside Hotel, The Gleneagles Hotel.

# EDZELL

## THE EDZELL GOLF CLUB

### COURSE DESCRIPTION:
Located in the foothills of the Grampian Mountains, the course is basically heathland, certainly with regard to the fine turf. A major tree-planting 25 years ago has given a parkland appearance. *Golf Monthly* magazine said of The Edzell: 'Golfers who are visiting the Angus area cannot afford to miss what is one of Scotland's true hidden gems.'
18 holes, 6,348 yards, par 71 (SSS 71). Amateur record 62.

### SIGNATURE HOLE:
FIFTEENTH ('The De'il's Neuk' 338 yards, par 4) With out of bounds on both sides, the drive can be daunting. Cross bunkers have to be avoided as have the greenside bunkers. If disaster happens then there's always the view to compensate.

## COURSE CARD

| HOLE | MEDAL YDS | PAR | FORWARD YDS | PAR | LADIES YDS | PAR | HOLE | MEDAL YDS | PAR | FORWARD YDS | PAR | LADIES YDS | PAR |
|---|---|---|---|---|---|---|---|---|---|---|---|---|---|
| 1 | 312 | 4 | 304 | 4 | 286 | 4 | 10 | 369 | 4 | 316 | 4 | 296 | 4 |
| 2 | 446 | 4 | 436 | 4 | 428 | 5 | 11 | 433 | 4 | 424 | 4 | 417 | 5 |
| 3 | 310 | 4 | 300 | 4 | 248 | 4 | 12 | 361 | 4 | 336 | 4 | 317 | 4 |
| 4 | 370 | 4 | 340 | 4 | 326 | 4 | 13 | 415 | 4 | 405 | 4 | 352 | 4 |
| 5 | 429 | 4 | 425 | 4 | 410 | 5 | 14 | 155 | 3 | 145 | 3 | 120 | 3 |
| 6 | 178 | 3 | 166 | 3 | 150 | 3 | 15 | 338 | 4 | 300 | 4 | 265 | 4 |
| 7 | 385 | 4 | 375 | 4 | 336 | 4 | 16 | 316 | 4 | 302 | 4 | 276 | 4 |
| 8 | 354 | 4 | 342 | 4 | 293 | 4 | 17 | 191 | 3 | 178 | 3 | 135 | 3 |
| 9 | 478 | 5 | 452 | 5 | 414 | 5 | 18 | 508 | 5 | 496 | 5 | 469 | 5 |
| Yds Out | 3,262 | | 3,140 | | 2,891 | | Yds In | 3,086 | | 2,902 | | 2,647 | |
| Total Yds | 6,348 | | 6,042 | | 5,538 | | | | | | | | |
| Total Par | 71 | | 71 | | 74 | | | | | | | | |

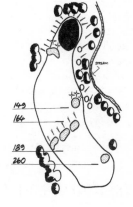

ADDRESS: High Street, Edzell, Angus DD9 7TF.
TELEPHONE: +44 (0)1356 648235.
FAX: +44 (0)1356 648094.
SECRETARY: Ian Farquhar +44 (0)1356 647283.
PROFESSIONAL: Alastair Webster +44(0)1356 648462.
E-MAIL: secretary@edzellgolfclub.demon.co.uk
VISITORS: Welcome all week. Societies weekdays and Sundays by arrangement.
GREEN FEES: £23 per round weekdays, £33 per day. £29 per round weekends, £43 per day.
CREDIT CARDS ACCEPTED: Visa/Mastercard.
CATERING: Restaurant and bar.
FACILITIES: Motorised buggies, trolley hire, club hire, changing-rooms, putting green, pro shop, practice ground, driving range.
LOCATION: Take B966 at north end of Brechin by-pass on A96. Continue 3½ miles to Edzell village. Midway between Dundee and Aberdeen.
LOCAL HOTELS: Airlie Arms Hotel, Carlogie House Hotel, Central Hotel, Glenesk Hotel, Kinloch House Hotel, Rosely Country House Hotel.

# FORFAR

## FORFAR GOLF CLUB

### COURSE DESCRIPTION:
Heathland course with tree-lined, undulating fairways. Founded in 1871 and

designed by James Braid.

18 holes, 6,052 yards, par 69 (SSS 70). Amateur record 61. Pro record 65.

**SIGNATURE HOLE:**

FIFTEENTH (412 yards, par 4) 'Braid's Best'. Dogleg right. Accurate drive required. Second shot over bunkers. Ground slopes right to left.

**COURSE CARD**

| HOLE | YDS | PAR | HOLE | YDS | PAR |
|------|-----|-----|------|-----|-----|
| 1 | 341 | 4 | 10 | 359 | 4 |
| 2 | 354 | 4 | 11 | 352 | 4 |
| 3 | 381 | 4 | 12 | 444 | 4 |
| 4 | 393 | 4 | 13 | 154 | 3 |
| 5 | 200 | 3 | 14 | 478 | 5 |
| 6 | 376 | 4 | 15 | 412 | 4 |
| 7 | 404 | 4 | 16 | 153 | 3 |
| 8 | 395 | 4 | 17 | 344 | 4 |
| 9 | 164 | 3 | 18 | 348 | 4 |
| *Yds* *Out* | 3,008 | | *Yds* *In* | 3,044 | |
| *Total* *Yds* | 6,052 | | | | |
| *Total* *Par* | 69 | | | | |

**ADDRESS:** Cunninghill, Arbroath Road, Forfar DD8 2RL.
**TELEPHONE:** +44 (0)1307 462120.
**FAX:** +44 (0)1307 468495.
**SECRETARY:** William Baird +44 (0)1307 463773.
**PROFESSIONAL:** Peter McNiven +44 (0)1307 465683.
**VISITORS:** Yes, 10 a.m. to 11.30 a.m. and 2.30 p.m. to 4 p.m., except on Saturdays.
**GREEN FEES:** £16 per round weekdays, £24 per day. £20 per round weekends, £32 per day.
**CATERING:** Bar.
**FACILITIES:** Trolley hire, putting green, pro shop, practice ground.
**LOCATION:** 1½ miles east of Forfar on A932.
**LOCAL HOTELS:** Airlie Arms Hotel, Alyth Hotel, Carlogie House Hotel, Rosely Country House Hotel.

# GLENALMOND

## GLENALMOND GOLF COURSE

COURSE DESCRIPTION:
Moorland course, founded in 1923, in grounds of Glenalmond College.
9 holes, 4,801 yards (for 18 holes) (SSS 68).

ADDRESS: Glenalmond, Perthshire.
TELEPHONE: +44 (0)1738 880270.
VISITORS: Members only.

# GLENSHEE

## DALMUNZIE GOLF COURSE

COURSE DESCRIPTION:
Challenging, hilly upland course – at 1,200 feet, one of the highest in Scotland.
Spectacular scenery with mountains rising 1,700 feet on either side. Reasonably
small greens. Well-maintained. Ideal for beginners and high handicappers.
9 holes, 4,198 yards (for 18 holes), par 60 (SSS 61).

COURSE CARD

| HOLE | FORWARD | | LADIES | |
| | YDS | PAR | YDS | PAR |
|---|---|---|---|---|
| 1 | 235 | 3 | 224 | 4 |
| 2 | 140 | 3 | 140 | 3 |
| 3 | 354 | 4 | 344 | 4 |
| 4 | 162 | 3 | 139 | 3 |
| 5 | 160 | 3 | 70 | 3 |
| 6 | 450 | 4 | 392 | 4 |
| 7 | 116 | 3 | 111 | 3 |
| 8 | 162 | 3 | 162 | 3 |
| 9 | 320 | 4 | 273 | 4 |
| *Yds* | 2,099 | *Yds* | 1,855 | |
| *Out* | | *In* | | |
| *Total Yds* | 2,099 | | | |
| *Total Par* | 30 | | | |

ADDRESS: Dalmunzie Estate, Spittal of Glenshee, Blairgowrie, Perthshire PH10
7QG.

TELEPHONE: +44 (0)1250 885226.
FAX: +44 (0)1250 885225.
E-MAIL: dalmunzie@aol.com
SECRETARY: Simon Winton.
VISITORS: Yes, any time except Sundays between 10.30 a.m. and 11 a.m.
GREEN FEES: £7 for 9 holes, £10 per day, £40 weekly.
CREDIT CARDS ACCEPTED: Visa/Mastercard.
CATERING: Restaurant and bar. Functions catered for.
LOCATION: Off A93, 2 miles north of Blairgowrie and 15 miles south of Braemar at
Spittal of Glenshee.
LOCAL HOTELS: Airlie Arms Hotel, Alyth Hotel, Ballathie House Hotel, Balrobin
Hotel, Bendarroch House Hotel, Callater Lodge, Carlogie House Hotel,
Dalmunzie House Hotel, Kinloch House Hotel, Newton House Hotel,
Parklands Hotel & Restaurant, Queens Hotel, Tayside Hotel, The Poplars
(Hotel).

# KENMORE

## KENMORE GOLF COURSE

COURSE DESCRIPTION:
Mildly undulating, testing moorland course for all abilities in magnificent
Highland setting. Good greens. Established in 1992.

9 holes, 6,052 yards (for 18 holes), par 70 (SSS 69). Amateur record A. Cooper
70.

COURSE CARD

| HOLE | YDS | PAR |
|------|------|-----|
| 1 | 392 | 4 |
| 2 | 316 | 4 |
| 3 | 170 | 3 |
| 4 | 560 | 5 |
| 5 | 160 | 3 |
| 6 | 445 | 5 |
| 7 | 171 | 3 |
| 8 | 404 | 4 |
| 9 | 408 | 4 |
| *Yds Out* | 3,026 | |
| *Total Yds* | 3,026 | |
| *Total Par* | 35 | |

ADDRESS: Kenmore, Aberfeldy, Perthshire PH15 2HN.

TELEPHONE: +44 (0)1887 830226.
FAX: +44 (0)1887 830211.
MANAGER: Robin Menzies.
VISITORS: Yes.
GREEN FEES: £12 per round weekdays, £18 per day. £13 per round weekends, £20 per day. 9 holes: £9 per round, £10 per day.
CATERING: Full catering.
FACILITIES: Trolley/buggy hire, putting green, pro shop, practice ground.
LOCATION: On A827. West of Kenmore, over bridge on right.
LOCAL HOTELS: Ballathie House Hotel, Balrobin Hotel, Bendarroch House Hotel, Kinloch House Hotel, Kenmore Hotel, The Poplars (Hotel).

## TAYMOUTH CASTLE GOLF CLUB

COURSE DESCRIPTION:
Flat parkland course surrounded by hills and beautiful scenery. Rated as one of the most scenic courses in the UK. Easy walking. Designed by James Braid and established 1923.

18 holes, 6,066 yards, par 69 (SSS 69). Course record 62.

COURSE CARD

| HOLE | YDS | PAR | HOLE | YDS | PAR |
|------|------|-----|------|-------|-----|
| 1 | 296 | 4 | 10 | 182 | 3 |
| 2 | 306 | 4 | 11 | 452 | 4 |
| 3 | 420 | 4 | 12 | 444 | 4 |
| 4 | 170 | 3 | 13 | 298 | 4 |
| 5 | 543 | 5 | 14 | 190 | 3 |
| 6 | 365 | 4 | 15 | 410 | 4 |
| 7 | 283 | 4 | 16 | 174 | 3 |
| 8 | 383 | 4 | 17 | 330 | 4 |
| 9 | 377 | 4 | 18 | 443 | 4 |
| *Yds Out* | 3,143 | | *Yds In* | 2,923 | |
| *Total Yds* | 6,066 | | | | |
| *Total Par* | 69 | | | | |

ADDRESS: Taymouth Castle, Kenmore, Perthshire PH15 2LE.
TELEPHONE & FAX: +44 (0)1887 830228.
VISITORS: Any time.
GREEN FEES: £20 per round weekdays, £32 per day. £22 per round weekends, £38 per day.
CATERING: Full service.
FACILITIES: Trolley/buggy hire, putting green, pro shop, practice ground.
LOCATION: 6 miles outside Aberfeldy on Killin Road (A827).
LOCATION: Ballathie House Hotel, Balrobin Hotel, Bendarroch House Hotel,

Kenmore Hotel, Kinloch House Hotel, The Poplars (Hotel).

# KIRRIEMUIR

## KIRRIEMUIR GOLF CLUB

### COURSE DESCRIPTION:
Wooded parkland course with narrow fairways and small greens. Demands accuracy. Founded 1908 and designed by James Braid.

18 holes, 5,510 yards, par 68 (SSS 67). Course record 62.

### SIGNATURE HOLE:
SEVENTEENTH (195 yards, par 3) 'Braid's Gem', designed by James Braid. Approach shot, if landed front left, should run around onto green.

### COURSE CARD

| HOLE | YDS | PAR | HOLE | YDS | PAR |
|------|-----|-----|------|-----|-----|
| 1 | 373 | 4 | 10 | 330 | 4 |
| 2 | 147 | 3 | 11 | 325 | 4 |
| 3 | 414 | 4 | 12 | 388 | 4 |
| 4 | 335 | 4 | 13 | 391 | 4 |
| 5 | 277 | 4 | 14 | 352 | 4 |
| 6 | 384 | 4 | 15 | 285 | 4 |
| 7 | 301 | 4 | 16 | 119 | 3 |
| 8 | 154 | 3 | 17 | 195 | 3 |
| 9 | 352 | 4 | 18 | 388 | 4 |
| Yds Out | 2,737 | | Yds In | 2,773 | |
| Total Yds | 5,510 | | | | |
| Total Par | 68 | | | | |

ADDRESS: Shielhill Road, Northmuir, Kirriemuir DD8 4LN.
TELEPHONE: +44 (0)1575 572144.
PROFESSIONAL: Karyn Dallas +44 (0)1575 573317.
VISITORS: Welcome, but restricted times at weekends. Phone in advance.
GREEN FEES: £20 per round weekdays, £26 per day. £25 per round weekends, £32 per day.
CATERING: Full service. Bar.
FACILITIES: Trolley hire, putting green, pro shop, practice ground.
LOCATION: 1 mile north, off B955.

LOCAL HOTELS: Airlie Arms Hotel, Alyth Hotel, Carlogie House Hotel, Castleton Park Hotel, Chapelbank Hotel, Rosely Country House Hotel.

# MONTROSE

## MONTROSE LINKS TRUST

### COURSE DESCRIPTION:

James Melville, golfer and scholar, may not figure prominently in the pantheon of Scottish golf, but it was his diary that proved the pedigree of this classic links of which Ben Crenshaw says: 'A magnificent stretch of marvellously natural ground which depicts how the game was born.' The game has been played here since 1562, more than 20 years before Mary Queen of Scots, golf's first lady player, met her untimely end. James, who entered St Andrews University as a 15 year old, recorded in his diary that in that year, at the age of six, he was taught 'how to use the glubb for goff'. That makes it one of Scotland's oldest golf venues. However, it is also one of the finest, with an array of challenging holes along narrow undulating fairways, although the Medal Course is only 18 holes these days (unlike back in 1866 when a round was over 25 holes). Resident professional Kevin Stables says: 'This is a classic Willie Park Jnr links course which requires good shot-making, particularly in the sea breezes which can change the whole character of the course daily.' From the 1st you get an idea what faces you, with the opening hole playing every inch of its 393 yards when you drive to the foot of the hill leaving a blind approach shot. There is a proliferation of gorse, gullies, valleys and mounds to be overcome before, at the 10th, it heads inland with the next six holes all demanding accurate iron play. You are welcomed back to the seashore by a tough par 3 of 233 yards which often requires a wood to clear the bunker on the left. Montrose keeps challenging you right to the end, with a final green well guarded by bunkers but with out of bounds awaiting that rush of adrenaline. Broomfield Course is flatter and easier.

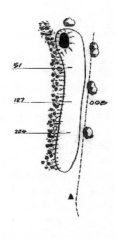

*Medal Course* – 18 holes, 6,496 yards, par 71 (SSS 72). Course record 63.

*Broomfield Course* – 18 holes, 4,800 yards, par 66 (SSS 63).

### SIGNATURE HOLE:

SEVENTEENTH ('Rashies' 416 yards, par 4) A truly testing hole on the Medal Course with out of bounds all down the right and trouble on the left. Your approach shot to an elevated green, cut into a gorse bank on the left, has to have the legs or else it is thrown off to the right.

## MEDAL COURSE CARD

| HOLE | MEDAL YDS | PAR | FORWARD YDS | PAR | LADIES YDS | PAR | HOLE | MEDAL YDS | PAR | FORWARD YDS | PAR | LADIES YDS | PAR |
|------|-----------|-----|-------------|-----|------------|-----|------|-----------|-----|-------------|-----|------------|-----|
| 1 | 393 | 4 | 379 | 4 | 368 | 4 | 10 | 379 | 4 | 368 | 4 | 333 | 4 |
| 2 | 388 | 4 | 378 | 4 | 357 | 4 | 11 | 441 | 4 | 434 | 4 | 339 | 4 |
| 3 | 155 | 3 | 150 | 3 | 137 | 3 | 12 | 176 | 3 | 140 | 3 | 131 | 3 |
| 4 | 365 | 4 | 350 | 4 | 334 | 4 | 13 | 320 | 4 | 307 | 4 | 292 | 4 |
| 5 | 292 | 4 | 276 | 4 | 226 | 4 | 14 | 416 | 4 | 401 | 4 | 379 | 5 |
| 6 | 490 | 5 | 479 | 5 | 416 | 5 | 15 | 542 | 5 | 522 | 5 | 492 | 5 |
| 7 | 370 | 4 | 357 | 4 | 302 | 4 | 16 | 233 | 3 | 226 | 3 | 192 | 3 |
| 8 | 331 | 4 | 299 | 4 | 270 | 4 | 17 | 416 | 4 | 378 | 4 | 398 | 4 |
| 9 | 443 | 4 | 420 | 4 | 330 | 4 | 18 | 346 | 4 | 339 | 4 | 326 | 4 |
| Yds Out | 3,227 | | 3,088 | | 2,740 | | Yds In | 3,269 | | 3,115 | | 2,882 | |
| Total Yds | 6,496 | | 6,203 | | 5,622 | | | | | | | | |
| Total Par | 71 | | 71 | | 73 | | | | | | | | |

ADDRESS: Traill Drive, Montrose, Angus DD10 8SW.

TELEPHONE: +44 (0)1674 672932.

FAX: +44 (0)1674 671800.

E-MAIL: secretary@montroselinks.co.uk

WEBSITE: www.montroselinks.co.uk

SECRETARY: Mrs Margaret Stewart.

PROFESSIONAL: Kevin Stables +44 (0)1674 672634.

VISITORS: Very welcome. Medal Course: Monday to Friday 9.30 a.m. to 12 noon and 1 p.m. to 4 p.m. Saturdays 2.30p.m to 3.30 p.m. Sundays after 10 a.m. No restrictions on Broomfield Course.

GREEN FEES: Medal Course: £28 per round weekdays, £38 per day. £32 per round weekends, £48 per day. Broomfield Course: £12 per round.

CREDIT CARDS ACCEPTED: Visa/Mastercard.

CATERING: Three golf clubs offer full catering plus bar and changing facilities.

FACILITIES: No motorised carts, trolley hire (£2), club hire (£10), no caddies, changing-rooms, putting green, pro shop, practice ground, coaching clinics available on request, memberships available.

LOCATION: Montrose lies approximately halfway between Dundee and Aberdeen. From the south follow the A90, turn off at Brechin and take the A935 to Montrose.

LOCAL HOTELS: Airlie Arms Hotel, Carlogie House Hotel, Corner House Hotel, Links Hotel, Park Hotel, Rosely Country House Hotel.

# MUTHILL

## MUTHILL GOLF CLUB

COURSE DESCRIPTION:
Parkland course of reasonably level terrain which can be challenging for all standards of golfer. Tight fairways, with out of bounds on six of the holes, and small well-bunkered greens. But the rough is never too penal and there are panoramic views from the top of the course.

9 holes, 4,700 yards (for 18 holes), par 66 (SSS 63). Amateur record 61.

SIGNATURE HOLE:
NINTH ('The Loaning' 205 yards, par 3) From an elevated tee, to a small, very difficult, well-bunkered green with threatening out of bounds on the right. Locals say that the green is 'not large enough to park a Fiesta on'.

COURSE CARD

| HOLE | YDS | PAR |
|------|------|-----|
| 1 | 224 | 4 |
| 2 | 186 | 3 |
| 3 | 268 | 4 |
| 4 | 274 | 4 |
| 5 | 144 | 3 |
| 6 | 395 | 4 |
| 7 | 322 | 4 |
| 8 | 332 | 4 |
| 9 | 205 | 3 |
| Yds Out | 2,350 | |
| Total Yds | 2,350 | |
| Total Par | 33 | |

ADDRESS: Peat Road, Muthill, Perthshire PH5 2DA.
TELEPHONE: +44 (0)1764 681523.
FAX: +44 (0)1764 681557.
E-MAIL: muthillgolf@lineone.co.uk
SECRETARY: Jim Elder.
VISITORS: Yes, any time.
GREEN FEES: £13 per round weekdays, £15 per day. £16 per round weekends. Weekly ticket £50.
CATERING: Meals.
FACILITIES: Trolley hire (£2), club hire (£5), changing-rooms, putting green, limited pro shop, memberships available.

LOCATION: 2 miles from Crieff on A822. At entrance to village turn right at bowling green. The course is ½ mile up Peat Road on the left.

LOCAL HOTELS: Arduthie Hotel, Balrobin Hotel, Drummond Arms Hotel, Muthill Village Hotel, Newton House Hotel, Parklands Hotel & Restaurant, The Gleneagles Hotel.

# PERTH

## CRAIGIE HILL GOLF CLUB

COURSE DESCRIPTION:
Challenging slightly hilly parkland course not for the faint-hearted. Views across the Tay Valley. Founded in 1909.

18 holes, 5,386 yards, par 66 (SSS 67). Pro record 63.

SIGNATURE HOLE:
THIRTEENTH ('Firton' 189 yards, par 3) From an elevated tee across wilderness to a small, well-bunkered green. Club selection is all important.

ADDRESS: Cherrybank, Perth PH2 0NE.
TELEPHONE: +44 (0)1738 624377.
FAX: +44 (0)1738 620829.
SECRETARY: Andrew Tunnicliffe +44 (0)1738 620829.
PROFESSIONAL: +44 (0)1738 622644.
VISITORS: Restricted on Saturdays. Telephone 3 days in advance.
GREEN FEES: £15 per round, £20 per day. £25 Sundays.
CATERING: Full service. Bar.
FACILITIES: Trolley hire, putting green, pro shop, practice ground,
LOCATION: 1 mile south-west of city centre, off A952.
LOCAL HOTELS: Balrobin Hotel, Lovat Hotel, Murrayshall Hotel, Newton House Hotel, Parklands Hotel & Restaurant, Queens Hotel, Royal George Hotel, Salutation Hotel, Tayside Hotel, The Gleneagles Hotel.

## KING JAMES VI GOLF CLUB

COURSE DESCRIPTION:
Perth's oldest course, established 1858. Parkland course situated on island in the middle of the River Tay. Easy walking.

18 holes, 6,038 yards, par 70 (SSS 69). Course record 62.

ADDRESS: Moncreiffe Island, Perth PH2 8NR.
TELEPHONE: +44 (0) 1738 625170.
FAX: +44 (0)1738 445132.
PROFESSIONAL: Tom Coles +44 (0)1738 632460.
VISITORS: Restricted on competition days. Closed to visitors on Saturdays. Contact

pro for bookings.

GREEN FEES: £17 per round weekdays, £23 per day. £20 per round Sundays, £30 per day.

CATERING: Full service. Bar.

FACILITIES: Trolley/buggy hire, putting green, pro shop, practice ground.

LOCATION: South-east of city.

LOCAL HOTELS: Balrobin Hotel, Lovat Hotel, Murrayshall Hotel, Newton House Hotel, Parklands Hotel & Restaurant, Queens Hotel, Royal George Hotel, Salutation Hotel, Tayside Hotel, The Gleneagles Hotel.

## MURRAYSHALL GOLF COURSE

COURSE DESCRIPTION:

A parkland course, with tree-lined fairways, which was opened in 1981 and has built a reputation for excellence. It has white sand bunkers, stone bridges and exciting water hazards and is set in 300 acres adjacent to the Murrayshall Country House Hotel.

18 holes, 6,446 yards, par 73 (SSS 71).

Also the Lynedoch course, opened in 2000: a shorter but hilly and possibly more demanding course.

18 holes, 5,359 yards, par 69.

ADDRESS: Murrayshall, Scone, near Perth PH2 7PH.

TELEPHONE: +44 (0)1738 551171.

FAX: +44 (0)1738 552595.

PROFESSIONAL: +44 (0)1738 552784.

VISITORS: Closed to visitors on Saturdays.

GREEN FEES: £27 per round weekdays, £35 per day. £30 per round weekends, £40 per day. Hotel residents £20 per round. Lynedoch: £18 per round weekdays, £20 weekends. Hotel residents £15 per round.

CATERING: Full service. Bar.

FACILITIES: Trolley/buggy hire, putting green, pro shop, practice ground, driving range, indoor golf clinic.

LOCATION: East of village, off A94.

LOCAL HOTELS: Balrobin Hotel, Lovat Hotel, Murrayshall Hotel, Newton House Hotel, Parklands Hotel & Restaurant, Queens Hotel, Royal George Hotel, Salutation Hotel, Tayside Hotel, The Gleneagles Hotel.

## NORTH INCH GOLF COURSE

COURSE DESCRIPTION:

Flat, open links course by River Tay to be upgraded to 18 holes in July 2001. Long established municipal course set in beautiful countryside. Reputation for excellent greens.

18 holes, 5,401 yards, par 68 (SSS 68). Course record 60.

SIGNATURE HOLE:
THIRTEENTH (352 yards, par 4) Too short an approach to the landing area from the right hand dogleg and another shot is required. Too far and your ball will end up in one of the many burns that cut across the course.

ADDRESS: off Hay Street, Perth PH1 5GD.
TELEPHONE: +44 (0)1738 475215.
FAX: +44 (0)1738 476410.
E-MAIL: gharbut@pkc.gov.uk
VISITORS: Contact in advance.
GREEN FEES: £6 per round weekdays, £7.50 weekends.
CATERING: Yes. Bar.
FACILITIES: Trolley hire, putting green.
LOCATION: North of Perth centre with the course situated on the west side of the Tay.
LOCAL HOTELS: Balrobin Hotel, Lovat Hotel, Murrayshall Hotel, Newton House Hotel, Parklands Hotel & Restaurant, Queens Hotel, Royal George Hotel, Salutation Hotel, Tayside Hotel, The Gleneagles Hotel.

# PITLOCHRY

## PITLOCHRY GOLF COURSE LTD

COURSE DESCRIPTION:
Hilly parkland course with lush turf and generous fairways and many natural hazards. A gradual climb over the first three holes is rewarded by the view from the 4th tee. Designed by Willie Fernie and established in 1908.

18 holes, 5,811 yards, par 69 (SSS 69).

ADDRESS: Golf Course Road, Pitlochry PH16 5QY.
TELEPHONE: +44 (0)1796 472792.
PROFESSIONAL: George Hampton.
VISITORS: Yes.
GREEN FEES: £14.50 per round weekdays, £22 per day. £19 per round weekends, £28.50 per day.
CATERING: Yes, all meals.
FACILITIES: Trolley/buggy hire, putting green, pro shop, practice ground.
LOCATION: North end of village off A924.
LOCAL HOTELS: Balrobin Hotel, Bendarroch House Hotel, Callater Lodge, The Poplars (Hotel).

# ST FILLANS

## ST FILLANS GOLF CLUB

COURSE DESCRIPTION:
Inland flat parkland course suitable for all standards of golfer, including the elderly. Designed by Willie Auchterlonie and founded in 1903. Beautiful mountain scenery.

9 holes, 5,796 yards (for 18 holes), par 68 (SSS 67) Amateur record 73.

## COURSE CARD

| HOLE | YDS | PAR |
|------|-----|-----|
| 1 | 337 | 4 |
| 2 | 462 | 4 |
| 3 | 272 | 4 |
| 4 | 420 | 4 |
| 5 | 272 | 4 |
| 6 | 224 | 3 |
| 7 | 453 | 4 |
| 8 | 171 | 3 |
| 9 | 287 | 4 |
| Yda Iut | 2,898 | |
| Total Yds | 2,898 | |
| Total Par | 34 | |

ADDRESS: South Loch Earn Road, St Fillans, Perthshire PH6 2NJ.
TELEPHONE: +44 (0)1764 685312.
SECRETARY: K. Foster.
VISITORS: Individuals any time. Parties by arrangement.
GREEN FEES: £12 per day weekdays. £16 per day weekends and bank holidays. Weekly ticket £50.
CATERING: Snacks and light meals, April to October.
FACILITIES: Trolley/buggy hire.
LOCATION: Off A85 at east end of village.
LOCAL HOTELS: Achray Hotel, Drummond Arms Hotel, Four Seasons Hotel, The Gleneagles Hotel.

# STRATHTAY

## STRATHTAY GOLF CLUB

### COURSE DESCRIPTION:
Wooded parkland course established in 1909. First three holes and the 9th are flat. The remainder are hilly, particularly the 5th and the 7th. Scenic views from the 6th and 8th tees.

9 holes, 4,086 yards (for 18 holes), par 62 (SSS 63).

### SIGNATURE HOLE:
FIFTH (256 yards, par 4) Green is hidden by a steep hill. If not cleared by your drive, the ball is likely to roll back down to the foot of the hill. Few succeed in getting over the top with their drive.

### COURSE CARD

| HOLE | YDS | PAR |
|------|-----|-----|
| 1 | 286 | 4 |
| 2 | 218 | 3 |
| 3 | 212 | 3 |
| 4 | 155 | 3 |
| 5 | 256 | 4 |
| 6 | 370 | 4 |
| 7 | 144 | 3 |
| 8 | 288 | 4 |
| 9 | 114 | 3 |
| *Yds Out* | 2,043 | |
| *Total Yds* | 2,043 | |
| *Total Par* | 31 | |

ADDRESS: Strathtay, Perthshire PH9 0PG.
TELEPHONE: +44 (0)1887 840211.
VISITORS: No visitors on Sundays from 12 noon to 5 p.m.
GREEN FEES: £10 per day. Juniors £5.
CATERING: At nearby hotel.
FACILITIES: Trolley hire, practice ground.
LOCATION: Eastern end of road to Weem, off A827.
LOCAL HOTELS: Ballathie House Hotel, Balrobin Hotel, Bendarroch House Hotel, Kinloch House Hotel, The Poplars (Hotel).

# TAYPORT

## SCOTSCRAIG GOLF CLUB

### COURSE DESCRIPTION:
Established in 1817, this course, although close to the sea, differs from traditional links courses in that it has heathland features with more trees than on most links courses. It has excellent greens and nestles in a drier and well-drained area providing a perfect golfing climate. An Open Championship final qualifying course.

18 holes, 6,550 yards, par 71 (SSS 72).

### SIGNATURE HOLE:
FOURTH (366 yards, par 4) Included in Henry Longhurst's 'Best 18 Holes of Golf', it is a hole that calls for accuracy off the tee and a second shot, with a short to medium iron, to a plateau green that is very difficult to hit.

### COURSE CARD

| HOLE | MEDAL YDS | PAR | FORWARD YDS | PAR | LADIES YDS | PAR | HOLE | MEDAL YDS | PAR | FORWARD YDS | PAR | LADIES YDS | PAR |
|------|-----------|-----|-------------|-----|------------|-----|------|-----------|-----|-------------|-----|------------|-----|
| 1 | 402 | 4 | 384 | 4 | 376 | 4 | 10 | 404 | 4 | 386 | 4 | 359 | 4 |
| 2 | 374 | 4 | 364 | 4 | 357 | 4 | 11 | 459 | 4 | 448 | 4 | 440 | 5 |
| 3 | 214 | 3 | 201 | 3 | 194 | 3 | 12 | 389 | 4 | 379 | 4 | 375 | 4 |
| 4 | 366 | 4 | 351 | 4 | 340 | 4 | 13 | 165 | 3 | 150 | 3 | 106 | 3 |
| 5 | 402 | 4 | 392 | 4 | 291 | 4 | 14 | 523 | 5 | 512 | 5 | 475 | 5 |
| 6 | 150 | 3 | 137 | 3 | 141 | 3 | 15 | 175 | 3 | 163 | 3 | 136 | 3 |
| 7 | 401 | 4 | 385 | 4 | 351 | 4 | 16 | 479 | 5 | 467 | 5 | 466 | 5 |
| 8 | 387 | 4 | 379 | 4 | 318 | 4 | 17 | 380 | 4 | 366 | 4 | 333 | 4 |
| 9 | 484 | 5 | 470 | 5 | 402 | 5 | 18 | 396 | 4 | 376 | 4 | 331 | 4 |
| Yds Out | 3,180 | | 3,063 | | 2,770 | | Yds In | 3,370 | | 3,247 | | 3,021 | |
| Total Yds | 6,550 | | 6,310 | | 5,791 | | | | | | | | |
| Total Par | 71 | | 71 | | 72 | | | | | | | | |

ADDRESS: Golf Road, Tayport, Fife DD6 9DZ.
TELEPHONE: +44 (0)1382 552515.
FAX: +44 (0) 1382 553130.
MANAGING SECRETARY: Barrie D. Liddle.
PROFESSIONAL: Stuart Campbell +44 (0)1382 552855.
VISITORS: Yes. 10 a.m. to 11.28 a.m. and 2.32 p.m. to 4 p.m. (Mondays to Fridays). 10 a.m. to 11 a.m. and 2.32 p.m. to 4 p.m. (Saturdays and Sundays).
GREEN FEES: £35 per round/day weekdays, £40 per round/day weekends.
CREDIT CARDS ACCEPTED: Visa/Mastercard.

CATERING: Restaurant and bar.

FACILITIES: Motorised buggies (£16), trolley hire (£3), club hire, changing-rooms, putting green, pro shop, practice ground, coaching clinics.

LOCATION: 10 miles north of St Andrews. Follow the A919 and B945 to Tayport, or 4 miles south-east of Dundee over the Tay Road Bridge.

LOCAL HOTELS: Old Manor Hotel, Rufflets Country House, Russacks Hotel, Russell Hotel, Sandford Country House Hotel, Scores Hotel, Seymour Hotel, St Michael's Inn.

# FIFE INCLUDING ST ANDREWS

# ABERDOUR

## ABERDOUR GOLF CLUB

### COURSE DESCRIPTION:
Parkland course running along the shore of the River Forth with views across the Forth to Edinburgh and beyond.

18 holes, 5,460 yards, par 67 (SSS 66). Course record 63.

### SIGNATURE HOLE:
FIRST (159 yards, par 3) Falls over 100 feet to the green, which is on a promontory into the Firth of Forth.

### COURSE CARD

| HOLE | YDS | PAR | HOLE | YDS | PAR |
|------|-----|-----|------|-----|-----|
| 1 | 159 | 3 | 10 | 530 | 5 |
| 2 | 159 | 3 | 11 | 340 | 4 |
| 3 | 343 | 4 | 12 | 163 | 3 |
| 4 | 287 | 4 | 13 | 251 | 4 |
| 5 | 359 | 4 | 14 | 318 | 4 |
| 6 | 365 | 4 | 15 | 171 | 3 |
| 7 | 163 | 3 | 16 | 449 | 4 |
| 8 | 458 | 4 | 17 | 354 | 4 |
| 9 | 394 | 4 | 18 | 197 | 3 |
| *Yds Out* | 2,687 | | *Yds In* | 2,773 | |
| *Total Yds* | 5,460 | | | | |
| *Total Par* | 67 | | | | |

ADDRESS: Seaside Place, Aberdour, Fife KY3 0TX.
TELEPHONE: +44 (0)1383 860080.
SECRETARY: John Train.
PROFESSIONAL: G. McCallum +44 (0)1383 860256.
VISITORS: Not Saturdays.
GREEN FEES: £19 per round. £30 per day.
CATERING: Full. Bar.
FACILITIES: Trolley hire, putting green, pro shop.
LOCATION: 6 miles south-east of Dunfermline.
LOCAL HOTELS: Kingswood Hotel, The Aberdour Hotel, Woodside Hotel.

# ANSTRUTHER

## ANSTRUTHER GOLF CLUB

### COURSE DESCRIPTION:
Seaside links course founded in 1890 and set in a picturesque old fishing village in the East Neuk of Fife. Kept in excellent condition. Some unusual holes and excellent par 3s. Suitable for golfers of all ages and experience. Magnificent views.

9 holes, 4,608 yards (for 18 holes), par 62 (SSS 63).

### SIGNATURE HOLE:
FIFTH ('The Rockies' 235 yards, par 3) The challenge of Anstruther is crowned by this hole that some say is the toughest par 3 in the country. Elevated tee, gorse banking and a knowe that obscures half of the green makes this an extremely difficult shot.

### COURSE CARD

| HOLE | YDS | PAR |
|------|-------|-----|
| 1 | 322 | 4 |
| 2 | 142 | 3 |
| 3 | 400 | 4 |
| 4 | 303 | 4 |
| 5 | 235 | 3 |
| 6 | 150 | 3 |
| 7 | 190 | 3 |
| 8 | 325 | 4 |
| 9 | 237 | 3 |
| *Yds Out* | 2,304 | |
| *Total Yds* | 2,304 | |
| *Total Par* | 31 | |

ADDRESS: Marsfield, Shore Road, Anstruther, Fife KY10 3DZ.
SECRETARY & FAX: +44 (0)1333 312283.
WEBSITE: www.eastneukwide.co.uk/anstergolf
SECRETARY: Graham Simpson.
VISITORS: Yes, most times.
GREEN FEES: £12 per round weekdays, £16 weekends.
CATERING: Bar, meals at weekends only.
FACILITIES: Trolley hire, changing-rooms, putting green, memberships available.
LOCATION: Entering Anstruther from the south on the A917, turn right at the Craw's Nest Hotel. Golf course at the bottom of the road.

LOCAL HOTELS: Craw's Nest Hotel, Old Manor Hotel, Rufflets Country House, Smugglers Inn, The Sporting Laird Hotel.

# BURNTISLAND

## BURNTISLAND GOLF HOUSE CLUB

COURSE DESCRIPTION:
Inland parkland course with generous fairways and good sea views.
18 holes, 5,965 yards, par 70 (SSS 70). Course record 62.

ADDRESS: Dodhead, Kirkcaldy Road, Burntisland KY3 9EW.
TELEPHONE: +44 (0)1592 873247.
MANAGER: +44 (0)1592 874093.
PROFESSIONAL: +44 (0)1592 872116.
VISITORS: Weekend play restricted. Book with pro.
GREEN FEES: £17 per round weekdays, £25 per round weekends.
CATERING: Full service. Bar.
FACILITIES: Trolley hire, putting green, pro shop, practice ground, driving range.
LOCATION: 1 mile east on B923.
LOCAL HOTELS: Inchview Hotel. Kingswood Hotel, The Aberdour Hotel.

# CARDENDEN

## AUCHTERDERRAN GOLF CLUB

COURSE DESCRIPTION:
Flat parkland course. Two or three testing holes.
9 holes, 5,250 yards (for 18 holes), par 66 (SSS 66). Course record 63.

ADDRESS: Woodend Road, Cardenden KY5 0NH.
TELEPHONE: +44 (0)1592 721579.
VISITORS: Any time, except from 7 a.m. to 11 a.m. and from 1 p.m. to 3 p.m. on Saturdays, and also some Sundays in season.
GREEN FEES: £10 per round weekdays, £19 per day. £14 per round weekends, £21 per day.
CATERING: Bar. Lunches by arrangement.
LOCATION: North of Cardenden on Kirkcaldy–Glenrothes road.
LOCAL HOTELS: Dean Park Hotel.

# COLINSBURGH

## CHARLETON GOLF CLUB

### COURSE DESCRIPTION:
Opened in 1994, this course is set in stunning parkland and surrounded by ancient trees and is claimed to be the 'most beautiful in the Kingdom of Fife'. Former US President George Bush said of his visit in 1994: 'From the minute I drove up to the wonderful Charleton Course, I was made to feel welcome and at home.' It is situated in the middle of the Charleton estate, which is owned by Baron St Clair Bonde: the family's 300-year-old ancestral home can be seen from many of the holes. There are large and heavily contoured greens and wide fairways to encourage the less accomplished player, but enough hazards to make it a true test of golf.

18 holes, 6,149 yards, par 72 (SSS 70).

9 holes, par 27.

### SIGNATURE HOLE:
SEVENTEENTH (287 yards, par 4) Called 'Ha Ha' for good reason, with a stone wall ditch in front of the green.

### COURSE CARD

| HOLE | MEDAL YDS | PAR | LADIES YDS | PAR | HOLE | MEDAL YDS | PAR | LADIES YDS | PAR |
|------|-----------|-----|------------|-----|------|-----------|-----|------------|-----|
| 1 | 380 | 4 | 373 | 4 | 10 | 364 | 4 | 361 | 4 |
| 2 | 265 | 4 | 248 | 4 | 11 | 344 | 4 | 323 | 4 |
| 3 | 402 | 4 | 358 | 4 | 12 | 265 | 4 | 175 | 3 |
| 4 | 475 | 5 | 455 | 5 | 13 | 557 | 5 | 534 | 5 |
| 5 | 120 | 3 | 114 | 3 | 14 | 368 | 4 | 355 | 4 |
| 6 | 443 | 5 | 408 | 5 | 15 | 318 | 4 | 268 | 4 |
| 7 | 264 | 4 | 246 | 4 | 16 | 375 | 4 | 349 | 4 |
| 8 | 177 | 3 | 166 | 3 | 17 | 287 | 4 | 271 | 4 |
| 9 | 376 | 4 | 357 | 4 | 18 | 369 | 4 | 354 | 4 |
| Yds Out | 2,902 | | 2,725 | | Yds In | 3,247 | | 2,990 | |
| Total Yds | 6,149 | | 5,715 | | | | | | |
| Total Par | 72 | | 71 | | | | | | |

ADDRESS: Charleton, Colinsburgh, Fife KY9 1HG.
TELEPHONE: +44 (0)1333 340505.
FAX: +44 (0)1333 340583.
E-MAIL: bonde@charleton.co.uk
WEBSITE: www.charleton.co.uk

SECRETARY: Jonathan Pattison.
PROFESSIONAL: Andy Hutton.
VISITORS: Yes, at all times.
GREEN FEES: £18 per round weekdays, £30 per day. £22 per round weekends, £36 per day.
CREDIT CARDS ACCEPTED: Visa/Mastercard.
CATERING: Restaurant and bar. Functions catered for.
FACILITIES: Motorised buggies (£16), Trolley hire (£2.50), club hire (£15), caddies by prior arrangement, changing-rooms, putting green, practice ground, driving range, pro shop, coaching clinics, memberships available (Full: £310, Country: £145, Overseas: £95).
LOCATION: Just north of Elie and 15 minutes south of St Andrews. From Edinburgh or Edinburgh Airport, follow signs to Forth Road Bridge ( M90). Exit junction 3. Follow signs to Kirkcaldy (A92). Exit Kirkcaldy East (A921). Follow signs to Leven and St Andrews ( A915). Go through Leven, Lundin Links and Upper Largo. Follow signs to Colinsburgh (A917). Turn left just before Colinsburgh.
LOCAL HOTELS: Charleton House, Golf Hotel, Old Manor Hotel, Lundith Links Hotel,The Elms.

# COWDENBEATH

## COWDENBEATH GOLF CLUB

COURSE DESCRIPTION:
Parkland course completed in 1988. Built on the site of the Dora coal mine. 9 holes, 6,552 yards (for 18 holes), par 72 (SSS 71). Course record 68.

ADDRESS: Dora Golf Course, Seco Place, Cowdenbeath KY4 9AD.
TELEPHONE: +44 (0)1383 511918.
VISITORS: Any time.
GREEN FEES: £7 weekdays, £8 weekends.
CATERING: Bar.
FACILITIES: Putting green, practice ground.
LOCATION: 6 miles east of Dunfermline.
LOCAL HOTELS: Woodside Hotel.

# CRAIL

## CRAIL GOLFING SOCIETY

COURSE DESCRIPTION:
The Crail Golfing Society was founded in 1786 and is the seventh oldest golfing society in the world. The present Balcomie Links course was designed by Old Tom

Morris in 1895 and is recognised as one of Scotland's classics. Recently Crail added a second course, the Craighead Links, which has proved to be a worthy neighbour of Balcomie. Both courses have stunning views across the North Sea to the distant mountains of Angus.

*Balcomie Links* (course card below) – Superbly maintained with magnificent greens, Balcomie is a beautiful course but a challenge. Several of the fairways wind alongside golden sandy bays and rocky outcrops of the Forth foreshore. Each hole has its own character and many are memorable including the 5th (Hell's Hole) and the back-to-back par 3 13th and 14th.

18 holes, 5,922 yards, par 69 (SSS 69).

*Craighead Links* – Designed in 1995 by American Gil Hanse and first played by the public in 1999, Craighead has wide sweeping fairways and large greens but features many of the best aspects of a classic links. It has many large bunkers and no two consecutive holes face the same direction.

18 holes, 6,728 yards, par 71 (SSS 73).

SIGNATURE HOLE:

FIFTH ('Hell's Hole' 459 yards, par 4) A dogleg right into prevailing wind across the North Sea. The question is, do you try to carry the beach or take the easy way round?

## BALCOMIE COURSE CARD

| HOLE | MEDAL YDS | PAR | FORWARD YDS | PAR | LADIES YDS | PAR | HOLE | MEDAL YDS | PAR | FORWARD YDS | PAR | LADIES YDS | PAR |
|------|-----------|-----|-------------|-----|------------|-----|------|-----------|-----|-------------|-----|------------|-----|
| 1 | 328 | 4 | 319 | 4 | 311 | 4 | 10 | 336 | 4 | 287 | 4 | 272 | 4 |
| 2 | 494 | 5 | 453 | 4 | 439 | 5 | 11 | 496 | 5 | 428 | 4 | 420 | 4 |
| 3 | 184 | 3 | 167 | 3 | 154 | 3 | 12 | 528 | 5 | 519 | 5 | 518 | 5 |
| 4 | 346 | 4 | 317 | 4 | 278 | 4 | 13 | 219 | 3 | 208 | 3 | 203 | 3 |
| 5 | 459 | 4 | 449 | 4 | 433 | 5 | 14 | 150 | 3 | 140 | 3 | 131 | 3 |
| 6 | 186 | 3 | 170 | 3 | 157 | 3 | 15 | 270 | 4 | 260 | 4 | 252 | 4 |
| 7 | 349 | 4 | 288 | 4 | 262 | 4 | 16 | 163 | 3 | 156 | 3 | 150 | 3 |
| 8 | 442 | 4 | 425 | 4 | 412 | 4 | 17 | 463 | 4 | 418 | 4 | 402 | 4 |
| 9 | 306 | 4 | 253 | 4 | 246 | 4 | 18 | 203 | 3 | 196 | 3 | 190 | 3 |
| *Yds* Out | 3,094 | | 2,841 | | 2,692 | | *Yds* In | 2,828 | | 2,612 | | 2,538 | |
| Total *Yds* | 5,922 | | 5,453 | | 5,230 | | | | | | | | | |
| Total Par | 69 | | 67 | | 69 | | | | | | | | | |

ADDRESS: Balcomie Clubhouse, Crail, Fife KY10 3XN.
TELEPHONE: +44 (0)1333 450686.
FAX: +44 (0)1333 450416.
E-MAIL: crailgolfs@aol.com
MANAGER: Jim Horsfield.
PROFESSIONAL: Graeme Lennie +44 (0)1333 450960.
VISITORS: Yes, all days from 9 a.m. to 12 noon and 1.30 p.m to 4.30 p.m. Advance

booking recommended.

GREEN FEES: £25 per round weekdays, £38 per day. £30 per round weekends, £48 per day.

CREDIT CARDS ACCEPTED: Amex/Visa/Mastercard.

CATERING: Restaurant and bar.

FACILITIES: Trolley hire (£3), club hire (£12), limited caddy service (£20), changing-rooms, putting green, pro shop, practice ground, coaching clinics.

LOCATION: 11 miles south-east of St Andrews on A917, then 2 miles from Crail to Fifeness.

LOCAL HOTELS: Balcomie Hotel, Craw's Nest Hotel, Denburn House B&B, Golf Hotel, Inn at Lathones, Old Manor Hotel, Rufflets Country House, The Sporting Laird Hotel.

# CROSSHILL

## LOCHORE MEADOWS GOLF COURSE

COURSE DESCRIPTION:
Inland, wooded lochside course with stream and superb views across Loch Ore and the County Park.

9 holes, 5,554 yards (for 18 holes), par 72 (SSS 71).

ADDRESS: Lochore Meadows Country Park, Crosshill KY5 8BA.

TELEPHONE: +44 (0)1592 414300.

VISITORS: Any time.

GREEN FEES: £5.40 for 9 holes, £8.60 for 18 holes, weekdays. £7.60 for 9 holes, £11.20 for 18 holes, weekends.

CATERING: Full.

FACILITIES: Putting green, practice ground.

LOCATION: 2 miles north of B920.

LOCAL HOTELS: Green Hotel.

# CUPAR

## CUPAR GOLF CLUB

COURSE DESCRIPTION:
Considered to be the oldest nine-hole course in Scotland, having been instituted in 1855. A very tricky, hilly, parkland course on land belonging to the National Trust on the side of the Hill of Tarvit. Hard walking but great views. Sloping fairways and cunningly positioned greens demand some accurate driving and very careful putting. The original course was at Tailabout Farm, laid out by the game's first professional, Allan Robertson of St Andrews. The club moved to its present

site in 1892 and, as you would expect, the clubhouse, opened in 1907, holds an impressive array of silverware.

9 holes, 5,074 yards (for 18 holes), par 68 (SSS 65). Course record 62.

### SIGNATURE HOLE:
EIGHTH (335 yards, par 4) Good positional drive required down and across side of a hill to set up the approach shot to small plateau green. Dogleg left cut into hillside. Tricky sloping green is protected by a large bunker on the right and out of bounds at the rear.

### COURSE CARD

| HOLE | MEDAL YDS | PAR | FORWARD YDS | PAR | LADIES YDS | PAR |
|------|------|-----|------|-----|------|-----|
| 1 | 184 | 3 | 138 | 3 | 135 | 3 |
| 2 | 259 | 4 | 250 | 4 | 239 | 4 |
| 3 | 277 | 4 | 257 | 4 | 250 | 4 |
| 4 | 319 | 4 | 273 | 4 | 279 | 4 |
| 5 | 391 | 4 | 368 | 4 | 363 | 4 |
| 6 | 142 | 3 | 120 | 3 | 121 | 3 |
| 7 | 373 | 4 | 343 | 4 | 337 | 4 |
| 8 | 335 | 4 | 310 | 4 | 259 | 4 |
| 9 | 257 | 4 | 225 | 3 | 219 | 4 |
| Yds Out | 2,537 | | 2,284 | | 2,202 | |
| Total Yds | 2,537 | | | | | |
| Total Par | 34 | | | | | |

ADDRESS: Hill of Tarvit, Cupar, Fife KY15 5JT.
TELEPHONE: +44 (0)1334 653549.
E-MAIL: secretary@cupargolfclub.freeserve.co.uk
SECRETARY: John M. Houston.
VISITORS: Yes, any day except Saturdays.
GREEN FEES: £15 per day. Weekly ticket £50. Juveniles £5. Families (2 adults/2 children) £30 a day.
CATERING: Restaurant and bar. Functions catered for.
FACILITIES: Trolley hire (£2), club hire (£5), changing-rooms, putting green, memberships available.
LOCATION: Follow Kirkcaldy–Glenrothes road out of Cupar and turn left onto Ceres Road. Car park on right after ½ mile on Ceres Road. 9 miles from St Andrews.
LOCAL HOTELS: Eden House Hotel, Kingswood Hotel, Newton House Hotel, Old Manor Hotel, Queens Hotel, Rufflets Country House, The Sporting Laird Hotel.

# ELMWOOD GOLF COURSE

COURSE DESCRIPTION:
Challenging parkland course, constructed in 1998 to the highest standards by Elmwood College – the top European college for Golf Management Studies. Elmwood has received several international awards in recognition of the outstanding work carried out on the course to enhance and improve the golf course environment. It offers a challenge to all golfers with a mixture of short par 4s and lengthy par 5s and two tough finishing holes. Set in around 50 hectares of gently undulating farmland with magnificent views of the Lomond Hills to the west and Hill of Tarvit to the south-east.

18 holes, 5,951 yards, par 70 (SSS 68).

COURSE CARD

| HOLE | MEDAL YDS | PAR | FORWARD YDS | PAR | LADIES YDS | PAR | HOLE | MEDAL YDS | PAR | FORWARD YDS | PAR | LADIES YDS | PAR |
|------|-----------|-----|-------------|-----|------------|-----|------|-----------|-----|-------------|-----|------------|-----|
| 1 | 343 | 4 | 321 | 4 | 319 | 4 | 10 | 266 | 4 | 261 | 4 | 256 | 4 |
| 2 | 512 | 5 | 501 | 5 | 491 | 5 | 11 | 526 | 5 | 489 | 5 | 485 | 5 |
| 3 | 174 | 3 | 168 | 3 | 160 | 3 | 12 | 156 | 3 | 131 | 3 | 117 | 3 |
| 4 | 455 | 4 | 440 | 4 | 431 | 5 | 13 | 313 | 4 | 293 | 4 | 286 | 4 |
| 5 | 306 | 4 | 287 | 4 | 274 | 4 | 14 | 329 | 4 | 302 | 4 | 291 | 4 |
| 6 | 404 | 4 | 382 | 4 | 370 | 4 | 15 | 301 | 4 | 287 | 4 | 280 | 4 |
| 7 | 184 | 3 | 178 | 3 | 162 | 3 | 16 | 272 | 4 | 253 | 4 | 250 | 4 |
| 8 | 410 | 4 | 397 | 4 | 396 | 4 | 17 | 447 | 4 | 430 | 4 | 408 | 5 |
| 9 | 128 | 3 | 121 | 3 | 116 | 3 | 18 | 424 | 4 | 412 | 4 | 405 | 5 |
| *Yds* Out | 2,917 | | 2,795 | | 2,719 | | *Yds* In | 3,034 | | 2,858 | | 2,778 | |
| *Total Yds* | 5,951 | | 5,653 | | 5,497 | | | | | | | | | |
| *Total Par* | 70 | | 70 | | 73 | | | | | | | | | |

ADDRESS: Stratheden, near Cupar, Fife KY15 5RS.
TELEPHONE: +44 (0)1334 658780.
FAX: +44 (0)1334 658781.
WEBSITE: www.elmwood.ac.uk
CLUBHOUSE & GOLF CO-ORDINATOR: Irene Jones.
VISITORS: Yes, any time.
GREEN FEES: £18 per round weekdays, £27 per day. £22 per round weekends, £31 per day. Reduced rates for seniors and juniors.
CREDIT CARDS ACCEPTED: Visa/Mastercard.
CATERING: Restaurant and bar. Functions catered for. Open to all, golfers and non-golfers alike.
FACILITIES: Motorised buggies, trolley hire, changing-rooms, putting green, practice ground.
LOCATION: 1 mile west of Cupar. Signposted from the A91 and A914. On M90 leave at junction 7 (southbound) or junction 8 (northbound) to join A91 in St

Andrews direction.

LOCAL HOTELS: Eden House Hotel, Kingswood Hotel, Newton House Hotel, Old Manor Hotel, Queens Hotel, Rufflets Country House, The Sporting Laird Hotel.

# DUNFERMLINE

## CANMORE GOLF CLUB

COURSE DESCRIPTION:
The club was founded in 1897 and has been at this undulating compact parkland course since 1902. Ben Sayers helped in laying out the 18-hole course in 1914. With some challenging par 3s, it is a good test of accuracy. Easy walking and only a few slopes to contend with.

18 holes, 5,376 yards, par 67 (SSS 66). Amateur record Robert Willme 61. Pro record Thomas Bjorn 65.

SIGNATURE HOLE:
ELEVENTH ('Quarry' 374 yards, par 4) Position of drive is important as the second shot is blind. Green lies in the quarry with a burn to the left of the green, then out of bounds. There is a bunker to the right on a steep slope.

COURSE CARD

| HOLE | MEDAL YDS | PAR | FORWARD YDS | PAR | LADIES YDS | PAR | HOLE | MEDAL YDS | PAR | FORWARD YDS | PAR | LADIES YDS | PAR |
|---|---|---|---|---|---|---|---|---|---|---|---|---|---|
| 1 | 257 | 4 | 250 | 4 | 237 | 4 | 10 | 375 | 4 | 358 | 4 | 340 | 4 |
| 2 | 398 | 4 | 388 | 4 | 369 | 5 | 11 | 374 | 4 | 335 | 4 | 333 | 4 |
| 3 | 352 | 4 | 340 | 4 | 314 | 4 | 12 | 195 | 3 | 190 | 3 | 120 | 3 |
| 4 | 155 | 3 | 148 | 3 | 144 | 3 | 13 | 188 | 3 | 185 | 3 | 183 | 3 |
| 5 | 337 | 4 | 327 | 4 | 310 | 4 | 14 | 347 | 4 | 343 | 4 | 338 | 4 |
| 6 | 351 | 4 | 341 | 4 | 326 | 4 | 15 | 184 | 3 | 178 | 3 | 173 | 3 |
| 7 | 143 | 3 | 139 | 3 | 137 | 3 | 16 | 258 | 4 | 251 | 4 | 243 | 4 |
| 8 | 334 | 4 | 326 | 4 | 286 | 4 | 17 | 430 | 4 | 421 | 4 | 412 | 4 |
| 9 | 375 | 4 | 371 | 4 | 331 | 4 | 18 | 323 | 4 | 243 | 4 | 240 | 4 |
| Yds Out | 2,702 | | 2,630 | | 2,454 | | Yds In | 2,674 | | 2,504 | | 2,382 | |
| Total Yds | 5,376 | | 5,134 | | 4,836 | | | | | | | | | |
| Total Par | 67 | | 67 | | 68 | | | | | | | | | |

ADDRESS: Venturefair Avenue, Dunfermline, Fife KY12 0PE.
TELEPHONE: +44 (0)1383 724969.
PROFESSIONAL: Jim McKinnon.
VISITORS: Yes, except Saturdays and specific Sundays.

GREEN FEES: £15 per round weekdays, £20 per day. £20 per round weekends, £30 per day. 10% discount on parties of 20 or more.
CATERING: Bar and meals. Functions catered for.
FACILITIES: Trolley hire, changing-rooms, putting green, practice ground, pro shop.
LOCATION: From Edinburgh and the south cross the Forth Road Bridge and take the M90 north to junction 3, then take the A907 into central Dunfermline.
LOCAL HOTELS: King Malcolm Thistle Hotel, Kingswood Hotel, The Aberdour Hotel.

## DUNFERMLINE GOLF CLUB

### COURSE DESCRIPTION:
Undulating parkland course with a clubhouse which is a 600-year-old category 'A' listed building. There are five par 3s and five par 5s.

18 holes, 6,126 yards, par 72 (SSS 70). Course record 65.

### SIGNATURE HOLE:
SIXTH (374 yards, par 4) Out of bounds right. Dogleg right.

### COURSE CARD

| HOLE | YDS | PAR | HOLE | YDS | PAR |
|------|-----|-----|------|-----|-----|
| 1 | 287 | 4 | 10 | 383 | 4 |
| 2 | 213 | 3 | 11 | 285 | 4 |
| 3 | 466 | 5 | 12 | 345 | 4 |
| 4 | 375 | 4 | 13 | 163 | 3 |
| 5 | 170 | 3 | 14 | 383 | 4 |
| 6 | 374 | 4 | 15 | 489 | 5 |
| 7 | 466 | 5 | 16 | 161 | 3 |
| 8 | 341 | 4 | 17 | 501 | 5 |
| 9 | 191 | 3 | 18 | 533 | 5 |
| *Yds Out* | 2,883 | | *Yds In* | 3,243 | |
| *Total Yds* | 6,126 | | | | |
| *Total Par* | 72 | | | | |

ADDRESS: Pitfirrane, Crossford, Dunfermline, Fife KY12 8QW.
TELEPHONE: +44 (0)1383 723534.
SECRETARY: R. De Rose
PROFESSIONAL: Steve Craig +44 (0)1383 729061.
VISITORS: Yes. Casual visitors Sunday to Friday, societies Monday to Friday. Members' guests all week.
GREEN FEES: £20 per round weekdays, £30 per day. £25 per round Sundays, £35 per day.
CATERING: Full catering all week. Bar.
FACILITIES: Trolley hire, putting green, pro shop, practice ground.
LOCATION: 3 miles west of Dunfermline on A994.

LOCAL HOTELS: Kingswood Hotel, Pitfirrane Arms Hotel, The Aberdour Hotel.

## PITREAVIE GOLF CLUB

COURSE DESCRIPTION:
Woodland course with undulating fairways and fairly fast greens. Panoramic view of River Forth valley. Testing golf.

18 holes, 6,086 yards, par 70 (SSS 69). Course record 65.

ADDRESS: Queensferry Road, Dunfermline, Fife KY11 5PR.
TELEPHONE & FAX: +44 (0)1383 722591.
PROFESSIONAL: Colin Mitchell +44 (0)1383 723151.
VISITORS: Welcome, except on competition days.
GREEN FEES: £19 per round weekdays, £24 per day. £26 per round weekends.
CATERING: Full service. Bar.
FACILITIES: Trolley hire, putting green, pro shop, practice ground.
LOCATION: 2 miles south-east of town on A823.
LOCAL HOTELS: King Malcolm Thistle Hotel, Kingswood Hotel, The Aberdour Hotel.

# ELIE

## THE GOLF HOUSE CLUB, ELIE

COURSE DESCRIPTION:
The Golf House Club was founded in 1875 but golf was first played here in 1750, although there are claims that its golfing history goes back almost 300 years earlier. The first official layout was around 1770. It's a delightful holiday links course, open and almost lacking in bushes and trees and without any par 5s. But plenty of variety is provided by the ever-changing wind. The local micro-climate means frost and snow-free winter golf. There are panoramic views over the Firth of Forth and it is very popular with golfers from Europe and North America making the pilgrimage to St Andrews. The legendary James Braid, five-times Open champion, learned to play here.

18 holes, 6,273 yards, par 70 (SSS 70). Course record 62.

SIGNATURE HOLE:
THIRTEENTH (380 yards, par 4) James Braid, who was born and learned his craft locally, called it 'the finest hole in all the country'. Played around the edge of West Bay to a long, narrow elevated green below the towering cliffs of Kincraig Point. Drive right to avoid a grassy hollow.

COURSE CARD

| HOLE | YDS | PAR | HOLE | YDS | PAR |
|------|-----|-----|------|-----|-----|
| 1    | 420 | 4   | 10   | 288 | 4   |
| 2    | 284 | 4   | 11   | 131 | 3   |

| | | | | | |
|---|---|---|---|---|---|
| 3 | 214 | 3 | 12 | 466 | 4 |
| 4 | 378 | 4 | 13 | 380 | 4 |
| 5 | 365 | 4 | 14 | 414 | 4 |
| 6 | 316 | 4 | 15 | 338 | 4 |
| 7 | 252 | 4 | 16 | 407 | 4 |
| 8 | 382 | 4 | 17 | 439 | 4 |
| 9 | 440 | 4 | 18 | 359 | 4 |
| *Yds* *Out* | 3,051 | | *Yds* *In* | 3,222 | |
| *Total* *Yds* | 6,273 | | | | |
| *Total* *Par* | 70 | | | | |

ADDRESS: Elie, Fife KY9 1AS.
TELEPHONE: +44 (0)1333 330301.
FAX: +44 (0)1333 330895.
E-MAIL: sandy@golfhouseclub.freeserve.co.uk
SECRETARY: Alexander Sneddon.
PROFESSIONAL: Robin Wilson.
VISITORS: Yes, but not on Sundays between May and September. A daily ballot for tee times is in operation in July and August.
GREEN FEES: £38 per round weekdays, £50 per day. £48 per round weekends, £60 per day. Weekly tickets: adult £130, junior £80; two-week tickets: £170, junior £120.
CREDIT CARDS ACCEPTED: Visa/Mastercard.
CATERING: Restaurant and bar.
FACILITIES: Trolley hire, club hire, changing-rooms, putting green, pro shop, practice ground, driving range, coaching clinics.
LOCATION: M90 from Forth Road Bridge to junction 3. A92 to Glenrothes. Turn right at second roundabout to A911 to Leven–Lundin Links–Upper Largo–A917 for ½ mile east to junction signposted for Elie. On entering Elie turn right at the church, then ½ mile to Golf Course Lane.
LOCAL HOTELS: Golf Hotel, Old Manor Hotel, The Elms, Victoria Hotel.

## ELIE SPORTS CLUB

COURSE DESCRIPTION:
Testing links course in superb condition for all ages and abilities. Perfect for beginners, improvers, children and retired golfers. Beautiful views over the Firth of Forth.
    9 holes, 4,306 yards (for 18 holes), par 64 (SSS 65).
SIGNATURE HOLE:
NINTH ('Home' 164 yards, par 3) Challenging downhill hole with scenic views.

COURSE CARD

| HOLE | YDS | PAR |
|---|---|---|
| 1 | 340 | 4 |

| | Yds | Par |
|---|---|---|
| 2 | 259 | 4 |
| 3 | 334 | 4 |
| 4 | 196 | 3 |
| 5 | 181 | 3 |
| 6 | 176 | 3 |
| 7 | 301 | 4 |
| 8 | 202 | 4 |
| 9 | 164 | 3 |
| Yds Out | 2,153 | |
| Total Yds | 2,153 | |
| Total Par | 32 | |

ADDRESS: Elie, Fife KY9 1AS.
TELEPHONE & FAX: +44 (0)1333 330955.
SECRETARY: Julien James.
PROFESSIONAL: Robin Wilson.
VISITORS: Yes, 7 days.
GREEN FEES: £9 per round/day. After 4 p.m. £5.50. Weekly ticket £36.
CREDIT CARDS ACCEPTED: Amex/Visa/Mastercard.
CATERING: Restaurant.
FACILITIES: Motorised buggies (£7.50), trolley hire (£2.50), club hire (£10), putting green, practice ground, pro shop, driving range, coaching clinics, memberships available.
LOCATION: 12 miles south of St Andrews in the East Neuk of Fife. Signs to course at main crossroads in village of Elie.
LOCAL HOTELS: Golf Hotel, Old Manor Hotel, The Elms, Victoria Hotel.

# FALKLAND

## FALKLAND GOLF CLUB

COURSE DESCRIPTION:
Well-kept parkland flat course with fast greens. Entrance to the course is not far from the walls of historic Falkland Palace.

9 holes, 5,216 yards (for 18 holes), par 68 (SSS 65). Course record 62.

ADDRESS: The Myre, Falkland, Fife KY7 7AA.
TELEPHONE: +44 (0)1337 857404.
VISITORS: Contact in advance.
GREEN FEES: £8 per round weekdays. £12 per round weekends.
CATERING: Bar.
FACILITIES: Trolley hire.

LOCATION: North of town on A192.
LOCAL HOTELS: Kingswood Hotel, Lomond Hills Hotel.

# GLENROTHES

## GLENROTHES GOLF COURSE

COURSE DESCRIPTION:
Testing parkland course with burn, which comes into play on the 11th, 12th, 13th and 18th holes. Wide fairways. Back nine hilly. Pleasant outlook to Lomond Hills and Firth of Forth.

18 holes, 6,444 yards, par 71 (SSS 71). Course record 67.

SIGNATURE HOLE:
THIRD (151 yards, par 3) Elevated tee to a raised green, 50 feet below and surrounded by bunkers. Anything from a wedge to a 2-iron depending on wind direction.

ADDRESS: Golf Course Road, Glenrothes, Fife KY6 2LA.
TELEPHONE: +44 (0)1592 758686.
SECRETARY: +44 (0)1592 754561.
VISITORS: Any time. Telephone in advance.
GREEN FEES: £12 per round weekdays, £20 per day. £15 per round weekends, £22 per day.
CATERING: Full service. Bar.
FACILITIES: Practice ground.
LOCATION: 35 miles north-east of Edinburgh. Junction 3 on M90, then A92 to Glenrothes.
LOCAL HOTELS: Balgeddie House Hotel.

# KINGHORN

## KINGHORN GOLF CLUB

COURSE DESCRIPTION:
Municipal links course 300 feet above sea level. Laid out by Old Tom Morris. Undulating and testing when the wind gets up.

18 holes, 5,269 yards, par 65 (SSS 66).

ADDRESS: Macduff Crescent, Kinghorn, Fife KY3 9RE.
TELEPHONE: +44 (0)1592 890345.
PROFESSIONAL: +44 (0)1592 890978.
VISITORS: Any time.

GREEN FEES: £11 per round weekdays, £14 per day. £14 per round weekends, £16 per day.
CATERING: Bar. Full services.
LOCATION: South side of town on A921.
LOCAL HOTELS: Dean Park Hotel, Kingswood Hotel, The Aberdour Hotel.

# KINNESSWOOD

## BISHOPSHIRE GOLF CLUB

COURSE DESCRIPTION:
Very testing, heathland course with views across Loch Leven and the Fife hills. Known by the locals as 'Coronary Hill'.
   9 holes, 4,540 yards (for 18 holes), par 62 (SSS 62).

ADDRESS: Kinnesswood, by Kinross, Fife, KY13.
TELEPHONE: +44 (0)1592 780203.
VISITORS: Yes.
GREEN FEES: £8 per round.
CATERING: Limited.
LOCATION: 3 miles east of Kinross off the M90.
LOCAL HOTELS: Lomond Country Inn, Scotlandwell Inn.

# KINROSS

## KINROSS GOLF CLUB

COURSE DESCRIPTION:
Two parkland tree-lined courses, both a tight challenge to the good golfer as well as the holiday golfer, on the banks of Loch Leven. Easy walking. The front nine of the Blue Course, which is longer and more demanding, is part of the original course. Unspoilt countryside further enhanced by planting of 15,000 additional trees. Owned by the Green Hotel.
   *Blue Course* – 18 holes, 6,456 yards, par 71 (SSS 71).
   *Red Course* – 18 holes, 6,257 yards, par 72 (SSS 70).

ADDRESS: Beeches Park, Kinross, Fife KY13 7EU.
TELEPHONE: +44 (0)1577 862237 or 863407.
PROFESSIONAL: Stuart Geraghty +44 (0)1577 865125.
VISITORS: Any time.
GREEN FEES: £17 per round weekdays, £27 per day. £27 per round weekends, £37 per day.
CATERING: Clubhouse and hotel.

FACILITIES: Trolley/buggy hire, putting green, pro shop, practice ground.
LOCATION: Off M90 at junction 6. Into Kinross, turn left at mini roundabout. Golf courses are directly across.
LOCAL HOTELS: Kingswood Hotel, Newton House Hotel.

# KIRKCALDY

## DUNNIKIER PARK GOLF CLUB

COURSE DESCRIPTION:
Municipal parkland course with few bunkers. Not hilly. Tree-lined rolling fairways. 18 holes, 6,601 yards, par 72 (SSS 72). Course record 65.

COURSE CARD

| HOLE | YDS | PAR | HOLE | YDS | PAR |
|------|-----|-----|------|-----|-----|
| 1 | 423 | 4 | 10 | 366 | 4 |
| 2 | 385 | 4 | 11 | 163 | 3 |
| 3 | 201 | 3 | 12 | 597 | 5 |
| 4 | 358 | 4 | 13 | 305 | 4 |
| 5 | 501 | 5 | 14 | 198 | 3 |
| 6 | 157 | 3 | 15 | 418 | 4 |
| 7 | 371 | 4 | 16 | 333 | 4 |
| 8 | 383 | 4 | 17 | 397 | 4 |
| 9 | 547 | 5 | 18 | 398 | 4 |
| *Yds Out* | 3,326 | | *Yds In* | 3,275 | |
| *Total Yds* | 6,601 | | | | |
| *Total Par* | 72 | | | | |

ADDRESS: Dunnikier Way, Kirkcaldy, Fife KY1 3LP.
TELEPHONE: +44 (0)1592 261599.
SECRETARY: A. Waddell.
PROFESSIONAL: Gregor Whyte +44 (0)1592 642121.
VISITORS: Societies by arrangement with secretary.
GREEN FEES: £15 per round weekdays, £23 per day. £19 per round weekends, £25 per day.
CATERING: Full facilities.
FACILITIES: Trolley hire, putting green, pro shop, practice ground.
LOCATION: From M90, join A92 for 9 miles. Leave at junction marked Kirkcaldy West. On B981, a mile from A92.
LOCAL HOTELS: Dean Park Hotel, Dunnikier House Hotel, Kingswood Hotel, The Aberdour Hotel.

# KIRKCALDY GOLF CLUB

**COURSE DESCRIPTION:**
One of the best kept courses in Fife, only 20 minutes from Edinburgh Airport. A challenging parkland layout, designed by Old Tom Morris in 1904. Set in 150 acres of a lovely rural setting with good views over surrounding countryside and the Firth of Forth.

18 holes, 6,038 yards, par 71 (SSS 69).

**SIGNATURE HOLE:**
SEVENTEENTH ('Mill Dam' 518 yards, par 5) A superb hole with a risky second shot from an elevated fairway to a green nestling across a burn. To go for it or not, that is the question.

**COURSE CARD**

| HOLE | MEDAL YDS | PAR | FORWARD YDS | PAR | LADIES YDS | PAR | HOLE | MEDAL YDS | PAR | FORWARD YDS | PAR | LADIES YDS | PAR |
|---|---|---|---|---|---|---|---|---|---|---|---|---|---|
| 1 | 330 | 4 | 300 | 4 | 300 | 4 | 10 | 278 | 4 | 263 | 4 | 263 | 4 |
| 2 | 230 | 3 | 230 | 3 | 224 | 3 | 11 | 382 | 4 | 347 | 4 | 347 | 4 |
| 3 | 332 | 4 | 323 | 4 | 323 | 4 | 12 | 536 | 5 | 530 | 5 | 472 | 5 |
| 4 | 390 | 4 | 390 | 4 | 360 | 4 | 13 | 153 | 3 | 145 | 3 | 132 | 3 |
| 5 | 540 | 5 | 525 | 5 | 515 | 5 | 14 | 430 | 4 | 420 | 4 | 361 | 4 |
| 6 | 335 | 4 | 309 | 4 | 309 | 4 | 15 | 319 | 4 | 310 | 4 | 310 | 4 |
| 5 | 130 | 3 | 120 | 3 | 120 | 3 | 16 | 359 | 4 | 359 | 4 | 304 | 4 |
| 8 | 329 | 4 | 300 | 4 | 300 | 4 | 17 | 518 | 5 | 518 | 5 | 518 | 5 |
| 9 | 307 | 4 | 310 | 4 | 310 | 4 | 18 | 140 | 3 | 140 | 3 | 140 | 3 |
| *Yds* Out | 2,923 | | 2,807 | | 2,761 | | *Yds* In | 3,115 | | 3,032 | | 2,847 | |
| *Total Yds* | 6,038 | | 5,839 | | 5,608 | | | | | | | | |
| *Total Par* | 71 | | 71 | | 72 | | | | | | | | |

**ADDRESS:** Balwearie Road, Kirkcaldy, Fife KY2 5LT.
**TELEPHONE & FAX:** +44 (0)1592 205240.
**SECRETARY:** Alistair Thomson.
**PROFESSIONAL:** Anthony Caira (Director of Golf) +44 (0)1592 203258.
**VISITORS:** Yes, every day except Saturdays.
**GREEN FEES:** £22 per round weekdays, £28 per day. £28 per round weekends, £36 per day.
**CATERING:** Restaurant and bar in newly refurbished clubhouse. Functions catered for.
**FACILITIES:** Motorised buggies, trolley hire, club hire, changing-rooms, putting green, practice ground, pro shop, coaching clinics, memberships available.
**LOCATION:** A90 to Forth Bridge. M90 to junction 3 (Halbeath interchange). Take A92 to Kirkcaldy. 'Kirk West' A910. Follow sign for town centre. Bear right at bottom of Oriel Road, past Laidlaws Garage. Turn right again at mini-roundabout, second exit at next roundabout with Beveridge Park on your right.

Just before the railway bridge, turn right into Balwearie Road.
**LOCAL HOTELS:** Dean Park Hotel, Dunnikier House, Kingswood Hotel, The Aberdour
Hotel, The Parkway Hotel, Victoria Hotel.

# LADYBANK

## LADYBANK GOLF CLUB

### COURSE DESCRIPTION:
Inland heathland course set amongst heather, Scots pine and silver birch in a
peaceful and secluded setting. A test of golf for the brave, with accuracy more
important than length. Established in 1879, the course was originally six holes and
designed by Old Tom Morris. It was expanded to nine holes in 1910 and eighteen
in 1961. The back nine remain relatively unchanged. Qualifying course for The
Open. Jack Nicklaus and Seve Ballesteros are both honorary members.

18 holes, 6,641 yards, par 71 (SSS 72). Amateur record Paul Stuart 63. Pro
record Mark Brooks 65.

### SIGNATURE HOLE:
NINTH (401 yards, par 4) Precise tee shot required on this right-to-left dogleg.
Long iron second shot against the prevailing wind into a large two-tier green.

### COURSE CARD

| HOLE | YDS | PAR | HOLE | YDS | PAR |
|------|-----|-----|------|-----|-----|
| 1 | 374 | 4 | 10 | 165 | 3 |
| 2 | 548 | 5 | 11 | 407 | 4 |
| 3 | 391 | 4 | 12 | 243 | 3 |
| 4 | 166 | 3 | 13 | 528 | 5 |
| 5 | 344 | 4 | 14 | 417 | 4 |
| 6 | 372 | 4 | 15 | 390 | 4 |
| 7 | 543 | 5 | 16 | 398 | 4 |
| 8 | 159 | 3 | 17 | 387 | 4 |
| 9 | 401 | 4 | 18 | 408 | 4 |
| *Yds Out* | 3,298 | | *Yds In* | 3,343 | |
| *Total Yds* | 6,641 | | | | |
| *Total Par* | 71 | | | | |

**ADDRESS:** Annsmuir, Ladybank, Cupar, Fife KY15 7RA.
**TELEPHONE:** +44 (0)1337 830814.
**FAX:** +44 (0)1337 831505.
**E-MAIL:** ladybankgc@aol.com
**SECRETARY:** David R. Allan.

PROFESSIONAL: Martin Gray +44 (0)1337 830725.
VISITORS: Without reservation Mondays to Fridays. Party bookings by arrangement.
GREEN FEES: £35 per round weekdays, £45 per day. £40 per round weekends.
CREDIT CARDS ACCEPTED: Visa/Mastercard.
CATERING: Full service with bar. Dining-room seats 80.
FACILITIES: Motorised buggies (£18), trolley hire (£2.50), club hire (£15), changing-rooms, putting green, pro shop, practice ground, coaching clinics.
LOCATION: ½ mile from A91/92 intersection on Kirkcaldy road (A92).
LOCAL HOTELS: Balgeddie Hotel, Kingswood Hotel, Lundin Links Hotel, Newton House Hotel, Old Manor Hotel, Queens Hotel, Rufflets Country House, Royal Hotel, The Sporting Laird Hotel.

# LESLIE

## LESLIE GOLF CLUB

COURSE DESCRIPTION:
Flat but undulating and challenging parkland course with a winding burn as a hazard.
9 holes, 4,686 yards (for 18 holes), par 63 (SSS 64). Course record 63.

ADDRESS: Balsillie Laws, Leslie, Fife KY6 3EZ.
TELEPHONE: +44 (0)1592 620040.
VISITORS: Contact in advance.
GREEN FEES: £9 per day, £11 weekends.
CATERING: By prior arrangement.
LOCATION: 10 miles east of M90 from junctions 5, 6 or 7.
LOCAL HOTELS: Balgeddie Hotel.

# LEUCHARS

## DRUMOIG HOTEL & GOLF COURSE

COURSE DESCRIPTION:
This is one of the most exciting developments in Scottish golf. A championship-style parkland course, designed by Dave Thomas and established in 1996, it is long and testing with lochside fairways and awesome quarry greens, which add up to quite a challenge. Lochs come into play on three holes and in particular the testing 9th hole with a difficult tee shot followed by a shot over water to the green. Two old whin quarries surround the 5th and 9th greens. It is also home to the Scottish National Golf Centre – Europe's premier indoor and outdoor practice facility. It includes a driving range, outdoor practice holes, indoor practice areas and the latest video swing technology with tuition available.

18 holes, 6,784 yards, par 71 (SSS 72).

**SIGNATURE HOLE:**
FIFTH ('East Quarry' 565 yards, par 5) A difficult par 5. Usually played into the prevailing wind, it requires a massive drive and a long iron just to reach the narrow opening to the green.

**ADDRESS:** Drumoig, by Leuchars, St Andrews, Fife KY16 0BE.
**TELEPHONE:** +44 (0)1382 541800.
**FAX:** +44 (0)1382 542211.
**E-MAIL:** drumoig@sol.co.uk
**WEBSITE:** www.drumoigleisure.com
**SECRETARY:** Christopher Walker.
**VISITORS:** At all times.
**GREEN FEES:** £25 per round weekdays, £45 per day. £30 per round weekends, £55 per day. Groups and societies welcome with discounted packages.
**CATERING:** Restaurant and bar. Functions catered for. Conferences, corporate golf, golf tour packages available.
**FACILITIES:** Motorised buggies (£17), trolley hire (£2), club hire (£12), changing-rooms, putting green, practice ground, memberships available, driving range, pro shop, coaching clinics.
**LOCATION:** On A914 between St Andrews (7 miles) and Dundee (4 miles). Follow A92 from Tay Road Bridge and turn left at Forgan roundabout. Drumoig is 1 mile down A914 on the left.
**LOCAL HOTELS:** Ballathie House Hotel, Kinloch House Hotel, Newton House Hotel, Old Manor Hotel, Queens Hotel, Rosely Country House Hotel, Rufflets Country House, Tayside Hotel, The Aberdour Hotel, The Sporting Laird Hotel.

## ST MICHAEL'S GOLF CLUB

**COURSE DESCRIPTION:**
Expanded to 18 holes in 1996. Undulating parkland course with trees and water hazard. Generous fairways but harder than it looks.
18 holes, 5,802 yards, par 70 (SSS 68). Amateur record 67.

**SIGNATURE HOLE:**
FIFTEENTH (157 yards, par 3) Elevated tee to raised green close to railway line.

**COURSE CARD**

| HOLE | YDS | PAR | HOLE | YDS | PAR |
|------|-----|-----|------|-----|-----|
| 1 | 415 | 4 | 10 | 352 | 4 |
| 2 | 168 | 3 | 11 | 360 | 4 |
| 3 | 341 | 4 | 12 | 156 | 3 |
| 4 | 443 | 4 | 13 | 391 | 4 |
| 5 | 307 | 4 | 14 | 486 | 5 |
| 6 | 337 | 4 | 15 | 157 | 3 |

| 7 | 176 | 3 | 16 | 337 | 4 |
|---|-----|---|----|-----|---|
| 8 | 261 | 4 | 17 | 265 | 4 |
| 9 | 502 | 5 | 18 | 348 | 4 |
| *Yds* *Out* | 2,950 | | *Yds* *In* | 2,852 | |
| *Total* *Yds* | 5,802 | | | | |
| Total | 70 | | | | |

**ADDRESS:** Leuchars, Fife KY16 0DX.

**TELEPHONE:** +44 (0)1334 839365.

**HONORARY SECRETARY & FAX:** +44 (0)1334 838666.

**VISITORS:** Any time, except Sunday mornings.

**GREEN FEES:** £20 per round weekdays, £28 per day, £22 per round weekends, £30 per day. 5 day ticket £60.

**CATERING:** All day if required.

**FACILITIES:** Trolley hire (£1), club hire, changing-rooms, putting green, memberships available.

**LOCATION:** On A919 St Andrews–Dundee road. 5 miles from St Andrews.

**LOCAL HOTELS:** Ballathie House Hotel, Kinloch House Hotel, Newton House Hotel, Old Manor Hotel, Queens Hotel, Rosely Country House Hotel, Rufflets Country House, St Michael's Inn, Tayside Hotel, The Aberdour Hotel, The Sporting Laird Hotel.

# LEVEN

## LEVEN LINKS GOLF CLUB

### COURSE DESCRIPTION:

A championship links, founded in 1820, used as a final qualifier for the Open Championship. A traditional Scottish links with undulating fairways, hills, out of bounds and a burn.

18 holes, 6,436 yards, par 71 (SSS 70). Amateur record 64. Pro record 63.

### SIGNATURE HOLE:

EIGHTEENTH (457 yards, par 4) – Green fronted by a burn.

### COURSE CARD

| HOLE | YDS | PAR | HOLE | YDS | PAR |
|------|-----|-----|------|-----|-----|
| 1 | 413 | 4 | 10 | 325 | 4 |
| 2 | 381 | 4 | 11 | 363 | 4 |
| 3 | 343 | 4 | 12 | 482 | 5 |
| 4 | 449 | 4 | 13 | 482 | 5 |
| 5 | 158 | 3 | 14 | 332 | 4 |
| 6 | 567 | 5 | 15 | 188 | 3 |

| 7 | 184 | 3 | 16 | 386 | 4 |
|---|-----|---|----|-----|---|
| 8 | 348 | 4 | 17 | 414 | 4 |
| 9 | 164 | 3 | 18 | 457 | 4 |
| *Yds* *Out* | 3,007 | | *Yds* *In* | 3,429 | |
| *Total* *Yds* | 6,436 | | | | |
| *Total* *Par* | 71 | | | | |

ADDRESS: Balfour Street, Leven, Fife KY8 4HS.

TELEPHONE: +44 (0)1333 428859 or 462096.

SECRETARY & FAX: +44 (0)1333 424229.

STARTER: +44 (0)1333 421390.

VISITORS: Any time, except Saturdays.

GREEN FEES: £28 per round weekdays, £40 per day. £30 per round weekends, £45 per day.

CATERING: Yes, full facilities.

FACILITIES: Trolley hire, putting green, pro shop, practice ground.

LOCATION: On main Kirkcaldy–St Andrews road. 10 miles east of Kirkcaldy on Leven Promenade.

LOCAL HOTELS: Caledonian Hotel, Lundin Links Hotel, Old Manor Hotel, Rufflets Country House, The Sporting Laird Hotel.

## SCOONIE GOLF CLUB

COURSE DESCRIPTION:

Pleasant inland parkland public course. Despite its proximity to the coast, it is parkland. Easy walking. Suitable for all ages.

18 holes, 5,456 yards, par 67 (SSS 66).

ADDRESS: North Links, Leven, Fife KY8 4SP.

TELEPHONE: +44 (0)1333 307007.

FAX: +44 (0)1333 307008.

PROFESSIONAL: +44 (0)1333 427437.

VISITORS: Any time.

GREEN FEES: £12 per round weekdays, £20 per day. £15 per round weekends, £22 per day.

CATERING: Full service.

FACILITIES: Trolley hire.

LOCATION: On coastal route between Kirkcaldy and St Andrews, close to Leven town centre.

LOCAL HOTELS: Caledonian Hotel, Lundin Links Hotel, Old Manor Hotel, Rufflets Country House, The Sporting Laird Hotel.

# LOCHGELLY

## LOCHGELLY GOLF CLUB

**COURSE DESCRIPTION:**
Relatively flat parkland course with fine views over the Lomonds and the Ochils. Easy walking.

18 holes, 5,491 yards, par 68 (SSS 67).

**ADDRESS:** Cartmore Road, Lochgelly, Fife KY5 9PB.
**TELEPHONE:** +44 (0)1592 780174.
**STARTER:** +44 (0)1592 782589.
**SECRETARY:** +44 (0)1383 512238.
**VISITORS:** Any time.
**GREEN FEES:** £12 per round weekdays, £18 per day. £21 per round weekends, £27 per day.
**CATERING:** Yes. Bar.
**FACILITIES:** Putting green.
**LOCATION:** West of town, off A910.
**LOCAL HOTELS:** Dean Park Hotel.

# LUNDIN LINKS

## LUNDIN GOLF CLUB

**COURSE DESCRIPTION:**
Principally links with four holes more akin to parkland. Every hole has the potential to ruin a card, even one that may seem an innocuous short par 4. Several holes have narrow burns crossing fairways. The old railway line provides an out of bounds area which runs through the course. Much praised for the quality of the greens which provide subtle borrows to test golfers of all levels.

18 holes, 6,394 yards. par 71 (SSS 71). Amateur record 64. Pro record 63.

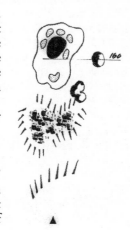

**SIGNATURE HOLE:**
FOURTEENTH (175 yards, par 3 ) Called 'Perfection' and you'll understand why when you survey the shot in front of you. From an elevated tee there is a magnificent view of the entire course and an outlook over the Firth of Forth. The green is virtually all carry with some impenetrable gorse bushes right on line with the flag.

The green is surrounded by five bunkers.

## COURSE CARD

| HOLE | YDS | PAR | HOLE | YDS | PAR |
|------|-----|-----|------|-----|-----|
| 1 | 424 | 4 | 10 | 353 | 4 |
| 2 | 346 | 4 | 11 | 466 | 4 |
| 3 | 335 | 4 | 12 | 150 | 3 |
| 4 | 452 | 4 | 13 | 512 | 5 |
| 5 | 140 | 3 | 14 | 175 | 3 |
| 6 | 330 | 4 | 15 | 418 | 4 |
| 7 | 273 | 4 | 16 | 314 | 4 |
| 8 | 364 | 4 | 17 | 345 | 4 |
| 9 | 555 | 5 | 18 | 442 | 4 |
| *Yds Out* | 3,219 | | *Yds In* | 3,175 | |
| *Total Yds* | 6,394 | | | | |
| *Total Par* | 71 | | | | |

ADDRESS: Golf Road, Lundin Links, Fife KY8 6BA.
TELEPHONE: +44 (0)1333 320202.
FAX: +44 (0)1333 329743.
WEBSITE: www.lundingolfclub.co.uk
SECRETARY: David Thomson.
PROFESSIONAL: David Webster +44 (0)1333 320051.
VISITORS: Yes. Monday to Thursday 9 a.m. to 3.30 p.m., Friday 9 a.m. to 3 p.m., Saturday after 2.30 p.m. (Societies limited to 32).
GREEN FEES: £32 per round weekdays, £40 per day. £40 per round Saturday afternoons only.
CATERING: Very welcome. Full facilities Tuesday to Saturday. Monday: hot soup, cold rolls.
FACILITIES: Trolley hire, 18-hole putting green, pro shop, practice ground, practice net.
LOCATION: A915 Kirkcaldy–St Andrews road. From Kirkcaldy, through Leven into Lundin Links. Turn right in dip, left, right and left.
LOCAL HOTELS: Crusoe Hotel, Lundin Links Hotel, Old Manor Hotel, Rufflets Country House, The Sporting Laird Hotel, Upper Largo Hotel.

# LUNDIN LADIES GOLF CLUB

### COURSE DESCRIPTION:

We can all tell horrendous stories of how the fairer sex are treated at some golf clubs where male chauvinism runs riot. Ladies are not allowed to use certain doors, banned from the bar or have to eat their lunch – sandwiches if they are lucky – in the car park. So it is with some relief that you turn up at Lundin Ladies Club, next door to the more famous Lundin Club, and find that far from getting their own back the ladies of Lundin are more generous and welcome golfers whatever their sex. There are limitations, of course. Men cannot become members and for understandable reasons are not encouraged to use the clubhouse apart from on special occasions. But for £80 they can become season ticket holders. Lundin Ladies is the only club so named in Scotland and one member says: 'I would think we are quite unique. We are completely run by ladies, there are no gentlemen in officialdom. I would like to think we are more tolerant. Men drive left and right but women golfers are always straight down the middle.' The parkland course dates back to 1891 and Lundin Ladies was founded in 1910. It has wide open fairways but is not as easy as it looks and is a fair test for even the most proficient of players. Lundin Ladies' members come from far and wide and at £180 per year new members are always welcome – as long as they play off the red tees.

9 holes, 4,730 yards (for 18 holes), par 68 (SSS 67).

SIGNATURE HOLE:
SECOND (262 yards, par 4) This fairway is home to the famous Standing Stones, which is an ancient burial ground.

COURSE CARD

| HOLE | YDS | PAR |
|------|-------|-----|
| 1 | 327 | 4 |
| 2 | 262 | 4 |
| 3 | 355 | 4 |
| 4 | 287 | 4 |
| 5 | 309 | 4 |
| 6 | 145 | 3 |
| 7 | 234 | 4 |
| 8 | 260 | 4 |
| 9 | 186 | 3 |
| Yds Out | 2,365 | |
| Total Yds | 2,365 | |
| Total Par | 34 | |

ADDRESS: Woodielea Road, Lundin Links, Fife KY8 6AJ.
TELEPHONE: +44 (0)1333 320832, 320022.
SECRETARY: Mrs Elizabeth Davidson.
VISITORS: Yes, both lady and gentlemen visitors are welcome. Restricted play on Wednesdays during season.
GREEN FEES: £10 per day weekdays, £12 per day weekends.
CATERING: No.
FACILITIES: Trolley hire, putting green.
LOCATION: Follow A915 to St Andrews and turn left at Royal Bank of Scotland in Lundin Links.

LOCAL HOTELS: Crusoe Hotel, Lundin Links Hotel, Old Manor Hotel, Rufflets Country House, The Sporting Laird Hotel, Upper Largo Hotel.

# MARKINCH

## BALBIRNIE PARK GOLF CLUB

### COURSE DESCRIPTION:
Scenic traditional parkland course with the natural contours being the inspiration behind the layout. Several interesting and challenging holes. Set within 140 acres of superb woodland, it was opened in 1983 and so has modern facilities.

18 holes, 6,210 yards, par 71 (SSS 70). Amateur records 67. Pro record 62.

### COURSE CARD

| HOLE | MEDAL YDS | PAR | FORWARD YDS | PAR | LADIES YDS | PAR | HOLE | MEDAL YDS | PAR | FORWARD YDS | PAR | LADIES YDS | PAR |
|---|---|---|---|---|---|---|---|---|---|---|---|---|---|
| 1 | 397 | 4 | 387 | 4 | 303 | 4 | 10 | 493 | 5 | 483 | 5 | 379 | 5 |
| 2 | 336 | 4 | 326 | 4 | 267 | 4 | 11 | 175 | 3 | 162 | 3 | 141 | 3 |
| 3 | 339 | 4 | 329 | 4 | 313 | 4 | 12 | 390 | 4 | 380 | 4 | 339 | 4 |
| 4 | 199 | 3 | 189 | 3 | 172 | 3 | 13 | 336 | 4 | 326 | 4 | 302 | 4 |
| 5 | 295 | 4 | 285 | 4 | 272 | 4 | 14 | 206 | 3 | 196 | 3 | 184 | 3 |
| 6 | 478 | 5 | 468 | 5 | 401 | 5 | 15 | 412 | 4 | 402 | 4 | 352 | 4 |
| 7 | 166 | 3 | 152 | 3 | 118 | 3 | 16 | 395 | 4 | 385 | 4 | 317 | 4 |
| 8 | 422 | 4 | 397 | 4 | 353 | 4 | 17 | 319 | 4 | 309 | 4 | 285 | 4 |
| 9 | 356 | 4 | 346 | 4 | 289 | 4 | 18 | 496 | 5 | 472 | 5 | 396 | 5 |
| Yds Out | 2,988 | | 2,879 | | 2,488 | | Yds In | 3,222 | | 3,115 | | 2,695 | |
| Total Yds | 6,210 | | 5,994 | | 5,183 | | | | | | | | |
| Total Par | 71 | | 71 | | 71 | | | | | | | | |

ADDRESS: Balbirnie Park, Markinch, Fife KY7 6NR.
TELEPHONE & FAX: +44 (0)1592 752006.
SECRETARY: Steve Oliver.
PROFESSIONAL: Craig Donnelly.
VISITORS: Yes, most of the time.
GREEN FEES: £25 per round weekdays, £33 per day. £30 per round weekends, £40 per day.
CREDIT CARDS ACCEPTED: Visa/Mastercard.
CATERING: Restaurant and bar (open from 9 a.m. to 10 p.m. during summer). Functions catered for. Full service.
FACILITIES: Motorised buggies (£20), trolley hire (£5 electric, £3 pull), club hire (£15), caddies on request, changing-rooms, putting green, practice ground, pro shop, coaching clinics, memberships available.

LOCATION: Just off the A92 at the junction for Markinch, 2 miles east of Glenrothes.

LOCAL HOTELS: Balbirnie House Hotel, Balgeddie House, Kingswood Hotel, Lundin Links Hotel.

# MILNATHORT

## MILNATHORT GOLF CLUB LTD

COURSE DESCRIPTION:

Undulating parkland course in tranquil setting. Lush and wide fairways with light rough which always gives you a shot no matter how far off course you stray. Ten excellent greens, two double. Twelve tees. Beware the 9/18th hole: with the prevailing wind, big hitters could land up in the clubhouse directly behind the green.

9 holes, 5,985 yards (for 18 holes), par 71 (SSS 69). Course record 65.

SIGNATURE HOLE:

SEVENTH (450 yards, par 4) Trying to get home in two causes all sorts of problems. Blind tee shot means that bunkers and trees can make for a difficult second shot.

COURSE CARD

| HOLE | YDS | PAR | HOLE | YDS | PAR |
|------|-----|-----|------|-----|-----|
| 1 | 408 | 4 | 10 | 408 | 4 |
| 2 | 326 | 4 | 11 | 342 | 4 |
| 3 | 285 | 4 | 12 | 285 | 4 |
| 4 | 140 | 3 | 13 | 146 | 3 |
| 5 | 378 | 4 | 14 | 378 | 4 |
| 6 | 495 | 5 | 15 | 495 | 5 |
| 7 | 450 | 4 | 16 | 489 | 5 |
| 8 | 203 | 3 | 17 | 203 | 3 |
| 9 | 277 | 4 | 18 | 277 | 4 |
| *Yds Out* | 2,962 | | *Yds In* | 3,023 | |
| *Total Yds* | 5,985 | | | | |
| *Total Par* | 71 | | | | |

ADDRESS: South Street, Milnathort, Fife KY13 9XA.

TELEPHONE: +44 (0)1577 864069.

EMAIL: milnathortgolf@ukgateway.net

HONORARY SECRETARY: A. Jones +44 (0)1577 864294.

VISITORS: Yes, apart from Saturdays. Advisable to phone in advance.

GREEN FEES: £12 per round weekdays, £18 per day. £14 per round weekends, £20 per day. Sundowner £6 weekdays, £7 weekends.

CATERING: Bar and bar meals.
FACILITIES: Changing-rooms, putting green, practice ground.
LOCATION: 1 mile north of Kinross. M90 junction 6 (north) or junction 7 (south).
LOCAL HOTELS: Jolly Beggars Hotel, Kingswood Hotel, Newton House Hotel.

# SALINE

## SALINE GOLF CLUB

COURSE DESCRIPTION:
Hillside parkland course with excellent turf and panoramic views.
   9 holes, 5,302 yards (for 18 holes), par 68 (SSS 66). Amateur record 63.

SIGNATURE HOLE:
EIGHTH (160 yards, par 3) Downhill. Must pitch on green. Very difficult if any
cross-wind, but best chance of hole in one.

### COURSE CARD

| HOLE | YDS | PAR |
|------|-------|-----|
| 1 | 279 | 4 |
| 2 | 314 | 4 |
| 3 | 166 | 3 |
| 4 | 289 | 4 |
| 5 | 372 | 4 |
| 6 | 378 | 4 |
| 7 | 329 | 4 |
| 8 | 160 | 3 |
| 9 | 364 | 4 |
| Yds Out | 2,651 | |
| Total Yds | 2,651 | |
| Total Par | 34 | |

ADDRESS: Kinneddar Hill, Saline, Fife KY12 9NF.
TELEPHONE: +44 (0)1383 852591.
SECRETARY: R. Hutchison +44 (0)1383 852344.
VISITORS: Unrestricted, except Saturdays and certain Sundays.
GREEN FEES: £9 weekdays. £11 per day Sundays.
CATERING: Bar and full service.
FACILITIES: Putting green, practice ground, practice nets.
LOCATION: Junction 4 off M90, 7 miles on B914 Dollar road.
LOCAL HOTELS: King Malcolm Thistle Hotel, Kingswood Hotel, The Aberdour Hotel.

# ST ANDREWS

## ST ANDREWS – THE OLD COURSE

### COURSE DESCRIPTION:

This is where it all started – the undoubted Home of Golf. Fittingly the venue for the 2000 Open Championship (won in record style by Tiger Woods), this traditional links course is the oldest in the world. Its layout is unique and challenging and its sense of history is overwhelming. To tread the turf of St Andrews, where in the thirteenth century shepherds played a form of golf, is a marvellous experience. Over 600 years, one simple track hacked through the bushes and heather has developed into six golf courses: the world-famous Old Course and its sister courses, The New, The Jubilee, The Eden, The Strathtyrum and The Balgove, all run by the St Andrews Links Trust. All are in effect public courses with several clubs allowed to play over them – the most famous of which is the Royal and Ancient (R&A), which was founded in 1754 and now governs the rules of golf everywhere in the world except the United States.

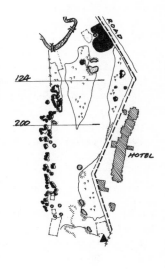

It is every golfer's dream to play the Old Course and if you are lucky enough to get the chance golf writer Michael McDonnell, a member of the R&A, gives this advice: 'One of the recurring charms of golf is that even the humble duffer can stand on the same hallowed ground where great deeds have been performed by past heroes and savour the challenge they experienced. It is a bond between champion and devotee few other sports can offer.

'There are moments when that awareness can be quite overwhelming and nowhere is the presence of past ghosts and great occasions more apparent than on the 1st tee of the Old Course at St Andrews because the game of golf, both in form and doctrine, was created upon this somewhat forbidding stretch of shore on the east coast of Scotland.

'The Old Course stands on the edge of a medieval town which was once the hub of the country's religious, academic and commercial affairs. The game itself has been played at St Andrews for at least five centuries. It is therefore unquestionably the Home of Golf. But, quite apart from being both shrine and spiritual Mecca for millions of golfers worldwide, the Old Course has extended an active influence on the game and the manner in which it is played. By definition a round of golf is conducted over 18 holes because in 1764 the players at St Andrews decided upon that number. And such was the influence of this 'auld grey toon' that in 1897 the Royal and Ancient Golf Club, one of several to play regularly over this public land, was given the responsibility of framing and maintaining the rules of the sport throughout most of the world.

'The Old Course exerts an even stronger hold because it has also defined the spirit of the game and its philosophies by establishing the fundamental doctrine that golf was never meant to be fair and consequently will always be a test of a player's character as well as personal skill. In a sense these enduring principles were determined by the bleak nature of the terrain from which the sea had receded and over which the ball was played. The uneven landscape which lacked definition, the hidden tracts of sand that formed penal hazards, as well as the constantly changing coastal weather conditions, all contributed to an exhaustive test of physical and mental stamina that is an intrinsic challenge.

'In truth the Old Course, which runs out and back along a peninsula, has to be played from memory, cruel experience and preferably with the wise counsel of a local caddie whose instructions must be observed to the letter and without question. The playing strategy is simple enough and demands a kind of stepping-stone approach in which various safe and pre-determined areas of the terrain are found en route to the massive, undulating greens.

'Sometimes the judicious line of attack ignores the intended flagstick in the distance because of the perils that lie in between. There is also a constant need for saint-like patience because temper and skill are tested to the limit, especially when a perfectly struck shot finds an uneven lie or is ambushed by a cavernous pot bunker. The old campaigners at St Andrews observe one golden rule: 'Never tease the bunkers'. In other words, these hazards must be given the widest possible berth because the ground around them invariably slopes in their direction, effectively making them much larger penalties than they appear. The other essential tenet is to find an immediate way out of a sand trap, even if that means playing out backwards as Australian Peter Thomson did when winning the Open Championship in 1955.

'What makes the Old Course such a complete test is that it combines the two basic elements of golf-course architecture in that it is both strategic and punitive. By definition the strategic concept demands positional play for the best results and provides proportionate rewards, while the punitive style imposes massive sanctions for the slightest deviation from the prescribed route.

'To stand on the 1st tee and aim an opening shot at that huge expanse of land which also includes the adjacent 18th fairway is to experience the strategic concept. The sharp line to the left will be safe enough, but then imposes a very difficult and long approach over the Swilcan Burn which menaces the front edge of the green. Thereafter, the Old Course remains both punitive and strategic in that the safe tee shot is played to the left and sometimes as far as the adjacent fairways to avoid the constant trouble on the right, but this tactic can make the approach more difficult – particularly to the seven huge greens that are shared by outward and inward holes. (Aim for the white flags on the outward nine and reds on the homeward stretch.)

'The overriding rule of play at the Old Course is that no matter how savage the setback or disaster, there is no good reason to surrender all hope. That said, the inward run presents a succession of challenges that can undermine the prospects of a reasonable score and tee shots must always be placed precisely to avoid escalating drama. From the 14th tee, the church spire in the distant town is the safe line on which to aim in order to pass to the right of the hazardous Beardies and find that level known as the Elysian Fields from where the second shot is directed left of Hell Bunker for a third stroke to the green. Pure stepping-stone stuff and essentially a double dogleg in open countryside.

'The mark of a great hole is the manner in which it makes players worry long before they reach it. Such is the awe in which the 17th – the Road Hole – is held. It is the most famous golf hole in the world. Some claim it is the best. The drive has to find a fairway over sheds and a wall to set up an approach to the green that is protected by the infamous Road Bunker at the front edge, while the road itself at the rear punishes any stroke that is too powerful. It contains the definitive elements of strategic and punitive golf and for lesser mortals is best played as a five to avoid heartbreak. Once completed, the ritual of the final tee shot remains and should be aimed towards the R&A clubhouse clock to avoid the right-hand out of bounds road – as well as houses and shops – which runs all the way to the green.

'No matter who you are, some local citizen will lean over the fence to watch how you tackle the Valley of Sin, that hollow in front of the green that has wrecked so many scores. The pitch and run can be risky if not played with confidence. The high wedge is safer although it may leave a downhill putt. But even if you miss, the journey is complete and you share an experience with all the great heroes of the past who strode the same fairways. At the Home of Golf, too. But try not to think about it on the 1st tee.'

18 holes, 7,125 yards (championship), 6,566 yards (medal), par 72 (SSS 72). Course record 62.

SIGNATURE HOLE:
SEVENTEENTH (455 yards, par 4) The Road Hole is the most famous hole in golf. Blind drive over hotel grounds. A very long second to an extremely narrow green with the road hard against the back edge and the fearsome Road Bunker front left.

COURSE CARD

| HOLE | CH'SHIP YDS | PAR | MEDAL YDS | PAR | HOLE | CH'SHIP YDS | PAR | MEDAL YDS | PAR |
|------|------|-----|------|-----|------|------|-----|------|-----|
| 1 | 376 | 4 | 370 | 4 | 10 | 379 | 4 | 318 | 4 |
| 2 | 413 | 4 | 411 | 4 | 11 | 174 | 3 | 172 | 3 |
| 3 | 397 | 4 | 352 | 4 | 12 | 314 | 4 | 316 | 4 |
| 4 | 464 | 4 | 418 | 4 | 13 | 430 | 4 | 398 | 4 |
| 5 | 568 | 5 | 514 | 5 | 14 | 581 | 5 | 523 | 5 |
| 6 | 412 | 4 | 374 | 4 | 15 | 456 | 4 | 401 | 4 |
| 7 | 388 | 4 | 359 | 4 | 16 | 434 | 4 | 351 | 4 |
| 8 | 175 | 3 | 166 | 3 | 17 | 455 | 4 | 461 | 4 |
| 9 | 352 | 4 | 307 | 4 | 18 | 357 | 4 | 354 | 4 |
| *Yds* Out | 3,545 | | 3,272 | | *Yds* In | 3,580 | | 3,294 | |
| *Total Yds* | 7,125 | | 6,566 | | | | | | |

| | | |
|---|---|---|
| *Total* | 72 | 72 |
| *Par* | | |

**ADDRESS:** St Andrews Links Trust, Pilmour House, St Andrews, Fife KY16 9SF.
**TELEPHONE:** +44 (0)1334 466666.
**FAX:** +44 (0)1334 479555. Links clubhouse: +44 (0)1334 466664.
**E-MAIL:** linkstrust@standrews.org.uk
**WEBSITE:** www.standrews.org.uk
**GENERAL MANAGER:** Alan McGregor.
**VISITORS:** All year apart from Sundays and by reservation or by ballot. Need to book well in advance. There is a daily ballot for play the next day but it does not always guarantee a game. Visitors must have handicap certificates or letter of introduction.
**GREEN FEES:** £90 per round.
**CREDIT CARDS ACCEPTED:** Visa/Mastercard.
**CATERING:** Restaurant and bar. Functions catered for.
**FACILITIES:** Trolley hire (only after 12 noon), club hire, caddies, changing-rooms, putting green, pro shop, practice ground, driving range.
**LOCATION:** A91 from Cupar. Once in town, take third turning on left into Golf Place and follow for 500 yards.
**LOCAL HOTELS:** Ballathie House Hotel, Kinloch House Hotel, Newton House Hotel, Old Manor Hotel, Queens Hotel, Rosely Country House Hotel, Rufflets Country House, Tayside Hotel, The Aberdour Hotel, The Sporting Laird Hotel.

## ST ANDREWS — BALGOVE COURSE

**COURSE DESCRIPTION:**
The course, which was upgraded and re-opened in 1993, is primarily for children, beginners and those who can manage only 9 holes.

9 holes, 1,520 yards, par 30.

**COURSE CARD**

| HOLE | YDS | PAR |
|---|---|---|
| 1 | 220 | 4 |
| 2 | 219 | 4 |
| 3 | 104 | 3 |
| 4 | 194 | 3 |
| 5 | 161 | 3 |
| 6 | 298 | 4 |
| 7 | 103 | 3 |
| 8 | 116 | 3 |
| 9 | 105 | 3 |
| *Yds Out* | 1,520 | |
| *Total Yds* | 1,520 | |

*The ninth at Turnberry – the most spectacular hole in Scottish golf, with a 50-foot drop from the championship tee (bottom left) to the rocks below. (Picture: Brian Morgan)*

*With undulating fairways like the fifth, Royal Dornoch must be one of the most beautiful courses in the world. (Picture: Brian Morgan)*

*Royal Troon's eighth, called the Postage Stamp, is perhaps the most famous par-three in the world, with a daunting tee shot to a small, well-guarded green.*
*(Picture: Brian Morgan)*

*The Home of Golf. The Royal and Ancient clubhouse provides the perfect backdrop to John Daly's Open Championship victory in 1995. (Picture: Andy Hooper,* Daily Mail*)*

*St Andrews' Road Hole 17th is for many the most difficult hole in golf. If you come up short of the green, you face the dilemma of getting over a cavernous bunker with not a lot of green to play with. Jack Nicklaus opted for putting around the bunker (right). Too strong and you're on the infamous road, faced with a similar shot knowing you could run through and into the bunker at the front.*
*(Top picture: Andy Hooper,* Daily Mail; *right picture: Stanley Hunter)*

*The Spectacles, the bunkers on the 14th at Carnoustie. Many a round has come to grief here. (Picture: Brian Morgan)*

*Jack Nicklaus regards the 146-yard 13th at Muirfield as a golfing gem. (Picture: Brian Morgan)*

| Total | 30 |
|-------|-----|
| Par   |    |

ADDRESS: St Andrews Links Trust, Pilmour House, St Andrews, Fife KY16 9SF.
TELEPHONE: +44 (0)1334 466666.
FAX: +44 (0)1334 479555.
LINKS clubhouse: +44 (0)1334 466664.
E-MAIL: linkstrust@standrews.org.uk
WEBSITE: www.standrews.org.uk
GENERAL MANAGER: Alan McGregor.
VISITORS: Yes, all year. Non-bookable.
GREEN FEES: £10 per round. Weekly ticket for Balgove only: £30.
CATERING: Restaurant and bar in Links clubhouse. Functions catered for.
FACILITIES: Trolley hire, club hire, caddies, changing-rooms, putting green, shop, practice ground, driving range.
LOCATION: Coming from Dundee, A91, follow signs. Coming from Edinburgh, A92, follow signs.
LOCAL HOTELS: Ballathie House Hotel, Kinloch House Hotel, Newton House Hotel, Old Manor Hotel, Queens Hotel, Rosely Country House Hotel, Rufflets Country House, Tayside Hotel, The Aberdour Hotel, The Sporting Laird Hotel.

## ST ANDREWS – EDEN COURSE

### COURSE DESCRIPTION:
Traditional links course laid out by H.S. Colt and opened in 1914. A good test with devilishly positioned bunkers and home of one of Scotland's oldest amateur tournaments, the Eden Trophy.
18 holes, 6,112 yards, par 70 (SSS 70).

### SIGNATURE HOLE:
SEVENTEENTH (432 yards, par 4) Running along the curve of the old railway, this is more of a banana than a dogleg. Out of bounds on the right. The line of the drive is on the most distant visible bunker. The green is reasonably deep, but the gap between the bunker on the left of the green and the out of bounds is tight.

### COURSE CARD

| HOLE | YDS | PAR | HOLE | YDS | PAR |
|------|-----|-----|------|-----|-----|
| 1 | 326 | 4 | 10 | 196 | 3 |
| 2 | 449 | 4 | 11 | 375 | 4 |
| 3 | 417 | 4 | 12 | 341 | 4 |
| 4 | 273 | 4 | 13 | 422 | 4 |
| 5 | 144 | 3 | 14 | 350 | 4 |
| 6 | 407 | 4 | 15 | 170 | 3 |
| 7 | 313 | 4 | 16 | 480 | 5 |
| 8 | 178 | 3 | 17 | 432 | 4 |
| 9 | 505 | 5 | 18 | 334 | 4 |

| | Yds | 3,012 | | Yds | 3,100 |
|---|---|---|---|---|---|
| | Out | | | In | |
| | Total Yds | 6,112 | | | |
| | Total Par | 70 | | | |

ADDRESS: St Andrews Links Trust, Pilmour House, St Andrews, Fife KY16 9SF.
TELEPHONE: +44 (0)1334 466666.
FAX: +44 (0)1334 479555.
LINKS CLUBHOUSE: +44 (0)1334 466664.
E-MAIL: linkstrust@standrews.org.uk
WEBSITE: www.standrews.org.uk
GENERAL MANAGER: Alan McGregor.
VISITORS: Yes, all year.
GREEN FEES: £28 per round weekdays. Weekly ticket: all courses except the Old, £190.
CREDIT CARDS ACCEPTED: Visa/Mastercard.
CATERING: Restaurant and bar in Links clubhouse. Functions catered for.
FACILITIES: Trolley hire, club hire, caddies, changing-rooms, putting green, shop, practice ground, driving range.
LOCATION: Coming from Dundee, A91, follow signs. Coming from Edinburgh, A92, follow signs.
LOCAL HOTELS: Ballathie House Hotel, Kinloch House Hotel, Newton House Hotel, Old Manor Hotel, Queens Hotel, Rosely Country House Hotel, Rufflets Country House, Tayside Hotel, The Aberdour Hotel, The Sporting Laird Hotel.

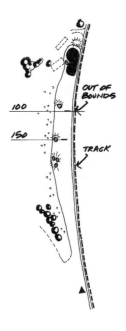

## ST ANDREWS – JUBILEE COURSE

### COURSE DESCRIPTION:
Traditional links course. First laid out in 1897 and upgraded to championship standard in 1989. A severe test. Catch the view of the 'auld grey toon' at sunset from the 18th tee.

18 holes, 6,805 yards, par 72 (SSS 73). A shorter version of the Jubilee Course is also available, known as the Bronze Course – 5,674 yards, par 69.

### SIGNATURE HOLE:
TWELFTH (538 yards, par 5) Shortest route hugs the edge of the left-hand dogleg. The placing of the second wood is critical. Too wide and you may need two or three more clubs to the green. Too tight and the mound to the left of the green and the bunker come into play. The green is 40 yards deep, so pin placement should be carefully assessed.

## COURSE CARD

| HOLE | YDS | PAR | HOLE | YDS | PAR |
|------|------|-----|------|------|-----|
| 1 | 454 | 4 | 10 | 411 | 4 |
| 2 | 336 | 4 | 11 | 497 | 5 |
| 3 | 546 | 5 | 12 | 538 | 5 |
| 4 | 371 | 4 | 13 | 188 | 3 |
| 5 | 162 | 3 | 14 | 438 | 4 |
| 6 | 498 | 5 | 15 | 356 | 4 |
| 7 | 373 | 4 | 16 | 428 | 4 |
| 8 | 369 | 4 | 17 | 211 | 3 |
| 9 | 192 | 3 | 18 | 437 | 4 |
| *Yds Out* | 3,301 | | *Yds In* | 3,504 | |
| *Total Yds* | 6,805 | | | | |
| *Total Par* | 72 | | | | |

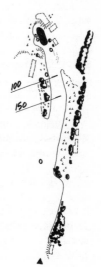

**ADDRESS:** St Andrews Links Trust, Pilmour House, St Andrews, Fife KY16 9SF.

**TELEPHONE:** +44 (0)1334 466666.

**FAX:** +44 (0)1334 479555.

**LINKS CLUBHOUSE:** +44 (0)1334 466664.

**E-MAIL:** linkstrust@standrews.org.uk

**WEBSITE:** www.standrews.org.uk

**GENERAL MANAGER:** Alan McGregor.

**VISITORS:** Yes, all year.

**GREEN FEES:** £37 per round. Weekly ticket: all courses except the Old, £190.

**CATERING:** Restaurant and bar in Links clubhouse. Functions catered for.

**FACILITIES:** Trolley hire, club hire, caddies, changing-rooms, putting green, shop, practice ground, driving range.

**LOCATION:** Coming from Dundee, A91, follow signs. Coming from Edinburgh, A92, follow signs.

**LOCAL HOTELS:** Ballathie House Hotel, Kinloch House Hotel, Newton House Hotel, Old Manor Hotel, Queens Hotel, Rosely Country House Hotel, Rufflets Country House, Tayside Hotel, The Aberdour Hotel, The Sporting Laird Hotel.

## ST ANDREWS – NEW COURSE

### COURSE DESCRIPTION:

Traditional links course, laid out by Old Tom Morris and opened in 1895. It's a tough test and has many of the features of the Old Course.

18 holes, 6,604 yards, par 71 (SSS 72).

259

SIGNATURE HOLE:
EIGHTEENTH (408 yards, par 4) The line is slightly left, but tempered by the rough edge bunker at driving range. The green is protected on the right by a single bunker and on the left by a pair backed up by gorse. If left, you should have a clear line to the pin. No trouble at the back, so play long for safety.

COURSE CARD

| HOLE | YDS | PAR | HOLE | YDS | PAR |
|------|-----|-----|------|-----|-----|
| 1 | 336 | 4 | 10 | 464 | 4 |
| 2 | 367 | 4 | 11 | 347 | 4 |
| 3 | 511 | 5 | 12 | 518 | 5 |
| 4 | 369 | 4 | 13 | 157 | 3 |
| 5 | 180 | 3 | 14 | 386 | 4 |
| 6 | 445 | 4 | 15 | 394 | 4 |
| 7 | 356 | 4 | 16 | 431 | 4 |
| 8 | 481 | 4 | 17 | 229 | 3 |
| 9 | 225 | 3 | 18 | 408 | 4 |
| Yds Out | 3,270 | | Yds In | 3,334 | |
| Total Yds | 6,604 | | | | |
| Total Par | 71 | | | | |

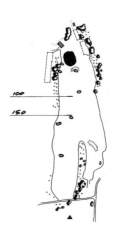

ADDRESS: St Andrews Links Trust, Pilmour House, St Andrews, Fife KY16 9SF.
TELEPHONE: +44 (0)1334 466666.
FAX: +44 (0)1334 479555.
LINKS CLUBHOUSE: +44 (0)1334 466664.
E-MAIL: linkstrust@standrews.org.uk
WEBSITE: www.standrews.org.uk
GENERAL MANAGER: Alan McGregor.
VISITORS: Yes, all year.
GREEN FEES: £42 per round weekdays. Weekly ticket: all courses except the Old, £190.
CREDIT CARDS ACCEPTED: Visa/Mastercard.
CATERING: Restaurant and bar in Links clubhouse. Functions catered for.
FACILITIES: Motorised buggies (only for senior citizens or medical certificate holders), trolley hire, club hire, caddies, changing-rooms, putting green, practice ground, driving range.
LOCATION: Coming from Dundee, A91, follow signs. Coming from Edinburgh, A92, follow signs.
LOCAL HOTELS: Ballathie House Hotel, Kinloch House Hotel, Newton House Hotel, Old Manor Hotel, Queens Hotel, Rosely Country House Hotel, Rufflets Country House, Tayside Hotel, The Aberdour Hotel, The Sporting Laird Hotel.

## ST ANDREWS — STRATHTYRUM COURSE

COURSE DESCRIPTION:
Opened in 1993, this is the newest course. Traditional links but with parkland features and few bunkers providing an enjoyable round.

18 holes, 5,094 yards, par 69 (SSS 70).

### COURSE CARD

| HOLE | YDS | PAR | HOLE | YDS | PAR |
|------|-----|-----|------|-----|-----|
| 1 | 332 | 4 | 10 | 297 | 4 |
| 2 | 324 | 4 | 11 | 447 | 5 |
| 3 | 154 | 3 | 12 | 317 | 4 |
| 4 | 261 | 4 | 13 | 148 | 3 |
| 5 | 456 | 5 | 14 | 317 | 4 |
| 6 | 125 | 3 | 15 | 270 | 4 |
| 7 | 295 | 4 | 16 | 125 | 3 |
| 8 | 165 | 3 | 17 | 326 | 4 |
| 9 | 345 | 4 | 18 | 390 | 4 |
| *Yds Out* | 2,457 | | *Yds In* | 2,637 | |
| *Total* | 5,094 | | | | |
| *Yds* | | | | | |
| *Total Par* | 69 | | | | |

ADDRESS: St Andrews Links Trust, Pilmour House, St Andrews, Fife KY16 9SF.
TELEPHONE: +44 (0)1334 466666.
FAX: +44 (0)1334 479555.
LINKS CLUBHOUSE: +44 (0)1334 466664.
E-MAIL: linkstrust@standrews.org.uk
WEBSITE: www.standrews.org.uk
GENERAL MANAGER: Alan McGregor.
VISITORS: Yes, all year.
GREEN FEES: £18 per round weekdays. Weekly ticket: all courses except the Old, £190.
CREDIT CARDS ACCEPTED: Visa/Mastercard.
CATERING: Full service in Links clubhouse. Bar.
FACILITIES: Motorised buggies (only for senior citizens or medical certificate holders), trolley hire, club hire, caddies, changing-rooms, putting green, shop, practice ground, driving range.
LOCATION: Coming from Dundee, A91, follow signs. Coming from Edinburgh, A92, follow signs.
LOCAL HOTELS: Ballathie House Hotel, Kinloch House Hotel, Newton House Hotel, Old Manor Hotel, Queens Hotel, Rosely Country House Hotel, Rufflets Country House, Tayside Hotel, The Aberdour Hotel, The Sporting Laird Hotel.

# THE DUKE'S COURSE

COURSE DESCRIPTION:

Classic, inland parkland course, which is a contrast to the Old Course and its neighbouring links courses that lie along the beach. The fairways are characterised by many small undulations and groups of small bunkers, often pot bunkers built into mounds. Designed by former Open champion Peter Thomson. Opened in 1995 and well worth a visit.

18 holes, 7,171 yards (championship), 6,649 yards (medal), par 72 .

COURSE CARD

| HOLE | CH'SHIP YDS | PAR | MEDAL YDS | PAR | LADIES YDS | PAR | HOLE | CH'SHIP YDS | PAR | MEDAL YDS | PAR | LADIES YDS | PAR |
|------|------|-----|------|-----|------|-----|------|------|-----|------|-----|------|-----|
| 1 | 517 | 5 | 479 | 5 | 459 | 5 | 10 | 429 | 4 | 403 | 4 | 374 | 4 |
| 2 | 448 | 4 | 421 | 4 | 345 | 4 | 11 | 510 | 5 | 478 | 5 | 447 | 5 |
| 3 | 156 | 3 | 140 | 3 | 128 | 3 | 12 | 212 | 3 | 192 | 3 | 134 | 3 |
| 4 | 439 | 4 | 404 | 4 | 358 | 4 | 13 | 397 | 4 | 366 | 4 | 339 | 4 |
| 5 | 375 | 4 | 343 | 4 | 300 | 4 | 14 | 472 | 4 | 435 | 4 | 408 | 4 |
| 6 | 565 | 5 | 510 | 5 | 455 | 5 | 15 | 533 | 5 | 501 | 5 | 471 | 5 |
| 7 | 467 | 4 | 431 | 4 | 400 | 4 | 16 | 429 | 4 | 410 | 4 | 390 | 4 |
| 8 | 212 | 3 | 185 | 3 | 149 | 3 | 17 | 191 | 3 | 177 | 3 | 140 | 3 |
| 9 | 415 | 4 | 393 | 4 | 327 | 4 | 18 | 404 | 4 | 381 | 4 | 353 | 4 |
| Yds Out | 3,594 | | 3,306 | | 2,919 | | Yds In | 3,577 | | 3,343 | | 3,055 | |
| Total Yds | 7,171 | | 6,649 | | 5,974 | | | | | | | | |
| Total Par | 72 | | 72 | | 72 | | | | | | | | |

ADDRESS: Craigtoun, St Andrews, Fife KY16 8NS.

TEL: +44 (0)1334 470214 or 474371.

PROFESSIONAL: John Kelly.

VISITORS: Any time.

GREEN FEES: £65 per round weekdays, £75 weekends.

CATERING: Full service from 7.30 a.m. to 10 p.m. Bar.

FACILITIES: Trolley/buggy hire, changing-rooms, putting green, pro shop, practice ground, chipping and bunker practice area.

LOCATION: 5 minutes from Old Course Hotel. Take the Craigtoun road from St Andrews and course is sign-posted on the left.

LOCAL HOTELS: Ballathie House Hotel, Kinloch House Hotel, Newton House Hotel, Old Course Hotel Golf Resort and Spa, Queens Hotel, Rosely Country House Hotel, Rufflets Country House, The Aberdour Hotel, The Sporting Laird Hotel.

# KINGSBARNS GOLF LINKS

COURSE DESCRIPTION:

The Kingsbarns course features dramatic sea views from each hole and a traditional links golf heritage dating from 1793. A challenging links experience awaits golfers as the course's spacious fairways roll and twist over dune ridges and hollows through Scottish heather and wispy rough along 1½ miles of scenic coastline near St Andrews. Kingsbarns truly 'embraces the sea'. The par-72 course extends to 7,126 yards for the championship tees. The 12th (see below) is the longest; the shortest is the 13th, a par 3 148 yards in length playing downhill to a small, well-bunkered green. The par-3 15th includes a forced carry over the foreshore for most of its 212 yards to a peninsula green jutting out into the North Sea. Sir Michael Bonallack, the former R&A secretary, has said of the course: 'Kingsbarns might well be one of the last true seaside links sites capable of development in Scotland. Mere words cannot convey just how extraordinary the place is. It must be seen to be believed. And once seen it will never be forgotten.'

18 holes, 7,126 yards, par 72. 6,652 yards from medal tees.

SIGNATURE HOLE:
TWELFTH (606 yards, par 5) Very challenging, with the sea hugging the fairway down the length of the hole on the left side. A green measuring 70 yards awaits your approach.

COURSE CARD

| HOLE | MEDAL YDS | PAR | FORWARD YDS | PAR | LADIES YDS | PAR | HOLE | MEDAL YDS | PAR | FORWARD YDS | PAR | LADIES YDS | PAR |
|---|---|---|---|---|---|---|---|---|---|---|---|---|---|
| 1 | 414 | 4 | 388 | 4 | 294 | 4 | 10 | 387 | 4 | 373 | 4 | 265 | 4 |
| 2 | 200 | 3 | 190 | 3 | 136 | 3 | 11 | 455 | 4 | 425 | 4 | 324 | 4 |
| 3 | 516 | 5 | 502 | 5 | 417 | 5 | 12 | 606 | 5 | 566 | 5 | 433 | 5 |
| 4 | 408 | 4 | 389 | 4 | 296 | 4 | 13 | 148 | 3 | 135 | 3 | 93 | 3 |
| 5 | 398 | 4 | 370 | 4 | 298 | 4 | 14 | 366 | 4 | 335 | 4 | 284 | 4 |
| 6 | 337 | 4 | 318 | 4 | 241 | 4 | 15 | 212 | 3 | 185 | 3 | 110 | 3 |
| 7 | 470 | 4 | 436 | 4 | 369 | 4 | 16 | 565 | 5 | 504 | 5 | 377 | 5 |
| 8 | 168 | 3 | 154 | 3 | 89 | 3 | 17 | 474 | 4 | 432 | 4 | 394 | 4 |
| 9 | 585 | 5 | 536 | 5 | 460 | 5 | 18 | 444 | 4 | 414 | 4 | 320 | 4 |
| Yds Out | 3,469 | | 3,283 | | 2,802 | | Yds In | 3,657 | | 3,369 | | 2,540 | |
| Total Yds | 7,126 | | 6,652 | | 5,342 | | | | | | | | |
| Total Par | 72 | | 72 | | 72 | | | | | | | | |

ADDRESS: Kingsbarns Golf Links, Kingsbarns, St Andrews, Fife KY16 8QD.
TELEPHONE: +44 (0)1334 460860.
FAX: +44 (0)1334 460877.
E-MAIL: info@kingsbarns.com
WEBSITE: www.kingsbarns.com
GENERAL MANAGER: Stuart McEwen.
PROFESSIONAL: David Scott.
VISITORS: Welcome every day, 7 days a week by advance reservation.
GREEN FEES: £125 per round weekdays/weekends, £185 per day.

CREDIT CARDS ACCEPTED: Amex/Visa/Mastercard.

CATERING: Restaurant and bar. All-day food and beverage available.

FACILITIES: Trolley hire (£4), club hire (£30), caddies (£30 + tip), changing-rooms, putting green, practice ground, pro shop, coaching clinics, driving range.

LOCATION:Take the A917 from St Andrews 6 miles along the coast to Kingsbarns. Once through the village, course entrance is on the left.

LOCAL HOTELS: Ballathie House Hotel, Kinloch House Hotel, Newton House Hotel, Old Manor Hotel, Queens Hotel, Rosely Country House Hotel, Rufflets Country House, Tayside Hotel, The Aberdour Hotel, The Sporting Laird Hotel.

# THORNTON

## THORNTON GOLF CLUB

### COURSE DESCRIPTION:

A scenic, easily walked parkland course bounded by the River Ore. Renowned for the condition of its greens. A challenge to every standard of golfer with as fine a finishing five holes as you'll find.

18 holes, 6,155 yards, par 70 (SSS 69). Amateur record 64.

### SIGNATURE HOLE:

FOURTEENTH ('Burn' 189 yards, par 3) River Ore runs to the left of the fairway and snakes around behind the green. Go left at your peril. Large bunker awaits on the right.

### COURSE CARD

| HOLE | MEDAL YDS | PAR | FORWARD YDS | PAR | HOLE | MEDAL YD | PAR | FORWARD YDS | PAR |
|------|-----------|-----|-------------|-----|------|----------|-----|-------------|-----|
| 1 | 347 | 4 | 336 | 4 | 10 | 399 | 4 | 333 | 4 |
| 2 | 366 | 4 | 336 | 4 | 11 | 401 | 4 | 384 | 4 |
| 3 | 208 | 3 | 195 | 3 | 12 | 421 | 4 | 410 | 4 |
| 4 | 399 | 4 | 388 | 4 | 13 | 530 | 5 | 498 | 5 |
| 5 | 428 | 4 | 413 | 4 | 14 | 189 | 3 | 178 | 3 |
| 6 | 465 | 5 | 456 | 5 | 15 | 359 | 4 | 348 | 4 |
| 7 | 189 | 3 | 170 | 3 | 16 | 244 | 4 | 228 | 4 |
| 8 | 398 | 4 | 387 | 4 | 17 | 291 | 4 | 268 | 4 |
| 9 | 125 | 3 | 120 | 3 | 18 | 396 | 4 | 381 | 4 |
| *Yds* *Out* | 2,925 | | 2,801 | | *Yds* *In* | 3,230 | | 3,028 | |
| *Total Yds* | 6,155 | | 5,829 | | | | | | |
| *Total Par* | 70 | | 70 | | | | | | |

ADDRESS: Station Road, Thornton, Fife KY1 DW.

**TELEPHONE:** +44 (0)1592 771111.

**FAX:** +44 (0)1592 774955.

**E-MAIL:** johntgc@ic24.net

**WEBSITE:** www.thorntongolfclubfife.co.uk

**SECRETARY:** B.S.L.Main.

**VISITORS:** Yes, except when competitions are being staged.

**GREEN FEES:** £17 per round weekdays, £27 per day. £25 per round weekends, £35 per day. Discounts on visiting groups of more than 20.

**CATERING:** Restaurant and bar. Functions catered for.

**FACILITIES:** Trolley hire, changing-rooms, putting green, practice ground, membership available.

**LOCATION:** 1½ miles off the A92 trunk road on the B9130, midway between Kirkcaldy and Glenrothes. Signposted on Main Street.

**LOCAL HOTELS:** Crown Hotel, Dean Park Hotel, Kingswood Hotel, Old Manor Hotel, Rescobie Hotel, Royal Hotel, The Aberdour Hotel, Travel Inn.

# CENTRAL INCLUDING STIRLING

# ABERFOYLE

## ABERFOYLE GOLF CLUB

### COURSE DESCRIPTION:
Hilly James Braid-designed parkland course with a variety of holes and scenic views. Established in 1890.

18 holes, 5,218 yards, par 66 (SSS 66).

### SIGNATURE HOLE:
FOURTH (271 yards, par 4) Good tee shot leaves a short uphill approach to a small green cut into the hillside.

### COURSE CARD

| HOLE | YDS | PAR | HOLE | YDS | PAR |
|------|-----|-----|------|-----|-----|
| 1 | 324 | 4 | 10 | 127 | 3 |
| 2 | 357 | 4 | 11 | 401 | 4 |
| 3 | 363 | 4 | 12 | 168 | 3 |
| 4 | 271 | 4 | 13 | 156 | 3 |
| 5 | 225 | 3 | 14 | 421 | 4 |
| 6 | 157 | 3 | 15 | 327 | 4 |
| 7 | 310 | 4 | 16 | 338 | 4 |
| 8 | 162 | 3 | 17 | 356 | 4 |
| 9 | 373 | 4 | 18 | 382 | 4 |
| Yds Out | 2,542 | | Yds In | 2,676 | |
| Total Yds | 5,218 | | | | |
| Total Par | 66 | | | | |

ADDRESS: Braeval, Aberfoyle FK8 3UY.
TELEPHONE: +44 (0)1877 382493.
SECRETARY: Roddy Steele +44 (0)1877 382638.
VISITORS: Welcome all times, some restrictions at weekends.
GREEN FEES: £15 per round weekdays, £20 per day. £20 per round weekends, £28 per day. Weekly ticket £60.
CATERING: Restaurant and bar, open all day +44 (0)1877 382809.
FACILITIES: Trolley hire (£1), changing-rooms, putting green.
LOCATION: 1 mile outside Aberfoyle on main Stirling road.
LOCAL HOTELS: Rob Roy Motor Inn, Forth Inn.

# ALLOA

## ALLOA GOLF CLUB

### COURSE DESCRIPTION:
Rolling parkland course, designed by James Braid in 1935, with tree-lined fairways set amongst the 150-acre Schawpark Estate. Ideal variety of all types of holes with spectacular views. A test for all discerning golfers and a challenging finish from the 15th.

18 holes, 6,229 yards, par 70 (SSS 71). Amateur record 63. Pro record 67.

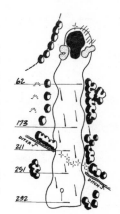

### SIGNATURE HOLE:
NINTH (467 yards, par 4) Panoramic views of the Ochil Hills and the Forth valley. Green guarded by two large bunkers.

### COURSE CARD

| HOLE | YDS | PAR | HOLE | YDS | PAR |
|------|-----|-----|------|-----|-----|
| 1 | 333 | 4 | 10 | 315 | 4 |
| 2 | 478 | 5 | 11 | 346 | 4 |
| 3 | 325 | 4 | 12 | 428 | 4 |
| 4 | 168 | 3 | 13 | 313 | 4 |
| 5 | 508 | 5 | 14 | 422 | 4 |
| 6 | 317 | 4 | 15 | 173 | 3 |
| 7 | 162 | 3 | 16 | 404 | 4 |
| 8 | 393 | 4 | 17 | 474 | 4 |
| 9 | 467 | 4 | 18 | 203 | 3 |
| *Yds Out* | 3,151 | | *Yds In* | 3,078 | |
| *Total Yds* | 6,229 | | | | |
| *Total Par* | 70 | | | | |

**ADDRESS:** Schawpark Course, Sauchie, Alloa, Clackmannanshire FK10 3AX.
**TELEPHONE:** +44 (0)1259 722745.
**E-MAIL:** bellville51@hotmail.com
**SECRETARY:** T. Crampton.
**PROFESSIONAL:** Bill Bennett +44 (0)1259 724476.
**VISITORS:** All days.
**GREEN FEES:** £24 per round weekdays, £34 per day. £28 per round weekends, £38 per day.
**CREDIT CARDS ACCEPTED:** Amex/Visa/Mastercard.

CATERING: Restaurant and bar. Functions catered for. Superb clubhouse with wonderful views.

FACILITIES: Trolley hire, club hire, changing-rooms, putting green, practice ground, pro shop, coaching clinics, memberships available.

LOCATION: From Kincardine, take the A977 then A907 into Alloa. At first large roundabout, take A908 for Tillicoultry. Take first exit at mini-roundabout and continue for 1 mile. Golf club is on the right just before the Schawpark Garage.

LOCAL HOTELS: Castle Campbell Hotel, Claremont Lodge Hotel, Dunmar House Hotel, Harviestoun Hotel, Kingswood Hotel, Royal Oak Hotel, The Aberdour Hotel.

# BRAEHEAD GOLF CLUB

COURSE DESCRIPTION:

Undulating parkland course with a fine variety of challenging holes. The only steepish hole is where the downhill par-3 8th is followed by the short uphill par-4 9th. The back nine is harder, particularly the 'Bermuda Triangle' around the 13th, 14th and 15th and the taxing final two holes. Good selection of par 3s. The 157-yard 6th is played from an elevated tee to a receptive green, but beware the pot bunker short on the left. The 8th is only seven yards longer but is often played into the prevailing wind. The 139-yard 11th has recently been remodelled and demands accuracy, but the 14th is the pick of the par 3s (see below). Spectacular views. The Ochil Hills are the backdrop to the north while the River Forth is to the south. To the west is the famous Wallace Monument. The magnificent panorama is completed by the distant mountains, Ben Lomond and Ben Arthur. Founded 1891.

18 holes, 6,052 yards, par 70 (SSS 69). Amateur record 64.

SIGNATURE HOLE:

FOURTEENTH (210 yards, par 3) Picturesque and challenging hole. Bunkers to the left and right will catch the slightly wayward shot, while out of bounds lurks to the rear.

COURSE CARD

| HOLE | MEDAL YDS | PAR | FORWARD YDS | PAR | LADIES YDS | PAR | HOLE | MEDAL YDS | PAR | FORWARD YDS | PAR | LADIES YDS | PAR |
|------|------|-----|------|-----|------|-----|------|------|-----|------|-----|------|-----|
| 1 | 350 | 4 | 337 | 4 | 323 | 4 | 10 | 467 | 4 | 443 | 4 | 400 | 4 |
| 2 | 332 | 4 | 325 | 4 | 319 | 4 | 11 | 139 | 3 | 126 | 3 | 116 | 3 |
| 3 | 356 | 4 | 341 | 4 | 331 | 4 | 12 | 518 | 5 | 508 | 5 | 359 | 4 |
| 4 | 297 | 4 | 293 | 4 | 289 | 4 | 13 | 400 | 4 | 395 | 4 | 390 | 5 |
| 5 | 344 | 4 | 309 | 4 | 302 | 4 | 14 | 210 | 3 | 187 | 3 | 183 | 3 |
| 6 | 157 | 3 | 151 | 3 | 144 | 3 | 15 | 376 | 4 | 370 | 4 | 366 | 4 |
| 7 | 505 | 5 | 452 | 5 | 448 | 5 | 16 | 270 | 4 | 252 | 4 | 206 | 4 |
| 8 | 164 | 3 | 136 | 3 | 133 | 3 | 17 | 467 | 4 | 444 | 4 | 425 | 5 |
| 9 | 273 | 4 | 264 | 4 | 256 | 4 | 18 | 427 | 4 | 414 | 4 | 392 | 5 |
| *Yds* *Out* | 2,778 | | 2,608 | | 2,545 | | *Yds* *In* | 3,274 | | 3,139 | | 2,837 | |

| *Total* | 6,052 | 5,747 | 5,382 |
| *Yds* | | | |
| *Total* | 70 | 70 | 73 |
| *Par* | | | |

ADDRESS: Cambus, by Alloa, Clackmannanshire FK10 2NT.
TELEPHONE: +44 (0)1259 725766.
FAX: +44 (0)1259 214070.
E-MAIL: clubhouse@braeheadgolfclub.fsnet.co.uk
SECRETARY: Paul MacMichael.
PROFESSIONAL: David Boyce +44 (0)1259 722078.
VISITORS: No restrictions, visitors advised to telephone in advance.
GREEN FEES: £18.50 per round weekdays, £24.50 per day. £24.50 per round weekends, £32.50 per day.
CATERING: Restaurant and bar. Full range of catering throughout the year. Functions catered for.
FACILITIES: Motorised buggies, trolley hire, club hire, changing-rooms, putting green, pro shop, practice ground, coaching clinics, ladies memberships available.
LOCATION: Well signposted on the A907, 1 mile west of Alloa.
LOCAL HOTELS: Castle Campbell Hotel, Dunmar House Hotel, Kingswood Hotel, Royal Oak Hotel, The Aberdour Hotel.

# ALVA

## ALVA GOLF CLUB

COURSE DESCRIPTION:
Sloping fairways and fast greens, some of which are on plateaux. Course founded in 1901, is at the foot of Ochil Hills.

9 holes, 4,846 yards (for 18 holes), par 66 (SSS 64). Parkland course record 62.

ADDRESS: Beauclerc Street, Alva FK12 5LH.
TELEPHONE: +44 (0) 1259 760431.
VISITORS: Any time, except during medal competitions and Thursday evenings (ladies' night).
GREEN FEES: £10 per round weekdays , £15 per day. £13 per round weekends. Weekly ticket (weekdays) £30.
CATERING: Bar and snacks only.
LOCATION: 7 miles from Stirling on A91 (Stirling–St Andrews road).
LOCAL HOTELS: Alva Glen Hotel.

# BALFRON

## SHIAN GOLF COURSE

COURSE DESCRIPTION:
Newly developed course with many interesting holes on upland pastures. Some hills.
  9 holes, 5,372 yards (for 18 holes), par 68 (SSS 67).

ADDRESS: Kepculloch Road, Balfron, Stirlingshire.
TELEPHONE: +44 (0)1360 440037.
VISITORS: Weekdays, last tee-off 4 p.m. At weekends, subject to competition restrictions.
GREEN FEES: £7 per round.

# BONNYBRIDGE

## BONNYBRIDGE GOLF CLUB

COURSE DESCRIPTION:
Inland course. Testing heathland but plays similar to links. Guarded greens. Easy
walking.
  9 holes, 6,060 yards (for 18 holes), par 72 (SSS 69).

ADDRESS: Larbert Road, Bonnybridge FK4 1NY.
TELEPHONE: +44 (0)1324 812822.
VISITORS: Must be accompanied by member. Contact in advance.
GREEN FEES: £10 per round weekdays.
CATERING: Bar, meals at weekends.
FACILITIES: Pro shop.
LOCATION: 1 mile north-east of Bonnybridge, off A883.
LOCAL HOTELS: Inchyra Grange Hotel, Royal Hotel.

# BRIDGE OF ALLAN

## BRIDGE OF ALLAN GOLF CLUB

COURSE DESCRIPTION:
Very picturesque and hilly moorland course in good condition. Established in
1895 and designed by Old Tom Morris. Overlooks Stirling Castle and the Wallace
Monument.
  9 holes, 5,120 yards (for 18 holes), par 66 (SSS 65). Course record 62 (men),
66 (ladies).

SIGNATURE HOLE:
FIRST (223 yards, par 3) Said by many to be the most difficult par 3 anywhere. Six-foot-high dyke 175 yards from tee.

ADDRESS: Sunnylaw, Bridge of Allan, Stirlingshire FK9 4LY.
TELEPHONE: +44 (0)1786 832332.
SECRETARY: Jim Black +44 (0)1786 813676.
VISITORS: Mondays, Wednesdays, Thursdays and Fridays.
GREEN FEES: £10 per round weekdays, £15 weekends.
CATERING: 7 days a week. Weekends only in winter. Bar.
FACILITIES: Trolley hire, putting green, small practice ground.
LOCATION: 1½ miles from Dunblane roundabout on M9. Follow signs for Bridge of Allan.
LOCAL HOTELS: Royal Hotel.

# CALLANDER

## CALLANDER GOLF CLUB

COURSE DESCRIPTION:
Inland wooded parkland course with panoramic views to Ben Ledi. Designed by Old Tom Morris in 1890.

18 holes, 5,151 yards, par 66 (SSS 66). Amateur record 61. Pro record 59.

SIGNATURE HOLE:
FIFTEENTH (135 yards, par 3) Down a narrow avenue of trees with bunkers to front and left of green.

COURSE CARD

| HOLE | YDS | PAR | HOLE | YDS | PAR |
|------|------|-----|------|------|-----|
| 1 | 348 | 4 | 10 | 179 | 3 |
| 2 | 199 | 3 | 11 | 179 | 3 |
| 3 | 329 | 4 | 12 | 404 | 4 |
| 4 | 321 | 4 | 13 | 324 | 4 |
| 5 | 163 | 3 | 14 | 224 | 3 |
| 6 | 372 | 4 | 15 | 135 | 3 |
| 7 | 250 | 4 | 16 | 365 | 4 |
| 8 | 296 | 4 | 17 | 478 | 5 |
| 9 | 232 | 3 | 18 | 333 | 4 |
| Yds Out | 2,530 | | Yds In | 2,621 | |
| Total Yds | 5,151 | | | | |
| Total Par | | 66 | | | |

ADDRESS: Aveland Road, Callander FK17 8EN.
TELEPHONE: +44 (0)1877 330090.
FAX: +44 (0)1877 330062.
E-MAIL: callandergc@nextcall.net
SECRETARY/MANAGER: Sandra Smart.
PROFESSIONAL: Allan Martin +44 (0)1877 330975.
VISITORS: Any time, but handicap certificates required on Wednesdays and Sundays.
GREEN FEES: £18 per round weekdays, £26 per day. £26 /£31 weekends. Seven day
    ticket £100.
CATERING: Full catering, bar facilities in season.
FACILITIES: Trolley hire, club hire, changing-rooms, putting green, pro shop, practice
    ground, membership available, coaching clinics.
LOCATION:16 miles north-west of Stirling on A84.
LOCAL HOTELS: Abbotsford Lodge Hotel, Myrtle Inn, Dreadnought Hotel.

# DOLLAR

## DOLLAR GOLF CLUB

COURSE DESCRIPTION:
Hillside course designed by Ben Sayers in 1906.
There are no bunkers, but small greens require
accurate shot-making. Overlooked by the
magnificent fifteenth-century Castle Campbell as
well as the Ochil Hills. Beautiful views along the
Devon Valley.

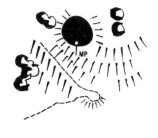

    18 holes, 5,242 yards, par 69 (SSS 66). Course
record 62.

▲

SIGNATURE HOLE:
SECOND ('Brae' 97 yards, par 3) Wedge shot uphill to a blind green. Not
difficult, but it can destroy a round if you fail to hit the green and the ball rolls
back down the slope.

COURSE CARD

| | MEDAL | | FORWARD | | LADIES | | | MEDAL | | FORWARD | | LADIES | |
|---|---|---|---|---|---|---|---|---|---|---|---|---|---|---|
| HOLE | YDS | PAR | YDS | PAR | YDS | PAR | HOLE | YDS | PAR | YDS | PAR | YDS | PAR |
| 1 | 196 | 3 | 185 | 3 | 162 | 3 | 10 | 153 | 3 | 152 | 3 | 152 | 3 |
| 2 | 97 | 3 | 80 | 3 | 71 | 3 | 11 | 449 | 4 | 449 | 4 | 445 | 4 |
| 3 | 254 | 4 | 206 | 3 | 219 | 4 | 12 | 519 | 5 | 418 | 4 | 401 | 4 |
| 4 | 331 | 4 | 278 | 4 | 219 | 4 | 13 | 320 | 4 | 288 | 4 | 278 | 4 |
| 5 | 307 | 4 | 285 | 4 | 293 | 4 | 14 | 302 | 4 | 186 | 3 | 207 | 4 |
| 6 | 331 | 4 | 315 | 4 | 306 | 4 | 15 | 288 | 4 | 253 | 4 | 252 | 4 |
| 7 | 306 | 4 | 299 | 4 | 296 | 4 | 16 | 296 | 4 | 273 | 4 | 257 | 4 |
| 8 | 308 | 4 | 290 | 4 | 279 | 4 | 17 | 303 | 4 | 287 | 4 | 298 | 4 |

| 9 | 200 | 3 | 188 | 3 | 180 | 3 | 18 | 282 | 4 | 273 | 4 | 258 | 4 |
|---|---|---|---|---|---|---|---|---|---|---|---|---|---|
| Yds Out | 2,330 | | 2,127 | | 2,024 | | Yds In | 2,912 | | 2,579 | | 2,548 | |
| Total Yds | 5,242 | | 4,706 | | 4,572 | | | | | | | | |
| Total Par | 69 | | 66 | | 68 | | | | | | | | |

ADDRESS: Brewlands House, Dollar, Clackmannanshire FK14 7EA.
TELEPHONE: +44 (0)1259 742400.
FAX: +44 (0)1259 743497.
E-MAIL: dollar.g.c.@brewlandshouse.freeserve.co.uk
WEBSITE: www.dollargolfclub.co.uk
SECRETARY: J. Brown +44 (0)1259 743581.
VISITORS: Seven days a week. Weekends by prior booking.
GREEN FEES: £13.50 per round weekdays, £17.50 per day. £22 weekends.
CATERING: restaurant and bar. Full service, except Tuesdays. Functions catered for.
FACILITIES: Trolley hire, club hire, changing-rooms, practice ground, memberships available.
LOCATION: North of town off A91.
LOCAL HOTELS: Castle Campbell Hotel, The Gleneagles Hotel.

# DRYMEN

## BUCHANAN CASTLE GOLF CLUB

COURSE DESCRIPTION:
Parkland course, designed by James Braid in 1936, in the grounds of Buchanan Castle. Braid's autograph of dogleg holes is well in evidence here. Fairly flat and true greens. Easy walking and good views.
   18 holes, 6,059 yards, par 70 (SSS 69).

SIGNATURE HOLE:
FIRST (396 yards, par 4) The first of Braid's doglegs. Two tall trees frame the corner of the dogleg right about 200 yards out from the tee. If you drive well to the left to open up the second shot, you find a diagonal of three bunkers squeezing out the left side of the green on the line of your approach.

ADDRESS: Drymen, Stirlingshire G63 0HY.
TELEPHONE: +44 (0)1360 660307.
FAX: +44 (0) 1360 870382.
E-MAIL: buchanancastle@sol.co.uk
SECRETARY: Richard Kinsella.
PROFESSIONAL: Keith Baxter +44 (0)1360 660330.
VISITORS: Yes, book by telephone.

GREEN FEES: £30 per round weekdays/weekends, £40 per day.
CREDIT CARDS ACCEPTED: Visa.
CATERING: Restaurant and bar. Functions catered for +44 (0)1360 660369.
FACILITIES: Trolley hire, club hire, changing-rooms, putting green, pro shop, practice ground, driving range, coaching clinics, membership available.
LOCATION: East side of Loch Lomond. 50 minutes north of Glasgow Airport, 30 minutes north of Glasgow on Aberfoyle road A81, A809.
LOCAL HOTELS: Buchanan Arms Hotel, Winnock Hotel.

## STRATHENDRICK GOLF CLUB

COURSE DESCRIPTION:
Testing, undulating parkland course, designed by Willie Fernie in 1901, with superb scenic views.
   9 holes, 4,982 yards (for 18 holes), par 66 (SSS 64). Amateur record 62.

SIGNATURE HOLE:
SEVENTH ('The Corner' 209 yards, par 3) Blind tee shot over ridge to a small green with a bunker to the left of the line and a bunker to the right front of the green. Out of bounds on the right.

ADDRESS: Glasgow Road, Drymen, Stirlingshire G63 0BY.
TELEPHONE: +44 (0)1360 660695.
SECRETARY: M. Gair.
VISITORS: Weekdays only (8.30 a.m. to 2.30 p.m.).
GREEN FEES: £12 per round weekdays, £15 per day.
FACILITIES: Changing rooms, putting green, memberships available.
LOCATION: From Glasgow A81 to Bearsden, then A809 to Drymen, 1 mile south of village on A811.
LOCAL HOTELS: Buchanan Arms Hotel, Winnock Hotel.

# DUNBLANE

## DUNBLANE NEW GOLF CLUB

COURSE DESCRIPTION:
Undulating parkland course. Founded in 1923.
   18 holes, 5,930 yards, par 69 (SSS 69). Amateur record 64. Pro record 66.

SIGNATURE HOLE:
ELEVENTH ('Ben Ledi' 181 yards, par 3) From the tee down to a green, which is guarded by six bunkers front and right with out of bounds on the left.

## COURSE CARD

| HOLE | MEDAL YDS | PAR | FORWARD YDS | PAR | LADIES YDS | PAR | HOLE | MEDAL YDS | PAR | FORWARD YDS | PAR | LADIES YDS | PAR |
|------|------|-----|------|-----|------|-----|------|------|-----|------|-----|------|-----|
| 1 | 324 | 4 | 307 | 4 | 306 | 4 | 10 | 402 | 4 | 365 | 4 | 359 | 4 |
| 2 | 418 | 4 | 403 | 4 | 385 | 5 | 11 | 181 | 3 | 170 | 3 | 146 | 3 |
| 3 | 190 | 3 | 177 | 3 | 162 | 3 | 12 | 381 | 4 | 321 | 4 | 317 | 4 |
| 4 | 296 | 4 | 283 | 4 | 268 | 4 | 13 | 378 | 4 | 361 | 4 | 343 | 4 |
| 5 | 357 | 4 | 346 | 4 | 334 | 4 | 14 | 160 | 3 | 149 | 3 | 134 | 3 |
| 6 | 503 | 5 | 478 | 5 | 467 | 5 | 15 | 322 | 4 | 291 | 4 | 289 | 4 |
| 7 | 162 | 3 | 156 | 3 | 144 | 3 | 16 | 195 | 4 | 182 | 3 | 160 | 3 |
| 8 | 422 | 4 | 404 | 4 | 315 | 4 | 17 | 366 | 4 | 363 | 4 | 320 | 4 |
| 9 | 386 | 4 | 379 | 4 | 374 | 4 | 18 | 492 | 5 | 445 | 5 | 433 | 5 |
| Yds Out | 3,058 | | 2,933 | | 2,755 | | Yds In | 2,872 | | 2,647 | | 2,501 | |
| Total Yds | 5,930 | | 5,580 | | 5,256 | | | | | | | | |
| Total Par | 69 | | 69 | | 71 | | | | | | | | |

ADDRESS: Perth Road, Dunblane, Perthshire FK15 0LJ.
TELEPHONE & FAX: +44 (0)1786 825281.
SECRETARY: John Dunsmore.
PROFESSIONAL: R. Jamieson +44 (0)1786 821521.
FAX: +44 (0)1786 821522.
VISITORS: Yes.
GREEN FEES: £22 per round weekdays, £36 per day. £36 per round weekends.
CATERING: Restaurant and bar. Functions catered for.
FACILITIES: Trolley hire (£1 per round), club hire, changing-rooms, putting green, pro shop, practice ground, coaching clinics.
LOCATION: 1 mile north off M9 at Fourways Roundabout.
LOCAL HOTELS: Dunblane Hydro, Stirling Arms Hotel.

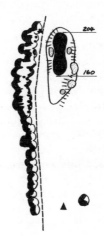

# FALKIRK

## FALKIRK GOLF CLUB

### COURSE DESCRIPTION:

Parkland course with streams and gorse, established in 1922 and designed by James Braid. Golfers are surprised by the degree of difficulty and the variety of holes. Several Roman burial plots have been found, the latest in 1975 – a sandstone grave below the 7th green containing the remains of a Centurion, a spearhead and the centre part of a shield.

18 holes, 6,230 yards (Championship tees), par 71 (SSS 70). Course record 66.

SIGNATURE HOLE:
SIXTH (351 yards, par 4) Stroke index 1. Dogleg left to an elevated green with out of bounds behind.

COURSE CARD

| HOLE | MEDAL YDS | PAR | FORWARD YDS | PAR | LADIES YDS | PAR | HOLE | MEDAL YDS | PAR | FORWARD YDS | PAR | LADIES YDS | PAR |
|---|---|---|---|---|---|---|---|---|---|---|---|---|---|
| 1 | 196 | 3 | 185 | 3 | 162 | 3 | 10 | 153 | 3 | 152 | 3 | 152 | 3 |
| 2 | 97 | 3 | 80 | 3 | 71 | 3 | 11 | 449 | 4 | 449 | 4 | 445 | 4 |
| 3 | 254 | 3 | 206 | 3 | 219 | 4 | 12 | 519 | 5 | 418 | 4 | 401 | 4 |
| 4 | 331 | 4 | 278 | 4 | 219 | 4 | 13 | 320 | 4 | 288 | 4 | 278 | 4 |
| 5 | 307 | 4 | 285 | 4 | 293 | 4 | 14 | 302 | 4 | 186 | 3 | 207 | 4 |
| 6 | 331 | 4 | 315 | 4 | 306 | 4 | 15 | 288 | 4 | 253 | 4 | 252 | 4 |
| 7 | 306 | 4 | 299 | 4 | 296 | 4 | 16 | 296 | 4 | 273 | 4 | 257 | 4 |
| 8 | 308 | 4 | 290 | 4 | 279 | 4 | 17 | 303 | 4 | 287 | 4 | 298 | 4 |
| 9 | 200 | 3 | 188 | 3 | 180 | 3 | 18 | 282 | 4 | 273 | 4 | 258 | 4 |
| Yds Out | 2,330 | | 2,127 | | 2,024 | | Yds In | 2,912 | | 2,579 | | 2,548 | |
| Total Yds | 5,242 | | 4,706 | | 4,572 | | | | | | | | |
| Total Par | 69 | | 66 | | 68 | | | | | | | | |

ADDRESS: Carmuirs, 136 Stirling Road, Camelon, Falkirk FK2 7YP.
TELEPHONE: +44 (0)1324 611061.
FAX: +44 (0)1324 639573.
SECRETARY: John Elliott +44 (0)1324 634118.
VISITORS: Weekdays. Societies weekdays and Sundays.
GREEN FEES: £15 per round weekdays, £20 per day. £30 Sundays.
CATERING: Full clubhouse facilities.
FACILITIES: Trolley/buggy hire, putting green, pro shop, practice ground.
LOCATION: 1½ miles north-west of Falkirk on A9.
LOCAL HOTELS: Inchyra Grange Hotel, Polmont Hotel.

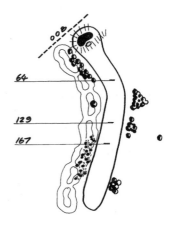

# POLMONT GOLF CLUB LTD

COURSE DESCRIPTION:
Hilly parkland course, founded in 1904, with tree-lined fairways. Small, tricky greens, well bunkered.

9 holes, 6,092 yards (for 18 holes), par 72 (SSS 70). Amateur record 70.

SIGNATURE HOLE:
FIRST (136 yards, par 3) Requires an accurate tee with bunkers to the right and left of the green.

COURSE CARD

| HOLE | MEDAL YDS | PAR | FORWARD YDS | PAR | LADIES YDS | PAR | HOLE | MEDAL YDS | PAR | FORWARD YDS | PAR | LADIES YDS | PAR |
|------|-----------|-----|-------------|-----|------------|-----|------|-----------|-----|-------------|-----|------------|-----|
| 1 | 136 | 3 | 185 | 3 | 140 | 3 | 10 | 220 | 3 | 185 | 3 | 140 | 3 |
| 2 | 452 | 4 | 419 | 4 | 353 | 4 | 11 | 453 | 5 | 419 | 4 | 353 | 4 |
| 3 | 412 | 4 | 354 | 4 | 349 | 4 | 12 | 373 | 4 | 354 | 4 | 349 | 4 |
| 4 | 323 | 4 | 307 | 4 | 288 | 4 | 13 | 323 | 4 | 307 | 4 | 288 | 4 |
| 5 | 193 | 3 | 194 | 3 | 197 | 3 | 14 | 194 | 3 | 194 | 3 | 197 | 3 |
| 6 | 375 | 4 | 325 | 4 | 286 | 4 | 15 | 375 | 4 | 325 | 4 | 286 | 4 |
| 7 | 476 | 5 | 475 | 5 | 422 | 5 | 16 | 481 | 5 | 475 | 5 | 452 | 5 |
| 8 | 340 | 4 | 328 | 4 | 279 | 4 | 17 | 340 | 4 | 328 | 4 | 279 | 4 |
| 9 | 308 | 4 | 308 | 4 | 269 | 4 | 18 | 318 | 4 | 308 | 4 | 269 | 4 |
| Yds Out | 3,015 | | 2,895 | | 2,583 | | Yds In | 3,077 | | 2,895 | | 2,613 | |
| Total Yds | 6,092 | | 5,790 | | 5,196 | | | | | | | | |
| Total Par | 72 | | 70 | | 70 | | | | | | | | |

ADDRESS: Manuelrigg, Maddiston, Falkirk, Stirlingshire FK2 0LS.
TELEPHONE: +44 (0)1324 711277.
FAX: +44 (0)1324 712504.
SECRETARY: Peter Lees.
VISITORS: Welcome any time, except Saturdays.
GREEN FEES: £8 per round weekdays. £15 per round Sundays.
CATERING: Restaurant and bar. Meals for parties by arrangement. Functions catered for.
FACILITIES: Changing rooms, putting green, practice ground, memberships available.
LOCATION: 4 miles south of Falkirk on the B805. First turn on right, past the Central Region Fire Brigade HQ, into Simpson Dive.
LOCAL HOTELS: Inchrya Grange Hotel, Polmont Hotel, Stakis Park Hotel.

# GRANGEMOUTH

## GRANGEMOUTH GOLF CLUB

COURSE DESCRIPTION:
Challenging undulating parkland course with excellent views of the Forth valley. Established 1973.

18 holes, 6,314 yards, par 71 (SSS 71).

SIGNATURE HOLE:
SEVENTH (216 yards, par 3) Tee shot over reservoir to an elevated green.

ADDRESS: Polmont Hill, Grangemouth, Stirlingshire FK2 0YE.
TELEPHONE: +44 (0)1324 711500.
PROFESSIONAL: Stuart Campbell +44 (0)1324 714355.
VISITORS: Contact in advance.
GREEN FEES: £12.50 per round weekdays, £20 per day. £14.50 per round weekends,
    £22 per day.
CATERING: Bar.
FACILITIES: Pro shop.
LOCATION: ½ mile north of M9 junction 4.
LOCAL HOTELS: Inchrya Grange Hotel, Lea Park Hotel.

# KILLIN

## KILLIN GOLF CLUB

COURSE DESCRIPTION:
Hilly parkland course. Very scenic, set in the Breadalbane Hills.
    9 holes, 5,016 yards, par 66 (SSS 65). Course record 61.

SIGNATURE HOLE:
FIFTH (97 yards, par 3) Called 'The Dyke', the small green is hidden behind a
stone wall. Bunkered left, right and behind.

### COURSE CARD

| HOLE | YDS | PAR |
|------|------|-----|
| 1 | 288 | 4 |
| 2 | 211 | 3 |
| 3 | 206 | 3 |
| 4 | 361 | 4 |
| 5 | 97 | 3 |
| 6 | 327 | 4 |
| 7 | 340 | 4 |
| 8 | 159 | 3 |
| 9 | 519 | 5 |
| *Yds Out* | 2,508 | |
| *Total Yds* | 2,508 | |
| *Total Par* | 33 | |

ADDRESS: Killin, Perthshire FK21 8TX.

TELEPHONE: +44 (0)1567 820312.
SECRETARY: S. Chisholm.
VISITORS: Yes. Visitor competition every Saturday.
GREEN FEES: £12 per round, £15 per day, including weekends.
CATERING: Yes, all meals.
FACILITIES: Trolley/buggy hire, putting green, pro shop, practice ground.
LOCATION: West end of Loch Tay on A827.
LOCAL HOTELS: Bendarroch House Hotel, Bridge of Lochay Hotel, Clachaig Hotel, Killin Hotel, The Poplars Hotel.

# KINCARDINE

## TULLIALLAN GOLF CLUB

COURSE DESCRIPTION:
Partially hilly parkland course renowned for its quality and true greens. Founded in 1902.
    18 holes, 5,982 yards, par 69 (SSS 69).

ADDRESS: Alloa Road, Kincardine FK10 4BB.
TELEPHONE: +44 (0)1259 730396.
PROFESSIONAL: Steven Kelly +44 (0)1259 730798.
VISITORS: Yes. Restrictions on Saturdays.
GREEN FEES: £15 per round weekdays, £25 per day. £20 per round weekends, £30 per day.
CATERING: Full services. Bar.
FACILITIES: Trolley hire, pro shop.
LOCATION: 1 mile north-west of village on A977.
LOCAL HOTELS: Kingswood Hotel, The Aberdour Hotel.

# LARBERT

## FALKIRK TRYST GOLF CLUB

COURSE DESCRIPTION:
Links course with sandy sub-soil, founded 1885. Mostly flat, tree-lined fairways. Large areas of gorse and whin bushes.
    18 holes, 6,053 yards, par 70 (SSS 69). Amateur record 62. Pro record 65.

### COURSE CARD

| HOLE | YDS | PAR | HOLE | YDS | PAR |
|------|-----|-----|------|-----|-----|
| 1    | 325 | 4   | 10   | 488 | 5   |
| 2    | 188 | 3   | 11   | 245 | 3   |

| | | | | | | |
|---|---|---|---|---|---|---|
| 3 | 347 | 4 | 12 | 298 | 4 |
| 4 | 201 | 3 | 13 | 162 | 3 |
| 5 | 337 | 4 | 14 | 361 | 4 |
| 6 | 412 | 3 | 15 | 175 | 3 |
| 7 | 544 | 5 | 16 | 503 | 5 |
| 8 | 257 | 4 | 17 | 357 | 4 |
| 9 | 418 | 4 | 18 | 435 | 4 |
| *Yds*<br>*Out* | 3,029 | | *Yds*<br>*In* | 3,024 | |
| *Total*<br>*Yds* | 6,053 | | | | |
| *Total*<br>*Par* | 70 | | | | |

ADDRESS: 86 Burnhead Road, Larbert FK5 4BD.
TELEPHONE: +44 (0)1324 562415.
FAX: +44 (0)1324 562091.
SECRETARY: R. Wallace +44 (0)1324 562054.
PROFESSIONAL: Steven Dunsmore +44 (0)1324 562091.
VISITORS: Weekdays only.
GREEN FEES: £16 per round, £25 per day.
CATERING: Restaurant and bar +44 (0)1324 570436.
FACILITIES: Trolley hire, putting green, pro shop, practice ground.
LOCATION: West of Stenhousemuir on A88.
LOCAL HOTELS: Airth Castle Hotel, Commercial Hotel, Plough Hotel, Stakis Park Hotel.

## GLENBERVIE GOLF CLUB

### COURSE DESCRIPTION:
Challenging parkland course set amidst mature trees and with outstanding views of the Ochil Hills. Glenbervie has twice hosted the British Boys' Championship and has been used for many years by the R&A as a regional qualifying venue for the Open Championship. The course has also been used to host the Scottish Professional Golfers' Championship.

18 holes, 6,423 yards, par 71 (SSS 70). Course record 64.

### SIGNATURE HOLE:
FOURTEENTH ('Braid's' 407 yards, par 4) Slightly uphill with the clubhouse in the background. It requires a good drive between a tree on the left and a bunker on the right to set up an approach shot to a sloping, two-tier green.

### COURSE CARD

| | MEDAL | | FORWARD | | LADIES | | | MEDAL | | FORWARD | | LADIES | |
|---|---|---|---|---|---|---|---|---|---|---|---|---|---|
| HOLE | YDS | PAR | YDS | PAR | YDS | PAR | HOLE | YDS | PAR | YDS | PAR | YDS | PAR |
| 1 | 356 | 4 | 346 | 4 | 342 | 4 | 10 | 168 | 3 | 149 | 4 | 134 | 3 |
| 2 | 534 | 5 | 493 | 5 | 469 | 5 | 11 | 331 | 4 | 270 | 3 | 266 | 4 |

| 3 | 332 | 4 | 315 | 4 | 297 | 4 | 12 | 424 | 4 | 403 | 5 | 401 | 4 |
|---|-----|---|-----|---|-----|---|----|-----|---|-----|---|-----|---|
| 4 | 153 | 3 | 148 | 3 | 138 | 3 | 13 | 198 | 3 | 172 | 3 | 171 | 3 |
| 5 | 386 | 4 | 360 | 4 | 299 | 4 | 14 | 407 | 4 | 395 | 4 | 351 | 4 |
| 6 | 401 | 4 | 375 | 4 | 345 | 4 | 15 | 506 | 5 | 472 | 5 | 468 | 5 |
| 7 | 211 | 3 | 180 | 3 | 183 | 3 | 16 | 373 | 4 | 356 | 4 | 340 | 4 |
| 8 | 339 | 4 | 316 | 4 | 277 | 4 | 17 | 500 | 5 | 486 | 5 | 431 | 5 |
| 9 | 436 | 4 | 419 | 4 | 399 | 5 | 18 | 368 | 4 | 327 | 4 | 307 | 4 |
| *Yds* *Out* | 3,148 | | 2,952 | | 2,749 | | *Yds* *In* | 3,275 | | 3,030 | | 2,864 | |
| *Total Yds* | 6,423 | | 5,982 | | 5,613 | | | | | | | | |
| *Total Par* | 71 | | 71 | | 72 | | | | | | | | |

ADDRESS: Stirling Road, Larbert FK5 4SJ.
TELEPHONE: +44 (0)1324 562605.
FAX: +44 (0)1324 551054.
E-MAIL: secretary@glenberviegolfclub.org
WEBSITE: www.glenbervie-golf-club.com
SECRETARY: Dr S.E. Hartley.
PROFESSIONAL: John Chillas +44 (0)1324 562725.
VISITORS: Monday to Friday up to 4 p.m.
GREEN FEES: £30 per round weekdays, £40 per day.
CREDIT CARDS ACCEPTED: Visa/Mastercard.
CATERING: Restaurant and bar.
FACILITIES: Trolley hire, changing-rooms, putting green, practice ground, pro shop.
LOCATION: 1 mile north of Larbert on A9. Junction 2 on M876
LOCAL HOTELS: Airth Castle Hotel, Commercial Hotel, Plough Hotel, Stakis Park Hotel.

# MUCKHART

## MUCKHART GOLF CLUB LTD

COURSE DESCRIPTION:
Situated at the foot of the Ochil Hills with a commanding outlook over the Forth Valley, the club was founded more than 90 years ago. The heathland course was upgraded to 18 holes in 1971 and a further nine holes were added to make it a 27-hole complex with the three separate nines – Arndean, Cowden and Naemoor – offering different challenging combinations. Each of the nine holes requires a different approach, demanding tactical awareness and a skilful touch.

*Arndean* – 9 holes, 2,835 yards, par 35.
*Cowden* – 9 holes, 3,251 yards, par 36.
*Naemoor* – 9 holes, 3,234 yards, par 35.
(Scorecard below shows 1–9 Naemoor, 10–18 Arndean.)

SIGNATURE HOLE:

Arndean FIFTH ('Top of the World' 361 yards, par 4) The views from the tee are stunning, looking westward down the Forth Valley and along the length of the Ochil Hills, with Stirling Castle and the Wallace Monument silhouetted against the background of the Trossachs mountains.

## COURSE CARD

| HOLE | MEDAL YDS | PAR | FORWARD YDS | PAR | LADIES YDS | PAR | HOLE | MEDAL YDS | PAR | FORWARD YDS | PAR | LADIES YDS | PAR |
|------|-----------|-----|-------------|-----|------------|-----|------|-----------|-----|-------------|-----|------------|-----|
| 1 | 331 | 4 | 321 | 4 | 296 | 4 | 10 | 288 | 4 | 278 | 4 | 270 | 4 |
| 2 | 404 | 4 | 378 | 4 | 350 | 4 | 11 | 307 | 4 | 287 | 4 | 275 | 4 |
| 3 | 223 | 3 | 194 | 3 | 135 | 3 | 12 | 290 | 4 | 290 | 4 | 280 | 4 |
| 4 | 345 | 4 | 339 | 4 | 255 | 4 | 13 | 168 | 3 | 165 | 3 | 156 | 3 |
| 5 | 311 | 4 | 289 | 4 | 273 | 4 | 14 | 361 | 4 | 361 | 4 | 361 | 4 |
| 6 | 457 | 4 | 436 | 4 | 396 | 4 | 15 | 195 | 3 | 192 | 3 | 157 | 3 |
| 7 | 190 | 3 | 176 | 3 | 158 | 3 | 16 | 530 | 5 | 469 | 5 | 469 | 5 |
| 8 | 562 | 5 | 533 | 5 | 460 | 5 | 17 | 487 | 5 | 475 | 5 | 475 | 5 |
| 9 | 411 | 4 | 394 | 4 | 328 | 4 | 18 | 209 | 3 | 201 | 3 | 195 | 3 |
| Yds Out | 3,234 | | 3,060 | | 2,661 | | Yds In | 2,835 | | 2,718 | | 2,638 | |
| Total Yds | 6,069 | | 5,778 | | 5,299 | | | | | | | | |
| Total Par | 70 | | 71 | | 72 | | | | | | | | |

ADDRESS: Drumburn Road, Muckhart, by Dollar, Clackmannanshire FK14 7JH.
TELEPHONE: +44(0)1259 781493.
FAX: +44 (0)1259 781544.
SECRETARY/MANAGER: A.B. Robertson/T. Naitby.
PROFESSIONAL: Keith Salmoni.
VISITORS: Yes.
GREEN FEES: £17 per round weekdays, £25 per day. £25 per round weekends, £35 per day.
CATERING: Restaurant and bar. Functions catered for.
FACILITIES: Trolley hire, club hire, changing-rooms, putting green, practice ground, pro shop, coaching clinics, memberships available.
LOCATION: On the A823 west of Kinross. A91 east of Dollar. South of village of Muckhart, 16 miles from Stirling.
LOCAL HOTELS: Gartwhinzean Hotel, Tormaukin Hotel, The Gleneagles Hotel.

# STIRLING

## AIRTHREY GOLF COURSE (UNIVERSITY OF STIRLING)

COURSE DESCRIPTION:
Short but challenging parkland par-3 course with Airthrey Castle providing a magnificent backdrop. Excellent views of Airthrey Loch and the Ochil Hills.
9 holes, 4,672 yards (for 18 holes) par 54 (SSS 54). Amateur record 23.

SIGNATURE HOLE:
SEVENTH ('Lochside' 145 yards par 3) Set around the banks of Airthrey Loch, this hole provides the ultimate challenge. A green built into the hillside, protected by water and trees, requires a full carry to the green.

ADDRESS: Airthrey Castle, University of Stirling, Stirling FK9 4LA.
TELEPHONE: +44 (0)1786 466901.
FAX: +44 (0)1786 466919.
E-MAIL: r.n.gowrie@stir.ac.uk
WEBSITE: www.stir.ac.uk
SECRETARY/MANAGER: Raleigh Gowrie.
VISITORS: Yes, municipal course open to everyone from 9.30 a.m. to dusk, 7 days a week.
GREEN FEES: £2.50 per round off peak, £4 peak. Season tickets available.
CATERING: Café bar in Airthrey Castle.
FACILITIES: Club hire, putting green, driving range, coaching clinics.
LOCATION: University of Stirling is based on the outskirts of Bridge of Allan. The course is positioned within the University campus.

## BRUCEFIELDS FAMILY GOLF CENTRE LTD

COURSE DESCRIPTION:
Interesting and challenging parkland course.
9 holes, 5,026 yards (for 18 holes), par 68 (SSS 68).

COURSE CARD

| HOLE | MEDAL | | FORWARD | |
| | YDS | PAR | YDS | PAR |
| --- | --- | --- | --- | --- |
| 1 | 279 | 4 | 276 | 4 |
| 2 | 407 | 4 | 393 | 4 |
| 3 | 164 | 3 | 146 | 3 |
| 4 | 260 | 4 | 254 | 4 |
| 5 | 477 | 5 | 466 | 5 |
| 6 | 136 | 3 | 122 | 3 |
| 7 | 300 | 4 | 265 | 4 |
| 8 | 307 | 4 | 299 | 4 |

| 9 | 183 | 3 | 176 | 3 | |
|---|---|---|---|---|---|
| Yds Out | 2,513 | | 2,397 | | |
| Total Yds | 2,513 | | | | |
| Total Par | 34 | | | | |

ADDRESS: Pirnhall Road, Bannockburn, near Stirling, FK6 8EH.
TELEPHONE: +44 (0)1786 818184.
FAX: +44 (0) 1786 817770.
VISITORS: Yes.
GREEN FEES: £14 per round weekdays, £16 per round weekends.
CATERING: Restaurant.
FACILITIES: Pro shop, driving range.

## STIRLING GOLF CLUB

COURSE DESCRIPTION:
Testing rolling parkland course with magnificent views of Stirling Castle and Ben Lomond and the Fintry Hills. Back in 1505 King James IV ordered 12 golf balls here for the Royal Games. Founded 1869.

18 holes, 6,498 yards, par 71 (SSS 71). Course record 65.

ADDRESS: Queens Road, Stirling FK8 3AA.
TELEPHONE : +44 (0)1786 464098.
SECRETARY: Gordon Easson.
PROFESSIONAL: Ian Collins +44 (0) 1786 471490.
VISITORS: Yes, Mondays to Fridays (9.30 a.m. to 3 p.m.).
GREEN FEES: £25 per round weekdays, £35 per day.
CREDIT CARDS ACCEPTED: Amex/Visa/Mastercard (only in pro shop).
CATERING: Restaurant and bar.
FACILITIES: Motorised buggies (£18), trolley hire (£3), club hire (£15), changing-rooms, putting green, pro shop, practice ground, coaching clinics.
LOCATION: ½ mile from from the town centre and 2 minutes from junction 10 on the M9 motorway.
LOCAL HOTELS: Golden Lion Hotel.

# TILLICOULTRY

## TILLICOULTRY GOLF CLUB

COURSE DESCRIPTION:
Undulating inland parkland course at foot of Ochil Hills. Hard walking. Founded 1899.

9 holes, 5,365 yards (for 18 holes), par 68 (SSS 66). Course record 61.

ADDRESS: Alva Road, Tillicoultry FK13 6BL.
TELEPHONE: +44 (0)1259 750124.
VISITORS: Contact in advance.
GREEN FEES: £12 per round, £16 weekends.
CATERING: Full service. Bar.
FACILITIES: Changing-rooms
LOCATION: 9 miles east of Stirling on A91.

# STRATHCLYDE INCLUDING AYR AND GLASGOW

# ABINGTON

## ARBORY BRAE GOLF CLUB

### COURSE DESCRIPTION:

This is a real step back in time. Played with hickory clubs and genuine hand-made gutta balls (or simulated gutty balls), Arbory Brae is a living example of the conditions and hazards that confronted the nineteenth-century inland golfer. Born from golf's famous 'boom' time in 1892, Abington was, and is again, a typical inland course where the hazards are essentially supplied by mother nature. Undulating contours are prominent throughout the course and the comparatively small greens give an ultimate challenge to any golfer. Hazards include grassy knolls through the green, bracken, rushes, and a network of penalising ditches from start to finish. This course will test the skill, patience, and perhaps the courage of the modern golfer. But most of all, it's fun. Pavilion contains extensive data/photography concerning the history of Clydesdale golf and golf history in general. Local golf historians are on hand most days to give advice and assistance.

9 holes, 1,858 yards, par 34 (SSS 33). Amateur record (9 holes) S. Callan 34, (18 holes) S. Callan 71.

### SIGNATURE HOLE

EIGHTH ('Priestgill' 186 yards, par 4) Requires a decision in the first instance. Do you go for it? Or do you play safe? The clever golfer would probably play safe with a mashie up the hill and into position for an accurate lob onto the green with the niblick and play out the par. The brave (foolhardy?) will have a crash with the brassie and hope for nothing but the best and then secure an excellent 3 – or maybe a 7.

### COURSE CARD

| HOLE | YDS | PAR |
|------|------|-----|
| 1 | 198 | 4 |
| 2 | 318 | 4 |
| 3 | 264 | 4 |
| 4 | 102 | 3 |
| 5 | 188 | 4 |
| 6 | 130 | 3 |
| 7 | 233 | 4 |
| 8 | 186 | 4 |
| 9 | 239 | 4 |
| *Yds* | 1,858 | |
| *Out* | | |
| *Total* | 1,858 | |
| *Yds* | | |

| | |
|---|---|
| *Total* | 34 |
| *Par* | |

**ADDRESS:** Coldchapel Road, Abington, South Lanarkshire ML12 6RW.
**TELEPHONE** +44 (0)1555 664634.
**E-MAIL:** whgl@morrissnr.freeserve.co.uk
**WEBSITE:** www.hickorygolf.co.uk
**MANAGERS:** Harry and Alfie Ward.
**VISITORS:** Welcome any time (booking of tee times is advised, especially weekends).
**GREEN FEES:** £22 for 18 holes, including hire of half set of hickory clubs. £25 for 18 holes, including hire of clubs; £16 for 9 holes, including hire of clubs. Weekly tickets/offers: Members' discounts on golf and merchandise. Details on request.
**CATERING:** Modest pavilion, but buffets can be arranged for small groups or catering can be organised at the nearby Bistro or Abington Hotel. Tea, coffee etc. available.
**FACILITIES:** Trolleys are prohibited on the course. (NB: trolleys not required, as the clubs are very light.) Club hire is inclusive of price, except when players brings their own hickory golf clubs. Cabin facility for changing shoes etc. Membership packages available (£50, £80).
**LOCATION:** From the M74 take exit 13 and follow signs for Abington village. Take a left at the Royal Bank of Scotland and cross over the railway line. Take left at the T-junction past the caravan site and the course is 200 yards away.
**LOCAL HOTELS:** Peebles Hotel Hydro.

# AIRDRIE

## AIRDRIE GOLF CLUB

**COURSE DESCRIPTION:**
Picturesque wooded parkland course with good views.
18 holes, 6,004 yards, par 69 (SSS 69). Course record 64.

**ADDRESS:** Rochsoles, Airdrie ML6 0PQ.
**TELEPHONE:** +44 (0)1236 762195.
**PROFESSIONAL:** Gregor Monks +44 (0)1236 754360.
**VISITORS:** Must contact in advance. Guests of members only at weekends and bank holidays.
**GREEN FEES:** £15 per round, £25 per day.
**CATERING:** Bar.
**FACILITIES:** Trolley hire, putting green, pro shop, practice ground.
**LOCATION:** 1 mile north on B802.
**LOCAL HOTELS:** Westerwood Golf & Country Club

## EASTER MOFFAT GOLF CLUB

COURSE DESCRIPTION:
Mixture of moorland and parkland. Founded in 1922.
    18 holes, 6,240 yards, par 72 (SSS 70).

ADDRESS: Mansion House, Plains ML6 8NP.
TELEPHONE: +44 (0)1236 842878.
PROFESSIONAL: Graham King +44 (0)1236 843015.
VISITORS: Weekdays only.
GREEN FEES: £15 per round, £20 per day.
CATERING: Bar.
FACILITIES: Pro shop.
LOCATION: 2 miles east, on old Edinburgh Road.
LOCAL HOTELS: Westerwood Golf & Country Club.

# ALEXANDRIA

## VALE OF LEVEN GOLF CLUB

COURSE DESCRIPTION:
Tricky parkland course on hillside with several holes overlooking Loch Lomond.
Members joke that to play here you need to have one leg shorter than the other.
    18 holes, 5,172 yards, par 67 (SSS 66). Amateur record Gordon Brown 60. Pro
record Eric Brown 63.

SIGNATURE HOLE:
SEVENTEENTH (178 yards, par 3) Looks down on Loch Lomond from an
elevated tee. Gorse to be carried. Three bunkers to the left of the green.

### COURSE CARD

| HOLE | YDS | PAR | HOLE | YDS | PAR |
|------|------|-----|------|-------|-----|
| 1 | 361 | 4 | 10 | 292 | 4 |
| 2 | 485 | 5 | 11 | 350 | 4 |
| 3 | 259 | 4 | 12 | 164 | 3 |
| 4 | 411 | 4 | 13 | 180 | 3 |
| 5 | 179 | 3 | 14 | 315 | 4 |
| 6 | 345 | 4 | 15 | 253 | 4 |
| 7 | 190 | 3 | 16 | 272 | 4 |
| 8 | 375 | 4 | 17 | 178 | 3 |
| 9 | 198 | 3 | 18 | 365 | 4 |
| *Yds* | 2,803 | | *Yds* | 2,369 | |
| *Out* | | | *In* | | |
| *Total* | 5,172 | | | | |
| *Yds* | | | | | |

| | |
|---|---|
| *Total* | 67 |
| *Par* | |

**ADDRESS:** Northfield Road, Bonhill, Alexandria G83 9ET.
**TELEPHONE:** +44 (0)1389 752351.
**E-MAIL:** secretary@valeoflevengolfclub.org.uk
**WEBSITE:** www.valeoflevengolfclub.org.uk
**PROFESSIONAL:** Barry Campbell +44 (0)1389 755012.
**VISITORS:** Any time, except Saturdays.
**GREEN FEES:** £16 per round weekdays, £24 per day. £20 per round weekends, £30 per day. Juniors £7 (£1.50 if introduced by a member).
**CATERING:** Full clubhouse and bar.
**FACILITIES:** Trolley, club hire, putting green, pro shop, memberships available.
**LOCATION:** A82 to Dumbarton, then Bonhill and Alexandria.
**LOCAL HOTELS:** Balloch Hotel, Lomond Park Hotel, Redcliffe House Hotel.

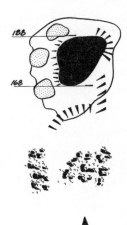

# ISLE OF ARRAN

## BRODICK GOLF CLUB

**COURSE DESCRIPTION:**
Short, very flat parkland/seaside course adjoining beach. Established in 1897, it's the first course from the ferry.
    18 holes, 4,405 yards, par 62 (SSS 62). Course record 60.

**ADDRESS:** Brodick, Isle of Arran KA27 8DL.
**TELEPHONE:** +44 (0)1770 302349.
**PROFESSIONAL:** Peter McCalla +44 (0)1770 302513.
**VISITORS:** Any time, except competition days. Contact in advance.
**GREEN FEES:** £14 per round weekdays, £19 per day. £17 per round weekends, £24 per day.
**CATERING:** Bar.
**FACILITIES:** Trolley hire, pro shop, practice ground.
**LOCATION:** North side of village.
**LOCAL HOTELS:** Auchrannie Country House Hotel, Kinloch Hotel.

## CORRIE GOLF CLUB

**COURSE DESCRIPTION:**
Short hilly, wooded moorland course, founded in 1892, with heather, rough and

tight fairways. Particularly challenging when the wind blows and the course changes character. High quality greens with hidden borrows. Very picturesque with stunning views across the Firth of Clyde into Argyll and westwards into local mountains. A haunt of red deer, birds of prey and hares. When the winds blow, it changes character. Established 1892.

9 holes, 3,896 yards (for 18 holes), par 62 (SSS 62). Amateur record 56.

SIGNATURE HOLE:

SIXTH ('Smearing House' 320 yards, par 4) Challenging hole sloping severely left to right and slightly uphill and usually against the prevailing wind. Daunting heather rough to the right.

COURSE CARD

| HOLE | MEDAL YDS | PAR | FORWARD YDS | PAR | LADIES YDS | PAR |
|------|-----------|-----|-------------|-----|------------|-----|
| 1 | 139 | 3 | 128 | 3 | 139 | 3 |
| 2 | 199 | 3 | 135 | 3 | 199 | 3 |
| 3 | 251 | 4 | 230 | 4 | 251 | 4 |
| 4 | 171 | 3 | 121 | 3 | 171 | 3 |
| 5 | 128 | 3 | 114 | 3 | 128 | 3 |
| 6 | 320 | 4 | 270 | 4 | 320 | 4 |
| 7 | 306 | 4 | 300 | 4 | 306 | 4 |
| 8 | 160 | 3 | 110 | 3 | 160 | 3 |
| 9 | 274 | 4 | 230 | 4 | 274 | 4 |
| Yds Out | 1,948 | | 1,638 | | 1,948 | |
| Total Yds | 1,948 | | | | | |
| Total Par | 31 | | | | | |

ADDRESS: Sannox, Brodick, Isle of Arran KA27 8JD.
TELEPHONE: +44 (0)1770 600403.
SECRETARY: G.E. Welford.
VISITORS: Yes, any time except Saturday afternoon.
GREEN FEES: £10 per day. Evening ticket £6. Weekly ticket £45; two-week ticket £70.
CATERING: Tea room open all day throughout summer (March to October).
FACILITIES: Changing-rooms, putting green, practice facilities.
LOCATION: 6 miles north of Brodick ferry port on A841 coastal road. Sharp left over bridge at Sannox.
LOCAL HOTELS: Blackrock Guest House, Corrie Hotel, Ingledene Hotel, Kinloch Hotel.

# LAMLASH GOLF CLUB

COURSE DESCRIPTION:
Challenging and undulating heathland course, designed by Willie Auchterlonie

and Willie Fernie and established in 1889. The views of the Holy Island from the 4th green are breathtaking.

18 holes, 4,640 yards, Par 64 (SSS 64). Amateur record: 60.

SIGNATURE HOLE:
SIXTEENTH (102 yards, par 3) Elevated tee. Green is protected by two bunkers at the front with a burn at the rear.

COURSE CARD

| HOLE | MEDAL YDS | PAR | FORWARD YDS | PAR | LADIES YDS | PAR | HOLE | MEDAL YDS | PAR | FORWARD YDS | PAR | LADIES YDS | PAR |
|------|-----------|-----|-------------|-----|------------|-----|------|-----------|-----|-------------|-----|------------|-----|
| 1 | 346 | 4 | 330 | 4 | 252 | 4 | 10 | 276 | 4 | 215 | 3 | 212 | 4 |
| 2 | 189 | 3 | 176 | 3 | 184 | 3 | 11 | 271 | 4 | 225 | 3 | 240 | 4 |
| 3 | 389 | 4 | 370 | 4 | 346 | 4 | 12 | 233 | 3 | 215 | 3 | 220 | 4 |
| 4 | 183 | 3 | 112 | 3 | 131 | 3 | 13 | 191 | 3 | 180 | 3 | 179 | 3 |
| 5 | 208 | 3 | 170 | 3 | 164 | 4 | 14 | 215 | 3 | 207 | 3 | 209 | 4 |
| 6 | 325 | 4 | 311 | 4 | 233 | 4 | 15 | 275 | 4 | 233 | 3 | 160 | 3 |
| 7 | 294 | 4 | 198 | 3 | 210 | 4 | 16 | 102 | 3 | 97 | 3 | 90 | 3 |
| 8 | 266 | 4 | 210 | 3 | 205 | 4 | 17 | 226 | 3 | 181 | 3 | 189 | 3 |
| 9 | 355 | 4 | 270 | 4 | 316 | 4 | 18 | 296 | 4 | 290 | 4 | 290 | 4 |
| *Yds* Out | 2,555 | | 2,147 | | 2,091 | | *In* | 2,085 | | 1,843 | | 1,789 | |
| *Total Yds* | 4,640 | | 3,990 | | 3,840 | | | | | | | | | |
| *Total Par* | 64 | | 59 | | 65 | | | | | | | | | |

ADDRESS: Lamlash, Isle of Arran KA27 8JU.
TELEPHONE & FAX: +44 (0)1770 600296; Starter +44 (0)1770 600196.
WEBSITE: www.arrangolf.net
SECRETARY: J. Henderson.
VISITORS: Yes, no restrictions.
GREEN FEES: £16 per day weekdays; £20 per day weekends.
CATERING: Restaurant and bar. Functions catered for.
FACILITIES: Motorised buggies (£12), trolley hire (£1.50), club hire (£10), changing-rooms, putting green, pro shop, memberships available.
LOCATION: 2½ miles south of Brodick ferry terminal; 1 hour from Ardrossan, North Ayrshire, by car ferry.
LOCAL HOTELS: Auchrannie Country House Hotel, Glenisle Hotel, Kinloch Hotel.

# LOCHRANZA GOLF CLUB

COURSE DESCRIPTION:
This reasonably level course (no cardiac hills), which was opened in 1991, is something different. Carefully designed to encourage good golf – driving is critical – it gives every shot options. There are six single greens and six large double greens, shaped fairways, doglegs, water hazards and more. Superb finish from the 16th

with the final testing hole, a 542-yard par 5, featuring the river on the elbow of the right-hand dogleg. Largely developed on the land as it lay. Scenically stunning. Extensive wildlife includes golden eagles overhead, red deer on the fairways and seals in the bay. The ruins of Lochranza Castle sit on a promontory in the middle of the sea loch.

18 holes, 5,487 yards, par 70 (SSS 70). Amateur record 72.

SIGNATURE HOLE:
SEVENTH ('Lochan' 255 yards, par 4) Played over a tree-line river to a 70-yard long green with a pond the full length on the right and mounds on the left.

COURSE CARD

| HOLE | YDS | PAR | HOLE | YDS | PAR |
|---|---|---|---|---|---|
| 1 | 445 | 4 | 10 | 375 | 4 |
| 2 | 284 | 4 | 11 | 265 | 4 |
| 3 | 194 | 3 | 12 | 225 | 3 |
| 4 | 150 | 3 | 13 | 119 | 3 |
| 5 | 281 | 4 | 14 | 286 | 4 |
| 6 | 343 | 4 | 15 | 371 | 4 |
| 7 | 255 | 4 | 16 | 268 | 4 |
| 8 | 267 | 4 | 17 | 315 | 4 |
| 9 | 502 | 5 | 18 | 542 | 5 |
| *Yds Out* | 2,721 | | *Yds In* | 2,766 | |
| *Total Yds* | 5,487 | | | | |
| *Total Par* | 70 | | | | |

ADDRESS: Lochranza, Isle of Arran KA27 8HL.
TELEPHONE: +44 (0)1770 830273.
FAX: +44 (0)1770 830600.
E-MAIL: golf@lochgolf.demon.co.uk
WEBSITE: www.arran.net
PROPRIETOR: I.M. Robertson.
VISITORS: April to October. All daylight hours.
GREEN FEES: £13 per round weekdays/weekends, £18 per day. Weekly ticket £55. £44 pre-booked fourball.
CATERING: Restaurant nearby.
FACILITIES: Trolley hire (£2), club hire (⅔ green fee), changing-rooms, putting green, memberships available.
LOCATION: Ferry from Ardrossan on Clyde coast, north of Irvine; 1 hour sailing to Brodick. Turn right 15 miles by road to Lochranza.
LOCAL HOTELS: Kinloch Hotel, The Lagg Hotel.

# MACHRIE BAY GOLF CLUB

COURSE DESCRIPTION:
Seaside links course on west coast of Arran. Designed by William Fernie.

9 holes, 4,400 yards (for 18 holes), par 66 (SSS 62). Amateur record 59. Pro record Walter Hagen (US Ryder Cup captain) 53.

SIGNATURE HOLE:
FIRST (315 yards, par 4) Shore to the right, road to the left. Both out of bounds.

COURSE CARD

| HOLE | MEDAL YDS | PAR | FORWARD YDS | PAR |
|------|------|-----|------|-----|
| 1 | 315 | 4 | 262 | 4 |
| 2 | 175 | 3 | 162 | 3 |
| 3 | 169 | 3 | 160 | 3 |
| 4 | 281 | 4 | 281 | 4 |
| 5 | 198 | 3 | 162 | 3 |
| 6 | 281 | 4 | 254 | 4 |
| 7 | 281 | 4 | 267 | 4 |
| 8 | 250 | 4 | 220 | 4 |
| 9 | 250 | 4 | 239 | 4 |
| *Yds Out* | 2,200 | | 2,007 | |
| *Total Yds* | 2,200 | | | |
| *Total Par* | 33 | | | |

ADDRESS: Machrie, Isle of Arran KA27 8DZ.
TELEPHONE: +44 (0)1770 850232.
SECRETARY: John Malesi.
VISITORS: Any time.
GREEN FEES: £8 for 18 holes.
CATERING: Meals, snacks, tea, coffee. No bar.
FACILITIES: Putting green, practice ground.
LOCATION: 9 miles from Brodick.
LOCAL HOTELS: Kinloch Hotel.

# SHISKINE GOLF & TENNIS CLUB

COURSE DESCRIPTION:
Unique 12-hole links course with magnificent outlook to the Mull of Kintyre. Next to the course is a cave in which the Scottish king, Robert the Bruce, supposedly came up with the famous adage 'If at first you don't succeed, try, try again.' Founded in 1896, the original nine-hole course was laid out by Willie Fernie of Troon. Fifteen years later Willie Park extended the course to 18 holes,

revising Fernie's layout in the process. Due to the intervention of the First World War, six of the new holes fell into disuse to leave the unique 12-hole layout as it is today. The course is crossed by two burns and has many distinguishing characteristics – including the longest par 5 on the island at 509 yards – and there are several blind holes. Has recently been included in the top 100 best courses in Britain.

12 holes, 2,823 yards (medal), 3,055 yards (championship), par 42 (SSS 41). Course record 38.

### SIGNATURE HOLE:
THIRD ('Crow's Nest' 117 yards, par 3) Aptly named. A daunting tee shot up and over a towering rocky cliff face.

### COURSE CARD

| HOLE | MEDAL YDS | PAR | LADIES YDS | PAR | HOLE | MEDAL YDS | PAR | LADIES YDS | PAR |
|---|---|---|---|---|---|---|---|---|---|
| 1 | 374 | 4 | 379 | 4 | 10 | 161 | 3 | 150 | 3 |
| 2 | 366 | 4 | 364 | 4 | 11 | 210 | 3 | 190 | 4 |
| 3 | 117 | 3 | 119 | 3 | 12 | 120 | 3 | 125 | 3 |
| 4 | 141 | 3 | 146 | 3 | | | | | |
| 5 | 200 | 3 | 212 | 4 | | | | | |
| 6 | 273 | 4 | 248 | 4 | | | | | |
| 7 | 161 | 3 | 150 | 3 | | | | | |
| 8 | 224 | 4 | 249 | 4 | | | | | |
| 9 | 476 | 5 | 483 | 5 | | | | | |
| Yds Out | 2,332 | | 2,350 | | Yds In | 491 | | 465 | |
| Total Yds | 2,823 | | | | | | | | |
| Total Par | 42 | | | | | | | | |

ADDRESS: Shiskine Shore Road, Blackwaterfoot, Isle of Arran KA27 8HA.
TELEPHONE: +44 (0)1770 860226.
FAX: +44 (0)1770 860205.
E-MAIL: info@shiskinegolf.com
WEBSITE: www.shiskinegolf.com
MANAGER: Fiona Crawford.
VISITORS: Yes, any time.
GREEN FEES: £13 per round weekdays, £20 per day. £16 per round weekends, £24 per day. Arran Golf Pass.
CATERING: Tea room (March to October) serves bar-type meals and snacks, but licensed.
FACILITIES: Motorised buggies (£10), trolley hire (£2), club hire (£8), changing-rooms, putting green, pro shop, memberships on application.
LOCATION: Off B880 at Blackwaterfoot. Turn right at the top of the pier. Go through Brodick and keep on to a junction where the main road goes 90 degrees right

to Corrie. Go on uphill for 11 miles until a Y junction and then take the right-hand fork through Blackwaterfoot.

LOCAL HOTELS: Kinloch Hotel, The Lagg Hotel.

## WHITING BAY GOLF CLUB

COURSE DESCRIPTION:
Hilly, testing links course.
   18 holes, 4,405 yards, par 63 (SSS 63). Course record 59.

SIGNATURE HOLE:
ELEVENTH (200 yards, par 3) Green is guarded by a tree with a burn at the back.

ADDRESS: Whiting Bay, Isle of Arran KA27 8QT.
TELEPHONE: +44 (0)1770 700487.
VISITORS: 8.45 a.m. to 9.30 a.m. weekdays. Also Sundays 11.45 a.m. to 1 p.m.
GREEN FEES: £13 per round weekdays, £17 per day. £25 weekends. £10 after 4 p.m.
CATERING: Bar.
FACILITIES: Trolley, buggy hire, putting green, pro shop.
LOCATION: North-west of village, off A841.
LOCAL HOTELS: Kinloch Hotel, The Lagg Hotel.

# AYR

## BELLEISLE GOLF CLUB

COURSE DESCRIPTION:
   *Belleisle Course* One of Britain's finest public courses. A championship parkland course opened in 1927 with beech trees and a burn influencing shots. A good short game is needed here with large undulating greens, several on plateaux, protected by bunkers. Beautiful sea views. Designed by James Braid.
   18 holes, 6,431 yards, par 71 (SSS 72). Amateur record K. Gimson 63. Pro record Jim Farmer 64.
   *Seafield Course* – A tight, hazardous course with some dangerous bunkers and smaller greens. A mixture of ten parkland and eight links holes. Wooded and rolling, it has only three holes that exceed 400 yards.
   18 holes, 5,481 yards, par 68 (SSS 67).

SIGNATURE HOLE:
Belleisle SIXTH ('The Lang Drap' 429 yards, par 4) A long sweeping hole which drops down to a small tight green protected by two large bunkers either side. Excellent views of the bay over to the Isle of Arran.

## BELLEISLE COURSE CARD

| HOLE | MEDAL YDS | PAR | FORWARD YDS | PAR | LADIES YDS | PAR | HOLE | MEDAL YDS | PAR | FORWARD YDS | PAR | LADIES YDS | PAR |
|---|---|---|---|---|---|---|---|---|---|---|---|---|---|
| 1 | 471 | 5 | 449 | 5 | 443 | 5 | 10 | 182 | 3 | 170 | 3 | 154 | 3 |
| 2 | 470 | 5 | 455 | 5 | 441 | 5 | 11 | 430 | 4 | 408 | 4 | 409 | 5 |
| 3 | 176 | 3 | 144 | 3 | 125 | 3 | 12 | 422 | 4 | 400 | 4 | 404 | 5 |
| 4 | 419 | 4 | 398 | 4 | 370 | 4 | 13 | 431 | 4 | 423 | 4 | 415 | 5 |
| 5 | 402 | 4 | 385 | 4 | 344 | 4 | 14 | 194 | 3 | 184 | 3 | 154 | 3 |
| 6 | 429 | 4 | 385 | 4 | 400 | 5 | 15 | 480 | 5 | 427 | 5 | 416 | 5 |
| 7 | 155 | 3 | 140 | 3 | 126 | 3 | 16 | 405 | 4 | 393 | 4 | 386 | 4 |
| 8 | 334 | 4 | 324 | 4 | 313 | 4 | 17 | 151 | 3 | 142 | 3 | 130 | 3 |
| 9 | 348 | 4 | 310 | 4 | 281 | 4 | 18 | 532 | 5 | 503 | 5 | 334 | 4 |
| *Yds* Out | 3,204 | | 2,990 | | 2,843 | | *Yds* In | 3,227 | | 3,050 | | 2,799 | |
| *Total Yds* | 6,431 | | 6,040 | | 5,642 | | | | | | | | |
| *Total Par* | 71 | | 71 | | 74 | | | | | | | | |

ADDRESS: Belleisle Park, Doonfoot Road, Ayr KA7 4DU.

TELEPHONE: +44 (0)1292 441258.

FAX: +44 (0)1292 442632.

SENIOR STARTER: Tom Coulter.

PROFESSIONAL: David Gemmell +44(0)1292 441314.

VISITORS: Any time after 9.36 a.m. Contact in advance.

GREEN FEES: *Belleisle:* £18 per round weekdays, £28 per day. £25 per round weekends, £35 per day. *Seafield:* £12 per round weekdays, £20 per day. £16 per round weekends, £258 per day. Three-day (Monday to Friday) passes £60. Five-day (Monday to Friday) passes £90.

CREDIT CARDS ACCEPTED: Visa/Mastercard.

CATERING: Restaurant and bar.

FACILITIES: Trolley hire (£2), club hire (£10), changing-rooms, putting green, practice ground, pro shop, coaching clinics, memberships available.

LOCATION: 2 miles south of Ayr on the A719.

LOCAL HOTELS: Belleisle House Hotel (overlooking course), The Abbotsford Hotel, Quality Friendly Hotel, Jarvis Caledonian Hotel.

## DALMILLING GOLF CLUB

COURSE DESCRIPTION:

Meadowland course with easy walking. The River Ayr and its tributary burns add interest to the early holes. Forgiving.

18 holes, 5,724 yards, par 68 (SSS 67).

## COURSE CARD

| HOLE | YDS | PAR | HOLE | YDS | PAR |
|---|---|---|---|---|---|
| 1 | 461 | 4 | 10 | 350 | 4 |

| 2 | 360 | 4 | 11 | 407 | 4 |
|---|---|---|---|---|---|
| 3 | 309 | 4 | 12 | 418 | 4 |
| 4 | 162 | 3 | 13 | 165 | 3 |
| 5 | 360 | 4 | 14 | 500 | 5 |
| 6 | 122 | 3 | 15 | 174 | 3 |
| 7 | 356 | 4 | 16 | 296 | 4 |
| 8 | 137 | 3 | 17 | 458 | 4 |
| 9 | 284 | 4 | 18 | 405 | 4 |
| *Yds Out* | 2,551 | | *Yds In* | 3,173 | |
| *Total Yds* | 5,724 | | | | |
| *Total Par* | 68 | | | | |

ADDRESS: Westwood Avenue, Ayr KA8 0QU.
TELEPHONE: +44 (0)1292 263893.
FAX: +44 (0)1292 610543.
PROFESSIONAL: Philip Cheyney.
VISITORS: Any time. Contact in advance.
GREEN FEES: £12 per round weekdays, £20 per day. £16 per round weekends, £28 per day. Three-day ticket (Monday to Friday) £60. Five-day ticket (Monday to Friday) £90.
CATERING: Bar.
FACILITIES: Trolley/buggy hire, pro shop.
LOCATION: 1½ miles east of town off A719.
LOCAL HOTELS: Carlton Toby Hotel.

# BALLOCH

## CAMERON HOUSE HOTEL & COUNTRY ESTATE

COURSE DESCRIPTION:
The Wee Demon Course is challenging with water hazards.
    9 holes, 4,532 yards (for 18 holes), par 64.

ADDRESS: Loch Lomond G83 8QZ.
TELEPHONE: +44 (0)1389 757211.
VISITORS: Residents only.
GREEN FEES: £15 per day.
CATERING: Full service. Bar.
FACILITIES: Trolley hire, practice nets.
LOCAL HOTELS: Cameron House Hotel.

# BARRHEAD

## FERENEZE GOLF CLUB

COURSE DESCRIPTION:
Hilly moorland course on Fereneze Braes with panoramic views over the Clyde Valley towards Glasgow and beyond. Founded in 1904, it is almost like a links course with tight fairways and fast and sloping greens, which call for the traditional bump and run approach shots.

18 holes, 5,962 yards, par 71 (SSS 71). Course record I.W. McMillan, T. Sclater 67.

SIGNATURE HOLE:
EIGHTEENTH (374 yards, par 4) Reputed to have been in the *Guinness Book of Records* as the longest hole in one in the UK. But not to be taken lightly, because it is a true test of character.

COURSE CARD

| HOLE | MEDAL YDS | PAR | FORWARD YDS | PAR | LADIES YDS | PAR | HOLE | MEDAL YDS | PAR | FORWARD YDS | PAR | LADIES YDS | PAR |
|------|-----------|-----|-------------|-----|------------|-----|------|-----------|-----|-------------|-----|------------|-----|
| 1 | 280 | 4 | 274 | 4 | 268 | 4 | 10 | 379 | 4 | 376 | 4 | 324 | 4 |
| 2 | 145 | 3 | 138 | 3 | 133 | 3 | 11 | 330 | 4 | 327 | 4 | 327 | 4 |
| 3 | 518 | 5 | 476 | 5 | 470 | 5 | 12 | 355 | 4 | 343 | 4 | 327 | 4 |
| 4 | 168 | 3 | 157 | 3 | 132 | 3 | 13 | 372 | 4 | 349 | 4 | 296 | 4 |
| 5 | 315 | 4 | 284 | 4 | 232 | 4 | 14 | 182 | 3 | 161 | 3 | 164 | 3 |
| 6 | 500 | 5 | 491 | 5 | 421 | 5 | 15 | 474 | 4 | 461 | 4 | 466 | 5 |
| 7 | 150 | 3 | 147 | 3 | 125 | 3 | 16 | 299 | 4 | 287 | 4 | 267 | 4 |
| 8 | 500 | 5 | 475 | 5 | 433 | 5 | 17 | 309 | 4 | 309 | 4 | 296 | 4 |
| 9 | 312 | 4 | 306 | 4 | 292 | 4 | 18 | 374 | 4 | 374 | 4 | 364 | 4 |
| Yds Out | 2,888 | | 2,748 | | 2,506 | | Yds In | 3,074 | | 2,987 | | 2,848 | |
| Total Yds | 5,962 | | 5,735 | | 5,354 | | | | | | | | | |
| Total Par | 71 | | 71 | | 72 | | | | | | | | | |

ADDRESS: Fereneze Drive, Barrhead, Glasgow G78 1HJ.
TELEPHONE: +44(0)141 881 1519.
E-MAIL: ferenezegolf@ic24.net
WEBSITE: www.ferenezegolf.ic24.net/index.htm
SECRETARY: Alex Johnston +44 (0)141 887 4141.
FAX: +44 (0)141 887 1103.
PROFESSIONAL: Stuart Kerr +44(0)141 880 7058.
VISITORS: Yes, on written request.
GREEN FEES: £20 per round. Weekday package: two rounds (including snack lunch,

high tea) £33.
CATERING: Yes. Bar.
FACILITIES: Trolley hire, putting green, pitching green, pro shop, practice ground (not adjacent to clubhouse).
LOCATION: 8 miles south of Glasgow city centre, off B774.
LOCAL HOTELS: Dalmeny Park Country House.

# BEITH

## BEITH GOLF CLUB

COURSE DESCRIPTION:
Inland, hilly parkland course with panoramic views. Established 1896.
18 holes, 5,641 yards, par 68 (SSS 68).

ADDRESS: Threepwood Road, Beith, Ayrshire KA15 2JR.
TELEPHONE & FAX: +44 (0)1505 506814.
SECRETARY: Mrs M. Murphy.
VISITORS: Yes.
GREEN FEES: On application.
CATERING: Bar and meals. Functions catered for.
FACILITIES: Changing-rooms, memberships available.
LOCATION: First left southbound on Beith by-pass (A737).
LOCAL HOTELS: Bowfield Hotel & Country Club.

# BELLSHILL

## BELLSHILL GOLF CLUB

COURSE DESCRIPTION:
Inland parkland course. Although most holes appear straightforward, there are enough out of bounds, fairway bunkers and small tree plantations to catch the unwary, especially in the prevailing westerly breeze. Most greens are well protected by bunkers and the sculptured fairways make accuracy a benefit.
18 holes, 6,315 yards, par 70 (SSS 69). Course record 67.

SIGNATURE HOLE:
NINTH (483 yards, par 5) Out of bounds to the left. A dogleg left to a generous green guarded by two large chestnut trees and a large fairway bunker. A good drive to right of centre opens up the green for big hitters. A birdie here is hard-earned.

## COURSE CARD

| HOLE | YDS | PAR | HOLE | YDS | PAR |
|------|-----|-----|------|-----|-----|
| 1 | 473 | 4 | 10 | 399 | 4 |
| 2 | 397 | 4 | 11 | 414 | 4 |
| 3 | 452 | 4 | 12 | 367 | 4 |
| 4 | 409 | 4 | 13 | 310 | 4 |
| 5 | 231 | 3 | 14 | 381 | 4 |
| 6 | 294 | 4 | 15 | 333 | 4 |
| 7 | 305 | 4 | 16 | 384 | 4 |
| 8 | 165 | 3 | 17 | 154 | 3 |
| 9 | 483 | 5 | 18 | 364 | 4 |
| *Yds Out* | 3,209 | | *Yds In* | 3,106 | |
| *Total Yds* | 6,315 | | | | |
| *Total Par* | 70 | | | | |

ADDRESS: Orbiston, Bellshill, Lanarkshire ML4 2 RZ.
TELEPHONE: +44 (0)1698 745124.
ADMINISTRATOR: Mrs L. Kennedy.
VISITORS: Contact administrator on arrival. Societies must book in advance.
GREEN FEES: £18 per round weekdays, £25 weekends. All-inclusive package includes morning coffee, midday snack and high tea.
CATERING: Yes. Bar.
FACILITIES: Putting green.
LOCATION: Exit 5 (A725) off M74 north or the A725 exit off the A8 east–west trunk road.
LOCAL HOTELS: Bothwell Bridge Hotel, Moorings House Hotel, Silvertrees Hotel.

# BIGGAR

## BIGGAR GOLF CLUB

COURSE DESCRIPTION:
Flattish, scenic parkland course in rolling border countryside.

18 holes, 5,537 yards, par 68 (SSS 67). Amateur record G Kerr 61. Pro record Paul Lawrie 63.

SIGNATURE HOLE:
NINTH (200 yards, par 3) Water hazard on the left and out of bounds on the right.

## COURSE CARD

| HOLE | YDS | PAR | HOLE | YDS | PAR |
|------|-----|-----|------|-----|-----|
| 1 | 254 | 4 | 10 | 130 | 3 |
| 2 | 407 | 4 | 11 | 408 | 4 |
| 3 | 294 | 4 | 12 | 425 | 4 |
| 4 | 412 | 4 | 13 | 201 | 3 |
| 5 | 159 | 3 | 14 | 353 | 4 |
| 6 | 317 | 4 | 15 | 368 | 4 |
| 7 | 161 | 3 | 16 | 482 | 5 |
| 8 | 504 | 5 | 17 | 252 | 4 |
| 9 | 200 | 3 | 18 | 210 | 3 |
| *Yds Out* | 2,708 | | *Yds In* | 2,829 | |
| *Total Yds* | 5,537 | | | | |
| *Total Par* | 68 | | | | |

ADDRESS: The Park, Broughton Road, Biggar ML12 6HA .
VISITORS: Any time. Prior booking on +44 (0)1899 220319.
GREEN FEES: £8.50 per round weekdays. £14.50 weekends.
CATERING: Full licence and catering. Pre-book on +44 (0)1899 220618.
FACILITIES: Trolley hire, putting green.
LOCATION: ½ mile from police station. Signposted off A702.
LOCAL HOTELS: Peebles Hotel Hydro, Shieldhill Hotel.

# BISHOPTON

## ERSKINE GOLF CLUB

COURSE DESCRIPTION:
Tight parkland course.
18 holes, 6,287 yards, par 71 (SSS 70).

ADDRESS: Golf Road, Bishopton, Renfrewshire PA7 5PH.
TELEPHONE: +44 (0)1505 862302.
PROFESSIONAL: Peter Thomson +44 (0)1505 862108.
VISITORS: Must be accompanied by member and have handicap certificate, but not at weekends.
GREEN FEES: £27 per round weekdays. £40 per day.
CATERING: Bar.
FACILITIES: Pro shop, changing-rooms, putting green, motorised buggies (£15).
LOCATION: ½ mile north-east off B815.
LOCAL HOTELS: Forte Posthouse.

# BOTHWELL

## BOTHWELL CASTLE GOLF CLUB

**COURSE DESCRIPTION:**
Inland, flat parkland course.
   18 holes, 6,243 yards, par 71 (SSS 70). Amateur record 63. Pro record 61.

**SIGNATURE HOLE:**
SIXTH (159 yards, par 3). Well protected green with a burn at the front and surrounded by five bunkers.

**COURSE CARD**

| HOLE | YDS | PAR | HOLE | YDS | PAR |
|------|-----|-----|------|-----|-----|
| 1 | 341 | 4 | 10 | 327 | 4 |
| 2 | 333 | 4 | 11 | 384 | 4 |
| 3 | 397 | 3 | 12 | 184 | 3 |
| 4 | 398 | 4 | 13 | 327 | 4 |
| 5 | 423 | 4 | 14 | 402 | 4 |
| 6 | 159 | 3 | 15 | 185 | 3 |
| 7 | 482 | 5 | 16 | 512 | 5 |
| 8 | 314 | 4 | 17 | 463 | 5 |
| 9 | 179 | 4 | 18 | 433 | 4 |
| *Yds Out* | 3,026 | | *Yds In* | 3,217 | |
| *Total Yds* | 6,243 | | | | |
| *Total Par* | 71 | | | | |

**ADDRESS:** Blantyre Road, Bothwell G71 8BR.
**TELEPHONE:** +44 (0)1698 853177.
**SECRETARY & FAX:** +44 (0)1698 854052.
**PROFESSIONAL:** Adam McCloskey +44 (0)1698 852052.
**VISITORS:** Tuesdays only. Tee off 9.30 a.m. and/or 2 p.m.
**GREEN FEES:** £24 per round, £48 per day.
**CATERING:** Full service. Bar.
**FACILITIES:** Trolley/buggy hire, putting green, pro shop, practice ground.
**LOCATION:** North-west of village, off B7071.
**LOCAL HOTELS:** Bothwell Bridge Hotel, Redstones Hotel, Silvertrees Hotel.

# BRIDGE OF WEIR

## THE OLD COURSE RANFURLY GOLF CLUB

**COURSE DESCRIPTION:**
Demanding and interesting inland course, situated on a hillside, with some very challenging holes, particularly the par-3 16th and 18th. New greenkeeping has recently made this a tighter test with graded rough and ever-improving greens.

18 holes, 6,061 yards, par 70 (SSS 70). Amateur record 65. Pro record 66.

**SIGNATURE HOLE:**
SIXTEENTH (199 yards, par 3) Aptly named 'The Mound', a hole that is either dramatic or dangerous depending on how you fare. It's a blind tee shot up a cliff face and for first-timers it is a case of hit and hope.

**COURSE CARD**

| HOLE | YDS | PAR | HOLE | YDS | PAR |
|------|------|-----|------|------|-----|
| 1 | 452 | 4 | 10 | 380 | 4 |
| 2 | 353 | 4 | 11 | 480 | 5 |
| 3 | 362 | 4 | 12 | 413 | 4 |
| 4 | 504 | 5 | 13 | 119 | 3 |
| 5 | 172 | 3 | 14 | 387 | 4 |
| 6 | 500 | 5 | 15 | 319 | 4 |
| 7 | 222 | 4 | 16 | 199 | 3 |
| 8 | 299 | 4 | 17 | 336 | 4 |
| 9 | 424 | 4 | 18 | 140 | 3 |
| *Yds Out* | 3,288 | | *Yds In* | 2,773 | |
| *Total Yds* | 6,061 | | | | |
| *Total Par* | 70 | | | | |

**ADDRESS:** Ranfurly Place, Bridge of Weir, Renfrewshire PA11 3DE.
**TELEPHONE & FAX:** +44 (0)1505 613214.
**E-MAIL:** secretary@oldranfurly.com
**WEBSITE:** www.oldranfurly.com
**SECRETARY:** Quintin McClymont.
**VISITORS:** Yes – weekdays.
**GREEN FEES:** £20 per round weekdays, £30 per day. Special offers for visiting parties/societies.
**CATERING:** Restaurant and bar. Functions catered for.
**FACILITIES:** Changing-rooms, putting green, practice ground.
**LOCATION:** 20 minutes south of Glasgow Airport. Follow signs for Irvine. Take Bridge of Weir/Johnstone slip road. Entering village fork left at bank. Second road on right.

LOCAL HOTELS: Gryffe Arms Hotel, Redcliffe House Hotel.

# THE RANFURLY CASTLE GOLF CLUB LTD

COURSE DESCRIPTION:
Magnificent inland, moorland course, hilly and open.

18 holes, 6,284 yards, par 70 (SSS 71). Amateur record W. Brown 65. Pro record A. Lockie 65.

COURSE CARD

| HOLE | YDS | PAR | HOLE | YDS | PAR |
|------|-----|-----|------|-----|-----|
| 1 | 319 | 4 | 10 | 294 | 4 |
| 2 | 393 | 4 | 11 | 441 | 4 |
| 3 | 490 | 5 | 12 | 381 | 4 |
| 4 | 269 | 4 | 13 | 370 | 4 |
| 5 | 139 | 3 | 14 | 185 | 3 |
| 6 | 403 | 4 | 15 | 389 | 4 |
| 7 | 184 | 3 | 16 | 347 | 4 |
| 8 | 461 | 4 | 17 | 411 | 4 |
| 9 | 383 | 4 | 18 | 422 | 4 |
| *Yds Out* | 3,044 | | *Yds In* | 3,240 | |
| *Total Yds* | 6,284 | | | | |
| *Total Par* | 70 | | | | |

ADDRESS: The Clubhouse, Golf Road, Bridge of Weir PA11 3HN.
TELEPHONE: +44 (0)1505 612609.
SECRETARY: Jack Walker.
PROFESSIONAL: Tom Eckford +44(0)1505 614795.
VISITORS: Casual visitors (golf club members) any weekday. Societies Tuesdays only.
GREEN FEES: £25 per round; £35 per day.
CATERING: Full catering available. Bar.
FACILITIES: Trolley hire, putting green, pro shop, practice ground.
LOCATION: From Glasgow Airport (5 miles), follow Irvine road and Bridge of Weir signs. Turn left immediately on entering village.
LOCAL HOTELS: Gryffe Arms Hotel, Redcliffe House Hotel.

# ISLE OF BUTE

## BUTE GOLF CLUB

COURSE DESCRIPTION:
Flat links course close to the sands of Stravannan with a number of natural hazards and gorse bushes.

9 holes, 4,994 yards (for 18 holes), par 68 (SSS 64).

ADDRESS: Kingarth, Isle of Bute PA20 9PF.
TELEPHONE: +44 (0)1700 83648.
SECRETARY: +44 (0)1700 504369.
VISITORS: Any time except Saturday mornings.
GREEN FEES: £6 per day.
LOCATION: 8 miles from Rothesay, off A845.
LOCAL HOTELS: Kingarth Hotel.

## PORT BANNATYNE GOLF CLUB

COURSE DESCRIPTION:
Opened in 1912 on the side of a hill above Port Bannatyne village, but no steep climbs. There are 13 holes – play the first 12 holes and then from the 1st to the 5th again before the 18th. Planning to extend the course to 18 holes. Small greens. Beautiful views to Cowal Hills, Kyles of Bute, the Firth of Clyde and Kintyre. A new clubhouse was opened in 1998 by former Walker Cup captain Charlie Green.

13 holes, 5,085 yards (for 18 holes), par 68 (SSS 65). Amateur record Jim O'Donnell 63.

SIGNATURE HOLE:
FIRST ('Burn' 362 yards, par 4) The longest hole on the course. A blind tee shot to a sloping fairway with 270 yards to the burn. From the yellow markers, the green is driveable (256 yards). Out of bounds on the right, slope of the hill runs towards out of bounds. Easiest way to play from yellow markers is 7-iron short of the burn and another iron to the small green.

COURSE CARD

| HOLE | MEDAL YDS | PAR | FORWARD YDS | PAR | LADIES YDS | PAR | HOLE | MEDAL YDS | PAR | FORWARD YDS | PAR | LADIES YDS | PAR |
|------|-----------|-----|-------------|-----|------------|-----|------|-----------|-----|-------------|-----|------------|-----|
| 1 | 362 | 4 | 256 | 4 | 232 | 4 | 10 | 164 | 3 | 121 | 3 | 118 | 3 |
| 2 | 304 | 4 | 289 | 4 | 285 | 4 | 11 | 274 | 4 | 269 | 4 | 266 | 4 |
| 3 | 330 | 4 | 316 | 4 | 309 | 4 | 12 | 296 | 4 | 229 | 4 | 179 | 4 |
| 4 | 187 | 3 | 177 | 3 | 155 | 3 | 13 | 362 | 4 | 256 | 4 | 232 | 4 |
| 5 | 320 | 4 | 302 | 4 | 295 | 4 | 14 | 304 | 4 | 289 | 4 | 285 | 4 |
| 6 | 289 | 4 | 283 | 4 | 273 | 4 | 15 | 330 | 4 | 316 | 4 | 309 | 4 |
| 7 | 297 | 4 | 230 | 4 | 224 | 4 | 16 | 187 | 3 | 177 | 3 | 165 | 3 |

| 8 | 287 | 4 | 277 | 4 | 269 | 4 | 17 | 320 | 4 | 302 | 4 | 295 | 4 |
| 9 | 253 | 4 | 239 | 4 | 232 | 4 | 18 | 219 | 3 | 178 | 3 | 169 | 4 |
| *Yds* *Out* | 2,629 | | 2,369 | | 2,284 | | *Yds* *In* | 2,456 | | 2,137 | | 2,018 | |
| *Total* *Yds* | 5,085 | | 4,506 | | 4,302 | | | | | | | | |
| *Total* *Par* | 68 | | 68 | | 68 | | | | | | | | |

ADDRESS: Bannatyne Mains Road, Port Bannatyne, Isle of Bute PA20 0PH.
TELEPHONE: +44 (0)1700 504544.
SECRETARY: I.L. MacLeod +44 (0)1700 502009.
VISITORS: Yes, almost always.
GREEN FEES: £10 per round weekdays, £13 per day. £15 per round weekends, £18 per day. Weekly ticket £25. Two-week ticket £40.
CATERING: Bar. Meals summer only. Functions catered for.
FACILITIES: Trolley hire, changing-rooms, memberships available.
LOCATION: Ferry to Rothesay. Port Bannatyne is 2 miles north of Rothesay. Follow signs to course. Alternatively, via A886 to Colintraive in Argyll. Then ferry (3 minutes) to Rhubodach on Bute. A886 (6 Miles) to Port Bannatyne.
LOCAL HOTELS: Ardmory House, Port Royal Hotel.

# ROTHESAY GOLF CLUB

COURSE DESCRIPTION:
Moorland course with magnificent views to the Kyles of Bute and the Clyde coast. A fairly hilly course, designed by James Braid and Ben Sayers. Two par 5s are challenging when the wind blows.

18 holes, 5,370 yards, par 69 (SSS 66). Course record 62.

COURSE CARD

| HOLE | YDS | PAR | HOLE | YDS | PAR |
| --- | --- | --- | --- | --- | --- |
| 1 | 265 | 4 | 10 | 262 | 4 |
| 2 | 401 | 4 | 11 | 145 | 3 |
| 3 | 342 | 4 | 12 | 304 | 4 |
| 4 | 200 | 3 | 13 | 170 | 3 |
| 5 | 273 | 4 | 14 | 254 | 4 |
| 6 | 514 | 5 | 15 | 276 | 4 |
| 7 | 359 | 4 | 16 | 515 | 5 |
| 8 | 204 | 3 | 17 | 372 | 4 |
| 9 | 268 | 4 | 18 | 246 | 4 |
| *Yds* *Out* | 2,826 | | *Yds* *In* | 2,544 | |
| *Total* *Yds* | 5,370 | | | | |
| *Total* *Par* | 69 | | | | |

ADDRESS: Canada Hill, Rothesay, Isle of Bute PA20 9HN.
TELEPHONE: +44 (0)1700 502244.
FAX: +44 (0)1700 503554.
PROFESSIONAL: James Dougal.
VISITORS: Yes, but pre-book for weekends.
GREEN FEES: £16 per day weekdays, £24 per day weekends.
CATERING: Bar. Catering by arrangement.
FACILITIES: Trolley hire, putting green, practice ground.
LOCATION: Off road to Kingarth.
LOCAL HOTELS: Ardmory House.

# CAMPBELTOWN

## DUNAVERTY GOLF CLUB

### COURSE DESCRIPTION:
Spectacularly scenic undulating seaside links course with great views of Ireland and the Mull of Kintyre. Players of all abilities will enjoy its springy turf. A well-kept course with small lush greens.

18 holes, 4,798 yards, par 66 (SSS 63). Course record 59.

### SIGNATURE HOLE:
ELEVENTH (266 yards, par 4) Dramatic long downhill drive.

### COURSE CARD

| HOLE | MEDAL YDS | PAR | LADIES YDS | PAR | HOLE | MEDAL YDS | PAR | LADIES YDS | PAR |
|------|-----------|-----|------------|-----|------|-----------|-----|------------|-----|
| 1 | 318 | 4 | 280 | 4 | 10 | 123 | 3 | 114 | 3 |
| 2 | 157 | 3 | 152 | 3 | 11 | 266 | 4 | 234 | 4 |
| 3 | 279 | 4 | 220 | 3 | 12 | 277 | 4 | 266 | 4 |
| 4 | 177 | 3 | 150 | 3 | 13 | 446 | 5 | 352 | 4 |
| 5 | 257 | 4 | 232 | 4 | 14 | 194 | 3 | 176 | 3 |
| 6 | 245 | 4 | 228 | 4 | 15 | 352 | 4 | 325 | 4 |
| 7 | 180 | 3 | 158 | 3 | 16 | 147 | 3 | 124 | 3 |
| 8 | 392 | 4 | 356 | 4 | 17 | 412 | 4 | 368 | 4 |
| 9 | 253 | 4 | 228 | 4 | 18 | 323 | 4 | 290 | 4 |
| Yds Out | 2,258 | | 2,004 | | In | Yds 2,540 | | 2,249 | |
| Total Yds | 4,798 | | 4,253 | | | | | | |
| Total Par | 66 | | | | | | | | |

ADDRESS: Southend, by Campbeltown, Argyll PA28 6RW.
TELEPHONE: +44 (0)1586 830677.

WEBSITE: www.redrival.com/dunaverty/
SECRETARY/MANAGER: David MacBrayne.
VISITORS: Welcome without restriction.
GREEN FEES: £12 per round, £18 per day. £45 per week.
CATERING: Teas/coffees and light snacks are available throughout the day. By prior arrangement, more substantial meals can be provided.
FACILITIES: Putting green, practice ground, shop.
LOCATION: 15 minutes by car from Campbeltown on the B842.
LOCAL HOTELS: Invercreran Country House Hotel, Kinloch Hotel, Seafield Hotel.

# MACHRIHANISH GOLF CLUB

### COURSE DESCRIPTION:

If it's true that Old Tom Morris took one look at this first-class natural links course lying along the shores of Machrihanish Bay and pronounced, 'The Almighty had golf in his eye when he created this place', then the Devil must have had a hand in planning the 1st hole. Machrihanish is perhaps the remotest golf course of championship standard in the British Isles. For many the Mull of Kintyre didn't exist until Paul McCartney sang about it. For some golfers it is a mystical test of every department of a golfer's game, but just a drive too far. True, it can be an expedition to get there overland, but once standing on that daunting 1st tee it is worth every mile. The first, a 423-yard par 4, has been voted the finest in the world. Not for Machrihanish the gentle start: it has you by the jugular from the off. You have a choice. Try to make the green in two and you have to risk a drive over the pounding Atlantic Ocean below – a 200-yard carry to an undulating fairway. Take the easier route right to the safety of the fairway and you have little chance of making your par. Machrihanish was founded as a 10-hole course in 1876 by a group of local dignitaries in Campbeltown. Three years later, four-times Open Championship winner Old Tom Morris redesigned it. In 1914 three-times Open Champion J.H. Taylor fashioned what is virtually today's 6,228-yard par-70 course. Little has changed to disturb the natural scenic beauty and inspiring challenge. If you survive that initiation then there are more tests to come as the outward nine follow the hills and hollows with many a blind shot along the sand dunes bordering the Atlantic. Each hole requires accurate tee shots and carefully chosen irons to reach the expertly maintained greens (including the 4th, a mere 123 yards, which is similar to Royal Troon's 'Postage Stamp'). The inward stretch is no less demanding. Two par 5s and three tricky par 3s, including the 233-yard 16th have to be negotiated until, within sight of the clubhouse, the Machrihanish Burn has to be driven while avoiding the out of bounds which borders the final two holes.

18 holes, 6,228 yards, par 70 (SSS 71).

### SIGNATURE HOLE:

FIRST (423 yards, par 4) As above.

## COURSE CARD

| HOLE | YDS | PAR | HOLE | YDS | PAR |
|------|-----|-----|------|-----|-----|
| 1 | 423 | 4 | 10 | 497 | 5 |
| 2 | 395 | 4 | 11 | 197 | 3 |
| 3 | 376 | 4 | 12 | 505 | 5 |
| 4 | 123 | 3 | 13 | 370 | 4 |
| 5 | 385 | 4 | 14 | 442 | 4 |
| 6 | 315 | 4 | 15 | 167 | 3 |
| 7 | 432 | 4 | 16 | 233 | 3 |
| 8 | 337 | 4 | 17 | 362 | 4 |
| 9 | 354 | 4 | 18 | 315 | 4 |
| Yds Out | 3,140 | | Yds In | 3,088 | |
| Total Yds | 6,228 | | | | |
| Total Par | 70 | | | | |

ADDRESS: Machrihanish, Campbeltown, Argyll PA28 6PT.
TELEPHONE: +44 (0)1586 810213.
FAX: +44 (0)1586 810221.
TEE RESERVATIONS: +44 (0)1586 810277.
E-MAIL: secretary@machrihanishgolfclub.co.uk
WEBSITE: www.machrihanishgolfclub.co.uk
SECRETARY: Anna Anderson.
PROFESSIONAL: Ken Campbell +44 (0)1586 810277.
VISITORS: Yes. Contact professional to reserve tee times.
GREEN FEES: £30 per round Sunday to Friday, £50 per day. £40 per round Saturdays, £60 per day.
CATERING: By arrangement with club steward.
FACILITIES: Trolley/buggy hire, gents and ladies club hire, putting green, pro shop, practice ground, caddies by advance notice.
LOCATION: Situated 160 miles from Glasgow on Kintyre peninsula. A82 to Tarbet on Loch Lomond, then A83 via Inveraray and Lochgilphead. 25 minutes by air from Glasgow Airport.
LOCAL HOTELS: Argyll Arms Hotel, Ardshiel Hotel, Balegreggan Country House, Invercreran Country House Hotel, Kinloch Hotel.

# CARDROSS

## CARDROSS GOLF CLUB

COURSE DESCRIPTION:
Undulating parkland course. Testing with good views. Has previously hosted the Scottish Professional Championship.

18 holes, 6,469 yards, par 71 (SSS 72). Course record 65.

ADDRESS: Main Road, Cardross G82 5LB.
TELEPHONE & FAX: +44 (0)1389 841754.
PROFESSIONAL: Robert Farrell +44(0)1359 841350.
VISITORS: Must not play at weekends unless introduced by a member. Contact professional in advance.
GREEN FEES: £25 per round, £35 per day.
CATERING: Yes. Bar.
FACILITIES: Trolley/ buggy hire, putting green, pro shop, practice ground.
LOCATION: In centre of village on A814.
LOCAL HOTELS: Commodore Toby Hotel.

# CARLUKE

## CARLUKE GOLF CLUB

COURSE DESCRIPTION:
Slightly hilly parkland course with views over the Clyde Valley. Tricky 11th hole which drops 150 feet to a green surrounded by four bunkers.
18 holes, 5,853 yards, par 70 (SSS 68). Course record 63.

ADDRESS: Mauldslie Road, Hallcraig ML8 5HG.
TELEPHONE: +44 (0)1555 771070 or 770574.
PROFESSIONAL: Richard Forrest +44 (0)1555 751053.
VISITORS: Not weekends. Must contact in advance.
GREEN FEES: £18 per round, £25 per day.
CATERING: Full service. Bar.
FACILITIES: Putting green, pro shop.
LOCATION: 1 mile west off A73.
LOCAL HOTELS: Popinjay Hotel.

# CARNWATH

## CARNWATH GOLF CLUB

COURSE DESCRIPTION:
Hilly parkland course with small greens.
18 holes, 5,943 yards, par 70 (SSS 69). Amateur record 63.

ADDRESS: 1 Main Street, Carnwath ML11 8JX.
TELEPHONE: +44 (0)1555 840251.
SECRETARY: W. Bruce.

VISITORS: Sundays, Mondays, Wednesdays and Fridays.
GREEN FEES: £22 per day weekdays. £30 per day Sundays and public holidays.
CATERING: Bar. Catering, except Tuesdays and Thursdays.
FACILITIES: Trolley hire, putting green.
LOCATION: On A70 west of village.
LOCAL HOTELS: Cartland Bridge Hotel

# CARRADALE

## CARRADALE GOLF CLUB

COURSE DESCRIPTION:
Very difficult heathland seaside course built on a promontory overlooking the Isle of Arran. Tiny greens and the terrain are the main hazards. Has been described as the most sporting nine-hole course in Scotland. Watch for wild goats on rocky outcrops.
   9 holes, 4,694 yards (for 18 holes), par 64 (SSS 64).

ADDRESS: Airds, Carradale, Argyll PA28 6RY.
TELEPHONE & FAX: +44 (0)1583 431378.
E-MAIL: carradalegolfclub@yahoo.co.uk
SECRETARY: Mrs Gail McIntosh.
VISITORS: Any time but check availability at weekends.
GREEN FEES: £10 per day.
CATERING: None on site but hotel adjacent.
FACILITIES: Trolley hire (£2), memberships available.
LOCATION: South side of village.
LOCAL HOTELS: Ashbank Guest House, Carradale Hotel, Dunvalanree Guest House, Invercreran Country House Hotel, Kinloch Hotel, Seafield Hotel.

# CLYDEBANK

## CLYDEBANK AND DISTRICT GOLF CLUB

COURSE DESCRIPTION:
Undulating parkland course with tree-lined fairways and well-bunkered greens. Established in 1905.
   18 holes, 5,823 yards, par 68 (SSS 68). Course record 64.

ADDRESS: Glasgow Road, Hardgate G81 5QY.
TELEPHONE: +44 (0)1389 873289 or 383832.
PROFESSIONAL: David Pirie +44 (0)1389 878686.
VISITORS: Weekdays only before 4 p.m. Round only. Contact pro.

GREEN FEES: £15 per round.
CATERING: Yes. Bar.
FACILITIES: Putting green, pro shop, practice ground.
LOCATION: 2 miles east of Erskine Bridge.
LOCAL HOTELS: Patio Hotel.

## CLYDEBANK MUNICIPAL COURSE

COURSE DESCRIPTION:
One of the most acclaimed municipal parkland courses in Scotland. Hilly with burn.
   18 holes, 5,349 yards, par 67 (SSS 67).

ADDRESS: Overtoun Road, Dalmuir G81 3RE.
STARTER: +44 (0)141 952 8698.
PROFESSIONAL: Stewart Savage +44 (0)141 952 6372.
VISITORS: Any time.
GREEN FEES: £6.55 weekdays, £7 weekends.
CATERING: Café available for functions.
FACILITIES: Trolley hire, pro shop.
LOCATION: 2 miles north-west of town centre.
LOCAL HOTELS: Patio Hotel.

# COATBRIDGE

## COATBRIDGE GOLF CLUB

COURSE DESCRIPTION:
Wooded parkland course built around two lochs. It offers a variety of golf with tight tree-lined fairways and open parkland.
   18 holes, 6,026 yards, par 69 (SSS 69).

ADDRESS: Townhead Road, Coatbridge ML5 2HX.
TELEPHONE: +44 (0)1236 428975.
PROFESSIONAL: George Weir +44 (0)1236 421492.
VISITORS: Any time, except before 2.30 p.m. weekends and after 5.30 p.m. weekdays.
   Course closed first Saturday of every month.
GREEN FEES: £5.10 per round weekdays, £7.60 weekends.
CATERING: Yes.
FACILITIES: Pro shop, 18-bay floodlit driving range.
LOCATION: 1¼ miles west of town centre.

## DRUMPELLIER GOLF CLUB

COURSE DESCRIPTION:
Undulating parkland course designed by Willie Fernie and established in 1894.
18 holes, 6,227 yards, par 71 (SSS 71). Amateur record 65. Pro record 62.

COURSE CARD

| HOLE | MEDAL YDS | PAR | FORWARD YDS | PAR | LADIES YDS | PAR | HOLE | MEDAL YDS | PAR | FORWARD YDS | PAR | LADIES YDS | PAR |
|---|---|---|---|---|---|---|---|---|---|---|---|---|---|
| 1 | 464 | 4 | 439 | 4 | 413 | 5 | 10 | 325 | 4 | 320 | 4 | 296 | 4 |
| 2 | 493 | 5 | 480 | 5 | 406 | 5 | 11 | 370 | 4 | 351 | 4 | 356 | 4 |
| 3 | 345 | 4 | 312 | 4 | 302 | 4 | 12 | 158 | 3 | 154 | 3 | 134 | 3 |
| 4 | 399 | 4 | 382 | 4 | 327 | 4 | 13 | 376 | 4 | 369 | 4 | 335 | 4 |
| 5 | 158 | 3 | 146 | 3 | 131 | 3 | 14 | 160 | 3 | 149 | 3 | 140 | 3 |
| 6 | 363 | 4 | 356 | 4 | 316 | 4 | 15 | 478 | 5 | 422 | 4 | 406 | 5 |
| 7 | 173 | 3 | 151 | 3 | 145 | 3 | 16 | 379 | 4 | 373 | 4 | 352 | 4 |
| 8 | 440 | 4 | 429 | 4 | 398 | 4 | 17 | 270 | 4 | 255 | 4 | 222 | 4 |
| 9 | 494 | 5 | 487 | 5 | 405 | 5 | 18 | 382 | 4 | 355 | 4 | 330 | 4 |
| *Yds Out* | 3,329 | | 3,182 | | 2,843 | | *Yds In* | 2,898 | | 2,748 | | 2,571 | |
| *Total Yds* | 6,227 | | 5,930 | | 5,414 | | | | | | | | | |
| *Total Par* | 71 | | 70 | | 72 | | | | | | | | | |

ADDRESS: Drumpellier Avenue, Coatbridge ML5 1RX.
TELEPHONE: +44 (0)1236 424139.
SECRETARY: William Brownlie +44 (0)1236 428723.
PROFESSIONAL: David Ross +44 (0)1236 432971.
VISITORS: Weekdays.
GREEN FEES: £22 per round, £30 per day.
CATERING: Yes. Bar.
FACILITIES: Trolley hire, putting green, pro shop, practice ground.
LOCATION: 8 miles east of Glasgow on A89.
LOCAL HOTELS: Georgian Hotel.

# ISLE OF COLONSAY

## COLONSAY GOLF CLUB

COURSE DESCRIPTION:
Challenging traditional links course on open machair. Established in mid-nineteenth century. Informal and with no facilities beyond bird watching and sunbathing.

18 holes, 4,775 yards, par 72 (SSS 72).

ADDRESS: Scalasaig, Isle of Colonsay, Argyll PA61 7YP.
TELEPHONE: +44 (0)1951 200316.
FAX: +44 (0)1951 200353.
VISITORS: Any time.
GREEN FEES: £10 per day weekdays/weekends.
CATERING: Colonsay Hotel, 2 miles from course.
LOCATION: 2 miles west on A870.
LOCAL HOTELS: Colonsay Hotel.

# CUMBERNAULD

## PALACERIGG GOLF CLUB

COURSE DESCRIPTION:
Municipal well-wooded parkland course, designed by Henry Cotton and opened in 1975. Good views over Cumbernauld to Campsie Hills.
   18 holes, 6,444 yards, par 72 (SSS 71). Amateur record 65. Pro record 66.

SIGNATURE HOLE:
FIFTEENTH ('Ca'canny' 409 yards, par 4) Player must decide to either carry burn at 240 yards or lay up short with their drive. The second shot is uphill to a sloping green with bunkers left, right and over the green.

COURSE CARD

| HOLE | MEDAL YDS | PAR | FORWARD YDS | PAR | LADIES YDS | PAR | HOLE | MEDAL YDS | PAR | FORWARD YDS | PAR | LADIES YDS | PAR |
|---|---|---|---|---|---|---|---|---|---|---|---|---|---|
| 1 | 426 | 4 | 366 | 4 | 373 | 4 | 10 | 383 | 4 | 350 | 4 | 338 | 4 |
| 2 | 405 | 4 | 379 | 4 | 355 | 4 | 11 | 338 | 4 | 303 | 4 | 278 | 4 |
| 3 | 394 | 4 | 370 | 4 | 353 | 4 | 12 | 344 | 4 | 329 | 4 | 298 | 4 |
| 4 | 349 | 4 | 370 | 4 | 353 | 4 | 13 | 308 | 4 | 265 | 4 | 232 | 4 |
| 5 | 503 | 5 | 470 | 4 | 459 | 5 | 14 | 314 | 4 | 305 | 4 | 282 | 4 |
| 6 | 161 | 3 | 137 | 3 | 115 | 3 | 15 | 409 | 4 | 333 | 4 | 309 | 4 |
| 7 | 540 | 5 | 519 | 5 | 425 | 5 | 16 | 222 | 3 | 205 | 3 | 190 | 3 |
| 8 | 157 | 3 | 148 | 3 | 121 | 3 | 17 | 342 | 4 | 316 | 4 | 304 | 4 |
| 9 | 360 | 4 | 329 | 4 | 272 | 4 | 18 | 489 | 5 | 477 | 5 | 474 | 5 |
| *Yds* Out | 3,295 | | 3,088 | | 2,826 | | *Yds* In | 3,149 | | 2,883 | | 2,655 | |
| *Total Yds* | 6,444 | | 5,971 | | 5,481 | | | | | | | | | |
| *Total Par* | 72 | | 71 | | 71 | | | | | | | | | |

ADDRESS: Palacerigg Country Park, Cumbernauld G67 3HU.

TELEPHONE: +44 (0)1236 734969.
FAX: +44 (0)1236 721461.
E-MAIL: palacerigg-golfclub@lineone.net
WEBSITE: www.palacerigggolfclub.co.uk
SECRETARY: David Cooper.
STARTER: J. Murphy.
VISITORS: Any time. Societies weekdays.
GREEN FEES: £7.90 per round weekdays, £10 per day. £10 per round weekends.
CATERING: Bar and meals. Functions catered for.
FACILITIES: Changing-rooms, putting green, practice ground, coaching clinics, memberships available – no joining fee.
LOCATION: From A80 or A73 into Cumbernauld then follow signs for Palacerigg Country Park. 2 miles south of Cumbernauld.
LOCAL HOTELS: Castlecary Hotel, Cumbernauld Travel Inn, Moodiesburn House Hotel, Westerwood Hotel.

# WESTERWOOD HOTEL GOLF & COUNTRY CLUB

### COURSE DESCRIPTION:
Undulating wooded, American-style moorland course with many water hazards. Designed by Seve Ballesteros and Dave Thomas and opened in 1989. After a takeover in 1999, £250,000 was invested to restore this championship course to its former glory. A good test of golf from the back tees with a good variety of quality holes, it is more enjoyable for those of lesser skills from the yellow tees (6,101 yards). Scenic course with great views of the Campsie Hills.

18 holes, 6,616 yards, par 72 (SSS 72). Amateur record 66. Pro record 65.

### SIGNATURE HOLE:
FIFTEENTH ('Waterfall' 165 yards, par 3) Over a burn with a 50-foot quarry wall behind the green. A single bunker to the right of the green and beyond that a lake. A waterfall cascades down the quarry wall and into the lake. Can be a card wrecker.

### COURSE CARD

| HOLE | MEDAL YDS | PAR | FORWARD YDS | PAR | LADIES YDS | PAR | HOLE | MEDAL YDS | PAR | FORWARD YDS | PAR | LADIES YDS | PAR |
|---|---|---|---|---|---|---|---|---|---|---|---|---|---|
| 1 | 513 | 5 | 486 | 5 | 451 | 5 | 10 | 365 | 4 | 337 | 4 | 300 | 4 |
| 2 | 232 | 3 | 208 | 3 | 170 | 3 | 11 | 188 | 3 | 173 | 3 | 140 | 3 |
| 3 | 334 | 4 | 306 | 4 | 262 | 4 | 12 | 308 | 4 | 295 | 4 | 274 | 4 |
| 4 | 492 | 5 | 455 | 5 | 408 | 5 | 13 | 197 | 3 | 175 | 3 | 138 | 3 |
| 5 | 385 | 4 | 356 | 4 | 332 | 4 | 14 | 526 | 5 | 495 | 5 | 450 | 5 |
| 6 | 366 | 4 | 329 | 4 | 293 | 4 | 15 | 165 | 3 | 147 | 3 | 114 | 3 |
| 7 | 417 | 4 | 369 | 4 | 330 | 5 | 16 | 416 | 4 | 388 | 4 | 361 | 5 |
| 8 | 180 | 3 | 168 | 3 | 142 | 3 | 17 | 427 | 4 | 371 | 4 | 345 | 5 |
| 9 | 555 | 5 | 525 | 5 | 486 | 5 | 18 | 550 | 5 | 518 | 5 | 435 | 5 |
| Yds Out | 3,474 | | 3,202 | | 2,894 | | Yds In | 3,142 | | 2,899 | | 2,557 | |

319

| | | | |
|---|---|---|---|
| *Total* *Yds* | 6,616 | 6,101 | 5,451 |
| *Total* *Par* | 72 | 72 | 75 |

ADDRESS: 1 St Andrews Drive, Cumbernauld G68 0EW.
TELEPHONE & FAX: +44 (0)1236 725281.
E-MAIL: westerwood@morton-hotels.com
SECRETARY: Fiona McKellan.
PROFESSIONAL: Alan Tait.
VISITORS: Yes, no restrictions.
GREEN FEES: £27.50 per round weekdays, £45 per day. £30 per round weekends, £50 per day. Hotel residents £20.
CREDIT CARDS ACCEPTED: Visa/Mastercard.
CATERING: Restaurant and bar, functions catered for, 4-star hotel (49 rooms) with excellent leisure centre.
FACILITIES: Motorised buggies (£20), trolley hire (£2.50), club hire (£15), changing-rooms, putting green, practice ground, pro shop, coaching clinics, memberships available.
LOCATION: Just off the main A80 Glasgow to Stirling road. Halfway between Glasgow and Stirling. Take the turn-off for Dullatur and Westerwood is 500 yards up the hill.
LOCAL HOTELS: Castlecary Hotel, Cumbernauld Travel Inn, Westerwood Hotel.

# ISLE OF CUMBRAE

## MILLPORT GOLF CLUB

### COURSE DESCRIPTION:

Island heathland course founded in 1888, making it one of the oldest established courses on the Firth of Clyde, and updated in 1913 by James Braid. Situated above the town of Millport, it is an excellent test of golf with outstanding views over the Firth. Not long but demands good shot-making. Out of bounds comes into play in the first seven holes and at the 2nd there is out of bounds right and left.

18 holes, 5,828 yards, par 68 (SSS 69). Amateur record 64.

### SIGNATURE HOLE:

TWELFTH ('Doo's Nest' 159 yards, par 3) From elevated tee down to a wide but difficult green. Generally plays into the wind. Spectacular views over the Firth of Clyde.

### COURSE CARD

| HOLE | MEDAL YDS | PAR | FORWARD YDS | PAR | LADIES YDS | PAR | HOLE | MEDAL YDS | PAR | FORWARD YDS | PAR | LADIES YDS | PAR |
|---|---|---|---|---|---|---|---|---|---|---|---|---|---|
| 1 | 307 | 4 | 307 | 4 | 265 | 4 | 10 | 345 | 4 | 337 | 4 | 328 | 4 |

| 2 | 323 | 4 | 305 | 4 | 315 | 4 | 11 | 384 | 4 | 332 | 4 | 332 | 4 |
|---|---|---|---|---|---|---|---|---|---|---|---|---|---|
| 3 | 402 | 4 | 357 | 4 | 364 | 5 | 12 | 159 | 3 | 150 | 3 | 141 | 3 |
| 4 | 162 | 3 | 145 | 3 | 141 | 3 | 13 | 449 | 4 | 438 | 4 | 427 | 5 |
| 5 | 227 | 3 | 197 | 3 | 197 | 4 | 14 | 342 | 4 | 321 | 4 | 312 | 4 |
| 6 | 312 | 4 | 261 | 4 | 256 | 4 | 15 | 418 | 4 | 394 | 4 | 386 | 5 |
| 7 | 373 | 4 | 368 | 4 | 373 | 5 | 16 | 160 | 3 | 117 | 3 | 110 | 3 |
| 8 | 303 | 4 | 303 | 4 | 303 | 4 | 17 | 449 | 4 | 438 | 4 | 418 | 5 |
| 9 | 313 | 4 | 280 | 4 | 280 | 4 | 18 | 400 | 3 | 299 | 4 | 272 | 4 |
| *Yds Out* | 2,722 | | 2,523 | | 2,499 | | *Yds In* | 3,106 | | 2,826 | | 2,726 | |
| *Total Yds* | 5,828 | | 5,349 | | 5,225 | | | | | | | | |
| *Total Par* | 68 | | 68 | | 74 | | | | | | | | |

ADDRESS: Golf Road, Millport, Isle of Cumbrae, North Ayrshire KA28 0HB.

TELEPHONE & FAX: +44 (0)1475 530306.

E-MAIL: secretary@millportgolfclub.co.uk

WEBSITE: www.millportgolfclub.co.uk

SECRETARY: D. Donnelly.

PROFESSIONAL: Hal Lee +44 (0)1475 530305.

VISITORS: At most times.

GREEN FEES: £20 per round weekdays, £25 per day. £25 per round weekends, £31 per day. Weekly ticket £60.

CREDIT CARDS ACCEPTED: Visa/Mastercard.

CATERING: Restaurant and bar. Functions catered for.

FACILITIES: Trolley hire, club hire, changing-rooms, putting green, pro shop, practice ground, coaching clinics, memberships available.

LOCATION: 7-minute ferry ride from Largs on Ayrshire coast. 4 miles from ferry to Millport town, course 1 mile from town.

LOCAL HOTELS: Brisbane House, Redcliffe House Hotel, Royal George Hotel.

# DALMALLY

## DALMALLY GOLF CLUB

COURSE DESCRIPTION:

Picturesque flat parkland course bounded to the north by the River Orchy. Lots of water hazards, 14 greenside bunkers. Course surrounded by mountains.

9 Holes, 4,528 yards (for 18 holes), par 64 (SSS 63). Course record 64.

SIGNATURE HOLE:

THIRD ('Orchy Splash' 175 yards, par 3) 140-yard carry over loop in River Orchy. Trees tight left from the tee and close to right of the green.

ADDRESS: 'Orchy Bank', Dalmally, Argyll PA33 1AS.
TELEPHONE: +44 (0)1838 200370.
SECRETARY: A.J. Burke.
VISITORS: Any time.
GREEN FEES: £10 per round/day.
CATERING: Light snacks. Bar by arrangement. Functions catered for.
FACILITIES: Trolley hire (£1.50), club hire (£5), changing-rooms, memberships available.
LOCATION: 2 miles west of village on A85 Oban–Tyndrum road.
LOCAL HOTELS: Glen Orchy Lodge Hotel.

# DOUGLAS WATER

## DOUGLAS WATER GOLF CLUB

COURSE DESCRIPTION:
Hilly course with small greens and undulating fairways.
   9 holes, 5,894 yards (for 18 holes), par 69 (SSS 69).

ADDRESS: Old School, Ayr Road, Rigside ML11 9NP.
TELEPHONE: +44 (0)1555 880361.
SECRETARY: Robert Paterson +44 (0)1698 792249.
VISITORS: Any time weekdays and Sundays. Competitions on Saturdays, normal restrictions.
GREEN FEES: £6 weekdays, £10 Sundays and public holidays.
FACILITIES: Putting green.
CATERING: Bar by prior arrangement. Snacks.
LOCATION: Junction 11 from M74, 7 miles south-west of Lanark.

# DULLATUR

## DULLATUR GOLF CLUB

COURSE DESCRIPTION:
Two undulating parkland/heathland courses with natural hazards. Originally established in 1896, the Carrickstone is 12 of the original 18 James Braid tree-lined holes of 1926 plus six new holes, designed by Dave Thomas. The Antonine, designed by Dave Thomas and opened in 1996, is narrower with small undulating greens, well guarded by large bunkers.
   *Carrickstone* –18 holes, 6,312 yards, par 70 (SSS 70).
   *Antonine* – 18 holes, 5,875 yards, par 69 (SSS 68).

SIGNATURE HOLE:
Carrickstone FIFTEENTH ('The Burn' 393 yards, par 4) Used to be a par 3 but was extended to a challenging par 4 in 1997. Drive from an elevated tee and a tricky approach to a green guarded by a burn and bunkers.

ADDRESS: 1a Glen Douglas Drive, Dullatur, Cumbernauld, North Lanarkshire G68 0DW.
TELEPHONE: +44 (0)1236 723230.
FAX: +44 (0)1236 727271.
SECRETARY/MANAGER: Carol Millar.
PROFESSIONAL: Duncan Sinclair.
VISITORS: Yes, apply in writing. Visitors are welcome at weekends but may not be able to play both courses on competition days.
GREEN FEES: £20 per round weekdays, £30 per day. £30 per round weekends, £35 per day.
CREDIT CARDS ACCEPTED: Visa/Mastercard.
CATERING: Restaurant and bar. Functions catered for.
FACILITIES: Motorised buggies, trolley hire, changing-rooms, putting green, pro shop, practice ground, coaching clinics, memberships available.
LOCATION: 1¼ miles north of the A80 at Cumbernauld.
LOCAL HOTELS: Castlecary House Hotel, Beefeater Travel Inn, Tinton Hotel.

# DUMBARTON

## DUMBARTON GOLF CLUB

COURSE DESCRIPTION:
Low-lying, very level parkland course with fine greens and some interesting holes – including the 356-yard 7th appropriately named the 'Punchbowl' because of its sunken green.
  18 holes, 6,027 yards, par 71 (SSS 69). Course record 64.

SIGNATURE HOLE:
EIGHTEENTH (339 yards, par 4 ) Played over water to a generous sloping green.

### COURSE CARD

| HOLE | YDS | PAR | HOLE | YDS | PAR |
|------|-----|-----|------|-----|-----|
| 1 | 337 | 4 | 10 | 422 | 4 |
| 2 | 376 | 4 | 11 | 510 | 5 |
| 3 | 332 | 4 | 12 | 155 | 3 |
| 4 | 158 | 3 | 13 | 334 | 4 |
| 5 | 355 | 4 | 14 | 310 | 4 |
| 6 | 267 | 4 | 15 | 307 | 4 |
| 7 | 356 | 4 | 16 | 489 | 5 |
| 8 | 186 | 3 | 17 | 386 | 4 |

| | | | | | | |
|---|---|---|---|---|---|---|
| 9 | 408 | 4 | 18 | 339 | 4 | |
| *Yds* | 2,775 | | *Yds* | 3,252 | | |
| *Out* | | | *In* | | | |
| *Total Yds* | 6,027 | | | | | |
| *Total Par* | 71 | | | | | |

ADDRESS: Broadmeadow, Dumbarton G82 2BQ.
TELEPHONE: +44 (0)1389 732830.
SECRETARY: +44 (0)1389 765995.
VISITORS: Not weekends and public holidays.
GREEN FEES: £22 per day.
CATERING: Yes. Bar.
FACILITIES: Putting green, practice ground.
LOCATION: ½ mile north of A814.
LOCAL HOTELS: Dumbuck Hotel.

# DUNOON

## COWAL GOLF CLUB

COURSE DESCRIPTION:
Founded in 1891, this heathland course overlooks the Firth of Clyde and Dunoon. Redesigned in 1934 by James Braid, it's an enjoyable test of golf. Wonderful views of the Isle of Arran and Ailsa Craig.

18 holes, 6,063 yards, par 70 (SSS 70). Amateur record 64. Pro record 63.

SIGNATURE HOLE:
FIFTH (191 yards, par 3) 'The Clumps' . Tricky tee shot to a well-bunkered green with a dyke to be carried.

COURSE CARD

| | MEDAL | | FORWARD | | LADIES | | | MEDAL | | FORWARD | | LADIES | |
|---|---|---|---|---|---|---|---|---|---|---|---|---|---|
| HOLE | YDS | PAR | YDS | PAR | YDS | PAR | HOLE | YDS | PAR | YDS | PAR | YDS | PAR |
| 1 | 430 | 4 | 424 | 4 | 421 | 5 | 10 | 320 | 4 | 300 | 4 | 300 | 4 |
| 2 | 422 | 4 | 420 | 4 | 369 | 4 | 11 | 333 | 4 | 332 | 4 | 330 | 4 |
| 3 | 376 | 4 | 369 | 4 | 301 | 4 | 12 | 336 | 4 | 316 | 4 | 316 | 4 |
| 4 | 380 | 4 | 369 | 4 | 320 | 4 | 13 | 483 | 5 | 425 | 4 | 415 | 5 |
| 5 | 191 | 3 | 177 | 3 | 165 | 3 | 14 | 165 | 3 | 153 | 3 | 141 | 3 |
| 6 | 295 | 4 | 285 | 4 | 267 | 4 | 15 | 381 | 4 | 355 | 4 | 308 | 4 |
| 7 | 308 | 4 | 300 | 4 | 265 | 4 | 16 | 341 | 4 | 333 | 4 | 301 | 4 |
| 8 | 296 | 4 | 290 | 4 | 213 | 4 | 17 | 371 | 4 | 363 | 4 | 356 | 4 |
| 9 | 171 | 3 | 166 | 3 | 139 | 3 | 18 | 464 | 4 | 414 | 4 | 398 | 5 |
| *Yds Out* | 2,869 | | 2,800 | | 2,460 | | *Yds In* | 3,194 | | 2,991 | | 2,865 | |

| | | |
|---|---|---|
| *Total* 6,063 | 5,791 | 5,325 |
| *Yds* | | |
| *Total* 70 | 69 | 72 |
| *Par* | | |

ADDRESS: Ardenslate Road, Dunoon, Argyll PA23 8IB.
TELEPHONE & FAX: +44 (0)1369 705673.
E-MAIL: secretary@cowalgolfclub.co.uk
WEBSITE: www.cowalgolfclub.co.uk
SECRETARY: Mrs W. Fraser.
PROFESSIONAL: Russell Weir.
VISITORS: Any time.
GREEN FEES: £22 per round weekdays, £35 per day. £32 per round weekends, £45 per day.
CATERING: Full, all day. Bar.
FACILITIES: Trolley/buggy hire, putting green, chipping and bunkered green, pro shop, practice ground.
LOCATION: 1 mile north of town.
LOCAL HOTELS: Enmore Hotel.

# EAST KILBRIDE

## EAST KILBRIDE GOLF CLUB

COURSE DESCRIPTION:
Inland wooded, parkland and hilly course. Very windy. Generous fairways and greens but some testing holes.
18 holes, 6,419 yards, par 71 (SSS 71).

ADDRESS: Chapelside Road, Nerston, East Kilbride G74 4PE.
TELEPHONE: +44 (0)1355 220913.
PROFESSIONAL: Willie Walker +44 (0)1355 222192.
VISITORS: By appointment. No weekends. Must be member of recognised golfing society.
GREEN FEES: £20 per round, £30 per day.
CATERING: Full service. Bar.
FACILITIES: Pro shop.
LOCATION: ¼ mile north, off A749.
LOCAL HOTELS: Bruce Swallow Hotel.

## LANGLANDS GOLF COURSE

COURSE DESCRIPTION:
Municipal moorland course.
18 holes, 6,202 yards, par 70 (SSS 70).

ADDRESS: Hurlawcrook Road, near Auldhouse, East Kilbride, G75 9DW.
TELEPHONE: +44 (0)1355 224685.
VISITORS: Any time
GREEN FEES: £8.75 weekdays, £9.95 weekends.
FACILITIES: Pro shop.
LOCATION: 2 miles south of East Kilbride town centre.
LOCAL HOTELS: Bruce Swallow Hotel.

## TORRANCE HOUSE GOLF COURSE

COURSE DESCRIPTION:
Municipal inland parkland course.
    18 holes, 6,415 yards, par 72 (SSS 71). Course record 71.

ADDRESS: Calderglen Country Park, Strathaven Road, East Kilbride G75 0QZ .
TELEPHONE: +44 (0)1355 248638.
PROFESSIONAL: John Dunlop.
VISITORS: Any time. Societies not weekends.
GREEN FEES: £8.75 per round weekdays. £9.95 weekends.
CATERING: Bar.
FACILITIES: Trolley/buggy hire, practice ground.
LOCATION: 1¼ miles south-east on A726.
LOCAL HOTELS: Bruce Swallow Hotel.

# ELDERSLIE

## ELDERSLIE GOLF CLUB

COURSE DESCRIPTION:
Undulating parkland course.
    18 holes, 6,300 yards, par 70 (SSS 70). Course record 61.

ADDRESS: 63 Main Road, Elderslie, near Glasgow PA5 9AZ.
TELEPHONE: +44 (0)1505 323956.
SECRETARY: Mrs A. Anderson.
PROFESSIONAL: Richard Bowman +44(0)1505 320032.
VISITORS: Yes, weekdays.
GREEN FEES: £21 per round, £28 per day.
CATERING: Yes. Bar.
FACILITIES: Trolley/buggy hire, putting green, pro shop, practice ground.
LOCATION: 3 miles from Glasgow Airport, 2 miles from M8 on A737.
LOCAL HOTELS: Lynnhurst Hotel.

# GALSTON

## LOUDOUN GOLF CLUB

### COURSE DESCRIPTION:
Relatively flat but testing parkland course, named on old maps as 'Gowf fields of Loudoun', situated in the picturesque Irvine Valley. Records indicate that 'The Gentlemen Gowfers of Loudoun' were playing here in 1773, 19 years after The Royal & Ancient Golf Club of St Andrews was formed.

18 holes, 6,016 yards, par 68 (SSS 69). Course record 64.

### SIGNATURE HOLE:
EIGHTEENTH ('Marsh' 302 yards, par 4) Many a score has been ruined on this hole. From an elevated tee, the big hitters are tempted to drive the green which is guarded by a bunker with a stream to the left and rear. The safe play is to position your tee shot to the right of the stream, which divides the fairway, and approach the green with a high iron shot.

### COURSE CARD

| HOLE | MEDAL YDS | PAR | FORWARD YDS | PAR | LADIES YDS | PAR | HOLE | MEDAL YDS | PAR | FORWARD YDS | PAR | LADIES YDS | PAR |
|------|-----------|-----|-------------|-----|------------|-----|------|-----------|-----|-------------|-----|------------|-----|
| 1 | 383 | 4 | 371 | 4 | 359 | 4 | 10 | 163 | 3 | 154 | 3 | 145 | 3 |
| 2 | 425 | 4 | 418 | 4 | 363 | 4 | 11 | 512 | 5 | 469 | 5 | 405 | 5 |
| 3 | 344 | 4 | 336 | 4 | 295 | 4 | 12 | 396 | 4 | 387 | 4 | 334 | 4 |
| 4 | 225 | 3 | 213 | 3 | 211 | 4 | 13 | 422 | 4 | 377 | 4 | 370 | 4 |
| 5 | 157 | 3 | 145 | 3 | 126 | 3 | 14 | 381 | 4 | 371 | 4 | 341 | 4 |
| 6 | 459 | 4 | 454 | 4 | 378 | 5 | 15 | 349 | 4 | 341 | 4 | 337 | 4 |
| 7 | 428 | 4 | 416 | 4 | 404 | 5 | 16 | 219 | 3 | 210 | 3 | 176 | 3 |
| 8 | 352 | 4 | 341 | 4 | 285 | 4 | 17 | 159 | 3 | 150 | 3 | 150 | 3 |
| 9 | 340 | 4 | 330 | 4 | 238 | 4 | 18 | 302 | 4 | 290 | 4 | 276 | 4 |
| Yds Out | 3,113 | | 3,024 | | 2,659 | | Yds In | 2,903 | | 2,749 | | 2,634 | |
| Total Yds | 6,016 | | 5,773 | | 5,293 | | | | | | | | |
| Total Par | 68 | | 68 | | 71 | | | | | | | | |

ADDRESS: Edinburgh Road, Galston, Ayrshire KA4 8PA.
TELEPHONE: +44 (0)1563 821993.
FAX: +44 (0)1563 820011.
E-MAIL: secretary@loudgowf.sol.co.uk
SECRETARY: W.F. Dougan.
VISITORS: Mondays to Fridays but not at weekends.
GREEN FEES: £20 per round weekdays, £30 per day. Special offers: Open Fairways, 2 Fore 1 (weekdays only and subject to availability).

CATERING: Restaurant and bar. Parties welcome by arrangement.
FACILITIES: Trolley hire, changing-rooms, putting green, pro shop, practice ground, driving range adjacent, coaching clinics adjacent.
LOCATION: From Glasgow, follow M77/A77 south to A719 and follow signs to Galston. Course is located on the A71 east of the village centre. From Ayr and Prestwick, follow A77 north to A71 junction at Kilmarnock. Take A71 east to Galston. The course is on this road. Glasgow 22 miles. Ayrshire coast 15 miles.
LOCAL HOTELS: Loudoun Mains, Strathaven Hotel, The Maxwood Hotel.

# ISLE OF GIGHA

## ISLE OF GIGHA GOLF CLUB

COURSE DESCRIPTION:
Meadowland course with wide fairways but very heavy rough. Easy walking. Scenic views over the Sound of Gigha.
   9 holes, 5,042 yards (for 18 holes), par 66 (SSS 65).

SIGNATURE HOLE:
FOURTH (300 yards, par 4) Narrow fairway with out of bounds on the right. Heavy rough to the left.

ADDRESS: Isle of Gigha, Argyll PA41 7AA.
SECRETARY: M. Tart +44(0)1583 505287.
VISITORS: Any time.
GREEN FEES: £10 per round.
CATERING: At Gigha Hotel.
LOCATION: Ferry from Tayinloan to Gigha. Course ½ mile north from PO.
LOCAL HOTELS: Gigha Hotel.

# GIRVAN

## BRUNSTON CASTLE GOLF CLUB

COURSE DESCRIPTION:
Sheltered, inland parkland course, designed by Donald Steel, set in one of the most scenic parts of Ayrshire. Course is bisected by River Girvan and includes a man-made lake.
   18 holes, 6,681 yards, par 72 (SSS 72). Amateur record 69. Pro record 63.

SIGNATURE HOLE:
SEVENTEENTH (184 yards, par 3) Requires an accurate tee shot as there is a horseshoe-shaped pond to contend with.

## COURSE CARD

| HOLE | MEDAL YDS | PAR | FORWARD YDS | PAR | LADIES YDS | PAR | HOLE | MEDAL YDS | PAR | FORWARD YDS | PAR | LADIES YDS | PAR |
|---|---|---|---|---|---|---|---|---|---|---|---|---|---|
| 1 | 414 | 4 | 387 | 4 | 331 | 4 | 10 | 323 | 4 | 319 | 4 | 253 | 4 |
| 2 | 413 | 4 | 361 | 4 | 339 | 4 | 11 | 362 | 4 | 358 | 4 | 264 | 4 |
| 3 | 384 | 4 | 336 | 4 | 295 | 4 | 12 | 426 | 4 | 369 | 4 | 367 | 4 |
| 4 | 338 | 4 | 290 | 4 | 238 | 4 | 13 | 519 | 5 | 515 | 5 | 459 | 5 |
| 5 | 215 | 3 | 191 | 3 | 156 | 3 | 14 | 355 | 4 | 345 | 4 | 336 | 4 |
| 6 | 533 | 5 | 484 | 5 | 429 | 5 | 15 | 351 | 4 | 316 | 4 | 297 | 4 |
| 7 | 408 | 4 | 359 | 4 | 344 | 4 | 16 | 397 | 4 | 349 | 4 | 345 | 4 |
| 8 | 176 | 3 | 172 | 3 | 133 | 3 | 17 | 184 | 3 | 170 | 3 | 128 | 3 |
| 9 | 497 | 5 | 456 | 5 | 418 | 5 | 18 | 386 | 4 | 350 | 4 | 387 | 5 |
| Yds Out | 3,378 | | 3,036 | | 2,768 | | Yds In | 3,303 | | 3,091 | | 2,868 | |
| Total Yds | 6,681 | | 6,127 | | 5,636 | | | | | | | | |
| Total Par | 72 | | 72 | | 74 | | | | | | | | |

ADDRESS: Golf Course Road, Dailly, Girvan, Ayrshire KA26 9GD.
TELEPHONE: +44 (0)1465 811471.
FAX: +44 (0)1465 811545.
E-MAIL: golf@brunstoncastle.co.uk
WEBSITE: www.brunstoncastle.co.uk
PROFESSIONAL: Stephen Forbes.
VISITORS: All times.
GREEN FEES: £26 per round weekdays, £40 per day. £30 per round weekends, £45 per day.
CREDIT CARDS ACCEPTED: Visa/Mastercard.
CATERING: Restaurant and two bars.
FACILITIES: Motorised buggies (£20), trolley hire (£2), club hire (£10), caddies (£25), changing-rooms, putting green, pro shop, practice ground, driving range, coaching clinics, memberships available.
LOCATION: 6 miles south-east of Turnberry.
LOCAL HOTELS: Annfield House Hotel, Kinloch Hotel, Malin Court Hotel, Redcliffe House Hotel, South Beach Hotel.

# GIRVAN GOLF COURSE

## COURSE DESCRIPTION:

Municipal course in two sections designed by James Braid. The first eight holes are links and run along the shores of the Firth of Clyde with Ailsa Craig as a backdrop. The rest are inland parkland, dissected by the river. Lush with wide fairways and minimal rough. Although only two holes are more than 400 yards, five of the par 3s are in excess of 200 yards to small greens. Not as easy as it might look.

18 holes, 5,064 yards, par 64 (SSS 64).

SIGNATURE HOLE:
EIGHTH ('Right Scunner' 243 yards, par 3) one of the longest Par 3s in Scotland made more difficult when played into prevailing wind. Plateau green with a bunker to the left and two to the right.

COURSE CARD

| HOLE | YDS | PAR | HOLE | YDS | PAR |
|------|-----|-----|------|-----|-----|
| 1 | 360 | 4 | 10 | 106 | 3 |
| 2 | 395 | 4 | 11 | 359 | 4 |
| 3 | 220 | 3 | 12 | 378 | 4 |
| 4 | 318 | 4 | 13 | 389 | 4 |
| 5 | 171 | 3 | 14 | 206 | 3 |
| 6 | 299 | 4 | 15 | 426 | 4 |
| 7 | 215 | 3 | 16 | 276 | 4 |
| 8 | 243 | 3 | 17 | 221 | 3 |
| 9 | 345 | 4 | 18 | 137 | 3 |
| *Yds Out* | 2,566 | | *Yds In* | 2,498 | |
| *Total Yds* | 5,064 | | | | |
| *Total Par* | 64 | | | | |

ADDRESS: Golf Course Road, Girvan, Ayrshire KA26 9HW.
TELEPHONE: +44 (0) 1465 714272.
STARTER: +44 (0)1465 714346.
FAX: +44 (0)1465 714346.
VISITORS: Any time.
GREEN FEES: £12 per round weekdays, £20 per day. £16 per round weekends, £28 per day. Three-day ticket (Monday to Friday) £60. Five-day ticket (Monday to Friday) £90.
CATERING: Bar.
FACILITIES: Putting green.
LOCATION: North of town, off A77.
LOCAL HOTELS: Annfield House Hotel, King's Arms Hotel, Kinloch Hotel, Malin Court Hotel, Redcliffe House Hotel, South Beach Hotel.

# GLASGOW

## ALEXANDRA PARK GOLF COURSE

COURSE DESCRIPTION:
A hilly, parkland course with lots of trees and some tricky par 3s.
9 holes, 4,016 yards (for 18 holes), par 60 (SSS 61).

SIGNATURE HOLE:
SEVENTH (217 yards, par 3) Attractive views of surrounding parkland.

COURSE CARD

| HOLE | YDS | PAR |
|------|-----|-----|
| 1 | 351 | 4 |
| 2 | 221 | 3 |
| 3 | 212 | 3 |
| 4 | 132 | 3 |
| 5 | 155 | 3 |
| 6 | 146 | 3 |
| 7 | 217 | 3 |
| 8 | 244 | 4 |
| 9 | 330 | 4 |
| *Yds Out* | 2,008 | |
| *Total Yds* | 2,008 | |
| *Total Par* | 30 | |

ADDRESS: Alexandra Park, Sannox Gardens, Glasgow G31 8SE.
SECRETARY: G. Campbell +44 (0)141 556 1294.
PROFESSIONAL: +44 (0)141 770 0519.
VISITORS: Any time. Must book 24 hours in advance.
GREEN FEES: On application.
FACILITIES: Practice ground.
LOCATION: 2 miles east of city centre off M8/A8.
LOCAL HOTELS: Courtyard Hotel.

# BEARSDEN GOLF CLUB

COURSE DESCRIPTION:
Started off as a parkland 9-hole course. Now has 16 greens (play to alternate greens at seven of the holes) and 11 teeing areas.
   16 holes, 6,014 yards (for 18 holes), par 68 (SSS 69). Course record 67.

COURSE CARD

| HOLE | MEDAL YDS | PAR | FORWARD YDS | PAR | LADIES YDS | PAR | HOLE | MEDAL YDS | PAR | FORWARD YDS | PAR | LADIES YDS | PAR |
|------|-----------|-----|-------------|-----|------------|-----|------|-----------|-----|-------------|-----|------------|-----|
| 1 | 304 | 4 | 291 | 4 | 285 | 4 | 10 | 304 | 4 | 291 | 4 | 268 | 4 |
| 2 | 428 | 4 | 420 | 4 | 408 | 5 | 11 | 455 | 4 | 444 | 4 | 438 | 5 |
| 3 | 366 | 4 | 332 | 4 | 319 | 4 | 12 | 350 | 4 | 316 | 4 | 303 | 4 |
| 4 | 455 | 4 | 377 | 4 | 367 | 4 | 13 | 449 | 4 | 370 | 4 | 361 | 4 |
| 5 | 206 | 3 | 201 | 3 | 195 | 3 | 14 | 137 | 3 | 131 | 3 | 122 | 3 |
| 6 | 398 | 4 | 319 | 4 | 312 | 4 | 15 | 391 | 4 | 312 | 4 | 308 | 4 |
| 7 | 170 | 3 | 149 | 3 | 143 | 3 | 16 | 156 | 3 | 149 | 3 | 133 | 3 |

| 8 | 327 | 4 | 319 | 4 | 369 | 4 | 17 | 327 | 4 | 319 | 4 | 309 | 4 |
| 9 | 373 | 4 | 364 | 4 | 339 | 4 | 18 | 418 | 4 | 406 | 4 | 362 | 5 |
| Yds Out | 3,027 | | 2,772 | | 2,657 | | Yds In | 2,987 | | 2,740 | | 2,622 | |
| Total Yds | 6,014 | | 5,512 | | 5,279 | | | | | | | | |
| Total Par | 68 | | 68 | | 71 | | | | | | | | |

ADDRESS: Thorn Road, Bearsden, Glasgow G61 4BP.
TELEPHONE: +44 (0)141 942 2351.
SECRETARY: J. Mercer +44 (0)141 942 2381.
VISITORS: Due to being basically a 9-hole course, very few societies can be accommodated. Visitors usually introduced by a member.
GREEN FEES: £10 per round, £15 per day.
CATERING: Full.
FACILITIES: Putting green, practice ground.
LOCATION: 6 miles north-west of Glasgow off A809.
LOCAL HOTELS: Burnbrae Hotel, Black Bull Thistle.

# BISHOPBRIGGS GOLF CLUB

### COURSE DESCRIPTION:
Inland, wooded parkland course, designed by James Braid as nine holes in 1907 and extended to 18 four years later. Not a long course by modern standards but plays far longer than its yardage.
18 holes, 6,041 yards, par 69 (SSS 69). Course record 63.

### SIGNATURE HOLE:
SEVENTH ('Firs' par 4) A slight dogleg right with out of bounds on both sides of the fairway. Bunkers guard the front left and right of the green. The most westerly point of the course provides views of the Forth and Clyde Canal.

ADDRESS: Brackenbrae Road, Bishopbriggs, Glasgow G64 2DX.
TELEPHONE: +44 (0)141 772 1810 or 8938.
FAX: +44 (0)141 762 2532
E-MAIL: bgcsecretary@dial.pipex.com
SECRETARY/MANAGER: Andrew Smith.
VISITORS: Monday to Friday – must contact in advance.
GREEN FEES: £20 per round £30 per day.
CATERING: Restaurant and bar (from light snacks to silver service).
FACILITIES: Changing-rooms, putting green, practice ground, waiting list for membership, pro shop.
LOCATION: 4 miles north of Glasgow on A803. Half a mile north-west of Bishopbriggs.
LOCAL HOTELS: Burnbrae Hotel, Black Bull Thistle.

# BLAIRBETH GOLF CLUB

**COURSE DESCRIPTION:**
A tight, difficult, hilly parkland course with a number of elevated greens.
18 holes, 5,518 yards, par 70 (SSS 68). Amateur record D. Orr 64.

**SIGNATURE HOLE:**
ELEVENTH (452 yards, par 5). From an elevated tee 200 feet down to a gully then a rise of 20 feet to green with heavy rough on the right and trees at the back.

**COURSE CARD**

| HOLE | YDS | PAR | HOLE | YDS | PAR |
|------|-----|-----|------|-----|-----|
| 1 | 268 | 4 | 10 | 228 | 3 |
| 2 | 356 | 4 | 11 | 452 | 5 |
| 3 | 264 | 4 | 12 | 167 | 3 |
| 4 | 186 | 3 | 13 | 223 | 3 |
| 5 | 383 | 4 | 14 | 299 | 4 |
| 6 | 377 | 4 | 15 | 541 | 5 |
| 7 | 501 | 5 | 16 | 303 | 4 |
| 8 | 277 | 4 | 17 | 122 | 3 |
| 9 | 247 | 4 | 18 | 324 | 4 |
| *Yds Out* | 2,859 | | *Yds In* | 2,659 | |
| *Total Yds* | 5,518 | | | | |
| *Total Par* | 70 | | | | |

**ADDRESS:** Fernbrae Avenue, Rutherglen, Glasgow G73 4SF.
**TELEPHONE:** +44 (0)141 634 3325.
**VISITORS:** By arrangement with secretary but not at weekends.
**GREEN FEES:** £18 per round weekdays, £22 per day.
**CATERING:** Available.
**FACILITIES:** Putting green.
**LOCATION:** 1 mile south of Rutherglen off Stonelaw Road
**LOCAL HOTELS:** Kings Park Hotel.

# BONNYTON GOLF CLUB

**COURSE DESCRIPTION:**
Challenging windy course surrounded by heather-covered moorland with tree-lined fairways, plateau greens, natural burns and well-situated bunkers.
18 holes, 6,255 yards, par 72 (SSS 71).

**ADDRESS:** Kirktonmoor Road, Eaglesham, Glasgow G76 0QA.
**TELEPHONE:** +44 (0)1355 302781.
**FAX:** +44 (0)1355 303151.

PROFESSIONAL: Kendal McWade +44 (0)1355 302256.
VISITORS: By prior arrangement.
GREEN FEES: £38 per day weekdays.
CATERING: Full service. Restaurant and bar.
FACILITIES: Trolley hire, club hire, changing-rooms, putting green, pro shop, practice ground, coaching clinics.
LOCATION: ¼ mile south-west of Eaglesham, off B764.
LOCAL HOTELS: Bruce Swallow Hotel.

## CAMBUSLANG GOLF CLUB

COURSE DESCRIPTION:
Sparsely wooded inland course.
9 holes, 6,072 yards (for 18 holes), par 70 (SSS 69).

ADDRESS: 30 Westburn Drive, Cambuslang, Glasgow G72 7NA.
TELEPHONE: +44 (0)141 641 3130.
VISITORS: Yes, but not at weekends.
GREEN FEES: £15 per round weekdays.
LOCAL HOTELS: Cambus Court Hotel.

## CATHCART CASTLE GOLF CLUB

COURSE DESCRIPTION:
Undulating, tree-lined parkland course.
18 holes, 5,832 yards, par 68 (SSS 68).

ADDRESS: Mearns Road, Clarkston, Glasgow G76 7YL.
TELEPHONE: +44 (0)141 638 0082.
PROFESSIONAL: Stephen Duncan +44 (0)141 638 3436.
VISITORS: Must have letter of introduction from own club.
GREEN FEES: £30 per round, £40 per day.
CATERING: Full service. Bar.
FACILITIES: Pro shop.
LOCATION: ½ mile south-west of Clarkston, off A726.
LOCAL HOTELS: Macdonald Thistle Hotel.

## CATHKIN BRAES GOLF CLUB

COURSE DESCRIPTION:
Inland moorland course. Loch at 5th hole.
18 holes, 6,208 yards, par 69 (SSS 69).

ADDRESS: Cathkin Road, Burnside, Glasgow G73 4SE.
TELEPHONE: +44 (0)141 634 6605.
PROFESSIONAL: Stephen Bree +44(0)141 634 0650.
VISITORS: Contact in advance and have handicap certificate. Not weekends.

GREEN FEES: £25 per round weekdays, £35 per day.
CATERING: Bar.
FACILITIES:Trolley hire, putting green, pro shop, practice ground
LOCATION: 1 mile south of Burnside on B759.
LOCAL HOTELS: Macdonald Thistle Hotel.

## CAWDER GOLF CLUB

COURSE DESCRIPTION:
Two parkland courses. Cawder is hilly with some testing holes. Keir is flat.
 *Cawder* – 18 holes, 6,295 yards, par 70 (SSS 71).
 *Keir* – 18 holes, 5,877 yards, par 68 (SSS 68).

ADDRESS: Cawder Road, Bishopbriggs, Glasgow G64 3QD.
TELEPHONE: +44 (0)141 772 5167.
PROFESSIONAL: Ken Stevely +44 (0)141 772 7102.
VISITORS: Contact in advance. Weekdays only.
GREEN FEES: £26 per round weekdays, £33 per day.
CATERING: Bar and full catering facilities.
FACILITIES: Pro shop.
LOCATION: 1 mile north-east of Bishopbriggs, off A803.
LOCAL HOTELS: Black Bull Thistle Hotel.

## CLOBER GOLF CLUB

COURSE DESCRIPTION:
Parkland course, fairly short with eight par 3s.
 18 holes, 5,098 yards, par 66 (SSS 65). Amateur record 62.

SIGNATURE HOLE:
FIFTH (119 yards, par 3) The Burn Hole is short but has out of bounds to the left and to the right, so the tee shot has to be accurate. There are trees left and right.

COURSE CARD

| HOLE | YDS | PAR | HOLE | YDS | PAR |
|------|-----|-----|------|-----|-----|
| 1 | 378 | 4 | 10 | 485 | 5 |
| 2 | 346 | 4 | 11 | 349 | 4 |
| 3 | 189 | 3 | 12 | 181 | 3 |
| 4 | 214 | 3 | 13 | 196 | 3 |
| 5 | 119 | 3 | 14 | 280 | 4 |
| 6 | 311 | 4 | 15 | 161 | 3 |
| 7 | 364 | 4 | 16 | 192 | 3 |
| 8 | 490 | 5 | 17 | 380 | 4 |
| 9 | 156 | 3 | 18 | 305 | 4 |
| *Yds* | 2,569 | | *Yds* | 2,529 | |
| *Out* | | | *In* | | |

| Total Yds | 5,098 |
| --- | --- |
| Total Par | 66 |

ADDRESS: Craigton Road, Milngavie, Glasgow G62 7HP.
TELEPHONE: +44 (0)141 956 1685.
PROFESSIONAL: Alan Tait +44 (0)141 956 6963.
SECRETARY: T. Arthur.
VISITORS: Weekdays before 4 p.m.
GREEN FEES: £15 per round.
CATERING: Yes.
FACILITIES: Trolley hire, putting green, pro shop.
LOCATION: From Milngavie Cross proceed along Clober Road for more than half a mile. Turn left into Craigton Road. Club is on left after 500 yards.
LOCAL HOTELS: Black Bull Thistle Hotel, Burnbrae Hotel.

## COWGLEN GOLF CLUB

COURSE DESCRIPTION:
Challenging and undulating parkland course with good views over Clyde Valley to Campsie Hills.
    18 holes, 5,976 yards, par 69 (SSS 69). Course record 63.

ADDRESS: Barrhead Road, Cowglen, Glasgow G43 1AU.
TELEPHONE: +44 (0)141 632 0556.
PROFESSIONAL: John McTear +44 (0)141 649 9401.
VISITORS: Welcome on weekdays if introduced by a member. Contact in advance. Handicap certificate. No weekends.
GREEN FEES: £22.50.
CATERING: Bar.
FACILITIES: Putting green, pro shop, practice ground, driving range.
LOCATION: 4½ miles south-west of Glasgow city centre on B762.
LOCAL HOTELS: Macdonald Thistle Hotel.

## CROW WOOD GOLF CLUB

COURSE DESCRIPTION:
James Braid-designed, tree-lined parkland course. Rolling fairways enjoy the scenic backdrop of the Campsie Fells. Good greens and fairways. Ideal for the budding star and high handicapper alike.
    18 holes, 6,261 yards, par 71 (SSS 71). Amateur record Dean Robertson 62. Pro record Colin Gillies 66.

SIGNATURE HOLE:
TENTH (291 yards, par 4) One of the most picturesque holes you could find. Although short, it has trees on either side and the Garnkirk Burn only 100 yards

or so from the tee. It can yield many birdies but also some horrific scores.

COURSE CARD

| HOLE | YDS | PAR | HOLE | YDS | PAR |
|------|-----|-----|------|-----|-----|
| 1 | 146 | 3 | 10 | 291 | 4 |
| 2 | 530 | 5 | 11 | 402 | 4 |
| 3 | 362 | 4 | 12 | 277 | 4 |
| 4 | 344 | 4 | 13 | 453 | 4 |
| 5 | 197 | 3 | 14 | 349 | 4 |
| 6 | 378 | 4 | 15 | 167 | 3 |
| 7 | 421 | 4 | 16 | 336 | 4 |
| 8 | 372 | 4 | 17 | 396 | 4 |
| 9 | 333 | 4 | 18 | 517 | 5 |
| *Yds* *Out* | 3,083 | | *Yds* *In* | 3,178 | |
| *Total Yds* | 6,261 | | | | |
| *Total Par* | 71 | | | | |

ADDRESS: Garnkirk House, Cumbernauld Road, Muirhead, Glasgow G69 9JF.
SECRETARY: Ian McInnes +44 (0)141 779 4954.
PROFESSIONAL: Brian Moffat +44 (0)141 779 1943.
VISITORS: Midweek, excluding public holidays and medal days.
GREEN FEES: £23 per round, £34 per day.
CATERING: Bar snacks and full meals.
FACILITIES: Trolley hire, putting green, pro shop, practice ground.
LOCATION: Take M80 from Glasgow towards Stirling. At the end of the motorway, the entrance is first left after 200 yards.
LOCAL HOTELS: Crow Wood House Hotel, Garfield Hotel, Moddiesburn House Hotel.

# DOUGLAS PARK GOLF CLUB

COURSE DESCRIPTION:
Parkland course with wide variety of holes.
18 holes, 5,957 yards, par 69 (SSS 69).

ADDRESS: Hillfoot, Bearsden, Glasgow G61 2TJ.
TELEPHONE: +44 (0)141 942 2220.
SECRETARY: Norman Nicholson +44 (0)141 942 1899.
PROFESSIONAL: David Scott +44 (0)141 942 1482.
VISITORS: Must be accompanied by a member. Contact in advance. Societies Wednesdays and Thursdays.
GREEN FEES: £22 per round, £30 per day.
CATERING: Bar.
FACILITIES: Trolley hire, pro shop.
LOCATION: East of Bearsden on A81.

LOCAL HOTELS: Black Bull Thistle Hotel.

# ESPORTA DOUGALSTON GOLF CLUB

COURSE DESCRIPTION:
Very picturesque championship course set in 300 acres of woodland with some mature tree-lined fairways and three ponds. Designed in 1975, the course makes full use of its natural attributes.

18 holes, 6,225 yards, par 71 (SSS 71). Amateur record 68. Pro record 65.

SIGNATURE HOLE:
SIXTH ('Stables' 191 yards, par 3) From an elevated tee downhill, with a burn in front of the green and a pond to the left side.

ADDRESS: Strathblane Road, Milngavie, Glasgow G62 8HJ.
TELEPHONE: +44 (0)141 955 2434.
FAX: +44 (0)141 955 2406.
SECRETARY: Johnathan Wallace.
EMAIL: johnathan.wallace@esporta.com
PROFESSIONAL: Craig Everett.
VISITORS: Welcome. Monday to Friday all day. Please phone for availablilty at weekends. Corporate and society packages.
GREEN FEES: £20 per round weekdays, £35 per day. £30 per round weekends.
CATERING: Wecoming clubhouse with restaurant and bar facilities all day. Functions catered for.
FACILITIES: Trolley hire (£2), club hire (£10), changing-rooms, putting green, practice ground, pro shop, coaching clinics, memberships available, health and fitness club, including swimming pool.
LOCATION: Just 10 minutes from Glasgow on the Milngavie–Strathblane road (A81).
LOCAL HOTELS: Burnbrae Hotel, Black Bull Thistle Hotel.

# GLASGOW GOLF CLUB (KILLERMONT)

COURSE DESCRIPTION:
If you're a member of Glasgow, you really get the best of both worlds – a pleasant parkland course at Killermont, featuring beech, chestnut and oak trees, and 30 miles away a second course, the demanding links of Glasgow Gailes on the Ayrshire course. Not surprisingly, membership to the club is much sought after and the waiting list is something like eight years. It was founded in 1787 by wealthy merchants and serving army officers, which makes it the ninth oldest in the world. To put it into historical context, many of its early members went off to fight in the Napoleonic Wars. Killermont doesn't have lady members and doesn't encourage visitors unless you're lucky enough to be the guest of a member. But if you get the chance to play this par-70, 5,977-yard course, designed by Old Tom Morris in 1904, it will be a joy and certainly not a war. It's perhaps best known for its somewhat eccentric start with an opening par 4 of only 273 yards and then a par 3 of almost the same distance (244 yards). The 3rd is a tough 405-yard par 4

uphill and the 5th, at 525 yards, is the longest hole on the course. It doglegs right to left off the tee and then switches left to right. The 19th hole is pretty impressive, too. The clubhouse, a former stately home built around the time of Trafalgar, houses a trophy collection that cannot be bettered anywhere.

18 holes, 5,977 yards, par 70 (SSS 69).

SIGNATURE HOLE:
TENTH (424 yards, par 4) Demands an accurate tee shot. Slightly left and you face an approach shot over trees to a green which slopes away from you. There are two cross-bunkers just short of the green and a greenside bunker on the left.

COURSE CARD

| HOLE | YDS | PAR | HOLE | YDS | PAR |
|------|-----|-----|------|-----|-----|
| 1 | 273 | 4 | 10 | 424 | 4 |
| 2 | 244 | 3 | 11 | 173 | 3 |
| 3 | 405 | 4 | 12 | 423 | 4 |
| 4 | 159 | 3 | 13 | 252 | 4 |
| 5 | 525 | 5 | 14 | 383 | 4 |
| 6 | 439 | 4 | 15 | 476 | 5 |
| 7 | 344 | 4 | 16 | 141 | 3 |
| 8 | 302 | 4 | 17 | 295 | 4 |
| 9 | 346 | 4 | 18 | 373 | 4 |
| Yds Out | 3,037 | | Yds In | 2,940 | |
| Total Yds | 5,977 | | | | |
| Total Par | 70 | | | | |

ADDRESS: Killermont, Glasgow G61 2TW.
TELEPHONE: +44 (0)141 942 2011.
FAX: +44 (0)141 942 0770.
SECRETARY: David Deas.
PROFESSIONAL: Jack Steven +44 (0) 141 942 8507.
VISITORS: With a member. Must have handicap certificate.
GREEN FEES: £50 per round weekdays.
CATERING: Full service. Restaurant and bar.
FACILITIES: Trolley hire, putting green, pro shop.
LOCATION: South-east of city, off A81.
LOCAL HOTELS: Black Bull Thistle Hotel.

# HAGGS CASTLE GOLF CLUB

COURSE DESCRIPTION:
A tricky wooded parkland course which has hosted a number of major championships, including the Scottish Open.

18 holes, 6,464 yards, par 72 (SSS 72). Amateur record 64. Pro record 62.

ADDRESS: 70 Dumbreck Road, Glasgow G41 4SN.
TELEPHONE & FAX: +44 (0)141 427 1157.
SECRETARY: Ian Harvey.
PROFESSIONAL: Jim McAlister +44 (0)141 427 3355.
VISITORS: By arrangement only. Monday to Friday. Handicap certificate required.
GREEN FEES: £30 per round, £44 per day.
CATERING: Yes.
FACILITIES: Trolley hire, putting green, pro shop, practice ground.
LOCATION: First slip road off M77 from M8.
LOCAL HOTELS: Sherbrooke Castle Hotel.

# HILTON PARK GOLF CLUB

## COURSE DESCRIPTION:
Two moorland courses set in extremely scenic surroundings near the West Highland gateway.

*Hilton* – 18 holes, 6,054 yards, par 70 (SSS 70). Amateur record A. McDonald, R. Fraser, B. Reid 65. Pro record 64.

*Allander* – 18 holes, 5,374 yards, par 69 (SSS 67). Amateur record 64. Pro record 63.

## SIGNATURE HOLE:
*Hilton*: FIFTH (422 yards, par 4): Stoke index 1.
*Allander*: FIFTH (372 yards, par 4) Particularly scenic.

## COURSE CARD

| HOLE | MEDAL YDS | PAR | FORWARD YDS | PAR | LADIES YDS | PAR | HOLE | MEDAL YDS | PAR | FORWARD YDS | PAR | LADIES YDS | PAR |
|------|------|-----|------|-----|------|-----|------|------|-----|------|-----|------|-----|
| 1 | 496 | 5 | 483 | 5 | 488 | 5 | 10 | 340 | 4 | 375 | 4 | 321 | 4 |
| 2 | 386 | 4 | 381 | 4 | 307 | 4 | 11 | 373 | 4 | 369 | 4 | 345 | 4 |
| 3 | 403 | 4 | 399 | 4 | 389 | 4 | 12 | 157 | 3 | 153 | 3 | 144 | 3 |
| 4 | 177 | 3 | 172 | 3 | 166 | 3 | 13 | 415 | 4 | 411 | 4 | 366 | 4 |
| 5 | 422 | 4 | 414 | 4 | 358 | 4 | 14 | 329 | 4 | 320 | 4 | 300 | 4 |
| 6 | 220 | 3 | 216 | 3 | 204 | 3 | 15 | 363 | 4 | 356 | 4 | 346 | 4 |
| 7 | 306 | 4 | 266 | 4 | 252 | 4 | 16 | 498 | 5 | 485 | 5 | 485 | 5 |
| 8 | 307 | 4 | 324 | 4 | 253 | 4 | 17 | 184 | 3 | 184 | 3 | 164 | 3 |
| 9 | 314 | 4 | 309 | 4 | 309 | 4 | 18 | 364 | 4 | 360 | 4 | 327 | 4 |
| Yds Out | 3,031 | | 2,964 | | 2,702 | | Yds In | 3,023 | | 3,013 | | 2,785 | |
| Total Yds | 6,054 | | 5,977 | | 5,197 | | | | | | | | |
| Total Par | 70 | | 70 | | 70 | | | | | | | | |

ADDRESS: Auldmarroch Estate, Stockiemuir Road, Milngavie, Dunbartonshire G62 7HB.
TELEPHONE & FAX: +44 (0)141 956 4657.

E-MAIL: info@hiltonparkgolfclub.fsnet.co.uk
SECRETARY: Mrs J. Dawson +44 (0)141 956 5124.
PROFESSIONAL: William McCondichie +44 (0)141 956 5125.
VISITORS: Yes, unrestricted on weekdays before 4 p.m. No weekends or public holidays.
GREEN FEES: £26 per round, £36 per day.
CATERING: Restaurant and bar. Functions catered for.
FACILITIES: Trolley hire (pull £1.50, electric £5), changing-rooms, putting green, pro shop, practice ground, driving range, coaching clinics.
LOCATION: 8 miles north-west of Glasgow on the A809.
LOCAL HOTELS: Black Bull Thistle Hotel, Kirkhouse Inn, West Highland Gate.

## KIRKHILL GOLF CLUB

COURSE DESCRIPTION:
Hilly, meadowland course designed by James Braid.
18 holes, 5,889 yards, par 69 (SSS 69). Course record 63.

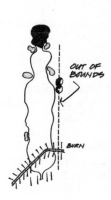

SIGNATURE HOLE:
FIRST (445 yards, par 4) Drive over Kirk Burn avoiding out of bounds on the right. Fairway narrows to the mouth of the green, which is guarded by bunkers right and left.

ADDRESS: Greenlees Road, Cambuslang, Glasgow G72 8YN.
TELEPHONE: +44 (0)141 641 8499.
PROFESSIONAL: Duncan Williamson +44 (0)141 641 7972.
VISITORS: Yes, midweek.
GREEN FEES: £20 per round, £32 per day.
CATERING: Yes.
FACILITIES: Putting green, pro shop, practice ground.
LOCATION: ½ mile north of A749, Rutherglen–East Kilbride road.
LOCAL HOTELS: Burnside Hotel.

## KNIGHTSWOOD GOLF COURSE

COURSE DESCRIPTION:
Flat and open parkland course with generous fairways.
9 holes, 5,584 yards (for 18 holes), par 68 (SSS 67).

SIGNATURE HOLE:
FIRST (442 yards, par 4) out of bounds on the right. Approach must be accurate. Bunkers front left, right and behind the green, which slopes away severely.

COURSE CARD

| HOLE | YDS | PAR |
|------|-----|-----|
| 1 | 442 | 4 |

| | | |
|---|---|---|
| 2 | 309 | 4 |
| 3 | 410 | 4 |
| 4 | 280 | 4 |
| 5 | 116 | 3 |
| 6 | 215 | 3 |
| 7 | 321 | 4 |
| 8 | 203 | 3 |
| 9 | 496 | 5 |
| *Yds Out* | 2,792 | |
| *Total Yds* | 2,792 | |
| *Total Par* | 34 | |

ADDRESS: Lincoln Avenue, Knightswood, Glasgow G71 5QZ.
STARTER: +44 (0)141 959 6358.
SECRETARY: +44 (0)141 954 6495.
VISITORS: Yes, without restriction. Book 24 hours in advance.
GREEN FEES: £3.20 for 9 holes, £6.40 for 18.
CATERING: Limited.
LOCATION: 4 miles west of city centre off A82.
LOCAL HOTELS: Jurys Glasgow Hotel.

## LENZIE GOLF CLUB

COURSE DESCRIPTION:
Founded in 1889. Parkland course. Prominent features include the old beech trees, which line some of the fairways, together with thorn hedges and shallow ditches. Extensive larch and fir plantations have also been created. A substantial practice area lies to the west of the 18th and beside a small loch. The course is relatively flat apart from a steep hill to the 5th green. From there is a fine view of the Campsie Hills to the north and beyond to Ben Lomond.

18 holes, 5,984 yards, par 69 (SSS 69). Amateur record 64. Pro record 63.

SIGNATURE HOLE:
FIFTH (343 yards, par 4) Small green on hilltop with out of bounds on the left.

COURSE CARD

| HOLE | YDS | PAR | HOLE | YDS | PAR |
|---|---|---|---|---|---|
| 1 | 307 | 4 | 10 | 500 | 5 |
| 2 | 286 | 4 | 11 | 431 | 4 |
| 3 | 433 | 4 | 12 | 462 | 4 |
| 4 | 350 | 4 | 13 | 400 | 4 |
| 5 | 343 | 4 | 14 | 159 | 3 |
| 6 | 140 | 3 | 15 | 370 | 4 |
| 7 | 363 | 4 | 16 | 425 | 4 |

| | | | | | |
|---|---|---|---|---|---|
| 8 | 205 | 3 | 17 | 152 | 3 |
| 9 | 286 | 4 | 18 | 372 | 4 |
| *Yds* | 2,713 | | *Yds* | 3,271 | |
| *Out* | | | *In* | | |
| *Total Yds* | 5,984 | | | | |
| *Total Par* | 69 | | | | |

ADDRESS: 19 Crosshill Road, Lenzie, Glasgow G66 5DA.
CLUB MASTER: +44(0)141 776 1535.
SECRETARY: +44 (0)141 776 6020.
PROFESSIONAL: Jim McCallum +44(0)141 777 7748.
VISITORS: Yes. Weekdays.
GREEN FEES: £18 per round, £26 per day.
CATERING: Yes. Clubhouse refurbished in 1996. Two dining-rooms. Bar snacks to à la carte dinners.
FACILITIES: Trolley/buggy hire, putting green, pro shop, practice ground.
LOCATION: South side of Lenzie on B819.
LOCAL HOTELS: Garfield Hotel, Moodiesburn House Hotel.

## LETHAMHILL GOLF COURSE

COURSE DESCRIPTION:
Municipal parkland course with many tree-lined holes. Excellent views over Hogganfield Loch.
18 holes, 5,859 yards, par 70 (SSS 68).

ADDRESS: 1240 Cumbernauld Road, Millerston, Glasgow G33 1AH.
TELEPHONE: +44 (0)141 770 0519 or to book 770 6220.
VISITORS: No restrictions. Book 24 hours in advance.
GREEN FEES: £6.50 per round/day.
CATERING: No.
LOCATION: 3 miles north-east of city centre on A80.
LOCAL HOTELS: Copthorne Hotel.

## LINN PARK GOLF CLUB

COURSE DESCRIPTION:
Undulating municipal parkland course with six par 3s in the outward half. Tight approaches into some greens due to well-placed bunkers.
18 holes, 5,132 yards, par 66 (SSS 65). Amateur record 61.

SIGNATURE HOLE:
TENTH (400 yards, par 4) Dogleg left. Out of bounds behind the green. Blind approach. Tree trouble left and right from the tee.

ADDRESS: Simshill Road, Glasgow G44 5EP.
TELEPHONE: +44 (0)141 637 5871.
SECRETARY: R. Flanagan.
VISITORS: Yes, any time.
GREEN FEES: £5.50. Book 24 hours in advance.
CATERING: No. Soft drink machine only.
LOCATION: South Glasgow. Near Castlemilk.
LOCAL HOTELS: Bruce Swallow Hotel.

## LITTLEHILL GOLF CLUB

### COURSE DESCRIPTION:
Reasonably flat municipal parkland course with some tree-lined fairways. One of the features is the 'Old Dyke' which cuts across several holes.
18 holes, 6,240 yards, par 70 (SSS 70).

ADDRESS: Auchinairn Road, Bishopbriggs, Glasgow G74 1UT.
TELEPHONE: +44 (0)141 772 1916.
VISITORS: Yes.
GREEN FEES: £7 per round.
CATERING: Snacks only.
LOCATION: 3 miles north of city centre.

## MILNGAVIE GOLF CLUB

### COURSE DESCRIPTION:
Scenic moorland course with beautiful views from the 5th tee especially. Short in yardage but plays its distance and is tricky with blind drives at the 9th and 10th.
18 holes, 5,818 yards, par 68 (SSS 68). Course record 59.

### SIGNATURE HOLE:
FIRST ( 359 yards, par 4) One of the most challenging anywhere. From the elevated tee, you have to drive over a burn and whins to a plateau fairway with out of bounds on the right and trees on the left. The fairway then doglegs left to a plateau green.

### COURSE CARD

| | MEDAL | | FORWARD | | LADIES | | | MEDAL | | FORWARD | | LADIES | |
|------|-----|-----|-----|-----|-----|-----|------|-----|-----|-----|-----|-----|-----|
| HOLE | YDS | PAR | YDS | PAR | YDS | PAR | HOLE | YDS | PAR | YDS | PAR | YDS | PAR |
| 1 | 359 | 4 | 356 | 4 | 304 | 4 | 10 | 361 | 4 | 352 | 4 | 315 | 4 |
| 2 | 162 | 3 | 158 | 3 | 158 | 3 | 11 | 313 | 4 | 299 | 4 | 275 | 4 |
| 3 | 333 | 4 | 323 | 4 | 315 | 4 | 12 | 175 | 3 | 170 | 3 | 167 | 3 |
| 4 | 446 | 4 | 442 | 4 | 414 | 5 | 13 | 380 | 4 | 376 | 4 | 371 | 5 |
| 5 | 294 | 4 | 287 | 4 | 277 | 4 | 14 | 372 | 4 | 339 | 4 | 328 | 4 |
| 6 | 133 | 3 | 117 | 3 | 105 | 3 | 15 | 462 | 4 | 460 | 4 | 459 | 5 |
| 7 | 423 | 4 | 417 | 4 | 401 | 5 | 16 | 197 | 3 | 193 | 3 | 168 | 3 |
| 8 | 333 | 4 | 316 | 4 | 310 | 4 | 17 | 394 | 4 | 390 | 4 | 372 | 4 |

| 9 | 374 | 4 | 361 | 4 | 329 | 4 | 18 | 307 | 4 | 296 | 4 | 245 | 4 |
|---|-----|---|-----|---|-----|---|----|-----|---|-----|---|-----|---|
| Yds Out | 2,857 | | 2,777 | | 2,633 | | Yds In | 2,961 | | 2,875 | | 2,700 | |
| Total Yds | 5,818 | | 5,652 | | 5,333 | | | | | | | | |
| Total Par | 68 | | 68 | | 72 | | | | | | | | |

**ADDRESS:** Laighpark, Milngavie, Glasgow G62 8EP.
**TELEPHONE:** +44 (0)141 956 1619.
**FAX:** +44 (0)141 956 4252.
**SECRETARY:** Ms S. McInnes.
**VISITORS:** Yes. Weekdays by prior arrangement with secretary.
**GREEN FEES:** £22 per round, £33 per day.
**CATERING:** Restaurant and bar. Functions catered for.
**FACILITIES:** Changing-rooms, putting green, practice ground, memberships available.
**LOCATION:** 7 miles north of Glasgow. A809 (Drymen road) to Craigton village. Turn right and follow road through farm to course (1½ miles).
**LOCAL HOTELS:** Burnbrae Hotel, Black Bull Thistle Hotel, West Highland Gate.

## MOUNT ELLEN GOLF CLUB

**COURSE DESCRIPTION:**
Short, but tricky, parkland course suitable for all handicaps. Four par 3s. No par 5s. 18 holes, 5,525 yards, par 68 (SSS 68). Amateur record 63. Pro record 61.

**COURSE CARD**

| HOLE | YDS | PAR | HOLE | YDS | PAR |
|------|-----|-----|------|-----|-----|
| 1 | 355 | 4 | 10 | 156 | 3 |
| 2 | 331 | 4 | 11 | 166 | 3 |
| 3 | 282 | 4 | 12 | 233 | 3 |
| 4 | 285 | 4 | 13 | 300 | 4 |
| 5 | 328 | 4 | 14 | 405 | 4 |
| 6 | 308 | 3 | 15 | 434 | 4 |
| 7 | 461 | 4 | 16 | 282 | 4 |
| 8 | 191 | 3 | 17 | 307 | 4 |
| 9 | 265 | 4 | 18 | 426 | 4 |
| Yds Out | 2,806 | | Yds In | 2,719 | |
| Total Yds | 5,525 | | | | |
| Total Par | 68 | | | | |

**ADDRESS:** Johnstone Road, Gartcosh, Glasgow G69 8EY.
**TELEPHONE:** +44 (0)1236 872277.
**FAX:** +44 (0)1236 872249.

SECRETARY: J. Docherty.
PROFESSIONAL: +44 (0)1236 872632.
VISITORS: Yes. Weekdays 9 a.m. to 4 p.m.
GREEN FEES: £16 per round, £25 per day.
CATERING: Full service.
LOCATION: 2 miles off Stirling road through Muirhead Cryston.
LOCAL HOTELS: Garfield House, Moodiesburn House Hotel.

# POLLOK GOLF CLUB

### COURSE DESCRIPTION:
Mature wooded, parkland course founded in 1892 and set in the Pollok Estate, which includes the Burrell Gallery and Pollok House. The holes are agreeably flat with well-drained turf. There are subtle undulations, making a choice of shot always available. Over 70 bunkers. Pollok describes itself as a 'club for gentlemen members'. The clubhouse has been recently extensively modernised.

18 holes, 6,358 yards, par 71 (SSS 70). Course record 62.

### COURSE CARD

| HOLE | MEDAL YDS | PAR | FORWARD YDS | PAR | HOLE | MEDAL YDS | PAR | FORWARD YDS | PAR |
|------|-----------|-----|-------------|-----|------|-----------|-----|-------------|-----|
| 1 | 383 | 4 | 367 | 4 | 10 | 394 | 4 | 366 | 4 |
| 2 | 330 | 4 | 320 | 4 | 11 | 387 | 4 | 373 | 4 |
| 3 | 373 | 4 | 347 | 4 | 12 | 167 | 3 | 152 | 3 |
| 4 | 333 | 4 | 315 | 4 | 13 | 355 | 4 | 332 | 4 |
| 5 | 372 | 4 | 357 | 4 | 14 | 400 | 4 | 368 | 4 |
| 6 | 173 | 3 | 142 | 3 | 15 | 493 | 5 | 476 | 5 |
| 7 | 502 | 5 | 481 | 5 | 16 | 329 | 4 | 317 | 4 |
| 8 | 386 | 4 | 351 | 4 | 17 | 157 | 3 | 142 | 3 |
| 9 | 428 | 4 | 420 | 4 | 18 | 396 | 4 | 382 | 4 |
| Yds Out | 3,280 | | 3,100 | | Yds In | 3,078 | | 2,908 | |
| Total Yds | 6,358 | | 6,008 | | | | | | |
| Total Par | 71 | | 71 | | | | | | |

ADDRESS: 90 Barrhead Road, Glasgow G43 1BG.
TELEPHONE: +44 (0)141 632 4351; +44 (0)141 632 1080.
FAX: +44 (0)141 649 1398.
E-MAIL: pollok.gc@lineone.net
WEBSITE: www.pollok.org
SECRETARY: Ian Cumming.
VISITORS: Mondays, Wednesdays, Fridays. Times by arrangement.
GREEN FEES: £32 per round weekdays, £42 per day. £40/£50 weekends.
CREDIT CARDS ACCEPTED: Visa.
CATERING: Restaurant and bar. Functions catered for.

FACILITIES: Free trolley hire, free club hire, changing-rooms, putting green, practice ground.

LOCATION: Going south on M77, exit Junction 2. At lights, go left for approximately a mile. Course is on left.

LOCAL HOTELS: Eglington Hotel, Forte Crest Hotel, Hilton Hotel, Macdonald Thistle Hotel, Tinto Firs.

## ROUKEN GLEN GOLF CENTRE

COURSE DESCRIPTION:
Well-maintained parkland course with wooded features suitable for all abilities. Designed by James Braid.
18 holes, 4,800 yards, par 64 (SSS 63).

ADDRESS: Stewarton Road, Thornliebank, Glasgow G46 7UZ.
TELEPHONE: +44 (0)141 638 7044.
PROFESSIONAL: Kendal McReid +44 (0)141 620 0826.
VISITORS: Welcome all week.
GREEN FEES: £9.50 per round weekdays, £16 per day. £11 per round weekends, £20 per day.
CATERING: Bar facilities.
FACILITIES: Shop, 18-bay floodlit driving range.
LOCATION: South side of city, 7 miles from Glasgow centre.
LOCAL HOTELS: Hilton Hotel, Marriott Hotel.

## SANDYHILLS GOLF CLUB

COURSE DESCRIPTION:
Inland course, slightly hilly. Excellent greens.
18 holes, 6,354 yards. SSS 70.

ADDRESS: 223 Sandyhills Road, Glasgow G32 9NA.
TELEPHONE: +44 (0)1698 282062.
VISITORS: Yes, but only with a member.
GREEN FEES: £17 per round, £27.50 per day.
CATERING: Yes.
LOCATION: On east boundary of city.
LOCAL HOTELS: Hilton Hotel, Marriott Hotel.

## THE EAST RENFREWSHIRE GOLF CLUB

COURSE DESCRIPTION:
Established in 1922. Only very minor alterations have been made to James Braid's original design. This basically undulating, moorland course is one of the finest in the West of Scotland, enjoying magnificent scenery and panoramic views over Glasgow and the Clyde Valley to the Campsie Fells to the north. The definition of many of the holes has been enhanced in recent years by copses of evergreen trees.

Pilmuir Dam lies between the 4th, 5th, 6th and 8th holes.

18 holes, 6,097 yards, par 70 (SSS 70). Amateur record David Orr 63. Pro record Colin Brooks 64.

## COURSE CARD

| HOLE | MEDAL YDS | PAR | LADIES YDS | PAR | HOLE | MEDAL YDS | PAR | LADIES YDS | PAR |
|---|---|---|---|---|---|---|---|---|---|
| 1 | 367 | 4 | 298 | 4 | 10 | 280 | 4 | 234 | 4 |
| 2 | 346 | 4 | 257 | 4 | 11 | 213 | 3 | 198 | 3 |
| 3 | 436 | 4 | 397 | 4 | 12 | 360 | 4 | 299 | 4 |
| 4 | 151 | 3 | 120 | 3 | 13 | 124 | 3 | 321 | 4 |
| 5 | 392 | 4 | 327 | 4 | 14 | 496 | 5 | 402 | 5 |
| 6 | 353 | 4 | 281 | 4 | 15 | 348 | 4 | 281 | 4 |
| 7 | 204 | 3 | 198 | 3 | 16 | 353 | 4 | 305 | 4 |
| 8 | 503 | 5 | 436 | 5 | 17 | 394 | 4 | 290 | 4 |
| 9 | 324 | 4 | 279 | 4 | 18 | 454 | 4 | 414 | 5 |
| *Yds* Out | 3,075 | | 2,587 | | *In* | *Yds* 3,022 | | 2,518 | |
| *Total Yds* | 6,097 | | 5,105 | | | | | | |
| *Total Par* | 70 | | 71 | | | | | | |

ADDRESS: Ayr Road, Pilmuir, Newton Mearns, Glasgow G77 6RT.

TELEPHONE: +44 (0)1355 500256.

FAX: +44 (0)1355 500323.

SECRETARY: A.L. Gillespie +44 (0)141 333 9989.

PROFESSIONAL: Stuart Russell +44 (0)1355 500206.

VISITORS: Yes by arrangement with the professional. Parties, Tuesdays and Thursdays – write to secretary.

GREEN FEES: £30 per round, £40 per day.

CATERING: Restaurant and bar. Functions catered for. Meals by arrangement, telephone +44 (0)1355 500258.

FACILITIES: Trolley hire, club hire, changing-rooms, putting green, practice ground, pro shop, coaching clinics.

LOCATION: 2 miles south of Newton Mearns on M77/A77 Glasgow–Kilmarnock road. Clubhouse is on the right.

LOCAL HOTELS: Macdonald Thistle Hotel.

# THE EASTWOOD GOLF CLUB

COURSE DESCRIPTION:

Scenic moorland course.

18 holes, 5,864 yards, par 68 (SSS 69). Amateur record 62.

SIGNATURE HOLE:
EIGHTH (480 yards, par 5) – Called 'Muckle Dicht', it's the hardest hole on the course.

COURSE CARD

| HOLE | YDS | PAR | HOLE | YDS | PAR |
|------|-----|-----|------|-----|-----|
| 1 | 385 | 4 | 10 | 173 | 3 |
| 2 | 247 | 3 | 11 | 431 | 4 |
| 3 | 360 | 4 | 12 | 335 | 4 |
| 4 | 153 | 3 | 13 | 159 | 3 |
| 5 | 233 | 3 | 14 | 451 | 4 |
| 6 | 325 | 4 | 15 | 142 | 3 |
| 7 | 383 | 4 | 16 | 353 | 4 |
| 8 | 480 | 5 | 17 | 385 | 4 |
| 9 | 481 | 5 | 18 | 388 | 4 |
| *Yds Out* | 3,047 | | *Yds In* | 2,817 | |
| *Total Yds* | 5,864 | | | | |
| *Total Par* | 68 | | | | |

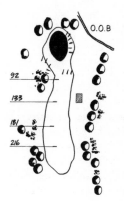

ADDRESS: Muirshield, Loganswell, Newton Mearns, Glasgow G77 6RX.
TELEPHONE: +44 (0)1355 500280.
PROFESSIONAL: Alan McGinness +44 (0)1355 500285.
VISITORS: Weekdays only.
GREEN FEES: £24 per round, £35 per day.
CATERING: Available.
FACILITIES: Trolley hire, putting green, pro shop, practice ground.
LOCATION: 3 miles south of Mearns Cross, just off the A77. Turn left at monument on road to Mearnskirk.
LOCAL HOTELS: Fenwick Hotel.

# WHITECRAIGS GOLF CLUB

COURSE DESCRIPTION:
Beautiful parkland course.
   18 holes, 6,230 yards, par 70 (SSS 70). Course record 65.
ADDRESS: 72 Ayr Road, Newton Mearns, Glasgow, G46 6SW.
TELEPHONE: +44 (0)141 639 4530.
SECRETARY: A. Keith.
PROFESSIONAL: Alistair Forrow +44 (0)141 639 2140.
VISITORS: Contact pro in advance and have handicap certificate. With a member only at weekends and bank holidays.

GREEN FEES: £28 per round, £35 per day.
CATERING: Full service. Bar.
FACILITIES: Trolley hire, putting green, pro shop, practice ground.
LOCATION: 1½ miles north-east on A77.
LOCAL HOTELS: Macdonald Thistle Hotel.

# WILLIAMWOOD GOLF CLUB

## COURSE DESCRIPTION:
James Braid-designed parkland, inland course. Fairly hilly with wooded areas. Small lake and pond.

18 holes, 5,878 yards, par 68 (SSS 69). Course record 61.

## SIGNATURE HOLE:
SECOND ('Sylvan' 209 yards, par 3) Requires an accurate tee shot through a gap in woodland to a well-bunkered green.

## COURSE CARD

| HOLE | MEDAL YDS | PAR | LADIES YDS | PAR | HOLE | MEDAL YDS | PAR | LADIES YDS | PAR |
|------|------|-----|------|-----|------|------|-----|------|-----|
| 1 | 386 | 4 | 368 | 4 | 10 | 427 | 4 | 415 | 3 |
| 2 | 209 | 3 | 145 | 3 | 11 | 201 | 3 | 133 | 4 |
| 3 | 357 | 4 | 345 | 4 | 12 | 162 | 3 | 154 | 4 |
| 4 | 129 | 3 | 121 | 3 | 13 | 254 | 4 | 245 | 4 |
| 5 | 408 | 4 | 374 | 4 | 14 | 448 | 4 | 360 | 3 |
| 6 | 429 | 4 | 345 | 4 | 15 | 352 | 4 | 305 | 4 |
| 7 | 189 | 3 | 185 | 3 | 16 | 387 | 4 | 344 | 3 |
| 8 | 345 | 4 | 342 | 4 | 17 | 391 | 4 | 348 | 4 |
| 9 | 385 | 4 | 375 | 5 | 18 | 419 | 4 | 410 | 4 |
| Yds Out | 2,837 | | 2,597 | | Yds In | 3,041 | | 2,661 | |
| Total Yds | 5,878 | | 5,258 | | | | | | |
| Total Par | 68 | | 71 | | | | | | |

ADDRESS: 690 Clarkston Road, Glasgow G44 3YR.
TELEPHONE: +44 (0)141 637 1783.
FAX: +44 (0)141 571 0166.
SECRETARY: Tom Hepburn.
PROFESSIONAL: Stewart Marshall +44 (0)141 637 2715.
VISITORS: Mondays to Fridays.
GREEN FEES: £30 per round weekdays, £40 per day.
CATERING: Restaurant and bar. Functions catered for.
FACILITIES: Trolley hire, changing-rooms, putting green, pro shop, practice ground, coaching clinics.
LOCATION: On the south side of Glasgow within 20 minutes drive of the city centre. Take

M77 from Glasgow signposted to Kilmarnock. After 4 miles take junction 3 (East Kilbride/Paisley) and follow signs to East Kilbride on the A726. Continue for 2½ miles. At third roundabout (Clarkston Toll) turn sharp left (signposted Glasgow) and within 100 yards the course will be seen on the left.

**LOCAL HOTELS:** Macdonald Thistle Hotel, Redhurst Hotel, Tinto Firs Hotel.

# WINDYHILL GOLF CLUB

**COURSE DESCRIPTION:**
Undulating, open parkland course with splendid views of Glasgow.
18 holes, 6,254 yards, par 71 (SSS 70). Amateur record 64. Pro record 67.

**SIGNATURE HOLE:**
TWELFTH (450 yards, par 4) Two-tier fairway and an elevated plateau green.

**COURSE CARD**

| HOLE | YDS | PAR | HOLE | YDS | PAR |
|---|---|---|---|---|---|
| 1 | 362 | 4 | 10 | 178 | 3 |
| 2 | 162 | 3 | 11 | 292 | 4 |
| 3 | 425 | 4 | 12 | 450 | 4 |
| 4 | 368 | 4 | 13 | 500 | 5 |
| 5 | 386 | 4 | 14 | 154 | 3 |
| 6 | 421 | 4 | 15 | 479 | 5 |
| 7 | 193 | 3 | 16 | 380 | 4 |
| 8 | 480 | 5 | 17 | 295 | 4 |
| 9 | 420 | 4 | 18 | 309 | 4 |
| *Yds Out* | 3,217 | | *Yds In* | 3,037 | |
| *Total Yds* | 6,254 | | | | |
| *Total Par* | 71 | | | | |

**ADDRESS:** Baljaffray Road, Bearsden, Glasgow G61 4QQ.
**TELEPHONE:** +44 (0)141 942 2349.
**FAX:** +44 (0)141 942 5874.
**SECRETARY:** A.B. Davidson.
**PROFESSIONAL:** Gary Collinson +44 (0)141 942 7157.
**VISITORS:** Most welcome, weekdays.
**GREEN FEES:** £20 per day.
**CATERING:** Yes. Bar.
**FACILITIES:** Trolley hire, putting green, pro shop, practice ground.
**LOCATION:** From Bearsden, take A809 to Baljaffray roundabout then B8050.
**LOCAL HOTELS:** Burnbrae Hotel, Black Bull Thistle Hotel.

# GLEDDOCH

## GLEDDOCH GOLF & COUNTRY CLUB

COURSE DESCRIPTION:
Parkland and heathland course with subtle undulations. Opened in 1975, it has spectacular views over the Firth of Clyde.
18 holes, 6,357 yards, par 72 (SSS 71).

ADDRESS: Langbank, Gleddoch PA14 6YE.
TELEPHONE: +44 (0)1475 540304.
FAX: +44 (0)1475 540459.
PROFESSIONAL: Keith Campbell +44 (0)1475 540704.
VISITORS: Contact in advance.
GREEN FEES: £30 per round weekdays, £40 weekends. Day tickets from £40.
CATERING: Full service. Bar.
FACILITIES: Pro shop.
LOCATION: B789 old Greenock road.
LOCAL HOTELS: Gleddoch House Hotel.

# GOUROCK

## GOUROCK GOLF CLUB

COURSE DESCRIPTION:
Challenging moorland course with hills and dells. Magnificent views of the Firth of Clyde.
18 holes, 6,512 yards, par 73 (SSS 73).

ADDRESS: Cowal View, Gourock PA19 6HD.
TELEPHONE: +44 (0)1475 631001.
PROFESSIONAL: Graham Clarke +44 (0)1475 636834.
VISITORS: By introduction or with a member. Societies welcome weekdays. Handicap certificate preferred.
GREEN FEES: £20 per round weekdays, £27 per day. £24 per round weekends.
CATERING: Full service. Bar.
FACILITIES: Trolley hire, putting green, pro shop, practice ground.
LOCATION: South-west of town off A770.
LOCAL HOTELS: Manor Park Hotel.

# GREENOCK

## GREENOCK WHINHILL GOLF CLUB

COURSE DESCRIPTION:
Public heathland course with private clubhouse and members. Well maintained but reasonably difficult.

18 holes, 5,506 yards, par 68 (SSS 68). Course record 64.

SIGNATURE HOLE:
FOURTH (459 yards, par 4) The toughest hole on the course.

COURSE CARD

| HOLE | YDS | PAR | HOLE | YDS | PAR |
|------|------|-----|------|-------|-----|
| 1 | 187 | 3 | 10 | 405 | 4 |
| 2 | 297 | 4 | 11 | 355 | 4 |
| 3 | 275 | 4 | 12 | 270 | 4 |
| 4 | 459 | 4 | 13 | 261 | 4 |
| 5 | 370 | 4 | 14 | 406 | 4 |
| 6 | 363 | 4 | 15 | 261 | 4 |
| 7 | 292 | 4 | 16 | 183 | 3 |
| 8 | 201 | 3 | 17 | 298 | 4 |
| 9 | 176 | 3 | 18 | 447 | 4 |
| *Yds Out* | 2,620 | | *Yds In* | 2,886 | |
| *Total Yds* | 5,506 | | | | |
| *Total Par* | 68 | | | | |

ADDRESS: Beith Road, Greenock PA16 9LN.
TELEPHONE: +44 (0)1475 724694.
SECRETARY: Raymond Kirkpatrick.
PROFESSIONAL: +44 (0)1475 721064.
VISITORS: Most days, except Saturdays.
GREEN FEES: £6.50.
CATERING: Maybe, if given plenty of time.
FACILITIES: Putting green.
LOCATION: Upper Greenock, off Dunlop Street towards old Largs Road. Off B7054.
LOCAL HOTELS: Manor Park Hotel.

## THE GREENOCK GOLF CLUB

COURSE DESCRIPTION:
Founded in 1890, the club offers two courses designed by former Open champion

James Braid. Testing moorland courses with trees defining many of the tight fairways and small undulating greens with the odd burn and bunker to catch the unwary. Panoramic views of the Clyde estuary.

*The Big Course* – 18 holes, 5,838 yards, par 68 (SSS 69). Amateur record 64. Pro record 65.

*The Wee Course* – 9 holes, 2,200 yards, par 32.

## COURSE CARD

| HOLE | MEDAL YDS | PAR | LADIES YDS | PAR | HOLE | MEDAL YDS | PAR | LADIES YDS | PAR |
|------|-----------|-----|------------|-----|------|-----------|-----|------------|-----|
| 1 | 330 | 4 | 255 | 4 | 10 | 210 | 3 | 185 | 3 |
| 2 | 306 | 4 | 272 | 4 | 11 | 412 | 4 | 328 | 4 |
| 3 | 138 | 3 | 127 | 3 | 12 | 364 | 4 | 324 | 4 |
| 4 | 446 | 4 | 420 | 5 | 13 | 177 | 3 | 172 | 3 |
| 5 | 480 | 5 | 383 | 4 | 14 | 371 | 4 | 285 | 4 |
| 6 | 259 | 4 | 235 | 4 | 15 | 416 | 4 | 411 | 5 |
| 7 | 210 | 3 | 197 | 3 | 16 | 147 | 3 | 111 | 3 |
| 8 | 336 | 4 | 293 | 4 | 17 | 414 | 4 | 370 | 4 |
| 9 | 447 | 4 | 422 | 5 | 18 | 375 | 4 | 364 | 4 |
| *Yds Out* | 2,952 | | 2,599 | | *Yds In* | 2,886 | | 2,559 | |
| *Total Yds* | 5,838 | | 5,148 | | | | | | |
| *Total Par* | 68 | | 71 | | | | | | |

**ADDRESS:** Forsyth Street, Greenock PA16 8RE.

**TELEPHONE:** +44 (0)1475 720793.

**E-MAIL:** info@greenockgolfclub.co.uk

**WEBSITE:** www.greenockgolfclub.co.uk

**PROFESSIONAL:** Stewart Russell +44 (0)1475 787236.

**EMAIL:** pro@greenockgolfclub.co.uk

**VISITORS:** May not play Saturdays. Contact in advance and have handicap certificates.

**GREEN FEES:** The Big Course: £20 per round weekdays, £28 per day. £25 per round Sundays, £35 per day. The Wee Course: £10 per round. 27-hole ticket: £25 weekdays, £30 Sundays.

**CATERING:** Superbly appointed clubhouse with restaurant and bar.

**FACILITIES:** Trolley hire, putting green, club hire (by prior arrangement), pro shop.

**LOCATION:** Set in the heart of Renfrewshire, the club is only 25 minutes from Glasgow Airport and is south-west of Greenock off the A770.

**LOCAL HOTELS:** Manor Park Hotel.

# HAMILTON

## HAMILTON GOLF CLUB

COURSE DESCRIPTION:
Inland parkland wooded course.
18 holes, 6,243 yards, par 70 (SSS 71). Course record 62.

ADDRESS: Carlisle Road, Ferniegair, Hamilton ML3 7TU.
TELEPHONE: +44 (0)1698 282872.
SECRETARY: +44 (0)1698 459537.
PROFESSIONAL: Maurice Moir +44 (0)1698 282324.
VISITORS: Not weekends. Contact in advance. Must be accompanied by a member.
GREEN FEES: £25 weekdays.
CATERING: Full service. Bar.
FACILITIES: Pro shop.
LOCATION: 1½ miles south-east of town on A72.
LOCAL HOTELS: Silvertrees Hotel.

## STRATHCLYDE PARK GOLF COURSE

COURSE DESCRIPTION:
Municipal wooded parkland course. Race course at top side of course. Nature reserve bands rest of the course. Small greens. Good views over to Strathclyde sailing loch.
9 holes, 6,260 yards (for 18 holes), par 72 (SSS 70). Course record 64.

SIGNATURE HOLE:
FOURTH (366 yards par 4) Drive downhill. Out of bounds on the right looking into bird sanctuary lake. Slight dogleg to the right around a small copse.

ADDRESS: Motehill, Hamilton, Strathclyde ML3 6BY.
TELEPHONE: +44 (0)1698 266155.
STARTER: +44 (0)1698 429350.
SECRETARY: Kevin Will.
PROFESSIONAL: W. Walker.
VISITORS: Municipal course. Any time. One week in advance booking system.
GREEN FEES: £2.70 per round weekdays. £3.40 per round weekends.
FACILITIES: Changing-rooms, putting green, pro shop, practice ground, driving range, coaching clinics, memberships available.
LOCATION: M74 exit junction 5 (Hamilton). Follow Rutherglen road signs through traffic lights and one roundabout. Turn right at second roundabout, pass ice rink and sports club.
LOCAL HOTELS: Holiday Inn, Travel Lodge.

# HELENSBURGH

## HELENSBURGH GOLF CLUB

### COURSE DESCRIPTION:
Challenging moorland course with panoramic views across Loch Lomond and the Clyde estuary.

18 holes, 6,104 yards, par 69 (SSS 70) Amateur and Pro records 64.

### SIGNATURE HOLE:
THIRD (182 yards, par 3) A tough par 3 with out of bounds on the left, woods beyond, wild moorland trees and a pond in front. Anything but a well-struck shot to a heavily bunkered green will be punished

### COURSE CARD

| HOLE | YDS | PAR | HOLE | YDS | PAR |
|------|------|-----|------|------|-----|
| 1 | 283 | 4 | 10 | 447 | 3 |
| 2 | 429 | 4 | 11 | 210 | 4 |
| 3 | 182 | 3 | 12 | 339 | 4 |
| 4 | 372 | 4 | 13 | 508 | 4 |
| 5 | 300 | 4 | 14 | 408 | 4 |
| 6 | 412 | 4 | 15 | 371 | 4 |
| 7 | 408 | 4 | 16 | 150 | 3 |
| 8 | 371 | 4 | 17 | 379 | 4 |
| 9 | 131 | 3 | 18 | 404 | 4 |
| *Yds Out* | 2,888 | | *Yds In* | 3,216 | |
| *Total Yds* | 6,104 | | | | |
| *Total Par* | 69 | | | | |

ADDRESS: 25 East Abercromby Street, Helensburgh G84 9JD.
TELEPHONE: +44 (0)1436 674173.
FAX: +44 (0)1436 671170.
SECRETARY: D. Loch.
PROFESSIONAL: David Fotheringham +44 (0)1436 675505.
VISITORS: Weekdays only.
GREEN FEES: £20 per round, £28 per day.
CATERING: Yes.
FACILITIES: Trolley hire, putting green, pro shop, practice ground.
LOCATION: A82 through Dumbarton and Cardross to Helensburgh. Turn right at traffic lights. Follow signs.
LOCAL HOTELS: Commodore Hotel.

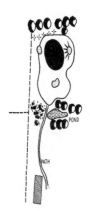

# HOLLANDBUSH

## HOLLANDBUSH GOLF CLUB

COURSE DESCRIPTION:
Moderately undulating municipal course. Tree-lined parkland on edge of moorland. The first half is flat, the second half hilly.
  18 holes, 6,200 yards, par 72 (SSS 70). Course record 63.

ADDRESS: Acretophead, Hollandbush, South Lanarkshire ML11 0JS.
TELEPHONE: +44 (0)1555 893484.
VISITORS: Any time.
GREEN FEES: £8.20 per round weekdays, £9.30 weekends.
CATERING: Full service. Bar.
FACILITIES: Trolley hire, pro shop, practice ground.
LOCATION: Off M74 between Lesmahagow and Coalburn.
LOCAL HOTELS: Strathaven Hotel.

# INNELLAN

## INNELLAN GOLF CLUB

COURSE DESCRIPTION:
Interesting undulating hilltop moorland course with panoramic views over the Firth of Clyde.
  9 holes, 4,686 yards (for 18 holes), par 64 (SSS 64). Course record 63.

SIGNATURE HOLE:
SIXTH ('Rubicon' 401 yards, par 4) Testing hole with out of bounds on the right. The first half of the hole slopes away from the out of bounds fence and the hole is dissected at 250 yards by a gorge.

COURSE CARD

| HOLE | MEDAL YDS | PAR | FORWARD YDS | PAR | LADIES YDS | PAR |
|------|------|-----|------|-----|------|-----|
| 1 | 367 | 4 | 367 | 4 | 345 | 5 |
| 2 | 184 | 3 | 184 | 3 | 184 | 3 |
| 3 | 167 | 3 | 134 | 3 | 134 | 3 |
| 4 | 160 | 3 | 160 | 3 | 160 | 3 |
| 5 | 289 | 4 | 187 | 3 | 231 | 4 |
| 6 | 401 | 4 | 401 | 4 | 339 | 5 |
| 7 | 269 | 4 | 199 | 3 | 199 | 4 |
| 8 | 201 | 3 | 198 | 3 | 198 | 3 |

| 9 | 305 | 4 | 295 | 4 | 262 | 4 | |
|---|---|---|---|---|---|---|---|
| Yds | 2,343 | | 2,125 | | 2,042 | | |
| Out | | | | | | | |
| Total | 2,343 | | | | | | |
| Yds | | | | | | | |
| Total | 32 | | | | | | |
| Par | | | | | | | |

ADDRESS: Knockamillie Road, Innellan, near Dunoon, Argyll PA23 7SG.
TELEPHONE: +44 (0)1369 830242.
SECRETARY: Andrew Wilson +44 (0)1369 702573.
VISITORS: Any time except Mondays after 4 p.m.
GREEN FEES: £8 for 9 holes weekdays/weekends, £12 per day. 25% discount for parties of 12 and over.
CATERING: Bar.
FACILITIES: Trolley hire, club hire, memberships available.
LOCATION: 4 miles south of Dunoon In Innellan, turn up Pier Road. At top of the hill turn left then first right up Knockamillie Road and follow signs to the clubhouse.
LOCAL HOTELS: Enmore Hotel, Osbourne Hotel.

# INVERARAY

## INVERARAY GOLF CLUB

COURSE DESCRIPTION:
Parkland course. Quite testing with views over Loch Fyne.
9 holes, 5,790 yards (for 18 holes), par 70 (SSS 68).

ADDRESS: Lochgilphead Road, Inveraray, Argyll, PA33.
TELEPHONE: +44 (0)1499 302079 or 302508.
LOCATION: 1 mile south of town.
VISITORS: Welcome.
GREEN FEES: £10 per round.
FACILITIES: Practice ground.
LOCAL HOTELS: Fernpoint Hotel.

# IRVINE

## GLASGOW GAILES

COURSE DESCRIPTION:
This championship links course with heather-lined fairways, superb turf, fine

greens and subtle qualities is the seaside course of the Glasgow Golf Club, which was established in 1787. The course was opened in 1892, making the Glasgow Club unique in having two courses 30 miles apart, although the current layout was completed in 1912 by Willie Park. It is a final qualifying course for the Open Championship.

18 holes, 6,539 yards, par 71 (SSS 72). Amateur record P. McKechnie 63. Pro record C. Gillies 64.

SIGNATURE HOLE:
FIFTH (536 yards, par 5) The toughest hole on the course a dogleg right with out of bounds down the right and strategically placed bunkers.

COURSE CARD

| HOLE | MEDAL YDS | PAR | FORWARD YDS | PAR | HOLE | MEDAL YDS | PAR | FORWARD YDS | PAR |
|------|-----------|-----|-------------|-----|------|-----------|-----|-------------|-----|
| 1 | 345 | 4 | 333 | 4 | 10 | 422 | 4 | 418 | 4 |
| 2 | 349 | 4 | 341 | 4 | 11 | 419 | 4 | 414 | 4 |
| 3 | 427 | 4 | 419 | 4 | 12 | 182 | 3 | 177 | 3 |
| 4 | 430 | 4 | 425 | 4 | 13 | 334 | 4 | 320 | 4 |
| 5 | 536 | 5 | 530 | 5 | 14 | 526 | 5 | 506 | 5 |
| 6 | 152 | 3 | 144 | 3 | 15 | 152 | 3 | 147 | 3 |
| 7 | 403 | 4 | 395 | 4 | 16 | 413 | 4 | 380 | 4 |
| 8 | 342 | 4 | 339 | 4 | 17 | 365 | 4 | 322 | 4 |
| 9 | 307 | 4 | 304 | 4 | 18 | 435 | 4 | 409 | 4 |
| Yds Out | 3,291 | | 3,230 | | Yds In | 3,248 | | 3,093 | |
| Total Yds | 6,539 | | 6,323 | | | | | | |
| Total Par | 71 | | 71 | | | | | | |

ADDRESS: Gailes, Irvine, Ayrshire KA11 5AE.
TELEPHONE: +44 (0)1294 311258.
FAX: +44 (0)1294 279366.
RESERVATIONS: Telephone: +44 (0)141 942 2011; Fax: +44 (0)141 942 0770.
E-MAIL: secretary@glasgow-golf.com
WEBSITE: www.glasgowgailes-golf.com
SECRETARY: David Deas.
PROFESSIONAL: Jack Steven +44 (0)1294 311561.
VISITORS: Yes, every day. Saturdays and Sundays, afternoon only.
GREEN FEES: £42 per round weekdays, £50 per day. £55 per round weekends (after 2.30 p.m. only).
CREDIT CARDS ACCEPTED: Visa/Mastercard.
CATERING: Restaurant and bar. Functions catered for.
FACILITIES: Motorised buggies (£20), trolley hire (£2), club hire (£20), caddies, changing-rooms, putting green, pro shop, practice ground.
LOCATION: 1 mile south of Irvine off A78 at Newhouse interchange.

LOCAL HOTELS: Annfield House Hotel, Hospitality Inn, Kinloch Hotel, Redcliffe House Hotel, South Beach Hotel.

## IRVINE GOLF CLUB

COURSE DESCRIPTION:
Very testing links/heathland, the Bogside course is used as a final qualifying course when the Open Championship is held at Royal Troon or Turnberry. Established in 1887 and designed by James Braid. Along with Royal Troon, will co-host the 2003 British Amateur Championship.

18 holes, 6,408 yards, par 71 (SSS 71). Amateur record A. Gourley 64. Pro record S. Martin 63.

SIGNATURE HOLE:
SIXTH ('Cannon Hill' 411 yards, par 4) Drive to the top of the hill with a second shot to a green guarded by bunkers and the river.

ADDRESS: Bogside, Irvine, Ayrshire KA12 8SN.
TELEPHONE: +44 (0)1294 275979.
FAX: +44 (0)1294 278209.
SECRETARY: W.J. McMahon.
PROFESSIONAL: Keith Erskine.
VISITORS: Weekdays, preferably by arrangement.
GREEN FEES: £35 per round weekdays, £45 per day. £45 per round weekends.
CATERING: Restaurant and bar.
FACILITIES: Trolley hire, caddies, changing-rooms, putting green, practice ground, pro shop, coaching clinics.
LOCATION: North on A78 (Irvine–Kilwinning road) and turn left for Bogside.
LOCAL HOTELS: Annfield House Hotel, Hospitality Inn, Kinloch Hotel, Redcliffe House Hotel, South Beach Hotel.

## RAVENSPARK GOLF CLUB

COURSE DESCRIPTION:
Flat and open parkland course. Well bunkered. Has hosted several national competitions.

18 holes, 6,429 yards, par 71 (SSS 71). Amateur record 65. Pro record 67.

SIGNATURE HOLE:
THIRD (452 yards, par 4) Stroke index 1.

COURSE CARD

| HOLE | YDS | PAR | HOLE | YDS | PAR |
|------|-----|-----|------|-----|-----|
| 1 | 343 | 4 | 10 | 508 | 5 |
| 2 | 380 | 4 | 11 | 394 | 4 |
| 3 | 452 | 4 | 12 | 412 | 4 |
| 4 | 158 | 3 | 13 | 398 | 4 |

| 5 | 400 | 4 | 14 | 346 | 4 |
|---|---|---|---|---|---|
| 6 | 365 | 4 | 15 | 185 | 3 |
| 7 | 339 | 4 | 16 | 313 | 4 |
| 8 | 282 | 4 | 17 | 347 | 4 |
| 9 | 398 | 4 | 18 | 409 | 4 |
| Yds Out | 3,117 | | Yds In | 3,312 | |
| Total Yds | 6,429 | | | | |
| Total Par | 71 | | | | |

ADDRESS: 13 Kidsneuk, Irvine, Ayrshire KA12 8SR.
TELEPHONE: +44 (0)1294 276467.
SECRETARY: George Robertson +44(0)1294 554617.
PROFESSIONAL: Peter Bond.
VISITORS: Any time, except before 2 p.m. on Saturdays (April to September).
GREEN FEES: £8.40 per round weekdays, £14 per day. £12.50 per round weekends, £19 per day.
CATERING: Full.
FACILITIES: Putting green, pro shop, practice ground.
LOCATION: 2 miles from Irvine. Irvine–Kilwinning main road, turn left at Irvine Royal Academy.
LOCAL HOTELS: Annfield House Hotel, Kinloch Hotel, Montgreenan Mansion House Hotel, Redcliffe House Hotel, South Beach Hotel.

# WESTERN GAILES GOLF CLUB

## COURSE DESCRIPTION:
Championship links course with views across the Firth of Clyde. Good greens, fine-bladed links turf, heather and sand dunes. Three burns cross the course. A trial of skill and strength and something of an endurance test. Established in 1897. Harry Vardon won the first major competition here in 1903 and since then it has played host to the Curtis Cup, PGA Championship, Seniors, Scottish and Boys' Championships, the Ladies' Home Internationals and is an Open Championship qualifying course. Sam McKinlay, the most eloquent of commentators on the game, once wrote: 'Western Gailes occupies a place in the affections of Scottish golfers that cannot be explained solely on the grounds of its undoubted quality, its superb situation, or the creature comforts which it furnishes. For Gailes represents to the true golfer, to the connoisseur of the game, something approaching the ideal in golf.'

18 holes, 6,714 yards, par 71 (SSS 73) from the championship tees, 6,639 yards from the medal tees. Amateur record R.A. Moscroft 65. Pro record Bernard Gallacher 65.

## SIGNATURE HOLE:
SIXTH (506 yards, par 5) Drive should be hit slightly across the fairway, which

points towards Troon harbour, to land in a series of humps and hollows. The second is played through a gap in the dunes and runs down to the fairway at a lower level. The golfer is left with a short iron which has to be accurate because the green, nestling in a hollow in the dunes, has a pronounced hump set into the middle of the right side.

## COURSE CARD

| HOLE | MEDAL YDS | PAR | FORWARD YDS | PAR | HOLE | MEDAL YDS | PAR | FORWARD YDS | PAR |
|------|-----------|-----|-------------|-----|------|-----------|-----|-------------|-----|
| 1 | 304 | 4 | 304 | 4 | 10 | 348 | 4 | 308 | 4 |
| 2 | 434 | 4 | 412 | 4 | 11 | 445 | 4 | 415 | 4 |
| 3 | 365 | 4 | 320 | 4 | 12 | 436 | 4 | 414 | 4 |
| 4 | 355 | 4 | 335 | 4 | 13 | 141 | 3 | 126 | 3 |
| 5 | 453 | 4 | 440 | 4 | 14 | 562 | 5 | 525 | 5 |
| 6 | 506 | 5 | 490 | 5 | 15 | 194 | 3 | 170 | 3 |
| 7 | 171 | 3 | 145 | 3 | 16 | 404 | 4 | 364 | 4 |
| 8 | 365 | 4 | 350 | 4 | 17 | 443 | 4 | 408 | 4 |
| 9 | 336 | 4 | 306 | 4 | 18 | 377 | 4 | 347 | 4 |
| *Yds Out* | 3,289 | | 3,102 | | *Yds In* | 3,350 | | 3,077 | |
| *Total Yds* | 6,639 | | 6,179 | | | | | | |
| *Total Par* | 71 | | 71 | | | | | | |

ADDRESS: Gailes, Irvine, Ayrshire KA11 5AE.

TELEPHONE: +44 (0)1294 311649.

FAX: +44 (0)1294 312312.

WEBSITE: www.westerngailes.com

VISITORS: Yes on Mondays, Wednesdays and Fridays (April 15 to September 28). Sundays only by approval of club manager. Must have handicap certificate.

GREEN FEES: £85 per round weekdays, £115 per day, including lunch. £90 per round Sundays 2.30–3.30 pm.

CREDIT CARDS ACCEPTED: Visa/Mastercard.

CATERING: Restaurant and bar. Lunch included in weekday green fees.

FACILITIES: Trolley hire (£2), caddies (£25+), changing-rooms, putting green, golf shop in bar, practice facilities, memberships available through secretary.

LOCATION: 3 miles north of Troon.

LOCAL HOTELS: Annfield House Hotel, Hospitality Inn, Kinloch Hotel, Marine Hotel, Redcliffe House Hotel, South Beach Hotel.

# ISLE OF ISLAY

## ISLAY GOLF CLUB

COURSE DESCRIPTION:
A championship seaside links opened on Islay in 1891. Golf's first £100 Open Championship was played here in 1901.
   18 holes, 6,226 yards, par 71 (SSS 70). Course record Iain Middleton 66.

SIGNATURE HOLE:
SEVENTH ('The Maiden', 395 yards, par 4) has a fearsome sandy ridge 100 yards from tee. Blind second shot to the green guarded by two bunkers.

ADDRESS: Machrie Hotel and Golf Course, Port Ellen, Isle of Islay, Argyll PA42 7AN.
TELEPHONE: +44 (0)1496 302310
E-MAIL: islaygolf@btinternet.com
WEBSITE: www.islay.golf.btinternet.co.uk
VISITORS: Yes, all year.
GREEN FEES: £35 per round, £40 per day.
CATERING: Full facilities at hotel.
FACILITIES: Trolley, club hire, caddies by arrangement, changing-rooms, membership available, putting green, shop, practice ground.
LOCATION: A846, 3½ miles north of Port Ellen.
LOCAL HOTELS: Machrie Hotel.

# JOHNSTONE

## COCHRANE CASTLE GOLF CLUB

COURSE DESCRIPTION:
Fairly hilly tree-lined parkland course. Two streams run through it, and there are views to the mountains in the north from the higher points of the course.
   18 holes, 6,226 yards, par 71 (SSS 71). Amateur record 65. Pro record 71.

SIGNATURE HOLE:
EIGHTH (554 yards, par 5) Drive from elevated tee with magnificent views to the mountains in the north.

COURSE CARD

| | MEDAL | | FORWARD | | LADIES | | | MEDAL | | FORWARD | | LADIES | |
|------|------|-----|------|-----|------|-----|------|------|-----|------|-----|------|-----|
| HOLE | YDS | PAR | YDS | PAR | YDS | PAR | HOLE | YDS | PAR | YDS | PAR | YDS | PAR |
| 1 | 166 | 3 | 156 | 3 | 287 | 4 | 10 | 346 | 4 | 338 | 4 | 287 | 4 |
| 2 | 332 | 4 | 325 | 4 | 265 | 4 | 11 | 361 | 4 | 352 | 4 | 350 | 4 |

| 3 | 454 | 5 | 415 | 4 | 363 | 5 | 12 | 394 | 4 | 363 | 4 | 326 | 4 |
| 4 | 428 | 4 | 420 | 4 | 395 | 5 | 13 | 348 | 4 | 340 | 4 | 330 | 4 |
| 5 | 500 | 5 | 476 | 5 | 446 | 5 | 14 | 167 | 3 | 147 | 3 | 112 | 3 |
| 6 | 156 | 3 | 147 | 3 | 126 | 3 | 15 | 423 | 4 | 418 | 4 | 392 | 4 |
| 7 | 331 | 4 | 321 | 4 | 308 | 4 | 16 | 486 | 5 | 480 | 5 | 432 | 5 |
| 8 | 554 | 5 | 554 | 5 | 470 | 5 | 17 | 164 | 3 | 158 | 3 | 122 | 3 |
| 9 | 211 | 3 | 203 | 3 | 168 | 3 | 18 | 405 | 4 | 399 | 4 | 294 | 4 |
| *Yds* *Out* | 3,132 | | 3,017 | | 2,684 | | *Yds* *In* | 3,094 | | 2,995 | | 2,645 | |
| *Total* *Yds* | 6,226 | | 6,012 | | 5,329 | | | | | | | | |
| *Total* *Par* | 71 | | 70 | | 72 | | | | | | | | |

ADDRESS: Scott Avenue, Craigston, Johnstone PA5 0HF.
TELEPHONE: +44 (0)1505 320146.
SECRETARY: J. Cowan
PROFESSIONAL: Stuart Campbell +44 (0)1505 328465.
VISITORS: Weekdays.
GREEN FEES: £17 per round, £25 per day.
CATERING: Full, except limited on Mondays.
FACILITIES: Trolley hire, putting green, pro shop, practice ground.
LOCATION: 5 miles west of Paisley, ½ mile off Beith road.
LOCAL HOTELS: Bird in the Hand Hotel, Lynnhurst Hotel.

# KILBIRNIE

## KILBIRNIE PLACE GOLF CLUB

COURSE DESCRIPTION:
Short but not easy inland parkland course. Easy walking. Good views of Place Castle and countryside.
18 holes, 5,400 yards, par 69 (SSS 67).

ADDRESS: Largs Road, Kilbirnie KA25 7AT.
TELEPHONE: +44 (0)1505 683398.
SECRETARY: +44 (0)1505 684444.
VISITORS: Any time except Saturdays.
GREEN FEES: £10 per round weekdays, £18 per day. £18 per round weekends.
CATERING: Bar.
FACILITIES: Putting green, practice ground.
LOCATION: 14 miles from Paisley, 1 mile west of Kilbirnie on A760.
LOCAL HOTELS: Annfield House Hotel, Elderslie Hotel, Kinloch Hotel, Redcliffe House Hotel, South Beach Hotel.

# KILMACOLM

## KILMACOLM GOLF CLUB

COURSE DESCRIPTION:
Situated on a plateau some 400 feet above sea level. Maximum use is made of natural hills and hollows, making this one of the most attractive moorland courses. Course demands accurate driving and well-judged second shots.
18 holes, 5,961 yards, par 69 (SSS 69).

ADDRESS: Porterfield Road, Kilmacolm, Renfrewshire PA13 4PD.
TELEPHONE: +44 (0)1505 872139.
SECRETARY: R. McDonald.
PROFESSIONAL: David Stewart.
VISITORS: Weekdays only. Must be accompanied by a member.
GREEN FEES: £20.50 per round. £30.50 per day.
CATERING: Full facilities available.
FACILITIES: Trolley hire, putting green, pro shop, practice ground.
LOCATION: South-east side of the town off A761.
LOCAL HOTELS: Gryffe Arms, Gleddoch House Hotel.

# KILMARNOCK

## ANNANHILL GOLF CLUB

COURSE DESCRIPTION:
Undulating municipal tree-lined parkland course.
18 holes, 6,269 yards, par 71 (SSS 70). Course record 66.

ADDRESS: Irvine Road, Kilmarnock KA1 2RT.
TELEPHONE: +44 (0)1563 521644.
SECRETARY: +44 (0)1563 525557.
VISITORS: Book at starter's office.
GREEN FEES: £12 per round weekdays, £20.25 per day. £17 per round weekends, £23.50 per day.
CATERING: By prior arrangement. Bar.
FACILITIES: Putting green, practice ground.
LOCATION: 1 mile west on A71.
LOCAL HOTELS: Annfield House Hotel, Chapeltoun House Hotel, Kinloch Hotel, Redcliffe House Hotel, South Beach Hotel.

## CAPRINGTON GOLF CLUB

COURSE DESCRIPTION:
Municipal parkland course with generous fairways and few hills. 18 holes, 5,718 yards, par 69 (SSS 68).

ADDRESS: Ayr Road, Kilmarnock KA1 4UW.
TELEPHONE: +44 (0)1563 523702.
VISITORS: Not on Saturdays.
GREEN FEES: £9.50 per round weekdays, £13.40 per round weekends.
CATERING: Bar.
FACILITIES: Pro shop.
LOCATION: 1½ miles south on B7038.
LOCAL HOTELS: Annfield House Hotel, Chapeltoun House Hotel, Kinloch Hotel, Redcliffe House Hotel, South Beach Hotel.

# KILSYTH

## KILSYTH LENNOX GOLF CLUB

COURSE DESCRIPTION:
Hilly moorland course, hard walking.
18 holes, 5,912 yards, par 70 (SSS 70). Course record 66.

ADDRESS: Tak Ma Doon Road, Kilsyth G65 0RS.
TELEPHONE: +44 (0)1236 824115 or 823089.
SECRETARY: +44 (0)1236 823213.
PROFESSIONAL: R. Abercrombie.
VISITORS: Contact in advance. No restrictions weekdays until 5 p.m. Not Saturdays but may play Sundays on application.
GREEN FEES: £14 per round weekdays, £24 per day. £16 per round weekends, £26 per day.
CATERING: Full service. Bar.
FACILITIES: Buggy hire, putting green, pro shop.
LOCATION: North side of town, off A803.
LOCAL HOTELS: Kirkhouse Inn.

# KIRKINTILLOCH

## HAYSTON GOLF CLUB

COURSE DESCRIPTION:
Undulating, tree-lined parkland course.

18 holes, 6,042 yards, par 70 (SSS 70). Course record 62.

ADDRESS: Campsie Road, Kirkintilloch G66 1RN.
TELEPHONE: +44 (0)141 776 1244.
SECRETARY & FAX: +44 (0)141 775 0273.
PROFESSIONAL: Steven Barnett +44 (0)141 775 0882.
VISITORS: Not at weekends. Contact in advance. Societies Tuesdays and Thursdays.
GREEN FEES: £18 per round, £25 per day.
CATERING: Full service. Bar.
FACILITIES: Trolley hire, putting green, pro shop, practice ground.
LOCATION: 1 mile north-west of town off A803.
LOCAL HOTELS: Kirkhouse Inn.

## KIRKINTILLOCH GOLF CLUB

COURSE DESCRIPTION:
Parkland course.
   18 holes, 5,269 yards, par 70 (SSS 66).

ADDRESS: Campsie Road, Kirkintilloch G66 1RN.
TELEPHONE: +44 (0)141 775 2387 or 776 1256.
VISITORS: Must be introduced by member.
GREEN FEES: £18 per round.
FACILITIES: Pro shop.
LOCATION: 1 mile north-west of town, off A803.
LOCAL HOTELS: Kirkhouse Inn.

# LANARK

## LANARK GOLF CLUB

COURSE DESCRIPTION:
Tough moorland course which is open to the prevailing wind. Club dates from 1851.
   18 holes, 6,306 yards, par 70 (SSS 71). Amateur record V. McInally 64. Pro record C. Maltman 62.
   9 holes, 1,562 yards, par 27 (SSS 28).

SIGNATURE HOLE:
EIGHTEENTH ('Home' 207 yards, par 3) Downhill to an elevated green.

**COURSE CARD**

| HOLE | MEDAL YDS | PAR | FORWARD YDS | PAR | LADIES YDS | PAR | HOLE | MEDAL YDS | PAR | FORWARD YDS | PAR | LADIES YDS | PAR |
|---|---|---|---|---|---|---|---|---|---|---|---|---|---|
| 1 | 354 | 4 | 350 | 4 | 340 | 4 | 10 | 149 | 3 | 139 | 3 | 141 | 3 |

| 2 | 459 | 4 | 447 | 4 | 433 | 5 | 11 | 398 | 4 | 390 | 4 | 389 | 5 |
| 3 | 395 | 4 | 385 | 4 | 345 | 4 | 12 | 357 | 4 | 386 | 4 | 342 | 4 |
| 4 | 446 | 4 | 430 | 4 | 406 | 5 | 13 | 358 | 4 | 348 | 4 | 311 | 4 |
| 5 | 312 | 4 | 288 | 4 | 250 | 4 | 14 | 388 | 4 | 378 | 4 | 367 | 5 |
| 6 | 368 | 4 | 352 | 4 | 345 | 4 | 15 | 458 | 4 | 445 | 4 | 361 | 4 |
| 7 | 135 | 3 | 125 | 3 | 125 | 3 | 16 | 333 | 4 | 307 | 4 | 301 | 4 |
| 8 | 525 | 5 | 510 | 5 | 515 | 5 | 17 | 302 | 4 | 290 | 4 | 291 | 4 |
| 9 | 362 | 4 | 335 | 4 | 287 | 4 | 18 | 207 | 3 | 202 | 3 | 205 | 3 |
| Yds Out | 3,356 | | 3,222 | | 3,032 | | Yds In | 2,950 | | 2,885 | | 2,702 | |
| Total Yds | 6,306 | | 6,107 | | 5,734 | | | | | | | | |
| Total Par | 70 | | 70 | | 74 | | | | | | | | |

ADDRESS: The Moor, Whitelees Road, Lanark ML11 7RX.
TELEPHONE & FAX: +44 (0)1555 663219.
E-MAIL: lanarkgolfclub@talk21.com
WEBSITE: www.lanarkgolfclub.org.uk
SECRETARY: George Cuthill.
PROFESSIONAL: Alan White +44 (0)1555 661456.
VISITORS: Monday to Friday, 9.15 a.m. to 3.45 p.m.
GREEN FEES: £26 per round. £40 per day.
CATERING: Full.
FACILITIES: Motorised buggies (£14), trolley hire (£3), changing-rooms, putting green, pro shop, practice ground.
LOCATION: East side of town off A73.
LOCAL HOTELS: Cartland Bridge Hotel.

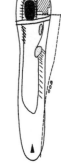

# LARGS

## INVERCLYDE NATIONAL GOLF TRAINING CENTRE

COURSE DESCRIPTION:
6 holes, training bunkers, driving range, video equipment for analysis.

ADDRESS: Burnside Road, Largs, Ayrshire KA30 8RW.
TELEPHONE: +44 (0)1475 674666.
VISITORS: Groups only. Two- and four-day courses. Bookings in advance on a residential basis.
GREEN FEES: On application.
LOCAL HOTELS: Annfield House Hotel, Kinloch Hotel, Redcliffe House Hotel, South Beach Hotel.

# LARGS GOLF CLUB

## COURSE DESCRIPTION:
Parkland and woodland course, which features winding
burns, lush fairways, tree-lined doglegs and undulating
greens. Situated in front of Kelburn Castle in the west of
Scotland on the Firth of Clyde, with scenic views over islands
of Cumbrae and Arran, it is a long-established private golf
club.

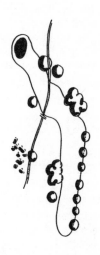

18 holes, 6,115 yards, par 70 (SSS 71). Amateur record
Charles White 64. Pro record 63.

## SIGNATURE HOLE:
TENTH (382 yards, par 4) Called 'Arran' because it has the
island as a backdrop, there is a spectacular avenue of trees on
this dogleg left demanding a placed tee shot which opens up
a plateau green. The second shot should be aimed to the left
edge of the green, as the ball will always come back round off
the slope.

## COURSE CARD

| HOLE | MEDAL YDS | PAR | FORWARD YDS | PAR | LADIES YDS | PAR | HOLE | MEDAL YDS | PAR | FORWARD YDS | PAR | LADIES YDS | PAR |
|------|-----------|-----|-------------|-----|------------|-----|------|-----------|-----|-------------|-----|------------|-----|
| 1 | 144 | 3 | 128 | 3 | 110 | 3 | 10 | 382 | 4 | 365 | 4 | 354 | 4 |
| 2 | 403 | 4 | 363 | 4 | 349 | 4 | 11 | 403 | 4 | 379 | 4 | 368 | 5 |
| 3 | 466 | 5 | 438 | 4 | 422 | 5 | 12 | 490 | 5 | 453 | 4 | 406 | 5 |
| 4 | 195 | 3 | 183 | 3 | 177 | 3 | 13 | 372 | 4 | 367 | 4 | 363 | 4 |
| 5 | 298 | 4 | 262 | 4 | 251 | 4 | 14 | 147 | 3 | 140 | 3 | 130 | 3 |
| 6 | 360 | 4 | 350 | 4 | 345 | 4 | 15 | 468 | 4 | 413 | 4 | 400 | 5 |
| 7 | 408 | 4 | 358 | 4 | 351 | 4 | 16 | 330 | 4 | 322 | 4 | 313 | 4 |
| 8 | 162 | 3 | 159 | 3 | 154 | 3 | 17 | 345 | 4 | 312 | 4 | 298 | 4 |
| 9 | 386 | 4 | 378 | 4 | 375 | 4 | 18 | 356 | 4 | 337 | 4 | 284 | 4 |
| Yds Out | 2,822 | | 2,619 | | 2,534 | | Yds In | 3,293 | | 3,088 | | 2,916 | |
| Total Yds | 6,115 | | 5,707 | | 5,450 | | | | | | | | |
| Total Par | 70 | | 68 | | 73 | | | | | | | | |

ADDRESS: Irvine Road, Largs, Ayrshire KA30 8EU.
TELEPHONE & FAX: +44 (0)1475 673594.
E-MAIL: secretary@largsgolfclub.co.uk
WEBSITE: www.largsgolfclub.co.uk
SECRETARY: D. MacGillivray.
PROFESSIONAL: K. Docherty +44 (0)1475 686192.
VISITORS: Yes any day. Prior booking required. Parties by arrangement Tuesdays and
   Wednesdays.

GREEN FEES: £30 per round weekdays, £40 per day. £40 per round weekends before 4 p.m.(£30 after 4 p.m.). Weekly tickets £110. Six-monthly tickets £275.
CATERING: Restaurant and bar.
FACILITIES: Trolley hire, club hire, changing-rooms, putting green, pro shop, practice nets, membership available.
LOCATION: Off Irvine Road (A78), 1 mile south of Largs.
LOCAL HOTELS: Annfield House Hotel, Brisbane House Hotel, Carlton Guest House, Elderslie Hotel, Haylie Hotel, Queens Hotel, Redcliffe House Hotel, Willow Bank Hotel.

## ROUTENBURN GOLF CLUB

COURSE DESCRIPTION:
Hilly heathland course, designed by James Braid, situated close to the Upper Firth of Clyde with fine views over Arran and the Cumbraes.
    18 holes, 5,650 yards, par 68 (SSS 67).

ADDRESS: Routenburn Road, Largs, Ayrshire KA30 8QA.
TELEPHONE: +44 (0)1475 687240.
PROFESSIONAL: Greig McQueen.
VISITORS: Any time.
GREEN FEES: £10 per round weekdays, £15 per round weekends.
CATERING: Full facilities, except Thursdays.
FACILITIES: Buggy hire, pro shop.
LOCATION: 1 mile north, off A78.
LOCAL HOTELS: Annfield House Hotel, Kinloch Hotel, Manor Park Hotel, Redcliffe House Hotel, South Beach Hotel.

# LARKHALL

## LARKHALL GOLF CLUB

COURSE DESCRIPTION:
Open inland parkland course ideal for players who enjoy a straightforward game. Only 12 bunkers and sand traps. No water hazards.
    9 holes, 6,700 yards (for 18 holes), par 72 (SSS 71). Course record 69.

ADDRESS: Burnhead Road, Larkhall ML9 3AB.
TELEPHONE: +44 (0)1698 881113.
VISITORS: Restricted Tuesdays and Saturdays. Phone in advance.
GREEN FEES: £7.25 weekdays, £8.50 weekends.
CATERING: Bar.
LOCATION: East side of town on B7019.
LOCAL HOTELS: Popinjay Hotel.

# LEADHILLS

## LEADHILLS GOLF CLUB

**COURSE DESCRIPTION:**
Highest course in Scotland at 1,500 feet above sea level. Testing hilly moorland course, with high winds.
9 holes, 4,354 yards (for 18 holes), par 66 (SSS 64).

**ADDRESS:** Leadhills, near Biggar, Lanarkshire ML12 6XR.
**VISITORS:** Any time.
**GREEN FEES:** £6 per day.
**LOCATION:** East side of village, off B797.
**LOCAL HOTELS:** Mennockfoot Lodge Hotel, Peebles Hotel Hydro.

# LENNOXTOWN

## CAMPSIE GOLF CLUB

**COURSE DESCRIPTION:**
Hillside course with extensive views over the central belt. Sporting, short, energetic and welcoming. Small greens and tricky lies make it more of a challenge than the yardage might suggest.
18 holes, 5,509 yards, par 70 (SSS 68). Amateur record M. Howat 70.

**SIGNATURE HOLE:**
SEVENTEENTH (165 yards, par 3) From an elevated tee, through trees left and right, to a green with bunkers left and right. The steep bank down from the putting surface right and long make it very difficult to get up and down.

**COURSE CARD**

| HOLE | YDS | PAR | HOLE | YDS | PAR |
|------|-----|-----|------|-----|-----|
| 1 | 262 | 4 | 10 | 250 | 4 |
| 2 | 182 | 3 | 11 | 252 | 4 |
| 3 | 330 | 4 | 12 | 194 | 3 |
| 4 | 355 | 4 | 13 | 278 | 4 |
| 5 | 386 | 4 | 14 | 191 | 3 |
| 6 | 478 | 5 | 15 | 380 | 4 |
| 7 | 380 | 4 | 16 | 477 | 5 |

| 8 | 245 | 4 | 17 | 165 | 3 |
|---|-----|---|----|-----|---|
| 9 | 291 | 4 | 18 | 413 | 4 |
| *Yds* | 2,909 | | *Yds* | 2,600 | |
| *Out* | | | *In* | | |
| *Total Yds* | 5,509 | | | | |
| *Total Par* | 70 | | | | |

ADDRESS: Crow Road, Lennoxtown G65 7HX.
TELEPHONE: +44 (0)1360 310244.
SECRETARY: J.M.Donaldson.
PROFESSIONAL: Mark Brennan +44(0)1360 310920.
VISITORS: Any time weekdays. Weekends by arrangement.
GREEN FEES: £16 per round weekdays, £25 per day. £22 per round weekends.
CATERING: Restaurant and bar.
FACILITIES: Changing-rooms, putting green, pro shop, practice ground, memberships available.
LOCATION: 10 miles due north of Glasgow at the foot of the Campsie Fells. Take the B822 Lennoxtown to Fintry road.

# LOCHGILPHEAD

## LOCHGILPHEAD GOLF CLUB

### COURSE DESCRIPTION:
Challenging parkland course in beautiful surroundings. Water hazards on five holes. Some tight fairways.

9 holes, 4,484 yards (for 18 holes), par 64 (SSS 63). Amateur record 58. Pro record 61.

### SIGNATURE HOLE:
FIFTH (177 yards, par 3) Aptly named the 'Graveyard'. A 177-yard carry to a slightly elevated green with trees on both sides and a sloping fairway

### COURSE CARD

| HOLE | YDS | PAR |
|------|-----|-----|
| 1 | 366 | 4 |
| 2 | 370 | 4 |
| 3 | 114 | 3 |
| 4 | 257 | 4 |
| 5 | 177 | 3 |
| 6 | 392 | 4 |
| 7 | 139 | 3 |
| 8 | 264 | 4 |

| 9 | 163 | 3 | |
|---|---|---|---|
| Yds | 2,242 | | |
| Out | | | |
| Total Yds | 2,242 | | |
| Total Par | 32 | | |

ADDRESS: Blarbuie Road, Lochgilphead, Argyll PA31 8LE.
TELEPHONE: +44 (0)1546 604230.
SECRETARY: A. Law +44 (0)1546 886302.
VISITORS: Any time, except during competitions.
GREEN FEES: £10 per day. Juniors £5.
CATERING: By arrangement for societies.
FACILITIES: Putting green, practice ground.
LOCATION: From church in Lochgilphead, take Manse Brae towards Argyll and Bute Hospital. Turn left before hospital grounds.
LOCAL HOTELS: Argyll Hotel, Invercreran Country House Hotel, Stag Hotel, Victoria Hotel.

# LOCHGOILHEAD

## DRIMSYNIE GOLF COURSE

COURSE DESCRIPTION:
Scenic course around the head of Loch Goil in the Argyll Forest Park. Not a course for big hitters – but plenty of problems for those wayward shots. Ideal for beginners and families.

9 holes, 3,678 yards (for 18 holes), par 60 (SSS 60).

SIGNATURE HOLE:
FIRST ('Manzini' 174 yards, par 3) Tee shot straight down toward the loch. Avoid the plantation on the right and the impressive Beech tree on the left. Better to be short, as overhitting will find you by the screen fence by the lochside road.

COURSE CARD

| HOLE | YDS | PAR |
|---|---|---|
| 1 | 174 | 3 |
| 2 | 188 | 3 |
| 3 | 233 | 4 |
| 4 | 177 | 3 |
| 5 | 246 | 4 |
| 6 | 151 | 3 |
| 7 | 138 | 3 |
| 8 | 223 | 3 |

| 9 | 309 | 4 |
|---|---|---|
| *Yds* | 1,839 | |
| *Out* | | |
| *Total* | 1,839 | |
| *Yds* | | |
| *Total* | 30 | |
| *Par* | | |

ADDRESS: Drimsynie Estate, Lochgoilhead, Argyll PA24.
TELEPHONE: +44 (0)1301 703247.
FAX: +44 (0)1301 703538.
E-MAIL: info@drimsynie.co.uk
WEBSITE: www.drimsynie.co.uk
SECRETARY: Leonard Gow.
VISITORS: Yes – all times.
GREEN FEES: £8 per round weekdays/weekends. Weekly tickets £30.
CREDIT CARDS ACCEPTED: Amex/Visa/Mastercard.
CATERING: Restaurant and bar in the grounds of Drimsynie House Hotel & Leisure
    Centre. Functions catered for.
FACILITIES: Club hire, changing-rooms.
LOCATION: A82 via Loch Lomond to Tarvert. A83 to Rest-and-be-thankful. B828 and
    B839 to Lochgoilhead. Follow sign for Carrick Castle, entrance to estate 300
    yards.

# LOCHWINNOCH

## LOCHWINNOCH GOLF CLUB

COURSE DESCRIPTION:
Hilly parkland course, founded in 1897, with testing holes situated on the edge of
a quiet conservation village beside the Barr and Semple lochs. Overlooking bird
sanctuary.
    18 holes, 6,243 yards, par 71 (SSS 70).

ADDRESS: Burnfoot Road, Lochwinnoch PA12 4AN.
TELEPHONE: +44 (0)1505 842153.
FAX: +44 (0)1505 843668.
PROFESSIONAL: Gerry Reilly +44 (0)1505 843029.
VISITORS: Not weekends and bank holidays unless accompanied by a member.
    Restricted on competition days.
GREEN FEES: £17 per round weekdays, £24 per day. Advance booking advised.
CATERING: Bar.
FACILITIES: Pro shop.
LOCATION: West of village, off A760.
LOCAL HOTELS: Bowfield Hotel and Country Club.

# LUSS

## LOCH LOMOND GOLF CLUB

### COURSE DESCRIPTION:

History tells us that many a man has died for his art – but a golf architect for his course? Tom Weiskopf almost did in creating one of the world's greatest courses along the bonnie, bonnie banks of Loch Lomond, which he considers his 'lasting memorial to golf'. One night the former Open champion stepped out to savour his handiwork and sank up to his chin in quicksand. Happily, he survived to complete, with partner Jay Morrish, 7,060 yards of an outstanding championship course that is ranked 44th in the top 100 courses of the world. When he first saw this tract of land, which was the ancestral home of the Clan Colquhoun, he admitted that it just 'blew me away' and if you had to pick a course that summed up the beauty of Scottish golf this could well be it. Framed by towering hills and bounded by the loch, the course winds

through an abundance of trees and wildlife without seeming to disturb a blade of grass. 'This is the finest golf course in Europe,' was Nick Faldo's verdict: 'It simply cannot be faulted. This is the standard all other European courses have to strive to attain.' Lush fairways, large beautifully manicured greens, the restored Rossdhu House as a clubhouse, it reeks of exclusivity. And exclusive, it is. The closest many can come to appreciating its style is watching on TV the European Tour compete here before the Open Championship. Only a member can invite you to play and even the members are not encouraged to over-golf, being reminded that it is 'intended as an international club for the occasional use of members and their guests and not meant as their primary club'. It starts gently enough to put you at your ease and soon you are marvelling at the difference of each hole. To pick out a favourite is difficult but there's the 6th – the longest hole in Scottish golf at 625 yards – but as it runs alongside the loch it's not a step too long. Then the 10th (see below). The 14th sorts out the men from the boys: go for the green, with over 250 yards' carry over the bog that almost claimed Weiskopf, or bale out to the fairway on the left. Then the 205-yard 17th, which is a classic par 3. Or the 18th finishing in front of the old castle. From the championship tees, it is a severe test for the very best of players, but from forward tees (and Weiskopf has offered a varied selection) the course is eminently playable for the less skilled. If you're lucky enough to play here, you won't be trying to recount the memorable holes – you'll be struggling to forget any one of the 18.

18 holes, 7,060 yards, par 71 (medal par 72, SSS 74).

### SIGNATURE HOLE:

TENTH (455 yards, par 4) Weiskopf says: 'Hitting the fairway is a must. The pond on the left does not really threaten the second shot, as it is much further from the big receptive green – which will accept long shots – than it looks.'

### COURSE CARD

| HOLE | CHAMPIONSHIP YDS | PAR | MEDAL YDS | PAR | HOLE | CHAMPIONSHIP YDS | PAR | MEDAL YDS | PAR |
|------|------|-----|-----|-----|------|------|-----|-----|-----|
| 1 | 425 | 4 | 400 | 4 | 10 | 455 | 4 | 425 | 4 |
| 2 | 455 | 4 | 410 | 4 | 11 | 235 | 3 | 215 | 3 |
| 3 | 505 | 5 | 465 | 5 | 12 | 415 | 4 | 380 | 4 |
| 4 | 385 | 4 | 360 | 4 | 13 | 560 | 5 | 560 | 5 |
| 5 | 190 | 3 | 175 | 3 | 14 | 345 | 4 | 330 | 4 |
| 6 | 625 | 5 | 580 | 5 | 15 | 415 | 4 | 385 | 4 |
| 7 | 440 | 4 | 440 | 4 | 16 | 480 | 4 | 510 | 5 |
| 8 | 155 | 3 | 155 | 3 | 17 | 205 | 3 | 185 | 3 |
| 9 | 340 | 4 | 340 | 4 | 18 | 430 | 4 | 415 | 4 |
| Yds Out | 3,520 | | 3,325 | | Yds In | 3,540 | | 3,405 | |
| Total Yds | 7,060 | | 6,730 | | | | | | |
| Total Par | 71 | | 72 | | | | | | |

ADDRESS: Rossdhu House, Luss, Dunbartonshire G83 8NT.
TELEPHONE: +44 (0)1436 860223.
FAX: +44 (0)1436 655500.
E-MAIL: info@lochlomond.com
WEBSITE: www.lochlomond.com
PROFESSIONAL: Colin Campbell.
VISITORS: May only play as guests of members.
CATERING: Full service. Bar.
FACILITIES: Putting green, pro shop, practice ground.
LOCATION: Only 25 minutes from Glasgow city centre. Take Luss turn-off on A82.
LOCAL HOTELS: Cameron House Hotel, Colquhoun Arms.

# MAUCHLINE

## BALLOCHMYLE GOLF CLUB

### COURSE DESCRIPTION:

Wooded undulating parkland course. Burns, out of bounds and small undulating greens guarded by bunkers provide a variety of shots for all handicaps.

18 holes, 5,972 yards, par 70 (SSS 69). Course record 65.

**SIGNATURE HOLE:**
ELEVENTH ('Clootie's Corner' 413 yards, par 4) A 90-degree dogleg right. To reach the dogleg requires a carry of 180 yards between trees on both sides and over a burn running across the fairway.

**ADDRESS:** Catrine Road, Mauchline, Ayrshire KA5 5AW.
**TELEPHONE:** +44 (0)1290 550469.
**FAX:** +44 (0)1290 553657.
**E-MAIL:** secretary@ballochmyle.freeserve.co.uk
**SECRETARY:** R. Leslie Crawford.
**VISITORS:** Yes, except Saturdays and bank holidays.
**GREEN FEES:** £20 per round weekdays, £30 per day. £25 per round weekends, £35 per day. Weekly ticket £100.
**CREDIT CARDS ACCEPTED:** Visa/Mastercard.
**CATERING:** Restaurant and bar. Functions catered for.
**FACILITIES:** Trolley hire, changing-rooms, putting green, practice ground.
**LOCATION:** 1 mile south-east on B705.
**LOCAL HOTELS:** The Royal Hotel.

# MAYBOLE

## MAYBOLE GOLF CLUB

**COURSE DESCRIPTION:**
Parkland course with breathtaking views of the Carrick Hills.
9 holes, 5,304 yards (for 18 holes), par 66 (SSS 66). Course record 64.

**ADDRESS:** Memorial Park, Maybole, Ayrshire KA19 7DX.
**TELEPHONE:** +44 01655 889770.
**VISITORS:** Any time.
**GREEN FEES:** £6 per round weekdays. £8 per round weekends.
**LOCATION:** 10 miles south of Ayr on Girvan road.
**LOCAL HOTELS:** Annfield House Hotel, Kinloch Hotel, Ladyburn Hotel, Redcliffe House Hotel, South Beach Hotel.

# MOTHERWELL

## COLVILLE PARK GOLF CLUB

**COURSE DESCRIPTION:**
Parkland course, designed by James Braid. First 9 mature, tree-lined. Back 9 more

open. Relatively flat. Founded 1923.

18 holes, 6,265 yards, par 71 (SSS 70). Amateur record 66. Pro record 65.

### SIGNATURE HOLE:
SIXTH (315 yards, par 4) Mature and tree-lined. Picturesque approach to a raised green.

### COURSE CARD

| HOLE | YDS | PAR | HOLE | YDS | PAR |
|------|-----|-----|------|-----|-----|
| 1 | 204 | 3 | 10 | 180 | 3 |
| 2 | 421 | 4 | 11 | 400 | 4 |
| 3 | 429 | 4 | 12 | 486 | 5 |
| 4 | 162 | 3 | 13 | 492 | 5 |
| 5 | 264 | 4 | 14 | 386 | 4 |
| 6 | 315 | 4 | 15 | 260 | 4 |
| 7 | 416 | 4 | 16 | 444 | 4 |
| 8 | 533 | 5 | 17 | 190 | 3 |
| 9 | 388 | 4 | 18 | 295 | 4 |
| *Yds* *Out* | 3,132 | | *Yds* *In* | 3,133 | |
| *Total Yds* | 6,265 | | | | |
| *Total Par* | 71 | | | | |

ADDRESS: Jerviston Estate, Merry Street, Motherwell ML1 3AP.
TELEPHONE: +44 (0)1698 263017.
FAX: +44 (0)1698 230418.
SECRETARY: +44 (0)1698 265378.
PROFESSIONAL: Alan Forrest +44 (0)1698 265779.
VISITORS: Welcome only as the guest of a member. Parties must book through secretary.
GREEN FEES: £20 per day.
CATERING: Full catering available.
FACILITIES: Putting green, pro shop, practice ground.
LOCATION: 1½ miles north-east from Motherwell Cross and railway station.
LOCAL HOTELS: Moorings Hotel.

# MUIRKIRK

## MUIRKIRK GOLF CLUB

### COURSE DESCRIPTION:
Moorland course established in 1991. Very scenic, with views of the 1,900-foot Cairn Table.

9 holes, 5,380 yards (for 18 holes), par 68 (SSS 67). Amateur record 70.

ADDRESS: Southside, Muirkirk, Cumnock, Ayrshire KA18 3RE.
TELEPHONE: +44 (0)1290 660184.
SECRETARY: Robert Bradford.
VISITORS: Welcome, seven days a week.
GREEN FEES: £9 per round/day.
CATERING: Meals.
FACILITIES: Changing-rooms, memberships available.
LOCATION: Muirkirk is situated on the main road (A74) between Edinburgh and Ayr.
It is 26 miles from Ayr, 52 miles from Edinburgh and 30 miles from Glasgow.

# ISLE OF MULL

## CRAIGNURE GOLF CLUB

### COURSE DESCRIPTION:
Natural and demanding seaside links course beside the Sound of Mull. First laid
out in 1895 and rebuilt in 1978. Holes face all points of the compass with terrific
views.
9 holes (18 tees), 5,233 yards, par 69 (SSS 66). Amateur record 72.

### SIGNATURE HOLE:
SIXTH (435 yards, par 4) From a tee set among pine trees at the highest point of
the course, the drive is inviting with pine trees and a circular water hazard 200
yards to the right awaiting a pushed shot. All along the left is a daunting lateral
water hazard to the bend of the dogleg. All but the wildly optimistic play the hole
as a par 5.

### COURSE CARD

| HOLE | MEDAL YDS | PAR | LADIES YDS | PAR | HOLE | MEDAL YDS | PAR | LADIES YDS | PAR |
|------|-----------|-----|------------|-----|------|-----------|-----|------------|-----|
| 1 | 255 | 4 | 239 | 4 | 10 | 303 | 4 | 239 | 4 |
| 2 | 270 | 4 | 256 | 4 | 11 | 260 | 4 | 258 | 4 |
| 3 | 255 | 4 | 233 | 4 | 12 | 233 | 4 | 233 | 4 |
| 4 | 328 | 4 | 227 | 4 | 13 | 342 | 4 | 227 | 4 |
| 5 | 121 | 3 | 115 | 3 | 14 | 120 | 3 | 115 | 3 |
| 6 | 435 | 4 | 392 | 4 | 15 | 392 | 4 | 392 | 4 |
| 7 | 490 | 5 | 264 | 4 | 16 | 444 | 5 | 254 | 4 |
| 8 | 211 | 3 | 168 | 3 | 17 | 217 | 3 | 165 | 3 |
| 9 | 305 | 4 | 291 | 4 | 18 | 252 | 4 | 191 | 3 |
| Yds Out | 2,670 | | 2,035 | | Yds In | 2,563 | | 2,085 | |
| Total Yds | 5,233 | | 4,170 | | | | | | |

| Total | 69 | 66 |
|---|---|---|
| Par | | |

ADDRESS: Scallastle, Isle of Mull PA65 6AY.
TELEPHONE & FAX: +44 (0)1680 300402.
E-MAIL: mullair@btinternet.com
SECRETARY: David Howitt.
VISITORS: Most times except when very occasional Sunday club matches are played.
GREEN FEES: £11 per round/day. Weekly ticket £40.
CATERING: Clubhouse open dawn to dusk. Washing facilities.
LOCATION: 1 mile from Oban to Mull ferry terminal (crossing 40 minutes) at Craignure. 3 miles from Lochaline ferry via A849 road to Tobermory.
LOCAL HOTELS: Invercreran Country House Hotel, Isle of Mull Hotel.

## TOBERMORY GOLF CLUB

COURSE DESCRIPTION:
A beautifully-maintained cliff-top course with small but good greens and no sand bunkers. Magnificent views over the Sound of Mull from all parts of the course. Founded in 1896.

9 holes, 4,890 yards (for 18 holes), par 64 (SSS 64). Amateur record G. Davidson 65.

SIGNATURE HOLE:
SEVENTH (142 yards, par 3) Difficult hole with out of bounds close on the right. Rocks behind and a steep slope in front of the two-tiered green.

COURSE CARD

| HOLE | YDS | PAR |
|---|---|---|
| 1 | 356 | 4 |
| 2 | 359 | 4 |
| 3 | 230 | 3 |
| 4 | 208 | 3 |
| 5 | 274 | 4 |
| 6 | 398 | 4 |
| 7 | 142 | 3 |
| 8 | 358 | 4 |
| 9 | 120 | 3 |
| Yds Out | 2,445 | |
| Total Yds | 2,445 | |
| Total Par | 32 | |

ADDRESS: Erray Road, Tobermory, Isle of Mull, Argyll PA75 6PS.
TELEPHONE: +44 (0)1688 302338.

FAX: +44 (0)1688 302140.
E-MAIL: tobgolf@fsmail.net
WEBSITE: www.tobermory.co.uk/golf
VISITORS: Yes, anytime except competitions.
GREEN FEES: £13 per day. Weekly ticket £50.
CATERING: Bar and meals.
FACILITIES: Trolleys (£2), club hire (£5), changing-rooms, putting green, practice
    ground, membership available
LOCATION: Above the town of Tobermory.
LOCAL HOTELS: Fairways Lodge, Invercreran Country House, Western Isles Hotel.

# NEW CUMNOCK

## NEW CUMNOCK GOLF CLUB

COURSE DESCRIPTION:
Testing parkland course, designed by Willie Fernie in 1901, overlooking loch.
    9 holes, 5,176 yards, par 68 (SSS 68). Course record 68.

SIGNATURE HOLE:
SECOND ('Road Hole', 387 yards, par 4). Starts at the highest point of the
course, driving down over a small burn with the road on the right. Second shot
uphill into the corner of the course to a small green.

ADDRESS: Lochill, New Cumnock, Ayrshire KA18 4PN.
TELEPHONE: +44 (0)1290 338848.
SECRETARY: John McGinn +44 (0)1290 338041.
VISITORS: Any time, except Sundays before 4 p.m.
GREEN FEES: £7 per day.
CATERING: Lochside House Hotel on the course.
LOCATION: North-west of New Cumnock on A76.
LOCAL HOTELS: Crown Hotel, Lochside House Hotel.

# OBAN

## GLENCRUITTEN GOLF CLUB

COURSE DESCRIPTION:
Picturesque, hilly parkland course, designed by James Braid in 1900, with many
elevated tees and greens. Beautiful isolated situation.
    18 holes, 4,500 yards, par 61 (SSS 63). Course record 55.

SIGNATURE HOLE:
FIRST (432 yards, par 4). Daunting! Second shot is blind, over a hill, to a saucer-shaped green.

ADDRESS: Glencruitten Road, Oban PA34 5PU
TELEPHONE: +44 (0)1631 562868.
SECRETARY: A. Brown +44 (0)1631 564604.
VISITORS: Yes, except Thursday afternoons, Saturdays and Sundays, which are competition days. Small groups can play at weekends by arrangement.
GREEN FEES: £16 per round weekdays, £19 per round weekends.
CATERING: Full service. Bar.
FACILITIES: Trolley hire, pro shop, practice ground.
LOCATION: One mile north-east of town centre, off A816.
LOCAL HOTELS: Barriemore Hotel, Invercreran Country House Hotel, Kilchrenan Hotel.

## ISLE OF ERISKA GOLF COURSE

COURSE DESCRIPTION:
New facility will upgrade to 9-hole links style course in 2002.
6 holes, 1,558 yards, par 22.

SIGNATURE HOLE:
THIRD (350 yards, par 4) Dogleg left to a well-bunkered green.

### COURSE CARD

| HOLE | YDS | PAR |
|------|-------|-----|
| 1 | 340 | 4 |
| 2 | 150 | 3 |
| 3 | 350 | 4 |
| 4 | 282 | 4 |
| 5 | 146 | 3 |
| 6 | 290 | 4 |
| *Yds Out* | 1,558 | |
| *Total Yds* | 1,558 | |
| *Total Par* | | 22 |

ADDRESS: Ledaig, Connel, by Oban, Argyll PA37 1SD.
TELEPHONE: +44 (0)1631 720371.
FAX: +44 (0)1631 720531.
E-MAIL: office@eriska-hotel.co.uk
WEBSITE: www.eriska-hotel.co.uk
VISITORS: Yes, phone for tee time.
GREEN FEES: £10 (includes soup).

FACILITIES: Trolley hire, club hire, changing-rooms, putting green, driving range, teaching academy.
LOCAL HOTELS: Eriska Hotel.

## ISLE OF SEIL GOLF CLUB

COURSE DESCRIPTION:
Challenging 9-hole course with several holes over water – two of them over the sea – and no bunkers.

ADDRESS: Balvicar, Isle of Seil, Argyll.
TELEPHONE: +44 (0)1852 300373.
VISITORS: Welcome.
GREEN FEES: £5 per day.
LOCATION: 9 miles south of Oban.
LOCAL HOTELS: Invercreran Country House Hotel.

# PAISLEY

## BARSHAW GOLF CLUB

COURSE DESCRIPTION:
Municipal parkland course, founded in 1920, with a variety of flat and hilly holes. No bunkers.
18 holes, 5,704 yards, par 68 (SSS 67). Course record 63.

ADDRESS: Barshaw Park, Glasgow Road, Paisley, Renfrewshire PA1 3TJ.
TELEPHONE: +44 (0)141 889 2908.
SECRETARY: W. Collins +44 (0)141 884 2533.
PROFESSIONAL: John Scott.
VISITORS: Any time.
GREEN FEES: £7.70 per round weekdays/weekends.
CATERING: Soft drinks only.
FACILITIES: Putting green.
LOCATION: ½ mile from Paisley town centre, heading for Glasgow.
LOCAL HOTELS: Brabloch Hotel, Watermill Hotel.

## RALSTON GOLF CLUB

COURSE DESCRIPTION:
Parkland course. 18 holes, 6,105 yards, par 71 (SSS 70). Course record 62.

ADDRESS: Strathmore Avenue, Paisley, Renfrewshire PA1 3DT.
TELEPHONE: +44 (0)141 882 1349.
FAX: +44 (0)141 883 9837.

SECRETARY: J. Pearson.
PROFESSIONAL: Colin Munro.
VISITORS: Not at weekends. Contact secretary.
GREEN FEES: £18 per round weekdays, £28 per day.
CREDIT CARDS ACCEPTED: Visa/Mastercard.
CATERING: Restaurant and bar. Functions catered for.
FACILITIES: Trolley hire, changing-rooms, putting green, practice ground, pro shop, coaching clinics.
LOCATION: 2 miles east of Paisley town centre, on A737.
LOCAL HOTELS: Crookston Hotel, Dean Park Hotel, Glynhill Hotel, Swallow Hotel, Watermill Hotel.

# THE PAISLEY GOLF CLUB

COURSE DESCRIPTION:
Windy moorland course with wide areas of gorse and heather. Most holes are tree-lined and there are breathtaking views over the Clyde Valley to Ben Lomond and beyond.

18 holes, 6,466 yards, par 71 (SSS 72). Course record 66.

SIGNATURE HOLE:
FIFTEENTH ('Silver Tassie' 200 yards, par 3) Requires an accurate high tee shot to a green framed by trees and guarded by bunkers.

ADDRESS: Braehead, Paisley, Renfrewshire PA2 8TZ.
TELEPHONE & FAX: +44 (0)141 884 3903.
E-MAIL: paisleygc@onetel.net.uk
CLUB ADMINISTRATOR: John Hillis.
PROFESSIONAL: Gordon Stewart +44 (0)141 884 4114.
VISITORS: By appointment, with handicap certificate.
GREEN FEES: £24 per round weekdays, £32 per day.
CATERING: Restaurant and bar. Functions catered for. By prior booking.
FACILITIES: Club hire (given notice), changing-rooms, putting green, pro shop, practice ground, coaching clinics.
LOCATION: Leave M8 at junction 27, to Paisley along Renfrew Road, nearside lane follow ring road through two sets of lights. Turn left at Causeyside Street, straight for 1½ miles. Turn right at Jet Garage into Glenburn Road. Turn left into Braehead Road.
LOCAL HOTELS: Glynhill Hotel & Leisure Club.

# PATNA

## DOON VALLEY GOLF CLUB

COURSE DESCRIPTION:
Undulating hillside parkland course. Has tight out of bounds and a number of water hazards. Little shelter on this course. Founded in 1927.

9 holes, 5,654 yards (for 18 holes), par 70 (SSS 69).

COURSE CARD

| HOLE | YDS | PAR |
| --- | --- | --- |
| 1 | 344 | 4 |
| 2 | 290 | 4 |
| 3 | 368 | 4 |
| 4 | 398 | 4 |
| 5 | 149 | 3 |
| 6 | 314 | 4 |
| 7 | 496 | 5 |
| 8 | 160 | 3 |
| 9 | 308 | 4 |
| *Yds Out* | 2,827 | |
| *Total Yds* | 2,827 | |
| *Total Par* | 35 | |

ADDRESS: Hillside, Patna, Ayrshire KA6 7JT.
TELEPHONE: +44 (0)1292 531607.
SECRETARY: Hugh Johnstone MBE +44 (0)1292 550411.
VISITORS: Welcome weekdays, weekends by arrangement.
GREEN FEES: £10 per round, £15 per day.
CATERING: Bar open in evenings on weekdays and all day weekends.
FACILITIES: Practice range.
LOCATION: 10 miles south of Ayr on A713.
LOCAL HOTELS: Parsons Lodge Hotel.

# PORT GLASGOW

## PORT GLASGOW GOLF CLUB

COURSE DESCRIPTION:
Undulating moorland course on hilltop overlooking the Clyde with views to the

Cowal Hills. Founded in 1895.
  18 holes, 5,712 yards, par 68 (SSS 68).

**ADDRESS:** Devol Road, Port Glasgow PA14 5XE.
**TELEPHONE:** +44 (0)1475 704181.
**VISITORS:** Weekdays until 3.55 p.m. Weekends by introduction.
**GREEN FEES:** £15 per round weekdays.
**CATERING:** Bar.
**FACILITIES:** Putting green, pro shop.
**LOCATION:** South-west of Glasgow and 1 mile south of Port Glasgow.
**LOCAL HOTELS:** Gleddoch House Hotel.

# PRESTWICK

## PRESTWICK GOLF CLUB

### COURSE DESCRIPTION:

If you are as interested in the history of golf as the playing of the game then Prestwick, the birthplace of the Open Championship on the west coast of Scotland, demands a visit. Here you will be walking in the footsteps of legends. Although when the Open was first played in 1860 it was over a 12-hole course of 3,799 yards, with a par in the mid-50s, the distinctive flavour of the Prestwick Old Course remains and seven of the original greens are in the same place.

Around the time America was preparing for the Civil War, the members of Prestwick – which had been founded nine years earlier – decided to hold an annual Open competition to find a successor to the great Allan Robertson. Nowadays the Open Championship is a multi-million pound event with the winner becoming a millionaire overnight and receiving world-wide acclaim. At the birth, the prize was an elegant red morocco belt, with anyone winning three times in succession getting to keep it.

The first Open had only eight entrants with Willie Park, from the east coast, carrying off the prize after rounds of 55, 59 and 60. Old Tom Morris was the professional at Prestwick and runner-up in the first championship. He later won the Open four times between 1861 and 1867, but it was his son, Young Tom, who made the belt his own, winning three in a row from 1868 to 1870. He was only 17 when he won his first title, carding a record score of 157 and recording the first official hole in one. The following year he broke 50 for the 12 holes and in achieving the hat-trick scored a 47.

With the influence of St Andrews and Muirfield growing, along with the need to be able to entertain large crowds, Prestwick staged its last Open in 1925. It is still a championship course though, having hosted the Amateur Championship in 1987.

Although the course expanded to 18 holes in 1883, you will still be playing in the divots of Old and Young Tom, facing the Pow Burn (which comes into play on several holes), humps and hillocks, deep bunkers, steep sandhills, and heather and gorse that they had to contend with. From the back tees, Prestwick is not the longest of courses at 6,544 yards, with a par of 71, but it is challenging.

Today's 1st hole is nowhere near as intimidating as in Young Tom's day. Now a mere 346 yards, it is certainly not easy with out of bounds and Prestwick Station and the railway on the right. There is a ruined church and graveyard beside the green. The vast Cardinal Bunker awaits on the 3rd and the 5th, called the 'Himalayas" is a testing 206-yard par 3. You have to play a blind tee shot over the burn then over a vast sand dune to a heavily bunkered green.

The 10th, a 454-yard hole, takes you towards the sea and there are magnificent views of Ailsa Craig and the Isle of Arran. The 460-yard 13th is played along a gully to a narrow, slanting green. The 391-yard 17th, the 'Alps' is the last major test before getting back to the haven of the clubhouse, involving a blind second shot over the 'Alps' to a green guarded by a huge bunker.

Whether playing, or just lunching at the vast table which stretches the length of the room with history all around you, take time to visit the stone cairn, close to the putting green, which is on the site of the original 1st tee. Imagine all those years ago Young Tom Morris – perhaps the first superstar of golf – facing the monster of the then 1st which stretched to 578 yards and ponder how, using hickory shaft and a gutty ball, he managed to hole out in three on what is now the 16th green.

Be prepared for a devilish test of golf, and if the wind and rain get up, the best of luck to you.

18 holes, 6,544 yards, par 71 (SSS 73).

## SIGNATURE HOLE:

THIRD (482 yards, par 5) With the Pow Burn running all down the right and the famous and huge Cardinal Bunker stretching the entire width of the fairway at the point of the dogleg, this is an outstanding hole. Once two good hits were needed to clear the bunker, but this is the age of the big hitters.

## COURSE CARD

| HOLE | YDS | PAR | HOLE | YDS | PAR |
|------|-----|-----|------|-----|-----|
| 1 | 346 | 4 | 10 | 454 | 4 |
| 2 | 167 | 3 | 11 | 195 | 3 |
| 3 | 482 | 5 | 12 | 513 | 5 |
| 4 | 382 | 4 | 13 | 460 | 4 |
| 5 | 206 | 3 | 14 | 362 | 4 |
| 6 | 362 | 4 | 15 | 347 | 4 |
| 7 | 430 | 4 | 16 | 288 | 4 |
| 8 | 431 | 4 | 17 | 391 | 4 |
| 9 | 444 | 4 | 18 | 284 | 4 |
| Yds Out | 3,250 | | Yds In | 3,294 | |
| Total Yds | 6,544 | | | | |
| Total Par | 71 | | | | |

ADDRESS: 2 Links Road, Prestwick, Strathclyde KA9 1QG.
TELEPHONE: +44 (0)1292 477404.
FAX: +44 (0)1292 477225.
E-MAIL: bookings@prestwickgc.co.uk
WEBSITE: www.prestwickgc.co.uk
SECRETARY: Ian T. Bunch (e-mail: secretary@prestwickgc.co.uk ).
PROFESSIONAL: Frank Rennie +44 (0)1292 479483; Fax: +44 (0)1292 477255.
VISITORS: Restricted. Not weekends or Thursday afternoons. Book well in advance.
GREEN FEES: £85 per round, £125 per day. Sundays (12–1pm and 3.30–4pm) £125.
CREDIT CARDS ACCEPTED: Visa/Mastercard.
CATERING: Restaurant and bar.
FACILITIES: Trolley hire (£3), club hire (£25), caddies (£25 + gratuity), putting green, pro shop, practice ground.
LOCATION: In town centre off A79.
LOCAL HOTELS: Annfield House Hotel, Parkstone Hotel, Redcliffe House Hotel, South Beach Hotel.

## PRESTWICK ST CUTHBERT GOLF CLUB

### COURSE DESCRIPTION:

The club was established in 1899 and moved to their existing course in 1963. Flat and partially wooded parkland with natural hazards. It includes nine doglegs, putting a premium on accurate driving. There are little up slopes before at least six of the greens, which are cunningly sloped with many two-tiered. Easy walking.

18 holes, 6,470 yards, par 71 (SSS 71). Course record 64.

### COURSE CARD

| HOLE | MEDAL YDS | PAR | FORWARD YDS | PAR | LADIES YDS | PAR | HOLE | MEDAL YDS | PAR | FORWARD YDS | PAR | LADIES YDS | PAR |
|------|-----------|-----|-------------|-----|------------|-----|------|-----------|-----|-------------|-----|------------|-----|
| 1 | 378 | 4 | 368 | 4 | 349 | 4 | 10 | 335 | 4 | 320 | 4 | 245 | 4 |
| 2 | 392 | 4 | 377 | 4 | 344 | 4 | 11 | 471 | 4 | 447 | 4 | 400 | 4 |
| 3 | 488 | 5 | 471 | 5 | 449 | 5 | 12 | 363 | 4 | 355 | 4 | 281 | 4 |
| 4 | 452 | 4 | 436 | 4 | 385 | 4 | 13 | 426 | 4 | 410 | 4 | 350 | 4 |
| 5 | 344 | 4 | 334 | 4 | 286 | 4 | 14 | 180 | 3 | 172 | 3 | 137 | 3 |
| 6 | 337 | 4 | 317 | 4 | 234 | 4 | 15 | 401 | 4 | 351 | 4 | 293 | 4 |
| 7 | 176 | 3 | 166 | 3 | 146 | 3 | 16 | 379 | 4 | 367 | 4 | 237 | 4 |
| 8 | 507 | 5 | 442 | 5 | 391 | 4 | 17 | 171 | 3 | 156 | 3 | 130 | 3 |
| 9 | 180 | 3 | 170 | 3 | 170 | 3 | 18 | 490 | 5 | 474 | 5 | 420 | 5 |
| Yds Out | 3,254 | | 3,081 | | 2,747 | | Yds In | 3,216 | | 3,052 | | 2,543 | |
| Total Yds | 6,470 | | 6,133 | | 5,290 | | | | | | | | |
| Total Par | 71 | | 71 | | 71 | | | | | | | | |

ADDRESS: East Road, Prestwick, Ayrshire, Strathclyde KA9 2SX.
TELEPHONE: +44 (0)1292 477101.

FAX: +44 (0)1292 671730.

E-MAIL: secretary@stcuthbert.co.uk

WEBSITE: www.stcuthbert.co.uk

VISITORS: Yes, but not at weekends.

GREEN FEES: £24 per round, £32 per day.

CATERING: Restaurant and bar.

FACILITIES: Trolley hire, changing-rooms, putting green.

LOCATION: From A77 take fourth exit at Whitletts roundabout for Heathfield. After passing two mini-roundabouts, take second right.

LOCAL HOTELS: Annfield House Hotel, Redcliffe House Hotel, South Beach Hotel, St Nicholas Hotel.

# PRESTWICK ST NICHOLAS GOLF CLUB

### COURSE DESCRIPTION:

Founded in 1851, this is an easy-walking links course with tight fairways.

18 holes, 5,952 yards, par 69 (SSS 69). Amateur record Gavin Lawrie 65. Pro record Tony Johnstone 63.

### SIGNATURE HOLE:

SECOND (172 yards, par 3) From elevated tee. Challenging and picturesque.

### COURSE CARD

| HOLE | YDS | PAR | HOLE | YDS | PAR |
|------|-----|-----|------|-----|-----|
| 1 | 342 | 4 | 10 | 165 | 3 |
| 2 | 172 | 3 | 11 | 498 | 5 |
| 3 | 281 | 4 | 12 | 139 | 3 |
| 4 | 420 | 4 | 13 | 456 | 4 |
| 5 | 406 | 4 | 14 | 412 | 4 |
| 6 | 326 | 4 | 15 | 276 | 4 |
| 7 | 454 | 4 | 16 | 379 | 4 |
| 8 | 360 | 4 | 17 | 301 | 4 |
| 9 | 338 | 4 | 18 | 227 | 3 |
| Yds Out | 3,099 | | Yds In | 2,853 | |
| Total Yds | 5,952 | | | | |
| Total Par | 69 | | | | |

ADDRESS: Grangemuir Road, Prestwick, Ayrshire KA9 1SN.

TELEPHONE: ++44 (0)1292 477608.

FAX: +44 (0)1292 678570.

SECRETARY: G. Thomson.

VISITORS: Yes. Weekdays and Sunday afternoons.

GREEN FEES: £30 per round weekdays, £35 Sundays.
CATERING: Full facilities in clubhouse refurbished in 1998.
FACILITIES: Trolley hire, putting green, golf shop.
LOCATION: From Prestwick town centre, along Main Street heading for Ayr. Right at traffic lights into Grangemuir Road.
LOCAL HOTELS: Annfield House Hotel, Parkstone Hotel, Redcliffe House Hotel, South Beach Hotel.

# RENFREW

## RENFREW GOLF CLUB

COURSE DESCRIPTION:
Tree-lined parkland course with featured rivers. Opened in 1973.
18 holes , 6,818 yards, par 72 (SSS 73).

SIGNATURE HOLE:
TWELFTH (315 yards, par 4) Short but tricky. Vibrant display of rhododendrons for part of the season.

### COURSE CARD

| HOLE | YDS | PAR | HOLE | YDS | PAR |
|------|-----|-----|------|-----|-----|
| 1 | 356 | 4 | 10 | 178 | 3 |
| 2 | 485 | 5 | 11 | 500 | 5 |
| 3 | 215 | 3 | 12 | 315 | 4 |
| 4 | 455 | 4 | 13 | 389 | 4 |
| 5 | 434 | 4 | 14 | 207 | 3 |
| 6 | 420 | 4 | 15 | 557 | 5 |
| 7 | 175 | 3 | 16 | 421 | 4 |
| 8 | 419 | 4 | 17 | 395 | 4 |
| 9 | 549 | 5 | 18 | 348 | 4 |
| Yds Out | 3,508 | | Yds In | 3,310 | |
| Total Yds | 6,818 | | | | |
| Total Par | 72 | | | | |

ADDRESS: Blythswood Estate, Inchinnan Road, Renfrew PA4 9EG.
TELEPHONE: +44 (0)141 886 6692.
FAX: +44 (0)141 886 1808.
SECRETARY: Ian Murchison.
VISITORS: Yes, Mondays, Tuesdays and Thursdays.
GREEN FEES: £25 per round weekdays, £35 per day.
CATERING: Restaurant and bar. Functions catered for.

FACILITIES: Changing-rooms, putting green, pro shop, practice ground.
LOCATION: Exit M8 at junction 26 or 27. Then A8 to Inchinnan. Turn off Inchinnan Road at the Normandy Hotel and follow a private road to the clubhouse.
LOCAL HOTELS: Dean Park Hotel, Glynhill Hotel, Normandy Hotel, Stakis Glasgow Airport Hotel.

# SHOTTS

## SHOTTS GOLF CLUB

COURSE DESCRIPTION:
Undulating moorland course, founded in 1895 and designed by James Braid. 18 holes, 6,205 yards, par 70 (SSS 70). Course record 63.

ADDRESS: Blairhead, Shotts, North Lanarkshire ML7 5BJ.
TELEPHONE: +44 (0)1501 820431 or 826628.
PROFESSIONAL: +44 (0)1501 822658.
VISITORS: Welcome weekdays, Saturdays after 4.30 p.m. and Sundays by prior arrangement.
GREEN FEES: £20 per round weekdays/weekends. Special packages for societies.
CATERING: Full service. Bar.
FACILITIES: Trolley/buggy hire, putting green, pro shop, practice ground.
LOCATION: Leave M8 at junction for B7057.
LOCAL HOTELS: The Hilcroft Hotel.

# SKELMORLIE

## SKELMORLIE GOLF CLUB

COURSE DESCRIPTION:
A short hilly moorland course but not to be underestimated. Originally designed by James Braid in 1891, it was upgraded from 13 to 18 holes in 1999. If anything, this has made it more challenging, with burns featuring in the five new holes. Seven pars 3s, but many of them difficult.
18 holes, 5,030 yards, par 65 (SSS 65).

SIGNATURE HOLE:
NINTH (396 yards, par 4) The first of the new holes and called 'Wright's Turf Dyke' after the captain, Nigel Wright, who put enormous effort into the development of the new holes. You drive from an elevated tee with trouble on both sides. A turf dyke before the green complicates the approach shot.

ADDRESS: Beithglass Road, Skelmorlie, Ayrshire PA17 5ES.

391

TELEPHONE: +44 (0)1475 520152.
WEBSITE: www.skelmorliegolf.co.uk
SECRETARY: Mrs A. Fahey +44 (0)1475 520774.
VISITORS: Weekdays and some Sundays. Not Saturdays during the season.
GREEN FEES: £14 per round weekdays, £18 per day. £15 per round Sundays, £21 per day.
CATERING: Bar open 11 a.m. to 11 p.m. Weekend and visiting parties.
LOCATION: Off A78, through Skelmorlie village.
LOCAL HOTELS: Manor Park Hotel, Redcliffe House Hotel.

# STEVENSTON

## ARDEER GOLF CLUB

COURSE DESCRIPTION:
Fairly hilly parkland course with fast greens and natural hazards. Established in 1880.
18 holes, 6,409 yards, par 72 (SSS 71). Course record 64.

SIGNATURE HOLE:
NINTH (339 yards, par 4) Trees on right, bunker on left. Burn meanders on right and crosses in front of two-tiered green.

ADDRESS: Greenhead, Stevenston KA20 4JX.
TELEPHONE: +44 (0)1294 464542.
SECRETARY: P. Watson +44(0)1294 465316.
PROFESSIONAL: G. Thomson +44(0)1294 601327.
VISITORS: Yes, except Saturdays and competition days.
GREEN FEES: £18 per round weekdays, £30 weekends.
CATERING: Full service.
FACILITIES: Putting green, pro shop, practice ground.
LOCATION: ½ mile off A78, Ayr to Greenock road.
LOCAL HOTELS: Bay Hotel, Hospitality Inn.

## AUCHENHARVIE GOLF CLUB

COURSE DESCRIPTION:
Although a seaside course, it is parkland not a links. Nine holes, but different tees for the back nine. Long and flat municipal course with narrow greens and water on the 3rd and 12th holes.
9 holes, 5,203 yards (for 18 holes), par 66 (SSS 66).

COURSE CARD

| HOLE | YDS | PAR | HOLE | YDS | PAR |
|------|-----|-----|------|-----|-----|
| 1 | 306 | 4 | 10 | 312 | 4 |

| | | | | | |
|---|---|---|---|---|---|
| 2 | 153 | 3 | 11 | 151 | 3 |
| 3 | 400 | 4 | 12 | 378 | 4 |
| 4 | 275 | 4 | 13 | 217 | 3 |
| 5 | 167 | 3 | 14 | 144 | 3 |
| 6 | 424 | 4 | 15 | 495 | 5 |
| 7 | 375 | 4 | 16 | 365 | 4 |
| 8 | 270 | 4 | 17 | 309 | 4 |
| 9 | 230 | 3 | 18 | 232 | 3 |
| Yds Out | 2,600 | | Yds In | 2,603 | |
| Total Yds | 5,203 | | | | |
| Total Par | 66 | | | | |

ADDRESS: Moorpark Road West, Stevenston, Ayrshire KA20 3HU.
TELEPHONE: +44 (0)1294 603103.
PROFESSIONAL: Bob Rodgers.
VISITORS: Six-day advance booking system.
GREEN FEES: £6.80 for 9 holes, £16 for 18.
CATERING: Full service. Bar.
FACILITIES: Trolley hire, putting green, pro shop, practice ground, driving range.
LOCATION: 12 miles north of Ayr.
LOCAL HOTELS: The Montgreenan Mansion House Hotel.

# STRATHAVEN

## STRATHAVEN GOLF CLUB

### COURSE DESCRIPTION:
Gently undulating, tree-lined, championship parkland course, 700 feet above sea level. Good challenge without being too strenuous. Founded in 1908 and designed originally as a nine-hole course by Willie Fernie.

18 holes, 6,224 yards, par 71 (SSS 71). Amateur record Robert Scott 65. Pro record David Huish 63.

### COURSE CARD

| HOLE | YDS | PAR | HOLE | YDS | PAR |
|---|---|---|---|---|---|
| 1 | 365 | 4 | 10 | 487 | 5 |
| 2 | 204 | 3 | 11 | 410 | 4 |
| 3 | 482 | 5 | 12 | 338 | 4 |
| 4 | 159 | 3 | 13 | 323 | 4 |
| 5 | 335 | 4 | 14 | 298 | 4 |
| 6 | 348 | 4 | 15 | 148 | 3 |
| 7 | 384 | 4 | 16 | 446 | 4 |

| 8 | 507 | 5 | 17 | 356 | 4 |
| 9 | 226 | 3 | 18 | 408 | 4 |
| *Yds* *Out* | 3,010 | | *Yds* *In* | 3,214 | |
| *Total* *Yds* | 6,224 | | | | |
| *Total* *Par* | 71 | | | | |

ADDRESS: Glasgow Road, Strathaven ML10 6NL.
TELEPHONE: +44 (0)1357 520421.
FAX: +44 (0)1357 520539.
SECRETARY: A. Wallace.
PROFESSIONAL: Matt McCrorie +44 (0)1357 521812.
VISITORS: Yes. Monday to Friday before 4 p.m. Handicap certificate required.
GREEN FEES: £25 per round weekdays.
CATERING: Restaurant and bar +44 (0)1357 520422.
FACILITIES: Trolley hire, putting green, pro shop, practice ground.
LOCATION: North-east side of town on A726.
LOCAL HOTELS: Strathaven Hotel, Springvale Hotel.

# STRONE

## BLAIRMORE & STRONE GOLF GLUB

COURSE DESCRIPTION:
Founded in 1896 and designed by James Braid, this undulating moorland and parkland course boasts spectacular views of the Clyde estuary.
  9 holes, 4,224 yards (for 18 holes), par 62 (SSS 62).

ADDRESS: High Road, Strone, by Dunoon PA23 8TJ.
TELEPHONE: +44 (0)1369 840676.
VISITORS: Yes, some restrictions Saturdays and Monday evenings.
GREEN FEES: £8 per day weekdays, £10 per day weekends. Weekly ticket £30.
CATERING: Bar facilities available.
LOCATION: 1 mile north of Strone on the A880, 5 miles north of Dunoon.

# TARBERT

## TARBERT GOLF CLUB

COURSE DESCRIPTION:
Hilly, wooded heathland course. Streams cross four fairways.

9 holes, 4,460 yards (for 18 holes), par 66 (SSS 63). Course record 62.

ADDRESS: Kilberry Road, Tarbert PA29 6XX.
TELEPHONE: +44 (0)1546 606896.
VISITORS: Not Saturday afternoons.
GREEN FEES: £10 per round, £15 per day.
LOCATION: 1 mile west of Tarbert on B8024.
LOCAL HOTELS: Stonefield Castle Hotel.

# TAYNUILT

## TAYNUILT GOLF CLUB

COURSE DESCRIPTION:
Undulating parkland course. Good views.
9 holes, 4,018 yards (for 18 holes). Par 64 (SSS 62).

ADDRESS: Laroch, Taynuilt, Argyll PA35 1JE.
SECRETARY: Murray Sim +44 (0)1866 822429.
VISITORS: Restricted play on Tuesday and weekends.
GREEN FEES: £10 per round/day.
FACILITIES: Changing-rooms.
LOCATION: 12 miles east of Oban on A85.
LOCAL HOTELS: Invercreran Country House Hotel.

# TIGHNABRUAICH

## KYLES OF BUTE GOLF CLUB

COURSE DESCRIPTION:
A short demanding course over open moorland, often wet and windy, with testing holes, small greens and wonderful views of the Kyles of Bute and Arran. Bunkers are not deemed necessary because of other dangers: burns and ditches, long carries over heather and whin and tough rough. A spare ball or ten should be carried, as should binoculars to view the plentiful wildlife.
9 holes, 4,814 yards (for 18 holes), par 68 (SSS 66). Course record 62.

SIGNATURE HOLE:
NINTH (188 yards, par 3) Tee up on the Cnoc (a small peak or hill) and play over a wide valley, with the burn running across, and over the access road to a raised flat green. Look back from the tee for a spectacular view of the Kyles of Bute 300 feet below.

## COURSE CARD

| HOLE | MEDAL YDS | PAR | FORWARD YDS | PAR | LADIES YDS | PAR |
|------|-----------|-----|-------------|-----|------------|-----|
| 1 | 110 | 3 | 110 | 3 | 110 | 3 |
| 2 | 343 | 4 | 333 | 4 | 273 | 4 |
| 3 | 260 | 4 | 197 | 4 | 207 | 4 |
| 4 | 329 | 4 | 329 | 4 | 229 | 4 |
| 5 | 278 | 4 | 201 | 3 | 205 | 3 |
| 6 | 402 | 4 | 402 | 4 | 365 | 4 |
| 7 | 254 | 4 | 234 | 4 | 236 | 4 |
| 8 | 243 | 4 | 206 | 4 | 244 | 4 |
| 9 | 188 | 3 | 178 | 3 | 162 | 3 |
| Yds Out | 2,407 | | 2,190 | | 2,005 | |
| Total Yds | 2,407 | | | | | |
| Total Par | 34 | | | | | |

ADDRESS: The Moss, Kames, Tighnabruaich PA21 2BE.
SECRETARY: Dr Jeremy Thomson.
VISITORS: All times, except Sundays between 9.30 a.m. and 1 p.m.
GREEN FEES: £8 per round/day weekdays. £10 weekends. Weekly tickets £40.
FACILITIES: Trolley hire, club hire, changing-rooms, memberships available.
LOCATION: From Dunoon (24 miles) take the B836 for 16 miles, then the A8003 to Tighnabruaich for eight miles. Turn west at seaside for 1 mile on B8000 to crossroads at Kames. Turn right for 400 yards. (signposted from Tighnabruaich).
LOCAL HOTELS: Kames Hotel, Kilfinan Hotel, Royal Hotel.

# TORRANCE

## BALMORE GOLF CLUB LTD

COURSE DESCRIPTION:
Founded in 1906 and designed by James Braid, this parkland course is set in beautiful countryside and offers fine views.
18 holes, 5,530 yards, par 66 (SSS 67). Course record 63.

ADDRESS: Golf Course Road, Balmore, Torrance, Stirlingshire G64 4AW.
TELEPHONE: +44 (0)1360 620240.
SECRETARY: +44 (0)1360 620284.
VISITORS: Contact in advance. Must be accompanied by a member.
GREEN FEES: £25 per round weekdays, £35 per day.
CATERING: Full clubhouse facilities.

FACILITIES: Putting green, practice ground.
LOCATION: 2 miles north of Glasgow on A807 off A803.
LOCAL HOTELS: Black Bull Thistle Hotel.

# TROON

## KILMARNOCK (BARASSIE) GOLF CLUB

COURSE DESCRIPTION:
Established in 1887, this relatively flat seaside course with much heather is a qualifying course for the Open Championship. It has great turf and small, fast greens and is more challenging than it might appear.

18 holes, 6,817 yards, par 72 (SSS 74). Amateur record 63. Pro record 68.
9-hole course, 2,756 yards.

COURSE CARD

| HOLE | MEDAL YDS | PAR | FORWARD YDS | PAR | HOLE | MEDAL YDS | PAR | FORWARD YDS | PAR |
|------|-----------|-----|-------------|-----|------|-----------|-----|-------------|-----|
| 1 | 506 | 5 | 501 | 5 | 10 | 357 | 4 | 346 | 4 |
| 2 | 392 | 4 | 376 | 4 | 11 | 396 | 4 | 385 | 4 |
| 3 | 425 | 4 | 365 | 4 | 12 | 439 | 4 | 387 | 4 |
| 4 | 159 | 3 | 149 | 3 | 13 | 377 | 4 | 355 | 4 |
| 5 | 366 | 4 | 336 | 4 | 14 | 185 | 3 | 170 | 3 |
| 6 | 154 | 3 | 143 | 3 | 15 | 428 | 4 | 413 | 4 |
| 7 | 439 | 4 | 427 | 4 | 16 | 490 | 5 | 475 | 5 |
| 8 | 539 | 5 | 519 | 5 | 17 | 406 | 4 | 401 | 4 |
| 9 | 383 | 4 | 371 | 4 | 18 | 376 | 4 | 365 | 4 |
| Yds Out | 3,363 | | 3,187 | | Yds In | 3,454 | | 3,297 | |
| Total Yds | 6,817 | | 6,484 | | | | | | |
| Total Par | 72 | | 72 | | | | | | |

ADDRESS: 29 Hillhouse Road, Barassie, Troon, Ayrshire KA10 6SY
TELEPHONE: +44 (0)1292 313920.
FAX: +44 (0)1292 313920 or 313824.
E-MAIL: barassiegc@lineone.net
WEBSITE: www.kbgc.co.uk
SECRETARY/MANAGER: D.D.Wilson.
PROFESSIONAL: Gregor Howie +44 (0)1292 311322.
VISITORS: Yes, Mondays, Tuesdays, Thursdays and Fridays p.m.
GREEN FEES: £40 per round, £60 per day.
CREDIT CARDS ACCEPTED: Amex/Visa/Mastercard.
CATERING: Restaurant and bar +44 (0)1292 311077.

**FACILITIES:** Trolley hire (£2), changing-rooms, putting green, pro shop, practice ground.
**LOCATION:** 2 miles north of Troon opposite Barassie railway station.
**LOCAL HOTELS:** Annfield House Hotel, Marine Hotel, Piersland Hotel, Redcliffe House Hotel, South Beach Hotel.

## ROYAL TROON GOLF CLUB

### COURSE DESCRIPTION:

Dramatic would perhaps be the best way to describe Royal Troon, which hosted the 1997 Open Championship. When the wind blows on the Old Course strange things can happen on this classic undulating links, which is full of bumps and hollows and rated amongst the world's best.

Founded in 1878 by 24 local enthusiasts, the course consisted of only five holes but it rapidly grew in stature and hosted the Open Championship five times between 1923 and 1989 – and every time there was high drama. No more so than in 1997 when the world expected the new golfing phenomenon Tiger Woods to follow up his runaway triumph in the US Masters with something special in Scotland. But it was another American, Justin Leonard, who took the honours pulling back Swede Jesper Parnevik's five-shot lead to win by three.

It was yet another American, Mark Calcavecchia, who executed a Houdini act to win the championship in 1989. First he holed out from deep rough on the 12th in the final round and then he birdied the 425-yard, par-4 18th to take the competition into extra time. Then at the 18th, the final hole in the four-hole play-off with Greg Norman and Wayne Grady, he hit an exquisite 5-iron again from deep rough and needed only a single putt to win. Earlier Norman, who had a final round 64, made a mark of his own, birdieing the first six holes.

Those golfing greats, Arnold Palmer and Jack Nicklaus, also go down in the history of the course. Palmer won the 1962 Open by six shots at the same time as Nicklaus, of all people, was taking a 10 at the 11th. High scores are not uncommon here. Royal Troon boasts both the longest and the shortest holes of any Open Championship. When you think of Troon you invariably think of the 8th, the 'Postage Stamp', which is the world's most famous par 3 and the Open's shortest at a mere 126 yards. Yet it can take anything from a 3-iron to a wedge depending on the wind. Some, however, have only happy memories of this devilish hole. In 1973, at the age of 71, Gene Sarazen holed his punched 5-iron then, as if to prove that this hole had no psychological terrors for him; the inventor of the sand wedge holed his second shot from a cavernous bunker in the next round.

Not everyone can look back with fondness on this par 3, though. In the same tournament, Palmer scored a seven there and in 1950 Herman Tissies, a German amateur, took 15 blows to get down.

When you prepare for your shot from a high tee with a troublesome gully between you and the green, it is hard to put all the problems facing you to the back of your mind. On the left is a hugh sandhill and the green is surrounded by five bunkers. Hitting into the crater bunker on the right approach could mean you going from bunker to bunker, as Herr Tissies did. With a green only 25 feet across at its widest point, from the tee it looks as big as a – well, a postage stamp.

The 6th is the longest in Open championship golf at 577 yards, and it is a dangerous hole. There being a slight dogleg to the right, the drive has to pitch on the upper half of the fairway which is tilted right to left. There are three bunkers positioned to catch the less than accurate drive. The second shot should be aimed slightly left to avoid a bunker on the right, ready for a pitch into a long narrow green with sand dunes on three sides. Miss the target and expect to have to do some exploring in the rough.

But this magnificent course is not just those holes. The 438-yard 10th is not the longest but it must rate the trickiest par 4 on the course. There is not a bunker on this hole but, from a low tee, you have to be long and straight to clear a range of sandhills. Get it wrong and you are in impenetrable rough. The plateau green falls sharply to the right. A bogey here is a result.

The 463-yard 11th is a par-4 in a championship and a fairly short par 5 in a modal, but don't let that fool you. In the prevailing winds it plays every inch and is reckoned to be the toughest hole on the course. Hit your drive left and you are in thick gorse; go right and you are out of bounds on the railway line, which runs the whole length of the hole and gets so close to the little green that the guard could almost punch your ticket without leaving his cab. Just to complicate matters, the fairway tightens almost to the narrowness of a Victorian lady's waist. Anything can happen here – and it usually does.

That gives you the flavour of Troon's testing finish, of which the 15th (457 yards, par 4) is the most difficult hole for most. The drive is slightly blind to a plateau fairway, with three bunkers in a landing area of about 30 yards, and the approach is to a well-guarded, sunken green.

Troon can be a terror and that's why you can expect a tale of the unexpected from any Open Championship contender there.

*Old Course* – 18 holes, 7,079 yards, par 71 (SSS 73). Course record Greg Norman 64.

*Portland Course* – Resembles moorland course but has the challenges of a links. 18 holes, 6,274 yards, par 71 (SSS 71).

SIGNATURE HOLE:

EIGHTH (126 yards, par 3) Called the 'Postage Stamp' because when you look down on it from the tee, the green, only 25 feet across at its widest point, looks no bigger than a postage stamp. This hole on the Old Course is the shortest hole in Open Championship golf, but also one of the deadliest.

## COURSE CARD

| HOLE | YDS | PAR | HOLE | YDS | PAR |
|------|-----|-----|------|-----|-----|
| 1 | 364 | 4 | 10 | 438 | 4 |
| 2 | 391 | 4 | 11 | 463 | 4 |
| 3 | 379 | 4 | 12 | 431 | 4 |
| 4 | 557 | 5 | 13 | 465 | 4 |
| 5 | 210 | 3 | 14 | 179 | 3 |
| 6 | 577 | 5 | 15 | 457 | 4 |
| 7 | 402 | 4 | 16 | 542 | 5 |
| 8 | 126 | 3 | 17 | 223 | 3 |
| 9 | 423 | 4 | 18 | 452 | 4 |
| *Yds Out* | 3,429 | | *Yds In* | 3,650 | |
| *Total Yds* | 7,079 | | | | |
| *Total Par* | 71 | | | | |

ADDRESS: Craigend Road, Troon, South Ayrshire KA10 6EP.

TELEPHONE: +44 (0)1292 311555.

SECRETARY: J.D. Montgomerie.

PROFESSIONAL: Brian Anderson +44 (0)1292 313281.

VISITORS: May not play Wednesdays, Fridays and weekends. Must write in advance, have introductory letter and handicap certificate of under 20. Ladies and under-18s may play only on the Portland.

GREEN FEES: £150 per day (includes a round on both courses, morning coffee and lunch).

CATERING: Full service. Bar.

FACILITIES: Trolley hire, putting green, pro shop, practice ground.

LOCATION: 3 miles from A77 (Glasgow–Ayr road). Follow signs for Prestwick Airport.

LOCAL HOTELS: Annfield House Hotel, Highgrove House Hotel, Lochgreen House Hotel, Marine Hotel, Piersland Hotel, Redcliffe House Hotel, South Beach Hotel.

# TROON MUNICIPAL GOLF COURSES

## COURSE DESCRIPTION:

These three links courses, two championship, lie alongside Royal Troon, Portland and Kilmarnock (Barassie) to form a group of six courses that totally surround the town of Troon.

*Lochgreen* – The most testing of the three, it favours long hitters. Has been used as an Open Championship qualifying course, and in 1962 a young Jack Nicklaus scored 78 and 66 here to qualify by one shot for the Open.

18 holes, 6,785 yards, par 74 (SSS 73).

*Darley* – Real challenge with hazards of heather, gorse and whin. Much tighter than Lochgreen.

18 holes, 6,360 yards, par 71 (SSS 72).

*Fullarton* – Ideal for beginners. Has eight par 3 holes, and the longest hole is the 441-yard 1st. Tight fairways and well-bunkered greens.

18 holes, 4,869 yards, par 64 (SSS 63).

## LOCHGREEN COURSE CARD

| HOLE | YDS | PAR | HOLE | YDS | PAR |
|------|-----|-----|------|-----|-----|
| 1 | 473 | 4 | 10 | 188 | 3 |
| 2 | 476 | 5 | 11 | 413 | 4 |
| 3 | 487 | 5 | 12 | 408 | 4 |
| 4 | 293 | 4 | 13 | 318 | 4 |
| 5 | 429 | 4 | 14 | 306 | 4 |
| 6 | 197 | 3 | 15 | 203 | 3 |
| 7 | 496 | 5 | 16 | 491 | 5 |
| 8 | 323 | 4 | 17 | 360 | 4 |
| 9 | 429 | 4 | 18 | 495 | 5 |
| *Yds Out* | 3,603 | | *Yds In* | 3,182 | |
| *Total Yds* | 6,785 | | | | |
| *Total Par* | 74 | | | | |

**ADDRESS:** Harling Drive, Troon, Ayrshire KA10 6NE.
**TELEPHONE:** +44 (0)1292 312464
**PROFESSIONAL:** Gordon McKinlay.
**VISITORS:** Any time.
**GREEN FEES:** *Lochgreen:* £18 per round weekdays, £28 per day. £25 per round weekends, £35 per day.
*Darley:* £15 per round weekdays, £25 per day. £20 per round weekends, £30 per day.
*Fullarton:* £12 per round weekdays, £20 per day. £16 per round weekends, £28 per day.
Five-day ticket (Monday to Friday) £90. Three-day ticket (Monday to Friday) £60.
**CATERING:** Full clubhouse facilities.
**FACILITIES:** Trolley hire, putting green, pro shop, practice ground.
**LOCATION:** In centre of Troon beside railway station.
**LOCAL HOTELS:** Annfield House Hotel, Crailea Hotel, Marine Hotel, Piersland Hotel, Redcliffe House Hotel, South Beach Hotel.

# TURNBERRY

## TURNBERRY HOTEL GOLF COURSES

**COURSE DESCRIPTION:**
The youngest of Scotland's Open Championship venues, but by no means

overshadowed by its rivals. The first 13 holes were laid out by Willie Fernie in 1903 and three years later it was the first hotel and golf complex in the world with the wealthy travelling down by train from Glasgow to visit.

It staged its first Open in 1977 and what a first championship that turned out to be – a head-to-head between Jack Nicklaus and Tom Watson, the two greatest players of the day. It was tagged the 'Duel in the Sun' and many still believe it to be the greatest ever finale to the championship.

Locals have a saying that if you can't see Ailsa Craig, the 1,208-foot high granite rock off the Ayrshire coast, it's raining; if you can, it's about to rain. They do a disservice to an area of Scotland that is home to a glorious course, which is amongst the best. Often when the rest of Britain is shivering in a freezing winter, the sun is shining on Turnberry and the temperature is mild. If you play Turnberry's Ailsa Course on one of those days with a light breeze coming in from the sea then there is nowhere you would rather be; play it in the rain and high winds and your step quickens towards the beckoning lights of the hotel, which is as magnificent as its two links courses.

During the Second World War, Turnberry was used as an airfield and many dunes were levelled and bunkers filled in. Part of the old runway remains and can be found if you play a particularly wayward shot. It looked like the end of Turnberry as a golf course, but thanks to the restoration work of Mackenzie Ross it reopened in 1951.

The first three holes are parallel and relatively flat and not the toughest of starts to an Open, although the 462-yard 3rd is directly into the wind, but the club golfer would be happy to come away with three par 4s even from the shorter medal tees.

With the short 4th, you now have a run of eight holes along the rugged coastline. It's 165 yards and not the hardest of holes but be careful not to go left or you could end up on the beach. There's another par 3 at the 6th and this is something else. It needs a hefty clout from the championship tee of 231 yards, or even the medal tee some ten yards shorter, to get up on top of a raised green. Three bunkers to the left with jungle farther left and a deep, deep bunker just in front for the drive that doesn't quite have the legs. Stray right and you'll find yourself at the bottom of a slope. Even if you make the green, it can be three-putt territory depending on pin placement.

The 7th, a classic 529-yard par 5 from the championship tees and possibly an even harder 475-yard par 4 from the medal markers, is regarded as the hardest hole on the course. Your tee shot has to carry a burn and be right to give yourself a decent second shot.

The 9th is Turnberry's 'Lighthouse' hole and one of the most photographed signature holes in the world. Even if you're not playing it, it is worth a stroll out to look at it. The rocks are 390 million years old and at that time there were several active volcanoes along this stretch of Ayrshire coast. From the green you can see the remains of Robert the Bruce's castle.

The 10th demands a solid strike and, if it's down the left of this 452 -yard hole, it could set you up for a birdie 3. From the 174-yard 11th, you head inland. The 13th has a tricky raised green, which is slower than any of the rest. The 15th, a 209-yard par 3, can be a cruel hole. Any error is heavily punished. With a ravine to the front, bunkers to the left and a huge drop to the right, you've got to hit the small green or else.

The 16th is called the Wee Burn, but it's not so wee. Not that long – 380 yards from the medal tees – it presents an intriguing approach shot. You often need a club more than you think to get over, because there is a danger of the ball rolling back into it.

Colin Montgomerie, who has his Links Golf Academy here, says: 'It's the finest links course in the world.' The hotel provides spectacular views of a breathtaking coastline and out to the Isle of Arran and the Mull of Kintyre and, on a clear day, all the way to Ireland. With the Ailsa and its new sister, the Kintyre, dominating Turnberry's 800 acres, a non-golfer could, from his hotel room, keep track of his partner's progress with a powerful pair of binoculars.

The old Arran course has been completely redesigned as the Kintyre by Donald Steel as a championship standard course. The new course incorporates Bains Hill, a stunning stretch of land extending to the coastline. In common with the Ailsa, the Kintrye offers undulating greens, tight tee shots, pot bunkers and thick Scottish rough. There are some excellent holes, especially the 8th with a drive from an elevated tee towards the sea and a blind second to the green set in a gully by the rocks.

If you've had a tough day on the links, you might be inclined to try your hand at the nine-hole pitch-and-putt course on the front lawns of the hotel. Be warned, it's tougher than you think – but then again that's Turnberry.

*Ailsa* – 18 holes, 6,976 yards (6,440 yards medal tees), par 70 (69 medal). Amateur record 70. Pro record 63.

*Kintyre* – 18 holes, 6,827 yards, par 72

## SIGNATURE HOLE:

*Ailsa Course*: NINTH (454 yards, par 4) The championship tee is perched out on a promontory of cliff with a sheer drop of 50 feet. Not for someone suffering with vertigo. The medal tee is some 40 yards further on, but still a spectacular tee shot. It takes a 200-yard drive from the championship tee just to reach the fairway and a white stone marker shows you where to aim for. If you are on this line, playing from the medal tees, you will have a shot of about 180 yards to a large green untroubled by bunkers.

## AILSA COURSE CARD

| HOLE | CHAMPIONSHIP YDS | PAR | MEDAL YDS | PAR | LADIES YDS | PAR | HOLE | CHAMPIONSHIP YDS | PAR | MEDAL YDS | PAR | LADIES YDS | PAR |
|---|---|---|---|---|---|---|---|---|---|---|---|---|---|
| 1 | 350 | 4 | 358 | 4 | 331 | 4 | 10 | 452 | 4 | 429 | 4 | 336 | 4 |
| 2 | 430 | 4 | 381 | 4 | 360 | 4 | 11 | 174 | 3 | 161 | 3 | 130 | 3 |
| 3 | 462 | 4 | 409 | 4 | 390 | 5 | 12 | 446 | 4 | 390 | 4 | 354 | 4 |
| 4 | 165 | 3 | 165 | 3 | 114 | 3 | 13 | 412 | 4 | 379 | 4 | 329 | 4 |
| 5 | 442 | 4 | 416 | 4 | 388 | 5 | 14 | 449 | 4 | 401 | 4 | 384 | 5 |
| 6 | 231 | 3 | 221 | 3 | 215 | 4 | 15 | 209 | 3 | 169 | 3 | 160 | 3 |
| 7 | 529 | 5 | 475 | 4 | 415 | 5 | 16 | 409 | 4 | 380 | 4 | 339 | 4 |
| 8 | 431 | 4 | 431 | 4 | 386 | 5 | 17 | 497 | 5 | 487 | 5 | 394 | 5 |
| 9 | 454 | 4 | 411 | 4 | 373 | 4 | 18 | 434 | 4 | 377 | 4 | 359 | 4 |
| *Yds* Out | 3,494 | | 3,267 | | 2,972 | | *Yds* In | 3,482 | | 3,173 | | 2,785 | |
| *Total Yds* | 6,976 | | 6,440 | | 5,757 | | | | | | | | |

| *Total* | 70 | 69 | 71 |
|---------|----|----|----|
| *Par*   |    |    |    |

ADDRESS: Turnberry, Ayrshire KA26 9LT.
TELEPHONE: +44 (0)1655 331000.
FAX: +44 (0)1655 331069.
E-MAIL: Turnberry @westin.com
WEBSITE: www.turnberry.co.uk
GOLF MANAGER: Brian Gunson.
PROFESSIONAL: Guy Redford.
VISITORS: Yes, all year round.
GREEN FEES: Ailsa: £130 per round weekdays. £175 weekends (£105 if hotel guest). Kintyre: £105 per round weekdays and weekends (£90 if hotel guest).
CREDIT CARDS ACCEPTED: Amex/Visa/Mastercard/Diners Club.
CATERING: Magnificent, well-appointed clubhouse with restaurant and bar. Functions catered for.
FACILITIES: Trolley hire (not permitted on Ailsa course), club hire, caddies, changing-rooms, putting green, pro shop, practice ground, driving range, coaching clinics, memberships available.
LOCATION: 15 miles south-west of Ayr on A77.
LOCAL HOTELS: Annfield House Hotel, Kinloch Hotel, Redcliffe House Hotel, South Beach Hotel, Turnberry Hotel.

# UDDINGSTON

## CALDERBRAES GOLF CLUB

COURSE DESCRIPTION:
Inland hilly, very tight, woodland course. Extremely difficult with out of bounds at almost every hole.
9 holes, 5,186 yards (for 18 holes), par 66 (SSS 67). Course record 65.

SIGNATURE HOLE:
FOURTH (434 yards, par 4) Demanding and long second shot to a green very high up with out of bounds to the left and right, only 5 yards from the green.

ADDRESS: 57 Roundknowe Road, Uddingston, Lanarkshire G71 7TS.
TELEPHONE: +44 (0)1698 813425.
SECRETARY: Seamus McGuigan.
VISITORS: Weekdays only.
GREEN FEES: £12 per day.
CATERING: Yes. Bar.
FACILITIES: Putting green, practice ground.
LOCATION: Beginning of M74, east of Glasgow next to Glasgow Zoo.
LOCAL HOTELS: Black Bear Travel Lodge.

# UPLAWMOOR

## CALDWELL GOLF CLUB LTD

COURSE DESCRIPTION:
Undulating parkland course founded in 1903.
   18 holes, 6,294 yards, par 71 (SSS 70). Amateur record 66. Pro record 63.

SIGNATURE HOLE:
THIRD (160 yards, par 3) Aptly named 'Risk an' Hope'. out of bounds on the right for the length of the hole. Long, narrow green.

COURSE CARD

| HOLE | YDS | PAR | HOLE | YDS | PAR |
|------|-----|-----|------|-----|-----|
| 1 | 395 | 4 | 10 | 311 | 4 |
| 2 | 422 | 4 | 11 | 391 | 4 |
| 3 | 160 | 3 | 12 | 345 | 4 |
| 4 | 304 | 4 | 13 | 360 | 4 |
| 5 | 516 | 5 | 14 | 280 | 4 |
| 6 | 382 | 4 | 15 | 131 | 3 |
| 7 | 422 | 4 | 16 | 395 | 4 |
| 8 | 331 | 4 | 17 | 547 | 5 |
| 9 | 196 | 3 | 18 | 406 | 4 |
| *Yds Out* | 3,128 | | *Yds In* | 3,166 | |
| *Total Yds* | 6,294 | | | | |
| *Total Par* | 71 | | | | |

ADDRESS: Uplawmoor, Renfrewshire, G78 4AU.
TELEPHONE: +44 (0)1505 850329.
FAX: +44 (0)1505 850604.
SECRETARY: H. Harper +44 (0)1505 850366.
PROFESSIONAL: Stephen Forbes +44(0)1505 850616.
VISITORS: Yes, but not at weekends or on local public holidays. Phone professional to book.
GREEN FEES: £20 per round. £28 per day.
CATERING: Yes. Not Thursdays.
FACILITIES: Trolley hire, putting green, pro shop, practice ground.
LOCATION: 5 miles south-east of Barrhead on A736, Glasgow–Irvine road.
LOCAL HOTELS: Dalmenny House Hotel, Uplawmoor Hotel.

# WEST KILBRIDE

## WEST KILBRIDE GOLF CLUB

COURSE DESCRIPTION:
Traditional flat seaside links, designed by Old Tom Morris, on the Firth of Clyde.
18 holes, 6,452 yards, par 71 (SSS 71). Course record 63.

ADDRESS: 33-35 Fullerton Drive, Seamill, West Kilbride, Ayrshire KA23 9HT.
TELEPHONE: +44 (0)1294 823911.
FAX: +44 (0)1294 829573.
E-MAIL: golf@westkilbridegolfclub.com
WEBSITE: www.westkilbridegolfclub.com
SECRETARY: Hamish Armour.
PROFESSIONAL: Graham Ross +44 (0)1294 823042.
VISITORS: Yes but not at weekends or public holidays. Parties over 8, Tuesdays and
    Thursdays only.
GREEN FEES: £25 per round weekdays, £38 per day.
CATERING: Restaurant and bar.
FACILITIES: Trolley hire, club hire, changing-rooms, putting green, pro shop, practice
    ground, coaching clinics on request.
LOCATION: On A78, Greenock–Ayr road.
LOCAL HOTELS: Elderslie Hotel, Redcliffe House Hotel, Seahill Hydro, South Beach Hotel.

# WISHAW

## WISHAW GOLF CLUB

COURSE DESCRIPTION:
Flat tree-lined parkland course, which was designed by James Braid and celebrated
its centenary in 1997. Bunkers on 17 greens.
18 holes, 6,073 yards, par 69 (SSS 69). Course record 64.

ADDRESS: 55 Cleland Road, Wishaw ML2 7PH.
TELEPHONE: +44 (0)1698 372869.
PROFESSIONAL: John Campbell +44 (0)1698 358247.
VISITORS: Welcome weekdays until 4 p.m. Not on Saturdays and by prior
    arrangement on Sundays. Handicap certificate required.
GREEN FEES: £13 per round weekdays, £22 per day. Sundays £26 per round.
CATERING: Full service. Bar.
FACILITIES: Trolley/buggy hire, putting green, pro shop, practice ground.
LOCATION: North-west of town, off A721.
LOCAL HOTELS: Popinjay Hotel.

# BORDERS INCLUDING HAWICK

# ASHKIRK

## THE WOLL GOLF COURSE

COURSE DESCRIPTION:
Challenging flat course set in peaceful and natural parkland of outstanding beauty on the Woll Estate. Opened in 1993. The Woll Burn plays a significant part on the 6th and 7th holes.

9 holes, 6,406 yards (for 18 holes), par 72 (SSS 71).

SIGNATURE HOLE:
SIXTH (300 yards, par 4) Requires an accurate tee-shot and perfect second over the Woll Burn.

ADDRESS: New Woll Estate, Ashkirk, Selkirkshire TD7 4NY.
TELEPHONE: +44 (0) 7957 873488 or +44 (0) 131 3370606
LOCATION: ¼ mile off the A7 at Ashkirk, which is situated on the A7 between Hawick and Selkirk.
VISITORS: Welcome.
GREEN FEES: £15 per day.
CATERING: Hot and cold drinks vending machines.
FACILITIES: Changing-rooms.
LOCAL HOTELS: Kings Arms Hotel, The Roxburghe Hotel & Golf Course

# COLDSTREAM

## THE HIRSEL GOLF CLUB

COURSE DESCRIPTION:
Winner of the 'Most Visitor-Friendly 18-hole Course in the Scottish Borders' in 1998. Beautifully situated parkland course with panoramic views of the Cheviot Hills. Truly a course not to be missed on a Borders visit. Each hole offers a different challenge and a scenic view. Founded 1948.

18 holes, 6,092 yards, par 70 (SSS 70).

SIGNATURE HOLE:
SEVENTH (170 yards, par 3) Demanding accuracy of flight and length from the tee is required to ensure carrying the river and stand a chance of a par.

## COURSE CARD

| HOLE | YDS | PAR | HOLE | YDS | PAR |
|------|------|-----|------|------|-----|
| 1 | 304 | 4 | 10 | 125 | 3 |
| 2 | 290 | 4 | 11 | 345 | 4 |
| 3 | 246 | 3 | 12 | 531 | 5 |
| 4 | 320 | 4 | 13 | 440 | 4 |
| 5 | 372 | 4 | 14 | 180 | 3 |
| 6 | 357 | 4 | 15 | 438 | 4 |
| 7 | 170 | 3 | 16 | 314 | 4 |
| 8 | 345 | 4 | 17 | 375 | 4 |
| 9 | 420 | 4 | 18 | 520 | 5 |
| *Yds Out* | 2,824 | | *Yds In* | 3,268 | |
| *Total Yds* | 6,092 | | | | |
| *Total Par* | 70 | | | | |

ADDRESS: Kelso Road, Coldstream TD12 4 NJ.
TELEPHONE: +44 (0)1890 882678.
SECRETARY & FAX: John Balfour +44 (0)1890 882233.
VISITORS: Yes. No restrictions.
GREEN FEES: £20 weekdays. £27 weekends.
CATERING: Bar snacks and full 48-seat restaurant.
FACILITIES: Trolley/buggy hire, putting green, pro shop, practice ground.
LOCATION: On A697 at west end of Coldstream.
LOCAL HOTELS: Collingwood Arms Hotel, Cross Keys Hotel, Kings Arms Hotel, Peebles Hotel Hydro, The Roxburghe Hotel & Golf Course, Tillmouth Park Hotel.

# DUNS

## DUNS GOLF CLUB

### COURSE DESCRIPTION:
Upland course suitable for both beginners and experienced players. Established in 1894, it is lightly hilly with a burn running through the course. No bunkers. Views south over the Tweed Valley to Cheviot Hills.
18 holes, 6,209 yards, par 70 (SSS 70).

### SIGNATURE HOLE:
FIFTEENTH (116 yards, par 3) Played from a high tee to a tiered green. Burn in front, burn behind. Not as easy as it looks.

## COURSE CARD

| HOLE | YDS | PAR | HOLE | YDS | PAR |
|------|-----|-----|------|-----|-----|
| 1 | 400 | 4 | 10 | 545 | 5 |
| 2 | 398 | 4 | 11 | 390 | 4 |
| 3 | 368 | 4 | 12 | 204 | 3 |
| 4 | 171 | 3 | 13 | 366 | 4 |
| 5 | 387 | 4 | 14 | 326 | 4 |
| 6 | 500 | 5 | 15 | 116 | 3 |
| 7 | 163 | 3 | 16 | 369 | 4 |
| 8 | 390 | 4 | 17 | 195 | 3 |
| 9 | 388 | 4 | 18 | 533 | 5 |
| *Yds Out* | 3,165 | | *Yds In* | 3,044 | |
| *Total Yds* | 6,209 | | | | |
| *Total Par* | 70 | | | | |

ADDRESS: Hardens Road, Duns, Berwickshire TD11 3NR.
TELEPHONE: +44 (0)1361 882194.
SECRETARY: Allan Campbell +44 (0)1361 882717.
VISITORS: Yes, without restriction. Ring clubhouse for bookings.
GREEN FEES: £16 per round weekdays, £19 per day. £19 per round weekends, £24 per day. Children £3 per round. Winter rates: £10 per round, children £2.
CATERING: Clubhouse and dining-room. Bar open all year.
FACILITIES: Trolley hire, practice ground.
LOCATION: 1 mile west of Duns, off A6105 Duns–Greenlaw road.
LOCAL HOTELS: Barniken House Hotel, Lauderdale Hotel.

# EYEMOUTH

## EYEMOUTH GOLF CLUB

### COURSE DESCRIPTION:
A superb course set on the rugged Berwickshire coast offering a true test of golf with a variety of spectacular and challenging holes on this 18-hole clifftop layout. Apart from the climb to the 1st tee, this is a flat seaside course. Fast greens constructed to US PGA specifications. Panoramic views.

18 holes, 6,520 yards, par 72 (SSS 72).

### SIGNATURE HOLE:
SIXTH (Par 3) Called 'Ah-still-no-ken' (roughly translated as 'I still don't know'). Played across the North Sea.

ADDRESS: The Clubhouse, Gunsgreenhill, Eyemouth, Berwickshire TD14 5HZ.

TELEPHONE: +44 (0)1890 750551.

BOOKINGS: +44 (0)1890 750004 .

PROFESSIONAL: Paul Terras.

VISITORS: Visiting parties and groups are very welcome on weekdays and weekends. The Club offers various package deals incorporating comprehensive and sensibly priced catering.

MEMBERSHIP: Vacancies still available – £250 per year for a Full Member, Country Membership 75% of full fee.

GREEN FEES: Weekdays £18 per round/£25 per day. Weekends £22 per round/£32 per day.

CATERING: Full Catering facilities from 9 a.m. through to approximately 6 p.m.

FACILITIES: Pro shop.

LOCATION: East of town, 8 miles north of Berwick-upon-Tweed, 46 miles from Edinburgh.

LOCAL HOTELS: Dolphin Hotel, Dunlaverock House Hotel, Press Castle Hotel, Ship Hotel.

# GALASHIELS

## GALASHIELS GOLF CLUB

COURSE DESCRIPTION:

A parkland course of two halves with a climb connecting them. Plateau greens and drystone dykes add to the challenge. Founded 1883.

18 holes, 5,185 yards, par 67 (SSS 66). Course record 61.

SIGNATURE HOLE:

FIRST (170 yards, par 3) Teeing off downhill towards town to a bunkered green with panoramic views. Out of bounds down the left.

COURSE CARD

| HOLE | YDS | PAR | HOLE | YDS | PAR |
|------|-----|-----|------|-----|-----|
| 1 | 170 | 3 | 10 | 272 | 4 |
| 2 | 244 | 4 | 11 | 121 | 3 |
| 3 | 524 | 5 | 12 | 376 | 4 |
| 4 | 460 | 5 | 13 | 230 | 3 |
| 5 | 150 | 3 | 14 | 359 | 4 |
| 6 | 432 | 4 | 15 | 277 | 4 |
| 7 | 246 | 3 | 16 | 304 | 4 |
| 8 | 357 | 4 | 17 | 275 | 4 |
| 9 | 217 | 3 | 18 | 171 | 3 |
| *Yds* *Out* | 2,800 | | *Yds* *In* | 2,385 | |
| *Total* *Yds* | 5,185 | | | | |

| Total | 67 |
|-------|-----|
| Par | |

ADDRESS: Ladhope Golf Course, off Ladhope Drive, Galashiels TD1 2DL.
TELEPHONE: +44 (0)1896 753724.
VISITORS: Any time, but weekends must be arranged through secretary.
GREEN FEES: £15 per round weekdays, £22 per day. £17 per round weekends, £24 per day.
CATERING: Full service available. Bar.
FACILITIES: Trolley hire.
LOCATION: ½ mile from town centre off A7 to Edinburgh.
LOCAL HOTELS: Abbotsford Arms Hotel, Cross Keys Hotel, Kings Hotel, Kingsknowes Hotel, Lauderdale Hotel, The Roxburghe Hotel & Golf Course.

## TORWOODLEE GOLF CLUB

COURSE DESCRIPTION:
Wooded parkland course running alongside River Gala. Testing, but fair, with tight fairways and small greens.
18 holes, 6,087 yards, par 70 (SSS 69). Course record 70.

SIGNATURE HOLE:
FOURTEENTH (546 yards, par 5) Elevated tee. Out of bounds on the right. Hole doglegs right with tight approach to the green.

### COURSE CARD

| HOLE | YDS | PAR | HOLE | YDS | PAR |
|------|-----|-----|------|-----|-----|
| 1 | 378 | 4 | 10 | 176 | 3 |
| 2 | 401 | 4 | 11 | 425 | 4 |
| 3 | 124 | 3 | 12 | 139 | 3 |
| 4 | 293 | 4 | 13 | 420 | 4 |
| 5 | 484 | 5 | 14 | 546 | 5 |
| 6 | 355 | 4 | 15 | 336 | 4 |
| 7 | 152 | 3 | 16 | 325 | 4 |
| 8 | 512 | 5 | 17 | 234 | 3 |
| 9 | 367 | 4 | 18 | 420 | 4 |
| Yds Out | 3,066 | | Yds In | 3,021 | |
| Total Yds | 6,087 | | | | |
| Total Par | 70 | | | | |

ADDRESS: Edinburgh Road, Galashiels, Selkirkshire TD6 9SR.
TELEPHONE: +44 (0)1896 752260.
VISITORS: All week, except during competitions.
GREEN FEES: £20 per round weekdays, £25 per day. £25 per round weekends, £30 per

day.

**CATERING:** Yes, except on Tuesdays.

**FACILITIES:** Trolley/buggy hire, putting green, pro shop, practice ground.

**LOCATION:** 2 miles from town centre on main Galashiels–Edinburgh A7 road.

**LOCAL HOTELS:** Burts Hotel, Cringletie House Hotel, Cross Keys Hotel, Kings Arms Hotel, Kingsknowes Hotel, Lauderdale Hotel, The Roxburghe Hotel & Golf Course.

# HAWICK

## HAWICK GOLF CLUB

### COURSE DESCRIPTION:

Founded in 1877, a well-bunkered gradually inclining hill course with challenging holes and spectacular views. The 388-yard 14th, looking towards Ruberslaw and the Cheviot Hills, offers a particularly spectacular view. Located on picturesque Vertish Hill in the heart of the Borders and the home of Pringle. Nick Faldo, who holds the professional course record of 64, Colin Montgomerie and Tony Jacklin are honorary members.

18 holes, 5,929 yards, par 68 (SSS 69).

### SIGNATURE HOLE:

SIXTH (445 yards, par 4) Stroke index 1.

### COURSE CARD

| HOLE | YDS | PAR | HOLE | YDS | PAR |
|------|-----|-----|------|-----|-----|
| 1 | 195 | 3 | 10 | 382 | 4 |
| 2 | 350 | 4 | 11 | 390 | 4 |
| 3 | 388 | 4 | 12 | 292 | 4 |
| 4 | 325 | 4 | 13 | 198 | 3 |
| 5 | 338 | 4 | 14 | 388 | 4 |
| 6 | 445 | 4 | 15 | 437 | 4 |
| 7 | 449 | 4 | 16 | 292 | 4 |
| 8 | 144 | 3 | 17 | 276 | 4 |
| 9 | 430 | 4 | 18 | 210 | 3 |
| Yds Out | 3,064 | | Yds In | 2,865 | |
| Total Yds | 5,929 | | | | |
| Total Par | 68 | | | | |

**ADDRESS:** Vertish Hill, Hawick, Roxburghshire TD9 0NY.

**TELEPHONE:** +44 (0)1450 372293

**SECRETARY:** J. Harley +44 (0)1450 374947

**VISITORS:** Daily without reservation but usually after 3 p.m. on Saturdays. First tee-off time on Sundays is 10.30 a.m.

**GREEN FEES:** £20 per round weekdays/weekends, £25 per day. Weekly tickets on request.

**CATERING:** Restaurant and bar. Functions catered for.

**FACILITIES:** Motorised buggies, trolley hire, club hire, changing-rooms, putting green, memberships available.

**LOCATION:** From north, A7 through town. Pass horse monument on left, proceed along Main Street. Turn left before roundabout, continue uphill then down to course. From south, A7 to roundabout then turn sharp right up hill.

**LOCAL HOTELS:** Cross Keys Hotel, Elm House Hotel, Elmsfield Hotel, Kings Arms Hotel, Kirklands Hotel, Lauderdale Hotel, Mansfield House Hotel, Peebles Hotel Hydro, The Roxburghe Hotel & Golf Course.

# INNERLEITHEN

## INNERLEITHEN GOLF CLUB

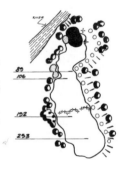

### COURSE DESCRIPTION:

Attractive course set in the Leithen valley with lovely view of the surrounding hills. Founded in 1886 and designed by three-times Open champion Willie Park of Musselburgh. A stream meanders through six holes and offers a challenge to all standards of golfers, yet it is easy walking.

9 holes, 6,056 yards (for 18 holes), par 70 (SSS 69). Course record 66.

### SIGNATURE HOLE:

FIRST (177 yards, par 3) Narrow entry to green with roadway on the right, a burn on front left and the Leithen Water at the back.

### COURSE CARD

| HOLE | YDS | PAR |
|------|-------|-----|
| 1 | 177 | 3 |
| 2 | 343 | 4 |
| 3 | 474 | 4 |
| 4 | 376 | 4 |
| 5 | 100 | 3 |
| 6 | 485 | 5 |
| 7 | 177 | 3 |
| 8 | 524 | 5 |
| 9 | 372 | 4 |
| *Yds* | 3,028 | |
| *Out* | | |
| *Total* | 3,028 | |

| | Yds | |
|---|---|---|
| Total | 35 | |
| Par | | |

ADDRESS: Leithen Water, Leithen Road, Innerleithen EH44 6NJ.
TELEPHONE: +44 (0)1896 830951.
VISITORS: Not necessary to book in advance.
GREEN FEES: £11 per round weekdays, £16 per day. £13 per round weekends, £19 per day.
FACILITIES: Putting green, practice ground.
CATERING: Bar open noon to 2.30 p.m. every weekday, usually offering light snacks. Special catering is available by arrangement.
LOCATION: A72 from Peebles (south) for 6 miles. At Innerleithen, left into Heriot Road. Golf course approximately ½ mile.
LOCAL HOTELS: Corner House Hotel, Traquair Arms Hotel.

# JEDBURGH

## JEDBURGH GOLF CLUB

### COURSE DESCRIPTION:
Undulating wooded parkland course, designed in 1889 by Willie Park. It has many natural and subtle hazards and, with small greens and tricky par 3s, provides a good test for golfers of all handicaps. No blind holes. Jedburgh propose a 9-hole extension in 2002.

9 holes, 5,555 yards (for 18 holes), par 68 (SSS 67). Amateur record 65. Pro record 63.

### SIGNATURE HOLE:
SEVENTH (417 yards, par 4) Longest hole on the course but it is downhill. Well protected by bunkers, a tee shot to the middle right will allow best access.

### COURSE CARD

| HOLE | YDS | PAR | HOLE | YDS | PAR |
|---|---|---|---|---|---|
| 1 | 302 | 4 | 10 | 302 | 4 |
| 2 | 314 | 4 | 11 | 314 | 4 |
| 3 | 381 | 4 | 12 | 381 | 4 |
| 4 | 197 | 3 | 13 | 197 | 3 |
| 5 | 184 | 3 | 14 | 184 | 3 |
| 6 | 337 | 4 | 15 | 337 | 4 |
| 7 | 417 | 4 | 16 | 417 | 4 |
| 8 | 320 | 4 | 17 | 320 | 4 |
| 9 | 309 | 4 | 18 | 342 | 4 |
| Yds | 2,761 | | Yds | 2,794 | |
| Out | | | In | | |

| | | | |
|---|---|---|---|
| *Total Yds* | 5,555 | | |
| *Total Par* | 68 | | |

**ADDRESS:** Dunion Road, Jedburgh TD8 6DQ.
**TELEPHONE:** +44 (0)1835 863587.
**SECRETARY:** G. McEwan.
**VISITORS:** Yes, weekdays before 5 p.m., weekends after 6 p.m.
**GREEN FEES:** £15 per round/day weekdays/weekends. Freedom of the Fairways (contact Scottish Tourist Board).
**CATERING:** Bar and catering facilities not full-time.
**FACILITIES:** Trolley hire, changing-rooms, putting green, memberships available.
**LOCATION:** 1 mile west of Jedburgh on B6358.
**LOCAL HOTELS:** Jedforest Hotel, Royal Hotel, The Roxburghe Hotel & Golf Course.

# KELSO

## KELSO GOLF CLUB

### COURSE DESCRIPTION:
Flat but testing parkland course within Kelso Racecourse. The Stank, a water hazard, crosses six holes.

18 holes, 6,046 yards, par 70 (SSS 70). Amateur record J. Thomas 64.

### SIGNATURE HOLE:
FIFTEENTH (176 yards, par 3 ) Tee shot to raised green protected by bunkers left and right and out of bounds behind the green.

### COURSE CARD

| HOLE | YDS | PAR | HOLE | YDS | PAR |
|---|---|---|---|---|---|
| 1 | 427 | 4 | 10 | 268 | 4 |
| 2 | 177 | 3 | 11 | 439 | 4 |
| 3 | 151 | 3 | 12 | 215 | 3 |
| 4 | 395 | 4 | 13 | 369 | 4 |
| 5 | 434 | 4 | 14 | 350 | 4 |
| 6 | 284 | 4 | 15 | 176 | 3 |
| 7 | 434 | 4 | 16 | 330 | 4 |
| 8 | 493 | 5 | 17 | 298 | 4 |
| 9 | 315 | 4 | 18 | 491 | 5 |
| *Yds Out* | 3,110 | | *Yds In* | 2,936 | |
| *Total Yds* | 6,046 | | | | |
| *Total* | 70 | | | | |

*Par*

ADDRESS: Golf Course Road, Kelso TD5 7SL.
TELEPHONE: +44 (0)1573 223009.
SECRETARY: J. Payne +44 (0)1573 223259.
VISITORS: Yes, by arrangement. Members only between 9 a.m. and 9.30 a.m.and
between 1 p.m. and 1.30 p.m.
GREEN FEES: £14 per round weekdays, £20 per day. £18 per round weekends, £27 per
day.
CATERING: Yes. Bar open 11 a.m. to 11 p.m.
FACILITIES: Trolley/buggy hire, putting green, practice ground.
LOCATION: 1 mile north-east of Kelso Square, off B6461.
LOCAL HOTELS: Cringletie House Hotel, Cross Keys Hotel, The Roxburghe Hotel &
Golf Course, King's Arms Hotel, Lauderdale Hotel.

## THE ROXBURGHE HOTEL & GOLF COURSE

COURSE DESCRIPTION:
Long, demanding championship course in mature woodland. Set in over 200 acres
of parkland surrounding the Roxburghe Hotel (formerly known as Sunlaws), a
Jacobean-style mansion built in 1853 which once played host to Bonnie Prince
Charlie. Hilly in parts with 80 bunkers and lakes on the 4th and 13th. Designed
by Dave Thomas to suit all standards of player and opened in 1997. Colin
Montgomerie said of it: 'The greens are immaculate and the picturesque course is
perfect to play for professionals and amateurs.'
18 holes, 7,111 yards, par 72 (SSS 75). Slope rating 140. Medal tees, 6,925
yards, par 72 (SSS 74). Slope rating 139.

SIGNATURE HOLE:
FOURTEENTH (571 yards, par 5) 'Viaduct' (above) runs alongside the River
Teviot. From an elevated tee you drive straight out towards the old Roxburghe
Viaduct.

COURSE CARD

| HOLE | MEDAL YDS | PAR | FORWARD YDS | PAR | LADIES YDS | PAR | HOLE | MEDAL YDS | PAR | FORWARD YDS | PAR | LADIES YDS | PAR |
|------|-----------|-----|-------------|-----|------------|-----|------|-----------|-----|-------------|-----|------------|-----|
| 1 | 421 | 4 | 385 | 4 | 347 | 4 | 10 | 469 | 4 | 439 | 4 | 338 | 4 |
| 2 | 396 | 4 | 373 | 4 | 316 | 4 | 11 | 526 | 5 | 504 | 5 | 408 | 5 |
| 3 | 364 | 4 | 352 | 4 | 318 | 4 | 12 | 399 | 4 | 385 | 4 | 323 | 4 |
| 4 | 188 | 3 | 177 | 3 | 158 | 3 | 13 | 216 | 3 | 183 | 3 | 164 | 3 |
| 5 | 546 | 5 | 537 | 5 | 489 | 5 | 14 | 523 | 5 | 511 | 5 | 475 | 5 |
| 6 | 382 | 4 | 360 | 4 | 336 | 4 | 15 | 177 | 3 | 159 | 3 | 134 | 3 |
| 7 | 520 | 5 | 486 | 5 | 467 | 5 | 16 | 394 | 4 | 385 | 4 | 352 | 4 |
| 8 | 181 | 3 | 171 | 3 | 148 | 3 | 17 | 398 | 4 | 355 | 4 | 329 | 4 |
| 9 | 403 | 4 | 384 | 4 | 287 | 4 | 18 | 422 | 4 | 400 | 4 | 292 | 4 |
| *Yds Out* | 3,401 | | 3,225 | | 2,845 | | *Yds In* | 3,524 | | 3,321 | | 2,815 | |

| | | |
|---|---|---|
| *Total* 6,925 *Yds* | 6,546 | 5,660 |
| *Total* 72 *Par* | 72 | 72 |

**ADDRESS:** Kelso, Roxburghshire TD5 8JZ.
**TELEPHONE:** +44 (0)1573 450331.
**FAX:** +44 (0)1573 450611.
**E-MAIL:** hotel@roxburghe.net
**WEBSITE:** www.roxburghe.net
**GENERAL MANAGER:** Stephen Browning.
**PROFESSIONAL:** Gordon Niven.
**VISITORS:** Yes. Official handicap certificates required (24 for men, 36 for ladies). Must pre-book. The owner, the Duke of Roxburghe, says: 'Once golfers have paid their green fee, they will be free to play from whichever set of tees they choose. I want them to enjoy themselves.'
**GREEN FEES:** £50 per round, £70 per day weekdays/weekends.
**CATERING:** Full catering. Bar.
**FACILITIES:** Trolley/buggy hire, changing-rooms, putting green, pro shop, practice ground, driving range.
**LOCATION:** From Kelso to Jedburgh. In village of Heiton, follow signs to course.
**LOCAL HOTELS:** Cringletie House Hotel, Cross Keys Hotel, The Roxburghe Hotel, Kings Arms Hotel, Lauderdale Hotel.

# LAUDER

## LAUDER GOLF CLUB

### COURSE DESCRIPTION:
Undulating moorland course on hillside. A fair test of golf with very good greens and stunning views of the Lauderdale Valley. Designed by Willie Park Jnr. Golf has been played here since 1896. Lauder are planning changes with the installation of a water feature, burn, waterfalls and pond, across the 1st fairway.

9 holes, 6,002 yards (for 18 holes), par 72 (SSS 69). Amateur record A. Lumsden 66. Pro record Willie Park Jnr 70.

### SIGNATURE HOLE:
SIXTH (150 yards, par 3) Called 'The Quarry', it is short but difficult. From the tee you cannot see the bottom of the flag and the ground slopes severely on all sides of a bowl-shaped undulating green, which demands careful reading.

### COURSE CARD

| HOLE | YDS | PAR |
|---|---|---|
| 1 | 374 | 4 |
| 2 | 353 | 4 |

| 3 | 252 | 4 |
| 4 | 351 | 4 |
| 5 | 405 | 4 |
| 6 | 150 | 3 |
| 7 | 482 | 5 |
| 8 | 368 | 4 |
| 9 | 266 | 4 |
| *Yds* *Out* | 3,001 | |
| *Total* *Yds* | 3,001 | |
| *Total* *Par* | 36 | |

ADDRESS: Galashiels Road, Lauder, Borders TD2 6RA.
TELEPHONE: +44 (0)1578 722240.
SECRETARY: Robert Towers.
VISITORS: Yes. Only restrictions are Wednesdays after 5 p.m and Sundays before noon.
GREEN FEES: £10 per round/day. Special offers: Freedom of the Fairways (contact Scottish Tourist Board).
CATERING: No. Local hotels.
FACILITIES: Changing-rooms, putting green, practice ground, memberships available.
LOCATION: From the A68, the road divides on either side of the Town Hall. Follow the signs to Galashiels. The golf course is signposted on the right about ½ mile from the town.
LOCAL HOTELS: Black Bull, Eagle Hotel, Lauderdale Hotel.

# MELROSE

## MELROSE GOLF CLUB

COURSE DESCRIPTION:
Set at foot of Eildon Hills. Undulating tree-lined fairways with splendid views and 11 tees. Founded 1880.
9 holes, 5,579 yards (for 18 holes), par 70 (SSS 68). Course record 61.

SIGNATURE HOLE:
FOURTH (343 yards, par 4) Dogleg left but the corner cannot be cut. Second to an elevated bunker-free green.

ADDRESS: Dingleton Road, Melrose TD6 9HS.
TELEPHONE: +44 (0)1896 822855, 822391.
VISITORS: Yes, but competitions have priority on all Saturdays and many Sundays (April to October). Ladies have priority on Tuesdays. Juniors have priority on

419

Wednesday mornings in the holidays.
**GREEN FEES:** £16 per round/day.
**CATERING:** Yes, by prior arrangement. Bar.
**FACILITIES:** Practice ground.
**LOCATION:** South side of town on B6359.
**LOCAL HOTELS:** Cringletie House Hotel, Cross Keys Hotel, Kings Arms Hotel, Lauderdale Hotel, The Roxburghe Hotel & Golf Course.

# MINTO

## MINTO GOLF CLUB

### COURSE DESCRIPTION:
Wooded parkland course with few sand bunkers. Not long but quite testing. Fine views.

18 holes, 5,453 yards, par 68 (SSS 67). Amateur record 63.

### SIGNATURE HOLE:
TWELFTH (267 yards, par 4) Short, steep uphill hole called 'Everest'. Drive through trees with an approach to a shelf green.

### COURSE CARD

| HOLE | YDS | PAR | HOLE | YDS | PAR |
|------|------|-----|------|-------|-----|
| 1 | 396 | 4 | 10 | 252 | 4 |
| 2 | 309 | 4 | 11 | 369 | 4 |
| 3 | 421 | 4 | 12 | 267 | 4 |
| 4 | 236 | 3 | 13 | 111 | 3 |
| 5 | 248 | 4 | 14 | 409 | 4 |
| 6 | 226 | 3 | 15 | 355 | 4 |
| 7 | 188 | 3 | 16 | 297 | 4 |
| 8 | 347 | 4 | 17 | 122 | 3 |
| 9 | 325 | 4 | 18 | 375 | 4 |
| *Yds Out* | 2,696 | | *Yds In* | 2,757 | |
| *Total Yds* | 5,453 | | | | |
| *Total Par* | 68 | | | | |

**ADDRESS:** Minto, Hawick TD9 8SH.
**TELEPHONE:** +44 (0)1450 870220.
**FAX:** +44 (0)1450 870126.
**SECRETARY:** I. Todd.
**VISITORS:** Very welcome. Phone for tee times.
**GREEN FEES:** £17 per round, £29 per day. £22 per round weekends. Discounts for

parties. Freedom of Fairways (contact Scottish Tourist Board).
CATERING: Full, except on Thursdays.
FACILITIES: Trolley/buggy hire, putting green, practice ground.
LOCATION: 5 miles north-east of Hawick. Leave A698 to Denholm.
LOCAL HOTELS: Cross Keys Hotel, Kings Arms Hotel, Lauderdale Hotel, Peebles Hotel Hydro, The Roxburghe Hotel & Golf Course.

# NEWCASTLETON

## NEWCASTLETON GOLF CLUB

COURSE DESCRIPTION:
Difficult moorland course on the side and on the top of Holm Hill. Not too great a strain on the legs. Small greens and slopes make putting interesting. Good views over Newcastleton.

9 holes, 5,483 yards (for 18 holes), par 69 (SSS 70).

SIGNATURE HOLE:
EIGHTEENTH (512 yards, par 5) Downhill dogleg left but trees make it difficult to cut the corner. Small green tucked away below a bank on the left.

### COURSE CARD

| HOLE | YDS | PAR | HOLE | YDS | PAR |
|------|-----|-----|------|-----|-----|
| 1 | 331 | 4 | 10 | 371 | 4 |
| 2 | 144 | 3 | 11 | 106 | 3 |
| 3 | 376 | 4 | 12 | 376 | 4 |
| 4 | 309 | 4 | 13 | 346 | 4 |
| 5 | 155 | 3 | 14 | 155 | 3 |
| 6 | 323 | 4 | 15 | 323 | 4 |
| 7 | 291 | 4 | 16 | 291 | 4 |
| 8 | 311 | 4 | 17 | 311 | 4 |
| 9 | 452 | 4 | 18 | 512 | 5 |
| Yds Out | 2,692 | | Yds In | 2,791 | |
| Total Yds | 5,483 | | | | |
| Total Par | 69 | | | | |

ADDRESS: Holm Hill, Newcastleton, Borders TD9 0QD.
TELEPHONE: +44 (0)1387 375257.
SECRETARY: F.J. Ewart.
VISITORS: Any time.
GREEN FEES: £10 per day.
CATERING: Meals available in hotels, 2 minutes from course.

FACILITIES: Changing-rooms, putting green, memberships available.
LOCATION: From Carlisle, M6 to junction 44, to A7 to Canonbie. 10 miles to
   Newcastleton.
LOCAL HOTELS: Grapes Hotel, Liddlesdale Hotel.

# PEEBLES

## PEEBLES GOLF CLUB

### COURSE DESCRIPTION:
Undulating parkland course – not totally flat, but the slopes are not unduly
demanding. Good-quality turf and greens. Founded in 1892. The present course
was first opened in 1908 and remodelled in 1933–34 by Harry Colt, who was also
responsible for Wentworth, Sunningdale and the Eden Course at St Andrews. The
original course on the south-west boundary of the town can still be seen, in
outline, for those interested in golfing history. Panoramic views.

   18 holes, 6,160 yards, par 70 (SSS 70). Course record 63.

### SIGNATURE HOLE:
SEVENTH ('Colts Choice' 135 yards, par 3) Named by the course architect,
Harry Colt.

### COURSE CARD

| HOLE | MEDAL YDS | PAR | FORWARD YDS | PAR | LADIES YDS | PAR | HOLE | MEDAL YDS | PAR | FORWARD YDS | PAR | LADIES YDS | PAR |
|------|-----------|-----|-------------|-----|------------|-----|------|-----------|-----|-------------|-----|------------|-----|
| 1 | 196 | 3 | 209 | 3 | 193 | 3 | 10 | 365 | 4 | 343 | 4 | 333 | 4 |
| 2 | 440 | 4 | 401 | 4 | 351 | 4 | 11 | 326 | 4 | 297 | 4 | 269 | 4 |
| 3 | 359 | 4 | 340 | 4 | 283 | 4 | 12 | 173 | 3 | 153 | 3 | 145 | 3 |
| 4 | 295 | 4 | 278 | 4 | 218 | 3 | 13 | 319 | 4 | 286 | 4 | 247 | 4 |
| 5 | 342 | 4 | 318 | 4 | 306 | 4 | 14 | 377 | 4 | 339 | 4 | 312 | 4 |
| 6 | 401 | 4 | 396 | 4 | 334 | 4 | 15 | 431 | 4 | 364 | 4 | 352 | 4 |
| 7 | 135 | 3 | 125 | 3 | 119 | 3 | 16 | 193 | 3 | 183 | 3 | 156 | 3 |
| 8 | 359 | 4 | 338 | 4 | 337 | 4 | 17 | 411 | 4 | 386 | 4 | 320 | 4 |
| 9 | 497 | 5 | 483 | 5 | 447 | 5 | 18 | 541 | 5 | 524 | 5 | 471 | 5 |
| Yds Out | 3,024 | | 2,888 | | 2,590 | | Yds In | 3,136 | | 2,875 | | 2,605 | |
| Total Yds | 6,160 | | 5,763 | | 5,195 | | | | | | | | |
| Total Par | 70 | | 70 | | 70 | | | | | | | | |

ADDRESS: Kirkland Street, Peebles EH45 8EU.
TELEPHONE: +44 (0)1721 720197.
E-MAIL: secretary@peeblesgolfclub.co.uk
WEBSITE: www.peeblesgolfclub.co.uk

SECRETARY: Hugh Gilmore.
PROFESSIONAL: Craig Imlach.
VISITORS: Yes, but check availability in advance.
GREEN FEES: £20 per round weekdays, £30 per day. £25 per round weekends, £35 per day. Discounts available for parties of 8 and 16.
CREDIT CARDS ACCEPTED: Visa/Mastercard.
CATERING: Restaurant and bar in a new clubhouse opened in 1998.
FACILITIES: Motorised buggies, trolley hire, changing-rooms, putting green, pro shop, practice ground, coaching clinics, memberships available.
LOCATION: North-west corner of the town, only 5 minutes' walk from the High Street.
LOCAL HOTELS: Cringletie House Hotel, Greentree Hotel, Kings Arms Hotel, Kingsmuir Hotel, Park Hotel, Peebles Hotel Hydro.

# SELKIRK

## SELKIRK GOLF CLUB

COURSE DESCRIPTION:
Set on the side of Selkirk Hill, undulating with heather and gorse-lined fairways and good greens. Offers a full range of shots. Exceptionally scenic. Founded in 1883 and designed by Willie Park.
 9 holes, 5,620 yards (for 18 holes), par 68 (SSS 67). Amateur record 60.

SIGNATURE HOLE:
EIGHTH (518 yards, par 5) Drive into narrow fairway flanked by heather slopes. Second shot sets up approach to the green, hidden behind grassy mounds. Dogleg to right.

ADDRESS: Selkirk Hill, Selkirk TD7 4NW
TELEPHONE: +44 (0)1750 20621.
SECRETARY: Alistair Wilson.
VISITORS: Yes, just turn up and play.
GREEN FEES: £16 per round/day weekdays/weekends.
CATERING: Book in advance. Bar open evenings and weekends in the summer.
FACILITIES: Trolley/buggy hire, putting green.
LOCATION: ½ mile south of Selkirk on A7.
LOCAL HOTELS: Heatherlie Hotel, Kings Arms Hotel, The Roxburghe Hotel & Golf Course, Woodburn Hotel.

# ST BOSWELLS

## ST BOSWELLS GOLF CLUB

### COURSE DESCRIPTION:

The course is situated close to village of St Boswells along the south bank of the River Tweed, which is renowned for its salmon fishing. On the opposite side of the river is Dryburgh Abbey, founded in 1150 and the burial place of Sir Walter Scott. The original course was laid out by Willie Park in 1899, who wrote: 'The turf is very good and resembles very much the turf to be found on seaside courses.' Unlike other Border courses, the terrain is flat and presents few difficulties other than the River Tweed, which is defined as a lateral water hazard.

9 holes, 5,274 yards (for 18 holes), par 68 (SSS 66).

### SIGNATURE HOLE:

SECOND (161 yards, par 3) A non-flat hole with a large green surrounded by bunkers and a drop into the 3rd fairway.

### COURSE CARD

| | MEDAL | | LADIES | |
|---|---|---|---|---|
| HOLE | YDS | PAR | YDS | PAR |
| 1 | 148 | 3 | 138 | 3 |
| 2 | 161 | 3 | 135 | 3 |
| 3 | 316 | 4 | 286 | 4 |
| 4 | 198 | 3 | 194 | 4 |
| 5 | 425 | 4 | 469 | 5 |
| 6 | 321 | 4 | 299 | 4 |
| 7 | 442 | 5 | 396 | 4 |
| 8 | 370 | 4 | 356 | 4 |
| 9 | 256 | 4 | 245 | 4 |
| *Yds Ou* | 2,637 | | | |
| *Total Yds* | 2,637 | | | |
| *Total Par* | 34 | | | |

ADDRESS: Braeheads, St Boswells, Melrose, Roxburghshire TD6 0DE.

TELEPHONE: +44 (0)1835 823527.

SECRETARY: J. Phillips.

VISITORS: Winner of the 'Most Visitor-Friendly 9-hole Course in the Scottish Borders' award in 1998. Weekdays 9 a.m. to 4 p.m.

GREEN FEES: £15 per round weekdays/weekends.

CATERING: Bar open at weekends and light refreshments are available or meals can be arranged if booked in advance.

LOCATION: Centre of the Borders, off A68.
LOCAL HOTELS: Buccleuch Arms, Cringletie House Hotel, Cross Keys Hotel, Kings Arms Hotel, Lauderdale Hotel, The Roxburghe Hotel & Golf Course.

# DUMFRIES & GALLOWAY
## INCLUDING DUMFRIES AND STRANRAER

# ANNAN

## POWFOOT GOLF CLUB

COURSE DESCRIPTION:
Compact seaside semi-links course on the Solway shore founded in 1903. Great views of hills of Cumbria and on a good day the Isle of Man. When the prevailing south-westerlies blow, it plays even longer. Designed by James Braid.
 18 holes, 6,255 yards, par 71 (SSS 71).

SIGNATURE HOLE:
SIXTEENTH (427 yards, par 4). Approach shot over a hill to a plateau green which falls away on all sides.

ADDRESS: Cummertrees, Annan DG12 5QE.
TELEPHONE & FAX: +44 (0)1461 700276.
PROFESSIONAL: Gareth Dick +44 ( 0)1461 700327.
VISITORS: Yes, weekends and between 2 and 4 p.m. on Saturdays and after 1 p.m. on Sundays.
GREEN FEES: £24 per round weekdays, £31 per day. £26 weekends.
CATERING: Yes. Bar.
FACILITIES: Trolley hire, putting green, pro shop, practice ground.
LOCATION: 15 miles south-east of Dumfries, off the B724.
LOCAL HOTELS: Cairndale Hotel.

# CASTLE DOUGLAS

## CASTLE DOUGLAS GOLF CLUB

COURSE DESCRIPTION:
Founded in 1905, an undulating parkland course with one very big hill.
 9 holes, 5,408 yards (for 18 holes), par 68 (SSS 66).

COURSE CARD

| HOLE | YDS | PAR |
| --- | --- | --- |
| 1 | 101 | 3 |
| 2 | 261 | 4 |
| 3 | 367 | 4 |
| 4 | 314 | 4 |
| 5 | 296 | 4 |
| 6 | 443 | 4 |

| 7 | 173 | 3 |
| 8 | 438 | 4 |
| 9 | 311 | 4 |
| Yds Out | 2,704 | |
| Total Yds | 2,704 | |
| Total Par | 34 | |

ADDRESS: Abercromby Road, Castle Douglas, DG7 1BB.
TELEPHONE: +44 (0)1556 502099.
SECRETARY: A. Millen.
VISITORS: Welcome.
GREEN FEES: £12 per day.
CATERING: During May to September. Bar meals available.
FACILITIES: Trolley hire, putting green, practice ground.
LOCATION: 400 yards from town centre on A713 to Ayr.
LOCAL HOTELS: Douglas Arms, Imperial Hotel, Kings Arms Hotel.

# COLVEND

## COLVEND GOLF CLUB

COURSE DESCRIPTION:
Extension to existing 9 holes opened in April 1997, making the course a challenging 18-hole scenic parkland course on the Solway coast with superb views over the Galloway Hills and the Solway Firth.

18 holes, 5,220 yards, par 68 (SSS 67).

SIGNATURE HOLE:
THIRTEENTH (183 yards, par 3) Downhill with the green between two trees. Ponds either side of the green.

COURSE CARD

| | MEDAL | | FORWARD | | LADIES | | | MEDAL | | FORWARD | | LADIES | |
|---|---|---|---|---|---|---|---|---|---|---|---|---|---|
| HOLE | YDS | PAR | YDS | PAR | YDS | PAR | HOLE | YDS | PAR | YDS | PAR | YDS | PAR |
| 1 | 258 | 4 | 241 | 4 | 253 | 4 | 10 | 253 | 4 | 221 | 4 | 214 | 4 |
| 2 | 118 | 3 | 109 | 3 | 119 | 3 | 11 | 371 | 4 | 282 | 4 | 282 | 4 |
| 3 | 360 | 4 | 340 | 4 | 307 | 4 | 12 | 431 | 4 | 393 | 4 | 383 | 5 |
| 4 | 171 | 3 | 160 | 3 | 117 | 3 | 13 | 183 | 3 | 122 | 3 | 166 | 3 |
| 5 | 318 | 4 | 290 | 4 | 299 | 4 | 14 | 413 | 4 | 391 | 4 | 384 | 4 |
| 6 | 335 | 4 | 328 | 4 | 335 | 4 | 15 | 513 | 5 | 500 | 5 | 434 | 5 |
| 7 | 365 | 4 | 318 | 4 | 328 | 4 | 16 | 139 | 3 | 104 | 3 | 110 | 3 |
| 8 | 192 | 3 | 173 | 3 | 163 | 3 | 17 | 226 | 4 | 188 | 4 | 214 | 4 |

| 9 | 300 | 4 | 293 | 4 | 285 | 4 | 18 | 274 | 4 | 263 | 4 | 257 | 4 |
|---|-----|---|-----|---|-----|---|----|-----|---|-----|---|-----|---|
| Yds Out | 2,417 | | 2,252 | | 2,222 | | Yds In | 2,803 | | 2,464 | | 2,454 | |
| Total Yds | 5,220 | | 4,716 | | 4,676 | | | | | | | | |
| Total Par | 68 | | 68 | | 69 | | | | | | | | |

ADDRESS: Sandyhills, Colvend, Dalbeattie, Kirkcudbrightshire, Dumfries & Galloway DG5 4PY.

TELEPHONE: +44 (0)1556 630398.

FAX: +44 (0)1556 630495.

SECRETARY: J.B. Henderson.

VISITORS: Any time.

GREEN FEES: £20 per day. £80 per week. Concession of £2 per head for parties of 10 or more.

CATERING: Restaurant and bar.

FACILITIES: Motorised buggies (£10), trolley hire (£2), changing-rooms, putting green, memberships available.

LOCATION: 6 miles from Dalbeattie on A710 Solway coast road from Dumfries.

LOCAL HOTELS: Baron's Craig Hotel, Cairngill Hotel, Clonyard Hotel, George Hotel, Pheasant Hotel.

# DUMFRIES

## CRICHTON GOLF CLUB

### COURSE DESCRIPTION:

Inland parkland course laid out on the side of a hill with many mature trees. From the first few holes there are magnificent views of Dumfries and the hills beyond. Across the road from the course is the Crichton Museum and Gardens.

9 holes, 5,952 yards (for 18 holes), par 70 (SSS 69). Amateur record W. Herd Jnr 64.

### SIGNATURE HOLE:

FIFTH (199 yards, par 3) out of bounds on the right. A sharp fall right to left provides for just one line to the green, which is surrounded by mature specimen trees.

### COURSE CARD

| HOLE | YDS | PAR |
|------|-----|-----|
| 1 | 350 | 4 |
| 2 | 380 | 4 |
| 3 | 339 | 4 |
| 4 | 323 | 4 |

| | | |
|---|---|---|
| 5 | 199 | 3 |
| 6 | 494 | 5 |
| 7 | 455 | 4 |
| 8 | 253 | 4 |
| 9 | 183 | 3 |
| *Yds* | | |
| *Out* | 2,976 | |
| *Total* | | |
| *Yds* | 2,976 | |
| *Total* | | |
| *Par* | 35 | |

ADDRESS: Bankend Road, Dumfries DG1 4TH.
TELEPHONE: +44 (0)1387 247894.
VISITORS: Yes, weekdays. Societies on application.
GREEN FEES: £12 per round.
CATERING: Bar and meals.
FACILITIES: Trolley hire, putting green, small shop, practice ground.
LOCATION: Dumfries, follow signs to hospital.
LOCAL HOTELS: George Hotel.

## DUMFRIES & COUNTY GOLF CLUB

COURSE DESCRIPTION:
Undulating parkland course alongside River Nith, where the great Scottish poet, Robbie Burns, was known to walk. Mature trees and double green at the 1st/6th. Founded in 1912 and designed by James Braid.
   18 holes, 5,928 yards, par 69 (SSS 69).

SIGNATURE HOLE:
FIFTH (374 yards, par 4) Called 'Spion Kop'. The river awaits a slice on the right. Second shot to the elevated green is hazardous.

ADDRESS: Nunfield, Edinburgh Road, Dumfries DG1 1JX.
TELEPHONE: +44 (0)1387 253585.
CLUBMASTER: +44 (0) 1387 249921.
PROFESSIONAL: Stuart Syme +44 (0)1387 268918.
VISITORS: Must contact in advance. May not play Saturdays.
GREEN FEES: £26 per round/day.
CATERING: Full services. Bar.
FACILITIES: Trolley hire, putting green, pro shop, practice ground.
LOCATION: 1 mile north-east off A701.
LOCAL HOTELS: Balmoral Hotel, Cairndale Hotel, Edenbank Hotel, George Hotel, Station Hotel.

## DUMFRIES & GALLOWAY GOLF CLUB

COURSE DESCRIPTION:
Challenging parkland course set in rolling countryside on the outskirts of Dumfries. Greens and fairways are kept in immaculate condition. The long 5th and 13th are very challenging holes, as is the short 12th with out of bounds on the right.

18 holes, 6,309 yards, par 70 (SSS 71).

ADDRESS: 2 Laurieston Avenue, Dumfries DG2 7NY.
TELEPHONE & FAX: +44 (0)1387 263848.
SECRETARY: T.M. Ross.
PROFESSIONAL: Joe Fergusson +44 (0)1387 256902.
VISITORS: Yes. Mondays, Wednesdays, Thursdays, Fridays and Sundays.
GREEN FEES: £26 per round/day weekdays, £32 weekends.
CATERING: Bar and meals.
FACILITIES: Trolley hire, club hire, changing-rooms, putting green, pro shop, practice ground, coaching clinics, memberships available.
LOCATION: West of town centre on A75.
LOCAL HOTELS: Balmoral Hotel, Cairndale Hotel, Edenbank Hotel, George Hotel, Station Hotel.

## THE PINES GOLF CENTRE

COURSE DESCRIPTION:
Built on a mixture of undulating grazing land, parkland and heathland on a 100-acre site with some significant water features, this is a fairly tight course and a challenge to golfers of all abilities. Many dogleg holes and interestingly positioned greens, which are kept in excellent condition. Easy walking course with only one major hill on one hole. Holes worth singling out are the 2nd (see below) and the 16th, a par 3 of 149 yards to a green with water on three sides and out of bounds on the right. Some 12,000 trees have been planted on a course completed in 1998.

18 holes, 5,920 yards, par 69 (SSS 69). Amateur record 71.

SIGNATURE HOLE:
SECOND ('Burnt Firs' 376 yards, par 4) A sharp dogleg to the right with out of bounds and trees on the right and out of bounds on the left. There's a carry of 200 yards to the corner, then an approach shot over a small rise to a green set in a glade of trees.

ADDRESS: Lockerbie Road, Dumfries DG13 PF.
TELEPHONE: +44 (0)1387 247444.
FAX: +44 (0)1387 249600.
E-MAIL: admin@pinesgolf.com
WEBSITE: www.btinternet.com/~pines
SECRETARY/MANAGER: Duncan Gray.
PROFESSIONAL: Brian Gemmell, James Davidson.

VISITORS: Yes, any time.
GREEN FEES: £14 per round weekdays/weekends, £18 per day. Weekly ticket £60. Visiting parties of more than 12, £12 per head.
CATERING: Restaurant (all home cooking and baking) and bar.
FACILITIES: Motorised buggies (£12), trolley hire (£2), club hire (£6), changing-rooms, putting green, extensive practice facilities and practice ground, 20-bay floodlit driving range, coaching clinics, memberships available.
LOCATION: Off A75 Dumfries bypass onto the A709 Lockerbie Road: 70 metres on left is the entrance.

# ECCLEFECHAN

## HODDOM CASTLE GOLF CLUB

COURSE DESCRIPTION:
Parkland holiday course surrounded by mature trees and bounded on one side by the River Annan. Short and testing, but an ideal course for beginners.
9 holes, 4,548 yards (for 18 holes), par 66 (SSS 66).

SIGNATURE HOLE:
FIFTH (301 yards, par 4). Dogleg left with the River Annan running the full length of the hole on the right. Green is guarded by mature hardwoods.

ADDRESS: Hoddom and Kinmount Estates, Hoddom Bridge, Ecclefechan, Dumfries & Galloway, DG11 1AS
TELEPHONE: +44 (0)1576 300251 or 300244.
VISITORS: Any time. No booking necessary.
GREEN FEES: £8 per round weekdays, £10 per round weekends.
CATERING: Restricted.
LOCATION: 2 miles south-west of Ecclefechan on B725.
LOCAL HOTELS: George Hotel.

# GATEHOUSE OF FLEET

## CALLY PALACE HOTEL GOLF COURSE

COURSE DESCRIPTION:
Designed by Tom Macaulay and opened in 1994, this challenging parkland course is for the exclusive use of hotel guests. Sculpted into the natural contours of the land, it features magnificent trees, hidden burns and Cally Lake. There are wonderful views of Cardoness Castle, Rutherford's Monument and the Fleet Estuary.
18 holes, 5,802 yards, par 70.

SIGNATURE HOLE:
FIFTEENTH ('Macaulay's Best' 504 yards, par 5) Tough long hole regarded as the
most difficult on the course.

## COURSE CARD

| HOLE | YDS | PAR | HOLE | YDS | PAR |
|------|-----|-----|------|-----|-----|
| 1 | 287 | 4 | 10 | 361 | 4 |
| 2 | 165 | 3 | 11 | 339 | 4 |
| 3 | 381 | 4 | 12 | 172 | 3 |
| 4 | 335 | 4 | 13 | 401 | 4 |
| 5 | 378 | 4 | 14 | 266 | 4 |
| 6 | 128 | 3 | 15 | 504 | 5 |
| 7 | 332 | 4 | 16 | 345 | 4 |
| 8 | 579 | 5 | 17 | 221 | 3 |
| 9 | 337 | 4 | 18 | 271 | 4 |
| *Yds Out* | 2,922 | | *Yds In* | 2,880 | |
| *Total Yds* | 5,802 | | | | |
| *Total Par* | 70 | | | | |

ADDRESS: Gatehouse of Fleet, Dumfries & Galloway DG7 2DL.
TELEPHONE: +44 (0)1557 814341.
FAX: +44 (0)1557 814522.
E-MAIL: enquiries@callypalace.co.uk
WEBSITE: www.callypalace.co.uk
VISITORS: Special golfing breaks.
FACILITIES: Motorised buggies, practice area, putting green.
LOCAL HOTELS: Anwoth Hotel, Cally Palace Hotel, Masonic Arms Hotel, Murray
    Arms Hotel.

# GATEHOUSE OF FLEET GOLF CLUB

COURSE DESCRIPTION:
Undulating course in excellent condition all year round. Winter greens are not
used, as the course drains very well. In an idyllic location with stunning views
inland to the Galloway Hills and out to sea to Wigtown Bay and the Isle of Man.
Recent improvements have included new tees for visitors. Green fees are excellent
value.
    9 holes, 5,042 yards (for 18 holes), par 66 (SSS 66).

SIGNATURE HOLE:
NINTH (165 yards, par 3) An extremely intimidating finishing hole which drops
almost 100 feet from tee to green. out of bounds to the left of the green, rough to
the right and bunkers below the green.

## COURSE CARD

| HOLE | MEDAL YDS | PAR | FORWARD YDS | PAR | LADIES YDS | PAR | HOLE | MEDAL YDS | PAR | FORWARD YDS | PAR | LADIES YDS | PAR |
|------|-----------|-----|-------------|-----|------------|-----|------|-----------|-----|-------------|-----|------------|-----|
| 1 | 211 | 3 | 206 | 3 | 198 | 4 | 10 | 211 | 3 | 206 | 3 | 198 | 4 |
| 2 | 354 | 4 | 338 | 4 | 345 | 4 | 11 | 354 | 4 | 338 | 4 | 345 | 4 |
| 3 | 320 | 4 | 288 | 4 | 230 | 4 | 12 | 320 | 4 | 288 | 4 | 230 | 4 |
| 4 | 322 | 4 | 316 | 4 | 313 | 4 | 13 | 322 | 4 | 316 | 4 | 313 | 4 |
| 5 | 131 | 3 | 120 | 3 | 116 | 3 | 14 | 131 | 3 | 120 | 3 | 116 | 3 |
| 6 | 549 | 5 | 532 | 5 | 546 | 5 | 15 | 549 | 5 | 532 | 5 | 546 | 5 |
| 7 | 280 | 4 | 272 | 4 | 267 | 4 | 16 | 280 | 4 | 272 | 4 | 267 | 4 |
| 8 | 189 | 3 | 186 | 3 | 183 | 3 | 17 | 189 | 3 | 186 | 3 | 183 | 3 |
| 9 | 165 | 3 | 160 | 3 | 158 | 3 | 18 | 165 | 3 | 160 | 3 | 158 | 3 |
| Yds Out | 2,521 | | 2,418 | | 2,356 | | Yds In | 2,521 | | 2,418 | | 2,356 | |
| Total Yds | 5,042 | | 4,836 | | 4,712 | | | | | | | | |
| Total Par | 66 | | 66 | | 68 | | | | | | | | |

ADDRESS: Gatehouse of Fleet, Dumfries & Galloway. Postal address: c/o 'Innisfree', Laurieston, Castle Douglas, Kirkcudbrightshire DG7 2PW.
TELEPHONE & FAX: +44 (0)1644 450260.
SECRETARY: Keith Cooper.
VISITORS: All year round, except Sunday mornings.
GREEN FEES: £10 per round/day. Weekly tickets £40.
CATERING: Several local hotels fulfil needs of golfers.
FACILITIES: Changing-rooms, putting green, memberships available (£85 per annum).
LOCATION: From A75 Dumfries–Stranraer trunk road, go into Gatehouse. At western end of Main Street (near Murray Arms/Tower), follow road to Laurieston. The course is a short distance up this road on the right.
LOCAL HOTELS: Anwoth Hotel, Cally Palace Hotel, Masonic Arms Hotel, Murray Arms Hotel.

# GRETNA

## GRETNA GOLF CLUB

### COURSE DESCRIPTION:
Parkland and not too hilly, a real test for enthusiastic and social golfer alike. Two par 5s. Extensive views over the Solway Firth and the Cumberland Hills.
9 holes, 6,430 yards (for 18 holes), par 72 (SSS 71). Course record 71.

### SIGNATURE HOLE:
FIRST (174 yards, par 3) Appears to be a nice gentle start, but do not be fooled.

COURSE CARD

| HOLE | YDS | PAR |
|------|-----|-----|
| 1 | 174 | 3 |
| 2 | 387 | 4 |
| 3 | 370 | 4 |
| 4 | 484 | 5 |
| 5 | 418 | 4 |
| 6 | 351 | 4 |
| 7 | 514 | 5 |
| 8 | 324 | 4 |
| 9 | 193 | 3 |
| *Yds Out* | 3,215 | |
| *Total Yds* | 3,215 | |
| *Total Par* | 36 | |

**ADDRESS:** Kirtleview, Gretna, Dumfries & Galloway, DG16 5HD.
**TELEPHONE:** +44 (0)1461 338464
**VISITORS:** Yes. Societies by prior arrangement.
**GREEN FEES:** £5 per 9 holes. £8 per day weekdays, £10 per day weekends.
**CATERING:** For parties, by prior arrangement.
**FACILITIES:** Trolley hire, driving range.
**LOCATION:** ½ mile west of Gretna. Well signposted from M74 and A75.
**LOCAL HOTELS:** Solway Lodge Hotel.

# KIRKCUDBRIGHT

## KIRKCUDBRIGHT GOLF CLUB

### COURSE DESCRIPTION:
Quite hilly parkland course with lovely views over the historic town of Kirkcudbright and the Dee estuary. Hard walking. Founded in 1893.
18 holes, 5,696 yards, par 68 (SSS 68). Amateur record 63.

### SIGNATURE HOLE:
TWELFTH (455 yards, par 5) Dogleg. Drive from elevated tee over a burn to a landing area guarded by three bunkers. Elevated green with vicious gorse behind.

COURSE CARD

| HOLE | YDS | PAR | HOLE | YDS | PAR |
|------|-----|-----|------|-----|-----|
| 1 | 331 | 4 | 10 | 342 | 4 |
| 2 | 390 | 4 | 11 | 334 | 4 |
| 3 | 295 | 4 | 12 | 455 | 5 |

| | | | | | |
|---|---|---|---|---|---|
| 4 | 143 | 3 | 13 | 190 | 3 |
| 5 | 427 | 4 | 14 | 326 | 4 |
| 6 | 134 | 3 | 15 | 263 | 4 |
| 7 | 385 | 4 | 16 | 179 | 3 |
| 8 | 487 | 5 | 17 | 405 | 4 |
| 9 | 206 | 3 | 18 | 404 | 4 |
| *Yds* *Out* | 2,798 | | *Yds* *In* | 2,898 | |
| *Total* *Yds* | 5,696 | | | | |
| *Total* *Par* | 68 | | | | |

ADDRESS: Stirling Crescent, Kirkcudbright DG6 4EZ.
TELEPHONE: +44 (0)1557 330314.
SECRETARY: Norman Russell.
VISITORS: Any time. Wednesday is gent's day.
GREEN FEES: £18 per round. £26 per day.
CATERING: Yes.
FACILITIES: Trolley hire, putting green.
LOCATION: Enter town from A75 on A713. Take fourth road on the left and course is straight ahead.
LOCAL HOTELS: Commercial Hotel, Royal Hotel.

# LANGHOLM

## LANGHOLM GOLF CLUB

COURSE DESCRIPTION:
Pleasant hillside course with commanding spectacular views over the rolling Border hills and south towards the Lake District. Rough is kept to a minimum with well-defined fairways and mature trees, as you would expect on a course founded in 1892.

9 holes, 6,180 yards (for 18 holes), par 70 (SSS 72). Amateur record 65.

SIGNATURE HOLE:
SEVENTH (334 yards, par 4) Tight drive with out of bounds on the left and trees on the right. Second shot needs touch of a draw if you are to hit and stop on the green, which is cut off by a large ravine.

COURSE CARD

| HOLE | MEDAL YDS | PAR | FORWARD YDS | PAR | YDS | LADIES PAR |
|---|---|---|---|---|---|---|
| 1 | 368 | 4 | 350 | 4 | 322 | 4 |
| 2 | 418 | 4 | 400 | 4 | 374 | 4 |

| 3 | 511 | 5 | 500 | 5 | 448 | 5 |
|---|-----|---|-----|---|-----|---|
| 4 | 172 | 3 | 156 | 3 | 156 | 3 |
| 5 | 333 | 4 | 300 | 4 | 323 | 4 |
| 6 | 412 | 4 | 410 | 4 | 311 | 4 |
| 7 | 334 | 4 | 310 | 4 | 238 | 4 |
| 8 | 391 | 4 | 380 | 4 | 317 | 4 |
| 9 | 151 | 3 | 130 | 3 | 106 | 3 |
| *Yds* Out | 3,090 | | 2,936 | | 2,595 | |
| *Total* *Yds* | 3,090 | | | | | |
| *Total* *Par* | 35 | | | | | |

ADDRESS: Whitaside, Langholm, Dumfries & Galloway, DG13 0JR.
TELEPHONE: +44 (0)1387 381247.
SECRETARY: +44 (0)1387 380673.
WEBSITE: www.langholmgolfclub.co.uk
E-MAIL: golf@langholmgolfclub.co.uk
SECRETARY: W. Wilson.
VISITORS: Always welcome at any time, but avoid Saturday afternoons. Course is open all year round and members will do their best to accommodate visitors.
GREEN FEES: £10 per round/day. Weekly ticket £30. 1st year half-price season ticket £42.50.
CATERING: Bar in recently refurbished clubhouse, meals by prior arrangement only.
FACILITIES: Changing-rooms, putting green, practice ground, memberships available.
LOCATION: Turn off Edinburgh–Carlisle road (A7) in Langholm at Post Office and follow signposts ¼ mile to the course
LOCAL HOTELS: Buck Hotel, Crown Hotel, Eskdale Hotel.

# LOCHMABEN

## LOCHMABEN GOLF CLUB

COURSE DESCRIPTION:
Attractive James Braid-designed parkland course occupying an historic area around Kirk Loch. Close by the second green is the site of a Bruce castle and when playing the third you can see the huge defensive ditch which helped protect the edifice. Excellent views.

18 holes, 5,377 yards, par 67 (SSS 66). Amateur record 62. Pro record 64.

SIGNATURE HOLE:
EIGHTH (120 yards, par 3) Tee shot across a corner of Kirk Loch demands an accurate short iron.

## COURSE CARD

| HOLE | YDS | PAR | HOLE | YDS | PAR |
|------|-----|-----|------|-----|-----|
| 1 | 314 | 4 | 10 | 143 | 3 |
| 2 | 188 | 3 | 11 | 425 | 4 |
| 3 | 190 | 3 | 12 | 522 | 5 |
| 4 | 311 | 4 | 13 | 445 | 4 |
| 5 | 359 | 4 | 14 | 343 | 4 |
| 6 | 404 | 4 | 15 | 141 | 3 |
| 7 | 291 | 4 | 16 | 426 | 4 |
| 8 | 120 | 3 | 17 | 328 | 4 |
| 9 | 295 | 4 | 18 | 132 | 3 |
| *Yds Out* | 2,472 | | *Yds In* | 2,905 | |
| *Total Yds* | 5,377 | | | | |
| *Total Par* | 67 | | | | |

ADDRESS: Castlehill Gate, Lochmaben, Lockerbie DG11 1NT.
TELEPHONE: +44 (0)1387 810552.
SECRETARY: J. Dickie +44 (0)1387 810713.
VISITORS: Weekdays unrestricted before 5 p.m. Weekends by arrangement.
GREEN FEES: £14 per round weekdays, £18 per day. £16 per round weekends, £22 per day.
CATERING: Yes. Bar.
FACILITIES: Putting green, practice ground.
LOCATION: 4 miles from Lockerbie, off A709.
LOCAL HOTELS: Balcastle Hotel, George Hotel, Queens Hotel, Somerton House Hotel.

# LOCKERBIE

## LOCKERBIE GOLF CLUB

COURSE DESCRIPTION:
Parkland course, upgraded from nine to eighteen holes in 1988, with fine views. Two or three water hazards and only pond hole in Dumfries & Galloway make it reasonably challenging.

18 holes, 5,614 yards, par 68 (SSS 67). Course record 64.

ADDRESS: Corrie Road, Lockerbie DG11 2ND.
TELEPHONE: +44 (0)1576 202462 or 203363.
SECRETARY: Jim Thomson.
VISITORS: Restricted Sundays. Contact in advance.
GREEN FEES: £18 per day weekdays. £22 per day Saturdays. £18 per round Sundays.
CATERING: Full facilities available April to October in modern clubhouse. Bar.

FACILITIES: Trolley hire, putting green, practice ground.
LOCATION: 12 miles east of Dumfries, off B7068.
LOCAL HOTELS: George Hotel, Kings Hotel, Queens Hotel, Ravenshill Hotel.

# MOFFAT

## THE MOFFAT GOLF CLUB

### COURSE DESCRIPTION:
Scenic moorland course, which is a great challenge for golfers of all abilities. Has some testing holes which become all the harder when the wind blows. Established in 1884 and designed by Ben Sayers. Set high in the Annandale Hills, it overlooks the town.

18 holes, 5,263 yards, par 69 (SSS 67). Amateur record 60.

### SIGNATURE HOLE:
NINTH (125 yards, par 3) Not the best but certainly the best-known hole on the course. Hitting over a towering rock face to an elevated green will remain in your memory for a long time.

### COURSE CARD

| HOLE | YDS | PAR | HOLE | YDS | PAR |
|------|-----|-----|------|-----|-----|
| 1 | 203 | 3 | 10 | 342 | 4 |
| 2 | 331 | 4 | 11 | 381 | 4 |
| 3 | 346 | 4 | 12 | 251 | 4 |
| 4 | 292 | 4 | 13 | 141 | 3 |
| 5 | 291 | 4 | 14 | 505 | 5 |
| 6 | 267 | 4 | 15 | 364 | 4 |
| 7 | 334 | 4 | 16 | 144 | 3 |
| 8 | 390 | 4 | 17 | 285 | 4 |
| 9 | 125 | 3 | 18 | 271 | 4 |
| *Yds* *Out* | 2,579 | | *Yds* *In* | 2,684 | |
| *Total* *Yds* | 5,263 | | | | |
| *Total* *Par* | 69 | | | | |

ADDRESS: Coatshill, Moffat DG10 9SB.
TELEPHONE: +44 (0)1683 220020.
SECRETARY: J. W. Mein
VISITORS: Any time, except Wednesdays after 3 p.m.
GREEN FEES: £18.50 per round weekdays, £20 per day. £28.50 per day weekends.
CATERING: Meals Monday to Friday 11 a.m. to 2.30 p.m. and 6 p.m. to 9 p.m.
Wednesdays 6 p.m. to 9 p.m. Weekends 11 a.m. to 8 p.m.

FACILITIES: Trolley hire, putting green, shop, club hire.

LOCATION: Leave A74 at Beattock. A701 to Moffat for a mile.

LOCAL HOTELS: Annandale Arms, Balmoral Hotel, Beechwood Country Hotel, George Hotel.

# MONREITH

## ST MEDAN GOLF CLUB

### COURSE DESCRIPTION:

Very tricky links course in Monreith Bay. Fairly fast greens. Founded in 1905. Magnificent views of Luce Bay, Scares Rocks bird sanctuaries, Mull of Galloway and the Isle of Man.

9 holes, 4,554 yards (for 18 holes), par 64 ( SSS 63). Course record 61.

Signature hole:

FOURTH (274 yards, par 4) Tee shot from an elevated tee towards the sea.

### COURSE CARD

| HOLE | MEDAL YDS | PAR | FORWARD YDS | PAR | LADIES YDS | PAR |
|------|-----------|-----|-------------|-----|------------|-----|
| 1 | 220 | 3 | 210 | 3 | 220 | 3 |
| 2 | 270 | 4 | 270 | 4 | 207 | 4 |
| 3 | 205 | 3 | 207 | 3 | 207 | 4 |
| 4 | 274 | 4 | 235 | 4 | 234 | 3 |
| 5 | 276 | 4 | 270 | 4 | 276 | 4 |
| 6 | 340 | 4 | 310 | 4 | 298 | 4 |
| 7 | 273 | 4 | 270 | 4 | 273 | 4 |
| 8 | 233 | 3 | 230 | 3 | 210 | 4 |
| 9 | 186 | 3 | 104 | 3 | 108 | 3 |
| Yds Out | 2,277 | | 2,105 | | 2,025 | |
| Total Yds | 2,277 | | | | | |
| Total Par | 32 | | | | | |

ADDRESS: Monreith, by Port William, Newton Stewart, Wigtownshire DG8 8NJ.

TELEPHONE: +44 (0)1988 700358.

SECRETARY: Peter Mellor.

VISITORS: Yes, when no competitions on.

GREEN FEES: £12 per round, £15 per day.

CATERING: Bar and meals. Clubhouse closed over the winter months. Limited opening for the rest of the year.

**FACILITIES:** Club hire, changing-rooms, putting green, memberships available.
**LOCATION:** 3 miles south of Port William, off the A747.

# NEW GALLOWAY

## NEW GALLOWAY GOLF CLUB

### COURSE DESCRIPTION:
Mixed woodland and moorland course founded in 1902 with excellent tees and first-class greens and no bunkers but many whins and gorse bushes. Some steep inclines. The 1st and 2nd fairways lead up to magnificent views over Loch Ken. All forms of wildlife abound.

9 holes, 5,006 yards (for 18 holes), par 68 ( SSS 67). Course record 63.

### SIGNATURE HOLE:
EIGHTH ('Lang Knowe' 367 yards, par 4) The hardest hole. Proceed from an elevated tee across a rocky bank to a fairway that slopes up and to the right, reducing the run of the ball and taking a sliced ball towards the rough and whins. Then a medium iron to a slightly elevated green.

### COURSE CARD

| HOLE | MEDAL YDS | PAR | FORWARD YDS | PAR | LADIES YDS | PAR |
|------|-----------|-----|-------------|-----|------------|-----|
| 1 | 302 | 4 | 199 | 3 | 216 | 4 |
| 2 | 252 | 4 | 242 | 4 | 252 | 4 |
| 3 | 358 | 4 | 292 | 4 | 292 | 4 |
| 4 | 133 | 3 | 117 | 3 | 120 | 3 |
| 5 | 377 | 4 | 373 | 4 | 325 | 4 |
| 6 | 256 | 4 | 256 | 4 | 256 | 4 |
| 7 | 121 | 3 | 106 | 3 | 106 | 3 |
| 8 | 367 | 4 | 348 | 4 | 367 | 5 |
| 9 | 337 | 4 | 337 | 4 | 337 | 4 |
| *Yds Out* | 2,503 | | 2,270 | | 2,271 | |
| *Total Yds* | 2,503 | | | | | |
| *Total Par* | 34 | | | | | |

**ADDRESS:** High Street, New Galloway, Castle Douglas, Kirkcudbrightshire, DG7 3RN.
**TELEPHONE:** +44 (0)1644 420737.
**E-MAIL:** webmaster@nggc.co.uk
**WEBSITE:** www.nggc.co.uk
**VISITORS:** Very welcome. Just turn up and play. Leave your money in the honesty box.

Sundays before 11 a.m or after 3.30 p.m. and not after 5 p.m. on Fridays.
**GREEN FEES:** £12.50 per day. £50 per week.
**CATERING:** Refreshments by arrangement.
**FACILITIES:** Changing-rooms, putting green, practice ground, memberships available.
**LOCATION:** South side of town on A762.
**LOCAL HOTELS:** Kenmure Arms, Cross Keys Hotel.

# NEWTON STEWART

## NEWTON STEWART GOLF CLUB

**COURSE DESCRIPTION:**
Parkland course with mature trees and excellent drainage so playable all year.
Basically on two levels with spectacular views of Galloway Hills and Solway Firth.
Its varying lay-outs have existed since 1896. Each hole is individual, with five par
3s a challenging feature. Greens have excellent surfaces with hidden borrows.

18 holes, 5,903 yards, par 69 (SSS 70). Amateur record 65.

**SIGNATURE HOLE:**
TENTH ('Gushet' 168 yards, par 3) Played from plateau tee to a bowl-shaped
green set in a slope above a burn in a small ravine.

**COURSE CARD**

| HOLE | YDS | PAR | HOLE | YDS | PAR |
|------|------|-----|------|------|-----|
| 1 | 346 | 4 | 10 | 168 | 3 |
| 2 | 360 | 4 | 11 | 520 | 5 |
| 3 | 177 | 3 | 12 | 197 | 3 |
| 4 | 371 | 4 | 13 | 523 | 5 |
| 5 | 426 | 4 | 14 | 405 | 4 |
| 6 | 175 | 3 | 15 | 328 | 4 |
| 7 | 353 | 4 | 16 | 345 | 4 |
| 8 | 383 | 4 | 17 | 164 | 3 |
| 9 | 337 | 4 | 18 | 325 | 4 |
| *Yds* *Out* | 2,928 | | *Yds* *In* | 2,975 | |
| *Total Yds* | 5,903 | | | | |
| *Total Par* | 69 | | | | |

**ADDRESS:** Kirroughtree Avenue, Minnigaff, Newton Stewart, Dumfries & Galloway
DG8 6PF.
**TELEPHONE & FAX:** +44 (0)1671 402172.
**E-MAIL:** enquiries@newtonstewartgolfclub.co.uk
**WEBSITE:** www.newtonstewartgolfclub.co.uk

SECRETARY: Michael Large.

VISITORS: Any time but prior booking advisable at weekends.

GREEN FEES: £20 per round weekdays, £23 per day. £23 per round weekends, £27 per day. Weekly ticket £100.

CATERING: Restaurant and bar. Functions catered for. Clubhouse open all year.

FACILITIES: Motorised buggies (£16), trolley hire (£2), club hire (£5), changing-rooms, putting green, practice ground, memberships available (entry £20, annual £165, country £100, associate £105).

LOCATION: Off A75 (Carlisle–Stranraer road)in Minnigaff village – signposted.

LOCAL HOTELS: Bruce Hotel, Creebridge House Hotel, Crown Hotel, Galloway Arms Hotel, Glencairn Hotel, Kirroughtree Hotel.

# WIGTOWNSHIRE COUNTY GOLF CLUB

## COURSE DESCRIPTION:

A links course (claimed to be the only true links in the south-west region) situated on the shores of the scenic Luce Bay with the Isle of Man visible on a clear day. Subtly sloping greens and changing sea breezes provide a test both for the high and low handicappers.

18 holes, 5,843 yards, par 70 (SSS 68). Course record 67.

## SIGNATURE HOLE:

TWELFTH ('Cunningham's best' 392 yards, par 4) Named after designer Gordon Cunningham, the former Scottish professional champion. Scenic dogleg right with out of bounds to the right and deep rough on the left. The second shot of approximately 160 yards is usually into the prevailing wind.

## COURSE CARD

| HOLE | MEDAL YDS | PAR | FORWARD YDS | PAR | LADIES YDS | PAR | HOLE | MEDAL YDS | PAR | FORWARD YDS | PAR | LADIES YDS | PAR |
|---|---|---|---|---|---|---|---|---|---|---|---|---|---|
| 1 | 332 | 4 | 324 | 4 | 324 | 4 | 10 | 332 | 4 | 326 | 4 | 273 | 4 |
| 2 | 350 | 4 | 294 | 4 | 294 | 4 | 11 | 294 | 4 | 283 | 4 | 277 | 4 |
| 3 | 402 | 4 | 358 | 4 | 358 | 4 | 12 | 392 | 4 | 368 | 4 | 363 | 4 |
| 4 | 301 | 4 | 284 | 4 | 284 | 4 | 13 | 152 | 3 | 141 | 3 | 134 | 3 |
| 5 | 162 | 3 | 154 | 3 | 152 | 3 | 14 | 341 | 4 | 319 | 4 | 313 | 4 |
| 6 | 491 | 5 | 481 | 5 | 401 | 5 | 15 | 372 | 4 | 362 | 4 | 352 | 4 |
| 7 | 363 | 4 | 349 | 4 | 342 | 4 | 16 | 325 | 4 | 317 | 4 | 308 | 4 |
| 8 | 300 | 4 | 294 | 4 | 289 | 4 | 17 | 196 | 3 | 187 | 3 | 182 | 3 |
| 9 | 341 | 4 | 330 | 4 | 281 | 4 | 18 | 397 | 4 | 397 | 4 | 343 | 4 |
| Yds Out | 3,042 | | 2,868 | | 2,725 | | Yds In | 2,801 | | 2,700 | | 2,545 | |
| Total Yds | 5,843 | | 5,568 | | 5,270 | | | | | | | | |
| Total Par | 70 | | 70 | | 70 | | | | | | | | |

ADDRESS: Mains of Park, Glenluce, Newton Stewart DG8 0NN.

TELEPHONE: +44 (0)1581 300420.
E-MAIL: wgc@glenluce.org.uk
WEBSITE: www.glenluce.org.uk/countygolfclub.htm
VISITORS: Yes, unrestricted except for competition and members' times.
GREEN FEES: £19 per round weekdays, £25 per day. £21 per round weekends, £27 per day. Seven-day weekly tickets £70 (juniors half price).
CATERING: Restaurant and bar. Parties should book in advance.
FACILITIES: Motorised buggies (£15), trolley hire (£1.50), club hire (£5), changing-rooms, putting green, pro shop (steward supplies equipment), practice ground, memberships available.
LOCATION: 8 miles east of Stranraer, off A75 Euroroute on the shores of Luce Bay.
LOCAL HOTELS: Glenbay Hotel, Glenluce Hotel, Kelvin Hotel, North West Castle Hotel.

# PORTPATRICK

## LAGGANMORE GOLF CLUB

COURSE DESCRIPTION:
Interesting parkland/heathland course lay-out with some testing holes. New course laid out on agricultural land. The 10th is a 608-yard, par 5.
  18 holes, 5,698 yards, par 69 (SSS 69).

SIGNATURE HOLE:
SEVENTH (476 yards, par 5) Blind water hazard causes many a problem.

ADDRESS: Lagganmore Farm, Portpatrick, Wigtownshire.
TELEPHONE: +44 (0)1776 810262.
VISITORS: Yes. Pay and play so no tee times booked.
GREEN FEES: £12 per round weekdays, £15 per round weekends.
CATERING: Bar and bar snacks.
FACILITIES: 8-bay floodlit driving range, changing-rooms, motorised buggies, trolley hire, club hire, membership available.
LOCATION: 1½ miles south-west of Portpatrick, off the A77.
LOCAL HOTELS: Crown Hotel, Downshire Arms Hotel, Dunskey Golf Hotel, Fernhill Hotel, Harbour House Hotel, Mount Stewart Hotel, North West Castle Hotel, Portpatrick Hotel, Waterfront Hotel.

## PORTPATRICK (DUNSKEY) GOLF CLUB

COURSE DESCRIPTION:
Links-type course set on the cliffs above Portpatrick overlooking the Irish Sea. An enjoyable test and very popular with visitors. *Golf World* magazine described it as 'the No. 1 holiday course in the south of Scotland'. Is a good test of golf, especially when the wind blows in from the sea. Three very demanding par 3s which,

although not long, require accurate tee shots. For example, the 165-yard 7th is uphill to a raised green and plays one club more than the yardage. There is a deep gully 30 yards in front of the green which falls away downhill to the left. Putting green has more slopes than one imagines. Portpatrick plan to extend the clubhouse for their centenary in 2003.

*Dunskey* – 18 holes, 5,908 yards, par 70 (SSS 69). Course record 63.

*Dinvin* – 9 holes, 1,504 yards, par 27 (SSS 27). Course record 23.

## SIGNATURE HOLE:

Dunskey: THIRTEENTH ('Sandseel' 293 yards, par 4) From the tee, which overlooks the North Channel, can be seen the Irish coast, Mull of Kintyre and, to the south, the Isle of Man. It is all downhill and the backdrop is Sandeel Bay and the rocky coastline. The green can be tricky.

## DUNSKEY COURSE CARD

| | MEDAL | | FORWARD | | LADIES | | | MEDAL | | FORWARD | | LADIES | |
|------|------|-----|------|-----|------|-----|------|------|-----|------|-----|------|-----|
| HOLE | YDS | PAR | YDS | PAR | YDS | PAR | HOLE | YDS | PAR | YDS | PAR | YDS | PAR |
| 1 | 393 | 4 | 387 | 4 | 388 | 5 | 10 | 329 | 4 | 319 | 4 | 206 | 3 |
| 2 | 375 | 4 | 331 | 4 | 308 | 4 | 11 | 163 | 3 | 138 | 3 | 129 | 3 |
| 3 | 544 | 5 | 534 | 5 | 513 | 5 | 12 | 388 | 4 | 370 | 4 | 368 | 4 |
| 4 | 160 | 3 | 156 | 3 | 126 | 3 | 13 | 293 | 4 | 285 | 4 | 280 | 4 |
| 5 | 405 | 4 | 365 | 4 | 362 | 4 | 14 | 293 | 4 | 293 | 4 | 291 | 4 |
| 6 | 382 | 4 | 345 | 4 | 329 | 4 | 15 | 101 | 3 | 99 | 3 | 99 | 3 |
| 7 | 165 | 3 | 160 | 3 | 152 | 3 | 16 | 393 | 4 | 379 | 4 | 306 | 4 |
| 8 | 377 | 4 | 288 | 4 | 272 | 4 | 17 | 301 | 4 | 285 | 4 | 243 | 4 |
| 9 | 311 | 4 | 298 | 4 | 247 | 4 | 18 | 535 | 5 | 506 | 5 | 503 | 5 |
| *Yds* *Out* | 3,112 | | 2,864 | | 2,697 | | *Yds* *In* | 2,796 | | 2,674 | | 2,425 | |
| *Total* *Yds* | 5,908 | | 5,538 | | 5,122 | | | | | | | | |
| *Total* *Par* | 70 | | 70 | | 70 | | | | | | | | |

ADDRESS: Golf Course Road, Portpatrick, Wigtownshire DG9 8TB.

TELEPHONE: +44 (0)1776 810273.

FAX: +44 (0)1776 810811.

E-MAIL: portpatrickgolf@aol.com

SECRETARY: J. Horberry.

PROFESSIONAL: K. Hughes.

VISITORS: Yes, all year round. Book in advance.

GREEN FEES: *Dunskey:* £25 per round weekdays, £35 per day. £30 per round weekends, £40 per day.

*Dinvin:* £10 per round, £15 per day.

CATERING: All day. Breakfast through to dinner.

FACILITIES: Trolley hire, putting green, golf shop, practice ground.

LOCATION: From North, A77 to Stranraer and to Portpatrick. From East, A 75 to Stranraer and to Portpatrick.

LOCAL HOTELS: Crown Hotel, Downshire Arms Hotel, Dunskey Golf Hotel, Fernhill Hotel, Harbour House Hotel, Mount Stewart Hotel, North West Castle Hotel, Portpatrick Hotel, Waterfront Hotel.

# SANQUHAR

## SANQUHAR GOLF CLUB

COURSE DESCRIPTION:
Established 1894, an inland parkland course with some challenging par 4s. Undulating but easy walking. Fine views.

9 holes, 5,594 yards (for 18 holes), par 70 (SSS 68). Course record 63.

SIGNATURE HOLE:
SIXTH ('Wull's Cairn' 149 yards, par 3) From elevated tee over a dip to an elevated green surrounded by bunkers.

COURSE CARD

| HOLE | MEDAL YDS | PAR | FORWARD YDS | PAR | LADIES YDS | PAR |
|------|-----------|-----|-------------|-----|------------|-----|
| 1 | 259 | 4 | 232 | 4 | 232 | 4 |
| 2 | 444 | 4 | 399 | 4 | 399 | 4 |
| 3 | 384 | 4 | 380 | 4 | 380 | 4 |
| 4 | 314 | 4 | 310 | 4 | 310 | 4 |
| 5 | 294 | 4 | 286 | 4 | 225 | 4 |
| 6 | 149 | 3 | 138 | 3 | 149 | 3 |
| 7 | 332 | 4 | 325 | 4 | 332 | 4 |
| 8 | 156 | 3 | 149 | 3 | 131 | 3 |
| 9 | 465 | 5 | 451 | 5 | 431 | 4 |
| Yds Out | 2,797 | | 2,670 | | 2,589 | |
| Total Yds | 2,797 | | | | | |
| Total Par | 35 | | | | | |

ADDRESS: The Euchan Course, Blackaddie Road, Sanquhar DG4 6JZ.
TELEPHONE: +44 (0)1659 50577.
SECRETARY: Doug Hamilton +44 (0)1659 66095.
VISITORS: Any time.
GREEN FEES: £12 per day weekdays, £15 weekends.
CATERING: Bar. Meals by arrangement.
FACILITIES: New locker rooms with showers, putting green, practice ground, disabled access to all parts.
LOCATION: 30 miles north of Dumfries, off A76.

LOCAL HOTELS: Blackaddie House Hotel, Glendyne Hotel, Nithsdale Hotel.

# SOUTHERNESS

## SOLWAY LINKS GOLF COURSE

COURSE DESCRIPTION:
New links type course laid out on agricultural land. Situated near the Solway Firth.
11 holes, 3,062 yards, par 41.

COURSE CARD

| HOLE | YDS | PAR | HOLE | YDS | PAR |
|------|------|-----|------|-----|-----|
| 1 | 410 | 4 | 10 | 220 | 3 |
| 2 | 82 | 3 | 11 | 305 | 4 |
| 3 | 270 | 4 | | | |
| 4 | 165 | 3 | | | |
| 5 | 154 | 3 | | | |
| 6 | 360 | 4 | | | |
| 7 | 486 | 5 | | | |
| 8 | 295 | 4 | | | |
| 9 | 315 | 4 | | | |
| *Yds Out* | 2,537 | | *Yds In* | 525 | |
| *Total Yds* | 3,062 | | | | |
| *Total Par* | 41 | | | | |

ADDRESS: East Preston Farm, Kirkbean, near Southerness.
TELEPHONE: +44 (0)1387 880323.
VISITORS: Yes, pay and play.
GREEN FEES: On application.
CATERING: None.
FACILITIES: Club hire.
LOCAL HOTELS: Cairndale Hotel, Clonyard Hotel, George Hotel, Paul Jones Hotel.

## SOUTHERNESS GOLF CLUB

COURSE DESCRIPTION:
Ask any golfing enthusiast to name a course that is one of Scotland's hidden gems
and Southerness will rank high on the list. Although Southerness has hosted
several national championships over the last 15 years, its location 15 miles south
of Dumfries has probably ruled it out of its fair share of prestigious events. But like
all good things, it's worth time and effort to experience the crisp, sandy turf and
rolling fairways and greens of a championship links course in superb condition

running along the Solway Firth coastline beneath the Galloway Hills. A relatively young course, it was designed by Mackenzie Ross (who rebuilt Turnberry's Ailsa course) and opened in 1947. In those days it was regarded as pretty difficult, with long carries to narrow fairways flanked by heather and gorse. Over the years the fairways have widened like a gourmet's waistband, the greens have expanded and the carries become perhaps fairer yet still daunting, but it's still a stunning test of shot-making as its standard scratch of 73 shows. In a recent *Golf World* survey of 1,000 courses in Britain and Ireland, Southerness came sixth for best value in golf. It is renowned for its long par 4s of which there are eight over 400 yards. Also, two of the five par 3s are more than 200 yards, but there is some respite in that the two par 5s – a mere 496 and 495 yards – offer birdie chances to keep your humour on an even keel.

18 holes, 6,566 yards, par 69 (SSS 73). Amateur record 65. Pro record 71.

## SIGNATURE HOLE:
TWELFTH (421 yards, par 4) Towards the sea and into the prevailing south-west wind. Strategically placed fairway bunkers shape this hole into a dogleg right and driving accuracy is paramount. The approach to an almost blind green up on a shelf demands concentration and self-belief. There are humps and bumps and bunkers to manoeuvre, and if you over-hit, the beach awaits you.

## COURSE CARD

| HOLE | MEDAL YDS | PAR | FORWARD YDS | PAR | LADIES YDS | PAR | HOLE | MEDAL YDS | PAR | FORWARD YDS | PAR | LADIES YDS | PAR |
|---|---|---|---|---|---|---|---|---|---|---|---|---|---|---|
| 1 | 393 | 4 | 372 | 4 | 350 | 4 | 10 | 168 | 3 | 141 | 4 | 141 | 3 |
| 2 | 450 | 4 | 405 | 4 | 361 | 4 | 11 | 390 | 4 | 371 | 4 | 282 | 4 |
| 3 | 408 | 4 | 383 | 4 | 376 | 4 | 12 | 421 | 4 | 387 | 4 | 385 | 4 |
| 4 | 169 | 3 | 132 | 3 | 128 | 3 | 13 | 467 | 4 | 436 | 4 | 430 | 5 |
| 5 | 496 | 5 | 479 | 5 | 433 | 5 | 14 | 458 | 4 | 416 | 4 | 409 | 5 |
| 6 | 405 | 4 | 367 | 4 | 357 | 4 | 15 | 217 | 3 | 195 | 3 | 187 | 3 |
| 7 | 215 | 3 | 215 | 3 | 176 | 3 | 16 | 433 | 4 | 414 | 4 | 407 | 4 |
| 8 | 371 | 4 | 342 | 4 | 262 | 4 | 17 | 175 | 3 | 164 | 3 | 149 | 3 |
| 9 | 435 | 4 | 404 | 4 | 392 | 5 | 18 | 495 | 5 | 480 | 5 | 423 | 5 |
| Yds Out | 3,342 | | 3,099 | | 2,829 | | Yds In | 3,224 | | 3,006 | | 2,793 | |
| Total Yds | 6,566 | | 6,105 | | 5,622 | | | | | | | | | |
| Total Par | 69 | | 69 | | 73 | | | | | | | | | |

ADDRESS: Southerness, Dumfries DG2 8AZ.
TELEPHONE: +44 (0)1387 880677.
FAX: +44 (0)1387 880644.
E-MAIL: admin@southernessgc.sol.co.uk
WEBSITE: www.Southernessgolfclub.com
SECRETARY: Bill Ramage.
VISITORS: Weekdays 10 a.m. to 12 noon, 2 p.m. to 5 p.m. Thursdays 11 a.m. to 1

p.m., 2.30 p.m. to 5 p.m. Weekends and bank holidays 10 a.m. to 11.30 a.m., 2.30 p.m. to 4.30 p.m. Handicap certificates required.

**GREEN FEES:** Winter rates: £18 per round weekdays, £25 per round weekends. Summer rates: £35 per day, weekdays; £45 per day weekends.

**CATERING:** Full catering and bar service.

**FACILITIES:** Trolley hire, putting green, shop, practice ground.

**LOCATION:** A710 from Dumfries, marked Solway coast. Follow Southerness sign after 15 miles.

**LOCAL HOTELS:** Cairndale Hotel, Clonyard Hotel, George Hotel, Paul Jones Hotel.

# STRANRAER

## STRANRAER GOLF CLUB

**COURSE DESCRIPTION:**
Undulating parkland course, with a burn (be wary) on the shores of Loch Ryan. This was the last course five-times Open champion James Braid designed. He died in 1951 before the course opened. Due to the mild climate in the south-west of Scotland, the course remains playable all year and is frost free on all but a few days.

18 holes, 6,308 yards, par 70 (SSS 72). Amateur record C. Findlay, J. Sproule 66.

**SIGNATURE HOLE:**
FIFTH (397 yards, par 4) From an elevated tee, the curved fairway skirts the shore of Loch Ryan. Strategically placed bunkers for tee shot.

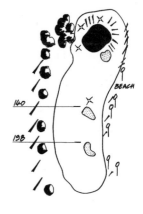

**COURSE CARD**

| HOLE | MEDAL YDS | PAR | FORWARD YDS | PAR | LADIES YDS | PAR | HOLE | MEDAL YDS | PAR | FORWARD YDS | PAR | LADIES YDS | PAR |
|---|---|---|---|---|---|---|---|---|---|---|---|---|---|
| 1 | 319 | 4 | 281 | 4 | 270 | 4 | 10 | 346 | 4 | 336 | 4 | 334 | 4 |
| 2 | 338 | 4 | 330 | 4 | 319 | 4 | 11 | 377 | 4 | 372 | 4 | 366 | 4 |
| 3 | 420 | 4 | 403 | 4 | 330 | 4 | 12 | 185 | 3 | 180 | 3 | 105 | 3 |
| 4 | 324 | 4 | 317 | 4 | 313 | 4 | 13 | 335 | 4 | 325 | 4 | 315 | 4 |
| 5 | 397 | 4 | 382 | 4 | 354 | 4 | 14 | 513 | 5 | 496 | 5 | 480 | 5 |
| 6 | 160 | 3 | 149 | 3 | 146 | 3 | 15 | 165 | 3 | 162 | 3 | 122 | 3 |
| 7 | 381 | 4 | 369 | 4 | 367 | 5 | 16 | 470 | 4 | 441 | 4 | 369 | 4 |
| 8 | 315 | 4 | 308 | 4 | 302 | 4 | 17 | 462 | 4 | 452 | 4 | 442 | 5 |
| 9 | 458 | 4 | 417 | 4 | 407 | 5 | 18 | 343 | 4 | 336 | 4 | 325 | 4 |
| *Yds* Out | 3,112 | | 2,956 | | 2,808 | | *Yds* In | 3,196 | | 3,100 | | 2,858 | |
| *Total Yds* | 6,308 | | 6,056 | | 5,666 | | | | | | | | |

| Total | 70 | 70 | 74 |
| --- | --- | --- | --- |
| Par | | | |

**ADDRESS:** Creachmore, Leswalt, Stranraer DG9 0LF.
**TELEPHONE:** +44 (0)1776 870245.
**FAX:** +44 (0)1776 870445.
**SECRETARY:** Bryce Kelly.
**VISITORS:** Weekdays 9.15 a.m. to 12.30 p.m., 1.30 p.m. to 5 p.m. Weekends 9.30 a.m. to 11.45 a.m., 1.45 p.m. to 5 p.m. Handicap certificates may be required.
**GREEN FEES:** £18 weekdays. £24 weekends.
**CATERING:** Full service and bar.
**FACILITIES:** Motorised buggies, trolley hire, club hire, caddies, changing-rooms, putting green, practice ground, memberships available.
**LOCATION:** 2 miles north of Stranraer on the Kirkcolm road.
**LOCAL HOTELS:** Fernhill Hotel, Kelvin House Hotel, North West Castle Hotel, Torrs Warren Hotel.

# THORNHILL

## THORNHILL GOLF CLUB

### COURSE DESCRIPTION:
Founded in 1893, this course is a delightful mixture of heathland and parkland set in the midst of the scenic southern uplands. It is worth walking the course for the scenery alone. Although reasonably short, it still proves a good test for the scratch golfer.

18 holes, 6,085 yards, par 71 (SSS 70). Course record 63.

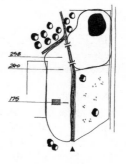

### SIGNATURE HOLE:
FOURTH (426 yards, par 4) Stroke index 1. A dogleg right with a burn on the right. An intimidating drive. Difficult second shot to a two-tiered green which has a collective bank on the right, falling sharply to the left.

### COURSE CARD

| HOLE | YDS | PAR | HOLE | YDS | PAR |
| --- | --- | --- | --- | --- | --- |
| 1 | 158 | 3 | 10 | 396 | 4 |
| 2 | 477 | 5 | 11 | 342 | 4 |
| 3 | 359 | 4 | 12 | 363 | 4 |
| 4 | 426 | 4 | 13 | 429 | 4 |
| 5 | 267 | 4 | 14 | 156 | 3 |
| 6 | 421 | 4 | 15 | 497 | 5 |
| 7 | 317 | 4 | 16 | 191 | 3 |

| 8 | 160 | 3 | 17 | 266 | 4 |
| 9 | 332 | 4 | 18 | 528 | 5 |
| *Yds* | 2,917 | | *Yds* | 3,168 | |
| *Out* | | | *In* | | |
| *Total* *Yds* | 6,085 | | | | |
| *Total* *Par* | 71 | | | | |

ADDRESS: Blacknest, Thornhill, Dumfriesshire DG3 5DW.
TELEPHONE: +44 (0)1848 330546.
SECRETARY: J. Crichton.
VISITORS: Any time, except open competition days.
GREEN FEES: £22 per day. £28 weekends and bank holidays.
CATERING: Full service available. Bar.
FACILITIES: Trolley/buggy hire, putting green, practice ground.
LOCATION: On A76 Dumfries–Kilmarnock road, 1 mile from the village cross.
LOCAL HOTELS: George Hotel, Gillbank Hotel.

# WIGTOWN

## WIGTOWN & BLADNOCH GOLF CLUB

COURSE DESCRIPTION:
Parkland course, part hilly, with several quite tricky holes. A haven for those seeking relaxing golf and a friendly atmosphere. From the 4th tee there are magnificent views of Wigtown Bay and across the Solway Firth to the hills of the Lake District.
    9 holes, 5,462 yards (for 18 holes), par 68 (SSS 67). Course record 61.

SIGNATURE HOLE:
THIRD (195 yards, par 3) Only the pin is visible from the tee. Out of bounds on the left. The fairway slopes from left to right with rough and trees on the right. Sloping green.

COURSE CARD

| | MEDAL | | LADIES | |
| HOLE | YDS | PAR | YDS | PAR |
| --- | --- | --- | --- | --- |
| 1 | 306 | 4 | 301 | 4 |
| 2 | 370 | 4 | 363 | 5 |
| 3 | 195 | 3 | 185 | 3 |
| 4 | 275 | 4 | 259 | 4 |
| 5 | 149 | 3 | 141 | 3 |
| 6 | 362 | 4 | 349 | 4 |
| 7 | 356 | 4 | 303 | 4 |

| 8 | 342 | 4 | 274 | 4 |
|---|-----|---|-----|---|
| 9 | 376 | 4 | 336 | 5 |
| *Yds* | 2,731 | | 2,511 | |
| *Out* | | | | |
| *Total* | 2,731 | | | |
| *Yds* | | | | |
| *Total* | 34 | | | |
| *Par* | | | | |

**ADDRESS:** Lightlands Terrace, Wigtown, Wigtownshire DG8 9DY.
**TELEPHONE:** +44 (0)1988 403354.
**HONORARY SECRETARY:** B. Kaye.
**VISITORS:** Yes, every day, except when open competitions.
**GREEN FEES:** £15 per round weekdays/weekends, £20 per day. Senior citizens and juniors half price. Honesty box in operation. Weekly ticket £50.
**CATERING:** Bar. Please phone for availability of bar/meals.
**FACILITIES:** Changing rooms, putting green, memberships available.
**LOCATION:** From roundabout on A75 at Newton Stewart take A714 to Wigtown. In Wigtown turn right and first left on St Agnew Crescent. Club is 100 yards on the right.
**LOCAL HOTELS:** Bladnoch Inn, Fordbank Hotel, Wigtown House Hotel.

# THE NORTHERN ISLES

# ORKNEY ISLES

## ORKNEY GOLF CLUB

COURSE DESCRIPTION:
Inland parkland course founded in 1889.
   18 holes, 5,411 yards, par 70 (SSS 67). Course record 65.

ADDRESS: Grainbank, Kirkwall, Orkney Isles KW15 1RD.
TELEPHONE: +44 (0)1856 872457.
VISITORS: Any time.
GREEN FEES: £10 per day.
CATERING: Lunch times during summer.
FACILITIES: Trolley hire, changing-rooms, putting green, practice ground.
LOCATION: At western boundary of Kirkwall.
LOCAL HOTELS: Kirkwall Hotel, Royal Hotel, Queens Hotel.

## STROMNESS GOLF CLUB

COURSE DESCRIPTION:
Seaside parkland course with a tight and tricky layout. Easy walking, but testing. Views of Scapa Flow. The main competition in the Stromness golfing year is the Stromness Open, which for the last 25 years has attracted an entry of up to 132 players from all parts of the UK and from countries such as Kenya, Canada, South Africa and Australia.
   18 holes, 4,762 yards, par 65 (SSS 63). Amateur record Graham Dunnett 61. Pro record 66.

SIGNATURE HOLE:
TENTH (163 yards, par 3) Played over former wartime gun emplacements. Out of bounds behind the green.

COURSE CARD

| | MEDAL | | LADIES | | | MEDAL | | LADIES | |
|------|-----|-----|-----|-----|------|-----|-----|-----|-----|
| HOLE | YDS | PAR | YDS | PAR | HOLE | YDS | PAR | YDS | PAR |
| 1 | 355 | 4 | 335 | 4 | 10 | 163 | 3 | 163 | 3 |
| 2 | 186 | 3 | 186 | 3 | 11 | 142 | 3 | 142 | 3 |
| 3 | 219 | 3 | 219 | 4 | 12 | 279 | 4 | 279 | 4 |
| 4 | 403 | 4 | 403 | 5 | 13 | 266 | 4 | 266 | 4 |
| 5 | 355 | 4 | 325 | 4 | 14 | 376 | 4 | 346 | 4 |
| 6 | 186 | 3 | 186 | 3 | 15 | 199 | 3 | 199 | 4 |
| 7 | 402 | 4 | 402 | 5 | 16 | 251 | 4 | 251 | 4 |
| 8 | 105 | 3 | 105 | 3 | 17 | 333 | 4 | 303 | 4 |

| 9 | 263 | 4 | 263 | 4 | 18 | 299 | 4 | 299 | 4 |
|---|-----|---|-----|---|-----|-----|---|-----|---|
| *Yds* | 2,454 | | 2,424 | | *Yds* | 2,308 | | 2,248 | |
| *Out* | | | | | *In* | | | | |
| *Total Yds* | 4,762 | | 4,672 | | | | | | |
| *Total Par* | 65 | | 65 | | | | | | |

**ADDRESS:** Ness, Stromness, Orkney Isles KW16 3DW.
**TELEPHONE:** +44 (0)1856 850772.
**E-MAIL:** enquiries@stromnessgc.co.uk
**WEBSITE:** www.stromnessgc.co.uk
**VISITORS:** Any time. All weekday mornings and afternoons are definitely available for visitors to play.
**GREEN FEES:** £15 per day. Juniors: £8 for a day (playing alone), £2 when playing with a paying adult.
**CATERING:** Lunches in summer.
**FACILITIES:** Disabled access.
**LOCATION:** 12 miles west of Kirkwall and south of town on A965.
**LOCAL HOTELS:** Royal Hotel, Queens Hotel, Kirkwall Hotel.

## WESTRAY GOLF CLUB

**COURSE DESCRIPTION:**
Interesting seaside links course. Easy walking, but watch out for the rabbit holes.
    9 holes, 4,810 yards (for 18 holes), par 66.

**ADDRESS:** Westray, Orkney Isles KW17 2DH.
**TELEPHONE:** +44 (0)1857 677373.
**TREASURER:** Billy Tulloch.
**VISITORS:** Any time.
**GREEN FEES:** £3 per day. £15 per week.
**CATERING:** No.
**LOCATION:** 1 mile north-west of Pierowall off B9066.
**LOCAL HOTELS:** Cleaton House.

# SHETLAND ISLES

## SHETLAND GOLF CLUB

**COURSE DESCRIPTION:**
Undulating moorland course founded in 1891. Wide fairways but hard walking. Burn runs full length of course and provides a natural hazard.
    18 holes, 5,800 yards, par 68 (SSS 68). Course record 68.

ADDRESS: PO Box 18, Lerwick, Shetland Isles ZE1 0YW.
TELEPHONE: +44 (0)1595 840369
VISITORS: Contact in advance.
GREEN FEES: £12 per day.
CATERING: Bar.
FACILITIES: Putting green.
LOCATION: 4 miles north of Lerwick on A970.
LOCAL HOTELS: Grand Hotel, Lerwick Hotel, Queens Hotel.

# WHALSAY GOLF CLUB

COURSE DESCRIPTION:
Most northerly golf course in Britain founded 1975. Moorland course, exposed with spectacular clifftop scenery. Fairways defined by marker posts.
 18 holes, 6,009 yards, par 70 (SSS 68). Course record 65.

SIGNATURE HOLE:
EIGHTEENTH (386 yards, par 4) Dogleg left around (or over) East Loch of Skaw.

COURSE CARD

| HOLE | YDS | PAR | HOLE | YDS | PAR |
|------|-----|-----|------|-----|-----|
| 1 | 401 | 4 | 10 | 381 | 4 |
| 2 | 399 | 4 | 11 | 398 | 4 |
| 3 | 150 | 3 | 12 | 529 | 5 |
| 4 | 311 | 4 | 13 | 202 | 3 |
| 5 | 140 | 3 | 14 | 342 | 4 |
| 6 | 337 | 4 | 15 | 346 | 4 |
| 7 | 165 | 3 | 16 | 510 | 5 |
| 8 | 482 | 5 | 17 | 175 | 3 |
| 9 | 355 | 4 | 18 | 386 | 4 |
| *Yds* *Out* | 2,740 | | *Yds* *In* | 3,269 | |
| *Total Yds* | 6,009 | | | | |
| *Total Par* | 70 | | | | |

ADDRESS: Skaw Taing, Island of Whalsay, Shetland Isles ZE2 9AA.
TELEPHONE: +44 (0)1806 566705.
SECRETARY: Charles Hutchison +44 (0)1806 566450.
VISITORS: Welcome any time.
GREEN FEES: £10 per day.
CATERING: By arrangement. New clubhouse built 1996.
FACILITIES: Changing rooms, putting green.
LOCATION: ½ hour's drive north from Lerwick, then ½ hour on ferry.

# THE WESTERN ISLES

# ISLE OF BARRA

## BARRA GOLF CLUB

COURSE DESCRIPTION:
The United Kingdom's most westerly course, established in 1992, with stunning views out over the Atlantic. On machair land, the natural turf provides an excellent playing surface. Greian Head in the north-west corner of Barra represents a triumph of local ingenuity over landscape with undulating fairways and rocky outcrops. Wire and post fencing to protect the greens from livestock are part of a unique golfing challenge. The 4th hole is a serious contender for the world's largest natural bunker. No clubhouse at present.

9 holes. 4,792 yards (for 18 holes), par 68 (SSS 64).

ADDRESS: Greian Head, Barra.
SECRETARY: Donald Mackinnon +44 (0)1871 810591.
E-MAIL: euan.scott@tesco.net
WEBSITE: www.isleofbarra.com/golf1.html
GREEN FEES: £5 per day, memberships available.
LOCAL HOTELS: Castlebay Hotel, Craigard Hotel.

# ISLE OF HARRIS

## ISLE OF HARRIS GOLF CLUB

COURSE DESCRIPTION:
This tight and devilishly difficult nine-hole links course on the Western Isles clings to the side of a hill running down to the Atlantic Ocean and the beautiful Scarista beach, whose white sands make Malibu look like a play-school sandpit. In the early '90s, Nick Faldo described it as one of the most beautiful settings for golf after depositing in the honesty box a signed £5 note, which was glazed and framed and – as the Faldo Fiver – is played for every year. Former cricketing greats, Richie Benaud and Allan Lamb, are members and it is believed that Sean Connery and Tom Watson have played the course. Harris is planning building a clubhouse with the income from a new release of life memberships. No play is allowed on the Sabbath but at all other times there is a typical Hebridean welcome. There is no other golfing experience quite like this. The 1st (282 yards, par 4) offers one of the most arresting sights in Scottish golf. Beyond the green is the island of Taransay and the North Harris hills on the right. To the left is Scarista beach and beyond the Atlantic. The 3rd (290 yards, par 4) has out of bounds on the left, while the 141-yard, par-3 4th demands precision play. Around the green to the left, longish grass and natural sand

creates a difficult recovery shot. Go too far right and you'll roll on and on down a steep hill to the valley below. The 5th (358 yards, par 4) is one of the most scenic of holes; it requires a straight drive to find the plateau just before the ditch and a well-executed approach to a green, guarded by bunkers to left and right. The 6th (247 yards, par 4) is a dogleg left which with a good strike can be driven, but if offline you could find the deep valley to the right from which recovery is difficult. The 142-yard, par-3 7th offers a little respite before the 201-yard, par-3 8th and to finish is a 483-yard par 5 which has bunkers awaiting your drive. The approach to the green needs to be accurate for dense rough lies left, very close to a difficult green.

9 holes, 4,864 yards (for 18 holes), par 68 (SSS 64).

## SIGNATURE HOLE:

SECOND (288 yards, par 4) Typical of a course that has been fashioned by nature. Although relatively short, it requires an accurate drive over the Ocean, chasm and rocks onto a fairway sloping sharply to the sea, then a blind second shot to a small green nestling in a hollow. The degree of difficulty is increased by the sometime gale-force winds sweeping in from the Atlantic.

## COURSE CARD

| HOLE | YDS | PAR |
|------|------|-----|
| 1 | 282 | 4 |
| 2 | 288 | 4 |
| 3 | 290 | 4 |
| 4 | 141 | 3 |
| 5 | 358 | 4 |
| 6 | 247 | 4 |
| 7 | 142 | 3 |
| 8 | 201 | 3 |
| 9 | 483 | 5 |
| Yds Out | 2,432 | |
| Total Yds | 2,432 | |
| Total Par | 34 | |

ADDRESS: Scarista Links, Isle of Harris, HS3 3DJ.
SECRETARY: Angus MacSween, 6 Urgha, Isle of Harris. +44 (0)1859 502331.
VISITORS: Any time, but no play on Sundays.
GREEN FEES: £10 per day (leave your money in the honesty box).
CATERING: No.
FACILITIES: Putting green, golf club hire.
LOCATION: 15 miles south of Tarbert on west coast. The Western Isles can be reached by car ferry from Ullapool (Wester Ross), which is approximately 1 hour 15 minutes from Inverness, to Stornoway (the drive from Stornoway to Scarista Golf Course takes approximately 1 hour 15 minutes). Or from Uig (Isle of Skye), which is approximately 2 hours 30 minutes from Inverness, to Tarbert,

and the course is 20 minutes' drive away. Or you can fly from either Glasgow or Inverness to Stornoway.

**LOCAL HOTELS:** Scarista House, Harris Hotel.

# ISLE OF LEWIS

## STORNOWAY GOLF CLUB

**COURSE DESCRIPTION:**
Parkland course, which is undulating but not too hilly, in the grounds of the Lewis Castle. Plenty of hazards for wayward shots including mature trees, heather and gorse. Excellent views of Stornoway Harbour and the Minch.

18 holes, 5,252 yards, par 68 (SSS 67). Amateur record Colin Macritchie 63. Pro record J. Farmer 65.

**SIGNATURE HOLE:**
ELEVENTH ('Dardanelles' 551 yards, par 5) Once described as amongst the top six most difficult holes in Europe, the tee shot has to be hit over a dip onto a steeply sloping fairway. Second shot is then played over a blind summit, using the war memorial as a guideline and with trees to the right and a heathery bank to the left.

**COURSE CARD**

| HOLE | MEDAL YDS | PAR | LADIES YDS | PAR | HOLE | MEDAL YDS | PAR | LADIES YDS | PAR |
|---|---|---|---|---|---|---|---|---|---|
| 1 | 362 | 4 | 362 | 5 | 10 | 180 | 3 | 150 | 3 |
| 2 | 484 | 5 | 427 | 5 | 11 | 551 | 5 | 470 | 5 |
| 3 | 173 | 3 | 166 | 3 | 12 | 295 | 4 | 252 | 4 |
| 4 | 347 | 4 | 265 | 4 | 13 | 266 | 4 | 266 | 4 |
| 5 | 315 | 4 | 271 | 4 | 14 | 309 | 4 | 309 | 4 |
| 6 | 278 | 4 | 200 | 4 | 15 | 143 | 3 | 143 | 3 |
| 7 | 274 | 4 | 269 | 4 | 16 | 362 | 4 | 257 | 4 |
| 8 | 332 | 4 | 200 | 4 | 17 | 230 | 3 | 191 | 3 |
| 9 | 142 | 3 | 101 | 3 | 18 | 209 | 3 | 138 | 3 |
| Yds Out | 2,707 | | 2,281 | | Yds In | 2,545 | | 2,176 | |
| Total Yds | 5,252 | | 4,457 | | | | | | |
| Total Par | 68 | | 69 | | | | | | |

**ADDRESS:** Lady Lever Park, Stornoway, Isle of Lewis H52 0XP.
**TELEPHONE:** +44 (0)1851 702240.
**E-MAIL:** admin@stornowaygolfclub.co.uk
**WEBSITE:** www.stornowaygolfclub.co.uk
**SECRETARY:** Huw Lloyd.

VISITORS: Any time, but no Sunday golf.
GREEN FEES: £20 per round weekdays/weekends. Weekly ticket £45.
CATERING: Modernised clubhouse with full facilities and bar.
FACILITIES: Trolley hire, club hire, changing-facilities, putting green, shop.
LOCATION: ½ mile out of town on the Tarbert road.
LOCAL HOTELS: Caberfeidh Hotel, Royal Hotel, Seaforth Hotel.

# ISLE OF NORTH UIST

## BENBECULA GOLF CLUB

COURSE DESCRIPTION:
Naturally flat course beside the Balivanich airfield. In good condition and, although subject to natural hazards such as rabbit scrapes, is a serious test for the discerning golfer featuring a few tricky holes. 18 tees.
    9 holes, 4,311 yards (for 18 holes), par 62 (SSS 62).

ADDRESS: Balivanich, Benbecula, North Uist, HS7 5LA.
SECRETARY: Iain Macrury +44 (0)1870 602126.
VISITORS: Welcome but not on Thursdays between 6 and 8 p.m.
GREEN FEES: £5 per day.
FACILITIES: Changing-rooms, practice area, driving range.
LOCAL HOTELS: Temple View Hotel, Longass Lodge Hotel, Creagorry Hotel.

# ISLE OF SOUTH UIST

## ASKERNISH GOLF CLUB

COURSE DESCRIPTION:
This course on the shores of the Atlantic Ocean was originally laid out by Old Tom Morris in 1891 on a site which he said was 'second to none in the various elements which go to make up a really good course'. Bracing air and the 18 tees give variety.
    9 holes, 5,042 yards (for 18 holes), par 68 (SSS 67). Course record 64.

ADDRESS: Lochboisdale, Isle of South Uist PA81 5SY.
TELEPHONE: +44 (0)1878 700541.
SECRETARY: Eric Cameron +44 (0) 1878 700401
EMAIL: eric.cameron@btclick.com
VISITORS: Any time.
GREEN FEES: £10 per day.
CATERING: Bar.
LOCATION: 5 miles north-west of Lochboisdale.
LOCAL HOTELS: Lochboisdale Hotel, Orasay Hotel.

# INDEX

# A

Aberdour Golf Club, Aberdour  224
Aberfeldy Golf Club, Aberfeldy  180
Aberfoyle Golf Club, Aberfoyle  268
Abernethy Golf Club, Nethy Bridge  121
Aboyne Golf Club, Aboyne  143
Aigas Golf Course, Beauly 84
Airdrie Golf Club, Airdrie  291
Airthrey Golf Course (University of Stirling), Stirling  285
Alexandra Park Golf Course, Glasgow  330
Alford Golf Club, Alford  143
Alloa Golf Club, Alloa  269
Alness Golf Club, Alness  82
Alva Golf Club, Alva  271
The Alyth Golf Club, Alyth  184
Annanhill Golf Club, Kilmarnock  365
Askernish Golf Club, Isle of South Uist  463
Anstruther Golf Club, Anstruther  225
Arbory Brae Golf Club, Abington  290
Arbroath Links Golf Course, Arbroath  185
Ardeer Golf Club, Stevenston  392
Auchenblae Golf Course, Auchenblae  144
Auchenharvie Golf Club, Stevenston  392
Auchmill Golf Club, Aberdeen  136
Auchterarder Golf Club, Auchterarder  187
Auchterderran Golf Club, Cardenden  226

# B

Baberton Golf Club, Edinburgh  39
Balbardie Park Golf Club, Bathgate  34
Balbirnie Park Golf Club, Markinch  250
Ballater Golf Club, Ballater  145
Ballochmyle Golf Club, Mauchline  376
Balmore Golf Club Ltd, Torrance  396
Balnagask Golf Course, Aberdeen  136
Banchory Golf Club, Banchory  148
Barra Golf Club, Isle of Barra  460
Barshaw Golf Club, Paisley  383
Bathgate Golf Club, Bathgate  34
Bearsden Golf Club, Glasgow  331
Beith Golf Club, Beith  303
Belleisle & Seafield Golf Courses, Ayr  299
Bellshill Golf Club, Bellshill  303

Benbecula Golf Club, Isle of North Uist  463
Biggar Golf Club, Biggar  304
Bishopbriggs Golf Club, Glasgow  332
Bishopshire Golf Club, Kinnesswood  239
Blair Atholl Golf Club, Blair Atholl  190
Blairbeth Golf Club, Glasgow  333
Blairgowrie Golf Club, Blairgowrie  191
Blairmore and Strone Golf Club, Strone  394
Boat of Garten Golf Club, Boat of Garten  85
Bonar Bridge/Ardgay Golf Club, Bonar Bridge  86
Bonnybridge Golf Club, Bonnybridge  272
Bonnyton Golf Club, Glasgow  333
Bothwell Castle Golf Club, Bothwell  306
Braehead Golf Club, Alloa  270
Braid Hills Golf Club, Edinburgh  40
Brechin Golf Club, Brechin  191
Braemar Golf Club, Braemar  151
Bridgend & District Golf Club, Linlithgow  61
Bridge of Allan Golf Club, Bridge of Allan  272
Brodick Golf Club, Isle of Arran  293
Broomieknowe Golf Club Ltd, Bonnyrigg  35
Brora Golf Club, Brora  87
Brucefields Family Golf Centre Ltd, Stirling  285
Brunston Castle Golf Club, Girvan  328
Bruntsfield Links Golfing Society Ltd (The), Edinburgh  50
Buchanan Castle Golf Club, Drymen  275
Buckpool Golf Club, Buckie  152
Burntisland Golf House Club, Burntisland  226
Bute Golf Club, Isle of Bute  309

# C

Caird Park Golf Club, Dundee  201
Calderbraes Golf Club, Uddingston  404
Caldwell Golf Club Ltd, Uplawmoor  405
Callander Golf Club, Callander  273
Cally Palace Hotel Golf Course, Gatehouse of Fleet  433
Cambuslang Golf Club, Glasgow  334
Cameron House Hotel and Country Estate, Balloch  301
Camperdown Golf Club, Dundee  201
Campsie Golf Club, Lennoxtown  371
Canmore Golf Club, Dunfermline  233
Caprington Golf Club, Kilmarnock  366
Cardross Golf Club, Cardross  313
Carluke Golf Club, Carluke  314
Carnegie Club (Skibo Castle), Dornoch  90

Carnoustie Golf Links – Buddon Links 195
Carnoustie Golf Links – Burnside Course 196
Carnoustie Golf Links – Championship Course 193
Carnwath Golf Club, Carnwath 314
Carradale Golf Club, Carradale 315
Carrbridge Golf Club, Carrbridge 89
Carrick Knowe Course, Edinburgh 40
Castle Douglas Golf Club, Castle Douglas 428
Castle Park Golf Club, Gifford 53
Cathcart Castle Golf Club, Glasgow 334
Cathkin Braes Golf Club, Glasgow 334
Cawder Golf Club, Glasgow 335
Cawdor Castle Golf Club, Nairn 118
Charleton Golf Club, Colinsburgh 227
Clober Golf Club, Glasgow 335
Clydebank and District Golf Club, Clydebank 315
Clydebank Municipal Course, Clydebank 316
Coatbridge Golf Club, Coatbridge 316
Cochrane Castle Golf Club, Johnstone 363
Colonsay Golf Club, Isle of Colonsay 317
Colvend Golf Club, Colvend 430
Colville Park Golf Club, Motherwell 377
Comrie Golf Club, Comrie 197
Corrie Golf Club, Isle of Arran 293
Covesea Golf Course, Lossiemouth 115
Cowal Golf Club, Dunoon 324
Cowdenbeath Golf Club, Cowdenbeath 228
Cowglen Golf Club, Glasgow 336
Craggan Golf Course, Grantown-on-Spey 103
Craibstone Golf Centre, Aberdeen 137
Craigentinny Golf Course, Edinburgh 41
Craigie Hill Golf Club, Perth 216
Craignure Golf Club, Isle of Mull 379
Craigmillar Park Golf Club, Edinburgh 41
Crail Golfing Society, Crail 228
Crichton Golf Club, Dumfries 430
Crieff Golf Club Ltd, Crieff 198
Crieff Hydro Golf Centre, Crieff 199
Crow Wood Golf Club, Glasgow 336
Cruden Bay Golf Club Cruden Bay 153
Cullen Golf Club, Cullen 154
Cupar Golf Club, Cupar 230

# D

Dalmally Golf Club, Dalmally 321

Dalmilling Golf Club, Ayr  300
Dalmunzie Golf Course, Glenshee  209
Deer Park Golf and Country Club, Livingston  63
Deeside Golf Club, Aberdeen  138
Dollar Golf Club, Dollar  274
Doon Valley Golf Club, Patna  385
Douglas Park Golf Club, Glasgow  337
Douglas Water Golf Club, Douglas Water  322
Downfield Golf Club, Dundee  202
Drimsynie Golf Course, Lochgoilhead  373
Drumoig Hotel & Golf Course, Leuchars  243
Drumpellier Golf Club, Coatbridge  317
Duddingston Golf Club, Edinburgh  42
Duff House Royal Golf Club, Banff  150
Dufftown Golf Club, Dufftown  156
The Duke's Course, St Andrews  262
Dullatur Golf Club, Dullatur  322
Dumbarton Golf Club, Dumbarton  323
Dumfries and County Golf Club, Dumfries  431
Dumfries and Galloway Golf Club, Dumfries  432
Dunaverty Golf Club, Campbeltown  311
Dunbar Golf Club, Dunbar  38
Dunblane New Golf Club, Dunblane  276
Dundas Parks Golf Club, South Queensferry  75
Dunecht House Golf Club, Dunecht  157
Dunfermline Golf Club, Dunfermline  234
Dunkeld and Birnam Golf Club, Dunkeld  205
Dunnikier Park Golf Club, Kirkcaldy  240
Dunning Golf Club, Dunning  206
Duns Golf Club, Duns  409
Durness Golf Club, Durness  94

# E

East Aberdeenshire Golf Centre Ltd, Balmedie  146
Easter Moffat Golf Club, Airdrie  292
East Kilbride Golf Club, East Kilbride  325
East Renfrewshire Golf Club (The), Glasgow  347
Eastwood Golf Club (The), Glasgow  348
Edzell Golf Club (The), Edzell  206
Elmwood Golf Course, Cupar  232
Esporta Dougalston Golf Club, Glasgow  338
Elderslie Golf Club, Elderslie  326
Elgin Golf Club, Elgin  95
Elie Sports Club, Elie  236
Eriska Golf Course (Isle of), Oban  382

Erskine Golf Club, Bishopton  305
Eyemouth Golf Club, Eyemouth  410

# F

Falkirk Golf Club, Falkirk  277
Falkirk Tryst Golf Club, Larbert  281
Falkland Golf Club, Falkland  237
Fereneze Golf Club, Barrhead  302
Forfar Golf Club, Forfar  207
Forres Golf Club, Forres  97
Fort Augustus Golf Club, Fort Augustus  97
Fortrose and Rosemarkie Golf Club, Fortrose  99
Fort William Golf Club, Fort William  98
Foulford Inn Golf Course, Crieff  200
Fraserburgh Golf Club, Fraserburgh  158

# G

Gairloch Golf Club, Gairloch  101
Galashiels Golf Club, Galashiels  411
Garmouth and Kingston Golf Club, Garmouth  102
Gatehouse of Fleet Golf Club, Gatehouse of Fleet  434
Gifford Golf Club, Gifford  54
Gigha Golf Club (Isle of), Isle of Gigha  328
Girvan Golf Course, Girvan  329
Glasgow Golf Club (Killermont), Glasgow  338
Glasgow Gailes, Irvine  358
Gleddoch Golf and Country Club, Gleddoch  352
Glen Golf Club, North Berwick  68
Glenalmond Golf Course, Glenalmond  209
Glenbervie Golf Club, Larbert  282
Glencorse Golf Club, Penicuik  72
Glencruitten Golf Club, Oban  381
The Gleneagles Hotel Golf Courses, Auchterarder  188
Glenisla Golf Centre, Alyth  182
Glenrothes Golf Course, Glenrothes  238
Gogarburn Golf Club, Newbridge  67
Golf House Club (The), Elie, Elie  235
Golspie Golf Club, Golspie  103
Gourock Golf Club, Gourock  352
Grangemouth Golf Club, Grangemouth  279
Grantown-on-Spey Golf Club, Grantown-on-Spey  104
Greenburn Golf Club, Fauldhouse  52
Greenock Golf Club (The), Greenock  353

Greenock Whinhill Golf Club, Greenock  353
Gretna Golf Club, Gretna  435
Gullane Golf Club, Gullane  55

# H

Haddington Golf Club, Haddington  59
Haggs Castle Golf Club, Glasgow  339
Hamilton Golf Club, Hamilton  355
Harburn Golf Club, West Calder  76
Harris Golf Club (Isle of), Isle of Harris  460
Hawick Golf Club, Hawick  413
Hayston Golf Club, Kirkintilloch  366
Hazlehead Public Courses, Aberdeen  138
Helensburgh Golf Club, Helensburgh  356
Helmsdale Golf Club, Helmsdale  105
Hilton Park Golf Club, Glasgow  340
The Hirsel Golf Club, Coldstream  408
Hoddom Castle Golf Club, Ecclefechan  433
Hollandbush Golf Club, Hollandbush  357
Hopeman Golf Club, Hopeman  106
Huntly Golf Club, Huntly  159

# I

Inchmarlo Golf Club, Banchory  149
Innellan Golf Club, Innellan  357
Innerleithen Golf Club, Innerleithen  414
Insch Golf Club, Insch  160
Inverallochy Golf Club, Inverallochy  161
Inveraray Golf Club, Inveraray  358
Inverclyde National Golf Training Centre, Largs  368
Invergordon Golf Club, Invergordon  107
Inverness Golf Club, Inverness  108
Inverurie Golf Club, Inverurie  162
Irvine Golf Club, Irvine  360
Islay Golf Club, Isle of Islay  363

# J

Jane Connachan Golf Centre, North Berwick  67
Jedburgh Golf Club, Jedburgh  415

# K

Keith Golf Club, Keith  163
Kelso Golf Club, Kelso  416
Kemnay Golf Club, Kemnay  164
Kenmore Golf Course, Kenmore  210
Kilbirnie Place Golf Club, Kilbirnie  364
Killin Golf Club, Killin  280
Kilmacolm Golf Club, Kilmacolm  365
Kilmarnock (Barassie) Golf Club, Troon  397
Kilspindie Golf Club, Aberlady  32
Kilsyth Lennox Golf Club, Kilsyth  366
Kinghorn Golf Club, Kinghorn  238
King James VI Golf Club, Perth  216
King's Acre Golf Course, Lasswade  60
Kingsbarns Golf Links, St Andrews  262
Kingsknowe Golf Club, Edinburgh  42
King's Links, Aberdeen  139
Kingussie Golf Club, Kingussie  111
Kinloss Country Golf Course, Kinloss  112
Kinross Golf Club, Kinross  239
Kintore Golf Club, Kintore  165
Kirkcaldy Golf Club, Kirkcaldy  241
Kirkcudbright Golf Club, Kirkcudbright  436
Kirkhill Golf Club, Glasgow  341
Kirkintilloch Golf Club, Kirkintilloch  367
Kirriemuir Golf Club, Kirriemuir  212
Knightswood Golf Course, Glasgow  341
Kyle of Lochalsh Golf Course, Kyle of Lochalsh  113
Kyles of Bute Golf Club, Tighnabruaich  395

# L

Ladybank Golf Club, Ladybank  242
Lagganmore Golf Club, Portpatrick  445
Lamlash Golf Club, Isle of Arran  294
Lanark Golf Club, Lanark  367
Langholm Golf Club, Langholm  437
Langlands Golf Course, East Kilbride  325
Largs Golf Club, Largs  369
Larkhall Golf Club, Larkhall  370
Lauder Golf Club, Lauder  418
Leadhills Golf Club, Leadhills  371
Lenzie Golf Club, Glasgow  342
Leslie Golf Club, Leslie  243

Letham Grange Hotel and Golf Course, Arbroath 186
Lethamhill Golf Course, Glasgow 343
Leven Links Golf Club, Leven 245
Liberton Golf Club, Edinburgh 43
Linlithgow Golf Club, Linlithgow 62
Linn Park Golf Club, Glasgow 343
Littlehill Golf Club, Glasgow 344
Lochcarron Golf Club, Lochcarron 114
Lochgelly Golf Club, Lochgelly 247
Lochgilphead Golf Club, Lochgilphead 372
Loch Lomond Golf Club, Luss 375
Lochmaben Golf Club, Lochmaben 438
Loch Ness Golf Course, Inverness 109
Lochore Meadows Golf Course, Crosshill 230
Lochranza Golf Club, Isle of Arran 295
Lochwinnoch Golf Club, Lochwinnoch 374
Lockerbie Golf Club, Lockerbie 439
Longniddry Golf Club, Longniddry 64
Longside Golf Club, Longside 166
Lothianburn Golf Club, Edinburgh 44
Loudoun Gowf Club, Galston 327
Luffness New Golf Club, Aberlady 33
Lumphanan Golf Club, Banchory 149
Lundin Golf Club, Lundin Links 247
Lundin Ladies Golf Club, Lundin Links 248
Lybster Golf Club, Lybster 117

# M

McDonald Golf Club, Ellon 157
Machrie Bay Golf Club, Isle of Arran 297
Machrihanish Golf Club, Campbeltown 312
Marriott Dalmahoy Hotel Golf & Country Club, Dalmahoy 37
Maybole Golf Club, Maybole 377
Meldrum House Golf Club, Oldmeldrum 170
Melrose Golf Club, Melrose 419
Melville Golf Centre, Lasswade 61
Merchants of Edinburgh Golf Club, Edinburgh 45
Millport Golf Club, Isle of Cumbrae 320
Milnathort Golf Club Ltd, Milnathort 251
Milngavie Golf Club, Glasgow 344
Minto Golf Club, Minto 420
Moffat Golf Club (The), Moffat 440
Monifieth Golf Links, Dundee 204
Montrose Links Trust, Montrose 213

Moray Golf Club, Lossiemouth  116
Mortonhall Golf Club, Edinburgh  46
Mount Ellen Golf Club, Glasgow  345
Muckhart Golf Club Ltd, Muckhart  283
Muirfield (The Honourable Company of Edinburgh Golfers), Gullane  57
Muirkirk Golf Club, Muirkirk  378
Muir of Ord Golf Club, Muir of Ord  117
Murcar Golf Club, Aberdeen  140
Murrayfield Golf Club Ltd, Edinburgh  46
Murrayshall Golf Course, Perth  217
Musselburgh Golf Club (The), Musselburgh  67
Musselburgh Links, The Old Course Musselburgh  65
Muthill Golf Club, Muthill  215

# N

Nairn Golf Club (The), Nairn  120
Nairn Dunbar Golf Club, Nairn  119
Newbattle Golf Club Ltd, Dalkeith  36
Newburgh-on-Ythan Golf Club, Newburgh  167
Newcastleton Golf Club, Newcastleton  421
New Cumnock Golf Club, New Cumnock  381
New Galloway Golf Club, New Galloway  442
Newmachar Golf Club, Newmachar  168
Newtonmore Golf Club, Newtonmore  123
Newton Stewart Golf Club, Newton Stewart  443
Niddry Castle Golf Club, Winchburgh  79
North Berwick Golf Club, North Berwick  69
North Inch Golf Course, Perth  217

# O

Old Course Ranfurly Golf Club (The),  Bridge of Weir  307
Oldmeldrum Golf Club, Oldmeldrum  170
Orkney Golf Club, Orkney Isles  456

# P

Paisley Golf Club (The), Paisley  384
Palacerigg Golf Club, Cumbernauld  318
Panmure Golf Club, Barry  190
Peebles Golf Club, Peebles  422
Peterculter Golf Club, Peterculter  171
Peterhead Golf Club, Peterhead  172

Pines Golf Centre (The), Dumfries  432
Pitlochry Golf Course Ltd, Pitlochry  218
Pitreavie Golf Club, Dunfermline  235
Polkemmet Country Park, Whitburn  79
Pollok Golf Club, Glasgow  346
Polmont Golf Club Ltd, Falkirk  278
Port Bannatyne Golf Club, Isle of Bute  309
Port Glasgow Golf Club, Port Glasgow  385
Portlethen Golf Club, Portlethen  172
Portobello Golf Club, Edinburgh  46
Portpatrick (Dunskey) Golf Club, Portpatrick  445
Powfoot Golf Club, Annan  428
Prestonfield Golf Club, Edinburgh  47
Prestwick Golf Club, Prestwick  386
Prestwick St Cuthbert Golf Club, Prestwick  388
Prestwick St Nicholas Golf Club, Prestwick  389
Pumpherston Golf Club, Pumpherston  74

# R

Ralston Golf Club, Paisley  383
Ranfurly Castle Golf Club Ltd (The), Bridge of Weir  308
Ratho Park Golf Club, Ratho  75
Ravelston Golf Club, Edinburgh  48
Ravenspark Golf Club, Irvine  360
Reay Golf Club, Reay  125
Renfrew Golf Club, Renfrew  390
Rosehearty Golf Club, Rosehearty  173
Rothes Golf Club, Rothes  174
Rothesay Golf Club, Isle of Bute  310
Rouken Glen Golf Centre, Glasgow  347
Routenburn Golf Club, Largs  370
Roxburghe Golf Course (The), Kelso  417
Royal Aberdeen Golf Club, Aberdeen  141
Royal Burgess Golfing Society of Edinburgh, Edinburgh  48
Royal Dornoch Golf Club, Dornoch  92
Royal Musselburgh Golf Club, Prestonpans  73
Royal Tarlair Golf Club, Macduff  166
Royal Troon Golf Club, Troon  398
Rutherford Castle Golf Club, West Linton  77

# S

St Andrews – The Old Course, St Andrews  253
St Andrews – Balgove Course, St Andrews  256

St Andrews – Eden Course, St Andrews  257
St Andrews – Jubilee Course, St Andrews  258
St Andrews – New Course, St Andrews  259
St Andrews – Strathtyrum Course, St Andrews  261
St Boswells Golf Club, St Boswells  424
St Fillans Golf Club, St Fillans  219
St Medan Golf Club, Monreith  441
St Michael's Golf Club, Leuchars  441
Saline Golf Club, Saline  252
Sandyhills Golf Club, Glasgow  347
Sanquhar Golf Club, Sanquhar  447
Scoonie Golf Club, Leven  246
Scotscraig Golf Club, Tayport  221
Seil Golf Club (Isle of Seil), Isle of Seil  383
Selkirk Golf Club, Selkirk  423
Shetland Golf Club, Shetland Isles  457
Shian Golf Course, Balfron  272
Shiskine Golf and Tennis Club, Isle of Arran  297
Shotts Golf Club, Shotts  391
Silverknowes Golf Club, Edinburgh  49
Skeabost Golf Club, Isle of Skye  127
Skelmorlie Golf Club, Skelmorlie  391
Isle of Skye Golf Club, Isle of Skye  126
Solway Links Golf Course, Southerness  448
Southerness Golf Club, Southerness  448
Spean Bridge Golf Club, Spean Bridge  127
Spey Bay Golf Club, Spey Bay  128
Stirling Golf Club, Stirling  286
Stonehaven Golf Club, Stonehaven  175
Stornoway Golf Club, Isle of Lewis  462
Stranraer Golf Club, Stranraer  450
Strathaven Golf Club, Strathaven  393
Strathclyde Park Golf Course, Hamilton  355
Strathendrick Golf Club, Drymen  276
Strathlene Golf Club, Buckie  152
Strathmore Golf Centre, Alyth  183
Strathpeffer Spa Golf Club, Strathpeffer  128
Strathtay Golf Club, Strathtay  220
Stromness Golf Club, Orkney Isles  456
Swanston Golf Club, Edinburgh  50

# T

Tain Golf Club, Tain  130
Tarbat Golf Club, Portmahomack  124
Tarbert Golf Club, Tarbert  394